Darwin's Orchestra

Darwin's Orchestra

An Almanac of Nature in History and the Arts

Michael Sims

A HENRY HOLT REFERENCE BOOK

Henry Holt and Company

New York

A Henry Holt Reference Book
Henry Holt and Company, Inc.
Publishers since 1866
115 West 18th Street
New York, New York 10011

Henry Holt® is a registered
trademark of Henry Holt and Company, Inc.

Published in Canada by Fitzhenry & Whiteside Ltd.,
195 Allstate Parkway, Markham, Ontario L3R 4T8.

Library of Congress Cataloging-in-Publication Data
Sims, Michael.
Darwin's orchestra: an almanac of nature in history
and the arts / Michael Sims.
p.   cm. — (A Henry Holt reference book)
Includes bibliographical references and index.
1. Animals in literature.   2. Animals in art.   I. Title.
II. Series.
PN56.A64S64   1997   96-25524
809'.9336—dc20   CIP

ISBN 0-8050-4220-2

Henry Holt books are available for special
promotions and premiums. For details contact:
Director, Special Markets.

First Edition—1997

DESIGNED BY PAULA R. SZAFRANSKI

Printed in the United States of America
All first editions are printed on acid-free paper.∞

1   3   5   7   9   10   8   6   4   2

For Chris.

What fun.

Contents

Why Thoreau Would
Not Like This Book

"Books," said the wild man of Walden, "should not be made from other books. The author should have *been there.*"

Well, I wasn't there. I was nowhere near Fairhaven Bay the day Thoreau's own campfire escaped its dry stump and burned 300 acres of woodland. Nor was I in Vienna for the elaborate funeral of Mozart's pet starling. I even missed one of my favorite moments in the history of science: Charles Darwin and his family testing the hearing of earthworms by playing for them the tin whistle, bassoon, and piano.

But others *were* there, and they have left us their stories—funny, heroic, tragic, wonderful stories. Therefore, this is a book made from other books. Not an anthology, but a collection of essays commemorating the role of nature in history and the arts. There's certainly no shortage of material. Dorothy Wordsworth and Benjamin Banneker kept diaries. Pliny the Younger and Rachel Carson wrote letters. We have "bills of mortality" documenting plague deaths, and ships' logs reporting mermaid sightings. Countless films and poems and paintings portray our world and fellow creatures. There are newspaper accounts and radio and television broadcasts. "A man will turn over half a library," Samuel Johnson observed, "to make one book." I like to imagine that his tone was less disapproving than Thoreau's.

While writing *Darwin's Orchestra,* I asked myself, Of all the splendid stories knocking at the door, which are eligible to enter this book? Pliny the Elder defined "nature" as everything not made by humans. I appealed to Webster and found as one definition "the sum total of all things in the physical universe." Unfortunately, that much elbow room doesn't help screen nominees for essay topics. So you may attribute the variety to my whims. The last passenger pigeon is here, and so is the warbler that helped doom Alger Hiss. Mr. Ed chats with the *Velociraptors* from *Jurassic Park,* Spider-Man rubs shoulders with Shakespeare. I wanted to talk about Easter and Halloween and other holidays. And I couldn't bear to leave out old monster movies. The diversity of nature is equaled only by the variety of human culture.

"When I make a word do a lot of extra work like that," Humpty-Dumpty said, "I always pay it extra." I may have to do that with my definition of natural history.

A Note on the Dates

"A calendar, a calendar! Look in the almanac."
—Bottom, in A MIDSUMMER NIGHT'S DREAM

This is a book of days. The calendar dictates its format. Following many of the essays, you will find a note recommending others on related topics. Natural events are chronicled on a relevant date—a particular visit of Comet Halley, for example, or an eclipse that halted a battle. The death of Francis Bacon symbolizes with a novelist's irony the man and his work; likewise, the birth of Omar Khayyám. However, a number of these essays are dated by internal evidence within a fictional work, such as November 1 for the film *The Thing* and May 9 for *Gulliver's Travels.* A handful of dates are approximations.

Under "Further Reading" you will find suggested sources for pursuing a topic, excluding those mentioned in the text.

And now the matter of dating. "I began this desperate Voyage," Lemuel Gulliver writes of his departure from the land of the Houyhnhnms, "on February 15, 1714–15, at 9 o'Clock in the Morning." That year date seems as if Gulliver wasn't sure when he left. Actually, in the time of Jonathan Swift, England's calendar marched to the beat of a different drummer. New Year's Day was March 25. In the rest of Europe, January 1 through March 24 already would have been 1715, but in England it was still 1714. Therefore, when referring to an event between those dates, one had to use both years. The problem is written in stone on the grave marker of John Evelyn: ". . . His Learned & usefull works fell asleep y^e 27th day of February 170^5/$_6$. . . ."

That sort of chaos is merely one example of the varying systems that make precisely dating events in history so iffy. There is also the matter of the differing Julian and Gregorian calendars (see the essay for October 4), not to mention the Chinese and Mayan and all the others. Furthermore, although most people on Earth are not Christians, the most widespread calendar, especially in the West, follows the Christian division of history into two segments, B.C. (before Christ) and A.D. (*anno Domini,* "in the year of the Lord"). Although this system is biased and awkward, it is prevalent, and I use it here.

Have I tried to align the various dates with our current definition of reality? No. I am simply commemorating events. Many are modern, even contemporary, and their dates are not questioned. Earlier ones are not always so definite. If something happens only once, but appears on two different calendars, and one calendar is eleven days behind the other—? No. It sounds like an algebraic word problem. I always hated those.

A Note on the Title

Creationists lament (or deny) Charles Darwin's discovery of a hairy cousin in the family tree, but evolution and ecology go hand in hand. Plants and animals breathe each other's breath because they grew up together. "Nothing in biology," the geneticist Theodosius Dobzhansky wrote, "makes sense except in the light of evolution." That's why Darwin appears several times in this book, even in the title. You can't look at biology, even at your pet cat or local songbirds, even at imaginative works of art that address the natural world, without seeing them differently because of him and his colleagues. Not only will you find here Darwin himself in the unforgettable role of conductor of a family band for an audience of earthworms (see the essay for October 10), but if ever natural scientists had an orchestra leader, it was the old man at Down House. I can imagine Jane Colden and J.-Henri Fabre and Maria Sibylla Merian in the orchestra, but only Charles Darwin could hold the baton.

The views of nature held by any people determine all its institutions.
—Emerson

Although there are many names, the arts are not separated;
and one kind of knowledge is not severed from another.
—Paracelsus

Day-by-Day Entries

1 January 1980

"The Far Side of Science"

In no other habitat could a zoologist find gong birds, insectosaurs, punk flamingos, and cow-intologists. A female praying mantis accuses another of devouring her husband. Alligators bob for poodles. In a bar, a male insect tries to pick up a female, with the old line that he has just metamorphosed and has only twenty-four hours to find a mate and breed before he dies. For fourteen years, this demented zoo could be found on the comics page of almost any U.S. newspaper. *The Far Side* began nationwide syndication in the United States on New Year's Day, 1980.

The cartoons that appeared on more refrigerators than any other also adorned more scientists' offices. Gary Larson drew ornithologists going through a mating dance when they met, delinquent astronomers monopolizing a telescope, animal behaviorists insulting fish to learn if they have feelings. No one had seen nature this way before, at least not in newspapers. "Something amazing has happened to the doors and bulletin boards of academic corridors in the natural sciences," Stephen Jay Gould wrote. "[Scientists] have spontaneously chosen Gary Larson as the national humorist of natural history."

THE FAR SIDE   By GARY LARSON

© 1985 FarWorks, Inc./Dist. by Universal Press Syndicate

11-7

"The picture's pretty bleak, gentlemen. ... The world's climates are changing, the mammals are taking over, and we all have a brain about the size of a walnut."

"A strange juxtaposing of things takes place that I don't understand," Gary Larson once said of his Far Side *cartoons. "It just happens."*

Sometimes artistic license permitted scientific heresy. Larson drew a polar bear disguising itself with a penguin mask, but the two are literally antipodal, polar bears in the Arctic and penguins in the Antarctic. One cartoon shows a male mosquito returning home after a hard day of infecting humans; in reality, only the female mosquito bites. Like countless movies and television programs, Larson also portrayed prehistoric humans coexisting with creatures that lived millions of years earlier. "I think there should be cartoon confessionals," Larson said, "where we could go and say things like, 'Father, I have sinned—I have drawn dinosaurs and hominids together in the same cartoon.' "

Larson's casual use of a precise scientific term such as "hominid" is typical. He seems as much biologist as cartoonist. As a child, he loved drawing and "science—specifically biology and, more specifically, when placed in a common jar, which of two organisms would devour the other." His countless pets included an alligator, iguanas, pigeons, insects, and tarantulas. His parents caught one snake just as it was vanishing into a davenport, and found a boa constrictor wrapped around the sewing machine.

Typically, Larson's cockeyed take on nature is a humbling experience for us humans. We do not come across as the paragon of animals. Larson won countless awards, and *The Far Side* became one of the most widely distributed cartoons in history. The California Academy of Sciences even mounted a 400-cartoon exhibition entitled "The Far Side of Science," which traveled to the Smithsonian and the American Museum of Natural History.

Larson's most bizarre accolade came in 1989. American entomologist Dale Clayton had been studying external parasites of birds and mammals, some of which are so host-specific that they can be used as identifying characteristics of a species. He discovered a hitherto unknown chewing louse found only on owls and named it *Strigiphilus garylarsoni*. Larson was pleased. Endlessly replicated, the creature adorns the endpapers of one of his books.

---

2 JANUARY 1912

Shaw's "Bad Natural History"

George Bernard Shaw began writing his play *Androcles and the Lion* on the second of January, 1912. Soon he was writing to a friend, "Do you know anyone who can play a lion well, with a practicable tail, for the Christian Martyr scene in the arena?" This was not one of his "larks," Shaw told a colleague. "It will fail unless it is presented as a great religious drama—with leonine relief."

In Aesop's fable, Androcles is a fugitive slave who aids a lion. They are captured together and taken to the city for use in a circus. When the emperor has the hungry lion set upon Androcles, it greets him ecstatically instead. Surprisingly, the appended moral is not about reaping the kindness one sows, but rather the sound natural history observation, "Gratitude is a quality not limited to Man."

Shaw's version takes place in the time of the Caesars. His Androcles is an animal-loving Greek tailor who predictably meets a lion in need of first aid. Its plight melts his already soft heart: "Did um get an awful thorn into um's tootsums wootsums? Has it made um too sick to eat a nice little Christian man for um's breakfast?" Androcles plucks out the thorn and dances away with the lion.

Androcles is a recent convert to Christianity, which naturally his wife considers atheism. The early Roman regard for this upstart cult is the background of the play, and the Christians' spectrum of zeal provides its philosophical weight. (Later, Shaw introduced the 43-page drama with a 101-page "Preface on the Prospects of Christianity.") Unwilling to renounce his new faith, the gentle Androcles protests, "I couldn't sacrifice to Diana: she's a huntress, you know, and kills things." True to the fable, when the lion appears, it recognizes Androcles and spares him. As they had in the forest, they embrace and waltz away. To a critic, Shaw replied, "I know that a dancing lion is bad natural history; but he is good nursery legend." He wrote *Androcles* partially in response to what he considered the patronizing tone of James Barrie's *Peter Pan,* but it offended too many parents to succeed as a children's play.

For background, Shaw and the man who was to play the lion went to the London Zoo. "At first it was a wretched business," Shaw wrote. "Nothing but furious terror & misery everywhere." A Siberian tiger roared at them, a lion tried to paw them. Then they visited the "maneless" lion, which, Shaw remarked, reminded him of the Trafalgar Square lions. "No nerves about *him.* He beamed on us most majestically. I put my hand into the cage and steamrollered him under the chin, and he nuzzled with his nose and chuckled and was prepared to take all the admiration that was going." Later, Shaw said that this particular lion made the story of Androcles credible.

Shaw was used to being misunderstood, but he was particularly amused by a letter from someone who had overheard a conversation at an American performance of *Androcles.* When one woman asked what on earth it all meant, another replied confidently, "It means just that we should be kind to animals."

The Doorman's Search for the Door

Juan is a young Cuban refugee who came to the United States during the Mariel boatlift in 1980. He works as the doorman of a Manhattan apartment building peopled with eccentrics. Juan himself is not exactly free of quirks. He has come to the conclusion that his daily job is merely metaphorical, that it is his mission to lead suffering humanity to the Door through which they can reach—well, what they may reach he doesn't know, but he feels that there is an urgent need to find this doorway to alternatives.

Juan is the protagonist of *The Doorman,* a 1991 fantasy by Cuban novelist Reinaldo Arenas. The animals in Juan's apartment building see a compatriot in him and ask him to help them escape from the evils of human society. They reveal that, like Mr. Ed, they know how to speak human language but seldom choose to. Storytellers throughout history have imagined many such versions of human-animal communication. They hate to settle for the reality, the chasm across which humans and animals speak, bark, gesture in sign language, and stare incomprehendingly.

Like so many animals in fiction, and in reality, these unwilling Manhattanites have many grievances against their supposed masters. Heading the revolution is the millionaire's rare Egyptian dog, said to be the last of her line, and named for a woman who supposedly kept the breed in her palace—Cleopatra. It is this dog that first approaches Juan to enlist him in the animals' cause. She behaves with great dignity except for when she chews up the doorman's copy of Sartre's *Being and Nothingness,* which she finds philosophically offensive.

The animals meet with Juan in the building's basement. They each express their complaints about humans and their hopes for the nature of the refuge the animals will seek from them. At this moment they sound both more self-centered and more realistic than the naive optimists who help launch the revolution at Orwell's Animal Farm. They are as divisive as any herd of human beings. The dove questions the whole plan. The turtle insists that the best place for them all is a lagoon. A rat opts for subways and caves, the goldfish for the open sea, the orangutan for the jungle. The black bear reveals that his master dyed him, that he is actually a polar bear, and demands that they immediately head for the frozen north. The rattlesnake suggests that he and his fellows, if they unite, can drive humans from their cities. No, says the rat, humans should be kept as domestic animals, producing garbage for the animals to eat. The ancient turtle disagrees. "To live for hatred," he declares, "is to live serving our enemy." He suggests that the animals go away and try to forget people. Naturally, but somewhat pathetically, it is a dog who insists that, without humans, animals are nothing.

On the night of January 3, 1991, Juan is caught with the animals and sent to an asylum. Somehow, the animals overcome their differences and unite to help Juan escape. Together they all head west across the continent. They aid each other in unfamiliar environments, at times hundreds of birds uniting to carry the others across mountains. Topeka farmers see a goldfish bowl passing overhead. In Tulsa, a woman glimpses a flying snake. Finally, the utopian beasts reach the Pacific Ocean and start south. Animals of every kind join them, from llamas to hornbills to sturgeon. "When they reached the Equator," Arenas wrote, "the thunderous stampede was deafening."

---

4 JANUARY 1939

A Prehistoric *Rite of Spring*

Igor Stravinsky completed his ballet *The Rite of Spring* (*Le Sacre du printemps*) in 1913. It is the dramatization of an ancient pagan rite. When Sergey Diaghilev's Ballets Russes premiered the work in Paris the next year, its unusual rhythms and harsh sounds were greeted with boos, insults, and even physical assaults on the musicians.

However, not only did the music become one of the touchstones of modernism, but it achieved a wide audience through an appropriately modern medium. In 1938, Walt Disney Productions was working on a collage of animation set to music, entitled *Fantasia.* The production team had been considering including a segment based upon Stravinsky's *Firebird*. Then, at a story conference, Disney asked, "Was there ever anything written on which we might build something of a prehistoric theme—with prehistoric animals?"

Someone suggested Stravinsky's *Rite of Spring* and played a recording of it. "This is marvelous!" Disney exclaimed. "It would be perfect for prehistoric animals." For $6,000, Disney bought the film rights from Stravinsky, and a contract was signed on January 4, 1939. Animators derived their inspiration from repeated listenings to Stravinsky's music, but the team had more than merely artistic goals. "From the outset," one of the art directors said later, "*Rite of Spring* was conceived as a scientific document."

When the film premiered in 1940, even an otherwise negative critic approved of "the geology lesson to Stravinsky's fine score." The segment begins with the viewer traveling through space, past stars and galaxies, to arrive at a molten Earth. On the young planet, lava bubbles and flows. Finally, water appears. Translucent single-celled amoebas float about and slowly evolve into more elaborate creatures. It is, as musicologist Deems Taylor says in introducing it, a "reproduction of what science thinks went on during the first few billion years of this planet's existence." The rhythms and sounds that offended the *Rite*'s first audience were perfect for the history of the Earth itself.

Most of *Fantasia*'s other segments feature anthropomorphized animals—centauresses so high-schoolish they should be popping bubblegum, the terminally cute dancing hippos, even The Mouse himself. However, Disney warned animators against disneyfying the dinosaurs: "Don't make them cute animal personalities. They've got small brains, y'know; make them real." (Actually, there might be a correlation between cuteness and relative cranial capacity, because most of the cute characters possessed disproportionately large heads.) Disney's artists enlisted the advice and support of paleontologists such as Barnum Brown, Julian Huxley, and Roy Chapman Andrews. A staffer later remembered that typical requests for information were along the lines of "Please provide anything and everything pertaining to the Permian Age through the Triassic which covers development from amphibians to earliest reptile forms."

Leopold Stokowski,* who conducted the score, suggested that if the film could "end with the most terrifying of the animals fighting and eating each other, people would gasp." *Tyrannosaurus* was an obvious nominee for that scene, and *Stegosaurus* was considered the worthiest opponent because of the four spikes on the end of its tail. The meek herbivores are feeding in the shallows when, heralded by dramatic music, *T. rex* appears. Every creature flees, and *Tyrannosaurus* grabs the running *Stegosaurus* by the tail. They battle to the death—the death of *Stegosaurus*, of course, for although his heavily armed tail gets in some good blows, it is no match for *Tyrannosaurus*'s dagger teeth. Stegosaurus falls to the ground. Slowly his tail stops slashing and his eyes close.

Originally, Disney intended to proceed with the story of evolution through "The Age of Mammals and the First Men" to "Fire and the Triumph of Man." However, fundamentalist Christians learned of the plan and threatened to cause an uproar. Disney scrapped the proposed section on human evolution and ended his evolutionary saga with the death of the dinosaurs.

See also the Pastorale ***segment of*** Fantasia, *11/2.*

---

* One of the Disney artists caricatured Stokowski as a "Stokisaurus," half arm-waving conductor and half dinosaur—with, naturally, a double tail.

Mr. Ed's Pedigree

A new character appeared on U.S. television on the fifth of January, 1961. Even in that land of favorite Martians and mothers reincarnated as cars, he stood out. He quoted Hamlet, spoke Latin, and imitated beatnik slang—but only in the presence of one person, Wilbur Post. The show was *Mr. Ed.* Wilbur's friend was a talking horse.

Before Mr. Ed there was Francis, a talking mule who starred in seven films between 1949 and 1956. Other than being articulate equine cousins, Ed and Francis had little in common. Unlike Ed, Francis would talk to others if necessary. Francis was a hard drinker, and Ed apparently a teetotaler. The Francis movies grew from a novel, Ed's series from a number of short stories by Walter Brooks, the author of the children's books about Freddy the Pig.

But Mr. Ed could trace his heritage farther back than that. In the Bible there is the story of Balaam, the diviner whose curse on the Israelites God turns into a blessing. Balaam is riding on an ass when an armed angel blocks the path. Although Balaam is blind to the manifestation, the ass not only sees the angel twice, but turns aside; and when the angel appears a third time and there is nowhere to turn, the ass falls to the ground. Balaam rewards the perceptive animal each time with blows from his staff. Finally, God gives the ass the power of speech, and it exclaims what might be the first words of many animals allowed to speak to humans: "What have I done unto thee?"

For all their dedication, neither Lassie nor Rin Tin Tin talked to their masters with more than a well-timed bark. The puzzled human response was usually along the lines of "What is it, girl? Is Timmy in trouble?" This was not conversation. Animals needed human speech. Of course, that hasn't always worked out well, either. Saki's character Tobermory, a cat who suddenly begins to speak at a cocktail party, has learned human language but without its attendant hypocrisy. Like Mr. Ed, he speaks his mind with little regard for human vanity.

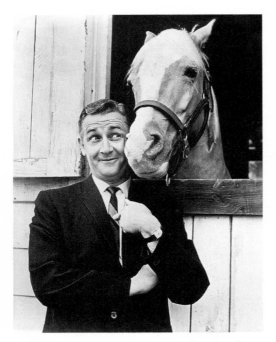

Like his predecessors, Balaam's ass and Francis the talking mule, Mr. Ed regarded the foolishness of human beings without enthusiasm. Ed is the one looking dignified. Courtesy of Ronald V. Borst / Hollywood Movie Posters

But is it only Ed who is talented? Perhaps, like the little girl Fern in *Charlotte's Web,* Wilbur Post is simply naive enough to listen to animals. Dr.

Dolittle was. He followed God's advice to Job—"Ask now the beasts, and they shall teach thee"—and took notes excitedly as Polynesia the parrot divulged "the Birds' ABC." And long before Ed spoke to Wilbur, those curious horse folk, the Houyhnhnms, were tutoring Lemuel Gulliver.

Unlike Dolittle, Charles Darwin studied the alien diversity of animal sounds and despaired: "It is not probable that any precise explanation of the cause or source of each particular sound . . . will ever be given." But that hasn't stopped us from trying. In the 1960s, before humans knew about the delphine aptitude for remembering series, John Lilly thought he had taught dolphins to count to ten. Since then, so many apes have learned sign language, they're ready for their own cable channel. The hordes of talking animals in fiction and fable hint at the human urge to communicate across the barriers of species. For example, hardly anyone can pass a parrot in a pet shop without speaking to it. One of Linnaeus's many pets was a parrot that sat on his shoulder and called out at lunchtime, "Twelve o'clock, Mr. Carl!" However, the bird was merely mimicking the frequent remark of one of the servants. If animals wouldn't speak to a man who devoted his life to cataloging nature, what chance do the rest of us have?

See also utopian animals, 1/3.

---

6 JANUARY 1806

Sacajawea and the Monstrous Fish

Sacajawea, the young Shoshone woman who accompanied the Lewis and Clark Expedition, has become more legendary than historical. There are more monuments in the United States to her than to any other woman in American history. Her name, which appears in eight spellings in the Lewis and Clark journals and other ways elsewhere, meant "Bird Woman." Heroic status, and the backlash against it, can obscure genuine contributions. Although Sacajawea was never, as legend claims, the Lewis and Clark Expedition's guide, she did act as one of the interpreters and was a skilled naturalist. It was a perfect combination, because President Thomas Jefferson had charged the expedition with performing both a natural and cultural survey while charting an overland passage to the Pacific.

Sacajawea was born in the late 1780s, in what is now Idaho. A band of Minitari (Hidatsa) captured her when she was still a child, and eventually a French-Canadian trapper and guide named Toussaint Charbonneau either bought or won her. Accompanied by Sacajawea and another "wife," Charbonneau encountered the already eighteen-month-old Lewis and Clark Expedition in late 1805. They hired him as interpreter because he could speak Minitari and other native languages, but they also needed someone who could speak Shoshone, and only Sacajawea fit the bill. Charbonneau was told to bring her (and their newborn child) along. Sacajawea was a member of the main party of the Lewis and Clark Expedition from April 1805 to August 1806. Again and again, she proved herself more courageous and resourceful than her husband, and she soon became a respected and valuable member of what was originally called "the Corps of Discovery."

Finally, the party neared the Pacific Ocean. Clark decided to winter there because they were running low on salt, which was not merely a tasty additive but an essential preservative. The party stopped before reaching the sea and built cabins. Shortly after New Year's Day, 1806, five men were sent on to the coast to boil down seawater and provide salt. The friendly locals gave the men whale blubber, which they took back with them to their primitive little fort. Cooked, the blubber turned out to be "tender and palatable, in flavor resembling the beaver." Several men prepared to return to the coast for more.

Sacajawea overheard these plans and complained. On Monday, January 6, Clark wrote in his guesswork spelling and punctuation:

> The last evening Shabano and his Indian woman was very impatient to be permitted to go with me, and was therefore indulged; She observed that She had traveled a long way with us to See the great waters, and that now that monstrous fish was also to be Seen, She thought it very hard that She Could not be permitted to See either (She had never yet been to the Ocian).

"So reasonable a request could not be denied," Lewis wrote in his own journal; "they were therefore suffered to accompany Captain Clark." With the rest of the party, and presumably with her child strapped on her back, Sacajawea trekked for thirty-five miles across creeks and up mountainsides to the site where the whale had beached. She saw the great water, but the natives had taken all the blubber and flesh off the "monstrous fish," leaving only a 100-foot skeleton. They would part with only a few pounds of oil and 300 pounds of blubber. "Small as this Stock is I prise it highly," Clark wrote in his journal, "and thank providence for directing the whale to us; and think him much more kind to us than he was to jonah, having Sent this monster to be *Swallowed by us* in Sted of *Swallowing of us* as jonah's did."

---

7 JANUARY 1963

Rachel Carson and Albert Schweitzer

"Man can hardly even recognize the devils of his own creation." Rachel Carson quoted the words of Albert Schweitzer in her 1962 call to arms against the dangers of pesticides, *Silent Spring*. She also dedicated the book to the polymath and humanitarian whose philosophy she found so inspiring.

Silent Spring is now considered a classic work of ecology, acknowledged as one of the roots of the environmental movement that blossomed in the United States in the 1960s. Thanks to the author's hybrid of science and art, it is also renowned as "nature writing." But, as more than one commentator has pointed out, its publication was greeted with the most outraged squeals heard since Charles Darwin's *Origin of Species* appeared a century earlier. The pesticide industry mounted a frantic campaign to deny Carson's claims, undermine her reputation, and even question her femininity.

However, to Carson's surprise, the acclaim balanced the abuse. As soon as sections of the book began appearing in the *New Yorker,* letters poured in. After President Kennedy's Science Advisory Committee published their corroboration of her claims, demands on Carson's time increased. Busier than ever, mourning her mother's death, serving as her nephew's guardian, she turned down most offers. She was also in considerable pain from cancer, with less than two years to live. But there were some honors she could not refuse. One was the Schweitzer Medal, awarded her by the Animal Welfare Institute on the seventh of January, 1963.

Years before, after Schweitzer won the 1952 Nobel Peace Prize, Carson had written about him to a friend, "I think he is an extremely significant figure. . . ." In 1961, she said that she hoped, if it weren't "too presumptuous a comparison," that *Silent Spring* might do for the subject of pesticides what Schweitzer had done for radiation in his Nobel Prize acceptance speech. Accepting the Schweitzer Medal, Carson explained why no award could please her more. "Dr. Schweitzer has told us that we are not being truly civilized if we concern ourselves only with the relation of man to man. What is important is the relation of man to all life."

Rachel Carson summed up her feelings about the strange appeal of the ocean in the last paragraph of her book *The Edge of the Sea:* "Contemplating the teeming life of the shore, we have an uneasy sense of the communication of some universal truth that lies just beyond our grasp. . . . The meaning haunts and ever eludes us, and in its very pursuit we approach the ultimate mystery of Life itself." Paul Brooks, Carson's editor and biographer, recalled one summer evening at her cottage on the Maine coast when they were working on a manuscript. After dinner, he and Carson examined snails, tube worms, and sponges under a microscope. Then Carson put them back into a pail. With a flashlight, she picked her way across the slippery rocks and returned the tiny creatures to their home in the sea. Brooks wrote: "This, I think, is what Albert Schweitzer . . . meant by reverence for life."

---

8 JANUARY 1951

"All Kinds of Murtherings"

Spaniards explored Bermuda in 1603. At night, they heard frightening, unnatural-sounding cries, which they took to be spirits. In time they discovered that the noises came from birds, which they killed and found tasty. In 1609, a hurricane wrecked the English ship *Sea Venture* off the Bermuda coast. Aboard was one William Strachey, who recorded the ten months spent trapped on the island. He, too, heard the birds that had frightened the Spaniards: "A kind of webbe-footed Fowle there is, of the bigness of an English greene Plover. . . ." Strachey said the marooned crew heard the birds on winter nights. They hovered in the air along the shore and "made a strange hollow and harsh howling. They call it of the cry which it maketh, a cohow."

For countless generations, the cahow (as we now spell it), or Bermuda petrel, fed in the Sargasso Sea and nested on the islets of Bermuda. Then came Europeans—accompanied, like witches with familiars, by hardy and aggressive rats. During the day, cahows fed at sea, and the rats dined upon their unattended eggs. In the early 1590s, ship crews released pigs that enthusiastically rooted up the nesting areas. By the time Strachey saw it, the cahow was in trouble, but it still seemed abundant. "There are thousands of these Birds," Strachey wrote, "and two or three Islands full of their Burrows, whither at any time . . . we could send our Cock-boat and bring home as many as would serve the whole Company."

For a few more years, the cahow seemed plentiful. Then, during the winter famine of 1614–15, countless birds were slaughtered. Soon a law forbade colonists to continue their "spoyle and havock of the Cahowes, and other birds, which already were almost all of them killed and scared away very improvidently by . . . all kinds of murtherings." These early conservation measures were too little and too late. By 1630, the cahow was gone.

Or so it seemed. Three centuries later, in 1906, someone discovered what was thought to be a previously unknown species of petrel on Bermuda's Castle Island. It matched reconstructions of the cahow that ornithologists had made from bones and old descriptions. Then, on January 8, 1951, a Bermuda conservationist named David Wingate discovered a few cahows nesting, as they always had, on rocky islets. The birds were still vulnerable to rats and other predators. They also had an avian competitor, the white-tailed tropic bird, which invades cahow nests during the day when the parents are at sea, and usually kills the chicks and commandeers the nest.

Wingate and others went so far as to build nest guards large enough to admit cahows but not the tropic birds. Slowly the cahow population grew. Then their breeding rate began to plummet, and ornithologists found that DDT had infiltrated even the remote Sargasso Sea in such quantities as to poison the fish on which the cahows fed. Only the 1972 ban on U.S. use of DDT gave the cahow another chance. Against all odds, the bird has survived in the past, perhaps only to face extinction now.

---

9 JANUARY 1872

"The Soul of the White Ant"

In 1937, a book was published in Africa. It was little recognized because it was written in Afrikaans, an Africanized dialect of Dutch at that time little known outside its native Transvaal (now a province of South Africa). Eugène Nielen Marais was more comfortable with English, but he had made a political commitment to the new language of his region, and insisted on writing in it. He died a year before the book appeared.

Eugène Marais was born on January 9, 1872, near Pretoria, which at the time was the capital of the Transvaal Republic. Marais's first noteworthy accomplishment was an award he received in school for reciting the entire catechism of the Church of England. Not all his subsequent activities were so warmly rewarded. He was tried for treason and acquitted. He worked as a controversial political journalist, a lawyer, an arms smuggler in the Boer War, a volunteer physician who never got a degree, and a self-taught naturalist. However, Afrikaners remember Marais primarily for his poetry and journalism. One of his poems, "Winter Nag," is now considered to have launched the vernacular Afrikaans movement.

Eugène Marais was a strange man, but then, *Die Siel van die Mier* ("The Soul of the White Ant") is a strange book. The ant of the title is actually the termite. Biologists remember Marais for his passionate conviction that the termitary—the colony of termites in their vast communal house—is a single animal. He was not speaking metaphorically. "I have taken great pains," he wrote, "to prove the termitary is a separate and composite animal in exactly the same way that a man is a separate and composite animal. Only the power of locomotion is absent." In Marais's scenario, soldier and worker castes are analogous to blood corpuscles. The colony's fungus gardens, tended deep in the bowels of the termite mound, are the liver and stomach. A queen in her gravid immobility is both the ovary and, by releasing pheromones like subliminal propaganda, the brain.

The social insects have played a curious role in modern biology. Termite society is too distinctive an adaptation to be ignored, although at times the notice has been rather silly. In 1935, British entomologist Herbert Noyes contrasted the vast number of abused, starving, and ill children in England with the tender loving care termite parents give their offspring. That's a bit of a stretch for an analogy, but a fine example of how termite society's stratified layers, with their rigid and enforced work assignments, appeal to some people. Like other animals who give their lives for a group, one African termite species raises questions about the role of altruism in nature. Its soldiers are armed with glandular secretions with which they entangle their opponents. Sometimes, in doing so, they contract the gland so violently that the insect's abdomen explodes, spraying the enemy with fluid but simultaneously committing suicide.

Since journals written in Afrikaans were conspicuously absent from the scientific centers of the world, Marais's work was little noted. Then, in 1926, the year after Marais's articles on termites first began appearing and years before they were gathered into a book, dramatist, naturalist, and future Nobel Prize winner Maurice Maeterlinck published a book entitled *The Life of the White Ant*. Marais's ideas, even his original terminology, appear in Maeterlinck's book. There were three countries in which Marais's articles would have been intelligible—the Transvaal, Holland, and Flanders. Born in Belgium, Maeterlinck was Flemish. Although he wrote separately on bees, there seems no doubt that Maeterlinck's termite book draws heavily upon an obscure volume by a little-known eccentric named Eugène Marais.

---

10 JANUARY 1951

Bedtime for Bonzo

Several roles from Ronald Reagan's film career supplied his political opponents with satirical ammunition. However, none was more popular with cartoonists and comedians than a sentimental comedy with a dash of garbled natural history, in which Reagan starred opposite a chimpanzee. *Bedtime for*

In Bedtime for Bonzo, *Ronald Reagan played a psychologist who is determined to prove that nurture is far more important than nature.* Courtesy of Ronald V. Borst / Hollywood Movie Posters

Bonzo premiered in Hollywood on January 10, 1951. "Having given a mule and an invisible rabbit a chance at film stardom," *Variety* remarked, "Universal now brings forth a stellar chimpanzee for a series of screen antics. . . ." The film came up so much during Reagan's political days that he learned to deflect jokes by making them first. During the 1980 campaign, a reporter asked him to autograph a studio still portraying him and Bonzo. He signed it, "I'm the one with the watch."

The issue that the film pretends to explore is one of the fundamental controversies in psychology and evolution. Usually summed up as "nature versus nurture," it addresses the respective roles of genetics and environment in human psychological development. Reagan plays a psychology professor named Peter Boyd, whose father was a thief. His dean fears the son will turn out like the father. Because he wants to keep his job and marry the dean's daughter, Boyd, author of *The Power of Environment,* secretly begins an experiment with a chimpanzee. He takes Bonzo into his home, to prove that "environment is all-important, that heredity counts for very little." Translation: Had his father been given a better start in life, he would not have run afoul of the law.

"What if," Boyd asks, "I could teach this monkey the difference between right and wrong?" (Technically, chimpanzees are apes, not monkeys.) Boyd hires a female assistant, and together they surround

Bonzo not with anything resembling chimpanzee life, but with a grotesque parody of the Fifties Ideal Family. They call each other Mama and Papa in front of the "child." Bonzo wears diapers, pajamas, and cowboy outfits. The nurse sings him lullabies.

Bedtime for Bonzo appeared only a quarter century after John B. Watson's famous behaviorist manifesto: "Give me a dozen healthy infants, well-formed, and my own specified world to bring them up in and I'll guarantee to take any one at random and train him to become any type of specialist I might select—doctor, lawyer, artist, merchant-chief, and, yes, even beggar-man and thief, regardless of his talents, penchants, tendencies, abilities, vocations, and race of his ancestors." It is curious that scientists who were determined to divorce humanity from a religious origin could be such rabid opponents of biological roots of behavior. The attempt to deny human beings any precultural biology led to extravagant claims. Zing Yang Kuo maintained that even sexual intercourse resulted from habits developed through imitation. "Behavior," he said flatly, "is not a manifestation of hereditary factors, nor can it be expressed in terms of heredity; it is the direct result of environmental stimulation."

Reagan's character comes to the same conclusion about Bonzo: "I feel justified in saying that Bonzo was motivated in everything he did by love for those who loved and protected him."

---

11 January 1844

"It Is Like Confessing a Murder"

"There are just as many species as there were in the beginning," the systematist Linnaeus proclaimed in the eighteenth century. "There is no such thing as a new species." He was convinced that species were merely the smallest unit of God's great static chain of being. That had been the assumption for a long time when Charles Darwin and his colleagues challenged it in the mid-1800s. However, the core of the idea of evolution—or, as it was called at first, "transmutation"—was that the species was not an immutable category, that animals and plants slowly changed into new forms to adapt to the demands of their environments.

Darwin thought that biology was lagging behind more progressive sciences. He was impatient with the paradox that "we can allow satellites, planets, suns, universe, nay whole systems of universe[s], to be governed by laws, but the smallest insect, we wish to be created at once by special act." It wasn't that religious thinkers regarded distant suns as any less God's creation than the fallen sparrow and the hairs on our heads. There was a simple reason that species needed to remain in their assigned cubbyholes. Once they began moving around, once their edges blurred into each other, the resulting confusion would begin to nibble away at the heavily fortified human classification. Darwin, and his opponents, foresaw that the realization that humans were a part of the game just like every other animal would ultimately refute the comfortable ancient assertion by Protagoras, "Man is the measure of all things." Of course, the location of Earth at the center of the solar system had once been an unshak-

The dapper simian in this Darwinian-era advertisement proves how readily we could see apes in human terms.

able tenet of science and religion, yet had gone the way of the dodo without taking society with it.

Biologists certainly didn't do away with the species. It is still the final, most narrow unit of biological classification (not counting less official designations such as subspecies and variety), defined as a population whose members are capable of freely interbreeding. Inability to breed, to exchange genetic information and produce fertile offspring, is the line of demarcation among species. However, as Emerson observed, "Nature ever flows; stands never still. Motion or change is her mode of existence." Boundaries blur and merge. Sometimes the placement of a creature in one category is debatable, and since no one enjoys debate more than scientists, each designation is examined and many are revised. If, for example, two or more groups formerly considered species are found breeding together, then they are reclassed from distinct species to races of a single species.

Following his informative five-year jaunt around the world aboard the *Beagle,* and his studies of our forced variations among domesticated animals, Charles Darwin had begun to doubt the fixity of species. He was not the first, but it was still a radical idea. On the eleventh of January, 1844, over seven years after his return to England, Darwin explained his position in a letter to his friend, botanist Joseph Hooker:

> I am almost convinced (quite contrary to the opinion I started with) that species are not (it is like confessing a murder) immutable. . . . I think I have found out (here's presumption!) the simple way by which species become exquisitely adapted to various ends.

Darwin felt like a murderer because he foresaw the "host of prejudices" his ideas would have to battle. His own wife was deeply religious and feared for his soul. He was plagued with the knowledge that aspects of his very lifework would pain her and many others. Although a reluctant convert to what his colleague Thomas Huxley would eventually label agnosticism, Darwin was no anti-Christian radical. He began his work agreeing with Herschel, who wrote that "we must not impugn the Scripture Chronology, but we *must* interpret it in accordance with *whatever* shall appear on fair enquiry to be the *truth* for there cannot be two truths." It was that elusive truth that Darwin was determined to follow to its lair, no matter in what ungodly territory it might lie.

See also Origin of Species, *11/24.*

Batman

Without their animal-inspired disguises, many comic book crime-fighters would be exposed as vigilantes with mask fetishes. A huge percentage of superheroines and -heroes either acquired their powers through some arcane interaction with an animal or chose one as their symbol and disguise. Most orders of Animalia are represented on the comic book roster. There are ornithological characters such as the Eagle, Owl, Falcon, and Hawkman. (Batman's sidekick Robin was named after Robin Hood, not after a songbird.) Mammalian crime-busters tend toward the feline, including Panther Woman, Black Cat, Black Panther, Wildcat, and Catman. Then there is the entomological brigade—Ant Man, Spider Queen, and, of course, Spider-Man; a colorful subgenre includes the Red Bee, Blue Beetle, and Green Hornet. More recent ones include Nite Owl and that hirsute X-man, Wolverine. These champions are constantly threatened by such villains as Zebra-Man, Catwoman, the Penguin, and the Octopus.

In 1939, in a DC comic book, a crime-fighter arrived sans superpowers. What he had was intelligence, strength, agility, and a persona. He had chosen the guise of a bat. Each hero's costume externalizes the animal relationship, and Batman wears a long dark bat-wing cape and a bat logo on his chest. His cowl has pointed bat ears, which actually look more like the feather-tuft "ears" of the great horned owl. This costume, which would elicit snickers in the real world, was supposed in the comic book universe to unnerve felons. In the canonical origin of Batman, young Bruce Wayne watches his parents gunned down by a hoodlum and vows to avenge their deaths. Years later, musing on the "superstitious, cowardly" nature of criminals, he decides he needs a disguise that will protect his real identity while striking terror into the hearts of evil-doers. Right on cue, a bat flies in the open window. "That's it!" Wayne exclaims. "I shall become a *bat!*" The campy TV series, which premiered on January 12, 1966, abandoned Batman's role as scary midnight vigilante. However, comic book artists gradually restored Batman's darker side—and therefore the point of the bat costume. It was maintained in Tim Burton's *Batman* movie in 1989, and later in the animated *New Adventures of Batman and Robin.*

Bob Kane, the creator of Batman, said he was inspired partially by the 1926 film *The Bat,* "in which the villain wore a batlike costume which was quite awesome." Fond of frequenting rooftops and standing where the light will cast his caped shadow across a wall, the homicidal maniac of *The Bat* genuinely seems an evolutionary forerunner of Batman. However, that sort of wardrobe already had a theatrical history. Dracula-type vampires on stage were wearing batlike capes as early as 1852, in the play *The Vampire.* Bats are even more important to vampire than to superhero lore.

A parody of Batman appears on the animated television series, *The Tick.* He has the huge, grotesque sound-gathering appurtenances of a real leaf-nosed or big-eared bat, and his name is Die Fledermaus, after Johann Strauss's opera. (Strauss's title means "The Bat." Germans describe the bat as a "flitter-mouse.") Less dutiful than his fellow bat-hero, Fledermaus takes his phone off the hook when the bat signal appears in the night sky, and he can usually be found hanging out at a diner with other super-anti-heroes.

The Twilight Barking

In the Book of Genesis, after creating all the many beasts of the earth, God wraps up his busy sixth day by making humans. He must have been alarmed when his last creation immediately began tinkering with the Garden. The Creator may have made the wolf and decided it was good, but humans were in his image, after all, and they too had imagination. They took the wolf and began to experiment, resulting in such unnatural progress as the cartoon physique of the dachsund, hip dysplasia in German shepherds, and the bark.

Coyotes yodel, wolves howl, and the crab-eating fox has raised whining to an art, but only domesticated dogs frequently bark. And not even all dogs, just those that we have nudged like bonsai toward some imagined ideal. For, through selective breeding, we created that particular canine attribute. The closer a dog is to its wild ancestry, the less it barks. In general, the Malamute, named for the Malimiut people who developed it from the Arctic wolf, does not bark. Nor does Africa's ancient breed, the basenji.

Occasionally those who live around dogs, and that includes millions of people who don't own one but can't seem to escape them, ask themselves how much information dogs communicate with that infernal noise. Scientists have their own analyses, but popular culture has expressed some opinions. One scenario appears in Dodie Smith's 1956 novel *One Hundred and One Dalmatians.* After that splendid villainess Cruella de Vil steals the pups of Pongo and Missis to make a Dalmatian-skin coat, the distraught parents drag their owners to the top of a hill and bark in every direction. "Anyone would think they were signaling," jokes one of their owners. They are. They are making use of the Twilight Barking, the daily canine network for news, gossip, and emergencies.

Walt Disney Productions released its animated adaptation of Smith's novel on January 13, 1961, and the barking that was amusing to read about became as annoying to listen to as that of real canines. However, because of it, England's resourceful dogs soon discover the hideout of the dognappers. The animal militia not only helps the pups escape but leads their parents to them.

How much information dogs can convey to *us* is a different issue. In Smith's book, the dogs decide their owners possess almost canine intelligence. They understand "the barks for 'Out, please!' 'In, please!' 'Hurry up with my dinner!' and 'What about a walk?' " Some other fictional dogs are even more talented at communicating with humans. Probably the best example is that hirsute heroine Lassie. When the little boy in the television series got stuck in some misadventure, he explained to Lassie exactly what was wrong and where to find help. Lassie would race away, find the neglectful parents, and bark. Comedian Andy Andrews parodied Lassie's linguistic talents: " 'Woof!' That would be all Lassie would say, but Ruth would respond in a very excited voice, 'Oh, my God, Paul, Timmy is down by the beaver pond stuck under a loblolly pine tree!' "

Lacking the famous collie's linguistic talents, the Dalmatians in Smith's book must rely upon the Twilight Barking for information, and battle Cruella de Vil without human assistance. Not surprisingly, they do just fine without us. Their communication network, after all, is superior to some of our own.

"Mainly about Birds and Beasts"

In the mid-1930s, T. H. White lived alone in a forest in England. His old gamekeeper's cottage possessed neither running water nor indoor plumbing, but it was in a stimulating animal community. Neighbors included badgers, carp, foxes, and owls. An equally diverse lot sometimes resided in his house: his setter bitch Brownie, two goshawks named Gos and Cully, two merlins (sparrow hawks) with Arthurian appellations but nicknamed Red and Black for their hoods, and an owl that White called Archimedes.

"Do you remember I once wrote a thesis on the Morte d'Arthur?" White asked a friend in a letter on January 14, 1938. A rereading had inspired him. "Anyway, I somehow started writing a book. It is not a satire. Indeed, I am afraid it is rather warm-hearted—mainly about birds and beasts." Ostensibly about the childhood of King Arthur, *The Sword in the Stone* absolutely teems with birds and beasts.

The goshawk Cully appears in the novel under his real name. Even though his brother Kay actually lost Cully, it is the young Arthur who stays in the forest all night to retrieve the falcon. White based this episode on an experience of his own. After six weeks of training the real Cully, White extended his tether an extra eighteen feet to give him room to move around. The old twine broke and the bird escaped.

It is during this search that Arthur encounters Merlyn. The magician's enchanted cottage seems a version of White's own cabin in the woods. It is full of animals—a corkindrill that winks at Merlyn in salutation even though it is stuffed, a white donkey, snakes in a terrarium, a wasp nest and a beehive, baby hedgehogs, a pair of badgers, and a nest of field mice.

When Merlyn takes off his pointed hat, an owl lands on his head, and the reader meets another creature that emigrated from White's life into his fiction. "We see so little company," Merlyn explains, "that Archimedes is a little shy of strangers." Elsewhere White described adopting a dying owl: "For the two days which his vitality left him, he would not leave me by an inch, and at night he slept on my head. . . ." White described *The Sword in the Stone* as a wish fulfillment, and in it not only does Arthur find the falcon that White lost, but the owl does not die.

White provided Arthur with the perfect tutor. "Education is experience," Merlyn tells him, "and the essence of experience is self-reliance." Most of these experiences require that Arthur be transformed into some sort of animal. First he becomes a young perch, swimming in the moat, learning about power from the king of the fish. Then Merlyn turns Arthur into a tethered hawk so he can spend the night with the other birds in the falconer's hutch, listening to the experts. For his third field trip, Arthur becomes an ant, and encounters everywhere the famous slogan "EVERYTHING NOT FORBIDDEN IS COMPULSORY." Ants' mindless obedience horrifies him.

Finally, Arthur has the honor of becoming an owl for a night and flying beside the venerable Archimedes. Although he doesn't know it yet, he is learning to be a king.

Josephine Baker's Menagerie

Expatriate American dancer and singer Josephine Baker declared that she had three passions—theater, children, and animals. Of the latter she said, "Animals interest me because they are as simple and as uncomplicated as babies." That simplification explains a great deal about Baker's attitudes toward both babies and animals. She was usually surrounded by both. Occasionally her pets did not get along with her numerous children. At times there were as many as thirty monkeys at one of her villas, and on one memorable occasion a female guenon (a member of a large group of long-tailed African monkeys) abducted Baker's infant adopted son from his cradle and escaped to a nearby park. The nurses were frantic until they found the baby, unharmed, tended by the monkey.

The stories about Josephine Baker and her animals seem endless. She had a pet pig named Albert and a chimpanzee named Ethel and a cheetah named Mildred. Some of the snakes she wore in her stage acts were pets. Early in her career, still unworldly, Baker housed her goldfish in a watery home she found handily provided in a hotel room. It turned out to be a bidet, and later she found it dry and full of dead fish.

One of the animals most famously associated with Baker was her pet leopard, Chiquita. Her adventures with the animal sound like Katharine Hepburn's in *Bringing Up Baby*. Baker received Chiquita from producer Henri Varna, owner of the Casino de Paris nightclub, who hired her for the 1930–31 season. An extravagant skit set in the African jungle needed a little extra color, and Varna provided the big cat for that purpose. In the gambling rooms and on the boardwalk at Deauville, the combination of the extravagantly attired Baker and her feline consort always caused a sensation. In an advertising poster, Baker sat naked except for feathers and pearls, with Chiquita beside her on her hind legs, proffering a bouquet to her mistress. Newspapers variously described Chiquita as a tiger, jaguar, and panther.

Baker once took Chiquita with her to the theater. The animal got loose and terrified the crowd, and the resulting publicity made all the papers. Another time, clad in feathers, Baker walked out to the audience and explained that before she could perform they must help her retrieve her pet monkey that had escaped and was somewhere in the building. The orchestra fell to their knees and looked under seats, calling, "Petit, petit, petit." An observer remarked that the musicians, on their knees and all facing the same way, resembled a scene in a mosque. After a while the monkey appeared and clung to the neck of a terrified woman until it could be peeled off of her.

On January 15, 1941, Baker was performing her classic "La Creole" dance number as the Nazis were approaching Paris. Friends informed her that there was a boat leaving France in two days, and that it might be the last one. A doctor faked a certificate declaring that Baker had a shadow on her lung and must get to a warmer climate as soon as possible. Typically, although it greatly complicated her escape, Baker refused to leave without her menagerie—monkeys named Glug Glug and Mica Gugusse, Bonzo the Great Dane, even a pair of white mice named Curler and Question Mark. Somehow she managed it. Animals in tow, she escaped Paris just before the Germans arrived.

"A Vast Golden Dragon"

"I find 'dragons' a fascinating product of imagination," J. R. R. Tolkien once informed a correspondent. A dragon plays a major role in his book *The Hobbit,* which was published in England in 1937. On January 16, 1938, the London *Observer* printed a letter signed "Habit," which asked several questions about the book, ending with, "And, by the way, is the hobbit's stealing of the dragon's cup based on the cup-stealing episode in *Beowulf?*" Tolkien replied that the Anglo-Saxon epic poem was one of his most valued sources.

In *Beowulf,* the hero's theft of the golden cup results in the dragon's rampage, which in turn culminates in Beowulf's last battle. The scene of Bilbo Baggins burgling proof of his courage from under the very nose of the sleeping dragon occupies only a page or so in *The Hobbit,* but it too is a pivotal action. Bilbo's first view of the dragon Smaug is fully in the tradition of the creature's forebears:

> There he lay, a vast golden dragon, fast asleep; a thrumming came from his jaws and nostrils, and wisps of smoke, but his fires were low in slumber. Beneath him, under all his limbs and his huge coiled tail, and about him on all sides stretching away across the unseen floors, lay countless piles of precious things, gold wrought and un-wrought, gems and jewels, and silver red-stained in the ruddy light. . . .

Much of the world's accumulated dragon lore appears in that description of the creature Bilbo names "Chiefest and Greatest of all Calamities." The dragon is huge, fiery, and bat-winged, and hoards gold with a passion reminiscent of the currently dominant species of mammal. Where, after all, does Smaug plan to *spend* his loot? This is not about the accumulation of wealth that will translate into power. Smaug already has power. This is about the mystical lure of gold. Tolkien didn't think much of the dragon in *Beowulf,* but admired "Fáfnir in the late Norse versions of the Sigurd-story . . ." and pointed out Smaug's debt

In this wooden incarnation from a nineteenth-century peasant-carving workshop, a dragon is shown being vanquished by Saint George. Vanderbilt University Fine Arts Gallery / Photo by Denny Adcock

to his ancestors. There are many of them, from the German epic *Nibelungenlied* to the Christian myth of Saint George to Kenneth Grahame's 1899 children's fantasy *The Reluctant Dragon*.

Dragons also appear in Greek mythology. In one story, the Delphic oracle demonstrates a novel approach to urban planning by advising Cadmus to follow a cow until it stops, then build a town there and name it Thebes. Cadmus finds the divinely ordained ungulate, but along the way he must kill a dragon. Afterward, Athena materializes and tells him to sow half of the dragon's teeth in the ground. When Cadmus does so, armed men—the *Spartoi*, "Sown Men"—grow from the soil before his eyes.

Still the legends live on. Anne McCaffrey writes a popular series of science fiction novels about a planet named Pern, where humans settle, forget their Earth origins, and manage to half domesticate an indigenous local animal that just happens to resemble the dragons of Earthlore. Jack Vance won a Hugo (science fiction's Oscar) with his novella *The Dragon Masters*, in which humans of the far future hybridize ever more monstrous dragonlike reptiles.

Some dragon stories may have prehistoric roots. For centuries at least, people around the world stumbled upon impossibly large bones and teeth and proclaimed them dragons'. They were, of course, fossils. In China, the bones frequently wound up as ingredients in medicines. At the turn of the century, a German naturalist delivered a trove of such pharmaceutical fossils to paleontologists, and the experts identified ninety species of prehistoric creature. A quarter of a century later, another naturalist searched such drugstores for fossils and discovered the extinct ape *Gigantopithecus*. As American anthropologist and science historian Richard Milner has asked, "Is it possible Round Table dragon-killers journeyed to purchase impressive 'battle trophies' at a far distant fossil quarry?"

---

17 January 1939

"Keep It Cute"

Just as the occasional glimpses of nudes that flickered across movie screens in the genre's infancy were soon verboten, so were the antics of animated characters circumscribed. In order to forestall government interference, Hollywood voluntarily imposed its own production code in 1930, proclaiming its concern was the effect of cinematic sex and violence on the morals of American youth.

The January 17, 1939, issue of *Look* ran an article entitled "Hollywood Censors Its Animated Cartoons." An accompanying illustration portrays a giant pair of scissors cutting between two frames of film. In the first frame, Petunia Pig and her boarfriend Porky chastely hold hands. In the second— the frame being snipped off—they have their fat little porcine muzzles plastered together, their trotters lifting off the ground in excitement. Leon Schlesinger, who produced Looney Tunes and other cartoons for Warner Brothers, is quoted reminding concerned American parents that cartoons are "primarily the favorite motion picture fare of children. Hence, we always must keep their best interests at heart by making our product proper for their impressionable minds." Nonetheless, by 1948, *The Saturday Review of Literature* was alarmed that the formerly lovable cartoon characters had evolved into "masks for human characters so violent and crude that they couldn't even be put on the screen in their natural form."

Even Mickey Mouse came under fire. He may be an avuncular straight man now, but he began his career as a wily rascal. The public demanded the evolution. Mickey first appeared in 1928, violently playing other animals as musical instruments in *Steamboat Willie.* By 1934 Disney was already complaining, "If we have Mickey kicking someone in the pants, we get a million letters from mothers scolding us for giving their kids the wrong idea." So Mickey was gradually tamed.

This anxiety about the behavior of fictional creations is only one reason for the evolution of cartoon characters to ever greater blandness. In the 1970s, in his column in *Natural History,* Harvard paleontologist Stephen Jay Gould addressed the increasingly youthful appearance and behavior of Mickey. Gould took his dial calipers and quantified the changes in Mickey's appearance over the years. It seems that interesting physical changes accompanied Mickey's moral growth. His snout grew thicker, and his impossibly round ears moved back, increasing the childlike proportion of his forehead. His legs were made fatter and shorter by dressing them in pants. The entire eye of the early Mickey became merely the pupil of the big later eye. In short, he grew younger.

Gould built his argument partially upon a 1950 paper by Konrad Lorenz, in which the Austrian ethologist had speculated upon the human response to "neoteny," an animal's retention of juvenile features in an adult form. It isn't uncommon. Some adult salamanders, for example, retain their gills and other larval characteristics after they reach adulthood. Lorenz theorized that juvenile proportions trigger in the adult human a nurturing response. He described exactly the characteristics toward which Mickey has evolved. Apparently we, like other animals, respond affectionately to those creatures that mimic the proportions of our own infants. We coo over kittens and puppies as readily as we do in response to human babies. And, in view of certain artificially evolved bug-eyed lap dogs, we seem to nudge even living creatures toward an ever more childlike "cuteness."

At times the trend has reached epidemic proportions. Over the years, American Saturday-morning cartoons recast in younger versions such formerly disreputable and (at least chronologically) mature scoundrels as Bugs Bunny and Daffy Duck. The Muppets reappeared as The Muppet Babies. Pound Puppies replaced Deputy Dawg. Felix the Cat regressed to Hello Kitty. And along the way, Mickey Mouse grew ever younger, ever "cuter." Mickey's transformation is merely a symptom of a trend begun even before Walt Disney himself advised his animators, "Keep it cute."

See also Mickey's premiere, 11/18.

"Afternoon of a Faun"

The Roman philosophical poet (or poetic philosopher) Lucretius insisted that centaurs were an impossibility because horses and humans have different life spans. The human torso would outlive its equine body, a circumstance that might be inconvenient for the top half of the creature. That same practical, built-in restriction would have prohibited the existence of a number of mythology's portmanteau creatures and deprived the arts of a whole herd of enduring characters. Merfolk, for example, were half human and half fish. Gryphons had the wings and head of an eagle on the body of a lion. One character whose halves were not so clearly demarcated, but who nonetheless partook of the nature of more than one creature, was that favorite bad boy of classical mythology, the faun. Basically, fauns were men, but they had the ears, horns, tail, cloven hooves—and carnal appetites—of goats.

Early in Ovid's *Metamorphoses,* Zeus describes the lesser deities of the Earth: "I have my demigods, my fauns and satyrs, my nymphs and rustic sprites of wold and wood. . . ." The Arcadian god Pan came to be confused with the Roman deity Faunus, who inspired woodland creatures who were then considered equivalent to Greek satyrs. Fauns, like satyrs, were part goat because that animal was considered the very embodiment of fecundity and wantonness. They were the attendants of Dionysus (Bacchus), god of wine and mystic ecstasy. Pan was thought to be the source of the unreasonable fear that sometimes overcame one in the wilderness—panic. His famous pipe, the syrinx, became in time the name of the voice apparatus of birds. The sister and wife of Faunus, Fauna, lends her name to the collective animal life of a specific region, just as the plants are named for the goddess Flora, who presided over everything that blooms.

The untamed, erotic nature of fauns has inspired some curious works of art. While unhappily working as a schoolteacher, Stéphane Mallarmé, the French essayist and poet who led the Symbolist movement, spent his off hours creating his famously difficult poetry—and, for a while, preoccupied with the image of a faun. His *L'Après-midi d'un faune* (The Afternoon of a Faun) appeared in 1876. In 1894, in that lovely way that works of art cross-fertilize and hybridize like living things, Mallarmé's poem inspired his countryman Claude Debussy to compose a work of his own. A symphonic work based upon such an extramusical topic is called a tone or symphonic poem; the genre includes Saint-Saëns's *Africa* and even Strauss's *Thus Spake Zarathustra.* Although apparently he intended to create a work with three movements, Debussy completed only the first part, which became the *Prelude to the Afternoon of a Faun,* in 1894. Impressed, Mallarmé told Debussy that the musical version of *Faun* "goes further into the nostalgia and light with subtlety, malaise, and richness."

But the family tree of Mallarmé's faun doesn't end there. It then appeared in the artistic medium best suited to its reputation for revelry. In Paris in 1912, the famed Ballets Russes premiered a ballet set to Debussy's score. True to the story's origins, Vaslav Nijinsky, in the title role, was so erotic one reviewer denounced his performance as "bestial." Soon the U.S. critics responded in kind. On the eighteenth of January, 1916, Debussy's *Faun* was among the works the Ballets Russes presented the day after their American premiere. Following that performance, the New York Police Department charged impresario Sergey Diaghilev with obscenity, and he had to defend the ballet before a judge. Thousands of years after they were first employed to symbolize the wilder shores of human behavior, fauns were still refusing to behave.

See also Lupercalia, 2/15; and Swan Lake, 2/20.

---

19 JANUARY 1840

The Search for the
Southern Continent

For many centuries, European maps were sprinkled with the frightening but evocative phrase *terra incognita,* "unknown land." However, the most famous and supposedly exotic of all these mysterious places was what Ptolemy, in the second century, called *Terra Australis Incognita,* the "Unknown Southern Land" at the bottom of the Earth. The mere thought of a lopsided geography offended classical notions of the symmetry of nature; if the Earth was round, as the ancients realized early on, then there must be other continents, as yet unknown, on the other side of the world. Ptolemy's term replaced that used by the Roman geographer Pomponius Mela, who had dubbed the region *Antichthon,* "Counter-Earth." In the Middle Ages, one sage insisted that if there was a Southern Continent, no creatures could live there because the six-month summer would burn them up.

Understandably, exploration of the region was slow to occur. It was many centuries after Ptolemy before seagoing vessels were capable of undertaking such a voyage. In the meantime, the whole region was frequently dismissed as an ancient dream. When Australia was discovered, it received a name meaning "southern," although it soon became clear that it was not the fabled land. Nor was New Zealand. Nonetheless, one English explorer optimistically insisted (without a shred of evidence) that the Southern Continent was larger than "the whole civilized part of Asia, from Turkey, to the extremity of China," and that "the scraps from this table would be sufficient to maintain the power, dominion and sovereignty of Britain. . . ."

Then, in three voyages from 1768 to 1779, England's Captain James Cook explored the southern seas. After the first voyage, Cook admitted, "I have faild in discovering the so much talk'd of southern continent (which perhaps do not exist) and which I my self had much at heart. . . ." Of his second voyage, Cook wrote, "Whether the unexplored part of the Southern Hemisphere be only an immense mass of water, or contain another continent, as speculative geography seemed to suggest, was a question which engaged the attention, not only of learned men, but most of the maritime powers of Europe." When he realized that South Georgia Island was truly an island and not part of the Southern Continent, he named it Cape Disappointment. Finally, sadly, Cook turned back to England. He had traveled farther south than anyone else on record, but he hadn't bumped into Antarctica.

That finally happened in early 1819. While sailing around Cape Horn on the southern tip of South America, William Smith, captain of an English merchant brigantine, ventured farther southward in the Drake Passage to circumvent the dangerous waters around the tip of Patagonia. At latitude 62°01′, he saw land about ten miles away. It was what is now called the South Shetland Islands. Back home, Smith's superiors ridiculed him for his "fanciful credulity." However, the American sealers—wealthy and greedy dealers in the valuable pelts of fur seals—realized the importance of Smith's claims. Even disputed, the new land's location was secret, and the sealers asked Smith to guide them. A patriotic Englishman, he refused. Soon, however, the American and other sealers were finding Antarctica on their own, and killing seals by the thousands.

From 1838 to 1842, Charles Wilkes led the first U.S. maritime scientific expedition. (He is also remembered for almost causing war with Britain in the "*Trent*" Affair" during the U.S. Civil War. He boarded the English mail steamer *Trent* and abducted two Confederate commissioners.) On January 19, 1840, Wilkes sighted that part of Antarctica now called Wilkes Land, on the opposite side of the continent from the South Shetland Islands, and claimed it for the United States. It was Wilkes who established that Antarctica was a continent. The slow rate of exploration of the least-known continent is demonstrated by how many of Wilkes's 180-odd nautical charts were used by the United States during World War II, a full century later. In a sense, of course, the South Land was never found. The barren, frozen wastes of Antarctica bear little resemblance to the fabled *Terra Australis Incognita.*

Mark Twain's Animals

Throughout his career, Mark Twain wrote about animals, from his celebrated frog to the monkeys of India. No creature was beneath his notice. His best-loved novel features vivid little scenes with animals.

Dan Beard's illustration from Mark Twain's Following the Equator *was originally captioned "An Honest Critic."*

Tom Sawyer releases his pet "pinch bug" in church, where a stray poodle learns the origin of the insect's name. Later Tom inhumanely administers Aunt Polly's fiery painkiller to the cat Peter, who tears around in a "frenzy of enjoyment."

However, Twain reported encounters with far more exotic animals than beetles and house cats. His travel books are spiced with zoological asides. More than once he traveled around the world, and in Sydney or Alahabad, San Francisco or Jerusalem, his eye saw every animal as a Mark Twain character. It was not exactly the objective eye of science. Twain imagined what it must have been like to be kicked by New Zealand's extinct ostrich-like bird, the moa. The cobra's bite, he said, "kills where the rattlesnake's bite merely entertains." He analyzed a dachsund's structural defects, claiming he couldn't classify the strange animal. He claimed the magpie lost its modesty when it discovered it was Australia's only musical bird, and said a flock of flying fish in bright sunlight "look like a flight of silver fruit-knives."

On the trip later recorded in *Following the Equator,* Twain reached India on the twentieth of January, 1896. The lieutenant governor of Lahore lent him transportation. "It was a fine elephant, affable, gentlemanly, educated. . . . I could easily learn to prefer an elephant to any other vehicle, partly because of that immunity from collisions, and partly because of the fine view one has from up there, and partly because of the dignity one feels in that high place, and partly because one can look in at the windows and see what is going on privately among the family."

In *A Tramp Abroad,* Twain had written of a raven that insulted him in the European woods. On this trip, he encountered "The Bird of Birds"—the Indian crow. He contrasted it with the American blackbird, which was noisy only "when holding religious services and political conventions in a tree." In contrast, the Indian crow was always raucous. "I never saw such a bird for delivering opinions. . . . And it is never a mild opinion, but always violent—violent and profane—the presence of ladies does not affect him."

Not surprisingly, Twain was always fascinated by the behavior of our closer cousins. He noted that sacred status had enhanced the vanity of temple monkeys. In Delhi, monkeys frequently entered the house. "Two of these creatures came into my room in the early morning . . . and when I woke one of them was before the glass brushing his hair, and the other one had my notebook, and was reading a page of humorous notes and crying." Twain threw something at the housebreakers, and he claimed they responded by throwing at him everything they could lift. Finally, when the monkeys went into the bathroom for more missiles, Twain was able to lock them out. "I did not mind the one with the hair-brush," he remarked, "but the conduct of the other one hurt me; it hurts me yet."

---

21 JANUARY 1852

The Battle of the Ants

"The ant," Stephen Vincent Benét wrote, "finds kingdoms in a foot of ground." There is no better example in literature than Henry David Thoreau's famous record of the battle of the ants. "One day, when I went out to my wood-pile, or rather my pile of stumps, I observed two large ants, the one red, the other much larger and black, fiercely contending with one another, and rolling over on the chips." Thoreau recorded this incident in his journal on the twenty-first of January, 1852, and later used it in the chapter "Brute Neighbors" in *Walden.*

"Looking further," Thoreau wrote, "I found to my astonishment that the chips were covered with such combatants, that it was not a *duellum* but a *bellum,* a war between two races of ants. . . ." Already the ground was strewn with tiny fallen soldiers. Naturally, Thoreau humanized the fighters, imagining infinitesimal bands playing martial songs, and that the ants were charged by their mothers to return with their shields or upon them. Three ants were fighting on a single wood chip, which Thoreau took indoors and covered with a glass tumbler. Through a magnifying glass, he could see that the ants had torn off each other's legs and antennae, and even ripped open one built-in breastplate. Finally the black one severed the heads of his opponents, but the bodiless jaws clung to him for half an hour.

People close to the Earth could not miss so widespread and energetic an animal as the ant, and therefore the insects play strong symbolic roles in our thinking. They were sacred to Ceres, Greek goddess of agriculture, because they taught humans to store food. In China, ants represented patriotism and subor-

A close-up of the sort of Lilliputian battlefield that Thoreau observed.

dination. That submersion of individuality was the very attribute that alarmed T. H. White. Merlyn, in White's *The Sword in the Stone,* transforms the young not-yet-king Arthur into an ant so that he can experience the horrors of mindless obedience.

Thoreau's isn't the only account of an ant war—although, for all his anthropomorphizing, his is more reliable than most. As Thoreau mentioned when he included the battle in *Walden,* sixteenth-century Swedish historian Olaus Magnus described a battle of ants after which the victor buried its own dead and left the enemy upon the battlefield. Scientists have not observed ants burying their dead, but although ants are slaves to instinct, occasionally they exhibit surprisingly "intelligent" behavior. After accumulating casualties on street-car tracks in Nicaragua, ants were observed tunneling under the tracks. When those tunnels were blocked, they created new ones before crossing.

Ants' violent tendencies can be observed in their armaments. The jaw-closing of *Odontomachus bauri,* for example, is the fastest movement measured in the animal kingdom, from a third of a millisecond to a full millisecond. Formerly the escape response of the cockroach, clocked at a now-sluggish forty milliseconds, seemed quick enough. A millisecond, after all, is one one-thousandth of a second. This lightning reflex alone shatters the myth of nature as peaceful. You need weaponry like that only if you live in a very bad neighborhood.

See also **Them!***, 6/15; and Darwin, 7/23; and his journal, 10/22.*

"What Kind of Monkey"

"I was born seven years after the start of the century," Loren Eiseley complained to his journal, "in the wrong time, the wrong place, and into the wrong family." An only child, his mother a stone-deaf prairie artist, his father an itinerant actor turned hardware store owner, Eiseley retained that sense of displacement and unfocused nostalgia all his life. He grew up a loner, drifting from hobo jungles to fossil expeditions. Sporadic study gradually built an education. Attention to his two loves, science and literature, eventually won him thirty-five honorary degrees. He wound up at the University of Pennsylvania, its most honored faculty member since Benjamin Franklin.

Eiseley was even elected to the National Institute of Arts and Letters, a rare honor for a scientist. But he was more than a scientist. He was a naturalist in the old-fashioned sense, one who embraced all of the natural world as his field of interest. He wrote two books on the evolution of our ideas about evolution, our changing views of nature and of ourselves, and our gradual realization that they are the same. He wrote an autobiography, too, and poetry. But he is best known for his volumes of informal essays, anecdotal meditations often inspired by numinous encounters with the world around him: a too-innocent fox cub, a broken-winged gull, a spider building a web near a streetlight to escape the winter cold.

Eiseley once wrote, "Every time a great scholar dies something unique vanishes out of the universe, a way of thinking that will never be expressed again." This was true of him. When he died in 1977 he left no heirs. No writer on nature and evolution can replace that combination of erudition and near-mystical insight that marked Eiseley's restless mind. He used a hermit crab as a metaphor for human evolution, noticed a man on a New York subway clinging to the strap with a hand like a gibbon's, described hillside wasp burrows as resembling the Valley of the Kings.

"Life is never fixed and stable," Eiseley wrote. He quoted the heretical axiom "God asks nothing of the highest soul but attention." He paid attention. He was an evolutionist, but he didn't assume that natural selection explains away all the intricacies of adaptation with which nature has filled the world. He guessed at the future as much as he reconstructed the past. "I am not nearly so interested in what monkey man was derived from," he wrote, "as I am in what kind of monkey he is to become."

"*Anthropomorphizing:* the charge of my critics," Eiseley wrote in his journal on January 22, 1970. "My countercharge: There is a sense in which when we cease to anthropomorphize, we cease to be men, for when we cease to have human contact with animals and deny them all relation to ourselves, we tend in the end to cease to anthropomorphize ourselves—to deny our own humanity."

---

23 JANUARY 1896

An Experiment at Kew

"The Royal Botanic Gardens, Kew" is the official name of the best-known botanical garden in the world. Primarily a botanical rather than a horticultural institution, England's Kew nonetheless became the oasis it is today through a determination to wed art to science. Definitions overlap: A botanical garden houses collections, both living and preserved, of plants organized by kinship; horticulture is the art and science of cultivating a garden. Kew covers all aspects, offering study in botany, horticulture, and landscape gardening. Orchids, roses, cacti, grasses, climbing plants—all are grown and studied at Kew. Its herbarium contains over 5 million specimens, and it possesses the world's largest collection of botanical books. Botanist Joseph Hooker, friend of Charles Darwin and director of Kew after his father's tenure, thought that the institution should be the center of information and final arbiter in matters botanical. (That great catalog, the *Index Kewensis,* still the standard in such matters, was originally funded by Darwin only months before he died, with instructions to his children to continue to support the project after his death.)

After his return from Captain Cook's first voyage round the globe in 1771, botanist Joseph Banks persuaded George III to send out plant collectors as England's scientific emissaries. Soon explorers began channeling the world's botanical riches back to London. From Kew, many plants were acclimatized and disseminated throughout the empire and the rest of the world. Kew-trained botanists founded the rubber industry and were the first to cultivate the tree from which we derive quinine, which until recently was our only ally against malaria.

Kew's crowning glory was, and perhaps still is, the Palm House. Constructed of iron and glass only a few years before the Crystal Palace that dominated the Great Exhibition of 1851, the Palm House's vast arches reminded many of Gothic cathedrals. The first palms established there in 1848 may have been brought back by Captain Bligh, whose notorious *Bounty* expedition was in Tahiti to transport breadfruit trees. Although at first it proved difficult to maintain the winter temperatures certain tropicals required, nowadays modern heating systems encourage even the African baobab and the coconut to flourish.

Since its founding, Kew has been supported as much by women as by men, from the first noble patroness to Victorian artist Marianne North, whose 832 plant paintings still reside there. But the gardeners had always been male. However, late-nineteenth-century England witnessed significant social changes, and finally the board of directors at Kew decided to bring their institution in tune with the times. On January 23, 1896, the *Daily Telegraph* reported, "A decided step toward the equalisation of the sexes has been taken by the director of Kew Gardens, who, as an experiment, has engaged two young ladies as gardeners. . . ." Certain old-timers were not thrilled. Then someone decided that the shock to masculine sensibilities would be cushioned if the uppity young women were to dress as boys. Therefore they worked the grounds in trousers and jackets. The director of Kew might have been forward-thinking, but there were limits.

See also Padua garden, 7/7.

----

24 JANUARY 1963

The Playboy Bunny

Many corporations employ animals as their mascots in order to capitalize upon a creature's established reputation or symbolism. When color was a wonderful new aspect of television, NBC chose as its logo the peacock, a bird famous for its brilliant plumage. An interstate bus line wisely chose as its emblem the famously fleet greyhound, over such unaerodynamic alternatives as, say, the Pekingese. Pocket Books chose a kangaroo as colophon to communicate to readers that its handy paperbacks were pocket-size.

Other companies' choices of animal mascot are more difficult to decipher. Take, for example, the Playboy rabbit. Famous mostly for timidity and fecundity, rabbits would seem to offer little positive cachet to a business trying to establish a debonair identity. In fact, when twenty-seven-year-old Hugh Hefner prepared to launch his own magazine in Chicago in the early 1950s, his tentative title was *Stag Party*. The first issue, with its notorious Marilyn Monroe calendar-pose centerfold, was almost ready for the printers when Hefner received a complaint about his title from lawyers representing a men's magazine called *Stag.* Last-minute brainstorming resulted in the new title *Playboy.* The fledgling magazine's art director hurriedly drew a logo—the now-famous rabbit.

The first issue of *Playboy* hit newsstands in 1953. Like his real counterparts, the corporate rabbit popped up unexpectedly here and there. The early smoking-jacket-attired version, lounging around his bachelor pad, bears an amusing resemblance to one of the ancient Chinese guardian spirits of the day and night. The figure called a *mao* watched over the period from 5:00 to 7:00 A.M. As portrayed in 2,000-year-old tiles, a *mao* wears a kimono and has the head of a rabbit. He is even in profile, with his ears, although shorter, at the same angle as Playboy's logo. Someday the coincidence will be attributed to aliens traveling back in time with copies of men's magazines.

Gradually, with the magazine's success, Hefner and his staff expanded into other venues. The first Playboy Club opened in 1960. Presumably inspired by the rabbit logo, the girlfriend of a staffer suggested that the waitresses in the new club dress as bunnies. Hefner refused, reportedly because he considered the rabbit a male symbol. But the girlfriend insisted reasonably that the rest of the world didn't assign rabbits a lone gender. Finally, Hefner okayed a mock-up of the first costume, which turned out to resemble a one-piece bathing suit plus rabbit ears and a fluffy little tail. At first the bunnies didn't wear the trademark collar, bow tie, and cuffs; a club-goer suggested those un-rabbity additions.

If it is possible to imagine anything more ridiculous than a Playboy bunny, it might be her counterpart had *Stag Party* remained the magazine's title. Probably she would have been called a "doe," and the same view of nature that thought of rabbits as particularly male might have approved antlers—strictly a buck's adornment—in place of rabbit ears. However, the choice of white-tailed deer would have permitted an even bigger and fluffier tail.

Understandably, many observers regarded the dressing up of women in rabbit costumes for the titillation of tired businessmen as a giant hop backward for feminism. A young reporter for the *New York Times* named Gloria Steinem went undercover as one of these leporine attendants. Her series of articles about the tribulations of pretending to be a human-rabbit hybrid began appearing in the *Times* on January 24, 1963.

Chinese New Year

As a consequence of the revolution the previous October, the year 1912 was a momentous one in China. The forced abdication of the boy emperor Xuantong ended the 267-year reign of the Qing (Manchu) Dynasty, and thus closed 2,000 years of imperial rule. China was declared a republic. Revolutionary changes that year included trial by jury and greater freedom for women.

Equally momentous was the establishment of a completely new calendar. The old one, like most calendars, was inadequately aligned with reality. It dated all the way back to the cultural and educational reforms of the Han Dynasty, which governed China from the third century B.C. to the third century

A.D. In 1912 China officially adopted the Gregorian calendar, which had been in use in much of the West since astronomers under the auspices of Pope Gregory XIII reformed the old Julian calendar in 1582. The Julian in turn was named for Julius Caesar, whose calendar reforms in the Roman Empire were roughly contemporaneous with the Han Dynasty's in China.

In spite of the adoption of a Western calendar, celebrations and traditions were still tied to the old one. Most Chinese continued to regard the New Year, for example, as coming at its old time, and celebrated accordingly. Many still do. What is called Chinese New Year falls on the first new moon between January 21 and February 19. In the old calendar, the year had 354 days, grouped in 12 lunar months, half with 29 days and half with 30. An awkward side effect of the discrepancy between nature and the Chinese calendar was the need to add a 13th month every 2½ years. The lesser discrepancy in the Gregorian requires the insertion of only an extra day every 4 years—Leap Day, February 29. Actually, measuring a year as 365¼ days long creates an annual surplus of over 11 minutes, which requires that 3 leap days in every 400 years should be suppressed.

In the Chinese calendar, years are grouped in twelve-year cycles. Each year of the cycle is named after an animal in the Chinese zodiac—rat, ox, tiger, hare, dragon, serpent, horse, ram, monkey, rooster, dog, and pig. The years fall in that order; the succession isn't random. According to tradition, the order of the animals in the cycle was determined by a cross-country race. The rat came in first, the ox second, and so on through the pig, which came in last. After the Year of the Pig comes another Year of the Rat, as the cycle begins anew. Al Stewart's famous rock song, "The Year of the Cat," employs an animal conspicuously absent from the Chinese cycle. In the informal Western hierarchy of animals, "The Year of the Rat" would not have made quite the same impression.

Chinese New Year celebrations frequently include children dressed as the twelve zodiacal animals. A prominent feature of the celebrations, whether or not it is the symbolic animal of that year, is the dragon. Generally regarded as a beneficent creature in Eastern folklore and mythology, as opposed to its evil, destructive reputation in the West, the dragon was one of the four Divine Creatures, along with the Phoenix, Tortoise, and Unicorn. As such it is the perfect creature to help optimistically usher in a new year.

See also the Gregorian calendar, 10/4.

---

26 JANUARY 1787

"A Much More Respectable Bird"

The bald eagle has been the symbol of the United States for so long that it is difficult to imagine another bird filling its role. To this day, the symbolic value of *Haliaeetus leucocephalus* is so cherished that some appeals for its preservation dwell upon its importance as a national emblem rather than its role in nature. In light of the eagle's current status, it is amusing to remember that its appointment was not unopposed. Benjamin Franklin disliked the eagle and nominated a dramatically different bird. On January 26, 1787, he wrote to his daughter:

> I wish the Bald Eagle had not been chosen as the Representative of our Country; he is a Bird of bad moral Character; like those among Men who live by Sharping and Robbing, he is generally poor, and often very lousy. The Turkey is a much more respectable Bird, and withal a true original Native of America.

Franklin's denunciation of the eagle was no sillier than other people's claims for its nobility. Both attitudes reflect the imposition of human values upon a natural world otherwise devoid of such judgments. However, there is no denying that Franklin's description of its habits was accurate. The majority of the bald eagle's diet consists of fish, and although it can catch them when circumstances demand such exertion, it prefers to find them dead upon the shore or steal from that much better fisherman, the osprey. It will also dine upon any other carrion that comes its way, but when necessary eats waterfowl, rodents, and even the occasional larger animal. As for being lousy, probably the bald eagle is no more infested with lice than any other bird, including the turkey.

Scattered all over the world, the 200-odd members of the vast family of Accipitridae count among their number birds as diverse as South Africa's eared vulture and Mexico's ornate hawk-eagle. Therefore the eagle in general is an ancient and well-established symbol. A sixth-century-A.D. mosaic from Constantinople portrays an eagle nobly battling an evil snake. One attends Zeus on Greek pottery from a thousand years earlier. The Roman consul Marius eliminated the legions' other badges—the wolf, horse, and Minotaur—and afterward Romans marched into war with eagle standards. Adolf Hitler addressed the crowds in Nuremberg from underneath the glaring Nazi eagle. It is interesting to note that, although the bald eagle's distinctive markings have made it an exclusively American symbol, its range includes Canada and even parts of Siberia.

On the other hand, numerous fossil forms dating as far back as the Oligocene testify to the American genesis of the turkey. There

If Benjamin Franklin had had his way, the turkey would have become the U.S. national bird and would now adorn coins, currency, and the presidential seal.

are two species, the lesser-known ocellated turkey of Central America, *Agriocharis ocellata,* and Franklin's darling, *Meleagris gallapavo,* which we call simply the wild turkey. It is, as he observed, "a true original Native of America." Hernán Cortés and his Spanish conquistadores found the Aztecs of Mexico domesticating turkeys early in the sixteenth century, and a few years later Coronado's men found them kept by the Pueblo Indians. The conquistadores brought turkeys back with them to Spain, whence they traveled quickly to the rest of Europe. When the first English settlers in the New World brought along domesticated turkeys, they were astonished to find the woods full of the wild variety.

"I suppose the opinion to be universal that the turkey is a native of America," Thomas Jefferson wrote in 1801. ". . . The book of every traveller, who came to America soon after its discovery, is full of accounts of the turkey and its abundance; and immediately after that discovery we find the turkey served up at the feasts of Europe, as their most extraordinary rarity." The turkey is still a favorite bird for feasts, especially at Christmas and Thanksgiving. Breeders have tinkered with the original stock, producing the smaller white turkey, which plucks more easily and grows a larger breast of succulent white meat. Having been denied the symbolic status that surrounds the eagle, the turkey has had to suffer nudging along more practical lines.

---

27 JANUARY 1987

Alligators in the Sewers

The encounter supposedly took place on East 123rd Street in Manhattan. Sixteen-year-old Salvatore Condulucci and his friends were shoveling the remains of a recent snowfall into an open manhole. Then, down in the darkness ten feet below the opening, something moved. Young Salvatore knelt and peered down into the murk, and was so surprised by what he saw he almost fell in. Something was breaking through the ice below.

The following day, the *New York Times* ran the story:

> **ALLIGATOR FOUND IN UPTOWN SEWER**
> Youths Shoveling Snow Into Manhole
> See the Animal Churning in Icy Water
> **SNARE IT AND DRAG IT OUT**
> Reptile Slain by Rescuers
> When It Gets Vicious—
> Whence It Came Is Mystery

The news story appeared in 1935. It may well be the original source for that perennial favorite piece of urban folklore, the alligators-in-the-sewers story. Oddly enough, there is one more bit of documentation. A former commissioner of sewers reported that the widespread stories of alligators under the city forced him to investigate. He claimed that he did, indeed, find alligators in the sewers in the 1930s. However, by 1937 he was declaring that his team had exterminated them.

The sheer unlikelihood of all this, from a biological point of view, doesn't curb the stories. How did the young reptiles survive their mad ride through the plumbing to the sewers? On what did they feed? How did the youngsters survive until they stumbled upon each other, mated, and begat a colony?

The story has achieved wide currency, along with a standard genesis for the problem: children bringing pets back from the Everglades and then releasing them. Thomas Pynchon incorporated the alligators-in-the-sewers scenario into his 1963 novel *V.,* adding that from long tenancy in that dark, subterranean world, they had become blind and albino. Those adaptations—the common fate of animals that adapt to caves—are part of the folklore. Many people claim that marijuana also thrives in the sewers, the result of millions of kilograms flushed down toilets during police raids. Like the alligators, the marijuana is said to be pale but hearty.

A 1973 children's book pictured the alligators disguising themselves as tourists and returning to Florida. By 1974, the story was so well known the *New Yorker* ran a parody in which they suggested that the "long, menacing objects" in New York City sewers were actually minisubs, "perhaps Bolivian." The next year, the legend was being analyzed in *Psychology Today.* But probably the best use of it was made by scriptwriter John Sayles, for Lewis Teague's 1980 film *Alligator.* The star not only survives flushing, but subsists on the corpses of animals killed in experiments and ingests enough hormones to grow to a monstrous size.

This sort of story is now called "urban folklore." On January 27, 1987, University of Utah folklorist Jan Brunvand began an urban folklore column in U.S. newspapers, introducing the term to thousands of people who were unaware that it was a field of study even if they collected "news of the weird" themselves. These stories, Brunvand said, never happen to anyone the storyteller knows, but to an FOAF, a Friend Of A Friend. Brunvand reported on many established pieces of folklore, from the Satanic-cult rumor that plagued Procter & Gamble in the early 1980s to the oft-repeated story of the ghostly hitchhiker. Many of his stories are about animals—a hairless dog bought on a Mexican vacation that was actually a rat, for example, or the Doberman that turns out to be choking on the fingers of a burglar who was locked in a closet. But none of his stories is better known than the classic tale of the alligators in the sewers.

---

28 JANUARY 1852

Animals in Fables

Some historians speculate that there was no such person as Aesop, that the later Greeks invented him as a source for already popular moralistic tales. However, the Greek historian Herodotus describes Aesop as a sixth-century-B.C. slave who once belonged to a man named Iadmon on the island of Samos. Legend has him, freed, meeting a violent death at Delphi while on a mission from King Croesus.

In the late 1800s, Brer Bear and Brer Rabbit joined a long line of animal characters that populated fables for our amusement and moral instruction.

Whether he lived or not, there is no denying that, just as practically every unsigned *ruba'i* in Persia was attributed to Omar Khayyám, so did every instructive Greek fable get filed under "Aesop."

Apparently the stories were originally passed on by word of mouth. Typically, Aesop's characters are animals, anthropomorphic stereotypes behaving with human motives. For those who can't distill a dramatization into a precept on their own, a moral at the end sums up the meaning. A well-known example is the story of the fox that couldn't reach a bunch of grapes and announced in disgust that they were probably sour anyway. That earns the moral "Any fool can despise what he cannot get," nowadays encapsulated in the phrase "sour grapes."

G. K. Chesterton remarked that characters in Aesop behave like pieces in a game of chess. Foxes are wily and lions brave, pigeons foolish, crows vain. They are some of the earliest of the symbolic animals that in time would populate medieval bestiaries and, more recently, play such roles as the noble eagle in U.S. and German military symbolism. The clichés seem almost primordial. Lions, for example, have so long been famed for their royal courage that, in *The Wizard of Oz,* one lacking it amuses merely by contrast.

Aesop inspired the medieval "beast epic," starring such characters as that clever rogue, Reynard the Fox, who reappeared as Brer Fox in the Uncle Remus stories. One of the earliest books published by England's first printer, William Caxton, was Aesop's *Fables.* Jean de La Fontaine's elegant verse adaptations took seventeenth-century France by storm. In Marianne Moore's celebrated translation, La Fontaine says he sings when Aesop's wand animates his lyre. One of Gotthold Ephraim Lessing's numerous contributions to the Enlightenment in Germany was his 1759 translation of Aesop.

Henry David Thoreau understood the alloy of example and maxim that reinforces animal fables. On the twenty-eighth of January, 1852, he wrote in his journal, "The world have always loved best the fable with the moral. The children could read the fable alone, the grown-up read both. . . . Cut off from Pilpay and Æsop the moral alone at the bottom, would that content you?" Pilpay, or Bidpai, wrote or collected Indian fables at least 1,500 years ago. In a similar vein was the *Gesta Romanorum* (Deeds of the Romans), which inculcated moral laws in the Middle Ages.

Aesop himself understood the vitality of his method and dramatized it in a fable about fables. Supposedly the Greek orator Demades was trying to hold the attention of a crowd, but his discourse was too abstract and they remained talkative. Finally, in desperation, he began again: "Ceres one day journeyed in company with a swallow and an eel." Demades paused. Everyone was listening.

"There Comes Poe with His Raven"

In the *Odyssey,* to alarm the suitors besieging Telemachus, Zeus sends two eagles tumbling across the sky. The man who is "keenest among the old at reading birdflight into accurate speech" tries to interpret the omen. A doubter scoffs:

> *Old man . . .*
> *Bird life aplenty is found in the sunny air,*
> *not all of it significant.*

By the time of Homer, bird life had long been considered significant. A subspecies of prediction called augury involved, along with divination from the entrails of sacrificial animals, prophesying from bird flight. Egyptian mythology embodied birds' importance by supplying them with human heads. The hieroglyph for birds corresponded to that of *Ba,* the soul, which flew away from the body after death. In heaven, Mohammed found the branches of the Tree of Life filled with beautiful and melodious birds—the souls of the faithful. Medieval alchemists thought augury a subtle language, depending sometimes on such details as whether the birds were swooping or soaring.

Understandably, such ready symbols have been popular in literature. Poetry alone includes Keats's nightingale, Shelley's skylark, and Coleridge's albatross. And on January 29, 1845, in a single long column on the back page of the *New York Evening Mirror,* Edgar Allan Poe added his contribution to the poetic aviary:

> *Once upon a midnight dreary, while I pondered, weak and weary,*
> *Over many a quaint and curious volume of forgotten lore . . .*

Such a dramatic and memorable work as "The Raven" invited parody. Shortly after its publication there appeared "The Turkey," "The Mammoth Squash," and even a version in which a temperance-minded owl repeatedly declines the offer of a drink with "Nevermore!" Poe's raven is still well enough known to have been parodied on a Halloween episode of the TV series *The Simpsons.*

Poe had been influenced by an earlier literary raven—Grip, companion to the title character in Charles Dickens's *Barnaby Rudge.* But *Corvus corvax* became Poe's personal totem. He was caricatured as a raven, even introduced as The Raven. Three years after the bird brought Poe his long-awaited fame, James Russell Lowell wrote:

There comes Poe with his raven like Barnaby Rudge,
Three-fifths of him genius and two-fifths sheer fudge.

Poe said the bird represented "Mournful and Never-ending Remembrance." He assigned his own meaning, but by choosing a raven over, say, a rufous-sided towhee, he was capitalizing upon millennia of symbolism. Ravens have a dark history. Like wolves, they were familiars of primitive gods of the dead. The first bird Noah sent out to reconnoiter after the Flood was a raven, but unlike its successor the pure-hearted dove, it failed. Imitating human speech, ravens symbolize prophecy: nature revealing its secrets. But their color made the prophecies baleful. Thomas Browne called ravens "ominous appearers."

Only now and then did ravens not play the villain. At God's request, they brought Elijah food in the wilderness. And when Odin's two ravens, Hugin (Thought) and Munin (Memory), returned to Valhalla, they perched on the old god's shoulder, like Poe's raven on the bust of Pallas, and told him what they had seen in the wide and wondrous earth.

---

30 JANUARY 1968

Planet of the Apes

When French novelist Pierre Boulle published *Planet of the Apes* in the United States in 1963, one reviewer said that it was descended from Swift and Verne. Jonathan Swift's literary genes are everywhere apparent, but the book's other ancestor is Voltaire. The absurd premise, heavy-handed moralizing, and coincidences all bear a family resemblance to *Candide*. Jules Verne was frequently humorous but seldom satirical, and he would have dismissed the unscientific cheek of Boulle, as he did the same tendency in H. G. Wells.

In the novel, three French astronauts land on a faraway planet and, because of its resemblance to Earth, christen it Soror, Latin for "sister." Here, apes run the world and humans are animals. The apes drive cars, fly planes, drink in nightclubs, and like names that begin with the letter *Z*. Males smoke pipes and run things; females blush and powder their simian noses. Tentatively reaching into outer space, the apes recently sent up a human in a satellite, but had to destroy the poor creature because they couldn't bring back the capsule. Most of Soror's flora and fauna are as obviously terrestrial as apes themselves, since Boulle's idea of an alien is a three-humped camel. This fable is so far removed from the aims of a realistic novel that one can't even scoff at evolution on another planet so strictly paralleling Earth's, the easy way out exploited ad nauseum by the scriptwriters of *Star Trek.*

Like Lemuel Gulliver, who is mistaken by the Houyhnhnms for one of the human Yahoos, the narrator (naturally named Ulysse) is captured with these mute human natives. The apes take him to the simian Institute for Advanced Biological Study, where a chimpanzee named Zira becomes his mentor. Boulle easily subverted human notions about evolution. Zira explains why, on Soror, humans have

The three kinds of apes that rule the postapocalyptic Earth of Planet of the Apes. *Chimpanzees are thinkers, orangutans administrators, and gorillas that essential Hollywood character—thugs.* Courtesy of Ronald V. Borst / Hollywood Movie Posters

remained animals. Merely bipedal and thus trapped on the ground, humans never developed a truly three-dimensional view of the universe. Thanks to being handicapped with only two stubby-fingered hands rather than the four nimble ones apes enjoy, humans were unable to use tools with any great dexterity. Apes, however, became quite handy. "Achievement followed," Zira says, "and it is thus we have raised ourselves to the level of wisdom."

In the 1968 film version of *Planet of the Apes,* three American astronauts *think* they have landed on another planet, but it turns out to be Earth in the future. The *New York Times* reviewer previewed the film on January 30, the day before its Hollywood premiere. He observed that, although the apes' makeup was convincing, the humans seemed like "Neanderthal flower children." The film is indeed very much of its era, with Charlton Heston at one point warning a teenage chimpanzee to never trust anyone over thirty. These apes solemnly intone such witticisms as "I never met an ape I didn't like" and "The proper study of apes is apes." Although we glimpse the Earthmen's naked posteriors, the other humans are clothed, which greatly reduces our perception of them as animals. And the apes' habitations—something between Neolithic and Art Nouveau—don't help the image of them as the dominant species, either. However, the film preserves Boulle's satirical point, which is that the planet of the apes looks familiar because it is our own.

Our Cousin in Space

Chimpanzees were enlisted in the space race from the first. The Soviet Union launched Earth's first artificial satellite, *Sputnik 1,* in 1957, the same year the United States optimistically began the Spacechimp Program. To predict the strains on humans under similar conditions, scientists started forty chimpanzees on a routine of intensive training. They flew. They spun in a centrifuge. They underwent simulated weightlessness. Several instrument panels yielded varying results depending upon how they were manipulated by the apes. In case patriotism and fame were not motive enough, wires in the feet of the space suit administered supposedly "mild" electric shocks when the subject performed unsatisfactorily.

There were precedents. As far back as 1783, the Montgolfier brothers sent animals up in balloons before risking the celestial atmosphere themselves. Numerous animals had already participated in the first few years of the Soviet-U.S. space race, primarily mice and rats. Two dogs died when a Soviet rocket burned.

How would chimps—and, by implication, humans—respond to the prolonged immobility required during space flight? One chimp was tested in flight simulation, in motionless solitary confinement, for fourteen days. He had already received almost 1,100 hours of training, but only 170-odd of that had been in simulated flight. After two weeks, he actually performed his tasks more efficiently than before, and within a day or so he regained his land legs. These tests implied that humans would do as well, but they also emphasized the intelligence of chimpanzees. This was news to many people. Jane Goodall had yet to go to Gombe, and this was before chimps learned sign language and long before their DNA turned out to be almost identical with our own.

The United States joined the Soviets in space on the last day of January 1958, with *Explorer I.* Exactly three years later, prior to risking the lives of human astronauts, the United States sent into space a Mercury-Redstone capsule containing a chimpanzee. His name was Ham. He was three years old and weighed 37½ pounds. A television camera watched his every move during the sixteen-minute flight, in which he went 155 miles into the sky at speeds of up to 5,000 miles per hour. After splashdown, Ham bobbed in the ocean for two hours, in a capsule that had begun to leak, before a Navy ship picked him up. Ham had proven that it really could be done, which suggested that humans too would survive ascent and descent. He was rewarded not with a ticker-tape parade but with lettuce, fruit, and handshakes all around. It was January 31, 1961.

Ham lived for many years after his moment of triumph. Sad to say, he did not retire in comfort. He went on to a lonely life in a cage at the National Zoo in Washington, D.C. Finally, in 1981, he was placed in the company of other chimpanzees at a North Carolina zoo. The pioneer astronaut died two years later.

See also the Montgolfiers' balloon, 9/19; and dogs in space, 11/3.

"As Remorseless as Nature"

"On February the First, 1887, the *Lady Vain* was lost by collision with a derelict when about the latitude 1° S. and longitude 107° W." With that, H. G. Wells began his most daring novel, *The Island of Dr. Moreau* (1896). Fresh from *The Time Machine* and not yet thirty years old, Wells was already a controversial author. Not everyone was thrilled with his new book. Mr. Wells, the *Times* suggested, was seeking ever more sensational topics. No, the *Guardian* editorialized, *Moreau* was worse than merely sensational; Wells seemed to be trying "to parody the work of the Creator of the human race, and cast contempt upon the dealings of God with his creatures."

After *Lady Vain* goes down, a freighter picks up survivor Edward Prendick, then abandons him near an uncharted island. The disquieting Dr. Moreau and his assistant rescue him. Moreau's crew are an eerie lot, long-bodied, tall, swathed in bandagelike clothing, their thighs "curiously twisted." When he learns that Prendick (like Wells himself) studied with the distinguished biologist T. H. Huxley, Moreau says, "As it happens, we are biologists here. This is a biological station—of a sort."

Prendick soon learns what is behind that masterpiece of understatement. Near his locked room, he hears the agonized screams of a puma that had been aboard the freighter. Soon he recalls old newspaper stories about "The Moreau Horrors," arcane work on blood transfusion and "morbid growths." Moreau is a vivisectionist, whose scandalous experiments on living animals led to his departure from England. Here on this secluded island, he continues his work. Finally he explains to Prendick: "These creatures you have seen are animals carven and wrought into new shapes." To Prendick's outrage, he replies, "The study of Nature makes a man at last as remorseless as Nature."

Moreau teaches his Beast-Folk a primitive moral code to try to control them. Prendick finds them chanting rules reminiscent of Kipling's Law of the Jungle: "Not to go on all-Fours; *that* is the Law. Are we not Men? Not to suck up Drink . . . eat Flesh or Fish . . . claw Bark of Trees. . . ." And then the warnings: "*His* is the House of Pain . . . the Hand that makes . . . the Hand that wounds. . . ." Still the creations regress. Animal traits slowly reappear. "Each time I dip a living creature into the bath of burning pain," Moreau complains, "I say: this time I will burn out all the animal, this time I will make a rational creature of my own."

In this scene from Island of Lost Souls, *the 1932 film of Wells's most controversial novel, mad vivisectionist Charles Laughton barely keeps at bay the not-quite-human results of his experiments on animals.* Courtesy of Ronald V. Borst / Hollywood Movie Posters

Finally, Wells makes his implications explicit. "A strange persuasion came upon me," Prendick says, "that, save for the grossness of the line, the grotesqueness of the forms, I had here before me the whole balance of human life in miniature, the whole interplay of instinct, reason, and fate, in its simplest form." Back in England, like Gulliver after living among the Yahoos of Houyhnhnm-land, Prendick can't adjust to human society. He sees people as merely "animals half-wrought into the outward image of human souls."

See also Lewis Carroll on vivisection, 2/12.

---

2 FEBRUARY

Groundhog Day

"Last Tuesday, the 2nd . . . was Candlemas day," Pennsylvania shopkeeper James Morris noted in his diary in February 1841, "the day on which, according to the Germans, the Groundhog peeps out of his winter quarters and if he sees his shadow he pops back for another six weeks nap, but if the day be cloudy he remains out, as the weather is to be moderate."

Variations on a rhyme about this superstition appear in many countries:

> *If Candlemas is fair and clear,*
> *There'll be two winters in the year.*

Candlemas (candle-mass) honors the traditional Hebrew purification ritual that, according to the second chapter of Luke, Mary underwent forty days after the birth of Jesus. Candles play an important symbolic role because of the words of Simeon, an old man in the temple who predicted the infant would be "a light to lighten the Gentiles." The Hebrews adapted many of their holy days to the dates of others they wished to replace. The timing of Candlemas may have grown from the torchlight processions accompanying the Roman festival of Ceres on the first day of February.

Nor were the Pennsylvania Germans the first to respect the meteorological expertise of animals emerging from hibernation. The Celtic festival of Imbolc was held on February 1. It survives as Ireland's Saint Bridget's Day, on which the hedgehog is supposedly as shadow-conscious as his American cousin. In Germany and England, the badger has the job. There is evidence that the oracle was originally the bear, which is honored in many cultures as a harbinger of spring, but declining numbers led to its replacement by other animals known for their winter sleep. In the Americas, the Ute, Crow, Blackfoot, and Kutenai all had versions of a bear dance to welcome the spring.

Whichever animal is observed, its emergence is of course a result, not a cause, of seasonal change. There are two main kinds of hibernators. Some remain dormant for extended periods of time and, with metabolic rates greatly reduced, subsist on stored body fat. Others awaken more frequently to dine on foods they brought indoors for the winter. The longer animals wait to emerge, the more hospitable the world to which they return, but the less time they will have to find a mate and produce offspring. Some animals emerge earlier than usual when winter ends early and sleep later when winter is long. People who lived closer to the earth were aware of these subtleties. They had to be.

Nowadays rituals that honor such observations seem merely quaint, because ceremonial acknowledgments of an awakening earth have been replaced by commercial publicity stunts. For example, every Groundhog Day, with great fanfare, locals pretend to consult Punxsutawney Phil, the groundhog named for his town in Pennsylvania. Actually, the current Phil spends most of his year in a nearby park, and is moved to an electrically heated burrow just for this event. Officials quietly decide in advance what will be announced as Phil's forecast on the second of February.

---

3 FEBRUARY 1579

"The Popular Errors"

During the early Renaissance in Europe, many of the most important naturalists were trained in medicine. The Italian Ulisse Aldrovandi; France's Pierre Belon; that amazing Swiss, Conrad Gesner; Guillaume Rondelet—all were professors of medicine or practicing physicians or both. Many other physicians also contributed to the natural history of their fellow creatures; most realized the two fields were one. One such scholar was the sixteenth-century French physician Laurent Joubert. Upon Rondelet's death, Joubert succeeded him as chancellor of the University of Montpellier. He was thirty-seven. He went on to become one of the most prestigious physicians of his time. Eventually, Catherine de Médicis called him to serve as her personal physician in Paris. All the while, he was gathering information on the ways of nature.

Joubert devoted much of his considerable energy and intelligence to planning a vast project entitled *Les Erreurs populaires* (The Popular Errors). He planned to include thirty books in the series, dealing with the entire spectrum of medical issues in his day—bloodletting, the role of wine in the diet, clean linen, the importance of rest during illness, the nature of various complaints. In the first volume, which appeared in 1578, Joubert denounced the sloppy thinking and barbaric practices of everyone from midwives to apothecaries. He presented his work as a long-overdue housecleaning in the medical field, and indeed fresh air blows through his charming writings.

Not surprisingly, this ambitious project was not completed when Joubert died in 1582. Three years earlier, however, he had published *La Seconde partie des erreurs populaires.* A dedicatory letter begging the approval of a patron is dated February 3, 1579. Under the original plan, this volume would have been devoted to Joubert's theories on what constituted the best regimen for preserving health, which would have included sections on clothing and maintaining one's environment. Since he had only a short time to live, it is fortunate that Joubert chose instead to present in his second book a great stew of bite-size pieces from the other proposed volumes.

The chapter titles alone are irresistible: "Against those who complain of hot nights in summer and yet sleep on a feather mattress with the windows closed," "Whether or not oysters and truffles make a man more lusty in the veneral [*sic*] act," the rather terrifying "That bloodletting can be used on pregnant women, children, and the elderly," and one relevant even now, "Why it happens frequently that patients who receive the most care most often die."

One section includes a number of what Joubert regarded as popular errors, along with questions and problems sent to him by others. Some are rational ponderings of nature's enigmas: "How every poisonous animal carries its own antidote; and why, if the animal dies, so too does its venom. Why is it that animals procreated from different species, such as mules, are sterile? Why is it that dogs always have a cold nose? Why do birds speak rather than other animals? Do the other animals dream, as man does?" Other topics seem strikingly medieval: "Why does one's voice become rough from being seen first by a wolf? When one has the plague, one must not blow on one's soup; and it is better to speak more often to God than to men."

In his section on animals, Joubert analyzed the origins of the misconception that viper young eat their way out of their mother, and explained that, unlike many snakes, they are simply born alive. He cleared away another birth myth by explaining that bears do not come into the world unformed, to be licked into bearness by their mothers, but rather are simply born "covered with slime," which the mother cleans off. Through a foray into etymology, he explained away the misapprehension that beavers bite off their own testicles because they know people hunt them for that organ. And, in a lovely refutation of myths about the supposedly nonflammable salamander, Joubert proclaimed his credo: "Experience (which is mightier than all the authority of the wisest in the world) teaches us that none of this is to be believed." The Middle Ages were over.

The Chinese Earthquake Weathercock

China has suffered a huge number of earthquakes over the centuries, and the long-standing tradition of scientific observation there has ensured that they are recorded in detail. Long ago, the scientific-minded were pondering this recurring problem and wondering if anything could be done to save lives and prevent the chaos that followed a quake. Unfortunately, the enemy was the treacherous earth itself.

Earthquake studies is an ancient field in China, and early in the second century A.D. an exceptional man contributed to it. One translation of his name is Chang Hêng. He was a poet, scholar, mathematician, painter, and astronomer royal to the ruling Han court. He was also a mapmaker whose works are considered to have founded scientific cartography. And, apparently an energetic fellow, he spent his spare time inventing things. In 132, seven years before his death, Chang presented a new invention to the court. It consisted of a closed urn ringed with eight bronze dragons that held little bronze balls in their mouths. Below each dragon was an open-mouthed bronze toad looking up expectantly. Chang explained that the device was an "earthquake weathercock." When a tremor shook the ground, a ball would fall from a dragon's mouth and land in a toad's. The clanging impact of the ball would alert an attentive seismologist that an earthquake had occurred. Supposedly its epicenter would be in the direction opposite that of the dragon that had spat the ball. Records mention a central column in the contrivance, and scholars agree that in order to be sensitive to tremors the alarm mechanism must have been an inverted pendulum with a weight at the top. Tests of carefully built reconstructions have proven that the earthquake weathercock responds to tremors, although the direction of the quake is not always opposite the fallen ball.

"Nothing like this," a history of the time declares, "had ever been heard of since the earliest records began." Understandably, the court did not immediately order the manufacture of bronze seismoscopes. (A seismograph documents the intensity of a quake. A seismoscope records only its occurrence.) Skepticism reigned until Chang's invention proved its usefulness. The history explains: "On one occasion one of the dragons let fall a ball from its mouth though no perceptible shock could be felt." No one could understand why this had happened. Then, a few days later, a messenger arrived in the capital with news of an earthquake in the Lung-Hsi region. "Upon this, everyone admitted the mysterious power of the instrument. Thenceforward it became the duty of the officials of the Bureau of Astronomy and Calendar to record the directions from which earthquakes came."

In time, Chang's invention was forgotten and had to be rediscovered all over again. Current technology greatly surpasses his, but its aim remains the same—the forecasting of earthquakes in order to reduce loss of life. Its value was made apparent in 1969. That year, a major quake struck the Bo Hai Province of northeastern China. As a result, much of nearby Liaoning Province soon was equipped with quake monitors. In January of 1975, the Earthquake Research Bureau predicted a massive quake within a month or two. Soon Liaoning began to experience an array of strange phenomena. Snakes emerged prematurely from hibernation. Cows and pigs fought among themselves. Radon measurements jumped; levels of groundwater rose and then fell. Wells spouted water or dried up.

For the first three days of February, increasingly violent tremors shook the region. At 10:30 on the morning of February 4, the government began a large-scale evacuation of the city of Haicheng. Nine hours later, an earthquake measuring 7.3 on the Richter scale struck the region. The loss of life was many times smaller than it would have been had the quake struck without warning.

That was the first time an earthquake was successfully predicted. Chinese and other seismologists hope to learn how to forecast them on a regular basis. Nowadays scientists employ the highest of high technology to monitor the Earth's spasms, but, sadly, none of it is adorned with bronze dragons and frogs.

See also the San Francisco earthquake, 4/18.

---

5 FEBRUARY 1967

The Andromeda Strain

What will be the nature of the first extraterrestrial life form to visit Earth? Never mind what we might meet if rashly we go Out There; what unfriendly foreigner might come and knock on our own door? Both scientists and science fiction writers find this question intriguing, with results as diverse as the SETI (Search for Extra-Terrestrial Intelligence) program and James Arness as a bloodthirsty plant-being in the film *The Thing.* In 1969, little more than a decade after the United States entered the space race, novelist Michael Crichton published a novel featuring a different kind of alien life—a microorganism. The unseen invader was brought back to Earth aboard a satellite and in time dubbed "the Andromeda Strain."

The Scoop program placed seventeen satellites in orbit around the earth, to collect extraterrestrial organisms and retrieve them for study. *Scoop I* found nothing extraterrestrial; *II* and *III* incinerated upon reentry; *IV* and *V* came back with a harmless contaminant of human skin, which reminded NASA to strengthen sterilization procedures; *VI* returned with an unknown single-celled organism, which was benign except for temporarily incapacitating female chickens. Then NASA launched *Scoop VII.* "The exact date is classified but it is believed to be February 5, 1967." After malfunctioning, that satellite is brought back to Earth near an isolated Arizona town named Piedmont. The town doctor opens it with a chisel, and within hours all but two Piedmont inhabitants are dead. The government recovers *Scoop VII* and, at the underground Wildfire installation in Nevada, analyzes the unknown life form that it carried.

Apparently the bacteria originally came from Earth. The likeliest danger to earthly organisms, scientists had theorized, was not a creature from another galaxy but rather one from home. Bacteria that originated on Earth may have drifted away from the surface just after the planet came out of the cosmic oven, to float in the upper atmosphere while terrestrial creatures evolved immunities to those bacteria with which they were familiar. Upon its return, it would be as dangerous as the microorganism that killed the Martians in H. G. Wells's *War of the Worlds* (1898).

Crichton reversed the plot device Wells used in that prototype of the alien invasion story. Wells killed off his invading Martians with a terrestrial bug. Their slaughter of humans and abandonment of their own dead fellows unite to create disease conditions. At the end, the narrator finds them *"dead—slain by the putrefactive and disease bacteria against which their systems were unprepared . . . slain, after all man's devices had failed, by the humblest things that God, in his wisdom, has put upon this earth."*

Probably Wells had tongue firmly in cheek during those last phrases, but the result for the Martians was the same whether the bacteria was a last-minute divine cavalry charge or purest happenstance. Disease germs had battled humans since life began. "By the toll of a billion deaths man has bought his birthright of the earth, and," Wells's narrator confidently asserts, "it is his against all comers. . . ." Seventy-two years later, in *The Andromeda Strain,* Michael Crichton was not so certain.

For other alien invasions, see 3/23 and 11/1.

---

6 February 1682

"An Imaginary River"

The Mississippi River has managed to stir the imaginations of all sorts of people. T. S. Eliot described it as a strong brown god that city dwellers had almost forgotten. Later, he wrote to a St. Louis newspaper about his youth there: "I feel that there is something in having passed one's childhood beside the big river which is incommunicable to those who have not." Samuel Clemens agreed. He spent much of his life writing about his experiences along the river near his birthplace in Florida, Missouri. Nowadays Florida's favorite son is the man who is always associated with the river. Even his nom de plume he owed to the Mississippi. "Mark twain!" was the riverboat pilot's cry to announce a depth of two fathoms, which guaranteed safe passage.

The word "Mississippi" derives from the Chippewa *mici zibi,* "large river." Affectionate but respectful nicknames include the Father of Waters and Big Muddy. The river has earned them. From a trickle heading south from Lake Itasca in Minnesota to the broad delta at the Gulf of Mexico is a distance of 2,340 miles. The Mississippi is the largest river in North America, draining all or part of thirty-one states and two provinces of Canada, a total area of about 1,200,000 square miles. In *Life on the Mississippi,* Twain described the river's drainage basin more colorfully as being "as great as the combined areas of England, Wales, Scotland, Ireland, France, Spain, Portugal, Germany, Austria, Italy and Turkey." He always knew how to perk up a dry statistic.

The French explorer René-Robert Cavelier, sieur de La Salle, was one of many who rode the Mississippi River into history. In his lifetime he was a Jesuit, an ex-Jesuit, a fur trader, a prisoner of the Sioux, and ultimately France's viceroy of North America. On February 6, 1682, La Salle and his fifty Frenchmen and natives first encountered the Mississippi. Two centuries later, that old black-water magic touched the romantic imagination of American historian Francis Parkman, and he described La Salle's first view of the river: "The travelers resumed their journey . . . and soon reached the dark and inexorable river, so long the object of their search, rolling, like a destiny, through its realms of solitude and shade." La Salle reached the Gulf of Mexico in 1682. Without consulting the residents of the already established nations, he presumed to claim the entire Mississippi Basin for Louis XIV and named it Louisiana.

Almost three centuries after La Salle's voyage, an Englishman named Jonathan Raban wrote about the river, "It is called the Mississippi, but it is more an imaginary river than a real one." In his native England, Raban first read *The Adventures of Huckleberry Finn* at the age of seven. "I hugged the idea of the huge river to myself. I exulted in the freedom and solitude of being afloat on it in my imagination." Thirty years later, in September of 1979, Raban tried to match the reality against his dream. He piloted a sixteen-foot aluminum boat from Minneapolis to the gulf and documented the trip in his book *Old Glory: An American Voyage*.

After he had put many miles and days behind him, Raban stayed for a while in St. Louis, T. S. Eliot's hometown and Mark Twain's old turf. One day he went to a museum and discovered that he was now qualified to appraise the works of the frontier genre painter George Caleb Bingham—not as an art critic, but as a seasoned traveler on The River. Bingham had succumbed to the Mississippi's lure in the mid-1800s. His popular paintings such as *Raftsmen Playing Cards* and *Jolly Flatboatmen in Port* now spoke to Raban in a language he could understand: "He had exactly caught the way the current twitched and folded over on itself, the leaden sheen of the water and the ruffled lights of the wind on it." The next day, Raban went on down the river.

---

7 FEBRUARY 1868

The First Missing Link

The fine-grained and porous limestone of the Solnhofen region, along the Altmühl River of Bavaria, has been quarried since the Romans used it to tile their baths. In time, it was discovered to be the perfect stone for the printing medium known as lithography. Then, in 1861, the stone demonstrated yet another virtue. It had perfectly preserved a creature that died when the quarry was a lagoon in the Jurassic Period, at least 150 million years ago.

Workmen in the quarry discovered a marvelously detailed impression of a fossil feather. The German paleontologist Hermann von Meyer was naturally intrigued by the find and decided to watch the quarry for further developments. He didn't have long to wait. Soon workers turned up a full, wonderfully preserved skeleton of the creature, which turned out to be about the size of a pigeon. It had a long bony tail, four unfused fingers, and—most important—distinct feathers. Meyer named it *Archaeopteryx* (ancient wing) *lithographica* (of the printing stone).

News of the find reached Richard Owen, London's premier anatomist and fossil expert. Immediately he dispatched a lieutenant to acquire it, even paying the scandalous sum of £450 for the prize. However, Owen was an implacable opponent of Darwinian evolution, and he refused to consider the creature a transitional form. He identified it as an anomalous bird. Not so, cried fellow paleontologist John Evans, who noticed that the jaw was not like that of a bird and held several teeth. Its importance to Darwin and evolution, Evans insisted, "must be evident to all."

The timing was fortuitous. In 1859, Darwin had predicted in the *Origin of Species* the eventual discovery of a protobird. In January of 1863, a friend informed him of the discovery of *Archaeopteryx,* this "sort of mis-begotten-bird-creature." Darwin himself had remarked about the scarcity of fossils that "the crust of the earth is a vast museum, but the

An early reconstruction of Archaeopteryx, *which came to be regarded as the first "missing link."*

natural collections have been imperfectly made. . . ." Not only was this new creature immediately seen as a missing link, but its degree of preservation was almost unprecedented. "The fossil bird," Darwin sighed, "is a grand case for me."

On the evening of February 7, 1868, Thomas Huxley, "Darwin's bulldog," addressed the distinguished gathered members of the Royal Institution. He informed them without hesitation that those scientists who thought evolution correct—"and I am one of them," Huxley declared—were firmly convinced that all the existing groups of animals had descended from a common ancestor. He painted a picture of that ancient Jurassic lagoon populated with a creature now called *Archaeopteryx,* a species caught in the very act of evolving from a reptile into a bird. The talk was hugely successful and was reprinted in numerous magazines.

Since then, other transitional forms have appeared. Not long after *Archaeopteryx* burst onto the scene, an obviously aquatic, penguinlike skeleton turned up in Kansas. It was named *Hesperornis,* and many specimens have been unearthed since. As recently as 1987, paleontologists in Mongolia discovered another animal that seems to be a transitional form between extinct reptiles and living birds. *Mononykus* was a turkey-sized creature with numerous birdlike characteristics. These subsequent discoveries only furthered what *Archaeopteryx* began. There are now a half-dozen fossil specimens demonstrating the evolutionary significance of the ancient winged creature of the printing stone.

Mary Stuart's Dog

Mary Stuart, queen of the Scots, was executed on the eighth of February, 1587, by order of her cousin Elizabeth I. It took two strokes of the ax to kill her, three to completely sever her head. When one executioner held Mary's head by the hair for the crowd to see, he was left holding what turned out to be a wig, as her head rolled across the scaffold. Then, under Mary's floor-length skirts, the executioners found her tiny terrier, which had walked along, hidden at her feet. As Marie Antoinette's little dog would attend her imprisonment two hundred years later, Mary's had comforted her during her long stay in the Tower of London. Coax as the attendants might, the dog "could not be gotten forth but by force." It lay down between Mary's head and shoulders, became drenched in her blood, and was taken away to be cleaned.

Mary Stuart, queen of Scots, before she lost her head. Her dog may be under her dress.

Terriers had been in Britain far longer than the Stuarts and the Tudors. After Julius Caesar's legions invaded the island in 55 B.C., they saw dogs following prey into burrows. Hence "terrier," from the Latin *terra,* "earth." Several biographers describe Mary's dog as a Skye terrier. If so, it wasn't called that at the time. The Isle of Skye is in the Hebrides, off the northwest coast of Scotland. In the 1600s, a Spanish ship wrecked on the rocks nearby, and its survivors included dogs that mated with the local terriers and produced what is now the Skye terrier. Mary's could have been its immediate ancestor. They are thought to have changed little in the 400 years since. Probably around ten inches tall and weighing twenty-odd pounds, Mary's dog was small enough to accompany her through the last moments of her life, even after her nurses had been held back from the scaffold.

Dogs in general were popular in England at the time. An entire chapter is devoted to them in Holinshed's *Chronicles,* that vast compilation from which Shakespeare mined his historical plays. "There is no country that may . . . compare with ours," the author boasted, "in number, excellency, and diversity of dogs." So prized were they even by expatriates that settlers in Virginia in 1619 outlawed the sale to the natives of dogs "of the English race."

In Holinshed, dogs fall into categories: "such as rouse the beast, and continue the chase, or springeth the bird, and bewrayeth [reveal] her flight by pursuit." They turned spits, guarded homes, even pulled plows. Macbeth used the many kinds of dogs to symbolize the assortment of men. Varieties produced by such husbandry later served Darwin as evidence that species are not fixed and have been manipulated by nature as they have by humans.

Most breeds have a celebrated attribute—intelligence, affection, tenacity. Skye terriers are still famed for their devotion. In Edinburgh there is a monument to Greyfriars Bobby, a Skye who spent his last decade guarding his master's grave. Mary's dog, too, was with her until the end.

For another celebrated terrier, see 7/3.

The Creature from the Black Lagoon

One of the curious ideas of past ages was that the seas contained watery analogues to every plant and animal native to land. A couple of creatures included in that category were the bishop-fish and the monk-fish. Sixteenth-century Swiss naturalist Conrad Gesner included in his *Icones Animalium* an illustration of the entirely imaginary bishop-fish. It portrays an animal standing on two froglike legs, with its scaly pointed head resembling a bishop's miter and its amphibian arms raised in a pose of blessing. "In our time," French naturalist Pierre Belon reported at about the same time, "there was caught, after a great storm, a sea monster to which all those who saw it straightway gave the name of Monk, for it had the face of a man, albeit rude and ungracious, the head close-shaven and smooth. On its shoulders, as it were, a monk's hood, with two long pinnate fins for arms, and the end of the body terminating in a long tail."

One of Gesner's contemporaries, French diplomat and poet Guillaume du Bartas, went even further in his *Divine Weekes and Works,* but circled back around to the aquatic clergy:

> Seas have . . . Rams, Calfs, Horses, Hares, and Hogs,
> Wolves, Lions, Urchins, Elephants and Dogs,
> Yea, Men and Mayds; and (Which I more admire)
> The mytred Bishop and the cowled Fryer. . . .

Long after humans abandoned the idea that the sea harbored a wet version of all things terrestrial, *The Creature from the Black Lagoon* premiered in Hollywood on February 9, 1954. The *New York Times* described the Creature as "made up terrifyingly enough to make a Grand Banks fisherman take up tat-

The Creature from the Black Lagoon *offered yet another variation on the monster-falls-in-lust theme.* Courtesy of Ronald V. Borst / Hollywood Movie Posters

ting." Actually, the title character looks remarkably like an evolutionary descendant of the bishop-fish, although the characteristic miter has evolved to a more secular-looking skull.

The movie was filmed in 3-D, perhaps to compensate for the lack of depth in the script. After finding the cheesiest fossil in filmdom sticking out of a sandbank at eye level, a scientist returns to the Black Lagoon with a research party. Naturally, the shy Creature becomes enamored of the scantily clad female scientist. The film's advertising poster proclaimed breathlessly, "Centuries of Passion Pent Up in His Savage Heart!" Originally, scriptwriter Harry Essex was offended when asked to adapt a story for a film with the ridiculous title of *The Creature from the Black Lagoon.* Then he decided to add "the 'Beauty and the Beast' theme. The whole idea was to give the Creature a kind of humanity—all he wants is to love this girl, but everybody's chasing him!"

The Creature's amorous intent was firmly in the tradition of King Kong's devotion to Fay Wray, and of the many Hollywood aliens that lusted uncontrollably after buxom, screaming women. Apparently other planets send out only libidinous male monsters to explore the universe. In reality, probably neither giant gorillas, aliens, nor reptilian living fossils would be smitten with desire for us. They might well be unable to distinguish human gender, and would, because of all the commotion, regard our entire species as animals on par with a yapping chihuahua.

For other monster movies, see 3/3, 3/23, 6/15, 7/16, and 11/1.

---

10 February 1774

"Man Can Live Under Water"

The earliest record of an artificial apparatus for breathing underwater appears in Aristotle's pioneer work of zoology, *The Parts of Animals,* from the fourth century B.C. He compared the elephant's "lengthened nostril" to the "instruments for respiration, through which [divers] can draw air from above the water, and thus remain for a long time under the sea. . . ." Later references to such apparatuses show up in unpredictable places, including twelfth-century German ballads. Not surprisingly, Chinese pearl divers developed methods of carrying air with them underwater, but most of them involved capturing air within a hood. That procedure enabled divers to stay down longer than if they were merely holding their breath, but it wasn't enough. It seemed that only a connection with the surface could allow extended dives. Inventors tried many variations on that theme. On February 10, 1715, an Englishman named Andrew Becker filed a patent for what is considered the first practical diving suit. To demonstrate its virtues, he dived into the Thames wearing it. Then, in 1819, German inventor Augustus Siebe fashioned the prototype for today's "deep-sea" diver's outfit, with a tube leading to the air above.

In Jules Verne's novel *Twenty Thousand Leagues Under the Sea,* Captain Nemo explains the shortcomings of Siebe's method when he invites the narrator, Pierre Arronax, to walk with him on the bottom of the ocean. "You know as well as I do, Professor, that man can live under water, providing he carries with him a sufficient supply of breathable air. In submarine works, the workman, clad in an impervious dress, with his head in a metal helmet, receives air from above by means of forcing pumps and regulators."

"That is a diving apparatus," Arronax says.

"Just so, but under these conditions the man is not at liberty; he is attached to the pump which sends him air through an india-rubber tube, and if we were obliged to be thus held to the *Nautilus,* we could not go far." Working within the carefree world of science fiction, Verne was free to envision a way around Siebe's limitations. Nemo explains that he has perfected an apparatus that allows safe travel underwater without remaining tethered to an air supply. It is a reservoir of pressurized air, carried upon the back like a knapsack, which provides breathable air for up to ten hours.

Verne published *Twenty Thousand Leagues Under the Sea* in 1870. Three-quarters of a century later, the device that Jules Verne envisioned was a reality. In 1936, at Le Mourillon, near Toulon, a twenty-six-year-old Frenchman named Jacques Cousteau donned swimming goggles for the first time. "I was a regular Navy gunner, a good swimmer interested only in perfecting my crawl style. The sea was merely a salty obstacle that burned my eyes." Goggles had been a familiar diving tool for centuries, but they were new to Cousteau. "Sometimes we are lucky enough to know that our lives have been changed. . . . It happened to me at Le Mourillon on that summer's day, when my eyes were opened on the sea."

Goggle-diving and spear-fishing were quite the rage along the French coast. From his involvement in that sport Cousteau met another diver named Emile Gagnan. They learned to adapt to changing air pressures down to the depths that sponge, pearl, and coral divers had been reaching for countless generations. But this was not enough. These dives could last only as long as the divers could hold their breath. Cousteau and Gagnan began to experiment with ways of carrying air with them. Finally, together, they invented the Aqua-Lung (also called the self-contained underwater breathing apparatus, or scuba).

The first manufactured prototype was shipped to them in June of 1943. It was similar to what Verne had envisioned. "We found an assembly of three moderate-sized cylinders of compressed air, linked to an air regulator the size of an alarm clock. From the regulator there extended two tubes, joining on a mouthpiece. With this equipment harnessed to the back, a watertight glass mask over the eyes and nose, and rubber foot fins, we intended to make unencumbered flights in the depths of the sea." With the addition of a relatively lightweight rubberized suit and artificial fins, Cousteau had achieved considerably greater freedom than even Nemo had managed. Even though France was occupied by the Nazis at the time, Cousteau and Gagnan logged 500 Aqua-Lung-assisted dives that summer and began to realize that a whole alien universe was open for exploration.

---

11 FEBRUARY 1910

Cometomania

The story appeared on the front page of the *New York Times*. The headline shouted, "COMET'S POISONOUS TAIL," followed by the slightly more calm "Yerkes Observatory Finds Cyanogen in Spectrum of Halley's Comet." Harvard astronomers announced receipt of a telegram in which the director of Yerkes reported his frightening discovery. However, added the Harvard people cautiously, they had not themselves photographed and analyzed the comet's spectrum.

"Cyanogen is a very deadly poison," the reporter said breathlessly, "a grain of its potassium salt touched to the tongue being sufficient to cause instant death." Cyanogen is a colorless gas, a member of that deadly family that includes chlorine. With potassium it forms potassium cyanide, a white crystalline compound whose almondlike odor is familiar to mystery readers. "The fact that cyanogen is present in the comet has been communicated to Camille Flammarion and many other astronomers, and is causing much discussion as to the probable effect on the earth should it pass through the comet's tail."

Flammarion was a prominent astronomer known especially for his studies of the surface of Mars and solar fluctuations. This was not the first time he had foretold doom; his 1893 book predicting an encounter with a comet was actually entitled *La Fin du Monde*. Apparently without evidence, Flammarion expressed the cheery opinion that, should Earth pass through the tail of the comet, in the reporter's words, "the cyanogen gas would impregnate the atmosphere and possibly snuff out all life on the planet." Four days later, on the eleventh of February, 1910, the *Times* downplayed the story, pointing out that astronomers insisted that comet tails were "of such almost inconceivable tenuity" as to be not only harmless but unnoticeable. "Only to ignorance or superstition are they alarming."

Of course, before cyanogen, other matters alarmed the ignorant and superstitious. In the

In 1857, a French cartoonist expressed a fear that has recurred several times since, most recently in 1994 when a comet struck Jupiter.

first century A.D., the Roman philosopher Seneca wrote that if an unusual comet appeared, "everyone wants to know what it is and, ignoring the other celestial phenomena, asks about the newcomer, uncertain whether he ought to admire or fear it. For there is no lack of people who create terror and predict dire meanings." Several possible dire meanings are summarized in the wonderful title of a single book published in 1684: *Cometomania. A Discourse of Comets: Shewing their Original [sic], Substance, Place, Time, Magnitude, Motion, Number, Colour, Figure, Kinds, Names, and*—and here we get to the meat of the matter—*more especially, their Prognosticks, Significations, and Presages.* The title page goes on with informative seventeenth-century garrulity: *Being a brief Resolution of a Seasonal Query, viz. Whether the Apparition of Comets be the Sign of Approaching Evil?* Apparently that's always the question. By the way, the query was seasonal because Comet Halley had come through only two years before.

Halley reached its closest approach to the Sun, its perihelion, in April of 1910. King Edward VII of England died in May, and newspapers reported the status of the comet in conjunction with the accession of King George V, remembering Shakespeare's words in *Julius Caesar*:

> *When beggars die, there are no comets seen;*
> *The heavens themselves blaze forth the death of princes.*

See also Comet Halley, 4/8.

"A Hell for Animals"

"Among the inferior professors of medical knowledge," Samuel Johnson remarked, "is a race of wretches, whose lives are only varied by varieties of cruelty." He was referring to practitioners of vivisection, experimental surgery on a living animal. The term comes from Latin words meaning "alive" and "cutting." Some saw it as a research method essential to science; others, as thinly disguised torture. It was already an old practice when Johnson railed against it. Vesalius vivisected during the Renaissance. In the seventeenth century, English physician William Harvey demonstrated his discovery of blood circulation on live animals.

In response to vivisection and many other forms of violence against animals, concerned English citizens formed the Royal Society for the Prevention of Cruelty to Animals (RSPCA) in 1824. It grew steadily more influential with the rising tide of compassion that, especially in the late 1800s, began to erode millennia of casual cruelty. Antivivisection was the first animal rights movement to achieve popular appeal. Prominent among its exponents was an Oxford don named Charles Lutwidge Dodgson. Sometimes he wrote to editors under his own name—adding his title, "Mathematical Lecturer," when relevant—and sometimes under his famous pseudonym, Lewis Carroll.

On February 12, 1875, the *Pall Mall Gazette* published Dodgson's response to someone else's letter. It was entitled "Vivisection as a Sign of the Times." A conservative theologian and a scholar in the bloodless field of mathematics, Dodgson sarcastically described vivisection as "a fair specimen of that higher civilisation which a purely secular state education is to give us." Of course, Dodgson weighted the balance in his favor by dismissing all vivisection as mere Frankensteinian curiosity. But his rhetoric was powerful: "Is the anatomist, who can contemplate unmoved the agonies he is inflicting for no higher purpose than to gratify a scientific curiosity, or to illustrate some well-established truth, a being higher or lower, in the scale of humanity, than the ignorant boor whose very soul would sicken at the horrid sight?" A chapter of the RSPCA asked and received permission to reprint Dodgson's letter as a pamphlet.

Dodgson didn't merely write letters. He also contributed funds. When a friend recommended a home for lost dogs, Dodgson first queried the organization to ask whether those dogs that had to be killed were, as was sometimes the case, sent instead to vivisection laboratories. The answer was no, and he contributed.

Later that year, the editor of the *Gazette* rejected Dodgson's article "Some Popular Fallacies about Vivisection," claiming he had never heard of most of the supposed fallacies. To his diary, Dodgson complained that of the thirteen mistaken notions he examined in his article, he had found seven in the man's own publication. Dodgson's article appeared instead in the *Fortnightly Review,* signed again with his famous pseudonym. Closing his letter, he foresaw a future "when the man of science looking forth over a world which will then own no other sway than his, shall exult in the thought that he has made of this fair green earth, if not a heaven for man, at least a hell for animals."

See also H. G. Wells on vivisection, 2/1.

---

13 FEBRUARY 1570

"This Serpent Is Extremely Cold"

When he died on February 13, 1570, Italian sculptor and soldier Benvenuto Cellini left behind an autobiography. It was not published until 1728, but has since become a classic of its genre. Among Cellini's many vivid stories is one of his first glimpse of a fabled animal. When he was five years old, his father saw in a fireplace "a little creature like a lizard, which was sporting in the core of the intensest coals." The elder Cellini sent for Benvenuto, pointed out the salamander, and boxed his son's ears. To the child's wailing he responded, "My dear little boy, I am not striking you for any wrong you have done, but only to make you remember that that lizard which you see in the fire is a salamander, a creature which has never been seen before by anyone of whom we have credible information." Apparently the abusive mnemonic worked.

Most information about salamanders, including Cellini's, has not been credible. Aristotle reported the allegation that salamanders put out fires by walking through them. Later, Pliny the Elder placed one in a fire to observe its quenching ability—and saved its ash for medications. Nonetheless, contrary to his own findings, he described the salamander as "a sort of lizard which seeks the hottest fire to breed in, but quenches it with the extreme frigidity of its body." Jonathan Swift condensed this:

> *Further, we are by Pliny told*
> *This serpent is extremely cold.*

Dioscorides, Pliny's contemporary and author of *De materia medica,* cast numerous salamanders into flames. They burned. But even that didn't rehabilitate the poor creature's reputation. Salamanders, the credulous declared, were so poisonous that if one even twined around the trunk of a tree, the fruit would become infected with its venom. Supposedly, 4,000 of Alexander the Great's men and 2,000 horses died when they drank from a stream into which a salamander had fallen. Medieval bestiaries used the salamander to symbolize unquenchable faith, like that which kept Shadrach, Meshach, and Abednego nonflammable in Nebuchadnezzar's furnace. In the "theory of elementals" by Cellini's contemporary Paracelsus, sylphs were associated with air, Nereids with water, gnomes with earth, and salamanders with fire.

One of the stories about the legendary medieval Christian king Prester John, who lived in the faraway land of Asia or Africa, claimed that his royal raiment was fireproof. Actually, the garments were more real than the man. Someone had discovered what was called "wool of salamander." A grayish mineral occurring in long threadlike filaments that can be woven into cloth, it was named from the Greek word for inextinguishable: *asbestos.* Prester John's salamanders, which lived in fire, built cocoons like silkworms, the threads of which were unwound and spun into a cloth. Arabs began to report fireproof clothes brought home by travelers. Marco Polo declared that "the true salamander is an incombustible substance found in the mountains of Tartary."

It is possible to trace the origins of this fabled skill. Salamanders do exude a milky fluid that can be poisonous to predators, although not to humans. They also hibernate in the hollows of fallen trees or standing deadwood. Probably their bedrooms frequently have become firewood. Thus the inhabitants would awaken in a fire and try to flee, with astonished humans peering at them, like the Cellini family, from beyond the flames.

---

14 FEBRUARY

Valentine's Day

The natural history of Valentine's Day can be found fossilized in literature. For centuries, it was an accepted fact of nature that birds chose their mates on February 14. Chaucer assumed it in *The Parlement of Foules:* "For this was Seynt Valentyne's day. / When every foul cometh ther to choose his mate." Never bothered by anachronisms, in *A Midsummer Night's Dream* Shakespeare allowed an ancient Greek to refer to the holiday thousands of years before it was established. Spying the quartet of sleeping lovers, Theseus jokes, "Saint Valentine is past. Begin these wood-birds but to couple now?"

Two love-preoccupied English poets dwelled at length upon the supposedly romantic birds. Robert Herrick included a complaint:

> Oft have I heard both youths and virgins say,
> Birds chuse their mates, and couple too, this day,
> But by their flight I never can divine
> When I shall couple with my Valentine.

Herrick's contemporary, John Donne, addressed the saint himself:

> Hail, Bishop Valentine! whose day this is;
> All the air is thy diocese,
> And all the chirping choristers
> And other birds are thy parishioners . . .

It's ironic that romantic love and the mating of birds had become linked with a Christian martyr. Two saints in the martyrology were supposedly killed under Claudius II, who ruled the Roman Empire in the third century. One was a physician and priest in Rome, the other a bishop at nearby Terni. Either both were named Valentine or they were the same person. Beheaded on 14 February, in 269 or 270, one of them was buried on that celebrated Roman road, the Flaminian Way. Later, a church was built on the site.

Usually when they came to power, Christians adapted existing holidays to their own purposes. In 494, the church converted that licentious Roman fertility festival, the Lupercalia, into the Feast of Purification of the Virgin Mary. Evidently, some of its associations also attached themselves to the Christian Candlemas; others adhered to Saint Valentine's Day, observed on what had been Lupercalia Eve. The trail is faint, but as usual the absence of facts didn't inhibit the mythmakers. One story solemnly claims that the ill-fated Valentine fell in love with his jailer's daughter and left a note for her signed, "From your Valentine." Another says he contributed anonymously to the dowries of poor girls to ensure their marriages. However the association originated, Valentine's Day has been celebrated as a lover's festival since at least the fourteenth century.

The notion that birds mate on a certain day is easier to understand. Frequently natural events are assigned unjustifiably precise dates. Swallows do not always return to Capistrano on the nineteenth of March, and groundhogs do not always emerge from their burrows on the second of February. At a time when human society and nature were inextricably entwined, when nature seemed only a mirror in which we could see ourselves, it must have seemed reasonable that the patron saint of romance would watch over lovers of any species.

For other holidays, see 2/2, 3/17, 3/24, 5/1, 10/31, and 12/25.

The Goat Song of
Julius Caesar

Early in Shakespeare's *Julius Caesar,* just before a soothsayer warns him to beware the Ides of March, Caesar instructs Mark Antony:

> *Forget not in your speed, Antonius,*
> *To touch Calphurnia; for our elders say*
> *The barren, touched in this holy chase,*
> *Shake off their sterile curse.*

Caesar's third wife, Calpurnia (Calphurnia, in the play), had borne him no heir, and he hoped she would become fertile at the annual festival of the Lupercal. It was 15 February 44 B.C.

Lupercus is thought to have been a fertility god worshiped in the Lupercal, the cave on the Palatine where, tradition claimed, a she-wolf had suckled Rome's legendary founders, Romulus and Remus. As was customary in Roman ritual, an animal was sacrificed, usually that notoriously ruttish beast, the goat. For barren Roman wives, the oracle of Juno prescribed sexual intercourse with goats, but in Caesar's time childless women—and sometimes men—were merely flailed with goatskin thongs. Caesar was asking Antony, who was to participate in the ritual, to flail his wife.

Hardy, almost omnivorous, producing milk and flesh and hide, goats were an important domestic animal. They occupy a house of the Zodiac and their horns adorn the winged Egyptian globe. Thor's chariot was drawn by goats. The word *tragedy* means literally "goat song," after the odes accompanying Dionysian sacrifices. Even the cornucopia comes from a goat. When Amalthea, the goat that suckled Zeus himself, broke her horn, he filled it with the earth's bounty: grains, fruits, flowers. In Leviticus, two goats are used in a purification ritual reminiscent of the Lupercalia. The first is sacrificed to expiate human sins, the second (the "scapegoat") symbolically laden with sins and then freed.

Goats' enthusiasm for copulation has long made them symbols of lust and fecundity. As early as the third century B.C., the Roman playwright Plautus was calling an aging lecher "an old goat." In time, possibly resulting from Hebrew distaste for Rome's decadent gods, the Judeo-Christian devil acquired caprine characteristics: horns, a tail, cloven hooves.

During the Lupercalia, these unfortunate symbolic animals were dressed for death, sanctified with a sprinkling of wine and meal, and offered in prayer. Then they were killed. The entrails were examined for omens, and if anything hinted that the gods might be displeased with this victim, another was killed—and others, if necessary, until all the signs were favorable. Then the meat was carefully butchered, with choice cuts offered to the god and the rest given to the celebrants.

Finally, the skins of the victims were cut into thongs called *februa,* "means of purification," from which we get February. Nobles of the priestly Order of Lupercus carried the whips. Sacrificial blood was smeared on their foreheads with a knife, then wiped off with wool moistened in milk. Dressed only in goatskin, the runners circled the boundary of the Palatine, striking the desperate women who jostled for position along the route. This was what Antony did, and presumably he struck Calpurnia. But she didn't become pregnant. And a month later, Caesar was dead.

See also Shakespeare, 3/15 and 8/22.

---

16 February 1939

Living Fossil

Charles Darwin coined an odd term in the *Origin of Species:* "living fossils." He was referring to those fugitives from time that have somehow outlived their fellows. Examples abound. Thomas Jefferson's hope that dinosaurs might lurk at the headwaters of the Mississippi proved vain, but the river is home to several "fossil" fish. In 1945 a dawn redwood, previously known only from fossil pollen, was discovered in central China. Ten years later, a primitive arthropod was found in the ooze at the bottom of Long Island Sound.

But these finds were preceded by a more dramatic one. In December of 1938, the young director of the natural history museum in East London, South Africa, went down to the docks to examine the day's catch. Marjorie Courtenay-Latimer found in the pile at the dock an odd-looking blue fish with unusual fin patterns. It was almost 5 feet long and weighed well over 100 pounds. She was unfamiliar with the species, but the armored scales and overall body shape told her it was primitive. She wrote to Professor J. L. B. Smith, the closest ichthyologist. From Courtenay-Latimer's sketch, Smith decided that she might have found a coelacanth. The great naturalist Louis Agassiz first described and named this creature—technically, like sharks, they aren't fish—in 1836, from fossil remains. It was a member of a primitive family thought to have died out at the end of the age of dinosaurs, 70 million years before.

Smith arrived to examine the fish on February 16, 1939. There are two stories about his arrival—his own and Courtenay-Latimer's. "Latimer was out for the moment," Smith wrote; "the caretaker ushered us into the inner room and there was the Coelacanth, yes, by God! Although I had come prepared, that first sight hit me like a white-hot blast and made me feel shaky and queer, my body tingled. I stood as if stricken to stone." In Courtenay-Latimer's version, she is present when Smith enters. "As he walked into my small office where I had the now mounted fish he said, 'I always KNEW somewhere, or somehow a primitive fish of this nature would appear.'"

Smith was so impressed because Courtenay-Latimer's discovery was as surprising as stumbling upon a living Stegosaurus. The past had come alive. Living species confirm or refute interpretations of fossils. Soft body parts are seldom preserved, so a chance to see them in the living animal is exciting. If body structure hasn't evolved much, then probably its function hasn't, either. Not only was the coelacanth an example of an extinct species; not only did it belong to a primitive group; but its group of lobe-finned fishes included the immediate ancestor of all land vertebrates, a fishy air-breathing land dweller of the Devonian Period, that early innovative time in which insects also developed.

Smith sent a sober little notice to the prestigious journal *Nature,* but it was scooped by the *Illustrated London News,* which trumpeted, "One of the Most Amazing Events in the Realm of Natural History in the Twentieth Century." Then the world press was onto the discovery. Suddenly the board of the little museum in East London was interested in the coelacanth. When Smith finally convinced them to let him take it away for study, they sent it under police escort.

Every one of the 200 or so specimens captured since has gone to researchers. Therefore, if this animal becomes truly extinct, it will be the first extinction traced directly to the curiosity of scientists. It has been suggested that, since scientists have now learned a great deal about coelacanths, they might try the radical policy of simply leaving them alone.

Animal Farm

"I am writing a little squib," George Orwell wrote to a friend on February 17, 1944, "which might amuse you when it comes out, but it is not so OK politically that I don't feel certain in advance that anyone will publish it." That awkward sentence is the first recorded mention of what would become *Animal Farm.* The same letter also contains the earliest glimmer of *1984*—Orwell's intention to write something along the lines of Yevgeny Zamyatin's dystopian novel *We.*

Orwell described *Animal Farm* to one publisher as "a little fairy story . . . with a political meaning." Several firms rejected the manuscript because that meaning was not in the spirit of the times. Few yet realized, or were willing to admit, the enormity of Joseph Stalin's crimes against humanity in Russia. Stalin had come a long way in the eyes of Europe since his pact with Hitler in 1939; for their heroism against the Nazis, the Russians were now lauded as heroes. When, at the height of pro-Russian sentiment, Orwell portrayed the nation as a farm run by animals, with Stalin as the vicious head pig, it seemed bad timing at best, if not treason. The book finally came out in 1946, and the early Cold War climate was more congenial to Orwell's thesis than had been that of the war years.

Animal Farm is no generalized swipe at tyranny that the Russians might have ignored. Many plot elements reflect Russian history. After the death of the pig Old Major, who preached the equality of animals and the need for an animal revolution, two other pigs struggle for control of the animals. The pig who winds up running Animal Farm, Napoleon, is a portrait of Stalin. Like Stalin, Napoleon betrays his alliances and obsesses on security. He is jealous, racist, and vain, demands conformity and worshipful obedience, and punishes with death both true opponents and those he finds it useful to portray as opponents.

Napoleon's partner in the revolution, Snowball, suffers the same fate as Stalin's archrival, Leon Trotsky. Together Napoleon and Snowball mastermind the rebellion, evicting czarlike Farmer Jones from Manor Farm so they can rename it Animal Farm and run it themselves. Then, just as Stalin ousted Trotsky after the death of Lenin, Napoleon vanquishes Snowball and rewrites his former comrade's role in the revolution. (As far as we know from Orwell's story, Snowball, unlike Trotsky, was not later assassinated.) At the end of the book, the uneasy truce between Napoleon and the two neighboring human farmers represents the Teheran Conference, at which Roosevelt, Churchill, and Stalin professed unity prior to the Allied invasion.

Orwell didn't mind controversy. "Liberty," he insisted, "is the right to tell people what they do not want to hear." Slogans could not replace dialogue; myths could not supplant reason. Orwell employed another animal image in his response to the uneasy fear of rocking the boat that he witnessed in skittish publishers: "Circus dogs jump when the trainer cracks the whip, but the really well-trained dog is the one that turns his somersault when there is no whip."

---

18 FEBRUARY 1930

Another Wanderer

Early civilizations were as familiar with the night sky as we are with the artificial lights that hide it from us. The ancient Greeks, for example, were so aware of the constant stars that they named any less-predictable visitors *planetes,* "wanderers." They recognized seven: the Sun, the Moon, Mercury, Venus, Mars, Jupiter, and Saturn. Earth was considered the center of the universe, definitely not a wanderer. Long after the true natures of the Sun, Moon, and Earth were recognized, the other five remained the only planets known. Then, in 1781, Uranus was discovered. Unexplained perturbations in its orbit led astronomers to predict yet another planet, and Neptune obligingly materialized in the 1840s.

Might other fugitive planets be lurking out there in the darkness? Some astronomers thought so. Already long ridiculed for his claim that Mars was inhabited by canal builders, American astronomer Percival Lowell switched obsessions and determined to locate another planet. Neptune's 248-year revolution hadn't crept far enough across the sky to offer its own orbit for analysis, so Lowell turned back to still-unexplained quirks in that of Uranus and predicted the mass and location of a "Planet X."

Lowell died without rehabilitating his reputation. In fact, he drew more laughter by reporting two comets that, in the light of publicity, turned into defects on the plates. However, after his death, his legacy—the Lowell Observatory in Flagstaff, Arizona—kept trying. Just as the older astronomers were tiring of the quest, a young man named Clyde Tombaugh applied for a job. He had no formal training, but he had built three telescopes, and his drawings of Jupiter and Mars were exquisite. They offered him a job working with a new telescope; when he arrived, he was assigned the search for Planet X. Like Lowell, Tombaugh used a machine called a blink comparator, which quickly alternated successive photographs of a part of the sky. Through it, stars remained motionless, but wanderers appeared to "jump."

After Lowell's death, researchers discovered that, ironically, he had overlooked photographic evidence of the unknown planet. In April 1929, Tombaugh also photographed a telltale jump, but didn't catch it. He kept going. "Blinking" a single plate took days, sometimes weeks. Then, on February 18, 1930, he was blinking January's plates, saw the telltale movement of a tiny dot of light, and exclaimed to himself, "That's it!"

Even though her bequest fight had kept a million dollars from the observatory, Percival Lowell's widow suggested that "her husband's" planet be named after herself. But the new planet was far too small to disturb another's orbit, so it couldn't have been Lowell's Planet X. Thus it did not wind up being named "Constance." At 3.7 billion miles from the Sun, forty times Earth's distance, so far out in the solar system that its own sun is just one more light in the starry sky, it was named for the lord of the underworld in Greek mythology—Pluto. Continuing this theme, when a satellite was discovered circling Pluto in 1978, it was named Charon, after Pluto's ferryman, who transported the dead across the River Styx to Hades.

---

19 FEBRUARY 1945

"A Four-Footed Evil Thing"

Only a few days after the firebombing of Dresden and the conference at Yalta, one of the strangest disasters of World War II took place off the west coast of Burma (now Myanmar). During the last weeks of 1944 and the first of 1945, British troops trapped over 1,000 Japanese infantry in an eighteen-mile-wide mangrove swamp between the Burmese mainland and the shore of Ramree Island in the Bay of Bengal. The Japanese commander had been optimistically awaiting reinforcements, only to learn that the British navy had intercepted them. Finally, in desperation, the Japanese soldiers sneaked into the swamp, braving the murky, waist-high water and mud in a last-ditch effort to dodge the British troops on the island proper. On February 19, 1945, as the Japanese fled, the British, in lightweight canvas boats, cut off escape routes and surrounded them.

What happened next sounds like it belongs in a Hollywood B-movie. However, among the many witnesses was a trained professional naturalist named Bruce Wright, who recounted the events in his 1962 book *Wildlife Sketches, Near and Far.* Apparently the gunfire and mortar shelling had driven the swamp's many crocodiles into the murky water, where they lurked with only their eyes and nostrils above the surface. Probably they were savoring one side effect of the battle—the smell of blood. When the tide went out, the Japanese troops were trapped in mud and a couple of feet of water. Then night fell. From their position in the bay safely outside the swamp, the British soldiers heard the screams of the Japanese when the crocodiles attacked them. The horrific scene lasted all night. No one knows how many Japanese soldiers the crocodiles killed. No doubt many men fell during the battle. Probably some drowned. But for whatever reasons, of the 1,000 soldiers who entered the swamp, only 20 came out alive.

Although that was the worst massacre of humans by animals on record, in a way it was not surprising. Crocodiles have long been recognized as one of the most dangerous carnivores on Earth. Periodically, crocodile autopsies reveal the torso of a missing villager or the claws of a cheetah. Death by crocodile appears to be singularly gruesome. They are unable to chew, and when their prey is larger than they can swallow, they tear it apart by grasping a limb and whirling around until they dismember the victim.

The Roman naturalist Pliny the Elder described the crocodile as "very greedy for human flesh," and "a four-footed evil thing, as dangerous on land as in the river. . . . Its length is generally more than thirty feet. . . . It is armed with talons and with a hide invincible against all blows." There is no indication that the crocodile is more greedy for human flesh than for that of other large animals such as cows. As for its evil nature, that of course is a slander that says a lot about us but nothing about crocodiles. However, Pliny is correct that the crocodile is potentially dangerous to human beings wherever it is found. Not that their behavior can be predicted. Some villages plagued with crocodiles are forced to fortify against them, while others seem to coexist comfortably with their reptilian neighbors. Pliny's claims of the crocodile's length seem excessive; reputable reports in this century do not exceed twenty-three feet. However, the six-foot skull of the fossil crocodilian *Phobosuchus* indicates that its total length would have been at least fifty feet, and in other respects it is practically indistinguishable from its living descendants. Also, crocodiles seem to continue growing as they age, so perhaps the old stories were not exaggerations after all.

See also alligators in the sewers, 1/27.

---

20 FEBRUARY 1877

Swan Lake

Swans play an eccentric role in the arts. In several ancient mythologies, there is a character called a swan maiden, who can be either bird or woman at will. For some reason, certain Greek gods liked to turn into swans—or, in those peevish little tantrums that make up half of mythology, turn others into swans. Ovid tells several swan stories in the *Metamorphoses.* In one which has been popular with painters throughout history, Zeus, the salacious and irresponsible king of the Greek gods, takes the form of a swan to seduce Leda.

In another story, the daughters of the sun witness the death of their brother, who dies while trying to drive their father's chariot across the sky. In their grief they turn into trees. A man named Cycnus witnesses this, and Apollo changes him into a swan. *Cygnus,* the Latin word for swan, is still around. It's the name of the constellation of the Swan, the birds' young are called cygnets, and *Cygninae* is a genus of swans. Because the swan was thought to sing a farewell song before dying, we have the phrase "swan song." Yet another of the many stories involving metamorphoses into these birds is the fairy tale of the ugly duckling.

One of the most recent and best known swan stories is not a poem or fable, but rather a dance. Even critics who dismiss his symphonies and concerti as banal and vulgar proclaim the perfection of Pyotr Ilich Tchaikovsky's ballet scores for *The Nutcracker, Sleeping Beauty,* and *Swan Lake.* However, at the time of his death in 1893, from cholera at the age of fifty-three, Tchaikovsky considered *Swan Lake* a failure. The first of several incarnations of *Lebedinoe Ozero* premiered at the Bolshoi Theater in Moscow on February 20, 1877. The conductor was not up to Tchaikovsky's innovative composition; he cut the score and replaced parts of it with bits from other ballets. The next few interpretations were equally unsuccessful.

The plot grew from the odd tradition of swan stories. When he comes of age, carefree Prince Siegfried's mother informs him that he must now choose a wife. She has helpfully arranged a lineup of nominees for his birthday party the following night. Siegfried is not pleased. A friend suggests that a swan-hunting party might be amusing diversion. The hunters go to a lake and find the birds led by a crowned female of great beauty—Odette, queen of the swans. In mime, she informs Siegfried that she is under the spell of that essential character, an evil magician. She must remain a swan, except between midnight and dawn, until a man loves her to the exclusion of all others. Naturally, the impulsive Siegfried vows to do just that. However, the magician dupes him with an Odette look-alike, and he promises to love *her.* When he realizes his mistake, Siegfried rushes to the lake and begs forgiveness of the true swan queen. Nearby, in the form of an owl, the magician watches. But his power is not enough to stop the devoted lovers, who dive together, triumphant, into the lake.

See also "Afternoon of a Faun," 1/18.

George Hale's Legacy

American astronomer George Ellery Hale left a considerable mark on his field. He isn't remembered for theories of the magnitude of Johannes Kepler or Isaac Newton, or for observations in the same league as William Herschel or E. E. Barnard, but for a different sort of legacy, one that also has a daily effect on his profession.

Hale was born in Chicago in 1868. After studying in Massachusetts and Berlin, he organized his first observatory, the Kenwood, in his hometown. While there he invented an instrument called a spectroheliograph. The spectroscope, a tool for direct observation developed in the mid–nineteenth century on principles dating all the way back to Newton's work with prisms, separates light into its component spectra for analysis. The early use of glass prisms, sometimes several in succession, was replaced in time by the diffraction spectroscope, which employs instead metallic mirrors or polished glass surfaces with thousands of machine-ruled grooves per inch. One that produces photographs is called a spectrograph. As its tripartite name indicates, Hale's spectroheliograph takes photographs of the sun's spectrum, employing a tiny range of wavelengths called monochromatic light.

In the early 1890s, while on the faculty of the University of Chicago, Hale began organizing the Yerkes Observatory, in Williams Bay, Wisconsin. While there, he founded the *Astrophysical Journal,* which still exists as the premier forum on astronomical physics and spectroscopy. More important, he built what was at the time the largest refracting telescope in the world, with a diameter of forty inches. There are two main kinds of optical telescopes (as opposed to radio telescopes, which gather invisible radiation). The refractor that Hale built at Yerkes was a much larger, far more sophisticated version of the simple tool Galileo used in the early 1600s. Refracting telescopes consist basically of a long tube, with a lens that collects incoming rays of light and focuses them at the other end of the tube, where a second lens magnifies the image. The lens diameter is important because the greater the instrument's light-gathering ability, the fainter the illumination it is able to perceive.

In 1904, Hale left Yerkes to organize the Mount Wilson Observatory, funded by the Carnegie Institution in Washington, D.C. There he directed the installation of a different kind of telescope. Unlike the refractor, the reflecting telescope doesn't have a light-gathering lens. It employs a concave mirror, usually positioned at the bottom of a tube, which reflects the light back up to a smaller mirror tilted at a 45° angle. The second mirror, in turn, projects the image into the viewing eyepiece. Isaac Newton designed the refractor to avoid problems that result from a lens's inability to focus all the colors of a spectrum at the same precise point, which resulted in a misleading phenomenon called chromatic aberration. Nowadays a few sophisticated instruments employ a combination of both refraction and reflection.

Hale resigned the directorship of Mount Wilson in 1928 and went to guide the construction of his magnum opus, high atop Mount Palomar near Pasadena, California. Today the 200-inch telescope at the Palomar Observatory is one of the most powerful reflecting telescopes in the world. A masterpiece of engineering, it is so perfectly balanced, with hydrostatic bearings so smoothly supporting its mechanism, that its entire 500 tons can be turned to follow the stars by an engine with only one-twelfth of a horsepower. Hale directed its construction until his death on February 21, 1938, but the instrument wasn't completed until a decade later. At its dedication in 1948, it was christened the George Ellery Hale Telescope.

---

22 FEBRUARY 1882

Jumbo Leaves England

Arabs captured the baby elephant, probably in Ethiopia, and sold him to an animal collector, who in turn shipped him to Europe. The Jardin des Plantes in Paris bought him in 1861. African elephants don't mature as quickly as their Indian cousins, and apparently his French keepers were frustrated that the baby was slow to attain elephantine proportions. They had a surplus of elephants but no rhinoceros, and when the London Zoological Society offered to trade a rhino for an elephant, Paris sent the baby. He was under five feet tall.

The English named him Mumbo Jumbo. The original Mandingo phrase *mama dyambo* referred to fearful medicine men, but "Mumbo Jumbo" had come to mean an idol, or anything dreaded; it has since eroded to merely describe confusing nonsense. In time the elephant reached a size worthy of fear, but by then his name had shrunk to Jumbo. He wasn't named Jumbo because he was large; "jumbo" came to mean large because of him.

Jumbo's popularity increased with his size. Hundreds of thousands of children rode in the howdah on his back, as he strolled the paths in Regent's Park for seventeen years. Young Winston Churchill was photographed with him; Theodore Roosevelt visited; the royal family doted on him. One man who rode Jumbo was America's brilliant promoter and shameless liar, P. T. Barnum.

Already famous in England as the man who brought Tom Thumb to amuse the young Queen Victoria, he returned in 1882. Naturally he coveted Jumbo, who by this time weighed 13,000 pounds and stood 12 feet tall at the shoulder. Expecting to be refused, Barnum's agent offered $10,000. The zoo accepted.

They had good reasons. Jumbo was obsessively attached to his keeper, Matthew Scott, and became violent whenever Scott left him. Also, he was likely to soon experience *musth* (from the Persian for "intoxicated"), a maddening glandular inflammation that afflicts some male elephants during mating season. Scott could accompany Jumbo to the United States, and Barnum's circus was undaunted by *musth.*

The zoo publicized the deal only after it was signed. Fanned by Barnum's agents, who knew there was no better free publicity than opposition, an outcry swept the country. Everyone from schoolchildren to the queen herself protested the sale of the realm's favorite animal. John Ruskin remarked in dismay that England was not in the habit of selling her pets. The public response reached a peak with Jumbo perfumes, hats, letterheads, cigars, and underwear. Restaurants offered everything from Jumbo fritters to Jumbo ice cream. A single day in the previous March, 214 people visited Jumbo; in the same period after the publicity, 4,626 came. Nonetheless, a court declared the deal valid.

Finally, the editor of the London *Daily Telegraph* sent a cable:

London, February 22, 1882

P.T. Barnum, New York:
> Editor's compliments. All British children distressed at elephant's departure. Hundreds of correspondents beg us to inquire on what terms you will kindly return Jumbo. Answer prepaid, unlimited.

Barnum refused:

> Fifty millions of American citizens anxiously awaiting Jumbo's arrival. My forty years' invariable practice of exhibiting best that money could procure makes Jumbo's presence here imperative. . . .

Jumbo himself didn't take his departure casually. As Scott led him through the zoo gate, he lay down in the street and wouldn't budge. Probably

English children take a last ride aboard Jumbo, with the elephant's beloved Matthew Scott driving.

Scott signaled him, but the public regarded the gesture as Jumbo's demonstration that he didn't want to leave his beloved England. Barnum cabled from the United States, "Let him lie there as long as he wants to. The publicity is worth it." Finally the wary elephant was tricked into a cage. A few weeks later he was in the United States.

See also Barnum's mermaid, 8/8.

---

23 FEBRUARY 1940

The Translation of Pinocchio and Bottom

The transformation of a human being into another creature is a common theme in the arts. Metamorphosis into an animal who represents one's true nature, however, is something of a specialized category. One particular version of that change appeared in three different mediums, hundreds of years apart.

In the wake of the fabulously successful *Snow White,* their first animated feature film, Walt Disney Productions commenced work on *Pinocchio.* After years of work, with the first five months scrapped completely in order to start over, the film was released February 23, 1940. Reviewers were ecstatic then as now, but the film has never achieved the widespread popularity of some of the sunnier tales. It is definitely Disney's darkest vision.

Those viewers who find the film emotionally violent should compare it with Carlo Collodi's 1882 novel. Pinocchio goes to sleep with his feet on the edge of the fireplace and awakens with them burned off. When the fox and cat attack him, he bites off the cat's paw. The Pinocchio in the book is a cocky little hoodlum who needs no help in allowing temptation to lure him from the straight and narrow. When Pinocchio expresses a desire to lead the life of a vagabond, the unnamed Talking-cricket warns him where such ambitions usually lead, and in a rage Pinocchio kills the insect with a wooden hammer.

One of the few points at which the book and film even intersect is the matter of Pinocchio's transformation into a donkey. In both, it is the culmination of the woe-unto-bad-little-boys theme. The boy Candlewick persuades Pinocchio to accompany him to the Land of Boobies, populated by boys from the age of eight to fourteen, where no one ever studies. After five days of "continual play and no study," Pinocchio scratches his head one morning and discovers that he has grown donkey ears. Candlewick is undergoing the same horrifying transformation.

> And their hands became hoofs, their faces lengthened into muzzles, and their backs became covered with a little gray hairy coat sprinkled with black. But do you know what the worst moment was for these two wretched boys? The worst and the most humiliating moment was when their tails grew.

The former boys are sold as beasts of burden. In the cinematic version, the Land of Boobies became the temptingly named Pleasure Island, where the boys smoke, drink, and play pool. The transformation scene is one of the most terrifying in any Disney film.

Pinocchio's transformation into an ass echoes that of another famous literary character—Nick Bottom, the weaver and part-time actor in Shakespeare's *Midsummer Night's Dream.* The mischievous fairy Robin Goodfellow (Puck) magically transforms Bottom while he is absent from the stage during the rehearsal of "the most lamentable comedy, and most cruel death of Pyramus and Thisby." When Bottom returns with his own head replaced by that of an ass, his fellow actors flee. "Bless thee, Bottom!" Quince exclaims. "Thou art translated." Bottom's translation into an ass-headed man is merely the physical manifestation of his dull-witted but well-meaning nature. Unlike Pinocchio, Bottom is blind to his transformation. However, when his friends desert him, he mutters a line the marionette might have used: "I see their knavery; this is to make an ass of me. . . ."

---

24 FEBRUARY 1902

Waiting for the Light and the Sea

"If a man wants to be an artist," Winslow Homer remarked to a friend early in his career, "he should never look at pictures." Although it was a rejection of tradition, that remark in itself exemplifies a theory of art. Homer's conviction that an American artist ought not dilute his native original vision with the art of the rest of the world embodied the patriotic biases of many of his fellow artists. Throughout his career Homer spent much of his time trying to attend to the world itself, to learn from nature how best to portray it. In 1862, he bought painting supplies "and started out into the country to paint from nature." When he finally went to sketch in the Louvre, he drew not the Old Masters, but the young women painting them.

Homer seldom discussed his methods, but he did remark that he always preferred "a picture composed and painted out of doors." This sounds like a manifesto. Plein-air painting was not yet the common procedure that would lead Degas to claim Monet's work always made him turn up his collar. The difference in Homer's approach and that of his contemporaries was apparent to both public and critics. As one of the latter wrote in 1879, Homer's watercolors bore "unmistakable marks of having been made outdoors in the summer and the sunlight."

After more than twenty years in New York City, where he quickly rose to the top of his profession as an illustrator for such periodicals as *Harper's Weekly,* Homer devoted himself to painting. He began producing his famous seascapes in 1890, after his move to the inhospitable northeast coast. From his home at Prout's Neck, ten miles south of Portland, Maine, he wrote to his brother, "I thank the Lord for this opportunity for reflection." The reflection resulted in a steady stream of paintings portraying the insignificance of human concerns, yet the nobility of the human struggle, against the indifference of the sea. Homer was determined to stand before nature and to stand alone. His largest painting, his first to be purchased by a museum, excludes human beings from the scene altogether.

As a periodic escape from the wilds of Maine, Homer journeyed to a dramatically different environment—Florida, Bermuda, and the Caribbean. And as he did so, he began to divide his subjects along the line of his mediums. Oils he reserved for the darker, thoughtful, more idea-driven northern seascapes. Watercolor, of which Homer is one of the recognized masters, became the medium for expressing a more spontaneous joy in the physical beauty of the world. Such watercolors as *Leaping Trout* and *A Wall, Nassau* are suffused with a delight that in the oils was usually muted and understated.

As time went on, Homer painted less. There were several reasons. One was his sense of his own position in the art market. He explained to a friend in 1905 that one new painting per year was "enough to fill the market." Scholars have noted that, as he aged, he reworked older paintings as frequently as he created new ones, as if his powers of invention might be flagging. But one factor in Homer's slow production of new paintings was his patient determination to wait until he had exactly what he wanted. Sometimes that took months. In March 1902, Homer wrote to a friend from his house at Prout's Neck: "It will please you to know that after waiting a full year, looking out every day for it (when I have been here) on the 24th of Feby, my birthday, I got the light and the sea that I wanted."

25 FEBRUARY 1807

Mammoth and Mastodon

In his sole published book, *Notes on Virginia,* Thomas Jefferson wrote at length of "the mammoth, or big buffalo, as called by the Indians. . . . From the accounts published in Europe, I suppose it to be decided that these are of the same kind with those found in Siberia." Jefferson was mistaken. The bones were indeed those of an extinct relative of the elephant, but they were not identical to the mammoth. As the French fossil expert Georges Cuvier pointed out, the teeth of Siberian mammoths differed considerably from those of their American cousins. Because of the rounded cone-shaped teeth of the latter, Cuvier proposed the name *mastodon,* "breast tooth." Nonetheless, Jefferson and others continued to refer to America's fossil elephant as a mammoth.

The word "mammoth" first appeared in 1694. It was originally an Anglicized version of a term used by the Ostyak of western Siberia. They described the vast quantities of fossil ivory that had been unearthed there during the seventeenth century as *mammout-tekoos.* The animal that presumably produced the ivory was called *mammout.* In time, of course, "mammoth" came to mean gigantic or otherwise impressive, and has almost been replaced by a related word, the name of a famously large elephant—Jumbo. Understandably, it was the size of these fossil tusks and bones that most impressed their first discoverers. No one yet realized the creatures' age. Large numbers of the fossil bones and teeth began to turn up in the late 1700s, inspiring a thriving trade in them over the next couple of centuries.

The woolly mammoth, one of the extinct elephantlike animals that once roamed the Earth.

Inevitably, similar bones were discovered in North America. In the early part of the century, however, when someone showed Cotton Mather a huge bone and tooth that had recently been unearthed, the Puritan parson had declared them proof of the biblical story of a former race of giants on the earth. In the spring of 1801, when American artist Charles Willson Peale learned that a farmer had found gigantic bones in a marl pit in New York two years before, he did not even consider the biblical-giant theory. He determined to excavate the creature. It took him several months, with numerous assistants, but he found relatively complete skeletons of more than one "mammoth." Like a modern paleontologist, he cautiously reconstructed the missing parts with casts from the other skeletons. Before featuring it as an exhibit in his natural history museum in Philadelphia, Peale hosted a Christmas Eve dinner for a dozen friends *inside* one reconstructed skeleton.

Other bones turned up. Several were found in Kentucky, at an ancient salt lick now preserved as Big Bone Lick State Park. On February 25, 1807, Thomas Jefferson wrote a letter to the American Philosophical Society demonstrating the lengths to which he would go to find out more about the creatures that fascinated him. "Being acquainted with Mr. Ross, proprietor of the big bone lick, I wrote to him for permission to search for such particular bones as the society might desire, and I expect to receive it in a few days." He had in his employ a man famous in a different context. "Captain Clarke (companion of Captain Lewis) who is now here, agrees as he passes through that country, to stop at the Lick, employ laborers, and superintend the search at my expense. . . ."

Almost two centuries after Peale and Jefferson enthused over mastodon bones, others are frequently unearthed. Like their cousins in North America, the mammoths of Asia and Europe help to create a picture of the world in the formative time of modern human beings. Mammoths still turn up regularly in Asia, frozen ever since the Ice Age. Soviet gold miners found an extraordinarily well preserved baby mammoth in 1977, while thawing permafrost. Apparently it had died at the age of six months or so, and after 10,000 years its body was perfectly preserved, all the way down to its blood cells and albumin. Its appearance, and even analysis of its blood serum, confirmed the predictions paleontologists had made based upon fossils and cave drawings. Eleven years later, again in Siberia, a ship captain found an even younger mammoth entombed in ice.

See also Jefferson's fight with Buffon, 10/2.

---

26 FEBRUARY 1979

"The End of the World Would Have to Feel Like This"

In 1979, American writer and naturalist Annie Dillard and her husband drove five hours from the coast of Washington to place themselves in the path of a solar eclipse. The next morning, with other intrepid early risers, they stood on a hill overlooking the Yakima Valley. February 26 dawned cloudy, but the sky soon cleared. Through welder's goggles, Dillard watched as a piece of the sun vanished.

"It was odd," Dillard wrote in *Tickets for a Prayer Wheel,* "that such a well-advertised public event should have no starting gun, no overture, no introductory speaker." For most of history, eclipses were terrifying reversals of that godlike and normally reliable monarch of the day. We now know, of course, that eclipses occur in natural cycles, when one celestial body blocks the view of or casts a shadow upon another. Nowadays astronomers are able to calculate the respective itineraries of Earth, the Moon, and the Sun, and such formerly terrifying phenomena have indeed become well-advertised public events. Television news programs allow the Sun a quick appearance sandwiched between the day's other celebrities.

Dillard remarked that, although everyone on that mountaintop in Washington knew of the Moon's role in the solar eclipse, Earth's satellite was not visible beforehand; the Sun's glare was too overwhelming. Then, suddenly present as a black disk, the Moon closed over the Sun. (Incidentally, February 26 was a Monday, from the Old English *monandæg,* "moon day.") It is one of the triumphs of astronomy and mathematics that nowadays the exact moment at which the Moon will cross the face of the Sun—or, in a lunar eclipse, the moment when the shadow of Earth will fall across the Moon—can be known in advance. And it isn't merely a recent accomplishment. Columbus may have saved his life by calculating the time of an eclipse, and one is known to have stopped a battle.

John Updike described his experience with an eclipse in a brief "Talk of the Town" essay in the *New Yorker.* In July of 1963, he stood in his yard in New England with his two-year-old daughter and watched a near-total solar eclipse. Sunlight dappled the ground with crescent shapes—all, Updike noted, curved in the same direction, from left to right. Later, that direction reversed. A neighbor warned him to go inside and avoid the dangerous rays from the sky. Instead he occupied his time burning trash. When the eclipse was over, Updike and his daughter went indoors. She was no more impressed by the predicted astronomical event than by the daily unscheduled miracles in her young life.

Updike said that he "felt a certain assurance evaporate forever under the reality of the sun's disgrace." Dillard agreed: "The sun was going, and the world was wrong." Observing the 1991 solar eclipse from La Paz, Mexico, American science writer William Sheehan summed up a response apparently felt by humans in the presence of this great mystery ever since we stared up at it from the African savannah: "The end of the world would have to feel like this."

See also Columbus's eclipse, 2/29; the eclipse that stopped a battle, 5/28; and a fictional eclipse, 6/21.

Owls with Human Heads

Real owls occupy a wide variety of territories, but fantasy is the only habitat of that renowned species, the wise owl. They flourish particularly in children's books. In *Mrs. Frisby and the Rats of NIMH,* by Robert C. O'Brien, the title character is a widowed mouse who desperately seeks help for her ill son. A crow who owes her a favor flies her to the distant, high-altitude home of "the owl." Trembling, she steps into his dark hollow-tree home and tells her story, and the owl proves to be worthy of his reputation. He provides a solution to her problem. For all his shyness, Archimedes, Merlyn's friend and housemate in *The Sword in the Stone,* has much raptor wisdom to share with the young king-in-training, Arthur.

Thanks to this impressive reputation, it is amusing when Owl, the old humbug in *Winnie-the-Pooh,* spells his name WOL and is very proud of Christopher Robin's notice on the door: PLEZ CNOKE IF AN RNSR IS NOT REQID. Like the faintheartedness of the Cowardly Lion, Owl's sham learning reverses a long-established tradition.

A quatrain from an 1875 issue of *Punch* explains just how the owl acquired its fabled wisdom:

> *There was an old owl liv'd in an oak*
> *The more he heard, the less he spoke;*
> *The less he spoke, the more he heard—*
> *O, if men were all like that wise bird!*

However, like most of our supporting players in the anthropocentric melodrama we have imagined nature to be, owls have not been limited to a single role. When not the sage, they have played the villain. One superstition, for example, claimed owls sucked the blood of infants. More often they are ill omens. "The owl shrieked at thy birth," Henry VI tells Gloucester, and designates that innocent bird call "an evil sign." Corroboration follows instantly, when Gloucester stabs him. In *Macbeth,* an owlet's wing becomes an ingredient in the witches' boiling, bubbling cauldron. Lover of darkness and desolation, a moping owl "complains" to the moon in Thomas Gray's *Elegy in a Country Churchyard.* This dark tradition is beautifully lampooned in a telegram sent to the title character of Max Beerbohm's novel *Zuleika Dobson:* "Deeply regret inform your grace last night two black owls came and perched on battlements remained there through night hooting at dawn flew away none knows whither awaiting instructions Jellings."

In the Bible, the owl is one of the birds God warns the Israelites they should hold in abomination among the fowls. Several times, Isaiah uses owls as symbols of uncleanness and desolation, as in a prediction of the downfall of Babylon: "And thorns shall come up in her palaces, nettles and brambles in the fortresses thereof: and it shall be an habitation of dragons, and a court for owls." Elsewhere, those two pariah animals were linked again when the unfortunate Job described himself as a brother to dragons and a companion to owls. Isaiah also links the owl with satyrs. The biblical prophets believed in a whole spectrum of legendary creatures, and mythologized the real ones.

Because of their many associations and their striking appearance, owls have been a popular model for visual artists. Picasso, for example, drew, painted, and sculpted innumerable representations of owls. One of the best portraits of Picasso shows him on the stairway of his studio in the Rue des Grands-Augustins in Paris, with his hand on one of two owl sculptures beside him. On February 27, 1953, at the pottery in Vallauris, he painted several terra-cotta sculptures of owls. One has the face of a woman, another of a bearded man. If they were oracular birds, they might as well have human heads.

---

28 FEBRUARY 1852

"An Elephantine Lizard"

London. Michaelmas Term lately over, and the Lord Chancellor sitting in Lincoln's Inn Hall. Implacable November weather. As much mud in the streets, as if the waters had but newly retired from the face of the earth, and it would not be wonderful to meet a Megalosaurus, forty feet long or so, waddling like an elephantine lizard up Holborn Hill. . . .

At first, a Charles Dickens novel seems an unnatural habitat for a dinosaur. In our own time the big lizards have evolved from oil company logos to Barney the purple platitudisaurus, and we think of them as twentieth-century discoveries. Yet *Megalosaurus* was already well known when the first monthly installment of *Bleak House* reached an eager public on February 28, 1852. It was discovered in England long before our current celebrity *Tyrannosaurus* was unearthed in the American West. When the Great Exhibition's Crystal Palace was moved from Hyde Park to Sydenham in 1851, among the highly publicized attractions in its new home were life-size models of dinosaurs. Tennyson had already worked *Megalosaurus* into his poetry. Later, H. G. Wells, Arthur Conan Doyle, even Thomas Hardy, would either refer to it or actually use it as a character in their fiction.

The existence of gigantic animal bones had been known for centuries. As early as 1676, one showed up in a book on the natural history of Oxfordshire. At that time, of course, the bones weren't recognized for what they were; they were considered the remains of giant beasts that God had allowed to perish in the biblical Flood. As his imagery indicates, Dickens wrote with that idea in mind.

An early view of some of the monsters whose bones were surfacing in the 1800s. Dinosaurs' posture, diet, and habitat are periodically reevaluated as new information and theories come along.

Whenever the animals lived, however they died, their bones kept surfacing—a jawbone here, a leg there, occasionally entire skeletons. Then, in 1818, the great French comparative anatomist Georges Cuvier visited England. In his time, museum collections of skeletons were growing quickly. Cuvier was capable of recognizing their kinship, and therefore he is considered to have founded the now-glamorous field of vertebrate paleontology. He examined bones found near Oxford and pronounced them reptilian. Four years later, fossils from Sussex were described and awkwardly reconstructed.

Finally, in 1824, Oxford geologist and theologian William Buckland proposed a name for these creatures: *Megalosaurus,* "giant lizard."

Soon the term "saurians" was invented to include *Megalosaurus* and its cousins. Not until 1841, at a meeting of the British Association for the Advancement of Science, did England's own premier anatomist, Richard Owen, coin the term by which we now know these animals: *Dinosaurus,* "terrible lizard." The word is no longer a biological classification, but its shortened form survives as a handy catchall.

Over 100 million years ago, during the late Jurassic Period, the *Megalosaurus* was the dominant carnivore in Europe, just as *Allosaurus* was in North America. They were about thirty feet long; Dickens, perhaps unwittingly, was close in his size estimate. Although his *Megalosaurus* is only an image, it was more than a passing fancy. *Bleak House* was a satire on the Court of Chancery, and Dickens foreshadowed his view of the antiquated system of civil law with that startling opening image—a dinosaur lumbering toward extinction.

See also Dickens's raven, 7/9.

---

29 February 1504

Columbus and His Angry God

Even though his third voyage to the New World ended in disaster, with Columbus himself shipped home in chains to Ferdinand and Isabella, the explorer did not retire. As soon as his patrons suspended the charges, he went back to sea, in command of four ships. He was certain that a passage through to the Indian Ocean was hiding, daring him to find it. Ferdinand and Isabella gave Columbus a letter of introduction to Vasco da Gama, who was then on his second voyage to India. They thought that, since the two explorers shared a destination—one coming from the east, one from the west—they might meet.

The fourth voyage was cursed with illness, storms, and finally mutiny. Columbus explored the coast of the Yucatán Peninsula, Nicaragua, and Honduras, all the way south to Panama. Meanwhile worms were riddling the ships' hulls, and sailors bailed water constantly just to remain afloat. In June of 1503, the European ships limped to the coast of Jamaica. At a port that Columbus himself had named Puerto Santa Gloria a decade before, they beached the two crippled vessels for repairs. They remained there for over a year.

Relations with the natives were amicable at first, but morale among the stranded Europeans plummeted. Finally, forty-eight mutineers confronted the gout-ridden Admiral of the Ocean Sea and took the canoes and departed. They went along the coast, claiming their pillaging was on Columbus's orders. The natives believed the mutineers and refused to provide provisions for Columbus and his remaining men. Apparently unable to fend for themselves, the Europeans were trapped.

One of the few books aboard the beached ships was a 1473 publication, *Ephemerides ab Anno 1475–1506,* by the German astronomer and mathematician Johannes Müller, who wrote under the pen name Regiomontanus. Fortunately, among the book's thirty years of astronomical predictions was an upcoming lunar eclipse, complete with illustrations of its progress. However, Columbus could not merely consult a table. Regiomontanus provided the time at which the eclipse was expected to occur in Nuremberg, but Columbus was in Jamaica. To correct for the distance from Nuremberg, Columbus first determined the latitude of the island. Then came the much more complicated and iffy calculation of longitude. Finally, to arrive at the time of the eclipse in that part of the world, he calculated the difference in both latitude and longitude between Jamaica and Nuremberg. Incidentally, because of a treaty with Portugal, Columbus misrepresented the time difference in his notes. He consistently disguised the location of his discoveries so that they would appear to be beyond the treaty's line of demarcation.

Through an interpreter, Columbus informed the natives that his god had punished the evil mutineers. Then he said that the Lord was angry with the natives for not providing food for the Spaniards, and pestilence and famine were nigh. Columbus warned them that three nights hence God would provide a sign of his disapproval on the face of the rising moon. Most of the natives were unimpressed. Some even laughed.

When, on the night of February 29, 1504, the friendly, normal moon actually began to disappear, the frantic islanders stormed Columbus's ships not with weapons but with food. They begged him to intercede with his deity, with whom he was obviously conversant. Columbus asked to be alone with his god and went to his cabin. When the moon began to reappear, he came out and announced that all would be well.

See also **Dillard and Updike**, *2/26;* **Medes versus Lydians**, *5/28; and* **Connecticut Yankee**, *6/21.*

"I Break the Lightning"

The Latin word for lightning is *fulgur,* and the Roman goddess Fulgora protected homes against thunderstorms. For centuries church bells often bore the inscription *Fulgura frango,* "I break the lightning." The faithful believed the music of such consecrated tools of the church banished evil spirits. The more scientifically minded told themselves that, since church bells were long established as the best defense, it must be that the sound somehow broke up the lightning's path.

Meanwhile, religious leaders found it difficult to explain why, just as plague killed as many priests as sinners, so did lightning not respect the house of God. Actually, churches were struck *more* often than other buildings. In earlier centuries, churches were routinely a city's tallest structures. Unfortunately, while aspiring to the heavens, they reached up and invited lightning to leap down from the clouds. A 1784 account in Munich reported that lightning had struck 386 church steeples in the past 33 years, killing 103 bell ringers. The bell tower of St. Mark's in Venice was struck twelve times in a 400-year period and burned to the ground three of those times. (The survival rate of bell ringers at St. Mark's is not recorded.) Then, in 1766, some innovative soul installed a lightning rod, and there was no further damage.

The lightning rod was the invention of that embodiment of curiosity at large, Benjamin Franklin. After experiments proved that lightning was indeed a naturally occurring form of the "electric fluid" scientists were manufacturing in Leyden jars, Franklin turned his practical mind to protecting against its ravages. A 1753 edition of his *Poor Richard's Almanack* contained an advertisement headed "How to secure Houses &c. from LIGHTNING." When religious leaders denounced this blasphemous attempt to dodge the hand of God, Franklin replied, "Surely the Thunder of Heaven is no more supernatural than the Rain Hail or Sunshine of Heaven, against the Inconveniences of which we guard by Roofs & Shades without Scruple."

On March 1, 1755, Franklin wrote to a friend that he had found satisfying proof of the value of his invention. "I saw an Instance of a very great Quantity of Lightning conducted by a Wire no bigger than a common Knitting Needle." Lightning had destroyed a church steeple below the section protected by a too-short rod. "Yet this is observable that tho' it was so small, as not to be sufficient to conduct the Quantity with Safety to its own Substance yet it did conduct it so as to secure all that part of the Building."

It was once a common misconception that lightning rods disarmed clouds and prevented lightning from occurring. Actually, they merely channel the flash into the ground. Meteorologists estimate that there are 2,000 thunderstorms occurring on earth at any given moment, generating lightning that strikes the earth an average of 40 million times annually. A flash of millions of volts, heating the air itself to 60,000°F, sometimes forms in the ground a vitrified column of fused earth. The Latin word for lightning lives on in its name—"fulgurite."

Olbers' Paradox

The German physician Heinrich Wilhelm Matthäus Olbers was born in 1758 and died on March 2, 1840. He was also one of those devoted, skilled amateur sky watchers with which the history of astronomy has been blessed. He converted the top floor of his house to an observatory and spent much of each night observing. Olbers left his mark on several areas of astronomy. He discovered five comets, one of which bears his name, and devised a method of determining a comet's orbit. He discovered the two asteroids Pallas and Vesta, and proposed the theory that asteroids resulted from the explosion of a planet. One of his most interesting accomplishments is what is now called "Olbers' paradox." It can be stated simply: If the universe is infinite and stars are strewn evenly throughout, there should be no nighttime. Astronomers of the time found the idea that the universe might not be finite, that it might have an end somewhere or might have had a specific beginning, distasteful.

Olbers was responding to an already old argument. In 1610, Galileo, whose telescope had revealed to him the vast number of stars invisible to the naked eye, argued in *Sidereus Nuncius* (usually translated as "The Starry Messenger") that the universe was infinite and so was the number of the stars. The German astronomer Johannes Kepler disagreed. In a letter to Galileo, he pointed out that if there were an infinite number of stars, the night sky would not be black, because wherever we look in the sky a star would ultimately meet our eye. The combined glow would be like a sky-wide sun. For that simple reason, Kepler concluded, the universe could not be infinite.

Early in the eighteenth century, English astronomer Edmund Halley replied to Kepler's objection. Perhaps, he suggested, light from far distant stars is so weakened during its long travel to us that we are unable to detect it. As many astronomers have pointed out, that solution won't work, because two of nature's quaint little laws cancel each other out. Halley was correct that the intensity of light decreases in proportion to the square of its distance. However, in an infinite universe, the volume of space also increases as the square of the distance, which means that the number of stars strewn out there would increase in the same proportion as their light would decrease. And we're back to a sky that ought to be brightly glowing instead of black.

There were two ways out of Olbers' paradox—if the universe is not old enough for all the light from distant stars to have reached us, or if it is not infinitely large. In the early twentieth century, two hundred years after Halley voiced his flawed solution, an American astronomer with the memorable name of Vesto Melvin Slipher analyzed the light emitted by a great many galaxies. He observed in their spectrographs the visual version of the Doppler effect, that law of physics by which the pitch of an approaching sound is higher than its pitch as it recedes. Slipher's figures indicated the ridiculous conclusion that everything in the universe was receding from us. However, this was not proof that the entire universe regarded us as *trayf*. At about the same time, before we could agonize over why we repelled everything in the cosmos, Edwin Hubble and Milton Humason discovered that galaxies aren't just retreating from us, they're all retreating from each other. The universe is expanding in every direction.

Astronomers determined the present locations of galaxies, and their relative velocities, and calculated the great cosmic explosion in reverse to estimate when it might have taken place. That explosion is now thought to have occurred about 15 billion years ago. This means that the universe is too young for the light from all the stars to have reached us and filled the sky with their glow. We call that explosion the Big Bang, and one of the interesting things about it is that it explains why the night sky is dark.

---

3 MARCH 1933

King Kong

Aboard the ship headed for Skull Island, the expedition leader defines his quarry as "neither beast nor man. Something monstrous, all-powerful. . . ." *King Kong* premiered on March 3, 1933. Over half a century earlier, in his *Explorations and Adventures in Equatorial Africa* (1861), French explorer Paul Du Chaillu described the gorilla similarly: a "hellish dream creature—a being of that hideous order, half-man, half-beast. . . ."

When the islanders kidnap Fay Wray and await Kong, finally we see the creature the actress later called her "tallest, darkest leading man." Kong rescues the would-be sacrifice. Little does he know how much trouble Wray will be. Simply trying to keep his love, he must outrun his rival from the ship, wrestle a *Tyrannosaurus* and a pterodactyl, and swat airplanes from a skyscraper. And still she scorns his advances.

As rickety as the lustful-gorilla theme always is, in *King Kong* it collapses. No matter what wantonness might be attributed to a normal-sized gorilla when his hormones get the best of him, surely a giant ape would prefer a girlfriend his own size. Kong looks like a big hairy Gulliver with a captive Lilliputian. Whatever may have happened to Wray's predecessors, this time Kong has love on his mind. In restored footage censored in the original release, Kong begins to strip off Wray's clothes, as if peeling fruit. He stops to sniff each article of clothing. He strokes her and sniffs his fingers. Oddly, it's a familiar scenario;

Kong's captor, whose greed destroys the giant ape, dodges responsibility by declaring, "It was Beauty killed the Beast." Granted, the big lug could be a bit pushy. Courtesy of Ronald V. Borst / Hollywood Movie Posters

gorillas have played the lecher in over sixty films—with, it is worth noting, such wholesome titles as *The Beast That Killed Women* (1965), *The Monster and the Girl* (1941), and *Bride of the Gorilla* (1951).

During the Middle Ages, apes were associated with many sins, but in time they specialized in those carnal appetites that so preoccupied the church. Their sexual reputation is everywhere. Katharina, the title character in Shakespeare's *Taming of the Shrew,* refers to the common notion that women who died spinsters would "lead apes in hell." A lusty baboon appears in one of the thousand and one tales Scheherazade tells to avoid the fate of the caliph's previous wives. Voltaire's Candide rescues two women from primate pursuers, only to find that the monkeys were their lovers. French animal sculptor Emmanuel Frémiet portrayed a gorilla with a naked woman under his arm, looking like Romulus stealing a Sabine bride.

"Every legend," Carl Denham, the expedition leader, insists, "has a basis of truth." Not this one. Male gorillas are simply not preoccupied with sex—not with female humans, not even with female gorillas. Behaviorist George Schaller witnessed gorillas copulating only twice in more than fifteen months of observing 169 individuals. Observers in both the wild and zoos report that male gorillas seem interested in sex only during the three or four days in which females are ovulating. Since females are usually pregnant or lactating, during which time they don't ovulate, males sometimes go up to a year without sex. To further explode the myth, the female chooses her partner, and both sexes seem affectionate before and after copulation. Perhaps this legend's "basis of truth" is our fear that we, too, may belong to "that hideous order, half-man, half-beast."

---

4 MARCH 1952

The Old Man and the Sea

As if the title alone didn't set the stage, Ernest Hemingway got to the point in the first sentence of *The Old Man and the Sea:* "He was an old man who fished alone in a skiff in the Gulf Stream and he had gone eighty-four days now without taking a fish." The old man goes off by himself to reestablish his manhood in a struggle against the natural world, all the while talking to himself like Hamlet. He talks to a warbler that lands on his fishing line. He talks to the fish. He even talks to his cut hand.

From La Finca Vigia, his home in Cuba, Hemingway began a letter to Scribner's (his publisher) on March 4, 1952, and completed it three days later. He enclosed it with the manuscript of *The Old Man and the Sea,* which, he declared flatly, was the best writing he had ever done, and possibly the best he would ever do.

A lifelong outdoorsman, Hemingway spoke with the authority of which he was so proud. He knew a turtle's heart will beat for hours after it is butchered and he knew what flying fish sound like. The old man in the story knows how to prepare lines with the hook buried deep inside the bait, and all the projecting part of the hook covered with fresh sardines. Although the book is filled with catalog-quality descriptions of bait and tackle and enough detail to serve as a how-to guide for the beginning philosophical fisherman, there is also much clear-eyed observation of nature.

Aboard his lonely boat, out of sight of land, pulled he knows not where by the huge fish he is hoping to tire, the old man has nothing to do but watch the world around him. Hemingway's attention to nature suffuses every page: "He loved green turtles and hawk-bills with their elegance and speed and their great value and he had a friendly contempt for the huge, stupid loggerheads, yellow in their armour-plating, strange in their love-making, and happily eating the Portugese men-of-war with their eyes shut." When the old man hears two porpoises around his boat in the night, he can tell, or at least imagines he can tell, the gender of each by its distinctive blowing sound.

Of course, being a Hemingway character, the old man can't simply love the natural world. He must conquer it. His creator made him a down-on-his-luck fisherman, not a naturalist. That was one reason that for Hemingwayphobes this, his last and shortest novel, was merely the same old story in the same old style, the style so easily parodied in the annual Bad Hemingway Contest: "I wish I could feed the fish, he thought. He is my brother. But I must kill him and keep strong to do it."

Hemingway had written to Charles Scribner, who had read what at that time was planned as part of a larger manuscript, that he was glad Scribner liked what he read but that he would have thought him a fool had he not. Apparently his confidence was well placed. *The Old Man and the Sea* won him his first Pulitzer, and two years later he received the Nobel Prize.

A "Majestic and Formidable Species"

Throughout the twentieth century, both professional ornithologists and amateur bird-watchers have monitored the ups and downs of the ivory-billed woodpecker. A 1917 bird book listed the ivorybill as "nearly" extinct. There have been scattered sightings since, but a 1994 guide says "probably" extinct. Formerly this largest and most striking woodpecker was common in the dense woodlands of both North America and Cuba. "I have seen entire belts of Indian chiefs closely ornamented with the tufts and bills of this species," Audubon wrote. Its skin also served "for the shot pouch of our squatters and hunters." But it wasn't hunting alone that devastated the population. Ivorybills ate wood-boring insects from deep in the inner bark of mature trees that had recently died, a specialized diet that became increasingly scarce as settlers cut the old hardwood forests.

Alexander Wilson, the Scottish immigrant whose *American Ornithology* preceded Audubon's *Birds of America,* called the ivorybill a "majestic and formidable species." In a letter headed "Savannah, 5 March 1809," he wrote to his mentor, fellow naturalist William Bartram, "As far north as Wilmington, in North Carolina, I met with the ivory-billed woodpecker." Today an ivory-billed woodpecker in Wilmington, North Carolina, would draw in birders from all over the world. At the time, though, nothing was known of their range or population. Wilson himself whittled away at the latter. In that era before cameras and binoculars, he acquired his specimens for drawings and paintings the same way Audubon did. He shot them. Wilson killed several ivorybills. Another "was only wounded slightly in the wing, and, on being caught, uttered a loudly reiterated and most piteous note, exactly resembling the violent crying of a young child; which terrified my horse so, as nearly to have cost me my life."

Wilson covered the bird and took it into Wilmington. Practically everyone he passed ran to see the crying infant. At a hotel, a crowd gathered, puzzled that they could find no child. As a joke, Wilson asked for a room for himself and his baby. Finally, to avoid being lynched as a baby-torturer, he uncovered the woodpecker, and everyone—except the poor bird—laughed.

Wilson planned to draw the woodpecker. He rented a room, left the bird there, and went out to tend his horse. While he was gone, the woodpecker did what woodpeckers do. It pecked wood. It clung to the window at ceiling level and hammered the wall. When Wilson returned, he found a fifteen-inch square cleared of plaster, and a hole in the wood underneath large enough for his fist. The bed was covered with plaster and wood chips. Wilson estimated that in another hour, the bird would have worked its way through the wall.

Yet Wilson was determined to care for the creature he had injured. He tied a string around the woodpecker's leg and secured it to the room's table. Then he went out in search of woodpecker food. Later, as he came back up the stairs, he heard the woodpecker hammering on the table—"on which," Wilson wrote, "he had wreaked his whole vengeance." Wilson had to pay for the wall and the table. If he shared any other rooms with woodpeckers, he doesn't mention it.

For more on Alexander Wilson, see 7/12.

"I'll Have a Starling"

"Let me not hear you speak of Mortimer," Henry warns Hotspur in *Henry IV, Part One.* After the king's departure, Hotspur rages to Worcester. At first he says he'll find the king asleep and "holla" in his ear the hated name. Then he has a brainstorm; for his revenge he'll get that scruffy ubiquitous cousin of the mynah, long famed for its mimetic abilities:

> *I'll have a starling shall be taught to speak*
> *Nothing but Mortimer, and give it him*
> *To keep his anger still in motion.*

Little did Shakespeare realize the effect of such a casual line. For, like Henry's anger, the starlings themselves are still in motion. They're everywhere. Long familiar in Europe, their presence in North America can be traced to that single reference in a play. Among the Shakespeare aficionados over the centuries was a wealthy New York drug manufacturer named Eugene Schieffelin. He was president of the Acclimatization Society, a group whose misguided goal was the importation into the United States of every species of bird mentioned in Shakespeare.

There were good reasons *not* to import the starling. Even though in Europe they were regarded by some as attractive—and useful, because they consumed huge quantities of grubs and insects—there was evidence that they could not be safely transplanted without getting out of hand. They had already been established in New Zealand for twenty years when Schieffelin brought them to the United States. It was well known that on that island the population had quickly grown out of proportion and caused extensive agricultural damage.

But the Acclimatization Society ignored the precedents. Already they had failed with chaffinches, skylarks, and nightingales, but they didn't give up. On the sixth of March, 1890, Schieffelin and company released forty pairs in Central Park. By summer the first nest had been found—under the eaves of the American Museum of Natural History. The birds quickly established a thriving colony. For the first few years they stayed around New York City, but gradually they began to wander. By 1959 starlings were being seen on the West Coast.

There are many reasons starlings have been so successful. They are strong and aggressive and willing to evict other birds inhabiting homes they covet. Unlike, say, passenger pigeons, they aren't particular about where those homes may be. Various factors increase their survival rate: several eggs per brood, at least two broods per season, both parents attending the brief incubation. Starlings can see far and near simultaneously, making them less susceptible to predators while foraging. They will eat almost anything—insects (half their diet), fruit, seeds, cattle feed, sandwich crumbs. Even their beaks are unusually strong and efficient. Most other species can close their mouths with speed and force to catch prey or grasp plants, but starlings can exert similar pressure when they open their beaks to pry apart seeds or tear into soil after insects.

Armed with such superlative adaptations, it isn't surprising that starlings have become the great avian success story, and their importation into the United States an ecological fable.

See also Mozart's starling, 5/27.

Scurvy

In his 1840 account of maritime life, *Two Years Before the Mast*, Richard Henry Dana described the sufferings of a fellow sailor afflicted with scurvy: "His legs swelled and pained him so that he could not walk; his flesh lost its elasticity, so that if it was pressed in, it would not return to its shape; and his gums swelled until he could not open his mouth." If allowed to go on long enough, depression, anemia, and lethargy were followed by death. "This disease is not so common now as formerly; and is attributed generally to salt provisions, want of cleanliness, the free use of grease and fat . . . and, last of all, to laziness."

We now know that scurvy actually resulted from vitamin C deficiency. Fruits and vegetables were conspicuously absent from sailors' diets. Shipboard victuals consisted of beer, bread, oatmeal, butter, and pease (meal made from peas, the source of "pease porridge" of nursery rhyme fame). To last even a brief voyage, meat had to be as salty as the briny deep itself, and one sailor complained that "Salt Beef & pork, without vegetables for 14 weeks running, would probably cure a Glutton. . . ."

Scurvy became a problem in the fifteenth century, when sea voyages grew long enough to cause dietary deficiencies. In the late 1490s, sailing around the Cape of Good Hope, Vasco da Gama lost over half his 160 men to scurvy. A few years later, while surveying the coast of Newfoundland, Jacques Cartier's scurvy-ridden crew would have suffered the same fate had the locals not saved their lives with a drink made from vitamin-rich spruce needles. Gradually observers noticed the relationship between the disease and plants. The island Curaçao received its name, which means "cure," from scurvy victims who ate fruit there and recovered. An English herb of the mustard family came to be called "scurvy grass."

In 1753, the physician to the British Royal Navy, James Lind, published *A Treatise of the Scurvy*, which reported dietary experiments suggesting that citrus fruits might cure the disease. One of the earliest to try to *prevent* scurvy was English navigator James Cook. On the seventh of March, 1776, he read a paper on the subject to the Royal Society. He reported that the *Resolution* carried raisins and sauerkraut for every sailor. He also kept fresh water, secured fresh meat, and provided greenery whenever possible, including a brew modeled after Cartier's spruce beer. In three years Cook lost not a single man to scurvy. For his work, the Royal Society presented him with the Copley Medal, awarded each year for "the most useful and most successful experimental inquiry."

Obviously, if Dana witnessed scurvy half a century later, Cook's idea did not take the world by storm. However, in 1795 the British navy finally required ships to carry enough lemons to provide every sailor with juice. Scurvy all but vanished from their ships. As the Napoleonic Wars loomed,

France was not so nutritionally armed; its army was greatly reduced by various ailments, scurvy prominent among them. Some historians attribute a measure of Britain's success in those conflicts to its sailors' swigging daily doses of citrus juice. Soon British vessels were called "lime-juicers," which earned their occupants the nickname Limey. By extension that word came to refer to all the English military, and, by World War II, to English citizens in general.

---

8 MARCH 1970

"Within Fitting Bounds"

"Chestnut Hill College in Pennsylvania asked me to talk about population," Isaac Asimov wrote to a friend on March 8, 1970. In various writings he had described in detail the inevitable horrors the planet would face if world leaders ignored the threat of overpopulation. With that in mind, Asimov prepared his "usual impassioned support of any and all means of birth control," and left for the college. Only when he arrived, however, did he learn that Chestnut Hill was a Catholic girls' school. The prospect of a middle-aged Jewish atheist preaching birth control to an audience of Catholic girls and nuns intimidated even Asimov. In a panic, he asked the student assigned to accompany him what he should do with his planned speech. She replied, "Give it exactly as you would give it elsewhere. We need it." So he did.

Asimov's discomfiture is typical of what advocates of population control have always faced. The earliest study of the effects of unlimited population growth was roundly condemned. The unsigned 50,000-word *Essay on the Principle of Population as It Affects the Future Improvement of Society* appeared in 1798. The author was a pessimistic English economist named Thomas Malthus, who wrote it partially to refute his father's utopian notions of the perfectability of society through redistribution of wealth. Malthus provided a sound mathematical model expressing the result of infinite population growth on finite resources. He concluded that the human population increases geometrically, but its resources arithmetically at best. (It was after reading Malthus that Carlyle branded economics "the dismal science.") Malthus's proposed solution—to teach men not to raise families until they have a guaranteed subsistence—seems just a bit inadequate to the task.

Malthus based his predictions of the result of human numbers on his observations of the effects of unlimited growth in nature. Charles Darwin read Malthus and turned the economist's observations of population pressure back on nature. Darwin, however, followed the implications of such competition to the inevitable changes in the competitors. The man who is considered the codiscoverer of the principle of natural selection, Alfred Russell Wallace, also credited Malthus with giving him insight into the role of competition for resources in what Malthus called "the struggle for existence." Wallace said that, after years of mulling over the problem, the idea of natural selection occurred to him while he wrestled with malarial fever in Malaysia. Tossing on his bed, he remembered Malthus's ideas about "positive checks" to population growth, and "there suddenly flashed upon me the idea of the survival of the fittest."

Of course, there was an awareness of the fecundity of nature before Malthus. Almost half a century earlier, Linnaeus wrote, ". . . I know not by what intervention of nature or by what law man's numbers are kept within fitting bounds." He went on to point out that disease and even war seemed most prevalent in larger populations, and theorized that nature had a built-in regulatory device that maintained what he so casually referred to as the "balance of nature." In 1750, one of Malthus's own sources, Benjamin Franklin, noted the tendency of breeding pigeons to reproduce as much as their artificial environment permitted. He observed that there is "no bound to the prolific nature of plants or animals but what is made by their crowding and interfering with each other's means of subsistence." As long ago as the fourth century B.C., Aristotle summed up the problem of population growth with a casual sentence in his *Historia Animalium*: "If the means of subsistence run short, creatures of like kind will fight together."

See also species, 1/11; and Origin of Species, 11/24.

---

9 MARCH 1796

Strange Bedfellows

The excesses of pet owners are legendary. We regard their indulgence and anthropomorphism with either amusement or scorn, depending upon our own relationship toward such animals. Dogs, especially, seem to inspire adulation in their supposed masters. In the seventeenth century, John Bunyan complained, "Some men cannot go half a mile from home but that they must have dogs at their heels." A contemporary was scandalized: "Over-familiar usage of any brute creature is to be abhorred." Apparently he feared that such usage might lead to unnatural unions between humans and beasts—a common enough occurrence, judging from the frequent admonitions against it.

Hunting dogs had the run of palatial homes—homes that had, as one observer complained, bones and excrement "as ornaments in the hall." In another special category were "ladies' lap dogs," which had to be small to be hugged to bosoms and dandled on knees. Many women took their miniaturized pets to church. Records of lightning strikes in churches, which were common among such tall buildings before the invention of the lightning rod, frequently list canine victims. With so many disorderly animals in the building, many churches were obliged to employ dog whippers to control them. Communion rails were originally designed to keep dogs away from the altar, inspiring one woman to carry her dog with her so they could smooch while she received communion.

It was (and is) not uncommon to find dogs sleeping with their owners. The pious denounced this as a sign of decadence. One seventeenth-century woman on her deathbed saw her dog and cried, "Good husband, you and I have offended God grievously in receiving many a time this bitch into our bed. . . ." She regretted that they had fawned over a mere animal when they would not so lovingly treat a fellow Christian. "The Lord give us grace to repent it."

However, dogs continued to share their owners' beds, as Napoléon Bonaparte learned to his chagrin. On the ninth of March, 1796 (which in the French Revolutionary calendar in use at the time was the nineteenth of Ventôse), the general married the widowed Joséphine de Beauharnais. When they went

Long before he faced Wellington, Napoléon Bonaparte was soundly defeated by another opponent—his wife's dog.

home to her house, Napoléon found Joséphine's bed already inhabited—not by one of her apparently numerous lovers, but by her pug, Fortuné.

Napoléon tried to evict the dog and failed. "I was told," he said later, "that one either had to sleep elsewhere or consent to the arrangement. This irked me somewhat, but I had to take it or leave it." The future emperor of France added, "I gave in." The dog, however, had not agreed to a truce. He bit the newcomer's knee. Napoléon once pointed out Fortuné and said to a visitor, "See that young upstart? He's my rival."

However, Napoléon may have got his revenge. The following summer, the extensive Bonaparte family assembled near Milan for the wedding of his sister. At the villa a mastiff was running free, and it killed Joséphine's beloved Fortuné. She got another. Shortly afterward, Napoléon found the cook training the mastiff away from the villa, out of regard for Joséphine's grief. "Nonsense," the general supposedly exclaimed. "Let him run where he wants. Perhaps he will get rid of this other one for me as well."

See also Joséphine's roses, 6/25.

The Call of the Wolf

Jack London didn't like the title *The Call of the Wild,* and neither did the *Saturday Evening Post,* which was about to begin serialization of it. London mentioned the title controversy to a publisher in a letter of March 10, 1903. Buck, the novel's canine protagonist, is half wolf, and London proposed *The Sleeping Wolf;* however, the magazine preferred simply *The Wolf.* In the end, the *Post* ran the story under the title with which millions of readers are now familiar. The following year, London wrote to the same publisher, describing his plan for a new novel. Not a sequel, he said, but a companion to *The Call of the Wild.* Referring to what would become *White Fang,* he wrote: "Instead of the devolution or decivilization of a dog, I'm going to give the evolution, the civilization of a dog—development of domesticity, faithfulness, love, morality, and all the amenities and virtues." Whatever his civilized traits, White Fang, too, would be close to his wolfish ancestors.

Again and again London returned to his favorite symbol—wolves. His own experience with the animal was limited, but he was moved by its ancient heritage as the symbol of wildness. "To the daughters of the wolf," reads the dedication to one collection, "who have bred and suckled a race of men." London published a story entitled "Brown Wolf," which was the name of his pet husky. His first book was *The Son of the Wolf,* and the captain in his novel *Sea Wolf* is named Wolf Larsen. London owned for a time a pet gray wolf. He called the huge home he designed, which burned two weeks before completion, Wolf House. At times London assumed the role himself, signing letters "Wolf." Even his bookmarks bore his personal totem: a wolf's head. The human characters in his stories are always snarling, baring their teeth, or leaping upon someone, and he described a crowd's response to a speech as "the growl of the pack" and "token of the brute in man."

Jack London's canine characters behave like his human ones. They fight, snarl, bite, growl, and generally reveal their feral origins.

London is one of the authors credited with foreseeing the approach of fascism, as portrayed in his book *The Iron Heel.* Interestingly, wolves were also the favorite symbol of the foremost fascist leader. During World War II, while Lon Chaney Jr. was portraying werewolves as the manifestation of some basic human dichotomy, Adolf Hitler was obsessing on wolves. His famous dog Blondi was a *Wolfshunde,* an Alsation; he named one of her pups "Wolf." Various military headquarters received lupine names—*Werwolf,* and *Wolfsschlucht,* "Wolf's Gulch"; the Volkswagen factory became *Wolfsburg.*

Hitler even felt his wolflike glory and destiny were symbolized in his name. "Adolf" derives from the old German "Athalwolf," which in turn was a combination of two other names, *Athal,* "noble," and *Wolfa,* "wolf." Therefore it isn't surprising that, early in his career, he chose as his political nom de plume "Herr Wolf," and later sometimes identified himself on phone calls as "Conductor Wolf." Perhaps the most disconcerting aspect of the preoccupation Hitler shared with Jack London is the Führer's habit of whistling the hit theme from *The Three Little Pigs,* "Who's Afraid of the Big Bad Wolf?"

See also The Wolf Man, *12/10.*

The First Miracle Drug

In 1906, a young Scot named Alexander Fleming received his medical degree from St. Mary's Hospital Medical School in London. He went on to conduct research in bacteriology there. His service in the medical corps during World War I did not halt his work, and he returned to St. Mary's in 1918 to resume research and teaching. Fleming was trying to find substances that would be toxic to bacteria without harming human beings. Three years after his return, he identified antibiotic agents in lysozyme, an enzyme found in some animals' tissues and secretions (such as saliva and tears).

Fleming began working with *Staphylococcus* bacteria. There are two species of staph, both common. They confine most of their ravages to the skin, but if they enter the bloodstream they can be deadly. In 1928, Fleming observed that spores of the green mold *Penicillium notatum* had contaminated an exposed culture of *Staphylococcus aureus,* leaving a ring around itself that was impressively bacteria-free. He investigated. After isolating the mold, he cultivated it in a fluid medium and found that whatever the substance was, it proved antibacterial even when diluted hundreds of times.

We now know that the several kinds of penicillin all attack bacteria the same way. They inhibit the enzymes that direct the bacterium's production of cell walls, and encourage the manufacture of other enzymes to traitorously begin the breakdown of the walls. For that reason, microorganisms that lack receptors in the walls of their cells already have a head start in resisting the drug. And, of course, microorganisms that lack cell walls entirely are not even threatened by penicillin.

In 1929, Fleming published his results. Over the next several years, he continued to try to perfect a method of producing the drug. In 1941, after years of work, a group of biologists at Oxford, led by Howard W. Florey and Ernst B. Chain, announced that they had developed a method of mass-producing penicillin. That year, Fleming was elected a fellow of the Royal Society, and in 1943 he was knighted. He shared the 1945 Nobel Prize for Physiology or Medicine with Florey and Chain. When Alexander Fleming died on March 11, 1955, he had lived long enough to see the widespread application and wonderful results of his discovery.

However, he left the stage before any of penicillin's negative results became apparent. Of course, as is true of most medicines, some people are allergic to the drug. But more important, in the brief time since the widespread use of penicillin began in the 1940s, some diseases have already developed strains resistant to the antibiotic. New strains appear so quickly because of the astonishingly high rate at which bacteria reproduce, and once they appear they waste no time spreading through the biosphere. Some epidemiologists fear that the overuse of antibiotics on humans and animals has destroyed many competing bacteria and opened up room for the stronger strains to reproduce wildly and eventually wreak havoc. A similar situation resulted from the widespread use of sulfa drugs to treat gonorrhea during World War II. The disease quickly developed antibiotic-resistant strains. Microorganisms' resistance to penicillin reminds some biologists of nature's response to the widespread use of pesticides, and may have similar long-lasting consequences.

The Greatest of Foreign Animals

Humans have held exotic animals captive for many reasons, including religious rituals, entertainment, and scientific curiosity. But one long-standing excuse has been royal ostentation. "It belongs to the position of the great," one observer noted, "to keep horses, dogs, mules, falcons and other birds, court-jesters, singers, and foreign animals." Royal menageries not only entertained the court, but often followed it in its travels to the countryside or even abroad.

Not surprisingly, one of the animals that had the misfortune to become a favorite royal symbol was the largest and strongest land mammal, the elephant. One vainglorious Roman liked to ride out to dinner astride his pet elephant. Charlemagne had several exotic animals in his palace, including an elephant he received from Harun ar-Rashid, the caliph of Baghdad glorified in the *Arabian Nights.* By the time of the Italian Renaissance, elephants were obligatory in the illustrious menageries of Florence, Milan, and Rome.

The most famous exploit of the Carthaginian general Hannibal was his trek through the Alps with a supply train of elephants, on his way to attack Rome.

The elephant flattered royal vanity. No stronger symbol of power could be found, simply because the price of acquiring and maintaining an elephant was so steep. Feeding alone could break the budget of a palace. Thus elephants became popular gifts between monarchs. When Henry IV of France learned that England's Queen Elizabeth coveted his elephant, he was only too glad to part with it. Likewise, after Cardinal Giovanni de' Medici became Pope Leo X, King Manuel of Portugal, a good Catholic and a good politician, thoughtfully sent him both an elephant and a rhinoceros. The latter didn't arrive; its ship foundered at sea. Lions and leopards from Florence, and bears from Hungary, had a better survival rate, and made their way to the new pontiff.

This particular Leo* is perhaps best known for his sale of indulgences to finance the rebuilding of St. Peter's, which provoked Martin Luther and led to the Reformation. But before he was a pope, Giovanni was a Medici. As the son of Lorenzo the Magnificent, patronage of the arts and sciences was in his blood. Ever since he returned from educational travel abroad, he had lived in more of a museum than a house. He encouraged arts and scholarship, but just as important to him was the royal menagerie.

So it is not surprising that Leo featured his new elephant in his pontifical procession on March 12, 1514. He sat surrounded by cardinals and a worshipful crowd. Ridden by a trained mahout, the pope's great symbol of his power approached at a respectful pace and stopped before him. At a signal from the mahout, it knelt. (Perhaps Leo was not surprised. Supposedly Saint Anthony's horse had knelt to receive communion. Did not Solomon himself declare that all creatures praise the Lord?) Then the elephant performed one of those pranks that, among circus trainers and zookeepers, give the elephant a reputation for a sense of humor. It turned to a nearby container of perfumed water, filled its trunk, and drenched the pontiff and his entourage.

See also Jumbo, *2/22.*

---

13 MARCH 1781

The First New Planet

An hour or two before midnight, on the evening of Tuesday, March 13, 1781, a musician named William Herschel sat in his house in Bath, England. He was not performing music, or teaching it, or engaged in any of the other ways he earned his living. He was exploring the sky through a telescope. Like so many musicians, he was interested in mathematics. Several years before, that interest had led to a study of geometrical optics, and thence very naturally to astronomy. For Herschel, it was not enough to be a harpsichordist, a violinist, and an oboist, not to mention the organist at the famed Octagon Chapel. He had set himself the goal of determining whether the unchanging firmament was indeed unchanging, or if it, like the planets, moved. He was determined, he wrote, "never to pass by" even the smallest segment of the sky "without due investigation."

---

* What's in a name? This famously pacific man surprised everyone by calling himself neither the devout *Pius* nor the gentle *Clemens,* but the more ferocious *Leo.*

Herschel was a patient, careful observer. On that fateful evening, he sat peering through his 6½-inch telescope and making notes. He wrote that he had seen "a curious either nebulous star or perhaps a comet." Clouds prevented observation over the next few nights. When the sky cleared, Herschel "looked for the comet or nebulous star, and found it is a comet, for it has changed its place." The members of the Bath Literary and Philosophical Society were soon treated to "An Account of a Comet," unaware that this was the first public mention of a wonderful discovery that would soon be known all over the world.

Because they were visible to the naked eye, five planets besides Earth were known to the ancients—Mercury, Venus, Mars, Jupiter, and Saturn. Those five were about to have to make way for a newcomer, for Herschel had found the planet he would ultimately name Uranus. With that name, Herschel continued the mythological family of planets named by the ancients. In Greek mythology, Uranus was the personification of the sky as a fertile element.

The extensive photographic records that now document the appearance of every corner of the sky were not available to Herschel and his colleagues. However, the planet's orbit could be calculated, and astronomers searched their hand-drawn star maps for formerly overlooked clues to the existence of Uranus. It turned out that earlier observers had seen Uranus, and even noted it on star maps. However, never imagining that there might be more wanderers than the five visible to the naked eye, they failed to recognize it as a planet. We now know that it had been recorded and either overlooked or misinterpreted more than twenty times, nine of them by a single astronomer, the Frenchman Pierre Charles Le Monnier. He was so mortified by the discovery that he could bring himself to mention in print only four of his previous sightings.

With the fame attending his identification of the sixth planet, Herschel was able to devote himself to his passion—astronomy. However, all his life he fought the claim that his discovery was "accidental." In the finest tradition of amateur contributions to science, it was by dint of his after-hours, unpaid studies that Herschel proved himself a professional observer. "Had I not seen it when I did," he later remarked, "I must inevitably have come upon it soon after, since my telescope was so perfect that I was able to distinguish it from a fixed star in the first minute of observation." And he added, "I had gradually perused the great Volume of the Author of Nature and was now come to the page which contained the seventh Planet."

---

14 MARCH 1890

Le Zig Zag

Étienne Léopold Trouvelot moved to the United States from France in 1857, at the age of thirty. Apparently he was fleeing Napoleon III's Second Empire. He settled in Medford, Massachusetts, near Boston, and in time built a career in entomology and, later, astronomy. Biographical details are sketchy, but it is known that soon after his arrival Trouvelot became enthusiastic about an old-world enterprise that many people were trying to establish in the New—sericulture, the cultivation of silkworms. Ever since 1619, colonial and then state governments had encouraged the ancient practice of silkworm farming, sometimes even going so far as to fine those who *didn't* cultivate silkworms. Land developers made money, as did importers of mulberries (the sole food of *Bombyx mori,* the silkworm), but many silkworm farmers went bankrupt.

For some reason, sericulture promoters remained optimistic. Then, in the middle of the nineteenth century, silkworms began to be plagued by a devastating disease. Sericulturists worldwide looked for other moths that could be crossed with *B. mori* to make a hardier insect. Étienne Trouvelot experimented with various American moths that at that time were classed in the same family as the silkworm, Bombycidae. Presumably he thought related moths would be likelier to interbreed with their potentially profitable cousin. None did, and that may have been because none of them were as closely related as entomologists then thought. Then Trouvelot went on a fateful trip. In 1866, he returned to Europe. He either brought back with him to the United States or later shipped specimens of a moth from his homeland. The French called it *le zig zag,* the Germans knew it as *Schwammspinner,* and in England it was the gypsy moth.

The gypsy moth's periodic outbreaks were well known in Europe and elsewhere. But that didn't stop Trouvelot from bringing them home to try to cross them with the silkworm. His hybridization failed. Along the way, apparently in either 1868 or 1869, some of the insects escaped from his house. Stories claim variously that Trouvelot's maid threw the eggs out when she was cleaning his room, that he left egg masses on a windowsill and the wind scattered them, and that caterpillars simply strolled away to explore the New World. More than a decade later, when a new tenant moved onto Trouvelot's property, he "found the shed in the rear of his house swarming with caterpillars."

In light of their subsequent ravages on the U.S. landscape, and the fortunes spent to eradicate them, the initial declaration of war against gypsy moths is comical. In 1889, the Medford Road Commission assigned $300 for putting inked bands on trees. With a growing awareness of the magnitude of the problem, the next year the price on the insects' tiny heads skyrocketed. On March 14, 1890, the Massachusetts legislature allocated $25,000 toward a showdown, then immediately doubled it. Since then, there have been countless attempts to eradicate gypsy moths.

Methods tried include the introduction of the moth's natural enemies and the distribution of millions of gallons of insecticides. All failed. Insecticides don't succeed in killing every individual in their targeted species. Like any of the more "natural" tribulations that might befall an insect, they leave behind the strongest and most resistant individuals. Having withstood their trial by fire, these hardy survivors proceed to be fruitful and multiply. In time, as they exhaust their resources, they move on. In this way, sprayings of poison are frequently counterproductive. They keep a species' population low enough that it doesn't attract the predators and epidemics that would normally limit a population out of bounds.

The problem is that gypsy moths in the United States are thousands of miles away from those natural enemies. Periodically there are outbreaks of them in their native range from Japan to Portugal, but the diseases and predators with which they evolved tend to limit the infestations' severity and duration. When Trouvelot imported gypsy moths into the United States in 1869, there was nothing around to stop them.

For another alien animal introduced into the United States, see 3/6.

"Constant as the Northern Star"

It is the Ides of March in Shakespeare's *Julius Caesar*. Unaware of the daggers hidden in the cloaks of the men around him, Julius Caesar is holding forth. As their pretense for surrounding the dictator, Metellus Cimber and others beg enfranchisement for Metellus's exiled brother. Caesar declines to reverse his decision, with one of his frequent allusions to his own fine character:

> *. . . I am constant as the northern star,*
> *Of whose true-fix'd and resting quality*
> *There is no fellow in the firmament.*

This is one of Shakespeare's worst scientific gaffes. The North Star is actually, in its own subtle way, as inconstant as the Moon. This speech doesn't appear in Plutarch's life of Caesar; the words and the sentiment belong to Shakespeare. Julius Caesar wouldn't have made the analogy, because during his time there was no North Star.

The star we call Polaris has a magnitude of 2.1, which places its brightness among the top two dozen or so stars, although in reality it is 6,000 times as luminous as the Sun. Since it is 680 light-years away, we are observing it as it looked that many years ago, in the time of Marco Polo. To us it seems to be the hub of the night sky, with the major constellations obediently circling around it. This is because of the rotation of Earth on its axis. An imaginary extension of our planet's axis, emerging from the North and South Poles, intersects the sky. We call these intersection points, directly above the poles on Earth, the North and South Celestial Poles. What is actually the rotation of Earth around its axis appears to us as the revolution of the stars around those celestial poles.

It so happens that near the North Celestial Pole is a relatively bright star. For that reason we call it Polaris, or the Pole Star, or the North Star. In reality, since it is a degree away from true north, it too revolves around the celestial pole, but this motion is not apparent to casual observers. In the Southern Hemisphere, Polaris's nearest equivalent is Sigma Octantis, which is barely visible without a telescope. Thus there is no true South Star.

It was the painstaking Greek astronomer Hipparchus, in the second century b.c., who noticed that the Sun doesn't return to the same position in the zodiac at every vernal equinox. It advances slowly westward. This is the result of Earth's rotation wrestling with the gravitational pull of the Sun and the Moon on Earth's equatorial bulge. Earth's axis is tilted 23½° to the plane in which the planet orbits. If the axis were perpendicular to that plane, we would have no seasons. With Earth tilted and spinning, like a giant top, its axis wobbles. That process is called the "precession of the equinoxes."

For Earth's axis to wobble a full circle takes 25,800 years, during which time the North Celestial Pole points to several different stars. In the time of Tutankhamen, for example, the closest thing to a

North Star was Thuban, the second-brightest star in the constellation Draco. During the reign of Julius Caesar, roughly 1,300 years later, there was no prominent star near the North Celestial Pole. Twelve thousand years from now, the closest nominee for North Star will be Vega, the brightest member of the constellation Lyra. And, finally, at the end of the cycle, Polaris will take its turn again.

See also Shakespeare and the Lupercalia, 2/15; and starlings, 3/6; and the Wars of the Roses, 8/22.

---

16 MARCH 1798

Smallpox

> The deviation of man from the stage in which he was originally placed by nature seems to have proved to him a prolific source of diseases. From the love of splendour, from the indulgences of luxury, and from his fondness for amusement he has familiarised himself with a great number of animals, which may not originally have been intended for his associates. . . .

In that moralizing tone, Edward Jenner began his first paper on vaccination. Then he launched into a description of certain diseases well known in the dairy country of his native Gloucestershire, England. One was an inflammation of the heel suffered by horses, and named by farriers "the grease." Jenner explained how anyone treating that ailment and then proceeding to milk a cow without proper hygiene would communicate the grease to the udder of the cow. The result would be an outbreak of pustules. "This disease has obtained the name of the cow-pox." Scientists later learned that the grease and cowpox are not the same, but that didn't invalidate the rest of Jenner's findings.

The effect of cowpox on the cows was bad enough, resulting in indisposition and reduced milk production. But there were also other effects. Those men and maids who had been milking infected animals soon found their hands developing inflammations, which in turn became pus-filled suppurations. Listlessness, headaches, and vomiting followed over the next few days. However, cowpox was not fatal. At this point in his paper, Jenner got to the real subject: "What renders the cow-pox virus so extremely singular is that the person thus affected is forever after secure from the infection of the smallpox. . . ." Jenner proceeded to document his claims with a number of case histories. Case XVIII, for example, was that of a five-year-old child named John Baker, whom Jenner inoculated on March 16, 1798, with matter taken from a pustule on the hand of an infected man.

Smallpox was an ancient and fearsome disease. When Rameses V died in twelfth-century-B.C. Egypt, his mummifiers preserved along with everything else the evidence that he suffered from smallpox. The disease killed Pocahontas and King Louis XV of France. Since it had long plagued the Old World, it helped resistant Europeans wipe out vulnerable native peoples of the New. Over the several thousand years of recorded history, smallpox has felled literally hundreds of millions of human beings.

Caused by a member of Orthopoxvirus, a nasty family of specialized poxes with such unlikely designations as monkeypox and buffalopox, it was eagerly infectious and frequently fatal.

The relationship between cowpox and smallpox did not occur to Jenner in a vision. It was a common belief among the local peasantry. It was Jenner, however, who thought to deliberately introduce small amounts of the material in the pustules of cowpox sufferers to prevent the much more dangerous smallpox. We now know that the introduction of the milder virus encourages the production of antibodies. In honor of Jenner's successful inoculations with cowpox virus, French chemist Louis Pasteur, who had been experimenting with other forms of inoculation, named the whole process "vaccination," from *vaccinus,* a Latin word meaning "of cows." Neither Pasteur nor Jenner originated the concept of inoculation, which, in primitive forms, had been a folk remedy throughout much of the East for centuries. Earlier in the eighteenth century, a Greek physician had reported successful inoculations through the method of touching a knife to a sufferer's sores and then scratching an uninfected person. At about the same time, Lady Mary Wortley Montague had her child inoculated in Turkey. But it was Edward Jenner who analyzed the nature of the problem and raised vaccination above the level of folk remedy.

Nonetheless, resistance to vaccination was ferocious. Jenner's first papers were rejected. Undaunted, in 1798 he published them in a book, *An Inquiry into the Causes and Effects of the Variolae Vaccinae, or Cow-Pox.* One memorable antivaccination cartoon from 1802 portrays Jenner inoculating an obviously frightened woman, while around them earlier victims cavort—people with small cattle-shaped excrescences erupting on their arms, from their ears and noses, even through their mouths. Slowly the medical community, and as a result their legislators, began to support the radical new notion. In 1807, vaccination became compulsory in Bavaria, and other nations followed. The last recorded case of smallpox occurred in Somalia in 1977.

Saint Patrick's Day

Why is Saint Patrick commemorated on March 17? Scholars disagree. However, they do agree that he converted the Irish pagans to Christianity during the first half of the fifth century. At that time, the Druids celebrated their vernal New Year rites with hilltop bonfires. Patrick, like many a shrewd missionary before him, knew to adapt the local customs to his own purposes. He Christianized the fires into an Easter observance.

Legend claims Patrick taught the Irish distillation and elevated the shamrock to a national symbol by using its three leaflets to demonstrate the nature of the Trinity: three spiritual parts that form one godhead. Distillation may have been Patrick's gift, but evidently the shamrock already represented a triad for the Druids—earth, sea, and sky. It also appeared in Celtic fertility rites.

The plant usually considered the Irish shamrock is the lesser yellow trefoil, *Trifolium mimus.* "Shamrock" comes from *seamrag,* the Gaelic name for the trefoil; its genus includes the common red and

Apparently, without Patrick, Ireland would be snake-infested, teetotaling, and overrun with insignificant clover. Two of the saint's supposed legacies are combined in the traditional Irish custom of "drowning the shamrock."

white clovers that carpet Britain and the United States. The trefoil is a common motif in ornamental architecture, and heraldry employs a threefold clover leaf complete with stem. That same silhouette appears in the suit of clubs in playing cards. Both the suit name and the word "clover" come from the Latin *clava,* "club," because the trefoil reminded someone of the three-knobbed club of Hercules.

Followers attributed supernatural feats to Patrick. An old Irish song honors his most famous:

> *The toads went pop, the frogs went hop, slap-dash into the water,*
> *And the snakes committed suicide to save themselves from slaughter.*

According to legend, Patrick drove the amphibians and reptiles from Ireland, like God banishing the serpent from the Garden of Eden. In 1187, Giraldus Cambrensis declared that in Ireland there were no tortoises, scorpions, or dragons. He was correct. In the earliest European guidebook, his famous *Fyrst Boke of the Introduction of Knowledge* (1548), Andrew Boorde added, "There is no Adder, nor Snake, no Toode, nor Lyzerd, nor no Euyt, nor none such lyke." He was mistaken. The island has one species each of toad, lizard, and newt—and one frog. True, there are no snakes.

Saint Patrick got the credit for the result of prehistoric climatic changes. During the last ice age, so much water was contained in ice that the sea levels sank. Dry land connected Ireland with England,

and England with the European mainland. As the ice melted, the seas isolated Ireland (c. 8000 B.C.) before filling the deeper channel between Britain and Europe (c. 5000 B.C.). Because their body temperature responds to their surroundings, reptiles and amphibians emigrated from the continent only after Britain became more hospitable. A few snakes reached England, but it was too late for Ireland.

Some natives claim that Patrick overlooked one venerable old serpent that lived in Lake Dilveen. He promised to return on the next Monday to banish it, too, but he forgot. Even now, once a week the old snake surfaces, peers around, and says, "It's been a long Monday, Patrick."

---

18 MARCH 1965

The Flat Earth

An American science writer told the story about how, after writing about astronomy for years, he finally viewed Earth's satellite through a telescope and exclaimed, "Good heavens, there *are* craters on the Moon!" A Soviet cosmonaut once experienced a similar revelation. On March 18, 1965, the Soviet Union launched *Voskhod 2*. Its pilot, Alexei Leonov, is remembered as the first human being to perform an extra-vehicular activity, or EVA, popularly known as a "space walk." Leonov exited the *Voskhod*'s airlock and, at the end of a tether, floated in space for just over twelve minutes. Far below him, on that green and blue jewel glowing against the black, was Africa. "In one glance I could see from Gibraltar to the Caspian Sea." And he was able to prove with his eyes what his brain already knew: "I looked down at the Earth, and the first thought that crossed my mind was 'The world is round, after all.'"

For centuries the knowledge that the Earth is round did indeed seem to defy the senses. "At one time, the earth was supposed to be flat," Vincent van Gogh wrote near the end of his life. "Well, so it is, even today, from Paris to Asnières. But that fact doesn't prevent science from proving that the earth as a whole is spherical. No one nowadays denies it." One who didn't deny it but who saw the paradox in the knowledge was George Bernard Shaw. "In the Middle Ages," he wrote in the preface to his play *Saint Joan*, "people believed that the Earth was flat, for which they had at least the evidence of their senses: we believe it to be round, not because as many as one per cent of us could give the physical reason for so quaint a belief, but because modern science has convinced us that nothing that is obvious is true. . . ."

The roundness of the Earth is not a recent discovery. Although jokes and cartoons portray Columbus worrying about sailing off the edge of the Earth, he and his sponsors could not have pursued their goal of a western route to the East without full realization of the sphericity of the planet. The evidence was there. The classic example of a ship's mast seeming to sink beneath the waves was enough for some people. The most difficult mental hurdle seems to have been the idea that those on the other side of the globe would be upside down. (These thinkers knew that *they* were certainly standing upright.) The third-century Christian writer Lactantius summed up this idea: "Can any one be so foolish as to believe that there are men whose feet are higher than their heads, or places where things may be hanging downwards, trees growing backwards, or rain falling upwards? Where is the marvel of the hanging gardens of Babylon if we are to allow of a hanging world at the Antipodes?" The word "antipodes" means "feet opposite."

Flat-earthers have actually claimed NASA went so far as to fake the Moon landings. The 1977 film *Capricorn One* exploits that notion, with NASA simulating the first flight to Mars by filming astronauts that are actually roaming the Southwest U.S. desert. And what, one might ask, would be the reason for such a complicated sham? The fanatic nineteenth-century flat-earth prophet John Hampden answered that when he denounced "that Satanic device of a round and revolving globe, which sets Scripture, reason, and facts at defiance."

In the twentieth century, there has been evidence enough for all but the most committed flat-earthers. In 1935, a photograph taken from a height of almost 14 miles clearly depicted the curvature of Earth's surface. In 1959, the *Explorer VI* satellite transmitted back home photographs, taken from almost 20,000 miles over Mexico, of a delicate sunlit crescent Earth against the blackness of space. Since 1961, when Soviet cosmonaut Yuri Gagarin first orbited the decidedly spherical Earth, countless others have experienced it for themselves—and most were as impressed as Alexei Leonov.

See also the view from the Moon, 7/20.

---

19 MARCH 1963

Birds Attack Bodega Bay

In 1963 birds invaded Hollywood. There was *The Yellow Canary, Sparrows Can't Sing,* even *Bye Bye Birdie.* And on March 19, Alfred Hitchcock's *The Birds* opened. Reviewers went into one of those feeding frenzies that have been described as a "delirium of interpretation." The film was an ecological fable of an avenging Mother Earth. No, it was an allegory of the classical Furies pursuing the wicked. *Variety* praised the novelty of its premise. *Time* said the film flapped to a plotless ending. Later, one critic said with a straight face, "the birds are best seen as an objective correlative of the arbitrariness of life."

However successful (or not) the film was as cinematic art, it was a memorable moment in the interaction of humans and other animals. Of course, Hitchcock either eschewed articulating or had never formed any philosophical stance behind the assault on Bodega Bay. But then he wasn't famous for portraying redeeming social values. "Ours not to reason why," he once said, "ours just to scare the hell out of people."

In *The Birds,* Hitchcock got what he was after. The vicious birds attack a children's birthday party, fly through a chimney to assault a group indoors, surround a woman in a phone booth, and strafe fleeing schoolchildren. Hitchcock used over 400 trick shots. Their success varied; in some scenes the birds and the people are clearly on separate films. One scene in which the birds attack Tippi Hedren required days of assistants throwing birds at her. She wound up with genuine injuries.

In the arts, as in life, nature had been unkind to humans before *The Birds.* Even the play of the same title by Aristophanes, although fantastical and satirical, derives from our fear that nature is fickle and its agenda not necessarily ours. Of course, science fiction movies from *Them!* to *Alien* deal with more monstrous creatures than the local songbirds. But it's more frightening to think that our everyday companions—creatures we erroneously perceive as our happy little friends—might turn on us.

"Logic," Hitchcock declared, "is dull." Therefore no explanation is advanced for the bloodthirsty birds. The meaningless attacks in this film are said to have spawned a genre. There have been numerous vengeful-nature films since, including such silliness as *Frogs,* or the giant bunnies in *Night of the Lepus* (both 1972). And the concept hasn't been confined to film. In Berton Rouché's novel *Feral,* abandoned cats on Long Island revert to a bloodthirsty wild state in which they attack summer residents. Stephen King's *Cujo* is about a homicidal dog.

Although Evan Hunter's adaptation expanded the human role, there was little more character development in Hitchcock's film than in Daphne du Maurier's original story. Hitchcock said the birds were the stars. As such, they got so much media coverage that the *New Yorker* remarked, "If this picture is a hit, the Audubon Society has an ugly public relations job on its hands."

---

20 MARCH 1345

Stars Blamed for the Plague

For a long time the word "plague," from the Latin for a severe blow, meant any epidemic fever that killed large numbers. There have been countless plagues throughout history—typhus, dysentery, influenza. The Greek anatomist Galen tells of fleeing an outbreak of what appears to have been smallpox. Such epidemics weakened the Roman Empire. Marcus Aurelius died during one.

But gradually the term has become almost synonymous with bubonic plague, the Black Death, which periodically ravaged Europe from the 1300s to the late 1700s. The literature of the time abounds in references to the disease. Boccaccio's travelers in the *Decameron* are fleeing plague. Daniel Defoe's *Journal of a Plague Year* recounts the horrors. When plague closed the London stages, Shakespeare wrote poems instead of plays. Many saw the mass deaths as punishment for humanity's sins, like the biblical plagues of locusts. However, as one observer noted, priests were smitten "as readily as whores," and among the best sources of information on the era are lists of plague-related clerical vacancies. Some reasoned that, if plague was the wrath of God, penance ought to help. Scourging became such a popular pastime it inspired a Brotherhood of Flagellants that finally had to be quelled by the pope. Dancing manias erupted—the tarantella, and the *danse macabre,* or "dance with death."

To their credit, some physicians of the time sought the plague's origins and cure. Unfortunately, while renouncing divine displeasure as a source, they turned to astrology, which at that time was still a common tool of the medical profession. They decided that the plague was caused by atmospheric pollution. This *miasma,* from a Greek word meaning a stain or pollution, was said to result from an unfortunate conjunction of Mars, Jupiter, and Saturn in the constellation Aquarius, at 1:00 P.M. on the twentieth of March, 1345.

It is now known that bubonic plague was actually spread by rats, especially black rats. A flea imbibing the blood of an infected rat would ingest the lethal bacteria. When its host rat died, it would prefer another rat, but with the rodent population also devastated, it was usually willing to settle for a human being.

Death from the plague was agonizing. It was called bubonic from bubo, the term for the characteristic swelling of lymph glands in the armpit or groin. Bubonic had two siblings, pneumonic and septicemic, both less common but more severe. The majority of bubonic sufferers died within five days of contracting the illness. Pneumonic plague attacked the lungs, and victims seldom lasted more than three days. The quickest killer was the septicemic strain, a blood poison that needed less than twenty-four hours to work.

Bubonic itself wasn't terribly infectious; filthy hovels and unwashed clothing simply incubated contagion. The urban poor were the most affected by the disease, but urban crowding in general was recognized as a factor. Not that this led to more hygienic attitudes. Actually, it led to greater divisiveness. Although even highborn urbanites were unwelcome outside the city, during one outbreak the royal court simply retreated to Windsor and banned trade with London.

---

21 MARCH 1885

"The Fit Ousting the False"

Because English-speaking birders have resisted attempts to teach them scientific names, the American Ornithological Union (AOU) and other organizations work toward a standardization of common names. That sounds like a contradiction in terms, since common names are the local designations that contain much of birding's colorful history. It is a contradiction that has inspired much debate among both backyard birders and professional ornithologists. In the 1880s, the fledgling AOU launched a journal to inform and unite its membership. English, Australian, and French ornithologists had named their birding journals, not surprisingly, after birds—*Ibis, Emu,* and *Alauda* ("Lark"), respectively. The AOU followed suit, and named their periodocal *The Auk,* after the flightless North American penguin that became extinct in the mid-1800s.

One of *The Auk*'s first campaigns was on behalf of standardized common names. On March 21, 1885, Canadian naturalist and writer Ernest Thompson Seton—who was also, among a long list of accomplishments, cofounder of the Boy Scouts of America—wrote a letter about the controversy.

> To the Editors of *The Auk:*
>
> The "powers that be," I understand, are preparing a "Check List" and revising the scientific and popular names of our birds.
>
> There is no doubt that scientific names are entirely in the hands of scientists, but it seems to be overlooked that popular names are just as completely in the hands of the people. Scientists may advise, but not dictate on this point.

Seton praised the stark, clear Anglo-Saxon names that had evolved from descriptions, such as thrush, hawk, and nightjar (which is now known, after its call, as the whippoorwill). In sharp contrast, he thought, were the "so-called popular, but really translated, scientific, spurious English names." His list of offensive terms included both those translated from Latin, such as semipalmated and gallinule, and those burdened with their discoverers' names, including Sprague's lark, Leconte's sparrow, and Baird's bunting. "[S]uch nomenclature," he wrote, "*cannot* stand the test of time." He complained that these names were artificial and nondescriptive, and thus would suffer the fate of the poorly adapted.

"As an example of the fit ousting the false," Seton wrote, "note how, in spite of the scientists, 'Veery' is supplanting 'Wilson's Thrush' throughout the length and breadth of the land." Seton's prediction on that point was correct; *Catharus fuscescens* is now known far and wide as the veery, a name apparently imitative of its call. Examples of helpfully descriptive common names appear among the veery's fellow thrushes—gray-cheeked (appearance), veery (song), wood (habitat), and hermit (behavior).

Another aspect of bird names that stirs controversy results from the great virtue of science—that it, unlike many other human constructs, is self-revising. This ongoing evolution is visible in any two subsequent editions of a birding field guide. For example, until the AOU revised the taxonomy (and thus, of course, the nomenclature) in 1980, North American field guides listed three species of eastern flicker—the yellow-shafted, the red-shafted, and the gilded. Each had its own Latin designation following the genus *Colaptes*. New editions list a single species with three geographical races. Ornithologists found that the populations were interbreeding, and were therefore, by the definition of the term, not separate species. The process was reversed in classifying juncos. The white-winged, slate-colored, Oregon, and gray-headed were lumped into a single species now called the dark-eyed junco.

The need for precise classification is small comfort to those sport-minded birders who accumulate life lists of the species they've seen. How can you keep track of your sightings if the experts keep changing the names around? Granted, the issue is not of earth-shaking significance, but it's one with which Ernest Thompson Seton would have sympathized. It, too, is a question of what's in a name.

---

22 MARCH 1971

Ecological Crimes

In his 1902 essay "A Defense of Detective Stories," G. K. Chesterton wrote of the genre, "It is the earliest and only form of popular literature in which is expressed some sense of the poetry of modern life." Mystery writers have always wrestled with crime and alienation, and a few sneaked in other topics along the way. However, one topic that took many years to worm its way into detective fiction was our relationship with our planet. The man who raised readers' ecological awareness was a California novelist and environmental activist named Kenneth Millar. Under the pen name Ross Macdonald, he wrote about private detective Lew Archer. Eventually his two interests merged. On March 22, 1971, *Newsweek* honored Millar's hybrid art with a gesture achieved by few writers, either mainstream or genre. He appeared on its cover.

Like many others, Kenneth Millar and his wife, crime novelist Margaret Millar, came to greater ecological awareness through birding, an experience she recorded in her book *The Birds and Beasts Were There.* They fought for the San Rafael Wilderness Act of 1964 and organized lobbies. He wrote articles, including "A Death Road for the Condor," about the government's attempt to build a road in a wilderness area populated by the few remaining condors. "The condor is our canary in the mine—the mine slowly filling with pollutants, which is a possible image of our world—and if the condor survives, perhaps we may, too."

In January of 1969, an explosion at an offshore drilling rig in Santa Barbara Channel spouted roughly a million gallons of crude oil into the sea. Another two million gallons leaked out in the next few months. The event helped to galvanize the U.S. environmental movement, and both Millars worked hard during the disaster, picketing, giving interviews, and cofounding GOO (Get Oil Out). Photographs show Kenneth Millar carrying a "Ban the Blob" sign. Afterward he wrote, "Our ease and confidence in our environment has cracked, slightly but permanently, like an egg."

If the spill was to have meaning, Millar felt, "that meaning would have to be created by the people on the scene." Therefore he placed the spill in the heart of his next novel, *Sleeping Beauty.* "I think I'll make this the first environmental mystery novel," he told a friend. He had already fictionalized the 1964 Coyote Canyon fire for his novel *The Underground Man,* but that disaster played a less symbolic role. In *Sleeping Beauty,* human violence blurs into ecological violence. Archer flies over the spill's damage: "An offshore oil platform stood up out of its windward end like the metal handle of a dagger that had stabbed the world and made it spill black blood." Throughout his novels, Macdonald interwove the story of human individuals, their generation, and their fellow creatures. "He belonged," he said of one young man, "to a generation whose elders had been poisoned, like the pelicans, with a kind of moral DDT that damaged the lives of their young."

Macdonald valued his conservation work as much as his mystery novels. He was pleased to learn that the *New York Times* had in its files a tentative obituary for him in which they described him as both "novelist and environmentalist."

---

23 MARCH 1955

Pod People

"There's something strange going on in Santa Mira."
—Dr. Miles Bennell, in *INVASION OF*
THE BODY SNATCHERS

The Body Snatchers, Jack Finney's novel about plantlike aliens that take over human bodies and minds, appeared in installments in *Collier's* in the mid-1950s. Film producer Walter Wanger liked it and hired Don Siegel to direct a film version. "*Invasion of the Body Snatchers* was the idea of some studio pod,"

Siegel said later. "The title I wanted was *Sleep No More*." A reference to Hamlet's to-kill-myself-or-not-to-kill-myself soliloquy, the rejected title embodied not only Siegel's concept of vigilance against conformity, but also his own lifelong insomnia. In the film, it meant that the pods couldn't take over victims' minds until they slept.

Filming began on the twenty-third of March, 1955. The human characters are the stars; no aliens appear other than in their pupal state as huge seedpods. What little money Siegel spent on special effects went mostly into the greenhouse scene, in which Kevin McCarthy's character, Dr. Miles Bennell, finds pods ripening with replicas of himself and Dana Wynter's character, Becky. Miles stabs his pod-self with a pitchfork, as if driving a stake through its heart. Science fiction often replaces that horror movie staple, demonic possession, with a more "scientific" occupancy by nonsupernatural tenants. Rooted in the same fear, each conforms to the predispositions of its genre. Robert A. Heinlein's *Puppet Masters,* to which Finney's novel has been compared, is another example.

Miles speculates on the origin of the pods. "It may be the result of atomic radiation on plant life, or animal life—some weird alien organism—a mutation of some kind." A reasonable guess, a decade after Hiroshima. Another character, however, after he becomes a pod and helps capture Miles, explains: "Seeds, drifting through space for years, took root in a farmer's field. From the seeds came pods, which have the power to reproduce themselves in the exact likeness of any form of life." The method by which the pods replace humans echoes the ancient idea of the homunculus, the notion that from conception the fetus was a complete miniature human being that simply grew larger inside the passive vessel of the female body.

The variety of analyses of the film is amusing. It's a leftist satire on Communist paranoia. It's a right-wing anti-Communist "Invasion of the Pinkos." (Never mind that the scriptwriter had been a Communist activist.) One critic obsessed on the similarity of the star's surname to that of a witch-hunting senator. Another insisted that the film was basically a "surrealistic projection" of Miles's fear of sex with Becky and claimed that, when Jack drops a bottle and cuts his hand, he is acting out his fear of castration, as proven by his tellingly "vulvaic" wound.

Apparently no early reviews mentioned a subtext. From the first, Siegel and his crew had been referring to conformists as "pods." The producer addressed the film's meaning in a speech to booksellers about the threat of censorship. "The film shows how easy it is for people to be taken over and to lose their souls if they are not alert and determined in their character to be free. Otherwise they will become mere vegetables—just pods."

See also the intellectual carrot, 11/1.

---

24 MARCH (DATE VARIES)

Easter

The Christian holy day of Easter falls on the first Sunday after the full moon that follows the vernal equinox, which means it can occur any time between March 22 and April 25. It commemorates the central tenet of the Christian faith, the bodily resurrection of Jesus Christ. Some sort of feast on Easter was an established custom by the second century after Christ's death, but there was considerable squabbling over the precise date. Just as there is no record of his birth date, so no one knows the date on which he died.

In the fourth century, the Roman emperor Constantine I converted to Christianity. (It was he who later moved the capital of the Roman Empire to Byzantium, which he renamed Constantinople.) The Edict of Milan in 313 established Christianity as not only legal but emperor-approved. A decade later, Constantine convened the first Council of Nicaea. It denounced the heretical teachings of Arianism, which denied the divinity of Christ, and established the date of an official annual celebration of Easter. However, not every one of the maverick factions of Christianity leaped upon Constantine's bandwagon. Britain's Celtic Church didn't accept the official date until the late seventh century, when King Oswy of Northumbria, at the Synod of Whitby, determined that the church of Northumbria was going to follow Roman notions rather than Celtic. Gaul held out even longer, until the time of Charlemagne, in the eighth century.

Many of Easter's customs are rooted in pagan celebrations. The very word "Easter" comes from the name of the Anglo-Saxon goddess of spring, Eostre. Not only was spring the perfect time to celebrate the resurrection of Jesus, but there were already several handy celebrations going on. Understandably, the early Christians always found it easier to replace an old holiday than to start a new one. As Pope Gregory I advised an agent, "From obdurate minds it is impossible to cut off everything at once." Just as Christmas was timed to coincide with the Roman Saturnalia at the winter solstice, and All Saints' Day substituted for the pagan harvest festivals, and Saint Patrick's Day elbowed out the Celtic New Year, so did Easter supplant the old ways of greeting the arrival of spring. With its return of flowers and birds and warmth, spring has always been the symbolic time of rebirth.

Much of the symbolism currently attached to Easter was derived from nature. Nowadays the holiday would not be the same without Easter eggs and Easter bunnies. Many cultures forbade the consumption of eggs during Lent, the time of penitence and fasting between Ash Wednesday and Easter that commemorates Jesus's hunger in the wilderness. Even the word "Lent" comes from the Anglo-Saxon *lencten,* meaning "spring." Their Lenten absence may have made eggs even more appealing when they began to be adopted as part of the Christian observance of Easter. The egg is an age-old symbol of hope and renewal, as expressed in the Latin proverb *Omne vivum ex vovo,* "All life comes from an egg." Coloring eggs is also an ancient rite. It seems to have been part of many ancient spring festivals. Because the custom is not mentioned in Europe before the 1400s, historians speculate that Crusaders brought the idea of colored Easter eggs home from the East.

Eggs were sacred to Eostre and to many other spring deities, and thanks to its shameless fecundity, so was the hare. There is a zoological distinction between the rabbit and the hare. The young of the former are born blind and naked, therefore helpless; the latter, clothed in fur and peering at the world. For that reason, the hare is likelier to be regarded as a harbinger of spring, but the distinction is not apparent in the cartoon biology of Easter. (By the way, recently taxonomists have determined that hares and rabbits bear only superficial resemblances to rodents, and they now proudly occupy their own order, Lagomorpha.) This convergence of two unrelated animals has led to the unlikely result that in the late twentieth century Easter can't be celebrated without the presence of a bunny carrying a basket of eggs.

Rousseau's Cats

In 1891, French painter Henri Rousseau submitted to the Salon des Indépendants the earliest of his many jungle paintings. Over four feet high and more than five feet wide, the painting *Surprise!* was filled with the primitive splendor that would ultimately gain the painter renown. Unlike some of his scenes of wild nature, this one isn't static. A tiger runs through a lush jungle, as wind and rain bend the trees and grasses, and lightning streaks across the ominous dark sky.

Rousseau was in his late forties. He had been painting for over a decade, and exhibiting in the Indépendants show at least half that time. His was not the placid view of nature seen in Monet's luminous haystacks, or the well-behaved parks that served Seurat as background to society. Not even the hot colors and sprawling Tahitians of his contemporary Gauguin conveyed a greater exoticism. At the time of the 1891 show, this exuberant view of nature was still drawing ridicule. One of the first reviewers to praise Rousseau, the twenty-six-year-old artist Felix Vallaton, wrote in response to *Surprise!*

Vallaton reviewed the Salon show in the March 25, 1891, issue of *Le Journal suisse.* "In spite of those doubled up with stifled laughter . . . Monsieur Rousseau becomes more and more astonishing each year, but he commands attention and, in any event, is earning a nice little reputation. . . . His tiger surprising its prey ought not to be missed; it's the alpha and omega of painting and so disconcerting that the most firmly held convictions must be shaken and brought up short by such self-sufficiency and childlike naïveté." It was part of Rousseau's naïveté that he didn't worry about whether his animals were likely to be found in the settings he provided for him. His nature had its own rules. He painted *An American Indian Struggling with an Ape* and the odd scene of *Horse Attacked by a Jaguar* deep in an impenetrable jungle. A monkey even sits dangling its feet in a stream, with what appears to be a fishing pole in its hands.

Rousseau was particularly drawn to the world's big cats. In the monumental *Sleeping Gypsy* (1897), he presented the haunting scene of a woman sleeping on the desert sands, dressed in a colorful burnoose, her mandolin nearby and a staring lion sniffing at her. On the frame Rousseau inscribed, "The feline, though ferocious, is loath to leap upon its prey, who, overcome by fatigue, lies in a deep sleep." A lion-jaguar hybrid lies like a sphinx underneath the moon in *Jungle with Lion.* There are two different paintings of tigers attacking buffalo. A gigantic, sensuously maned lion appears in Rousseau's crowded homage to the Indépendants show.

Paradoxically, most of Rousseau's more violent scenes of nature red in tooth and claw grew from prosaic sources. In the 1910 canvas *Forest Landscape with Setting Sun,* a jaguar attacks a human figure below an orange orb. Rousseau's model for the pose was a picture in the 1910 photographic album *Bêtes sauvages* ("Savage Beasts"). However, in the photograph, the semidomesticated animal is merely rearing up at its trainer, who, like the figure in Rousseau's version, tries to turn away. Even when his inspirations were more mundane, Rousseau's imagination transported them to strange and dangerous lands. Several animals in *The Hungry Lion* of 1905 were probably inspired by mounted animals in Paris's Museum of Natural History, but the characters in his picture do not behave as if stuffed. In his catalog note for the painting, Rousseau demonstrated the unnatural but romantic juxtapositions that pervade his art: "The hungry lion, throwing himself upon the antelope, devours him; the panther stands by awaiting the moment when he, too, can claim his share. Birds of prey have ripped out pieces of flesh from the poor animal that sheds a tear!"

---

26 MARCH 1835

"The Great Black Bug of the Pampas"

Diseases acquire their common names from many sources. The filovirus Ebola is named for a river in Zaire, and Marburg for a town in Germany. "Legionnaires' disease" was so named because it was first recognized when it devastated a convention of American Legion veterans in Philadelphia, and as a consequence its scientific name is now *Legionella.* Sometimes the first well-known victims have the dubious honor of their names forever attaching to an ailment, as in Lou Gehrig's disease. Occasionally disease researchers wind up with diseases named after them. Carlos Ribeiro Justiniano Chagas was one of those.

Chagas was a Brazilian physician and bacteriologist. In 1909, he identified the microorganism *Trypanosoma cruzi* and described the illness now referred to as Chagas' disease. Trypanosomes are single-celled blood parasites that infest not only human beings but a number of other vertebrates. They are, as epidemiologists say, the "causative agent" of several diseases. For example, they are blamed for an infectious anemia called surra, the South African livestock ailment nagana, sleeping sickness, and, as of 1909, Chagas' disease. *T. cruzi* damages intestinal nerve tissue and the heart muscle, revealing itself in both intestinal ailments and cardiac disorders. Like many such afflictions (sleeping sickness and nagana are both transmitted by the tsetse fly), Chagas' disease is transmitted by an insect, in this case the South American species *Triatoma infestans.*

In 1959, Israeli parasitologist Saul Adler suggested a possible origin for the disorders that plagued Charles Darwin after his return from the *Beagle* voyage. According to *The Voyage of the "Beagle,"* on March 26, 1835, Darwin was in Argentina.

> At night I experienced an attack (for it deserves no less a name) of the *Benchuca,*
> a species of Reduvius, the great black bug of the Pampas. It is most disgusting
> to feel soft wingless insects, about an inch long, crawling over one's body.
> Before sucking they are quite thin, but afterwards they become round and
> bloated with blood, and in this state are easily crushed.

The insect known in Darwin's time as *Benchuca* is now named *Triatoma infestans* and recognized as the primary carrier of *Trypanosoma cruzi.* Darwin went on to describe the foolhardy ways the men amused themselves.

One which I caught at Iquique (for they are found in Chile and Peru) was very empty. When placed on a table, and though surrounded by people, if a finger was presented, the bold insect would immediately protrude its sucker, make a charge, and if allowed, draw blood. No pain was caused by the wound. It was curious to watch its body during the act of sucking, as in less than ten minutes it changes from being as flat as a wafer to a globular form.

Although not causing pain, the bite of the insect may have been transmitting *T. cruzi.* Saul Adler pointed out that some of Darwin's symptoms were consistent with those of Chagas' disease. Darwin's illnesses take up almost as much place in his diaries and letters as do his scientific studies. Some biographers leaped upon the notion that the illnesses had a physical cause, referring to suggestions of psychogenic origins as "unflattering." Others still regarded most of Darwin's problems as probably the result of internal turmoil from the evolutionist's worries about the reception and impact of his work.

There is no question that Chagas' disease is a debilitating and long-lasting affliction. It does manifest itself in long-term intestinal problems, which Darwin certainly reported. However, if Darwin contracted Chagas' disease from the great black bug of the pampas, why did he show no signs of it over the next year and a half of the voyage, until after he returned to England and began work on his controversial theories? The rest of his life, he suffered from painful illnesses, whether of physical or psychological origin. The consensus nowadays is that Darwin probably did not contract Chagas' disease, but it is one of those minor historical mysteries the final answer to which we may never know.

---

27 MARCH 1724

Naming Weeds after Christian Women

Jane Colden was born on March 27, 1724, at the family estate of Coldengham, near Newburgh in the colony of New York. She was the second daughter of ten children. In a time when education was usually reserved for men (and only white men, at that), Colden was educated at home by her father, pioneer Colonial naturalist Cadwallader Colden.

Young Jane was fortunate that her brain was appreciated, in whatever patronizing way. In a letter to a colleague in Leiden in 1755, her father described her: "I have a daughter who has an inclination to reading and a curiosity for natural philosophy." Fearing that her curiosity might not be enough to overcome the intellectual shortcomings of her gender, he avoided a difficult foreign language. "I took the pains to explain Linnaeus's system and put it in English for her use. She is now grown very fond of the study and understands in some degree Linnaeus's characters." Of course, old Cadwallader's reasoning was firmly of his time. "I thought that botany is an amusement which may be made agreeable for the ladies who are often at a loss to fill up their time. Their natural curiosity and the pleasure they take in the beauty and variety of dress seem to fit them for it."

However, Colden's father was able to overcome his own prejudices. He not only trained her, he enthusiastically notified colleagues around the world of her accomplishments, even going so far as to overstate them. His network of fellow scientists admired her expertise and exploited her willingness to assist by asking her to collect specimens for them. Visitors to the father-and-daughter team of botanists included well-known naturalists John Bartram and Peter Kalm. Another described the female Colden as "a Florist and Botanist" who "has discovered a great number of Plants never before described and has given their Properties and Virtues, many of which are found useful in Medicine, and she draws and colors them with great beauty."

Jane Colden contributed greatly to the *Plantae Collinghamiae,* the first work on the flora of New York. She collected, identified, and drew 340 plants for her own book, *The Flora of New York.* Soon a copy resided in the British Museum, purchased by the president of the Royal Society. Finally, after being considered too choosy by her sisters, she married at the age of thirty-five. In the seven years or so remaining to her, she lived a mostly unbotanical but apparently happy life as Mrs. William Farquhar. In 1766, not quite forty-two years old, she died while giving birth.

Colden's interests were hardly those considered proper for the women of her time. A London naturalist suggested to Linnaeus that he assign a certain plant the species name *coldenella* in honor of the impressive and helpful young woman in America. After all, there was already a *coldenia* named for her father. When Colden's aunt heard of the proposition, she is said to have exclaimed in outrage, "What! Name a weed after a Christian woman!" Linnaeus himself may have shared that opinion. Quaker naturalist Peter Collinson of London suggested to Linnaeus that he name at least some plant for "the first lady that has so perfectly studied your system." There were countless opportunities to do so, including a few plants Colden herself discovered, but Linnaeus declined. Still, although she may not be remembered in latinizations of her name, Jane Colden is not forgotten.

---

28 MARCH 1941

The Death of the Moth

"I'm going to live the life of a badger," Virginia Woolf wrote in her diary, "nocturnal, secretive . . . alone in my burrow at the back." She habitually expressed herself in such animal imagery. Her path to the sea was a snail's walk; she must treat her nervous system "like a pampered pug dog"; she felt as drowsy as a bear; a friend was sandy as a cat. "Frog's weather," she called a downpour. In correspondence she addressed her husband as "Dearest Mongoose, darling Mongoose," and signed letters to Vita Sackville-West with the name of a kind of lemur, "Bosman's Potto." She spoke of her mind as "the most capricious of insects—flitting, fluttering."

That last image leads directly to Woolf's favorite zoological symbol, the moth. Her interest in lepidoptera seems to date from the many butterfly and moth hunts with her father during childhood. As a girl, she recorded an outing in her diary with an artist's appreciation and a collector's cold zeal: "By the faint glow we could see the huge moth—his wings open, as though in ecstasy, so that the splendid crimson of the underwing could be seen—his eyes burning red, his proboscis plunged into a flowing stream of treacle. We gazed one moment on his splendor, & then uncorked the bottle." In Woolf's novel *Jacob's Room,* the narrator describes herself as "vibrating, like the hawk moth, at the mouth of the cavern of mystery." Woolf's later work *The Waves* was originally titled *The Moths.* Her sister's name, Vanessa, prompts the appearance of several moths from that family, including *Vanessa atalanta,* the red admiral, a favorite of another lepidoptera-preoccupied novelist, Vladimir Nabokov. Even Woolf's image for how she prepared to write each morning is in this vein; she began by "tapping [her] antennae in the air vaguely." Significantly, in Woolf's essay "Reading," moths represent the imagination itself.

Decades later and an ocean away, a moth became for Annie Dillard a symbol of a world in which "implacable realities hold sway." In *A Pilgrim at Tinker Creek,* and again in *An American Childhood,* she described witnessing as a child a Polyphemus moth emerging from its cocoon. It happened while she was at school, and the teacher placed the insect in a Mason jar. Trying to unfold its new, wet wings, it found itself too cramped in the tight space. Soon the wings dried without ever having unfolded. At recess, Dillard saw the crippled, hunchbacked moth creeping across the asphalt. Just as the moths of Virginia Woolf's childhood remained with her, so did this afflicted one permanently capture Annie Dillard's imagination: "The Polyphemus moth never made it to the past; it . . . is still crawling down the driveway, crawling down the driveway hunched, crawling down the driveway on six furred feet, forever."

When writing that description, Dillard may have remembered an essay by Virginia Woolf, "The Death of the Moth." What makes the four-page description of a moth's final hours stand out is the depth of Woolf's empathy: "The possibilities of pleasure seemed that morning so enormous and so various that to have only a moth's part in life, and a day moth's at that, appeared a hard fate, and his zest in enjoying his meager possibilities to the full, pathetic. . . . Watching him, it seemed as if a fibre, very thin but pure, of the enormous energy of the world had been thrust into his frail and diminutive body." The moth's death throes come to represent the struggle of any creature, including ourselves, against our strongest and most mysterious opponent. "O yes, he seemed to say, death is stronger than I am." That essay was published in book form in 1942—posthumously. The year before, on March 28, 1941, the fifty-nine-year-old author had waded into the River Ouse near her famous Bloomsbury home and drowned herself.

See also Nabokov, the lepidopterist, 6/12.

Archy's New Outlook

On the twenty-ninth of March, 1916, Don Marquis wrote in "The Sun Dial," his column in the *New York Sun,* "We came into our room earlier than usual in the morning, and discovered a gigantic cockroach jumping about upon the keys." It was an opening reminiscent of Kafka's in *The Metamorphosis:* "As Gregor Samsa awoke one morning from uneasy dreams he found himself transformed in his bed into a gigantic insect."

George Herriman's portrait of Archy, the former poet now reincarnated as a cockroach, hard at work.

Marquis said he watched as the cockroach threw himself head first against the typewriter keys. The poor creature couldn't manage capitals, and it took all his might to shift lines, but he kept going. When he crawled away, exhausted, Marquis inspected his work:

expression is the need of my soul
i was once a vers libre bard
but i died and my soul went into the body of a
    cockroach
it has given me a new outlook on life

. . . leave a piece of paper in your machine
every night you can call me archy

Both vers libre and reincarnation were in the air. Although it was being denounced as a modern abomination, actually free verse's reliance upon what Ezra Pound called the "sequence of musical phrase" to break free of traditional metrical patterns dates to the King James translation of the Psalms. And the creator of Sherlock Holmes was leading a resurgence of interest in reincarnation, séances, and immaterialism in general. Marquis said in his introduction that the soul of spiritualist Madame Blavatsky had passed into a white horse, so why couldn't a poet's enter a cockroach? Reborn or not, the skeptical insect says he never ran across any of that ectoplasm that Sir Arthur Conan Doyle talked about.

Archy the cockroach isn't the only character who has been around before. The scruffy body of the alley cat Mehitabel houses the transmigrated soul of Cleopatra. She has had her ups and downs, but she remains "*toujours gai.*" Another cat carries around the tortured soul of medieval poet François Villon. There is the parrot who knew Shakespeare and claims that "Bill" sat around moaning that he might have been a poet if only he had stayed away from the theater. Dickensian characters include Freddy the Rat, a former literary critic who now simply eats the work he doesn't like; the batrachocentric toad Warty Bliggens; and the worm and beetle who philosophize in the belly of a robin that has just eaten them, until Mehitabel eats the robin.

The Archy columns eventually became three books. A novelist and playwright, Marquis is, as he feared, in danger of being remembered as "the creator of a goddam cockroach." He employed animal characters as they had been used since Aesop—to satirize human behavior. However, Aesop's industrious ants and shiftless grasshoppers were, as Chesterton remarked, like so many chess pieces. Marquis infused his creations with life and individuality, with his own take on the brevity and smallness of life. They lived. They still live, and they still answer Archy's own question:

> *human wandering through the zoo*
> *what do your cousins think of you*

Black Beauty

April 1878. A hearse and carriages of mourners gather before a house near Norwich, England. "Bearing reins," or "check-reins," force the horses to hold their heads high as they await departure for the cemetery. Upstairs, the mother of the deceased glances out the window, notices the horses' unnatural posture, and exclaims, "Oh, this will never do!" She hurries downstairs, and a minute later a man removes the bearing reins of all the horses in the procession.

Her mother's action would have pleased Anna Sewell, who spent much of her life battling the abuse of horses. Only five months before her death at the age of fifty-eight, she published *Black Beauty*, subtitled "The autobiography of a horse, Translated from the original equine." It was only one in a growing genre of animal stories. Probably Sewell had read *The Adventures of a Donkey* (1815), in which the narrator, Jemmy, converses with other animals. Beauty had his pal Merrylegs; Jemmy had a mentor named Balaam, after the articulate ass in the Bible. Probably Sewell encountered other talking animals, such as the cab horses in George MacDonald's recent *At the Back of the North Wind* (1871).

Anna Sewell was born on the thirtieth of March, 1820, in Yarmouth, where she developed an interest in horses before she was ten years old. Apparently Beauty was based upon her brother's carriage horse, Black Bess. At the age of fourteen, Anna was running home in the rain and fell. In her diary, she described the accident in equine terms: "My ankles are twisted like the leg of the wagonhorse who fell on the frozen cobbles last year and had to be shot." Beauty's life is likewise ruined in youth, when he falls and injures his knees and suddenly is no longer a gentleman's prize. After her fall, Anna was crippled, and finally became bedridden. After his, Beauty plummets down the social scale, winding up one of the notoriously mistreated London cab horses. Sewell became one of those Victorian invalids whose life was dominated by her mother. Beauty winds up cared for by a kindly former owner.

Sewell's own kindness was legendary. As a Quaker child, she kept from a man the blackbird he had shot in her garden with the words, "Thee cruel man, thee shan't have it at all." Friends who rode in her cart—her only means of transportation as her legs failed completely—reported that she held the reins gently, trusting the horse to know the way, and saying such things as "Now thee must go a little faster; thee would be sorry for us to be late at the station" and "Now thee shouldn't walk up this hill. Don't thee see how it rains?"

Sewell's imagination lifted *Black Beauty* above the level of a sermon, but her aim was social rather than artistic: "to induce kindness, sympathy, and an understanding treatment of horses." A particular evil she battled was the bearing rein. Eventually only undertakers could still use it, as they had tried to in 1878, on the day Sewell was buried. In 1914 it was finally abolished.

---

31 MARCH 1870

The Donkey and the Elephant

Symbolic animals have been a mainstay of political cartooning since the genre evolved. The American eagle, like the Russian bear and even the English bulldog, embodies the hopes or fears of a group defining itself or someone else. Terrorists are portrayed as sharks and street gangs become wolf packs. Some of the symbols are more enduring, others topical. For a long time, the popular conception of a dinosaur might depict anything grown too old and outmoded to survive. However, since being portrayed in *Jurassic Park* as nimble and ravenous, *Velociraptor* has even represented small businesses outmaneuvering the lumbering giants.

No one used animals to personify individuals, organizations, and concepts more successfully than pioneer political cartoonist Thomas Nast. He began publishing in *Frank Leslie's Illustrated Newspaper* when he was fifteen, in 1855. Nast found little stimulus in the feeble history of political cartooning in the United States, which consisted mostly of intricate and pompous allegories. His own approach borrowed from John Tenniel's work in *Punch,* Gustave Doré's illustrations, and Honoré Daumier's caricatures that so plagued the reign of Louis Philippe.

In 1867, Nast began fighting the political machine of William Marcy "Boss" Tweed and his graft-ridden "Tweed ring" of coconspirators who controlled New York City politics. Unlike most of the Tweed-manipulated press, two voices expressed the public outrage: *Harper's Weekly,* where Nast was a staff artist until 1886, and, beginning with a change of leadership in 1870, the *New York Times.* By then, Tammany Hall controlled much of the state; even the governor was a figurehead. The daily *Times* was a

In 1870, cartoonist Thomas Nast gave the donkey its enduring role as a symbol of the Democratic party.

much greater threat to the Tweed ring than the weekly *Harper's*. Tweed unsuccessfully offered the publisher $1 million to behave himself.

Then, in early 1870, the *Times* ran a Nast cartoon entitled "A Live Jackass Kicking a Dead Lion." The lion was Edwin M. Stanton, Lincoln's secretary of war, who died late in 1869. The jackass was specifically the Democratic press but more generally Democratic attitudes. It was the first time a donkey represented the Democratic party. Nast himself used the symbol numerous times over the next few years, and by then it was popular with other cartoonists, too potent in the public imagination to abandon.

By this time Tweed considered Nast such a problem that he honored his work in a way few caricaturists have experienced. On March 31, 1870, a bill in the state legislature denounced Nast's work as "vulgar and blasphemous." Tweed supposedly said, "I don't care

In 1874, the elephant was assigned the job of representing the Republicans and was thrown into the editorial arena with the Democratic donkey. The two animals have been warring ever since.

what they print about me; most of my constituents can't read, anyway. But them damn pictures—"

Undeterred, Nast kept drawing cartoons. Of course, sometimes they didn't employ animals at all; some didn't even concern politics. One series fashioned the American image of Santa Claus. But his cartoons of animals ensure his fame. He drew the Tammany Tiger prowling the streets and frightening the populace, and portrayed Tweed and company as loathsome vultures. Not satisfied with creating a symbol for the Democratic party, in November of 1874 he completed his political zoo when he established the elephant as the Republican symbol. It had already appeared in that role once or twice, most notably around 1860, in one of Abraham Lincoln's campaign posters. But it was Nast, with his genius for animal characters, who gave both the donkey and the elephant their enduring political identities.

"From the Common Earth"

"The smallest fact," Thomas Huxley wrote in the late nineteenth century, "is a window through which the infinite can be seen." In similar or more convoluted phrasing, that conviction is a commonplace of both scientific and religious thinking. Everything connects, the theory goes, and at least the traces of those connections ought to be visible from anywhere in the chain. One fact through which we may glimpse the whole universe and our own place in it is the basic truth that our elements, the atoms and molecules that compose us, were born in the hearts of stars, ultimately tracing back to the original explosion that seems to have created our universe. Scientists have proven that the unity of nature is not a metaphysical abstraction.

"We forget," Loren Eiseley wrote, "that nature itself is one vast miracle transcending the reality of night and nothingness. We forget that each one of us in his personal life repeats that miracle." Poets and mystics, scientists and philosophers, all have expressed this idea of the unity of nature. George Gaylord Simpson, an American evolutionist, said it in precise scientific terms: "Life and its environment are interdependent and evolve together." Walt Whitman declared that he incorporated gneiss, coal, long-threaded moss, fruits, grains, and esculent roots. Eiseley remarked that "we, who are last year's dust and rain, have risen from that dust to look about with the devised crystal of a raindrop before we subside once more into snow and whirling vapor." We are the elements contemplating themselves.

Edward FitzGerald's Omar Khayyám saw this sort of oneness all about him.

> Then said another—"Surely not in vain
> My Substance from the common Earth was ta'en,
>   That He who subtly wrought me into Shape
> Should stamp me back to common Earth again."

In a similar vein, Thomas Hardy wrote in his poem "Transformations":

Portion of this yew
Is a man my grandsire knew,
Bosomed here at its foot:
This branch may be his wife,
A ruddy human life
Now turned to a green shoot.

Donald Culross Peattie was a writer and naturalist who was firmly convinced that such matters should remain in the forefront of our thoughts. In his Whitmanesque way, he tried in his various works to embrace the whole of creation. One of his best-known books was *An Almanac for Moderns,* published in 1935. In an essay for every day of the year, he emphasized the spiritual impact of the scientifically observed facts of nature. The entry for April 1 addresses the issue that so moved Eiseley and Hardy:

> I say that it touches a man that his blood is sea water and his tears are salt, that the seed of his loins is scarcely different from the same cells in a seaweed, and that of stuff like his bones are coral made. I say that physical and biologic law lies down with him, and wakes when a child stirs in the womb, and that the sap in a tree, uprushing in the spring, and the smell of the loam, where the bacteria bestir themselves in darkness, and the path of the sun in the heaven, these are facts of first importance to his mental conclusions, and that a man who goes in no consciousness of them is a drifter and a dreamer, without a home or any contact with reality.

---

2 APRIL 1961

John Steinbeck and the Mohole

Scientists discovered the layers of the earth below us by analyzing earthquake records. Seismic waves ricochet from one layer to another, creating a kind of X ray of the Earth. The Croation geophysicist Andrija Mohorovicic studied seismic records and discovered a layer between the crust and mantle of the earth. It was named the "Mohorovicic discontinuity," which is usually abridged to the "Moho." Scientists' plan in the 1960s to drill down to that layer was called Project Mohole. The directors offered the job of historian on their great adventure not to a scientist but to a writer who, a year later, would win the Nobel Prize—John Steinbeck.

Steinbeck had reluctantly refused to chronicle a survey of the Great Barrier Reef because it was too soon after his third marriage. But Mohole he could not resist. Steinbeck was one of the few novelists of his time interested in the natural sciences. The protagonist of *Cannery Row* is a marine biologist and with biologist Ed Ricketts, Steinbeck wrote *The Log of the "Sea of Cortez,"* about their rambles in the

Gulf of Mexico. Some critics lamented Steinbeck's demeaning portrayal of humans as part of the natural world. Others thought him an ecologist disguised as a novelist.

Life entitled Steinbeck's article about Mohole "High Drama of Bold Thrust through Ocean Floor." Geologists had decided to drill at sea. Moho can be 20 miles below the surface on land, but is sometimes only 3 miles or so below the bottom of the ocean. A redesigned Navy barge, carrying a flock of scientists, "waddled like a duck" to a site "44 miles west of Guadalupe and 220 miles south of San Diego." Motors at each corner of the barge enabled the pilot, monitoring sonar screens, to nudge his ship in various directions. If the barge, and thus the drilling derrick, drifted too far, the long pipe would snap, and its recoil could endanger ship, crew, and mission. Finally, the scientists informed the drillers of their united task: "to read the world's history as you would read the rings of a tree."

Drilling began in late March. Echo-mapping indicated the ocean bottom was 12,000 feet below. There were mishaps and disappointments, but on the twenty-eighth the drill touched bottom. The first sample contained what appeared to be out-of-place Miocene fossils. "Everything is new about this, everything a discovery," Steinbeck wrote. "A lot of textbooks will have to be rewritten."

At 600 feet they struck hard rock. On Easter Sunday, April 2, 1961, the team "brought up a great core of basalt, stark blue and very hard with extrusions of crystals exuding in lines—beautiful under a magnifying glass." No one had seen the second layer before, and the experts guarded the core as if it were treasure. Steinbeck asked for a sample. He was refused, so he stole a tiny fragment. Later the chief scientist secretly gave him a piece, and, feeling guilty, Steinbeck surreptitiously returned his pilfered memento.

See also Steinbeck and Charley, 9/27.

---

3 APRIL 1974

The Super Outbreak

"From the far north they heard a low wail of the wind, and Uncle Henry and Dorothy could see where the long grass bowed in waves before the coming storm. There now came a sharp whistling in the air from the south, and as they turned their eyes that way they saw ripples in the grass coming from that direction as well." L. Frank Baum wasted no time in launching Dorothy on her great adventure; a tornado strikes the Kansas farm in chapter one of *The Wonderful Wizard of Oz.* Aunt Em yells for Dorothy to run for the cellar. With her dog Toto in her arms, the girl tries to obey, but she hasn't reached the trapdoor when the house begins to rise.

Victor Fleming's 1939 film version might have taken its title from another movie out that year, *Gone with the Wind.* His tornado lifts other objects besides Dorothy's house. Judy Garland sees outside the window a cow, two men rowing a boat, and even the witchy, Toto-hating neighbor still pedaling furiously on her bicycle. (Of course, in the film, the entire ride turns out to be a dream.) Decades later, a group of tornado researchers remembered the book and film when they named a 400-pound collection of instruments designed to study tornadoes while they were occurring. They called it the Totable Tornado Observatory, or TOTO.

"In the middle of a cyclone the air is generally still," Baum wrote, "but the great pressure of the wind on every side of the house raised it up higher and higher, until it was at the very top of the cyclone; and there it remained and was carried miles and miles away as easily as you could carry a feather." Baum published this first of his fourteen *Oz* books in 1900, when Midwesterners still called tornadoes "cyclones." From the Greek *kykloun,* the word means "to go around," as do "twister" and even "tornado," from the Spanish verb *tornar,* "to turn." However, usage has shifted. "Cyclone" still refers to winds around a low-pressure area, but is now used mostly in reference to huge oceanic storms.

Tornadoes are an inland phenomenon. If a twister doesn't touch land, it's called a funnel cloud. Scientists are still trying to determine just why tornadoes form, or, in other words, what makes them twist. Unstable winds launching powerful updrafts, considerable moisture supplying a storm system, the requisite spin from the lower layers of air—all are required to create the right conditions. Meteorologists attribute many U.S. tornadoes to violent skirmishes between hot and cold air masses over the Great Plains. That vast flat area is why tornadoes seem as American as *The Wizard of Oz.* They are both stronger and more numerous in North America than on any other continent; roughly 800 form annually. The "tornado alley" across the flat prairies of the United States is centered next door to Dorothy's home state, in Oklahoma, the world capital of tornadoes. The most destructive flurry of tornadoes on record anywhere in the world, called the Super Outbreak, lasted two days, beginning April 3, 1974. It produced 127 tornadoes that killed more than 300 people and injured over 6,000.

Although she may be the only one named after a storm, Dorothy Gale isn't the only character in the arts to be transported by a twister. In American folktales, Pecos Bill, the Paul Bunyan of the Southwest, rides a twister as if it were a wild bronco. In Walt Disney's 1935 short cartoon *The Band Concert* (the debut of Mickey Mouse in color), Mickey conducts an all-animal orchestra. The musicians are approaching the "Storm" section of the *William Tell* Overture when a tornado picks them up and whirls them in the air. Mickey continues to conduct, and no musician misses a note.

Real tornadoes can be equally imaginative. During the 1974 outbreak, a single half-mile-wide tornado touched down in Xenia, Ohio. It lifted freight cars from a moving train and tossed them aside, then hurled two buses through a school wall and onto an auditorium stage only moments after students had been evacuated. Tornadoes have been known to lift cars, boats, mobile homes—and, yes, even houses. Dorothy was lucky. Even after landing on a witch, her home remained intact.

See also hailstorm, 5/8; and hurricanes, 7/24 and 9/7.

---

4 APRIL 1882

Rearing Orange Ants in China

In the West, biological pest control is a recent innovation, still derided by the profit-conscious manufacturers of chemical pesticides. However, the concept is not new. As long ago as the fourth century, Chinese gardeners employed biological pest controls in their orchards. Mandarin oranges were susceptible to attack by various predators, including caterpillars and ants. For a long time, this probably seemed like an unavoidable side effect of cultivating oranges, perhaps even simply the will of the gods. Then some astute but forever nameless amateur entomologist observed a ferocious enemy of these creatures. Soon the Chinese were sending into battle legions of an unwitting ally, the yellow citrus killer-ant, *Oecophylla smaragdina.*

Over the centuries, numerous Chinese accounts of this form of biological pest control have accumulated. Hsi Han's *Records of the Plants and Trees of the Southern Regions* (A.D. 304) includes the first mention. He said that in the markets of Chiao-Chih one could find carnivorous ants sold in bags of rush matting. The bags were attached to branches and leaves, with the ants inside in their nests. "The ants," Hsi Han wrote, "are reddish-yellow in colour, bigger than ordinary ants. These ants do not eat the oranges, but attack and kill the insects which do."

By 1130, when Chuang Chi-Yü published his *Miscellaneous Random Notes,* clever entrepreneurs had invented other methods of trapping the ants. The distribution of these insects had developed into its own established trade, with the vendors collecting and selling them to fruit farmers. Their method of gathering the ants was not pretty: "They trap them by filling hogs' or sheep's bladders with fat and placing them with the cavities open next to ants' nests. They wait until the ants have migrated into the bladders and then take them away. This is known as 'rearing orange ants.' "

Hundreds of years later, a book entitled *Miscellanies from the Southern Regions,* which Wu Chen-Fang published in 1600, described the method by which the ants were deployed throughout the battlefield. Trees were "connected to each other by bamboo strips to facilitate the movement of the large ants which ward off insect pests. The ants build nests among the leaves and branches in the hundreds and thousands."

Apparently the first Western mention of the Chinese use of this insect was in a little-known paper by H. C. McCook, published in the *North China Herald* on April 4, 1882. Needless to say, few Western scientists noticed it. Then, when canker devastated Florida citrus groves early in the twentieth century, the U.S. Department of Agriculture delegated a plant physiologist to research oranges that would resist the plague. In China, he discovered one of the secrets of that country's success with citrus fruits. He was perhaps the first Westerner to witness the predatory orange ants going about their business—ignoring the cherished oranges themselves, preying upon fruit-eating insects, and running back and forth from tree to tree via bamboo pedestrian walkways high above the ground.

---

5 APRIL 1839

The Philosophy of Storms

"Everybody talks about the weather, but nobody does anything about it." Usually that quip is attributed to Mark Twain. Actually, his friend Charles Dudley Warner, who cowrote *The Gilded Age,* said it. It's a great line, but it isn't true. For centuries people have been trying to do something about the weather.

In the Sermon on the Mount, while reminding the crowd to love their enemies, Jesus says that God "sendeth rain on the just and on the unjust." The earliest known prose work, the fifth-century-B.C. *History* by Herodotus, reports that the Egyptians also considered rain a whim of the gods. However, they thought of the Nile as more reliable: "[H]earing that the whole land of the Hellenes [the Greeks] has rain and is not watered by rivers as theirs is, they said that the Hellenes would at some time be disappointed of a great hope and would suffer the ills of famine."

For many centuries to follow, those without recourse to a periodically flooding river pursued methods of rainmaking. Most thought rain was determined by a deity, and begging for precipitation involved strange rites. The Hopi rain dance required participants to hold live snakes in their mouths. In some cultures, dancers whirled in circles to inspire the wind. Countless drought-plagued mortals implored and cajoled their local gods, sacrificed animals, analyzed portents—all, presumably, to no avail. "But methought it lessened my esteem of a king," Samuel Pepys once remarked to his diary, "that he should not be able to command the rain."

In Philadelphia in 1839, the April 5 issue of the *National Gazette and Literary Register* carried the first recorded proposal for a nonsupernatural attempt at rainmaking. A man named James P. Espy suggested that in an appropriately humid atmosphere, large fires would generate updrafts that might encourage cumulus clouds to form rain. Espy is remembered as the author of a classic of meteorology with the wonderful title *The Philosophy of Storms*.

Others pursued different methods. In 1871, Edward Powers published a book entitled *War and Weather,* in which he confirmed an observation made by Plutarch 1,800 years earlier: "It is a matter of current observation that extraordinary rains pretty generally fall after great battles." Powers thought his experience in the Civil War confirmed the theory that battle sounds induced precipitation. With balloons, he and his crew lifted explosives into the higher atmosphere and detonated them. The results were inconclusive.

However, that didn't inhibit "rainmakers," who took to the county-fair circuit. As often happens, the shysters tarnished the reputation of the serious experimenters. Still, the scientists persisted. One distributed electrically charged grains of sand in the air above clouds. No rain fell. In fact, the sand-sprinkled clouds dissipated. One scientist observed that savannah brushfires in Africa were followed by rain, and another got the bright idea of burning vast quantities of oil—as much as three metric tons per minute—to create convection. That worked. It worked so well he created a small tornado.

Then, in 1946, Vincent J. Schaefer released roughly 1.5 kilograms of solid carbon dioxide (dry ice) pellets into a stratocumulus cloud over the Berkshire Mountains in Massachusetts. Within minutes snowflakes began to form. Although the methods are still under development and the applications under debate, it had finally happened. A man had done something about the weather.

See also lightning, 3/1.

"The Deadliest Snake in India"

"Pray be precise as to details," Sherlock Holmes instructs Helen Stoner when she consults him on April 6, 1883. Arthur Conan Doyle didn't follow his own brainchild's advice; "The Adventure of the Speckled Band" is chock-full of errors. But it features one of the more interesting murder weapons in the genre—a snake. Of course, snakes abound in literature, from the "subtil" serpent who beguiled Eve to Aesop's ungrateful vipers. Although Cleopatra supposedly committed suicide by asp, Conan Doyle was probably the first to use a snake for homicide. Not the last, though. Rex Stout's first Nero Wolfe mystery was *Fer-de-Lance,* in 1934.

After years in India, Helen Stoner's stepfather, Grimesby Roylott, returned to England with several exotic animals, including a swamp adder—"the deadliest snake in India," according to Holmes. Roylott murdered Stoner's sister by putting the snake in her bedroom. But before he can kill Stoner, she consults the great detective. Thus Holmes and Watson are hiding in Stoner's room when Roylott deploys the snake a second time. Lashing at it as it climbs down a bell rope, Holmes drives it back through the air vent and hears Roylott's scream when the snake turns upon its master. Holmes paraphrases Ecclesiastes: ". . . the schemer falls into the pit which he digs for another."

On the train back to London, Holmes explains to Watson that after the snake killed his stepdaughter, Roylott recalled it by whistling. Trained to return for a reward of milk, the snake climbed back up the bell rope, leaving no clues in the locked room except tiny puncture marks and the dying woman's cryptic reference to a "speckled band."

Unfortunately, there is no snake called a swamp adder. Also, however sensitive they may be to vibrations, snakes are deaf; they do not come when you whistle. Nor do they covet milk. And neither of the two kinds of snake venom can cause death within ten seconds. These inconsistencies have led experts with too much time on their hands to consider all known poisonous snakes in India, and finally to expand to other habitats. Finding that the speckles don't match the hissing, or that the puncture marks don't match the size, some have suggested that there were two or more snakes. One theory, carefully cut to fit all the story's claims, employs a bizarre hybrid of the Indian cobra and the Mexican gila monster.

Even the snake's acrobatics have been disputed. Not that snakes don't climb. Some do. Thoreau tells an anecdote about a tree-climbing black snake, for example. But they climb by wedging into nooks and crannies, not by wrapping around objects. Even if one slid down a dangling bell rope, it couldn't retreat by the same unstable route. In his 1910 stage adaptation of the story, Doyle used an uncooperative rock boa in the title role. It hung like a sausage and moved only when pinched. When a critic mistakenly dismissed this bit of *théâtre vérité* as "palpably artificial," Doyle replaced the real snake with a more convincing fake one.

See also "Silver Blaze," 9/25; and **The Hound of the Baskervilles,** *10/15.*

God's Fondness for Beetles

Shakespeare's reference to "the poor beetle, that we tread upon" seems just a bit anthropocentric. Beetles are found in a greater variety of shapes and in a wider spectrum of habitats than any other creature. Even insects as diverse and sophisticated as ants or butterflies can't keep up with them. Beetles possess two pairs of wings, from which trait derives the name of the order, Coleoptera, from the Greek *koleos,* "sheath," and *pteron,* "wing." The hard outer wings, called elytra, protect the more fragile inner pair, then lift out of the way to allow flight. The tropical rhinoceros beetle is the heaviest insect in the world, and the smallest beetles are barely visible to the naked eye.

One of the remarks attributed to the British biologist J. B. S. Haldane concerns these diversified creatures. It is said that when someone asked him what his lifelong study of nature had revealed about God, Haldane replied, "An inordinate fondness for beetles." That pithy version may be apocryphal, but he definitely made the reference. On April 7, 1951, Haldane addressed the British Interplanetary Society. Beetles were germane because they are so prevalent on Earth. Haldane pointed out that there are only 8,000 species of mammals on this planet, contrasting dramatically with the 400,000 known species of beetles. He concluded that if there is a Creator, he has "a special preference for beetles," and therefore they were the type of creature most likely to be awaiting us on some other planet. We already know that they inhabit some rather fantastic places. In L. Frank Baum's first *Oz* book, the Tin Woodman accidentally treads upon a beetle and, in his grief over killing a fellow creature, cries until his jaw hinges rust.

Beetles were a particular passion of Charles Darwin. He came of age at the beginning of the Victorian preoccupation with nature study that would send amateur naturalists scurrying across fen and moor in search of curiosities. At Cambridge, young Charles fell in with a crowd of nature enthusiasts. They spent untold hours beetle chasing. In these endeavors, Darwin revealed the vigor and persistence that were to be the admiration of the *Beagle* crew a few years later. Once he even buried a dead snake, only to dig it up later to collect flesh-eating beetles from the corpse. "No poet ever felt more delight at seeing his first poem published," Darwin wrote later, "than I did at seeing in Stephens' *Illustrations of British Insects* the magic words, 'captured by C. Darwin, Esq.' " A schoolmate caricatured Darwin as a top-hatted young man, waving his butterfly net, astride a beetle large enough to star in a 1950s monster movie. The caption was "Go it Charlie!"

A good example of the adaptability of the order Coleoptera is that odd species, the dung beetle, in this illustration by E. J. Detmold.

In his autobiography, Darwin told of an occasion on which he found one prized beetle, then a second, and soon afterward a third. His hands were full when he encountered the third, so he freed one hand by putting a beetle in his mouth. "Alas it ejected some intensely acrid fluid, which burnt my tongue so that I was forced to spit the beetle out, which was lost, as well as the third one." A little lesson in etymology might have saved Darwin pain. The word "beetle" comes from the Anglo-Saxon *bitle,* which in turn evolved from *bitan,* from which we get another common word—"bite."

---

8 APRIL 1910

"Oh! Halley's, Where Are Thou?"

"I came in with Halley's Comet in 1835," Mark Twain said in 1909. "It is coming again next year, and I expect to go out with it. It will be the greatest disappointment of my life if I don't." Twain liked to speak, as Einstein would later, as a personal acquaintance of the God in whom he did not believe. "The Almighty," he went on, "has said, no doubt: 'Now here are these two unaccountable freaks; they came in together, they must go out together.' Oh, I am looking forward to that."

Not everyone expected such a momentous event to accompany the return of Comet Halley, but few people other than astronomers looked forward to it. One wit who seemed eager contributed a poem to the April 8, 1910, issue of *Punch:*

> *No more I feel the potent spell*
> *of Jupiter or Mars,*
> *Or know the magic peace that fell*
> *Upon me from the Stars,*
> *A fiercer flame—a Comet Love*
> *Consumes my spirit now;*
> *I cry to you in heavens above,*
> *"Oh! Halley's, where are thou?"*

That anonymous versifier was right about Halley outshining all other celestial phenomena. It has been doing that every three-quarters of a century or so since long before humans were around to watch. The earliest record of it dates from 1059 B.C. A drawing of the 684 arrival appears in the famous *Nuremburg Chronicle,* a history of Earth from Creation to the book's publication in 1493. As if determined to further the reputation of comets as portents, Halley dropped by for the Norman conquest of England in 1066; several figures in the Bayeux Tapestry are pointing at it. The Florentine painter Giotto witnessed the 1301 visit. He employed it as the Star of Bethlehem in his *Adoration of the Magi,* where it streaks over the heads of the gift-laden Wise Men. (Some scholars have nominated Halley as the original light in the east, but its closest visit was roughly 11 B.C., and, as we now reckon such things, Jesus was born in roughly 6 B.C.) Pope Calixtus called the 1456 comet "an agent of the devil," and English diarist John Evelyn blamed the 1618 visit for the Thirty Years' War.

James Thurber was fourteen when Comet Halley came by in 1910. "Nothing happened," he reported, "except that I was left with a curious twitching of my left ear after sundown and a tendency to break into a dog trot at the striking of a match or the flashing of a lantern." Unlike Thurber, most people take comets very seriously. In 1991, already years away from its latest visit to our neighborhood, Halley suddenly spewed a

A drawing after the original Bayeux Tapestry, which was completed shortly after the Norman invasion of Britain in 1066. It depicts Halley's visit that year, which was seen as a portent.

dust cloud 200,000 kilometers wide, which made it seem 300 times brighter. Instantly, even in the age of the Hubble Space Telescope and the space shuttle, comet fear blossomed like a hardy perennial. An advertisement in a London newspaper declared that Halley had reversed its orbit and was returning to Earth—"Unexpectedly! Now!"

Mark Twain, who adopted Halley as his personal symbol, would have loved that. The story of the comet accompanying Twain's birth and death sounds ridiculous, but it's true. He was born in November of 1835, only two weeks after Halley reached perihelion (its closest approach to the Sun). He died in April of 1910, the very day after perihelion. Of course, no one knows how many other people's births and deaths roughly coincided with Halley's rather lengthy visits. But the most famous example has become part of the considerable mythology surrounding Mark Twain. His wish had come true. It was as if the comet had come back for him.

See also Cometomania, *2/11.*

---

9 APRIL 1626

The Death of Francis Bacon

"He that dies in an earnest pursuit," Francis Bacon wrote, "is like one that is wounded in hot blood, who for the time scarce feels the hurt." One of Bacon's own earnest pursuits killed him. He was following the motto he had proposed for scientific investigation: Don't just recycle what the classical writers said about the world; go out into the world and see for yourself.

In late March 1626, as he rode through the snowy streets of London, Bacon was thinking about the retarding effect of cold on putrefaction. John Aubrey later heard the story from Bacon's former secretary, the philosopher Thomas Hobbes: "As he was taking the air . . . snow lay on the ground, and it came into my Lord's thoughts, why flesh might not be preserved in snow, as in salt. . . . They alighted out of the coach and went into a poor woman's house . . . and bought a hen, and made the woman exenterate [evis-

123

cerate} it, and then stuffed the body with snow, and my Lord did help to do it himself. The snow so chilled him that he immediately fell so extremely ill, that he could not return to his lodgings. . . ."

Apparently stricken with either pneumonia or bronchitis, Bacon lay in the earl of Arundel's house. From bed Bacon dictated a letter to his absent host: "My very good Lord, I was likely to have had the fortune of Caius Plinius the elder, who lost his life trying an experiment about the burning of the mountain Vesuvius. For I was also desirous to try an experiment or two. . . ."

In Bacon's time, such a use for ice was a radical concept, even though people have always gathered and stored snow and ice, often at great expense. As early as 1700 B.C., a king of what is now a corner of Iraq boasted of being the first ruler on the Euphrates to build an ice house. But ice's preservative powers were seldom applied to food; it was mostly for cooling drinks. Food was usually eaten immediately or salted and stored. Only after Bacon's time did food refrigeration become a goal. Samuel Pepys noted in his diary forty-odd years later that Baltic merchants were claiming that chickens could last all winter if preserved in ice.

By the end of the next century, ice houses were common on English estates. Soon they were built alongside rivers to store fish. Then ships were equipped to carry ice for preserving catches at sea. The first mechanical refrigeration device was introduced in 1755, but the technology wasn't practical for a long time to come. Two and a half centuries after Bacon's death, Mark Twain could still say, "Ice was jewelry. Only the rich could wear it."

Bacon's experiment killed him. He died early on Easter Sunday, April 9, 1626, at the age of sixty-five. It's a shame he wasn't alive in 1799, when Russian scientists reported discovering frozen mammoths whose flesh, after thousands of years, was well enough preserved to feed the camp's dogs.

---

10 APRIL 1872

Arbor Day

Resolved,

That April 10, 1872, be and the same is hereby especially set apart and consecrated for tree planting in the State of Nebraska, and that the State Board of Agriculture hereby names it Arbor Day.

The Nebraska legislature also offered incentives for tree planting. A $100 premium would go to the agricultural society of the county that "properly" planted the largest number of trees. The individual who single-handedly did the most to assuage Nebraska's tree shortage would receive $25 worth of agricultural books.

The ancient word *arbor*, Latin for "tree," is still gainfully employed in such words as arboreal (living in or associated with trees), arboretum (a garden of trees), and arborvitae (the "tree of life," a popular ornamental conifer). But those specialized uses failed to bring the word widespread recognition in the United States. It took a national tree-oriented holiday to do that.

Arbor Day was the brainstorm of Nebraska City newspaper editor Julius Sterling Morton. Soon after he and his wife settled on the treeless plains of Nebraska in 1855, he decided that what the prairie needed was trees. They would prevent the soil from blowing away, provide windbreaks, and eventually supply much-needed lumber. Morton planted many trees himself, then began to preach the virtues of arboriculture. At first his idea was slow to catch on. This was, after all, long before anyone coined the term "conservationist." However, when Morton joined the Nebraska Board of Agriculture, he proposed that a specific day be set aside to boost statewide awareness of the need for trees. A realist, he added the proviso for incentives.

Apparently the nudges proved effective. It is said that a million trees were planted in Nebraska on that first Arbor Day. Over the next sixteen years these pioneer arboriculturists planted some 350 million more. In 1885, the Nebraska legislature resolved that henceforth Arbor Day would be an annual event, to be celebrated on Morton's birthday, April 22. Two years after the first observance in 1872, Tennessee and Kansas adopted Arbor Day. Other states followed, creating, if not a legal holiday, at least an annual observance. In 1882, Ohio timed their observance to coincide with a national meeting there of the American Forestry Congress. The response was so enthusiastic, especially among schoolchildren, that the next year the organization voted to pursue an annual observance in the nation's schools. That is still where the most enthusiastic celebrations occur, fueled by environmentally minded displays, contests, and pageants. In some states, Arbor Day is now a legal holiday, although observances and even the date varies from state to state. England began observing Arbor Day in the year of Queen Victoria's jubilee, 1887. Spain began an annual Fiesta del Arbol in 1896.

In time, Morton's estate became an arboreal showplace, and now boasts over 160 kinds of trees. At his home, inevitably named Arbor Lodge, there is a plaque bearing an inscription:

> *Other Holidays Repose upon the Past—*
> *Arbor Day Proposes for the Future*

See also Earth Day, 4/22; and John Chapman's birthday, 9/26.

Praising the Cherry Blossoms

One of the revered plants in Japanese prose and poetry—along with the bamboo, lotus, and plum blossom—is the cherry. It represents, among other things, richness and prosperity. Its blossoms appear before its leaves, and in some places these early arrivals represent humanity born naked and vulnerable into the world, to enjoy our brief flowering before falling and rejoining the earth. For example, in a famous poem by the eighteenth-century haiku master Buson, fallen cherry blossoms have revealed a temple in among the trees. The twelfth-century poet Saigyo, one of the founders of Zen-influenced nature poetry, saw cherry blossoms reflected in water and wrote famously of fishermen rowing through blossoms.

In the 1600s, Matsuo Munefusa, known as Basho, included memorable descriptions of cherry trees in his wonderful little book of travel and meditation, *Narrow Road to the Interior.* Once, when Matsuo and his companions were coming down from the summit of Moon Mountain, they decided to rest upon a rock. A nearby cherry tree, only three feet tall and almost buried in snow, was optimistically holding its new buds upward. Matsuo's friend Gyoson Sojo wrote, "So sad, blossoming cherry, you have no one to admire you." Recording that, Matsuo added, "It's all here, in these tiny blossoms!"

Sojo's comment resembles an anonymous old Japanese poem that nicely sums up the appreciation of this particular tree:

> *So high in the mountains,*
> *You must be lonely,*
> *blossoming cherry:*
> *no one to sing your glory.*
> *I will praise you if I can.*

One writer who came late in this tradition was Higuchi Natsuko. She was born in 1872, four years after the establishment of Emperor Matsuhito ended centuries of shogun rule and launched what is now called the Meiji Restoration. Edo, the capital of the Tokugawa Shogunate, had just been renamed Tokyo. From an early age Higuchi proved remarkably precocious, and in time she became the first important female writer of the new Japan, under the pseudonym Higuchi Ichiyo. Cherry blossoms were both a familiar part of her life and a favorite symbol. Her early short story "Flowers at Dusk" ends with an image worthy of haiku: "There was no wind in the air, but the cherry blossoms fell beneath the shadows of the leaves. In the evening sky, the temple bell resounded."

When she died of tuberculosis at the age of twenty-four, Higuchi left behind stories, essays, literally thousands of poems, and several volumes of diary. Like many young artists, when feeling betrayed by people, battered by life, or merely confused by hormones, she turned to nature. On April 11, 1891, she recorded in her diary a gathering held at the home of a friend, in honor of the newly flowering cherry trees. It was a day of celebration. The university boat races were under way on the Sumida River, and on its banks Higuchi and her friends "held a little poetry match," much of it on the theme of the beauty of the blossoming cherries. The setting sun lit up blossoms falling from the cherry trees. Then fireworks exploded in the evening sky. Finally nothing was visible through the mist rising above the river except other celebrants' picnic bonfires. "As we left the cherry arbor and boarded rickshaws to take us home," Higuchi wrote in her diary, "light rain began to fall."

"The Animals in This Neighborhood"

The Author of the following Letters takes the liberty, with all proper deference, of laying before the public his idea of parochial history, which, he thinks, ought to consist of natural productions and occurrences as well as antiquities.

With that, Gilbert White introduced the 110 letters that comprise *The Natural History and Antiquities of Selborne,* a chatty celebration of his village in Hampshire, fifty miles southwest of London. The first 44 are addressed to Thomas Pennant, a prominent Welsh naturalist, and the rest to another naturalist, a Bristol lawyer named Daines Barrington. It was Barrington who suggested to White that his vivid, informative letters would make a charming book. Posterity deemed the natural productions and occurrences more interesting than the antiquities, and in most of the more than 200 editions and translations that have appeared, the latter have vanished from both book and title.

"What make ye of Parson White of Selborne?" Thomas Carlyle asked a friend, and offered his own answer: "He copied a little sentence or two *faithfully* from the inspired volume of nature." American nature writer John Burroughs, who made a pilgrimage to Selborne, said of White, "He did not seek to read his own thoughts into nature but submitted his mind to her with absolute frankness and ingenuousness." Unlike some other parson-naturalists, White believed observation should replace superstition in the study of nature.

White was not a "trained" naturalist, but few were, in a time when education consisted primarily of several years of marinating in the Greek and Latin classics. White once lamented to Barrington, "It has been my misfortune never to have had any neighbours whose studies have led them towards the pursuit of natural knowledge; so that, for want of a companion to quicken my industry and sharpen my attention, I have made but slender progress in a kind of information to which I have been attached from my childhood." That complaint is disingenuous; White's "progress," as he well knew, was by no means slender. He was one of the earliest naturalists to explore territoriality in birds, and his account of the life of swifts was the most complete until the mid-twentieth century. He differentiated between birds formerly considered the same species. His observations of earthworms helped inspire Darwin's.

In the letters, White debated whether birds deal with winter by "hiding" or by migrating, and speculated on why other birds are willing to incubate the larger eggs of the cuckoo and even become foster parents for its offspring. He informed Pennant that he would send to Wales for identification the body of a "falco"—a peregrine falcon, he learned later. "I found it nailed up at the end of a barn, which is the countryman's museum." White also speculated on the identity of what appeared to be two species of "water-rats." One was probably the brown (Norway) rat, which at that time had been in England for perhaps forty years, quickly subduing the indigenous black rat. On April 12, 1770, he wrote in his fifth letter to Barrington, "When we meet, I shall be glad to have some conversation with

127

you concerning the proposal you make of my drawing up an account of the animals in this neighborhood." This is the first mention of what would become *The Natural History of Selborne.*

---

13 APRIL 1984

The Human Family Album

At the height of the creationist resurgence in the United States, evolutionary scientists from around the world gathered at the American Museum of Natural History in New York for a conference entitled "Paleoanthropology, the Hard Evidence." To hold the largest fossil reunion in history required international cooperation. France sent one of the earliest examples of modern humans, the Cro-Magnon. Both lighter and heavier forms of *Australopithecus,* called *gracilis* and *robustus,* came from South Africa, as did the famous Taung Child. Pakistan sent *Sivapithecus,* a senior participant at 8 million years old. Even the oldest known hominoid, Egypt's 33-million-year-old *Aegyptopithecus,* was there.

The crowd included Donald Johanson, who discovered the ancient fossil nicknamed Lucy, and even Jean Auel, author of the popular series of "prehistoric" novels that began with *Clan of the Cave Bear.* Mary Leakey, widow of Louis Leakey and matriarch of paleoanthropology's first family, was there. Her equally famous son, Richard, was not, nor did he permit Kenya's original fossils to participate. For various reasons, mostly political, some other countries could not or would not contribute. Peking Man remained in China. Even the important and famous Lucy didn't attend. Some non-American curators

An early representation of the similarities between the skeletons of ourselves and our near relatives.

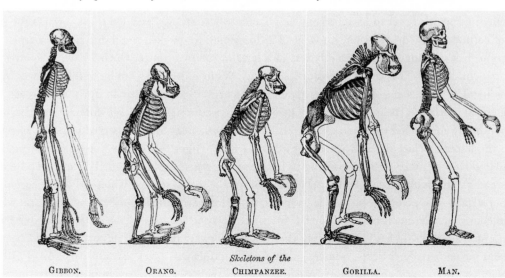

GIBBON.   ORANG.   *Skeletons of the* CHIMPANZEE.   GORILLA.   MAN.

complained that the exhibit was obviously aimed at the creationists and refused to participate in a controversy that didn't concern them.

Although absent fossils were represented by casts, mostly these were the irreplaceable original bones. Since not even the half-million-dollar insurance policies could replace them, both scientists and curators worried about security. Given the antievolution tone of the Reagan years, terrorism seemed distinctly possible. Breakage, accidental or deliberate, would be tragic. Some of the bones flew first class with their curators to be met by police escorts and limousines. The museum staff took extra precautions. Could a bump destroy years of work? Special carts were constructed and the route through the museum smoothed. Would fundamentalists attempt vandalism? The bones wound up resting in shock-resistant and bulletproof display cases.

Finally, the forty-odd fossils were in one room. These individuals had lived and died thousands of miles and sometimes millions of years apart. Countless seasons had come and gone while their bones lay in the earth. Now, exhumed, they became a family album wherein paleontologists could seek resemblances to themselves. One scientist said that working there was like discussing theology in a cathedral. The hushed tones and tense excitement led more than one person to remark on the similarity to ancestor worship.

Nonspecialists were equally fascinated. The museum opened its doors for the public exhibition, "Ancestors: Four Million Years of Humanity," on the thirteenth of April, 1984. The line of visitors stretched a quarter of a mile—in the rain. Visitors included businesspeople, teenagers, retirees, anyone who realized that the exhibit was *Roots* for the entire human species. Over the next few months nearly half a million people came, like pilgrims to a shrine, to commune with their ancestors.

See also Neandertals, 6/2; Lucy, 11/30; and Piltdown, 12/18.

The Song of the Cuckoo

Sumer is icumen in,
Lhude sing cuccu!

Apparently written by a monk at Reading Abbey in England in the thirteenth century, the "Cuckoo Song" is still performed there every spring. It doesn't describe lewd singing; "lhude" or "hlud" is the old Anglo-Saxon form of "loud." In modern English the lines would be, "Summer is a-coming in, loudly sing cuckoo." The cuckoo has long been one of the harbingers of spring in Europe. In traditional English folklore, the bird was supposed to return from its winter migration on April 14, along with the nightingale.

The cuckoo's name comes from the Old or Middle French *cucu* and imitates the bird's song, a sound that apparently no poet can resist. "O Cuckoo!" cried William Wordsworth to the disembodied sound. "Shall I call thee bird, / Or but a wandering voice?" Thomas Gray described a warbler as singing its own song in response to the cuckoo's. Edmund Spenser happily referred to the cuckoo as a merry messenger of spring. At the other end of the seasons and the emotional spectrum, Matthew Arnold thought "the cuckoo's parting cry was . . . 'The bloom is gone, and with the bloom go I.' "

The English poets were writing about the common cuckoo, *Cuculus canorus.* Only the males loudly sing "cuckoo." It is their vernal advertisement of their merits as nest mates, and presumably a declaration of territory to their fellow suitors. Or perhaps they're complaining about their long flight. Those cuckoos that nest in Europe migrate to central Africa, and natives of Asia overwinter in the East Indies.

A strange aspect of the bird's reputation appears in Shakespeare's parody of courtliness, *Love's Labour's Lost.*

> *When daisies pied and violets blue*
> *And lady-smocks all silver-white*
> *And cuckoo-buds of yellow hue*
> *Do paint the meadows with delight,*
> *The cuckoo then, on every tree,*
> *Mocks married men; for thus sings he,*
> *Cuckoo;*
> *Cuckoo, cuckoo; O, word of fear,*
> *Unpleasing to a married ear!*

According to Samuel Johnson, a cry of "Cuckoo!" would warn a husband that an adulterer was coming (the reverse seems likelier), and the word began to apply to the husband himself. The result is an interesting term based upon the cuckoo's name, "cuckold," referring to a man whose wife has committed adultery. Shakespeare uses it in *Othello,* when Desdemona asks, "Who would not make her husband a cuckold to make him a monarch?"

Apparently the word results from a moralistic interpretation of a perfectly natural phenomenon. Some species of cuckoos, the common European one especially, practice what ornithologists call brood parasitism. Rather than raising their own young, they lay their eggs in the nests of other birds. Usually they choose a bird whose eggs resemble their own, sometimes removing one from the nest to make room for their replacement. Some hosts recognize the alien egg and abandon the nest. But many do not. Illustrations of the cuckoo in ornithology books frequently depict the vaudeville scene of a smaller bird feeding a Brobdingnagian cuckoo. Soon after it hatches, the foster fledgling simply shoves other eggs out of the nest. Robbed of their natural family, the host birds are faced with the nightmare of trying to feed a child that is sometimes several times larger than themselves. Ornithologists do not understand why some species reject cuckoo eggs and others accept them.

There are 120-odd species of cuckoos, including a red-winged one in Asia, North America's yellow-billed and black-billed, and the emerald and the black species of Africa. Even the legendary roadrunner of Mexico and the southwestern United States is a cuckoo. Almost half of them are brood parasites. In North America, the black-billed and yellow-billed cuckoos are not so parasitical as their Eurasian cousins, although they occasionally parasitize each other. Another bird that behaves with similar abandon is the cowbird—which, not surprisingly, is sometimes called the cuckold.

See also the nightingale, 5/12.

15 April 1912

"Iceberg Right Ahead!"

Although the White Star Line never claimed the *Titanic* was unsinkable, articles about the ship recklessly did so from the first. Actually, it wasn't as safe as ocean liners once had been, because for half a century competition had encouraged the gradual abandonment of many early safety features. The legend persists nonetheless, because of its perfect moral. The shipbuilders' pride went before their fall— theirs and the lives of over 1,500 passengers and crew. That it was the great ship's maiden voyage lent the disaster an even more bitter irony. Not for nothing did Greek dramatists and poets dwell upon "hubris," overweening pride, and the inevitable "ate," the gods' revenge.

Actually, the worst maritime disaster in history was the result of human irresponsibility, not divine displeasure. The captain received numerous warnings of ice ahead and to the north, and ignored them. The wireless, later a crucial navigational aid, was at that time still a novelty reserved for emergencies. Between England and New York, the *Titanic* passed a ship returning from Halifax. Its captain reported heavy pack ice. A mild northern winter had left glaciers melting and breaking at a dangerous rate.

The formation of icebergs, called "calving," can be initiated by collision between an iceberg and a glacier, cracks in the ice that fracture into more cracks, or even tidal fluctuations. Glaciers and ice shelves produce icebergs when they extend out over the sea and begin to break apart. Two kinds of icebergs result. Those produced by glaciers are called simply glacier or irregular icebergs, and they can be thousands of years old. Pinnacled, domed, or block-shaped, their size varies enormously, and because they are formed of dense glacial ice it is they that inspired the truism that 90 percent of an iceberg is underwater. The Arctic's other main type of iceberg comes mostly from the Ward-Hunt Ice Shelf in northern Canada. Called tabular because they are generally flatter and smoother than their irregular kin, they are also larger, like mountains floating in the sea. The very word "iceberg" probably comes from the Danish *ijsberg,* "ice mountain."

Because they aren't produced at sea but only wind up there, icebergs consist of fresh- rather than saltwater, although frequently they are attended by floating chunks of sea ice. Ships are now equipped with radar and sonar, and experts track iceberg movements, greatly reducing the risk of collision. Nowadays the greater hazard is to offshore drilling sites. When a berg threatens a drilling platform or its pipes, tugboats come and, like sheepdogs, herd the ice away, either by nudging or by tugging.

The *Titanic* was not the first ship to go down in the iceberg fields of the Grand Banks off Newfoundland, but with its international publicity it was the decisive one. A few minutes before midnight, a crewman rang the alarm bell and shouted, "Iceberg right ahead!" Half a minute later, with its 46,000 tons moving at 22½ knots—38 feet per second—the *Titanic* struck the iceberg. The ship sank less than three hours later, in the early hours of April 15, 1912.

"My Friend the Pig"

It seems to be the fate of pigs to supply the lowest of animal comparisons. James Cagney ruined "dirty rat" as a term of opprobrium, but no one has yet made "filthy pig" a signature phrase. "Pig" was once the worst term one could shout at a police officer, beating "fuzz" by several orders of magnitude. Feminists also found it a handy descriptive term, with or without the adjective "chauvinist." A certain proverb must have been invented by someone who assumed the object farthest down the aesthetic spectrum from a silk purse is a sow's ear. "Swinish" is a most opprobrious adjective, and the lowest rung on the scale of housing is "sty." Only that vain Muppet, Miss Piggy, seems unaware of this reputation.

Porcine terminology is rampant. Some of it makes sense, such as pig-leather footballs being called pigskins. At other times it gets out of hand. We can save our money in a piggy bank. We can go the whole hog, pig out, or go hog wild. For its legendary appetite, Ambrose Bierce assigned the pig the fake Latin name, *Porcus omnivorous.* Apparently it is possible to be run down by a pigheaded, pigtailed road hog hauling pig iron. Incidentally, the exclamation "In a pig's eye!" originally referred to the opposite end of the pig's anatomy.

In the Bible, the lot of swine is not a happy one. When Jesus is about to exorcise the devils that possess the Gadarenes (or Gergesenes), he agreeably takes the advice of the devils themselves and casts them into a herd of swine, the whole bunch of which then dash off a cliff into the sea. In his Proverbs, Solomon coins one of his less tasteful similes: "As a jewel of gold in a swine's snout, so is a fair woman which is without discretion." It is during the Sermon on the Mount that Jesus advises his listeners to avoid casting their pearls before swine. From these last two remarks, we get the impression that pigs are ugly and not terribly discerning.

Not so, cried W. H. Hudson, the English naturalist. In his essay "My Friend the Pig," Hudson wrote, "I have a friendly feeling toward pigs generally, and consider them the most intelligent of beasts, not excepting the elephant and the anthropoid ape—the dog is not to be mentioned in this connection." With that assessment some biologists agree. Hudson maintained that the pig is a forest animal that is not naturally drawn to filth and mire. He became acquainted with a pig that lived near

Thomas Nast employed pigs to represent abusive police officers long before the term occurred to 1960s college students.

him on the Wiltshire downs, and took to greeting it and feeding it apples and elderberries. Then, Hudson recounted with a clear-eyed lack of regret, as he passed by one day he saw the pig's owner carting it off, squealing, with its legs bound (the origin of the term "hog-tied").

The pig's usual fate, of course, is to be eaten. Charles Lamb discussed it with great glee in his essay "A Dissertation upon Roast Pig." Salivating particularly over the thought of young suckling roasted to perfection, Lamb exclaimed, "Pig—let me speak his praise—" That is the fate from which the heroic spider saves Wilbur, in E. B. White's *Charlotte's Web.* Like Hudson, White admired pigs. As he recorded in his essay "Death of a Pig," he once fought hard for the life of an animal that he had originally planned to fatten and slaughter.

On April 16, 1968, White replied to a student who had asked specifics about why and how he wrote the essay. "The death of this animal moved me, heightened my awareness. To confront death, in any guise, is to identify with the victim and face what is unsettling and sobering." Elsewhere, White wrote: "My involvement with suffering and death became great, but I was pursued by the shadows of the irony (or perhaps idiocy) of a man's desire to save the life of a creature he had every intention of murdering."

---

17 APRIL 1610

Henry Hudson

Little is known about the life of the English explorer Henry Hudson. His date and place of birth are lost. No portraits exist, and no descriptions of his appearance. We know that he was married to a woman named Katherine, and that they had three sons. However, if we know little of Hudson the man, quite a bit is recorded about his accomplishments. Captain John Smith wrote, "The bounds of *America* doth stretch many thousand miles: into the frozen partes whereof one Master *Hutson* an English Mariner did make the greatest discoverie of any Christian I knowe of. . . ." Smith was exaggerating, but Hudson's four voyages did broaden the knowledge of the extent of the New World.

One of the overriding concerns of North American exploration in the sixteenth and seventeenth centuries was the search for a northwest passage, a sea route connecting the Atlantic and Pacific Oceans through the Arctic Ocean. Although many ships tried and many sailors lost their lives, it would be the mid-1800s before anyone could prove that such a passage actually existed. Not until 1969 did a commercial vessel actually navigate the hazardous Northwest Passage, and it was an ice-breaking oil tanker.

Long before this was known, Hudson was one of many explorers charged with finding a sea route to the wealth of the East Indies and Cathay. He was not a man with a dream. He was a mariner-for-hire, exploring for both English and Dutch concerns. His first voyage for the "islands of spicery" began in the spring of 1607, when he left England in the tiny ship *Hopewell,* with only eleven sailors. On that occasion, he was employed by the English Muscovy Company, which yearned for a more profitable route to the East. The next year he was off again, for the same company. His widely varying routes are apparent in this voyage, because this time he reached Novaya Zemlya, an island of Arctic Russia. His

Henry Hudson's situation as his crew abandoned him and others (including his son) was every bit as bad as this melodramatic illustration implies.

third voyage came in 1609, when the Dutch East India Company hired him to renew his search. Aboard the *Halve Maen* ("Half Moon"), he discovered the Hudson River and sailed into it as far as what is now Albany.

On his fourth and what turned out to be his final voyage, Hudson was again employed by his native land. He left England as captain of the *Discoverie* on April 17, 1610. By June the ship was at Greenland. He passed through what is now called the Hudson Strait and entered Canada's vast body of water called Hudson Bay. Around the third week of June, 1611, Hudson's crew mutinied and set him and eight others adrift without provisions.

The men had been rebellious throughout the voyage and the preceding winter had been difficult. One imaginative illustration protrays Hudson as a bearded, beatific, even Mosaic figure set adrift in a small boat, with the inhospitable glacier-infested northern waters behind him. His young son sits in the floor of the boat at his father's knee, looking up beseechingly. However romanticized that portrayal may be, it is safe to assume that the reality was bad enough. The mutineers returned to England, and some told their stories, but no one knows what became of Henry Hudson.

---

18 APRIL 1906

The San Francisco Earthquake

The San Andreas Fault, and the system of faults linked to it, emerges from under the Pacific Ocean north of San Francisco, at Cape Mendocino, and runs under much of California all the way down the Baja Peninsula. It marks the uneasy meeting place of the Pacific plate and the North American plate, two chunks of the earth's relatively thin, brittle crust that slowly move atop the less solid mantle. (The study of these movements is called "tectonics," from a Greek root meaning "to build.") The Pacific plate moves northwest sometimes as much as an inch per year, which makes it strain against the North American plate. The strain accumulates, and at irregular intervals it is released in the form of an earthquake.

The most famous of San Andreas tension-releasers occurred around San Francisco, on April 18, 1906, when an earthquake struck at 5:12 A.M. It lasted for over a minute, and the earth was calm again. There was little vertical displacement, but in some places the ground moved sideways as much as 20 feet. One witness compared the movement to a "terrier shaking a rat." Tremors were felt in Oregon, 750 miles to the north, and in Nevada, 300 miles to the east.

It would be another thirty years or so before Charles Richter and Beno Gutenberg would perfect the Richter scale of earthquake magnitude. However, seismologists have formulated retrospective estimates of the quake's magnitude, based upon descriptions and damage. They fluctuate on either side of 8.0. For comparison, a common, garden-variety quake of 6.3 magnitude (there are as many as a hundred or so in that range annually around the

A reconstruction of the havoc from the 1906 San Francisco earthquake, by a witness.

world) releases something like 50 times the energy of the atomic bomb that destroyed Hiroshima. The Richter scale doesn't measure magnitude on a linear scale; it is exponential. Each full point represents 50 times the power of the preceding. A quake registering 8.0 is 50 times as powerful as one of 7.0, and therefore 2,500 times as powerful as one of 6.0. The result at the surface depends upon the combination of magnitude, duration, and depth underground.

The San Francisco earthquake was severe enough to cause great damage, but it didn't break any world records. The resulting fire, however, was the worst in the country's history. Even the blaze that ravaged London in 1666 burned only one-sixth as wide an area. Almost 500 city blocks, a total of over 2,800 acres, were completely leveled. At least 450 people were killed.

Jack London was there when the quake struck, and he wrote an eyewitness report for the newspapers. "San Francisco is gone!" it began. "Nothing remains of it but memories and a fringe of dwelling houses on the outskirts. . . . Within an hour after the earthquake shock the smoke of San Francisco's burning was a lurid tower visible a hundred miles away." Exactly twenty-four hours after the quake, London sat on the steps of a residence in the exclusive Nob Hill neighborhood. "With me sat Japanese, Italians, Chinese, and Negroes—a bit of the cosmopolitan flotsam of the wreck of the city." Together they watched two great walls of flame approaching. Nature can be a great leveler. The owner of the house said calmly, "Yesterday morning, I was worth six hundred thousand dollars. . . . The flames will be here in fifteen minutes."

Picasso's Doves

Pablo Picasso's interest in doves dated back to his childhood. His father, the Spanish painter José Luis Blasco, kept doves, and his surviving portrayals of them are sensitive if not inspired. One of young Pablo's own sketches of pigeons survives from 1890, when he was nine. The birds in the drawing perch, fly, and feed their tiny young. Even at this early date they bear a strong family resemblance to the famous dove of peace Picasso would paint many years later.

Picasso kept doves at several of his villas, and the birds appeared in works throughout his life. In *Child Holding a Dove* (1901), the child gently cups the bird in praying hands. The baby in *Child with Pigeons* (1943) sits on the floor holding a rattle while two pigeons occupy the armchair beside him. Picasso created metal cutouts of doves, and one of a metal dovelike bird imprisoned in a wooden cage. In early 1947, amid representations of owls and mythological creatures, Picasso began working on lithographs of his favorite birds.

Partially as a symbol of his opposition to Franco's Fascism in his native Spain, Picasso had joined the Communist party in 1944. Hard-liners, already displeased with Picasso's "decadent" art, soon condemned him for his unflattering portrait of Stalin. He had drawn the dictator's forelock as a proletarian cap. "Those fools!" he exclaimed. "Now they don't want Marshal Stalin to be a proletarian!" In 1949, Louis Aragon, the writer and surrealist who had commissioned the Stalin portrait, came to Picasso's Paris studio in search of a symbol for the peace movement. Picasso allowed him to choose whatever he liked, and Aragon finally enthused over a series of sketches of pigeons: "Those beautiful doves . . . that's just what is needed for peace."

Aragon departed with the drawing. Picasso then exclaimed, "Poor old Aragon! His dove is a pigeon. . . . And as for the gentle dove, what a myth that is! There's no crueller animal. I had some here, and they pecked a poor little pigeon to death because they didn't like it. They pecked its eyes out, then pulled it to pieces. . . . How's that for a symbol of Peace?"

Ornithologists do not distinguish between pigeons and doves, but in common usage the more slender birds are called doves. However, Picasso was right about their violent tendencies. As every backyard bird-watcher knows, doves are not pacifists. Fortunately for the World Peace Congress, their reputation was better known than their true behavior. In his studies of aggression, the Austrian animal-behaviorist Konrad Lorenz once left two doves in a spacious cage. When he returned, the male was lying on the floor. "In the middle of this gory surface, like an eagle on his prey, stood the second harbinger of peace. Wearing that dreamy facial expression that so appeals to our sentimental observer, this charming lady pecked mercilessly with her silver bill in the wounds of her prostrated mate."

Picasso's pigeon drawing soon appeared on the poster announcing the Communist-sponsored World Peace Congress scheduled to open in Paris in April. Almost immediately it acquired the title *Dove of Peace*. That image has been reproduced so widely that it has become a cliché, if not kitsch, adorning everything from a Paul Robeson album to dormitory walls. On the day the World Peace Congress opened, April 19, 1949, with his dove posters papering the city, Picasso's lover, Françoise Gilot, gave birth to a daughter. Picasso, typically, had chosen the conference over accompanying Gilot to the hospital. When he finally arrived, he and Gilot named the baby Paloma, the Spanish word for "dove."

See also dove symbolism, 8/29.

"A Question of Monsters"

For six months and 17,000 leagues, Captain Nemo has held French zoologist Pierre Arronax, his servant Conseil, and Canadian harpooner Ned Land prisoner aboard the *Nautilus.* On April 20, 1868, the submarine is passing near the Bahamas. This day's dramatic encounter in Jules Verne's 1870 novel *Twenty Thousand Leagues under the Sea* became the most thrilling scene in Walt Disney's 1954 film version—the fight with the giant squid.

"I will never believe that such animals exist," Land declares. At first Professor Arronax himself dismisses stories of the legendary size and ferocity of the giant squid. "You know what to make of legends in the matter of natural history," he says. "Besides, when it is a question of monsters, the imagination is apt to run wild."

But at that time they hadn't seen the giant squid outside the submarine's porthole. "Before my eyes was a horrible monster, worthy to figure in the legends of the marvelous. . . . Its eight arms, or rather feet, fixed to its head, that have given the name of cephalopod to these animals, were twice as long as its body, and were twisted like the furies' hair." Captain Nemo explains that the jaws of the creature are entangled in the propeller. The submarine rises to the surface, and as a hatch opens, giant tentacles slither in. One grabs a crewman. Outside, there is chaos—men screaming, tentacles thrashing. Arronax estimates the creature's weight at 4,000–5,000 pounds. Its flesh isn't hard enough to detonate Nemo's electric bullets, so the crewmen attack with hatchets. The sailor vanishes over the side.

Arronax links the giant squid with a legendary Scandinavian sea monster, the kraken. He mentions Erik Pontoppidan, who said in his *Natural History of Norway* that this animal "may be reckoned of the Polype, or of the Starfish kind." Arronax says *poulp,* the French word for octopus, from the Latin *polypus* ("many-foot"). Another Frenchman claimed a "*poulpe colossal*" tried to drag a three-masted ship underwater. In the first century A.D., Pliny the Elder wrote of an enormous many-armed monster that rose from the sea to feast upon salted fish in Spanish curing ponds. The locals killed it. The corpse, Pliny claimed, weighed 700 pounds, with a head the size of a 90-gallon cask. One twentieth-century witness described a horrific battle between a sperm whale and an adversary almost as large—a giant squid. There is no question that sperm whales, which eat squid, have been found with monstrous sucker marks on their skins.

Surprisingly, such stories may not be beyond the bounds of possibility. Other than the jellyfish *Cyanea,* giant squid are the largest—and apparently the most ferocious—known invertebrate. Estimates of the upper size limit of the giant squid *Architeuthis* reach absurd lengths, but the largest con-

A squid captured alive off the coast of Newfoundland and later exhibited at the New York Aquarium.

firmed size is about 55 feet. Those versatile tentacles surround the mouth and direct food into it, and are actually a modified foot. From that characteristic derives the class name, Cephalopoda, which means "head-foot."

The class also contains one mollusk with an external shell, the well-known chambered nautilus. Presumably Nemo named his ship after that of Robert Fulton, who invented the first practicable submarine around the beginning of the nineteenth century. Fulton derived the name from *nautilos,* the Greek word for sailor, the same etymology as that of the chambered nautilus. It seems that, on that busy day in 1868, the *Nautilus* encountered a ferocious cousin of the nautilus.

See also kraken, 8/10; and octopus, 9/18.

---

21 APRIL 1948

The Death of Aldo Leopold

A few books emerge from their times and become milestones in cultural evolution. Now and then a work of natural history is awarded the retrospective status of "classic" for its impact on our thinking about our world. Gilbert White, whose 1787 *Natural History of Selborne* is the first example of modern nature writing, was determined to see the world clearly, without the anthropomorphism that wrapped nature in a fog of superstition and fable. In 1854, Henry David Thoreau, in *Walden,* resolved to see nature deeply, as an eternal Garden of Eden where even a crotchety pencil-maker might stroll with his personal god. Because of its graceful style and vision of a unified nature, Rachel Carson's *Silent Spring* (1962) remains not just an important social document but a monument of nature writing.

Another book that has achieved masterpiece rank is *A Sand County Almanac,* by Aldo Leopold. Published in 1949, a year after its author's death, it gradually drew readers, but became a best-seller with its paperback re-release, timed to fuel the dawning ecological awareness of the 1960s. The book's conservationist stance is apparent in the rejected alternative titles: *Great Possessions, Our Mounting Loss, This We Lose.* But it's Leopold's wonderful writing that gives it staying power. His admiration for the ways of the wild was rooted firmly in personal experience, and his essays are more psalms of appreciation than sermons about what must be done.

Leopold believed that conservation was first a matter of conscience, not legislation. "Obligations have no meaning without conscience, and the problem we face is the extension of the social conscience from people to land." And he summed up his approach with a typical epigram: "A conservationist is one who is humbly aware that with each stroke he is writing his signature on the face of the land."

On the morning of Wednesday, April 21, 1948, Aldo Leopold got up before dawn. He checked the status of several spring plants, counted the migrating geese, and noted all of his observations in his journal. Around midmorning, he detected smoke. A neighbor's trash fire had escaped and burned their farmyard. It was heading toward the Leopold place. A forester and lifelong woodsman, Leopold knew what to do. He and his family spread out. The daughter ran to call the fire department and the Forestry Service. With a backpack fire pump, Leopold dampened the ground while his wife stamped out ashes with a wet broom.

When daughter and wife reunited about noon, they realized neither had seen Leopold for at least an hour and a half. When they found him, he was lying on his back with his hands folded across his chest. Apparently he had had a heart attack and lay down to recover and died. The flames had leaped over his body and gone on. If Leopold could have chosen, he might have picked just such a death—quiet, unobserved, but working to protect the land he loved. A colleague eulogized a few days later, "The cause of conservation has lost its best friend."

---

22 April 1970

Earth Day

The "environmental movement" in the United States may be said to have come of age on a sunny day in the spring of 1970. Across the nation, 20 million Americans gathered in public to celebrate the earth and protest its abuse. The event was billed as the first Earth Day. It was April 22.

To their own surprise, those who understood ecological intricacies and those who dismissed them as irrelevant were finding themselves united by a common emotion—fear. That mythical quantity, the "average American," had begun to wonder about all those poisons showing up on the nightly news, and about the pollution breeding illness in more and more people around them and finally even in themselves. Then the Santa Barbara oil spill in 1969 generated a new interest in ecology.

The Nixon administration still regarded the environmental movement as a passing fad. They were correct in perceiving conservationists as unable to present a unified front. Unlike other civil rights movements during the era, conservation had no charismatic central leader. Factions quibbled among themselves regarding priorities and methods. The organizers of Earth Day tried to demonstrate to political leaders and anticonservation business groups the combined voting and lobbying power behind that occasionally divisive phalanx.

Of course, committed individuals were already making a difference, as they had since the days of Theodore Roosevelt. Maine Democrat Edmund Muskie was pushing environmental legislation. Stuart Udall, secretary of the interior under both Kennedy and Johnson, was fighting for a more thoughtful approach to the wilds, not least with his own book, *The Quiet Crisis.* The time was definitely ripe. Then Democratic senator Gaylord Nelson conceived the idea of Earth Day. Interestingly, established conservation organizations, such as the Audubon Society and the Sierra Club, hardly participated. Indeed, as they viewed the enthusiasm from the position they had always occupied until then—on the sidelines—they were astonished. Could this really be happening? Did that many people out there *care?*

Earth Day is credited with inspiring the national awareness that led to such milestones of U.S. legislation as the Endangered Species Act, the Clean Water and Clean Air Acts, and even the Toxic Substances Control Act. The national festivities on that day proclaimed changing times. "That was the important objective and achievement of Earth Day," Senator Nelson said later. "It showed the political and opinion leadership of the country that the people cared, that they were ready for political action, that the politicians had better get ready, too."

The attitude of the time is summed up in a paperback published just in time for the first Earth Day, *Ecotactics: The Sierra Club Handbook for Environment Activists.* An editor's note defined the title as "*n. pl.* the science of arranging and maneuvering all available forces against enemies of the earth." April 22 was one day after the birthday of John Muir, whose early work had meant so much to the beginnings of conservation in America. *Ecotactics* quotes Muir's famous line that became a banner for ecology: "When we try to pick out anything by itself, we find it hitched to everything else in the universe."

See also Arbor Day, 4/10.

---

23 APRIL 1949

The Cat Bill

Illinois governor Adlai Stevenson was a busy man in 1949. He spoke out against anti-Communist paranoia, served as a character witness for Alger Hiss, and negotiated his divorce. Legislation crossing his desk dealt with Chicago's organized crime, old-age pensions, and Sabbath ordinances. But few bills attracted as much amused interest as one promoted by bird lovers and approved by their elected representatives. Stevenson wrote a memorable letter to the state senate on the twenty-third of April, 1949.

"I herewith return, without my approval, Senate Bill No. 93 entitled 'An Act to Provide Protection to Insectivorous Birds by Restraining Cats.' This is the so-called 'Cat Bill' . . ."

Stevenson's complaints about the proposed law included the statement that "it is in the nature of cats to do a certain amount of unescorted roaming." Then, "This legislation . . . ," he reminded the senators, "has, over the years, been the source of much comment—not all of which has been in a serious vein. . . . I cannot believe there is a widespread public demand for this law. . . ."

Stevenson conceded that "we are all interested in protecting certain varieties of birds." That adjective is telling. As the idea of protecting various animals evolved in Europe after the Renaissance, favored species status was awarded for a variety of criteria. Some were questionable. After robins became a favorite in England, wrens were sometimes protected because they were thought to be the robins' wives, just as cuckoos were considered hawks in summer plumage. In a seventeenth-century poem, a robin boasts that humans don't hurt him because it would bring them ill luck. Gradually species were added to the protected list for reasons other than superstition.

British naturalist W. H. Hudson gave considerable thought to "the army of cats" that plague songbirds. Half a century before Stevenson, he devoted an entire chapter in his *Birds of London* to "The Cat Question." Speaking of managed urban birds, Hudson wrote, ". . . so long as cats are allowed to range about the parks these species cannot be said to be properly protected." Although he also warned against both the irresponsible bird fancier and the casually destructive "rough," nonetheless cats were "the deadliest enemy of the birds which are of most value—the resident species that sing most of the year, and that nest in low bushes close to the ground." Hudson concluded that concerned citizens must "look to the County Council."

Obviously Illinois bird lovers agreed. However, Adlai Stevenson foresaw a dilemma. "The problem of cat *versus* bird is as old as time. If we attempt to resolve it by legislation who knows but what we may be called upon to take sides as well in the age-old problem of dog *versus* cat, bird *versus* bird, or even bird *versus* worm. In my opinion, the State of Illinois and its local governing bodies already have enough to do without trying to control feline delinquency. For these reasons, and not because I love birds the less or cats the more, I veto and withhold my approval from Senate Bill No. 93."

---

24 April 1498

"Of Christians and of Spices"

In 1497, King Manuel I of Portugal assigned to a young navigator named Vasco da Gama the task of finding a route around Africa to India. Da Gama sailed down the west coast of Africa and around the Cape of Good Hope. Battling storms and mutinies, he proceeded up the east coast of Africa to Malindi, in what is now Kenya. In April of 1498, da Gama prepared to depart from Africa and proceed with the rest of his assignment. "We left Malindi on Tuesday, the 24th of the month, for a city called Calecut, with the pilot whom the king had given us. . . ." The Hindu pilot navigated the ship northeastward across what is now called the Arabian Sea to the coast of India. Twenty-three days after departure, the crew sighted land. In time, they were greeted by two "Moors" (Muslims) from Tunis, who spoke Castilian and Genoese. Da Gama wrote:

> The first greeting that he received was in these words: "May the Devil take thee! What brought you hither?" They asked what he sought so far away from home, and he told them that we came in search of Christians and of spices.

The Portuguese found more spices than Christians. Da Gama's mission, a sea route from Europe to India for the spice trade, was one of the all-consuming obsessions of fifteenth-century Europe. The arduous and expensive route in use at the time involved shipping goods across the Indian Ocean to Syria or Egypt, where they had to be slowly carried across the Isthmus of Suez, shipped across the Mediterranean to Venice, and trekked through the Alps. Whichever nation managed the coup of a route to the spice suppliers would become the most powerful in Europe. That is why Portugal, a tiny nation on the edge of the Mediterranean, briefly ruled the waves.

The Crusades, from the eleventh through the thirteenth centuries, had made Europe aware of the culture of the "Orient," by which they meant at first the Arabic civilizations. The impact of Arabic culture upon more primitive medieval Europe has been compared to the effect of Greek civilization on agrarian Rome. From the East came the knowledge of seafaring and astronomy that enabled such men as da Gama to venture away from their coastlines. Without the sophisticated Arabic numbering system, the new rising merchant class could not have developed the detailed bookkeeping that underlay the expansion of capitalism. Although the trade in luxuries had little effect on the vast majority of the huddled poor, it enabled the more fortunate upper classes to further separate themselves from their subjects. The cold and spartan castles of Europe began to be furnished with fine fabrics and furniture.

But the most valued of all luxury items were spices. Many plant products are described as spices, including nutmeg, cinnamon, pepper, and clove. But heading the list was pepper. Some historians explain away the European hunger for spices as the need to preserve food in the days before refrigeration. Another answer may appear in the German language, where spices are included with intoxicants and stimulants in the category called *Genussmittel,* "articles of pleasure." However, to medieval Europeans, spices were more than preservatives and tasty additives. For those who could afford them, spices had also come to represent the exotic, the mystery of the East. They were the very definition of luxury. The market for spices grew as the new merchant class began to emulate the ways of the aristocracy. And, as demand rose, prices became exorbitant.

Da Gama's voyage and its aftermath brought disaster to the native civilizations. It began the European exploitation of the established civilizations and ended a long period of flourishing trade among the nations bordering the Indian Ocean. But nothing could stop the European drive for more spices and less expensive ways to acquire them. Vasco da Gama gave Portugal the ability to supply the demand. The consequences were not considered important. It was merely business as usual.

"I An't Got No Frog"

Jim Smiley was a gambling man. He bet on the outcome of chicken fights, where a "straddlebug" might be going, even whether Parson Walker's wife would survive her illness. He bet on the hind-leg-holding ability of his bull pup Andrew Jackson, until he pitted the poor dog against an opponent that had lost its hind legs in a mill accident. But most famously of all, he bet that his frog Dan'l Webster could outjump any other frog in Calaveras County.

Mark Twain's first well-known story, "Jim Smiley and His Jumping Frog," was published in the *New York Saturday Press* in November 1865. It was the paper's last issue, for which Twain claimed credit. Soon American novelist and critic James Russell Lowell called the story "the finest piece of humorous writing ever produced in America." Twain himself, who had already written better works, dismissed it as a "villainous backwood sketch." Book publication was announced on April 25, 1867, in an unappetizing advertisement in the *New York Times:* "The Jumping Frog will to-day jump down the popular throat." *The Celebrated Jumping Frog of Calaveras County, and Other Sketches* sold well.

"Smiley," Twain wrote, "was monstrous proud of his frog, and well he might be, for fellers that had traveled and been everywheres, all said he laid over any frog that ever *they* see." All a frog lacks is education, Smiley is convinced, and he works hard to educate Dan'l Webster. Therefore Dan'l always wins. Then comes the day a stranger isn't impressed, and Smiley bets him forty dollars that his frog can outjump any frog in the county. The stranger responds with a line that gamblers were soon quoting: ". . . I an't got no frog; but if I had a frog, I'd bet you." Smiley tramps off to the swamp to catch a frog for the newcomer. While he's gone, the stranger spoon-feeds Dan'l quail shot until the poor creature can't move. The outcomes of both the contest and the story are inevitable.

In 1894, Henry Van Dyke asked Twain if he knew the age of the jumping frog story. When Twain confidently said forty-five years, Van Dyke sent him a Greek textbook by Henry Sidgwick that contained a brief fable entitled "The Athenian and the Frog." In Greek, it began: "An Athenian once fell in with a Boeotian who was sitting by the roadside looking at a frog . . ." The Boeotian frog winds up filled with stones rather than quail shot. Rather than considering the story a venerable piece of folklore, Twain decided that history had repeated itself.

Years later, Twain met Sidgwick. He learned that the professor, thinking Twain's story similar to Aesop's stories, had adapted it in Greek, not expecting anyone to be misled by what was merely

An early representation of Jim Smiley's frog, looking dyspeptic as his rival jumps away.

an academic exercise. Frogs appear in several of Aesop's fables. One tries to blow himself up as big as an ox; another leads astray an innocent mouse. Sidgwick thought old Dan'l Webster would fit right in.

See also Mark Twain and animals, 1/20; Halley's Comet, 4/8; **Connecticut Yankee, 6/21; *and*** *grieving pet, 12/26.*

---

26 APRIL 1882

Darwin's Funeral

Born in 1809 on the same day as Abraham Lincoln, Charles Darwin lived past the births of Freud and Picasso. His life spanned a time of enormous change—world exploration, the beginnings of the Industrial Revolution, great wars, and not least the acceptance of his own revolutionary ideas. By the time of his death, he was a scientific and popular icon. The reviled scoundrel of the "monkey theory" had become the revered elder statesman of English science. Nothing so clearly shows this evolution of opinion than Darwin's burial in Westminster Abbey.

A simian-looking Darwin holds up a mirror for a cousin. It was what that reflection said about humanity that bothered people, long after Darwin died.

Darwin wanted to be buried in Downe, the village twenty miles south of London where he spent the last forty-odd years of his life. His family and the other villagers also wanted him to rest on the land he loved. But world stature demanded world-class gestures of appreciation. Darwin's neighbor John Lubbock, a scientist and Member of Parliament, asked the dean of Westminster for permission to bury Darwin in the esteemed abbey. The dean telegraphed his full approval.

With the eyes of the world upon them, religious leaders seized this opportunity to profess themselves free of rancor. "[T]rue Christians," declared the *Standard,* "can accept the main scientific facts of Evolution just as they do of Astronomy and Geology, without any prejudice to more ancient and cherished beliefs." The High Church *Morning Post* conceded that "we who cannot respect all his theories can admire [Darwin's] life." For his integrity and kindness, the *Church Times* went so far as to label the deceased agnostic "a Christian gentleman."

The *Pall Mall Gazette* declared that Darwin belonged in the abbey more than many of the statesmen who were already there. "The bustle of daily politics is for the most part but dusty sterility compared with the vast effects of the labours of the thinker who from his tranquil hilltop in his little Kentish village shook the world." As the London *Times* remarked about the funeral, "The Abbey needed it more than it needed the Abbey."

The funeral took place on April 26, 1882. Pallbearers included Lubbock himself; Thomas Huxley, whose ferocious support had earned him the label "Darwin's bulldog"; botanist Joseph Hooker; Alfred Russell Wallace, whose independent arrival at the concept of natural selection prompted his and Darwin's joint paper in 1858, and nudged Darwin to finally publish the *Origin* the next year; an earl and two dukes; the president of the Royal Society; and the United States minister to England, a poet and scholar named James Russell Lowell. Among the mourners were London's lord mayor, members of the Royal and Linnaean and other scientific societies, representatives from other countries, and at least one novelist—Thomas Hardy.

During the funeral, Darwin's son William felt a draft. Having inherited both a fear of illness and a disregard for public opinion, he placed his gloves atop his balding head and left them there for the rest of the ceremony. The choir sang Handel's "His body is buried in peace, but his name liveth evermore." One of the abbey's organists had composed for the occasion a hymn from Proverbs that could have been Darwin's motto in life: "Happy is the man that findeth wisdom, and getteth understanding."

---

27 April 1941

The Swastika

At the Salzburg Conference in 1920, Hitler adopted the swastika as the official banner of the National Socialist German Workers' Party—the National-Sozialistische Deutsche Arbeiterpartei, of which Nazi was originally a contraction. In 1933 it became the Reich flag, and two years later it was declared the only national flag of Germany. The swastika became a sacred icon. When Baldur von Schirach wrote the anthem for the Hitler Youth, *Unsre Fahne flattert uns voran* ("Our Flag Flutters before Us"), he included the line, "The flag is greater than death."

Soon the swastika flag was fluttering over other countries. On April 27, 1941, for example, Athens fell to the Nazis. The Germans raised over the ancient capital of Greece what most did not realize was an even more ancient symbol. In his speeches, Hitler referred to the swastika as a symbol of resurrection, which for him meant the restoration of a mythical "pure" Germany. But the swastika was a widespread symbol thousands of years before the brief vicious reign of the Third Reich. The Nazis called their emblem the *Hakenkreuz*. The term *swastika* comes from the Sanskrit words *su* ("well"), *asti* ("being"), and the suffix *ka*, and simply means "well-being."

There are variations on the shape. In India, when the symbol's arms turn clockwise, it is called a swastika; when they turn counterclockwise, it is a *sauwastika*. The "ogee swastika," which has rounded arms as if they were flexible and twirling, is also a common symbol. The swastika shows up in one form or another in cultures around the world and throughout history. Fifth-millennium-B.C. Sumerian pottery portrays stylized silhouettes of four women with their feet together at the center of a circle and their heads pointing outward, each with three strands of hair blowing to the right—the shape of a turning swastika. A ninth-century Sanskrit manuscript drawing shows Buddha with a swastika symbol on the robe across his chest. Heinrich Schliemann found spindles bearing the swastika in the ruins of Troy. The familiar pattern appears on a pre-Columbian vase from Arkansas, coins from Gaul and mosaics from Rome, Mycenean wooden buttons, even an Iron Age spear.

Some symbols recur again and again across cultures because they passed from one to another. Others are widespread because they are based upon universal observation—the round circles of the sun and moon, for example. The swastika is prevalent in too many widely separated cultures around the globe to have traveled from one to another. It seems to have arisen spontaneously. Many archaeologists interpret the swastika as a diagrammatic representation of the cycle of the sun in the sky. However, there are other possible origins. Carl Sagan and Ann Druyan, in their 1985 book *Comet,* speculated "[v]ery tentatively" that the swastika may be an ancient representation of a comet. Pliny the Elder described one comet as having "a very rapid motion, like a circle revolving on itself." There are other descriptions of comets as rotating. We do not always see comets in their classic flowing-hair profile. (The word "comet" comes from the Latin *coma,* "hair.") Sometimes the view is from an oblique angle, or even looking down upon the axis of rotation.

Sagan and Druyan pointed out a fascinating piece of evidence. In China, in the third or fourth century B.C., astronomers painted on silk an atlas of the various forms of comets. Archaeologists found it in a Han Dynasty tomb at Mawangdui, near Changsha, in the 1970s. There are twenty-nine comets depicted, categorized by both appearance and ill effects. The comets are simplified and stylized, drawn with sure brush strokes, without the symbolic paraphernalia that accompanies many Western portrayals. At the time this atlas was compiled, China already had an ancient tradition of precisely recorded astronomical observations. Comets are shown with their tales curving, fragmenting, and bushing. The last one in the list is a swastika.

---

28 APRIL

Bilbo Baggins Has an Adventure

The hobbit stands on his doorstep, contentedly blowing smoke rings. The wizard looks him over and says, "I am looking for someone to share an adventure that I am arranging, and it's very difficult to find anyone."

Bilbo Baggins laughs. "I should think so—in these parts! We are plain quiet folk and have no use for adventures. Nasty disturbing uncomfortable things! Make you late for dinner!"

The reader immediately suspects that Bilbo Baggins will soon find himself late for dinner. He does indeed. Bilbo's wild adventures read, not surprisingly, like the tribulations of his literary forebears. A scholar and philologist who read Icelandic, Greek, Spanish, and other languages, J. R. R. Tolkien patterned Bilbo's escapades after the great adventure stories of the past—Homer's *Odyssey,* Virgil's *Aeneid,* the Norse *Elder Edda,* the German *Nibelungenlied.* He wrote most of *The Hobbit* while a professor of Anglo-Saxon at Oxford.

Adventuring away from one's quiet little hobbit-hole is always dangerous, but Middle-Earth is populated with characters from European literature and folklore, including elves, giants, dwarfs, goblins, trolls, and dragons. Many of them consider hobbits choice morsels, and one misadventure follows another. While fleeing from the evil, cave-dwelling goblins, Bilbo and the dwarfs are treed by the monsters' allies, evil wolves called Wargs. Then the heroes are rescued by the Lord of the Eagles, who commands his subjects to fly down and grab them. One of the monsters they encounter now seems reminiscent of a 1950s horror film: Giant spiders capture them. Wrapped in silk and stacked like firewood, the terrified heroes listen to the spiders' comments, such as, "You were quite right, the meat's alive and kicking." Most dramatically of all, they must battle the fire-breathing dragon, Smaug.

Supposedly, *The Hobbit* takes place "long ago in the quiet of the world, when there was less noise and more green." Although Tolkien didn't specify his locale's modern name, it is obviously Europe, and much of it is the English countryside, just as many of the customs and values of hobbits are decidedly English. Tolkien was not bothered by anachronisms. This Edenic world is cluttered with modern inventions, but they are those of which Tolkien himself was fond.

In the first chapter, Bilbo is standing on the doorstep of his hobbit-hole, admiring the day and blowing smoke rings from his pipe. Unfortunately, while tobacco was common among the pre-Columbian South Americans long before, it didn't arrive in Europe until the end of the fifteenth century. Perhaps the hobbit was smoking marijuana. When Bilbo wants to get rid of Gandalf for talking about such dangerous things as adventures, he invites him to tea the next day, which is Wednesday. Tea came to Europe from China as late as the 1600s, and "Wednesday" is from "Wodin's Day," in honor of the chief Germanic god Wodin. Bilbo serves his uninvited guests such various stored foods as pork, beef, chicken, and even pickles. And the dwarfs expect Bilbo to meet them at 11:00 sharp, perhaps thousands of years before such punctuality was even possible, much less a virtue. This particular obstacle to the suspension of disbelief is reminiscent of the striking clock that Brutus hears in Shakespeare's *Julius Caesar,* over a thousand years before such mechanisms existed.

Tolkien was aware of the discrepancies. "Some of the modernities found among [the hobbits] (I think especially of *umbrellas*) are probably, I think certainly, a mistake, of the same order as their silly names. . . ." One of the more jarring anachronisms is Tolkien's reference to a date phrased in modern terms. Gandalf says to Thorin Oakenshield, the leader of the dwarfs, "And Thrain your father went away on the twenty-first of April, a hundred years ago last Thursday. . . ." From that remark, incidentally, it is apparent that Bilbo departs on his adventure on April 28.

See also dragons, 1/16.

From Fur to Nylon

In the beginning we didn't need clothing. We had fur. Then, gradually, our own body hair dwindled to vestigial patches. It still protected the head, and, clustered strategically, held certain bodily scents, but it no longer provided much in the way of warmth. However, we were a clever species. With a revolutionary tool that would later be called imagination, we were able to figure out that if another animal's body covering would keep it warm, it would also keep *us* warm. We also had another handy tool, opposable thumbs, and with them we proceeded to rob animals of their own coverings.

Five-inch-tall figures carved from Siberian mammoth ivory 20,000 years ago portray individuals clad in heavy fur suits. Contemporaneous sites reveal such artifacts as eyed needles made of bone, ivory beads, and traces of leather clothing, including shoes and caps. Then came another innovation. The recent discovery of a small cave at Nahal Hemer in the arid Judaean desert revealed linen dating back roughly 8,500 years. Spun from the fibers of the flax plant, apparently linen was one of the earliest natural materials exploited for human benefit. A wooden model of a weaving shop, from Egypt's Eleventh Dynasty (roughly 2,000 B.C.), depicts a number of activities, including women processing flax. We will never know who first thought to weave together a number of short plant fibers into a longer one, and to create from them a flexible fabric to protect the body. It was a brilliant innovation.

Flax grows up to four feet high, and the length of its fibers provided a head start over the use of cotton fibers, which come in tiny tangled bunches. (Hemp, by contrast, grows up to sixteen feet tall, and naturally its long fibers were woven into rope.) Different climates encourage the growth of different plants. Cotton would become the most important crop in nineteenth-century North America. Numerous other materials have been used in similar ways, including human hair, which grows to a greater length than that of most other animals. Wool has long been a favorite. Like our own hair, wool grows quickly and can be sheared without harming the bearer. Wool's insulating virtues are apparent on the animals it naturally protects from harsh environments.

Flax, cotton, wool, and other plant and animal fibers have long been cultivated. With the Industrial Revolution in Europe came the mechanization of cloth production. The cotton gin, spinning jenny, and power loom revolutionized the manufacture of textiles. Still, the raw materials were derived from nature and were limited by nature's ability to produce them. We kept trying to create better variations on natural fibers. In attempts to mimic silk, inventors created such products as cellulose acetate and cellulose nitrate.

Then along came a material that would revolutionize the textiles industry. While working in the laboratories of E. I. du Pont de Nemours and Company in Delaware, an American chemist named Wallace Hume Carothers began looking for a way to replace natural fibers with artificial ones. By 1930 he was certain he was on the right track, and a few years later there was no question that he was developing a revolutionary product. It was a superpolymer, a synthetic material manufactured—in one of those industrial transmutations that would delight a medieval alchemist—basically from coal, water, and air.

Highly elastic, with a strength out of all proportion to its size, it could be fashioned into sheets, filaments, bristles, and fibers, which gave it almost unlimited applications in plastics and textiles. Carothers applied for a patent in the spring of 1937. Three weeks later, on April 29, 1937, he committed suicide, and the patent rights to one of the most famous un-natural textiles reverted to the company.

Soon the new product would astonish the world with its seemingly endless applications, from paintbrushes to parachutes, from fishing lines to stockings. Du Pont proceeded to manufacture a great deal of it. Apparently they simply manufactured the word for it, too. "Nylon" did not come from a combination of *New York* and *Lon*don, as some have speculated, or from *ni*trogen plus a futuristic suffix. It is simply, as the dictionaries say, an arbitrary formation, like the product itself, both its name and its character divorced from the natural history of its predecessors.

---

30 APRIL 1844

Thoreau Burns the Woods

That cranky iconoclast Henry Thoreau was not the most sociable of men, but now and then someone got along with him and became his friend. This small circle included for a time Edward Hoar, son of Concord, Massachusetts's most prominent citizen. On April 30, 1844, home from his senior year at Harvard, Hoar went canoeing with Thoreau to the headwaters of the Sudbury River.

The two young men planned to stop and cook the fish they'd caught, but they discovered they hadn't brought matches. They had to beg one from a shoemaker they passed. When they kindled a fire in a dry stump that was surrounded by even drier grasses, sparks leaped eagerly to the grass. The fire quickly raced out of control. Both men went for help, Hoar in the canoe, Thoreau on foot.

The first man Thoreau met declared the fire "none of his stuff" and drove on; later the fire hit his own land and, ironically, burned several cords of his firewood. The second man he encountered owned the woods then burning. He went with Thoreau to the fire, but it was already too much for them and the farmer returned to town for help. Thoreau stayed behind, exhausted after running two miles. Helpless before a wall of flame that was spreading every moment, he climbed Fair Haven Cliff, the better to watch the spectacle. He could hear clanging bells gathering volunteers to the village. When there were enough to help, Thoreau came back down and joined them in digging trenches and setting backfires.

Naturally, the townsfolk were furious. There were threats of prosecution, but they weren't followed up. Hoar's father unofficially paid some damages. Likewise, no names were mentioned in the editorial that estimated more than $2,000 worth of damage to over 300 acres of woodland. But everyone knew who the culprits were. For years afterward, Thoreau was mocked with whispers of "Woodsburner!"

It is telling that Thoreau didn't mention the fire in his journal, that repository for every passing thought, until six years later. In 1850 he still had the incident on his mind and devoted five pages to it. "I had felt like a guilty person," he wrote, "—nothing but shame and regret." Then he tried to rationalize his actions and undermine the opprobrium from his fellow citizens. "What could I do alone against a front of flame nearly half a mile wide?" And he included one of his frequent reminders to himself of his own superiority: "I felt I had a deeper interest in the woods, knew them better and should feel their loss more, than any or all of them. The farmer whom I had first conducted to the woods was obliged to ask me the shortest way back, through his own lot." The journal even records a statement belied by the very account itself: "It has never troubled me from that day to this more than if the lightning had done it."

See also Thoreau and warring ants, 1/21; and Darwin, 7/23; and his journal, 10/22.

May Day

During the reign of Queen Elizabeth I, a rising group of religious dissidents was determined to purify the Church of England of its Catholic influence. In 1583 they published an *Anatomie of Abuses.* Therein these "Puritans" also took offense at numerous aspects of English society that had nothing to do with Catholicism, including such seemingly innocuous artifacts as maypoles. "Stinckying idols," they called them, and charged that around them May Day celebrants "leape and daunce, as the heathen did." At best, to this humorless crowd, such pagan revelry was frivolous; at worst, blasphemous.

Late in the factious reign of Charles I, the English Parliament solemnly declared that "all and singular Maypoles that are, or shall be erected, shall be taken down." Of course, the people simply observed the spring rites secretly until the Restoration of Charles II in 1660. Then, to the clamorous approval of the citizenry, Charles erected a 134-foot cedar maypole, the tallest ever.

The Puritans were so obsessed with maypoles because May Day embodied threatening pre-Christian traditions. On the first of May, the Celts held the feast of Beltane, the time to light hilltop bonfires, apparently to encourage the vernal sun. Traces of another holiday persisted: the Floralia, which was observed over the last days of April and on the first of May. Flora was the Roman goddess of flowers, and one of the spring deities. During the Floralia, girls wound temple columns with flowers, just as children later wound maypoles with garlands. Related customs migrated to Charles's birthday, Oak Apple Day.

Distaste for heathen rites accompanied the Puritans to the New World. Thomas Morton scandalized the good people of Plymouth in 1627, when he erected an eighty-foot maypole at his plantation, Merry Mount. Rumor had it that he and his "cohorts" danced around it—with the natives, no less. John Endecott, later governor of Massachusetts, ordered the pole chopped down. He renamed Merry Mount "Mount Dagon," after the Philistine idol whose temple Samson suicidally destroyed. A fish-bodied Mesopotamian deity, Dagon was himself probably another agricultural god.

Perhaps the best-known work of art linked to May Day is Shakespeare's *A Midsummer Night's Dream.* The events don't actually take place on Midsummer Day, June 24, or even on its equally celebrated eve. Shakespeare used the term "midsummer night's dream" to refer to the general madness associated with such wild festivities. We know when the incidents take place because Theseus explicitly says of the four lovers, "No doubt they rose up early to observe / The rite of May . . ." Also, Hermia dismisses the skinny and made-up Helena as "a painted maypole."

The subsequent history of Charles's controversial maypole is interesting. Naturally, its base finally rotted, and it was cut in 1717. Isaac Newton, of all people, bought it. He took it to his place in Essex, where he used it to support his 124-foot telescope—another worldly function that probably upset the Puritans.

---

2 May 1945

One Perfect Rose

"If Jove wished to give the flowers a queen," the Greek poet Sappho wrote, "the rose ought to be crowned." The earliest known portrayal of the queen of flowers, on a fresco in the ruins of Minos's palace on what is now Crete, is at least 3,500 years old. That's ancient in human terms, but fossil roses go back 40 million years.

Roses have represented both divinity and sensuality, and a spectrum from the evanescence of life to the blood of Adonis, Jesus, and Mohammed. In Roman funerary gardens, they symbolized the returning spring, and thus resurrection. In time, their beauty and ephemeral life made roses into the very emblem of love and romance. Chaucer chose this symbol for his *Legend of Cleopatra:* "And she was fair as is the rose in May."

This popularity led gardeners to breed an ever wider variety of roses. However, because they understood little about genetics, their work was slow and haphazard. Roses were generally small-blossomed and short-lived. Then, in the early eighteenth century, Chinese breeders introduced tea roses, so called for their tealike scent. Gardeners bred these with a group of hybrids called, because they bloomed more than once per season, perpetuals. These mixes resulted in what are now the most popular roses, the famous hybrid teas.

By the twentieth century, Dorothy Parker could complain that it was always her fate to receive from admirers nothing but "one perfect rose." Florists deserve credit for the widespread availability of those perfect roses; they were breeding hybrid teas when gardeners were scorning them. Florists worried less about a rose's appearance in a flower bed, and more about its individual beauty and hardiness. Finally, one perfect rose brought florists and gardeners together—a cultivar (cultivated variety) called "Peace."

Like most of the 1,400 or so teas introduced during the preceding century, Peace was French. It was bred by Francis Meilland, who, with his father, Antoine, also created another florists' favorite, the rich red "Baccara." Myths surround Peace's birth. Legend claims that the Nazis reached France in 1942 just as Meilland, working in the family gardens near Lyons, discovered what his crossbreeding had created; that he sneaked bud wood to the American consul, who smuggled it out of the country; and that Meilland knew nothing of the plant's fate until after the war.

The reality is less cinematic. Meilland himself said he simply mailed bud wood to Germany, Italy, and the United States in the summer of 1939. Four years of careful trials had developed a hardy, vigorous plant with large yellow flowers edged in pink, whose blooms remained richly colored from the moment they opened until they died. Even its foliage was ornamental. Considered huge at the time, it spawned most of our current hardy, large-blossomed roses. Meilland named it "Mme. Antoine Meilland." In Germany it was called originally "Gloria Dei" and in Italy "Gioia." In the United States, the rose was introduced on the day Berlin fell to the Allies, 2 May 1945, and thus acquired its best-known name: "Peace."

See also Joséphine's roses, 6/25; and flowers, 7/30.

---

3 MAY 1849

"Gold They Say Is Very Abundant"

In early 1848, shortly before the wild territory of California was scheduled to become a state, a carpenter named James Wilson Marshall was building a sawmill near Sacramento. He noticed a telltale glint among the particles in the refuse water and bent down to examine it more closely. When he stood up he exclaimed the historic words, "Boys, I believe I have found a gold mine!" The men informed the owner of the mill, one Mr. Sutter, and the rush was on. A year later, a judge in California described the new way of life: "The farmers have thrown aside their plows, the lawyers their briefs, the doctors their pills, the priests their prayer books, and all are now digging gold." In 1852, Congress authorized the construction of a West Coast branch of the U.S. mint in San Francisco.

A young man from Missouri named Bennet Clark was among those gold-struck adventurers in 1849. He quit his job and, in company with twenty-three other men, headed west. On May 3, as Clark prepared to leave what is now Kansas City, Missouri, he wrote in his diary, "Finally we broke up camp and started on our long and toilsome journey." His vision of the trip would prove to be accurate. Both the people and the stock suffered from thirst. The mules became so hungry they ate the wagon covers. Death was everywhere. The train passed graves; companions died along the way; Clark saw beside one trail a human skull penciled with names of passersby. Stories of bandits in California were not encouraging. "We regret to hear these reports but if we knew them to be true & a return was practicable (which is not) we would still go on." And Clark stated the most important fact of his life at that moment: "Gold they say is very abundant." After all his troubles, Clark became ill in Nevada, and he was forced to sail home from San Francisco without ever seeing the gold fields. However, his diary exemplifies the lengths to which people are willing to go when gold has captured their imagination.

The promise of gold was the American dream. It was one of the primary lures that drew Europeans to the New World. From the moment the first invaders returned with their loot, Europe buzzed with the news of the gold that Cortés stole from the Aztecs and Pizarro from the Incas. In 1595, when Walter Raleigh returned to England from a trip to Venezuela, he told stories of a mountain of pure gold. He said that Venezuela's monarch was called *El Dorado,* "the Gilded One." In England in 1605, a character in the play *Eastward Hoe* did his part to enhance the vision of the promised land: "Why man, all their dripping pans and their chamber pots are pure gold, and all the prisoners they take are fettered in gold." One of the troubles that befell the English settlement at Jamestown, Virginia, was that many of the immigrants were untrained gentlemen adventurers. Their minds danced not with plans of wresting a home from the wilderness but with visions of picking up Montezuma's gold from the ground.

Bennet Clark was only one of countless adventurers dreaming of gold. It had drawn his ancestors to America. It was only natural that now, in 1849, it would draw their descendants westward.

---

4 MAY 1825

The Birth of Doubting Thomas

"The birth of Themistocles," Plutarch wrote of that Athenian statesman, "was somewhat too obscure to do him honor." Themistocles, however, demonstrated Plutarch's comment elsewhere, that "there is no beginning so mean, which continued application will not make considerable." One of the preeminent scientists of the nineteenth century, a man who rose above his humble beginnings to carry the banner of the new scientific thinking into the twentieth century, proved that old adage again. He was Thomas Huxley.

Doubting Thomas Huxley, scientist, freethinker, and, eventually, "Darwin's bulldog."

Although he had many other social and scientific interests, for his passionate defense of the ideas of his friend Charles Darwin, Huxley became known as "Darwin's bulldog." Because Huxley's name is so often linked with Darwin's, it is instructive to contrast their respective backgrounds. Darwin was born to the gentry, his father a successful physician, his grandfather a famous poet and scientist. His father sent him through Cambridge and even medical school, and upon his return from the *Beagle* voyage set him up with an income for life. Darwin was able to experiment, correspond, and revolutionize science from the comfort and solitude of his study.

Thomas Huxley, on the other hand, was born in a dingy room over a butcher's shop in the little village of Ealing, in Middlesex. It was May 4, 1825.

"Why I was christened Thomas Henry, I do not know," Huxley wrote; "but it is a curious chance that my parents should have fixed for my usual denomination upon the name of that particular Apostle with whom I have always felt most sympathy." A freethinker in both scientific and religious matters, he happily remained a doubting Thomas to the end of his days.

Huxley's father was a teacher. Young Thomas was educated at home until he was eight, when he began attending the school where his father taught. His formal education ended when his father lost his job and removed the family to his hometown, Coventry. Although he had had little formal education, Huxley later won a scholarship to medical school and began his scientific career as assistant surgeon aboard HMS *Rattlesnake*.

Over the years, Huxley demonstrated expertise in a variety of disciplines. He wrote lucidly and entertainingly about the wonders of science, and championed science education for the masses. He became president of the Royal Society and a lecturer and professor at numerous institutions. If the circumstances of Huxley's birth were too obscure to do him honor, his rise above them was just the opposite. He did not forget those he outgrew. He became a champion of numerous social causes, especially the commitment to providing education for the common people. In time he went on to be an influential member of the first school board in London.

But above all, Huxley was a scientist, one of the most influential of his era. Although initially doubting the validity of Darwin's ideas on natural selection, Huxley was won over by the sheer undeniability of the evidence. As a consequence he championed the *Origin of Species* from the moment of its publication in 1859. In 1870, the newly minted Johns Hopkins University in Baltimore, Maryland, invited him to the United States to christen the world's first institution to emphasize the teaching of the sciences. A single sentence from one of his essays exemplifies both his philosophy and his way with an analogy: "Science is nothing but trained and organized common sense, differing from the latter only as a veteran may differ from a raw recruit: and its methods differ from those of common sense only as far as the guardsman's cut and thrust differ from the manner in which a savage wields a club."

See also Pope Huxley, 11/4.

The Breadfruit Voyages

By order of George III, a member of England's House of Lords wrote to the Lords commissioners of the Admiralty on the fifth day of May, 1787. "The Merchants and Planters interested in His Majesty's West India possessions have represented that the Introduction of the Bread Fruit Tree into the Islands in those Seas to constitute an Article of Food would be very essential Benefit to the Inhabitants. . . ." The Admiralty was instructed to outfit a ship and send it to the Society Islands, "where according to the accounts which are given by the late Captain Cook . . . the Bread Fruit Tree is to be found in its most luxuriant state."

Naturally, the inhabitants the Crown wished to benefit were not the natives of the West Indies, but rather the European merchants and planters. The Society Islands were what we now call Micronesia, especially Otaheite (Tahiti). The motivating force behind the expedition was botanist Joseph Banks. Now president of the Royal Society, Banks had accompanied Captain James Cook on the first of his voyages around the world. In Tahiti they found the breadfruit tree. There are two kinds of breadfruit, both members of the Moraceae family, but it is the Micronesian rather than the African that had a major historical impact.

A warty football-size fruit, breadfruit was as valuable to the islanders as the olive tree was to the people of the Mediterranean region. Too starchy and pulpy to be eaten raw, it was boiled in coconut milk, dried and ground into flour and baked, and even pickled by burial in the sand. The trunk of the tree could be made into planks or hollowed out as canoes. West Indian planters thought breadfruit might adapt well to the Caribbean and develop into a good food for their slaves, and they had long lobbied Banks to pursue the matter.

The Admiralty assigned the task of transporting breadfruit to the *Bethia,* which at eighty-seven feet long and twenty-four feet wide was the smallest ship in the navy. Overhauled and rechristened, it sailed into history under its new name—the *Bounty.* Under its captain, Lieutenant William Bligh, and Mate Fletcher Christian were a skeleton crew of officers and more sailors than there was room for. Those conditions helped provoke the most famous mutiny in history.

The *Bounty* entered Matavai Bay, Otaheite, in late October of 1788, eleven years after Cook's last visit—and Bligh's, since he was master on Cook's ship, the *Resolution.* Bligh issued strict orders to keep mum about their mission. The *Bounty* didn't load breadfruit until it proved to grow well in small pots; then the hold was stuffed with it. After twenty-three weeks on Otaheite, the *Bounty* sailed for the West Indies. Three weeks later, Bligh awoke one morning with a pistol at his head. He and eighteen men who chose him over the mutineers were put in an open launch and abandoned to the whims of Neptune. Incredibly, they survived. Bligh returned to Tahiti in 1791 and completed his original assignment of transplanting breadfruit from Tahiti to the West Indies.

---

6 MAY 1949

Rejoicing in the Bee

"What sort of insects do you rejoice in, where *you* come from?" the Gnat asks Alice in *Through the Looking-Glass.* When Alice admits that she doesn't really rejoice in any insect, she is speaking for the majority of human beings. However, there is one insect that, while certainly having its unpopular aspects, has nonetheless inspired occasional rejoicing. History has been accompanied by the sound that Tennyson described as the "murmuring of innumerable bees."

That same history does not record who first risked the stings of outraged bees for a taste of honey. A 6,000-year-old rock painting from Spain portrays a man scooping honey from a bees' nest in a tree-top while the disgruntled insects fly about. Roughly 2,500 years ago, during the Fifth Dynasty in Egypt, someone carved on a stone in the temple at Abu Ghorab a scene demonstrating the progress in honey gathering that had transpired in the intervening centuries. A number of men work around a group of hives, gathering honeycombs, dropping pieces into a pot, and straining honey into a jar. Their hives, incidentally, were hollow cones of dried mud.

The attitude of the Spartans, that honey was not a food for free men, is atypical. In most cultures sweet, golden honey has been highly prized. At one time, Romans expressed the uncomfortable-sounding wish, "May honey drip on you." By some perverse quirk of the imagination, the Egyptians decided that not all of this delicacy should go to the people, who would merely eat it. Much was set aside for the gods. A twelfth-century-B.C. document from the reign of Ramses III lists 31,092 jars of honey offered to the gods—an amount estimated at 15 tons, or a year's production from 5,000 hives. What actually happened to it, considering the unlikelihood of Anubis and Bast smearing it on divine croissants, is not recorded.

Of course, bees have other interesting attributes besides their ability to produce honey. They are, for one thing, famously busy. It naturally occurred to Samuel Johnson to describe Tom Birch's conversation as "brisk as a bee." Because they are seldom seen lounging about the yard, bees are universally lauded by proponents of the work ethic. The seventeenth-century English hymnist (and platitudist) Isaac Watts, in his poem "Against Idleness and Mischief," was lost in admiration:

> *How doth the little busy bee*
> *Improve each shining hour,*
> *And gather honey all the day*
> *From every opening flower!*

How exactly are bees accomplishing all this commendable labor? In the early years of the twentieth century, Austrian biologist Karl von Frisch set out to answer that question. First he proved, contrary to the opinion of a rival scientist, that not only did bees perceive color, they even preferred light in the ultraviolet range. They were making use of all sorts of visual cues invisible to us. Frisch learned that bees distinguish tastes through organs in the tips of their legs. And then he learned his most famous revelation. A paint-marked bee drank from one of Frisch's sugar-water dispensers, then returned to the hive and performed an aerial dance. Apparently excited, another bee accompanied the first to the sugar water. In time Frisch analyzed a variety of such "dances," slowly decoding the ancient language of the bees.

Another man who studied bees for knowledge rather than honey was the Belgian playwright and poet, Maurice Maeterlinck. When he died on May 6, 1949, Maeterlinck left behind a considerable literary legacy, including a Nobel Prize and *Pelleas and Melisande,* upon which Debussy based his opera. But to naturalists his greatest creation was a little book he published in 1901 entitled *The Life of the Bee.* It is as much poetry as science, and the combination promoted it from apiculture tract to literature. At one point Maeterlinck wrote of the insect in which he rejoiced, "To him who has known them and loved them, a summer where there are no bees becomes as sad and empty as one without flowers or birds."

The Orange Wench

Upon the Restoration of Charles II to the throne of England in 1660, after the repressive Puritan interlude, actors found themselves again welcome in London. Old, boarded-up theaters reopened, and new ones appeared. The King's Company soon found their quarters too small and built a spacious new playhouse in Covent Garden. Thomas Killigrew opened the King's Theatre on May 7, 1663, with Beaumont and Fletcher's comedy, *The Humorous Lieutenant.*

Earlier that year, for a fee of six shillings and eight pence daily, the King's Company granted to a widow named Mary Meggs permission to sell in their new theater "oranges, lemons, fruits, sweetmeats, and all manner of fruiterers and confectioners wares." Meggs immediately hired three smart, attractive girls to hawk those wares. Six days a week, baskets in hand, their job was to stroll among the rowdy theater-goers and entice them to spend the extravagant prices of theater snacks—sixpence, for example, for the popular new "China" oranges. The name was accurate. After the original cultivation of citrus fruits in northern Burma and Assam, whence they spread to India, China, and Malaysia, various kinds of oranges are thought to have emerged from China.

A girl named Eleanor Gwynn joined Meggs's staff either when the theater opened or soon afterward. She was thirteen years old. In a few years Nell Gwynn established herself as a comedienne in Drury Lane and eventually wound up as the mistress of the king. (However, having already had two lovers named Charles, she called the king not Charles the Second but her Charles the Third.) Those critics who denounced "pretty, witty Nellie" as a lowborn whore frequently began their recitation of her ignoble career with her youth spent selling oranges in the theater. "Anybody might know she had been an orange wench," a rival murmured, "by her swearing."

It was a new profession. Oranges came to England relatively late, near the end of the sixteenth century, long after they were established elsewhere in the world. Roman paintings and mosaics portray oranges, along with limes and other fruits. Apparently the Romans cultivated groves of citrus more for the aroma they exude, and for the supposed fumigant properties of their wood when burned, than for their fruits. Orange and other citrus trees smell like lemons because their leaves all contain the same compound, limonene.

The several categories of citrus fruits include mandarins, lemons, oranges, limes, grapefruit, kumquats, citrons, and pomelos. Botanists describe anywhere from 8 to 145 species, depending upon the criteria employed. The lines are difficult to draw because most members of the citrus clan hybridize with incestuous abandon. For example, the tangelo is a hybrid of the grapefruit and mandarin, or the pomelo and mandarin; the Meyer's parents are an orange and a lemon. Many citrus fruits contain more than one embryo, resulting in numerous seedlings whose eventual fruit may vary unpredictably.

Nowadays, in the United States, most of the oranges used in juice are grown in Florida. California provides the majority of the fresh whole oranges. Its climate not only encourages both more acid and sugar, but even produces a thicker rind that is more resistant to damage during shipping. After only bananas and grapes, citrus are now the third-largest fruit crop in the world—just as popular in England, for example, as in their native Asia. Orange Nell helped launch a revolution.

---

8 May 1784

"The Flail of the Lashing Hail"

Hail is one of the least-common forms of precipitation, but it can also be one of the most dangerous. On May 8, 1784, a hailstorm battered a two-mile-wide area along the Wateree River in South Carolina. Many of the hailstones were as large as baseballs. Countless livestock died, and there were numerous human casualties, including, according to the *South Carolina Gazette,* "several negroes" working in the fields. In April of 1890, a hailstorm bombarded Baltimore with stones anywhere from two inches in diameter to "as large as a man's fist," according to the city's weather bureau. "There was a sound like the roll of musketry, and the storm burst suddenly upon the city with an almost deafening roar as the hail stones rained down upon the tin roofs and crashed into windows."

Farmers have long been aware of the damage that hail can cause. Entire crops can be utterly destroyed in minutes. As early as 1880, the Tobacco Growers' Mutual Insurance Company in Connecticut issued hail insurance on growing tobacco crops. In 1910, the North Dakota legislature approved hail insurance. There were over a thousand policies issued the first year, and the paid losses greatly surpassed the accumulated premiums. Naturally, losses to buildings and equipment have always been high. Many people who will never encounter a tornado or hurricane have had to file insurance claims when hail vandalized an automobile or shattered household windows.

Hail researchers—a narrow specialty if there ever was one—do not lead normal lives. When a storm is handy, they rush into it and gather hailstones for study. Once upon a time, that consisted primarily of collecting the fallen stones by hand, as if harvesting windfall apples. Hail usually falls in warm weather, and in order to gather their subjects before they melt the scientists must be in the storm. Frequently that results in pummelings.

Witches conjuring up hail, from De lanijs et phitonicis mulieribus, *by Ulrich Molitor, 1489.*

However, some simple but helpful aids have been invented, such as one weather researcher's van with a funnel in the roof to gather hailstones for −70°F storage. This sort of research requires that laboratories be kept cold enough to preserve the hailstones so that they can be examined under a microscope. Only that way can they be sliced and their layers analyzed to determine just how they are formed.

Such research has revealed that often hail has the same genesis as sleet. It begins as raindrops that freeze solid on their way from cloud to ground, sometimes melting and then getting caught in an updraft and blowing back up and freezing again. Some hailstones, however, have few layers because they remained suspended between updraft and gravity while they grew. On occasion hailstones form around ice crystals rather than around raindrops. Just as amazing as the force of the hail is the strength of the updrafts required to lift, sometimes again and again, chunks of ice the size of cherries or golf balls or even oranges.

Percy Bysshe Shelley's 1819 poem "The Cloud" nicely expresses the power and transience of this strange form of precipitation:

> *I wield the flail of the lashing hail,*
> *And whiten the green plains under,*
> *And then again I dissolve it in rain,*
> *And laugh as I pass in thunder.*

---

9 May 1711

A Voyage to the Houyhnhnms

Lemuel Gulliver's wanderlust was not satisfied by his enlightening sojourns in Lilliput, Brobdingnag, and Laputa. After only five months home, he left his "poor Wife big with Child" and sailed on the aptly named *Adventure.* Soon he found himself in perhaps the strangest land of all. In Lilliput, Gulliver had been a giant; in Brobdingnag, as tiny as one of the Borrowers. On the fourth voyage, he was an animal in a land of intelligent horses.

Jonathan Swift began *Travels into several Remote Nations of the World* (1726), which we now call *Gulliver's Travels,* as a satire on the travel writers who routinely duped the credulous eighteenth-century public. But, as usual, he satirized humanity in general. Gulliver's deadpan assertion that his "principle Design was to inform, and not to amuse" echoes Swift's own motto: "to vex the world rather than divert it." Over the years, Part Four has frequently been the least popular. Its savage ironies hit close to home.

After a mutiny, Gulliver is marooned on an island on May 9, 1711. He finds himself in a land of rational horses named Houyhnhnms (pronounced, one would never guess, WHIN-ums). "The Word *Houyhnhnm,* in their Tongue, signifies a *Horse;* and in its Etymology, *the Perfection of Nature."* That etymology lampoons most cultures' tendency to see themselves as the center of creation. On this island, humans are not the beauty of the world, nor even the paragon of animals. But they *are* animals.

Swift has great fun inverting the human-horse relationship. The Houyhnhnm leader asks if there are creatures like him in Gulliver's country. The Englishman replies that "in Summer they grazed in the Fields, and in Winter were kept in Houses . . . where Yahoo Servants were employed to rub their Skins smooth, comb their Manes, pick their Feet, serve them with Food, and make their Beds." Aha, the Houyhnhnm responds; obviously the horses are the masters and the Yahoos merely attendants.

These Yahoos are suspiciously reminiscent of Gulliver's own species back home. Only his clothes and hat disguise him—until the Houyhnhnms find him sleeping without them, and his resemblance to Yahoos is unmistakable. Thanks to Swift, "Yahoo" now means a lout or bumpkin. He may have taken the word from similarly named peoples in Africa or the Caribbean, or it may simply be an extension of the derisive interjection "Yah!"

But what inspired the creation of these degenerate characters? They seem almost prehuman.

Mr. Gulliver meets and greets the ruler of the Houyhnhnms, from a French edition published in 1797.

Certainly Swift wasn't thinking in evolutionary terms; no human fossils would be recognized as such for over a century. Of course, Swift found humanity's own lowly nature disgusting. But also he must have known the tales of improbable humanlike creatures European travelers encountered late in the previous century, animals that turned out to be the gorilla and orangutan. From the first, the discovery of the anthropoid apes disturbed Europeans. That very adjective comes from *anthropo,* "human," and *eidos,* "resembling." The resemblance was too close for comfort, and Jonathan Swift may have exploited it in *Gulliver's Travels.*

---

10 MAY 1907

The Wind in the Willows

A friend of Kenneth Grahame's remembered him standing on a footbridge and calling to an animal on the bank below with a whistle as "sweet and imperative as any pipe of Pan." Grahame explained: "There's a water rat down there . . . ; he's quite a friend of mine. Evidently he's gone on some excursion. I shall hear about it one day." Elsewhere he wrote to someone about what the rabbits were doing that day, adding, "I have it from one of themselves." An innocent affectation, this pretense of communicating with his wild neighbors, but it hints at Grahame's way of looking at nature. As readers of his 1908 novel, *The Wind in the Willows,* might guess, he found animals more congenial than his fellow humans.

In the spring of 1907, Grahame and his wife were on holiday during the fifth birthday of their son Alastair. However, that didn't stop the doting father from continuing his practice of telling his son animal stories. On the tenth of May, he wrote the first of the letters that grew into one of the world's best-loved children's books. Grahame first described the gifts they had sent. Then, without preamble, he launched into Toad's adventures. Apparently he had already been telling Alastair the stories. "Have you heard about the Toad? He was never taken prisoner by brigands at all. It was all a horrid low trick of his. . . ." Toad finds a party that has just motored down from London and simply steals one of their cars. The letter ends, "I fear he is a bad low animal."

Grahame wrote installments in the adventures on the stationery of a succession of vacation hotels. Fortunately, Alastair's nanny kept the letters. Grahame hadn't published a book since 1898, and publishers were eager to see anything he wrote. However, after he was persuaded to add to the letters to form a novel, editors firmly rejected the result. Mole and Ratty and Toad were slow to find a home.

When they did, the reviewers were no more thrilled than editors had been. *The Wind in the Willows* differed too much from the nostalgic sketches of childhood in Grahame's previous books. Some reviewers faulted the book for failing at what it didn't even attempt. *The Times Literary Supplement* complained that "as a contribution to natural history the work is negligible." The literal-minded reviewer couldn't understand why a mole would be whitewashing his burrow, and thought that of all animals a water rat would be the least likely to row about in a boat. Another critic deplored errors "which (I am sorry to say) will win no credence from the very best authorities on biology." Even those who liked the book refused to accept it as a simple tale. Arnold Bennett called it "an urbane exercise in irony at the expense of the English character and of mankind."

Of course, while the book does star animals, and there is a genuine understanding of their natural history interwoven with their outrageous adventures, Grahame wasn't trying to write like a naturalist. He had his own aims. He was writing about friendship and innocence and an ideal world to which he admitted he longed to escape. Mostly he ignored reviewers, but he remarked to a friend, "A large amount of what Thoreau called life went into the making of many of those playful pages."

---

11 May 1935

4M Sings His Way into History

Margaret Morse was born in 1883 in Amherst, Massachusetts, and was taking notes on birds by the age of nine. In college, on her Wednesdays off from Mount Holyoke, she explored the countryside with a female friend, on foot and by canoe. When her parents worried, she carried a revolver—which, of course, made them worry more. Her master's thesis on bobwhite feeding behavior revealed that a single bird could eat 75,000 insects and 5 million weed seeds in a season, but that pleased her parents less than her marriage to a promising pharmaceutical student named Blaine Nice. For years Margaret Nice devoted herself to her children, even published at least one paper annually on their language development. Then, at the age of thirty-six, she realized she missed the study of nature.

Later, living near Columbus, Ohio, she began studying song sparrows, whose scientific name, *Melospiza melodia,* means the "melodious song finch." She worked mainly in what she called the "wild neglected piece of flood plain" outside her back door, observing in minute detail the daily lives of several generations. One way Nice tried to remain objective with her subjects was to give them scientifically remote names. Occasionally whimsy crept in, as when she named two mating nest mates after Wagner's incestuous siblings, Siegmund and Sieglinde. However, the fourth male she studied she coolly called 4M, and he became her favorite.

For years 4M returned to his third-of-an-acre territory in Nice's backyard. Then, on Saturday, May 11, 1935, he entered ornithological history. Beginning at 4:44 A.M., with hardly a pause, he sang for almost exactly fifteen hours, until seven minutes after sunset—2,305 times. Notebook in hand, Nice was there for all of them; her children brought her breakfast and lunch outdoors.

Although the local bird club excluded women, Nice was attracting attention elsewhere. Because of her family life and because much of her fieldwork took place so near her home, Nice was often dismissed as a mere housewife, an amateur bird-watcher. In reality, besides her advanced degrees, she published 250-odd articles and over 3,000 reviews. She became a fellow of the American Ornithological Union and editor of *Bird-Banding.* Fluent in French and German, she reviewed foreign publications. French ornithologist Jean Delacour said Nice's work on song sparrows was "perhaps the most important contribution yet published to our knowledge of the life of a species." And the great Nobel Prize–winning animal behaviorist Konrad Lorenz called Nice the founder of ethology (animal behavior studies).

A German scientist wrote to Nice about her beloved 4M: "May he reach a Biblical age!" He did. Nice last heard him sing on Thanksgiving Day, 1935. He had had eleven mates and had outlived seven of them. On the date of his farewell performance, he was at least eight-and-a-half years old. For a song sparrow, it was a venerable, even a biblical, age.

---

12 MAY 1819

"Such Sweet Lowd Musick"

In his dictionary of 1755, Samuel Johnson defined the nightingale as "A small bird that sings in the night with remarkable melody; Philomel." The Anglo-Saxon *nightingale* means literally "singer of the night." That nocturnal urge is considered the bird's defining characteristic. Portia, in *The Merchant of Venice,* says that if the nightingale sang during the day it would be considered no more musi-

The nightingale, alias Philomel.

cal than the wren. Actually, nightingales *do* sing in the daytime, but their evening concerts made their reputation.

The bird's other name, Philomel, is older. In Greek mythology, King Tereus rapes his wife's sister, Philomela. When she vows that her voice will fill the woods and move the rocks to pity, Tereus cuts out her tongue. Naturally the sisters unite to wreak bloody revenge. As they flee, some unnamed god who ought to have interfered earlier changes them into birds. In the original version, Philomela became a swallow and her sister Procne a nightingale, but in time those roles reversed. The nightingale, famed for its sorrowful midnight lament, acquired the nickname Philomel. Pliny the Elder later claimed that swallows avoided the city of Bizyes, "because of the crimes of Tereus." Of course, he also said that nightingales modulate their voices to sing soprano, mezzo, or baritone.

In a poem to his wife, Samuel Taylor Coleridge addressed the nightingale as Philomel, calling the bird "the Minstrel of the Moon." Years later, on May 12, 1819, he wrote to a friend about an unpleasant occasion on which he had listened to the birds without enjoying their music. Indigestion kept him up, and he was "qualmy and twitchy" from the effects of a cathartic called calomel. He quoted a joke he made to himself that night about the noisy nightingales: "Ah! PHIlomel! ill do thy strains accord with those of CALomel!"

Coleridge's contemporary John Keats wrote about nightingales in several poems. The spring of 1819 was a productive time for the young poet. Within the space of a couple of weeks he wrote his odes on indolence, melancholy, and—probably the best-known work of art concerning these birds—the nightingale. Keats was staying with his friend Charles Brown, and a nightingale was nesting near the house. "Keats felt a tranquil and continual joy in her song," Brown wrote later, "and one morning he took his chair from the breakfast-table to the grass-plot under a plum-tree, where he sat for two or three hours." When Keats came indoors, he had a few sheets of paper that expressed "his poetic feeling on the song of our nightingale."

There are several tuneful birds called nightingales—a Chinese nightingale, neotropical nightingale thrushes, a West Indian mockingbird. Usually, however, the name refers to a particular family of Old World thrushes, especially the Eurasian nightingale, *Erithacus megarhynchos*. Its melodious cousins include the American robin and hermit thrush. Still, although Tex Beneke's tenor sax was a good substitute, it is unlikely that a nightingale ever sang in Berkeley Square. Americans don't get to hear what Izaak Walton praised in his *Compleat Angler*: "The Nightingale . . . breathes such sweet lowd musick out of her little instrumental throat, that it might make mankind to think Miracles are not ceased."

See also Keats's laurel, 6/10; and Coleridge's albatross, 11/13.

The Trumpet of the Swan

E. B. White's third children's book is the story of the friendship between two creatures—a trumpeter swan named Louis, who is born without a voice, and a boy named Sam Beaver. Sam helps Louis learn to read and write, and ever afterward the swan carries a slate and chalk on a cord around his neck. After Louis's father breaks into a music store to steal a trumpet for his musically challenged son, Louis goes to work to pay for the damages. *The Trumpet of the Swan* is less moving than *Stuart Little* and *Charlotte's Web*, but it is more adventurous. Louis works as a trumpeter in a Canadian boys' camp, on swan boats in Boston's Public Garden, and in Philadelphia in both a nightclub and the zoo.

In an essay entitled "A Boy I Knew," White wrote nostalgically of himself in the third person: "This boy felt for animals a kinship he never felt for people. . . . He kept pigeons, dogs, snakes, polliwogs, turtles, rabbits, lizards, singing birds, chameleons, caterpillars and mice." White won three prizes from magazines before he was fourteen, and the single poem and two brief prose pieces all concern animals. In *The Trumpet of the Swan,* some of Sam's diary entries, in which he wonders why a fox barks or how a bird automatically understands nest building, come from White's own journal, which he began at the age of eight. As an adult, his letters teemed with animal stories—a man who almost sat on a porcupine in a dark outhouse, a neighbor whose ministrations to an injured catbird including massaging its feet, White's own punning contest with his wife about how an alligator might deal with a swallowed beer bottle. Friends, of course, understood this love of all things wild. One of them annually celebrated spring by sending White praying mantis egg cases.

In the early stages of the book, White wrote to a friend, "How would you like to do some sleuthing for an aging fiction writer?" Then he requested detailed information on the Philadelphia Zoo, home of the first trumpeter swan cygnets hatched in captivity. The correspondent provided details, including photos of the swans, but was unimpressed with the calls of the trumpeters. White reminded him that no less an authority than Audubon had praised the talent that earned the trumpeter swan its name. After publication, a friend congratulated White. He replied: "I'm glad you like my kooky little swan story. It took a lot of gall to write it, as I have never in my life laid eyes on a Trumpeter Swan, either in or out of captivity."

The story of Louis and Sam reached the first slot on the *New York Times* list of best-selling children's books in 1971, just ahead of a book White had published nineteen years before, *Charlotte's Web*. That year, asked to coauthor a concert for children to be performed by the Philadelphia Orchestra, White distilled his new book for Benjamin Lees's score. The first performance was on May 13, 1972.

See also **Charlotte's Web,** *5/24.*

The Ship of the Desert

Some slanderous wit once observed that the camel looks like a horse that was designed by a committee. Ambrose Bierce accented the camel's grotesqueness when he defined it as "a quadruped . . . of great value to the show business." Actually, the camel owes its popularity in arid regions to those innovative but goofy-looking adaptations. Little moisture is lost through perspiration; the temperature must be around 125°F before the camel even sweats. Long legs lift it above the hottest layer of air, and huge feet work like snowshoes to keep it from sinking into sand. Camels can drink twenty-five gallons of water in ten minutes. Rather than stored in the hump, as folklore claims, the water is distributed throughout the body tissues and held in the red blood corpuscles, which can expand to 240 times their normal size. The hump holds the camel's fat supply, and when it doesn't receive food it begins to consume its stored resources. At the end of a long journey, camels look emaciated, and their humps are slack.

Camels evolved in North America, along with horses, at about the same time that elephants' ancestors evolved in Africa. Approximately 2.5 million years ago, all three crossed what is now the Bering Strait, via the land bridge that joined Asia and North America at the time. Early protoelephants such as mammoths came to America, and horses and camels went to Asia and on down to Africa. Some American protocamels went south and evolved into the wild guanaco and vicuña, from which humans developed the domesticated llama and alpaca.

The camel died out in North America, but on the other side of the world it thrived. In India and Mongolia it developed into the two-humped Bactrian camel, and in North Africa and the Middle East it became the dromedary. After humans came on the scene and domesticated camels, caravans of up to 12,000 of the beasts transported kola nuts, dates, ivory, gold, and that "prince of commodities," salt, to trading posts. Without camels, the Sahara would have been an insurmountable barrier between nations. Both African and Asian history would be dramatically different.

Then, in the mid-nineteenth century, the same adaptations that make the camel the "ship of the desert" in the East inspired some Americans to bring it back to their continent. The U.S. Army was experiencing considerable difficulty providing supplies to its more isolated outposts, such as San Antonio. Someone came up with the idea of importing camels for use in the deserts of the Southwest. The first shipment of thirty-four arrived on May 14, 1856, and forty-one more came a year later.

For several reasons, camels didn't adjust well to North America. They had been away from their ancient homeland for millions of years and had evolved highly specialized adaptations to the desert conditions of Africa and Asia. American deserts were rocky and jagged, not the cushiony sandy expanses to which camels had adapted. (They got along fine in the flat wastes of Australia.) Also, seasoned mule-drivers found their new charges both uncooperative and embarrassing. When Rebel soldiers captured Yankee camels during the Civil War, they freed them in the desert. Other camels were imported. One could be seen hauling wood in Virginia City, Nevada, in the 1870s, and another

After camels were imported into the United States in the nineteenth century, they were employed in a wide variety of jobs, including mowing the grass in New York's fledgling Central Park.

stomped a woman to death in Arizona in 1883. Here and there, curious documentary evidence survives. For example, Brownsville, Texas, once had an ordinance prohibiting camels on the street.

---

15 MAY 1943

The Bats of War

"The project seems silly," Louis Fieser confided to his diary. And then he added the fateful word: "But . . ."

Fieser was responding to a proposed new weapon. Los Angeles dentist Lytle Adams had a plan to help the United States win World War II. He wanted the government to send thousands of incendiary bombs to ignite small fires in Germany and Japan. His brainstorm was the method by which the bombs would be transported to their targets: bats. Yes, according to the Adams plan, obliging little bats would carry bombs with them when they sought roosts under eaves and in attics. Homes and factories alike would be reduced to ash. The war would be over in no time.

How would the military get the bats to their destinations? Simple—refrigeration. They would keep the bats on ice, in artificially induced hibernation, until the planes were over Tokyo. Dumped out asleep and wearing tiny parachutes, the bats would awaken during their fall, roost as usual under eaves, and then chew through the cords that secured their burdens. Automatic timers would do the rest. Those bats that did not shed the bombs in time would simply give their lives for their country.

Adams had been returning from Carlsbad Caverns when he learned of Pearl Harbor. He thought of the millions of bats he had just seen emerging from the caves every evening, and he had his patriotic vision. He took it to Washington, D.C., where the idea climbed all the way up to Franklin Roosevelt, who was intrigued by it. The project took off. Zoologists brought in to conscript bats included Harvard's prominent mammalogist, Donald Griffin. He was one of the first scientists to demonstrate bats' use of sonar, which was far more useful in winning the war than using bats as bombers. For the bomb itself they got chemist Louis Fieser, who soon forgot the doubts expressed to his diary. Inevitably, the work was stamped TOP SECRET.

Unfortunately, the bats did not respond cordially to refrigeration. Workers tested the poor animals' carrying capacity, speculated on the best altitude from which to parachute them, and tried to determine at what height they might emerge from hibernation. The first group didn't emerge at all. They fell to the ground—dead. When the first tests with conscious bats and live bombs were held on May 15, 1943, the brass turned out to witness the demonstration. Planes dropped bats over the site. During the proceedings someone noticed that an administration building was on fire. The next casualty was a general's car. Then an observation tower burned.

For some reason, Fieser now considered the project "very promising." New tests were arranged. Mock-ups of German and Japanese houses were burned. More bats were killed. Realizing bats could be released from ships, the Navy expressed interest. But, after $2 million had been spent on two-and-a-half years of work, what had become Project X-Ray was finally tabled as unfeasible.

---

16 May 1913

Mr. Pennock and
Mr. Williams

Among his several jobs, Charles Pennock was Delaware's state ornithologist, and curator of oology (the study of eggs, especially bird eggs) for the Philadelphia Academy of Sciences, to which he donated his own formidable collection. He was famous for his exhaustive Christmas bird census, and for his convincing imitations that lured birds near, especially his ability to converse with owls. A member of the American Ornithologists Union, and popular as an authoritative and congenial field companion, he kept track of many aspects of bird life and wrote well-received articles about them.

But Pennock was a restless man, working in various fields, changing jobs frequently. Once he went off for several days without telling his wife and children; later his absence was attributed to amnesia from "inflammatory rheumatism."

In the spring of 1913, Pennock attended a meeting of the Delaware Valley Ornithological Club as usual. But the next day, May 16, Mrs. Pennock began calling friends because her husband hadn't come home after the meeting. A fellow club member recalled that, as they left the meeting, Pennock had remarked that he didn't feel well. The police's missing-persons bulletin yielded no result. Soon bird societies were listing Pennock as a "Deceased Member (Disappeared)."

It was six years before Pennock's family and colleagues learned what happened to him. That night in May 1913 he felt overworked and depressed. After the meeting, he caught the train as usual, but instead of going home to the Philadelphia suburbs, he went to Florida. With $100 in his pocket, he drifted down to a little town south of Tallahassee called St. Marks. There bearded family man Charles Pennock metamorphosed into clean-shaven bachelor John Williams.

And there, while supporting himself as bookkeeper, part-time lighthouse attendant, and notary public, Pennock began sending in reports on local birds. He could abandon family and friends, but not his beloved birds. Near the gulf and the confluence of the Wakulla and St. Marks Rivers, surrounded by mudflats and marshes, the area was popular with birds migrating across the gulf. It was ideal for ornithology.

Pennock's devotion to his passion finally betrayed his new identity. A formerly unknown professional-quality birder, suddenly sending in reports from the backwater of St. Marks, attracted some attention, but there was no reason to link him with the disappearance of Charles Pennock. Then, in those days before typewriters became common, a former colleague recognized Pennock's handwriting on an article signed "John Williams." He mentioned this to Pennock's brother-in-law, who journeyed down to St. Marks.

Pennock seemed almost glad to see someone who recognized him. Soon he was back in his old life, with his family in Philadelphia, and with his colleagues at the bird club meetings. Later he even showed the astonishingly forgiving Mrs. Pennock where John Williams had lived. Ornithological journals wrestled with their indexes, dropping John Williams, and restoring to the ranks the formerly deceased Charles Pennock.

---

17 MAY 1988

"Fortune-Telling by the Stars"

"It is the stars," the Earl of Kent declares in *King Lear*. "The stars above us, govern our conditions." Apparently Ronald and Nancy Reagan agreed. In the spring of 1988, former White House chief of staff Donald Regan published *For the Record,* his memoir of working with the Reagans. In it he revealed that the First Lady consulted California astrologer Joan Quigley before approving the president's schedule. Like most astrologers, Quigley wisely avoided prediction and relied instead upon fortune-cookie advice such as "March 19–25 no public exposure" and "Feb 20–26 be careful." At first, to the public outcry over this revelation, Reagan merely said, "I'll be damned if I'll just stand by and let them railroad my wife." Finally, he started issuing denials, and on May 17 the *New York Times* ran the memorable headline "Not a Slave to the Zodiac, Reagan Says."

If he was a slave to the stars, Reagan wasn't alone, as indicated by the astrology column in virtually every newspaper and many magazines. Even our casual speech reveals long-held convictions about the heavens. *Disaster* comes from the Greek for "bad star." *Influenza* refers to the influence of the stars, and *consider* means "with the planets." Apparently human beings have always been preoccupied with, as the subtitle of a seventeenth-century book on comets expressed it, "this grand Question, Whether any certain Judgements and Predictions concerning future Events, can be made from the Observation of the Heavenly Bodies."

Astrology's basic premise is that the positions of the planets and stars at one's birth profoundly influence character and personality. This power is determined, among lesser factors, by the position of the sun in the zodiac, an imaginary section of the sky that extends for eight degrees on either side of the apparent path of the sun against the background of the stars. The word "zodiac" is from the Greek for "band of animals." Astrology began with some ancient insomniac's notion of what a group of stars resembled—a goat, perhaps, or a scorpion. Seven constellations represent animals (ram, bull, crab, lion, scorpion, goat, and fish), three people (twins, a virgin, a water bearer), and one a hybrid (usually the archer Sagittarius is portrayed as a centaur). The only inanimate sign is Libra, "the Scales." The supposed influence of these constellations manifests itself differently for each sign of the zodiac, based upon the mythological origins of the constellation, such as the lionlike strength and courage attributed to those born under the sign of Leo.

In reality, the twelve zodiacal constellations occupy unequal portions of the sky. Aries, for example, is far smaller than Virgo. But astrologers have done away with the constellations entirely and replaced them with "signs," which are equally proportioned. The sun doesn't spend an equal amount of time in each constellation; sometimes it sweeps across one and barely grazes the next. Much of the time the sun is in the *sign* Scorpio, it is actually crossing the unzodiacal *constellation* Ophiuchus. There are other irregularities that, if astrology had any validity, ought to dramatically affect one's fate.

Of course, the stars in, say, the constellation Taurus are only grouped in a bull-like composition from our vantage point in our corner of the galaxy. Seen from anywhere else in the universe, the arrangement would be completely different, and would lose that crucial connect-the-dots resemblance to terrestrial creatures. From some far-distant planet, other creatures may view our star as the tail of the constellation Spreading Fungus, but it is unlikely they base their important decisions on fables about us.

Not everyone has fallen for astrology's claims. Thomas More's Utopians, for example, were skeptical: "But as for astrology—friendships and quarrels between the planets, fortune-telling by the stars, and all the rest of that humbug—they've never even dreamt of such a thing." Perhaps in some future Utopia more people will concur with Shakespeare's Cassius, who would have disagreed with Ronald Reagan's astrological leanings:

> The fault, dear Brutus, is not in our stars,
> But in ourselves. . . .

See also North Star, 3/15; Persian astrology, 5/18; and star symbolism, 10/9.

---

18 May 1048

Omar Khayyám's Birthday

The precise date of countless historical events simply cannot be determined. Calendars varied from nation to nation and frequently they were unreliable to begin with. In war, victors sometimes imposed their calendars on the vanquished. Before the spread of literacy, which led to the more careful record-keeping of recent centuries, many births went unrecorded. However, for an odd reason, we know the birthdate of one Persian astronomer.

In 1859 there appeared in London an anonymous translation of a group of Persian poems almost unknown outside their homeland. Nowadays it is said that *The Rubáiyát of Omar Khayyám* is the second best known translation into English from another language, behind only the King James Bible. Actually a mix of Khayyám and himself, Edward FitzGerald's "translation" misrepresents much of the poet. Still, while such revered Persian masters as Rumi and Hafez are little known in the West, it is thanks to FitzGerald that a relatively minor poet is a household word.

For centuries, Khayyám's birth date was a matter of speculation. An early biographical work contained a precise astrological chart, but scholars overlooked or ignored it. Then, in 1941, Swami Govinda Tirtha published his analysis of the chart. Apparently Omar Khayyám was born shortly after sunrise on the morning of May 18, 1048. Astronomers at the Institute of Theoretical Astronomy at the Soviet Academy of Sciences confirmed Govinda's findings. Other historians determined at least to their own satisfaction that Khayyám lived until 1131. Those calculations yield a lifetime of eighty-three years, which confirms contemporary reports that Khayyám survived to a ripe old age.

That Khayyám's birth date could be determined from his horoscope is amusing. Astronomy has long since justifiably disowned astrology as its evil twin, but at the time the two were a single discipline. If astrologers were going to claim that the positions of the celestial bodies influenced one's life, they first had to determine those positions very precisely. Khayyám himself was one of those hybrid scientists. In a twelfth-century compendium of information on various professions, Khayyám shows up with the astrologers. Although an increasing number of *rubá'iya* were attributed to him after his death, from a few dozen at first to a peak of a thousand or so in the seventeenth century, his contemporaries don't mention his poetry. In his lifetime he was known as a mathematician, a physician, a judge of the subtleties of the "Truth" (the Koran), and a prominent astronomer.

In 1074, the Saljuq Sultan Jalalu al-Din Malikshah summoned him to Isfahan to help revise the Persian calendar, used in what is called either the Maleki or Jalali Era. We know that Khayyám also worked with other distinguished astronomers on the design of a new observatory. In spite of his profession, he seems to have been skeptical of astrology. Once, when he was ordered to predict the best time for a royal hunting expedition, he used as his guide not the stars but a weather forecast, whose sunny hunting days won him still more respect. Not that his record was perfect. He once incurred lifelong enmity by mistakenly predicting a prince's illness would be fatal.

---

19 MAY 1953

"An Expensive Meal and a Happy One"

Among his other duties, Moses was the ancient Hebrews' dietitian. In Leviticus, speaking through Moses, God declares numerous animals unclean, including both those that "cheweth the cud, but divideth not the hoof" and vice versa. He forbids snails, moles, and tortoises. Certain insects are allowed—beetles, grasshoppers, and (fortunately for John the Baptist, who survived on them in the Judean desert) locusts. Birds are a separate category. "And these are they which ye shall have in abomination among the fowls . . ." The list includes nineteen birds and the bat, which the ancients considered a bird. However, not wanting his people to starve, God charitably adds, "Of all clean birds shall ye eat."

Biblical injunctions were largely abandoned during the Reformation, with the excuse that Christ's appearance on Earth repealed the old Hebrew laws. A 1634 banquet for Charles I included herons and storks, two birds expressly prohibited by Moses. "It would be curious to trace the revolutions of fashion in the article of eatables," eighteenth-century naturalist Thomas Pennant observed. Times had changed so much that he could ask, "What epicure first rejected the seagull and heron?"

As England prospered, larger animals achieved food status; beef, for example, became popular only after oxen were no longer needed as draft animals. In time, smaller birds didn't seem worth the effort to kill and prepare. Cultural inhibitions arose. By the 1840s an Englishman traveling in Italy could be horrified to find the locals cooking and eating songbirds: "What! Robins! Our household birds! I would as soon eat a child." In hungry nations, hunters depleted the songbird populations. English novelist Tobias Smollett rode mile after mile in France "without hearing the song of blackbird, thrush, linnet, gold-finch, or any other bird whatsoever." It was mostly the demand for their flesh that exterminated passenger pigeons in the United States.

Those Italian peasants who offended the Englishman ate not only robins, but also starlings and other birds the English considered "unwholesome." Starlings are unpopular in most parts of their vast range, as food or as anything else. But here and there an adventurous gourmet considers them tasty. Nero Wolfe, the detective in Rex Stout's series of mystery novels, is one such connoisseur. On the day that begins the case recorded as *The Golden Spiders*—May 19, 1953—Wolfe and his faithful Watson, Archie Goodwin, are eating a dinner that some readers find distasteful. "Each year around the middle of May . . . ," Archie records, "a farmer . . . shoots eighteen or twenty starlings, puts them in a bag, and gets in his car and drives to New York . . ." The birds are bound for the kitchen of Wolfe's private chef, Fritz Brenner. "It is an expensive meal and a happy one . . ."

Frequently birds' diets determined their edibility. That's why scavengers were unclean. However, a change in diet could earn a change in status; young rooks, for example, could be eaten if fed grain. Wolfe could have sent Archie out on West 35th Street to bag a dirty city starling. But no, they had to come from the country, where they had fed on appropriate foods.

See also Nero Wolfe and the fer-de-lance, 10/24.

---

20 May 1515

Dürer's Rhinoceros

One of Albrecht Dürer's most influential images is his 1515 woodcut of a rhinoceros. At the time, elephants were common in Europe in the menageries of the powerful, but the rhino was still an exotic creature few people had encountered. Dürer himself didn't actually see the animal he was portraying; he elaborated upon a sketch by another artist. In his version, the hide seems to be made of layers of armor, and on its withers the animal bears an imaginary second horn. This drawing's unmistakable descendants show up in Flemish tapestries, on Meissen porcelain, even on the bronze door of the Pisa Cathedral. Today the original is reproduced on everything from posters to computer mouse pads.

At the end of the fifteenth century, Vasco da Gama's sea route around the southern tip of Africa opened the way for Portuguese colonies to plunder India. Treasures flooded into Portugal. Soon European spice merchants abandoned Venice for Lisbon. The ruler of the Indian province of Gujarat, Muzafar II, gave a live rhinoceros to the new Portuguese governor, who sent the beast on to his sovereign, King Manuel I, back home in Portugal.

Laden with spices, the Portuguese ship *Nostra Senhora da Ajuda* returned from an eighteen-month round trip to India on May 20, 1515. Down in the hold with the myrrh, sandalwood, and indigo was the governor's gift to Manuel, the first rhinoceros to reach Europe alive since the third century. The ship docked at the shore of the Tagus River near Lisbon, below the fortress of Belem. This is worth noting because the earliest European portrayal of the rhino is carved on a column of the Belem fortress, facing out to sea.

King Manuel was pleased with the rhinoceros. He amused himself by pitting it against an elephant, to test Pliny's claim in his *Natural History* that elephants and rhinos were deadly enemies. Without bloodshed, triumph was awarded the rhino. It didn't have to prove its bravery, because the terrified elephant turned and ran.

During 1515 an artist, probably the Moravian painter Valentim Fernandes, sketched and painted the rhinoceros in Lisbon. His portrayals made their way to Albrecht Dürer in Nuremburg. A painter, engraver, and scientist, Dürer also designed armor. He took Fernandes's portrayal a step further, making the rhinoceros into a heavily protected pachyderm with overlapping layers of armor, like a military vehicle. The German word for the rhino was *Panzernashorn,* from an old word for armor, *Panzer,* which would later be applied to German armored military divisions in World War II.

In March of 1514, Manuel had given Pope Leo X an elephant, and now he decided to send the pontiff his rhinoceros. The rhino departed Lisbon in December 1515, on a ship loaded with various treasures, including golden goblets and silver tankards. The poor beast was overdressed, wearing a green velvet collar with gilt roses and carnations, and a gilded iron chain. On its way to Rome, in a severe storm just off the northwestern coast of Italy, the ship sank. Having come so far and inspired so much artwork, Dürer's rhinoceros drowned without the artist ever having met his model.

---

21 MAY 1787

Horse Power

In Greek mythology, the sea god Poseidon and that mutiltalented goddess Athena disputed over the honor of naming the capital of the region of Greece known as Attica. The other gods tired of the squabble and proclaimed that the city should bear the name of the deity who provided the most useful gift to humanity. Athena created the olive tree, most versatile of plants, and Poseidon the horse, most versatile of animals. Athena won, and Athens was named after her, but the horse ran a close second in the list of nature's most valuable gifts.

An interesting episode in the intertwined story of humans and horses occurred in the United States in 1787. On the twenty-first of May, the state of Maryland granted a monopoly to a man named Oliver Evans. He was to have the exclusive statewide right to develop several mechanical projects that he had proposed. They included an arrangement of automatic, water-driven conveyor belts for a grain mill, and "a steam carriage for the purpose of conveying without the aid of animal force." It was a revolutionary concept. Animals had been the primary source of both transportation and hauling since before the beginning of written history. Certainly in Evans's time the sheer animal force of horses provided most forms of overland transportation.

Evans was exploiting the work of Scottish inventor James Watt, whose radical improvements to the steam engine were quickly revolutionizing industry. The dependence upon horses for so much of the power to drive civilization is indicated by a term Watt coined. After estimating the pulling power of dray horses, Watt declared that the measure of the rate of performing work was to be called "horsepower." One horsepower would be equivalent to 33,000 "feet pounds per minute," the force required to raise 33,000 pounds at the rate of one foot per minute. In time, Watt's own name was assigned to a unit of measure of electrical power, and another way of defining a single horsepower was that it equaled 746 watts. There are now variations for specific instances, such as brake horsepower and indicated horsepower, but the basic term has remained. Even today, before choosing an automobile or a riding lawn mower, prospective buyers compare the horsepower of rival machines.

In time, horses provided the animal force behind a related form of transportation in the United States. A gas-powered streetcar appeared in Rhode Island in 1873, and an electric one began operation in Baltimore in 1885. However, long before that, a horse-drawn streetcar went into service. Horses had been used before to pull train cars on railroad tracks, but in New York City, in 1832, for 12½ cents apiece, thirty passengers could ride in the first horse-drawn streetcar. Although it had been almost half a century since Evans received his monopoly, he had failed to supplant animal power as the motive force of civilization. He adapted his steam engine to various industrial applications, but it was never used in transportation. One reason it didn't replace horses was that Evans was

One side effect of the invention of motorized transport was horses' eventual release from thousands of years of backbreaking toil.

forbidden to drive it on the Pennsylvania Turnpike. The authorities worried that the contraption would frighten the horses.

Singing Insects

Our generic slang for insects, "bug," comes from the Middle English *bugge,* meaning a specter or hobgoblin, which survives in such terms as "bogeyman" and "bugaboo." (This usage is imprecise; there is an entire order of insects, Hemiptera, called "true bugs.") However, we have always had a sneaking affection for those insects said to sing. Actually, of course, insects have no voice, because they lack an organ for it. Like creatures in *Alice* or *Fantasia,* they are musical instruments that play themselves. Some crickets and grasshoppers rub wings together or tap legs against wing ridges as if playing the violin or xylophone. Cicadas are percussionists; they vibrate drumlike membranes on their undersides.

These forms of musical apparatus predate frogs and birds and most of earth's other noise-making animals. There are references to them throughout history. A Greek legend tells of a musician who broke a string on his lyre but was able to continue playing because a cicada sat on the instrument and sounded the missing note. Plato spoke of the music of insects. One of the few dissenting voices is that of Hercules, who was awakened by cicadas and begged Zeus to quiet them. Walt Whitman, on the other hand, admired the sounds produced by both "locusts" (cicadas) and katydids: "I thought the morning and evening warble of birds delightful; but I find I can listen to these strange insects with just as much pleasure." Hawthorne said of crickets, "If moonlight could be heard, it would sound like that." Eventually someone noticed that only males make the sound, prompting one ancient Greek to remark that cicadas were lucky because their wives were silent.

Like so many other animals, singing insects have been absorbed into our culture. To the Chinese, their life cycle symbolized eternal life: apparent death followed by metamorphosis into a new form. Athenian men wore dagger-shaped hairpins with cicadas carved on the handles. Some homeowners kept watch crickets because they stopped chirping if a stranger crept into the house. Many wound up housed in decorative cages, some of which were very expensive and even furnished with elegant beds. Songs and poems were written about pet crickets, and tombs erected in their honor. It was said that emperors had entire orchestras of insects singing different notes. Commoners simply enjoyed crickets' music or thought it a good omen.

Singing insects are still honored in celebrations around the world. Every spring Florence, Italy, hosts the Festa del Grillo, the Cricket Festival. It takes place on the Christian holiday known as Ascension Day, the date of which varies because it is traditionally held forty days after Easter, another variable holiday. Like Easter, it is a spring festival of resurrection, here honored in part with the crickets' renewed joyful noise after the silence of winter. And in late May in Japan, another celebration honors singing insects—the Festival of Fudo Temple. Fanciers stroll among cages, listen to the inhabitants and to the spiels of the salespeople, and carry crickets home. There, as it did long before humans took notice, the diminutive orchestra fills the air with its ancient music.

See also plagues of locusts, 8/7; The Cricket in Times Square, *8/28; and* The Cricket on the Hearth, *12/20.*

---

23 MAY 1938

Birds in a Time Capsule

In the year 2938, historians—assuming there are any at the time—are supposed to open the time capsule buried at the 1938 New York World's Fair. Among more tangible mementos of the early twentieth century, they will find an issue of *Life* dated May 23, 1938. Errol Flynn is on the cover, and inside is such trademark whimsy as a photograph of nuns drawing a male nude in art class. A browser will also find more chilling documentation of our century: Adolf Hitler and Benito Mussolini admiring a huge Fascist demonstration in Rome, Spanish dictator Francisco Franco seated on a magnificent throne. But rivaling the space devoted to world leaders are several pages of color paintings of spring birds by thirty-year-old Roger Tory Peterson.

Peterson was already prominent in his field. Over the next few decades, he would become world famous as an ornithologist, artist, writer, and lecturer. A cartoon from the 1960s depicts two birds in a tree observing a bird-watcher peering at them; one says, "Say, isn't that Roger Tory Peterson?"

Peterson's hobby seems to have moved steadily toward a career, beginning in childhood in Jamestown, New York. When his father told him to mow the lawn, young Roger protested that a yard left wild would invite more birds. His seventh-grade teacher encouraged him to copy bird pictures from Junior Audubon Club leaflets. He corrected his biology teacher when she claimed the snowy egret was extinct. Under his photo in his high school yearbook was the prophetic note, "Woods! Birds! Flowers! Here are the makings of a great naturalist." Later, he studied at art schools, painted commercially, and spent summers as a nature counselor at a camp in Maine.

A Field Guide to the Birds, the first of a series that would become a publishing phenomenon and make Peterson a wealthy man, appeared in 1934. The original illustrations had to run a gauntlet: Could famed birder Ludlow Griscom identify each species from across the room? He could. The guide was rejected by several publishers who underestimated depression-era willingness to pay the hefty $2.75 when other guides were available for a dollar. But to many birders, after Peterson came along, there were no other guides. His simplified, schematic paintings and drawings have brought more people to bird-watching than any other inducement. The growth of bird-watching, and birders' almost inevitable appreciation of the ecological web to which each bird contributes, is considered the most important boost to the conservation movement in this century.

Naturally, Peterson was intrigued by the thought of his work resting in a time capsule for a thousand years. "The historian who studies this issue [of *Life*] in 2938," he said, "will learn not only about a world and its leaders edging toward World War II, but will also learn that the spring migration of birds was a week earlier in the year of 1938. Wars and their leaders come and go, but the birds will probably be performing their yearly ritual more or less on schedule."

Charlotte's Web

E. B. White lavished more attention on a spider than on any other character in his three children's books. "I didn't like spiders at first," White wrote to a fifth-grade class, "but then I began watching one of them, and soon saw what a wonderful creature she was and what a skillful weaver." He named her Charlotte.

At first White thought the tenant of his barn was a Grey Cross spider, *Aranea sericata.* His reference said it had formerly been *Epeira sclopetaria,* and he named his fictional character Charlotte Epeira. When he learned that she was actually the aptly named "barn spider," *Araneus cavatica,* she became Charlotte A. Cavatica. Zoologists have since altered the species name to *cavaticus,* to match the gender of the genus. The initial stood not for the genus but for the family, Aranea, from the Latin for "spider."

White studied spiders for a year before writing *Charlotte's Web.* After finding one book helpful, he visited its author with a list of questions. He made notes on arachnid anatomy and diagrammed the web-spinning process. Even Charlotte's story of her cousin who caught a fish in his web isn't fanciful; spiders have caught mice, birds, even snakes. Much of her behavior comes from White's own observations. He watched the real Charlotte spin an egg sac and deposit eggs, then took spider and sac with him to the city, where he left them on his dresser. Weeks later hundreds of baby spiders emerged and strung lines everywhere. The *Araneus* genus comprises over 1,500 species of orb-weaving spiders, and thanks to White's research, Charlotte behaves like a member in good standing. She works mostly at night. She produces hundreds of eggs and dies afterward. The eggs hatch in the spring, and the spiderlings travel by "ballooning," floating on gossamer lines of web.

Charlotte knew her talents. In the book, Wilbur, the pig, boasts, "I could spin a web if I tried," and she merely replies, "Let's see you do it." Spider silk is wonderful stuff. A fibrous protein extruded in liquid form, it solidifies immediately. It is incredibly strong and versatile, and only spiders' antagonistic personalities prevent their commercial exploitation in the manner of silkworms.

White's attention to detail extended to advising the illustrator, Garth Williams. He sent Williams one book on spiders and recommended others. In a letter to his editor on May 24, 1952, White complimented the jacket design, remarked that the goose looked snakelike, and addressed the portrayal of Charlotte. The "mussy Charles Addams attic web," while acceptable for the cover, was unlike Charlotte's own. He liked her "smooth, silk-stocking legs," although he knew that each was covered in tiny hairs. Williams drew numerous faces for Charlotte, but White rejected them; she remains a tiny, distant figure, except for one close-up in which White himself gave her two dots for eyes.

White's fascination with spiders lasted all his life. "When I get sick of what men do," he wrote, "I have only to walk a few steps in another direction to see what spiders do . . . This sustains me very well indeed . . ."

The River Horse

The habitat of the hippopotamus is apparent in its name, which comes from two Greek words, *hippos,* "horse," and *potamos,* "river." (Its scientific name, *Hippopotamus amphibius,* is therefore somewhat redundant.) Of course, the hippo is not a member of the horse family. It is a cousin of the pig—and, scholars think, the inspiration for the Behemoth in the Book of Job:

> *Behold, Behemoth,*
> > *which I made as I made you;*
> > *he eats grass like an ox. . . .*
> *Under the lotus plants he lies,*
> > *in the covert of the reeds and in the marsh.*
> *For his shade the lotus trees cover him;*
> > *the willows of the brook surround him.*
> *Behold, if the river is turbulent he is not frightened;*
> > *he is confident though Jordan rushes against his mouth.*

The hippopotamus has been a familiar animal in its native Africa throughout human habitation there. It appears in Roman and Egyptian paintings. Pliny described it as "even mightier than the crocodile," although, as Job noted of the Behemoth, it is a vegetarian. Pliny also wrote that a hippopotamus was once displayed, with five crocodiles, in an artificial lake in Rome.

No other hippos are on record as having been exhibited in Europe for many centuries. Then, in 1849, the viceroy of English-controlled Egypt, Abbas Pasha, sent a hunting party along the White Nile, near Khartoum in what is now the Sudan. Near the island of Obaysch, the hunters killed a female hippopotamus. Its calf was found hiding nearby, and, after a struggle in which it was scarred with a boat hook, it was captured. Considering its initial abuse, the orphan's subsequent royal treatment is ironic. Escorted by Nubian soldiers, the hippo was presented to the British consul general, who then sent him on to the Zoological Society of London. An Arab named Hamet Safi Cannana was hired as keeper. The hippo was named after the island where he was captured.

Obaysch arrived in London on May 25, 1850. The English had never seen anything like him, and he became the talk of the town. A week later, English geologist Gideon Mantell wrote that he had been "to the Zoological Gardens in the Regent's Park to see the live Hippopotamus just arrived. He is a fine lively young animal, and was gambolling in the water with great glee. His Arab keeper in attendance." In 1822, Mantell had discovered the *Iguanodon,* the first creature to be recognized as a "dinosaur." When Mantell submitted its teeth and bone fragments for identification, the French fossil expert Baron Cuvier misidentified the *Iguanodon* bones as those of a fossil hippopotamus. Perhaps, as he gazed upon the Zoological Society's new prize, Mantell remembered that error.

A week after Mantell's visit, Emma Darwin, Charles's wife, wrote to a friend, "I suppose the Hipp. causes a great run upon the gardens," because Charles's brother had asked him for tickets and they were already difficult to acquire. London's premier zoologist Richard Owen, the man who coined the word "dinosaur," naturally trotted over for a look at Obaysch. He described the hippo's arrival: "On arriving at the gardens, the Arab walked first out of the transport van, with a bag of dates over his shoulder, and the beast trotted after him, now and then lifting up its huge grotesque muzzle and sniffing at its favourite dainties, with which it was duly rewarded on entering its apartment."

Obaysch appeared in a number of guises, including Harry Furniss's illustration for Lewis Carroll's Sylvie and Bruno.

Although his star faded as other animal celebrities came to town, Obaysch was the public's darling for several years. *Punch* nicknamed him HRH (His Rolling Hulk). One of the hit popular songs of the time was "The Hippopotamus Polka." Naturally, one of the hippo's most obvious traits was his ability to eat astonishing quantities of food, especially his porridge of maize and milk. Lewis Carroll lampooned Obaysch's famous appetite in *Sylvie and Bruno:*

> *He thought he saw a Banker's Clerk*
> *Descending from the bus:*
> *He looked again, and found it was*
> *A Hippopotamus:*
> *"If this should stay to dine," he said,*
> *"There won't be much for us!"*

See also Jumbo, 2/22.

---

26 MAY 1684

Noah's Ark

On Trinity Monday, the twenty-sixth of May, 1684, Bishop Sir Thomas Ken preached to Londoners a sermon on a matter both theological and zoological. According to John Evelyn's diary, Ken gave "a very learned discourse about the dimensions of the Ark, compar'd with other vessells of antient and later times, to obviate severall objections of Atheistical persons. . . ."

Speculating on the accommodations and social life of the animals aboard Noah's Ark has long been a favorite game of persons both atheistical and not. One illustration of the ark from the early 1800s shows both interior and exterior views and is labeled "Shewing the Apartments assigned to the several Creatures therein contained, and to the keeping of the Food they lived on." Recognizable larger animals include elephants, giraffes, elk, and what appear to be a pair of unicorns. Some animals do not show up. Sir Walter Raleigh insisted that hyenas, for example, were not aboard the boat. They were obviously an unnatural hybrid, and Noah had saved only pure-blooded creatures.

Over the centuries, as knowledge accumulated, devout naturalists found themselves wrestling with the problem of Noah's floating zoo. The ark's dimensions were the first obstacle. In the Bible, God warns Noah of the impending Flood,* and offers some boat-building tips: "The length of the ark shall be three hundred cubits, the breadth of it fifty cubits, and the height of it thirty cubits . . . With lower, second, and third stories shalt thou make it." A cubit equaled about 18 inches. Therefore the ark was roughly 450 feet long, 75 feet wide, and 45 feet tall. That might have accommodated the relatively few species known to the Israelites, and even the several hundred recognized at the time of the King James Version of the Bible in 1611. But with world exploration the list of species grew almost daily. Furthermore, Noah had to stock enough food for an entire year or so in the ark, and the tendency of certain carnivores to prey upon their fellow passengers would require that they be segregated.

Meanwhile, geology was pushing the age of the Earth ever further back. Fossils surfaced in depressing abundance and were proving dramatically different from living animals. Biblical literalists proposed that such bones were evidence of a series of creations, with God destroying each round before going on to the next. With the vast time scale proposed by Charles Lyell in his 1831 *Principles of Geology,* however, the aim of reconciling geology with the Bible began to erode for good. By midcentury, as far as most scientists were concerned, Noah's Ark was sailing out of history and into myth. Of course, strict creationists disagreed, and many still do. As late as 1938, a Deluge Geological Society formed in California,

When fossils, such as the Iguanodon *here charmingly reconstructed, began to threaten the biblical age of the earth, literalists protested that they were animals that had perished in the Flood.*

* God warns the 480-year-old Noah 120 years in advance. Noah lives to be 950, only 19 years short of the record set by his cousin Methuselah, who dies the year of the Flood.

occupying itself with such tasks as a Footprint Research Committee that sought evidence of the contemporaneity of human and dinosaur tracks.

A few believers suggested that the problem with Noah's Ark was that sacred tenet of creationism, the fixity of species. If God created all animals and plants and they haven't changed since, the ark was too small to accommodate them. However, a rejection of the fixity of species would make Noah's Ark more reasonable, because it would allow that many animals had been created since the Flood.

The story of the ark ends strangely. Repeatedly, God informs Noah that the purpose of taking aboard two of every animal is "to keep them alive." Noah does so. When the dove returning with the olive branch indicates that the waters have receded, Noah and his cramped passengers disembark. Then, after carefully safeguarding God's creatures for months, Noah immediately designates several of them as sacrifices and kills them.

---

27 MAY 1784

Mozart's "Musical Joke"

Spring 1784. Wolfgang Amadeus Mozart was thirty-one. In mid-April he noted in his diary the completion of his new Piano Concerto in G Major (K. 453). On May 27, he passed a pet shop. Probably he did a double take, because from inside the shop a bird was whistling a section of his new concerto, a work not yet performed in public.

Mozart rushed inside. The singer was a caged starling, which the composer purchased on the spot. At home he recorded in his diary both the odd incident and the bird's song. Except for a sharp G and grace notes, the song was identical with the first five measures of the allegretto of his new concerto. Mozart added the note, *Das war schön!* ("That was beautiful!")

The mimetic talents of starlings are legendary. Pliny said that they mimicked both Greek and Latin, practicing diligently and speaking in ever longer sentences. Samuel Pepys wrote in his diary that he had heard a starling "which do whistle and talk the most and best that ever I heard anything in my life." Researchers tell wonderful stories about these birds. After hearing the sentence once the day before, a starling asked clearly, "Does Hammacher Schlemmer have a toll-free number?" While undergoing treatment for an infection, one kept crying out, "I have a question!"

Starlings are certainly also able to imitate music, but it seems they mix it up. Recently one in a lab kept linking portions of "Rockabye Baby" and the *William Tell* Overture. Since such modifications tend to creep into starlings' imitations over time, the precision and length of the fragment from Mozart's concerto indicates the imitation was a fairly new one. Had Mozart visited the shop before? Frequently he whistled and hummed to himself. Did the starling hear him? It has also been suggested that Mozart got the theme from the starling, but the diary entries seem to rule that out, unless Mozart bought the bird only after plagiarizing it.

For its remaining three years of life, the bird delighted Mozart. His devotion to it may explain a little mystery. Perhaps the master's least-understood work is *Ein musikalischer Spass* ("A Musical Joke"), the first work entered in his diary after the death of his father and the starling, in 1787. Plagued with false starts and awkward transitions, stopping suddenly, it has been considered a parody of incompetent composition and performance. But some scholars now think the style of the piece resembles the madhouse repertoire of, yes, a starling.

At the starling's funeral, which took place only a few days after the death of his father, Mozart and a procession of veiled mourners gathered at the bird's graveside and sang hymns. Then the bereaved Wolfgang read a eulogy:

> *A little fool lies here*
> *Whom I held dear—*
> *A starling in the prime*
> *Of his brief time . . .*

It went on to detail the bird's charms and virtues. A few days later, after working on it off and on for three years—exactly the time the starling lived with him—Mozart finished his "Musical Joke." ***See also Shakespeare's starling, 3/6.***

---

28 MAY 585 B.C.

A Failing Sun Halts a Battle

The word "eclipse" comes from the Greek *ekleipsis,* meaning a failing or a forsaking, from two earlier words meaning "to leave out." This occasional failure of those reliable and worshiped orbs up there has always inspired fear in human beings. Whether it was the Moon vanishing or turning red, or, worse yet, the Sun becoming dark, the sudden change was terrifying. "Their cause was hidden by the rarity of their occurrence," as Pliny the Elder observed of other celestial phenomena, "and for this reason they are not understood." He added parenthetically that humans aren't the only ones who fear eclipses; so do apes and other animals.

It would be odd if there were no eclipses. Our planet revolves around the Sun once a year, and the Moon around Earth twelve times as often. All three astronomical bodies are in roughly the same plane; indeed, that plane is called the "plane of the ecliptic." Eclipses occur in regular cycles. A lunar eclipse results when the shadow of Earth falls across the Moon, a solar eclipse when the Moon blocks our view of the Sun. Astronomers are able to calculate the periodicity of eclipses and forecast them well in advance. The reliability of such phenomena was an early hint of the natural laws that underlie the apparent whims of the gods.

It is no more difficult to calculate the occurrence of eclipses in the past than to predict them in the future. Therefore, thanks to astronomers, historians know the first event in history that can be precisely dated. In the sixth century B.C. in Asia Minor, in what is now Turkey, the river Halys separated the two states of Media and Lydia. Their respective rulers, Cyaxeres and Alyattes, had been fighting a half-hearted war against each other for a couple of years. Finally, on the twenty-eighth of May in 585 B.C., their armies met at the River Halys to settle the matter. Unknown to their strategists, and hidden by the glare of the sun, the moon was moving into position overhead. During the battle, there was a total eclipse of the Sun. Apparently everyone present regarded this as a straightforward message from the gods, and they stopped the battle. Instead of fighting for control of the region, the two nations negotiated peace.

Nor is that the only historical significance of that day. The solar eclipse of 585 B.C. is sometimes mistakenly described as the event that launched science as a way of examining the world. It has even been said that Greek philosophy began then. At the time there lived in Miletus, in Ionia, a man named Thales, now called one of the Seven Sages of the Ancient World. Aristotle described him as the founder of natural philosophy. He sought answers to his questions about the universe not in revelation or decree but in the physical universe itself. Pliny reported that Thales, "in the fourth year of the 48th Olympiad, predicted an eclipse which occurred two years later in the reign of Alyattes."

Alas, tradition seems to have attributed more to Thales than he actually could have accomplished. Most contemporary science historians agree that he could not possibly have possessed the astronomical knowledge to predict the eclipse of 585 B.C. Perhaps Thales made a lucky guess, the accuracy of which was exaggerated in retrospect. It's a good thing no one predicted the event to either Alyattes or Cyaxeres. No doubt they would have used the knowledge to their own advantage. Their response to the unforeseen eclipse proves that this battle, like so many others, could have been stopped at a moment's notice had the opposing leaders only desired it.

For other eclipses, see 2/26, 2/29, and 6/21.

"Goddess Mother of the World"

In 1852, Chief Computer Radhanath Sikdar exclaimed to the surveyor general of India, "Sir, I have discovered the highest mountain in the world." He was referring to a peak in northeastern Nepal on the Tibet-Nepal border. The locals called the summit Qomolangma, "Goddess Mother of the World," and the survey party knew it as Peak XV. In 1865, the English named the entire mountain after a former surveyor general, Sir George Everest.

The chief computer didn't have a simple task. The question of the tallest mountain is still debatable. In measuring a mountain, does one figure outward from the center of the Earth or upward from sea level? The former method would award the honor of tallest wrinkle on our planet's surface to the Ecuadorian mountain Chimborazo; the latter, to Mount Everest. Chimborazo is only 20,577 feet above sea level, but it is situated over the Earth's equatorial bulge. That makes it over 7,000 feet farther from the center of the planet than the topmost peak of Everest. However, most mountain climbers and geographers measure a mountain's height upward from sea level, and therefore Mount Everest is generally considered the highest peak on our planet.

As a result of that first survey, Everest's official height became 29,002 feet. A century later, an Indian party raised that 26 feet, and later a Chinese group raised the estimate another 15 inches. A final determination is unlikely. Geologists estimate that some parts of the Himalayas are rising at a rate of perhaps a few feet per century, with some other areas possibly sinking.

As soon as explorers realized Everest's preeminence, they yearned to climb it. However, Buddhists revere the peak, and the Dalai Lama withheld permission to explore it until 1920. Not that it was easy even then. Everest reaches two-thirds of the way up through the Earth's atmosphere. It is a land of scant oxygen and yearlong ice. Expeditions, each with more advanced equipment, tried and failed to scale the summit, and observers became pessimistic about the success of each new attempt.

The fabled Everest was finally scaled by an expedition led by Tenzing Norgay and Edmund Hillary. Tenzing was a Sherpa—a native Nepalese people famous for their mountaineering skills—and Hillary a New Zealander. When they walked into the camp of their waiting comrades, they were greeted with Eastern and Western congratulations. As the blue-jacketed figures approached, their colleagues rushed to meet them, to shake their hands and pound their backs and take their photographs. The conquerors posed arm-in-arm, Tenzing smiling broadly, Hillary trying to keep his face appropriately controlled. An observer was reminded of the account of a proper Brit on an earlier expedition: "We so far forgot ourselves as to shake hands on the summit." Tenzing's fellow Sherpas did not forget themselves. They approached him with respect and bowed with their hands clasped. One bent his forehead to touch Tenzing's hand.

Tenzing and Hillary told their story. They had reached the snow-covered summit at 11:30 A.M., May 29, 1953. Hidden above the jagged stone ridge that appeared to be the summit was what Hillary described as "a symmetrical, beautiful snow-cone summit." To pose for a photograph by Tenzing, Hillary removed his oxygen mask without harm. Hillary then took the camera and recorded Tenzing holding aloft several flags, including the United Nations', Great Britain's, and that of his native Nepal. After months of preparation and weeks of climbing, they spent only fifteen minutes on the summit before starting back down.

---

30 MAY 1667

Mad Madge at the Royal Society

In 1667, when Margaret Cavendish, duchess of Newcastle, hinted that she expected an invitation to the Royal Society, there was consternation in that all-male company. A half century before, Francis Bacon had published his revolutionary plea for a new learning founded upon observation of nature rather than upon reinterpretation of classical texts. The embodiment of Bacon's dream, the Royal Society, was only seven years old. Members felt they already drew enough satirical fire from the ballad singers in the streets without inviting a woman to attend.

And *such* a woman. "Mad Madge," she was called, and a "Great Atheistical Philosophraster," and even Newcastle's "illustrious whore." A female contemporary said one could find saner people in Bedlam. Samuel Pepys confided to his diary that he thought the duchess "a mad, conceited, ridiculous woman." These remarks were inspired by Cavendish's unseemly interest in the natural sciences. She was also the first Englishwoman to write for publication—several volumes on natural philosophy, in both prose and verse.

Privileged, childless, with a supportive husband and a brother-in-law who invested much energy in her education, Cavendish managed a room of her own in a time when women hardly even had lives of their own. "Women," she wrote, "live like bats or owls, labour like beasts, and die like worms." Not Mad Madge. She wrote stories in which women held positions of power on exotic adventures. Her analysis of gender inequality was denounced in every quarter. Another acquaintance, the philosopher Thomas Hobbes, influenced her toward what was considered atheism. She thought God probably existed, but that he didn't serve as a hands-on administrator of nature, which was "altogether Material." And, finally, she wrote candidly in English, which was more provocative than, say, Newton's circumspect Latin.

The meeting of May 30, 1667, was one of the best attended in the society's history. Cavendish entered with her usual flourish. She liked to wear her own extravagant designs, sometimes with servants matching. This time it took six attendants just to carry her train. Pepys strained for a better view. Yes, she was "a good, comely woman," but her outfit was "antick."

Unwilling hosts or not, the fellows gave a good show. First they weighed air. With microscopist Robert Hooke assisting, chemist Robert Boyle used his famous air pump to remove the air from a container, which was then weighed. When the air was restored, the container was two ounces heavier. They mixed colors because Boyle thought color a topic to interest the more domestic gender. Two transparent liquids, sulfuric acid and aniseed oil, were combined to produce "Heat and Smoak and a Blood-Red colour." A sixty-pound lodestone was shown disturbing a compass seven feet away.

The Royal Society inclined toward observation and measurement. Cavendish herself, like her family friend Descartes, was more theoretical. With Galileo discovering worlds in the sky and Leeuwenhoek finding ecosystems in his mouth, enthusiasm for the new instruments alarmed Cavendish. She warned that science might become too narrow-minded and experimental if hobbled by the limits of technology.

---

31 May 1786

The Affair of the Diamond Necklace

The scandal helped inspire the French Revolution. In 1785, a young woman convinced the gullible Cardinal Prince Louis de Rohan that Marie Antoinette desired the clandestine purchase of a fabulous diamond necklace originally designed for Louis XV's favorite, Madame du Barry. Eager to restore his faded prestige at court, the cardinal pledged his credit for the necklace. Everything was fine until the jeweler produced the cardinal's signed notes and requested payment. Although many French observers didn't believe her, Marie Antoinette declared that she had neither desired the necklace nor received it. In the very act of holding Assumption Day religious services for Louis XVI and his queen, de Rohan was arrested.

The Affair of the Diamond Necklace caught the imagination of many writers. Alexandre Dumas *père* wrote an entire novel about it. Thomas Carlyle, in his epic history of the French Revolution, rose to new heights of sarcastic parentheses as he gleefully depicted the pettiness and greed of the French aristocracy. One florid meditation concerned the nature of the jewels themselves: "But to tell the various Histories of those various Diamonds, from the first making of them; or even, omitting all the rest, from the first digging of them in the far Indian mines! How they lay, for uncounted ages and aeons . . . silently imbedded in the rock; did nevertheless, when their hour came, emerge from it, and first behold the glorious sun smile on them, and with their many-coloured glances smiled back on him."

This particular necklace consisted of 647 smiling diamonds weighing a total of 2,800 carats, and arranged in an elaborate pattern of strands. Carlyle must have agreed with Pliny's comments on such jewels: "Therein Nature reaches its utmost concentration and in no department does she arouse more wonder. . . . Consequently, for very many people a single precious stone can provide a matchless and perfect view of nature."

Diamonds inspire in humans not only wonder but greed. To Marilyn Monroe and the other husband hunters in the film *Gentlemen Prefer Blondes,* they are a girl's best friend. Ian Fleming's definition is less debatable: Diamonds are forever. They are forever because they are the hardest naturally occurring substance on Earth. They are composed of pure carbon. Of course, so is the graphite in pencils. The two substances don't share identical properties because carbon is an allotropic element, which means it can exist in more than one form without changing its basic nature. A material's characteristics, its "behavior," depend upon how its atoms are arranged. In diamond molecules, the carbon atoms are much more securely linked with each other than in the looser structure of graphite.

Experiments indicate that to make a diamond the earth must bake carbonaceous material at a temperature of at least 5,000°F at a pressure of over 1 million pounds per square inch. Volcanoes then deliver the prized crystals to the surface, or at least within reach of it, in molten magma. When the magma cools, huge plugs called "diamond pipes" form in its crust, with the diamonds contained in a bluish rock called kimberlite. Sometimes diamonds are found far from their pipes, carried away by glacial or fluvial (stream or river) erosion.

Although diamonds don't lie around on the ground like acorns, their value results not so much from true rarity as from an imposed scarcity. Therefore these ancient chunks of carbon can be exchanged for different symbols of value—for pieces of other prized natural substances such as gold or silver, or for printed pieces of paper, or nowadays for numbers in a computer. Human beings have always imposed such arbitrary values on aspects of nature, with unpredictable side effects. The case of the credulous cardinal is a perfect example. Although de Rohan was acquitted on May 31, 1786, his entrapment in *L'Affaire du Collier* destroyed his career.

The Naming of Names

On the first day of June, 1870, while drawing the illustrations for *Through the Looking-Glass,* John Tenniel wrote Lewis Carroll with questions about Alice's railway journey. The scene appears in Chapter Three. Shortly after passing through the Looking-Glass, Alice finds herself aboard a train. Her fellow passengers include a Goat; a Beetle; a ticket agent peering at her through telescope, binocular, and microscope; and a gentleman dressed in white paper, who appears to be British politician Benjamin Disraeli, whom Tenniel portrayed similarly in the humor magazine *Punch.* To add to Alice's confusion, a tiny sad voice murmurs in her ear, "I know you are a friend. . . . And you wo'n't hurt me, though I *am* an insect."

This chatty Gnat points out the local insects—the Rocking-horse-fly, Snap-dragon-fly, and Bread-and-butter-fly—and he and Alice begin to talk about names. The Gnat asks about the insects Alice knew back home. "I can tell you the names of some of them," she says.

> "Of course they answer to their names?" the Gnat remarked carelessly.
>
> "I never knew them to do it."
>
> "What's the use of their having names," the Gnat said, "if they won't answer to them?"
>
> "No use to *them,*" said Alice; "but it's useful to the people that name them, I suppose. If not, why do things have names at all?"

It is a fine question. "What's in a name?" Juliet asks Romeo. A rose by any other name *would* smell as sweet, but if it lacked any name at all, others would not know to which sweet-smelling flower we were referring. A hint of the power of names can be found in the slang term for "name" popular during the CB-radio craze of the 1970s—"handle." Because of that power, some birders are content to merely identify a bird's species, without moving on to an awareness of its place in the world, because the identification alone seems enough.

In Genesis, the origin of the names of animals is straightforward: "And out of the ground the LORD God formed every beast of the field, and every fowl of the air; and brought *them* unto Adam

Peter Newell's 1902 illustration of Alice chatting with the Looking-Glass Gnat.

to see what he would call them: and whatsoever Adam called every living creature, that *was* the name thereof." Then along came the Swedish systematist Linnaeus and placed creatures in categories. As he himself observed, "God created, but Linnaeus classified."

We call Linnaeus's system of naming "binomial nomenclature." It is a universal language. Written in Latin, scientific names exhibit no bias toward a particular nation, or at least not one still in existence. Binomial nomenclature works like a person's surname and given name, except that there may be tens of thousands of John Smiths, but there will be only one *Sturnus vulgaris.* The first word, always capitalized, designates the genus, a group of related species. The second distinguishes the species, the unique taxonomic group to which this particular individual belongs. By this system, the genus name of John Smith would be Smith, and his species name John, but there could not be any other John Smith anywhere in the world.

Had Alice been an entomologist, she might have tried to classify the Looking Glass insects. Take, for example, the Bread-and-butter-fly. She could assume that this was merely its local name. Since "its wings are thin slices of bread-and-butter, its body is a crust, and its head is a lump of sugar," it is obviously unrelated to the lepidoptera of the world back home. Therefore Alice would have the pleasure of introducing to the scientific community a new species, perhaps named something like *Paniptera cephalosaccharum,* meaning "sugar-headed bread-wing." And unlike the animals back home, it would answer to its new name.

---

2 JUNE 1857

A New Man

L'homme fossile n'existe pas! [Fossil man does not exist!]

—Baron Georges Cuvier,
early nineteenth century

Neandertals* were the first fossil humans to be recognized as such. Consequently their name is wonderfully apt. When seventeenth-century hymnist Joachim Neumann, vicar and organist at St. Martin's Church in Düsseldorf, signed his compositions in Greek, Neumann ("New Man") came out Neander. Later, the citizenry named their valley after the local celebrity: Neanderthal, "New Man Valley."

In August 1856, quarrymen in the Neander Valley blasted open two limestone-rich caves and found some odd bones: a heavy skull with low brow ridges, equally robust thigh bones, part of a pelvis, ribs, a shoulder. The foreman figured it was a bear skeleton, but he gave it to a local schoolteacher and amateur naturalist, Johann Karl Fuhlrott.

At that time, few fossil humans were known, and none seemed dramatically different from us. Nonetheless, apparently Fuhlrott suspected that he had found a new man. He consulted a professor of anatomy at the University of Bonn, Hermann Schaafhausen, who would in time become a resolute Darwinian. On June 2, 1857, at the general meeting of the Natural History Society of Prussian Rhineland and Westphalia, Fuhlrott described his discovery. Schaafhausen then presented his analysis of the skeleton, beginning with his conviction that the skull exhibited "a natural conformation hitherto not known to exist." In 1864 the bones became the first to be named a new species, *Homo neanderthalensis,* since demoted to a subspecies, *H. sapiens neanderthalensis.*

The discovery was not immediately applauded. Skeptics claimed the skeleton belonged to a sufferer from brain disorders, or a "half-crazed" wild man, or even a Cossack who died during Napoléon's retreat from Moscow. As late as 1872, Rudolf Virchow, the founder of modern pathology, insisted that the Neander Valley skeleton was that of a contemporary middle-aged arthritis sufferer who had received "stupendous" blows to the head. As vehemently antievolution as Schaafhausen was pro-, Virchow delayed the identification of numerous fossil humans by dismissing them as merely diseased.

The appearance, the *idea,* of Neandertals hit Victorian society with an uproar that has been compared with savages bursting in upon a sewing circle. The Neander Valley skeleton was unearthed three years before Darwin published the *Origin of Species.* Having so long traced their ancestry back to Adam, and thence to God, shocked genealogists described their long-lost cousin as "uncouth" and "repellant," unworthy of "the glorious title 'Homo sapiens.' "

Since then, the bones of over 350 Neandertals have been unearthed, from Poland to the Iberian Peninsula, and across the globe as far as western Asia. Actually, the Neander Valley specimen wasn't the first discovered, only the first identified. Around 1830, the skull of a small child was found in Belgium, but it wasn't correctly identified for almost a century; and in 1848 a skull was discovered in Gibraltar. Since that fateful day in the Neander Valley quarry, paleontologists have found many skeletons more primitive than the Neandertals. The realization of the true nature of the eerie bones, however, began when Fuhlrott's bear skeleton turned out to be a new man.

See also Lucy, 11/30; and Piltdown, 12/18.

---

* In the twentieth century, the spelling "Neanderthal" has been changed to "Neandertal" to reflect the actual German pronunciation of the word.

"The Sly Rhinocerot"

"We are now to discourse of the second wonder in nature," Conrad Gesner began, in Edward Topsell's majestic 1607 translation of Gesner's *Historia Animalium,* "namely of a beast every way admirable, both for the outward shape, quantity, and greatnesse, and also for the inward courage, disposition, and mildnes." Gesner had already installed the elephant at the top of his hierarchy. In second place he put the rhinoceros. He admired it partly for its uniqueness, "differing in every part from all other beasts, from the top of his nose to the tip of his taile, the eares and eies excepted, which are like Beares." Topsell added candidly, "as the beast is strange and never seene in our countrey, so my eye-sight cannot adde any thing to the description."

Of course, the rhinoceros was known in its native lands thousands of years before European naturalists began pontificating about it. When the Tatar warlord Timur-i-leng (Timur the Lame, "Tamerlane") conquered India, a prince of Delhi commanded his elephants and rhinoceroses to kneel before the new lord. At the time rhinos were beasts of burden, taught to carry howdahs like elephants. Sadly, a popular sport of the time was watching rhinos battle to the death in gladiatorial bouts with other animals.

Because of their size and armor, rhinoceroses were often pitted against each other or against other animals in battles to the death.

Pliny the Elder claimed that the rhinoceros and the elephant despised each other, and that when they met they naturally fought to the death. Not everyone agreed. Some writers maintained that the rhino was not always the victor; others, that the two animals were not even enemies. Pliny claimed that "when the Beast comes near the Elephant to fight with him, he always first whets his Horn upon the Stones." Toward the end of the fifteenth century, after Portugal had conquered much of India, an Indian prince gave a rhinoceros to the Portugese governor of his region. The governor passed the beast on to his country's ruler, King Manuel I. Manuel thought it would be a pleasant diversion to test Pliny's claims about the animosity between the elephant and the rhinocerous. On June 3, 1515, he pitted one against the other. Topsell commented on the outcome: "It is confidently affirmed that when the Rhinocerot which was at Lisborne was brought in the presence of an Elephant, the Elephant ran away from him." As a seventeenth-century translation of a poem by Guillaume du Bartas said of the elephant,

> But his huge strenth nor subtil witt can not
> Defend him from the sly Rhinocerot.

This notion of animosity between the first and second wonders of the world slowly faded. Sixteenth- and seventeenth-century painters portrayed the rhinoceros and elephant sauntering up the gangplank of Noah's Ark with no sign of squabbling. In an illustration for his 1675 *Arca Noe,* the German Jesuit Athanasius Kirchner depicted them comfortably ensconced in adjacent cabins.

The aspect of the rhinoceros that most caught the attention of Marco Polo was its single horn. (There are actually two kinds of rhinoceroses, one with a single horn and one with two.) He wrote that unicorns were common animals in Sumatra, which he called Java the Less. "The head resembles that of a wild boar, and they carry it ever bent towards the ground. They delight much to abide in mire and mud. 'Tis a passing ugly beast to look upon, and is not in the least like that which our stories tell us as being caught in the lap of a virgin." It is the rhino's fearsome weapon that has placed it on the endangered list. The magical-minded have attributed formidable healing and aphrodisiac powers to almost all animal horns, from the rhino to the narwhale, another creature killed so that its horn could be passed off as an alicorn (a unicorn's horn). The greedy have always been willing to prey upon the gullible, and the result has been the loss of countless thousands of rhinoceroses around the world. However, at least they are no longer pitted against each other for the amusement of the bloodthirsty.

See also Dürer's rhino, 5/20.

---

4 JUNE 1940

Lassie

On June 4, 1940, an aristocratic collie in a Hollywood kennel gave birth to a litter of pups. The line was carefully bred, back to Old Cockie, England's first great collie. When one pup was found to have

Lassie Jr., son of the first Lassie, with one of his television costars, Jon Provost as Timmy. Courtesy of Ronald V. Borst / Hollywood Movie Posters

large eyes and the disfiguring white blaze that breeders were trying to eliminate, he was considered pet quality and sold without being registered.

One day a trainer was asked to teach the eight-month-old pup, now named Pal, to stop barking and chasing motorcycles. Rudd Weatherwax had trained Asta for the *Thin Man* movies and Daisy for the *Blondie* series, but he couldn't make a living solely in film. He trained countless dogs, always watching for the next Rin Tin Tin or Strongheart. With all the gentleness and positive reinforcement for which he was known, Weatherwax couldn't halt Pal's motorcycle chasing, but he stopped the barking. The dog was bright and friendly. Weatherwax received him in payment for a debt, but because there was no interest in collies in Hollywood, he sent Pal on extended loan to a friend's ranch.

Meanwhile, there in Los Angeles, novelist and playwright Eric Knight wrote a book inspired by his own beloved collie, Toots, a famously gifted dog who understood numerous hand signals. When Knight returned to his native England to report on depressed areas for the *Saturday Evening Post,* he witnessed poverty-stricken Yorkshire families being forced to sell their prized collies. That became the kernel of a 1938 *Post* story, which he expanded into the novel *Lassie Come-Home.* When Weatherwax learned that MGM intended to film the book, he spent ten dollars overcoming his friend's newfound affection for Pal. MGM rejected Pal in favor of a beautiful award-winning bitch, but they hired Weatherwax as trainer and Pal as stunt dog.

Louis Mayer slated *Lassie* as a grade B black-and-white featuring two unknown children, Roddy McDowall and Elizabeth Taylor. Necessarily budget-minded, the director capitalized on a flood by rushing dogs and crew to the scene. "Lassie jumps in the river," the script read, "swims across the stream, and comes out exhausted." The star wouldn't enter the water, so Weatherwax persuaded the director to try the stunt dog. Pal didn't hesitate. He swam the torrent and climbed out and lay still. Only when Weatherwax signaled did he stand and shake off the water. The crew had used the only film handy: color. Mayer was so impressed he promoted *Lassie* to the A list. The man who had discovered Garbo and Valentino knew a star when he saw one.

Asta, Daisy, and Rin Tin Tin attended the premiere to salute their colleague. *Lassie Come Home* (MGM dropped the hyphen) was one of the most popular films of 1943. A reviewer called the male dog "Greer Garson in furs." Lassie's autograph was so in demand that rubber stamps were made from a plaster cast of Pal's paw for signing publicity photographs. Soon breeders began restoring the white blaze to collies' faces.

See also Asta, 7/3.

"Eighteen Hundred and Froze to Death"

The year 1816 began in New England with no hint of the cold to come. January's temperatures were not abnormally low, and February was actually warmer than usual. March went by without a hint of trouble. April, however, was 3° colder than what records had established as "normal." May continued the trend, with a mean temperature of under 53°F. Finally, by noon on the fifth of June, the temperature had risen to a respectable 83°F, and there was talk that the long weird spring was over.

Then, within hours, the temperature plummeted 40°. The next day snow fell, and the high was in the mid-40s. Over the next few weeks, as summer refused to arrive, the weather killed early crops, migrating birds, and even shorn sheep. All over New England, snow was falling. In late August, the temperature was in the 30s. When winter arrived, it was as if it had never left.

That winter finally gave way to the perfectly normal spring of 1817. Soon 1816 acquired the nickname "the year without a summer," and eventually old-timers referred to it as "Eighteen Hundred and Froze to Death." The first periodical to regularly furnish meteorological data in the United States, the *North American Review,* predicted that "The very singular seasons of 1816 will long be remembered."

The scientific-minded speculated that the Ice Age had returned; the religious worried that God was punishing America. New churches sprang up. "The alarm and depression so wrought upon the feelings of the community," a New York historian wrote, "that a religious revival ensued." So did a mass exodus. That year, Indiana alone recorded 42,000 new settlers, and the following year marks the beginning of the first major migration to the Middle West from New England.

At the time many natural philosophers blamed the cold summer on sunspot activity. It is true that in May and June sunspots were so conspicuous that they could be seen through smoked glass without a telescope. However, nowadays meteorologists attribute the unseasonable weather to several volcanic eruptions that occured prior to that eerie season. Soufrière, a volcano on the island of St. Vincent in the West Indies, erupted in 1812. Mayon, in the Philippines, followed two years later. And in 1815, only the year before the unsummery summer, the Indonesian island of Sumbawa was devastated when Tambora blew its top.

Volcanoes' effect on the weather isn't theoretical; it has been observed as recently as the eruptions of Mount St. Helens in 1980 and Pinatubo in 1991. It isn't the gritty volcanic ash that irritated eyes after Mount St. Helens that affects long-term weather. Precipitation quickly washes that to the earth. It is the sulfur dixoide gas ejected into the upper atmosphere. After El Chichón erupted in Mexico in 1982, clouds of sulfuric acid were shot all the way to the stratosphere and blocked as much as 5 percent of the sunlight reaching the earth. The year before the cold summer of 1816, Tambora alone, in the most powerful eruption in historical times, threw an estimated 50–100 cubic miles of material into the air, producing hazy red sunsets for months.

Naturally, the effects of such widespread volcanic dust and gases were not limited to North America. An English newspaper predicted, "It will ever be remembered by the present generation that the year 1816 was a year in which there was no summer." Elsewhere in Europe, weather was steadily gloomy and rainy. On the shore of Lake Geneva in Switzerland, in June of 1816, foul weather trapped four travelers from England—Mary Shelley; her husband, Percy Bysshe Shelley; Lord Byron; and Byron's physician and hanger-on, John Polidori. "Incessant rain," Mary Shelley wrote, "often confined us to the house for days." Finally, bored, they agreed to each try to write a ghost story. Two years later, Mary Shelley published hers. *Frankenstein* is yet another legacy of the year that had no summer.

---

6 JUNE 1841

The Soundless Moonlight

Long before its light was acclaimed by poets, the Moon was simply a handy form of illumination. Although the timing of Easter at the vernal equinox was designed to replace pagan spring festivals, its scheduling on the first Sunday after the full moon was intended to illuminate the nighttime pilgrimages of the faithful. The Lunar Society, that loose affiliation of eighteenth-century intellectuals that included Joseph Priestley and Erasmus Darwin, was so named because the monthly meetings were scheduled to provide illumination for late-goers, especially if they were tipsy.

In *A Midsummer Night's Dream,* when the bumpkin thespians are rehearsing "The most Lamentable Comedy, and most Cruel Death of Pyramus and Thisby," they run up against a problem. The question, director Quince points out, is how "to bring the moonlight into a chamber: for, you know, Pyramus and Thisby meet by moonlight." Snout asks, "Doth the moon shine that night we play our play?" The ever helpful Bottom cries, "A calendar, a calendar! Look in the almanac. Find out moonshine, find out moonshine." Elsewhere, as Bottom massacres the role of Pyramus, he utters a memorable description of the night without moonlight: "O grim-look'd night! O night with hue so black! O night, which ever art when day is not! O night, O night! alack, alack, alack." (Corin in *As You Like It* has a grasp of astronomy fully equal to Bottom's. "A great cause of the night," the old shepherd confides, "is lack of the sun.")

However, although the Moon may have illuminated the paths of pilgrims, lunatics, and Charles Darwin's grandfather, it is the grandeur of its light that we remember, not the wattage. Moonlight has inspired some diverse comparisons. In the *Aeneid,* as he recounts for Dido the role of the hollow horse ("pregnant with enemies") in the fall of Troy, Aeneas describes the Achaean soldiers approaching the city in "the friendly silence of the soundless moonlight." Nineteen centuries later, Nathaniel Hawthorne compared moonlight to the nocturnal serenade of crickets. Another century and more would pass before the American naturalist Edwin Way Teale would list what he most wanted to experience in nature during his last day on Earth. He, too, mentioned crickets, along with other sights and sounds, "but more than any of them the moon and the light of the moon—shining on breaking waves along the shore, extending a path across a forest lake, glittering on crystalline fields of winter snow—the moon bringing to the world and the nighttime the never-ending wonder and magic of its light."

In "the friendly silence of the soundless moonlight," Trojan soldiers learn the hard way to beware of Greeks bearing gifts.

It is hard to imagine how moonlight could be regarded in a negative sense, except perhaps by burglars, but Alfred, Lord Tennyson managed it. In one of its stranger cameos, moonlight exemplifies the smug sexism of the Victorian era. The lines appear in "Locksley Hall."

> *Woman is the lesser man, and all thy passions match'd with mine,*
> *Are as moonlight unto sunlight, and as water unto wine.*

Tennyson was not only in tune with his times, but with celestial similes throughout history. Many cultures have considered the Moon female. The notion survives in literature, from Titania's description of the Moon as "the governess of floods" (Shakespeare alone could have kept the Moon gainfully employed as poetic imagery) to Christina Rosetti's famous poem, in which she asked, "Is the moon tired? / She looks so pale. . . ."

Ralph Waldo Emerson used the feminine pronoun when he referred to the Moon. On June 6, 1841, he remarked to his journal that he sometimes tired of his house and neighborhood because of their shortcomings. However, when he saw them by moonlight he changed his mind. "This very street of hucksters and taverns the moon will transform to a Palmyra, for she is the apologist of all apologists, and will kiss the elm trees alone and hides every meanness in a silver-edged darkness." In his essay "History," Emerson expressed the effect of moonlight even more forcefully: "The man who has seen the rising moon break out of the clouds at midnight has been present like an archangel at the creation of light and of the world."

See also Moon landing, 7/20; the far side of the Moon, 10/7; and fictional trips to the Moon, 10/14.

La Cucaracha

The war-weary doctors on *M*A*S*H* raced them. Dracula's pal Renfield munched them. From their Spanish name, *la cucaracha,* derives the English word for an animal despised by most other human beings—"cockroach." Appropriately, these insects have a family name un-euphonious enough to have been coined by Dickens: Blattidae. It claims (reluctantly, one imagines) more than 3,000 species. Cockroaches share the order Orthoptera with crickets, grasshoppers, mantids, and those Wonderland insects called walking sticks. The order's name means "straight wing" and comes from the way they fold them. With impressive style, their hard outer wings protect membranous hind wings; however, most species seldom if ever fly.

The flat, hard body, with its bullet-shaped head, seems created by the Pentagon on the most advanced principles of evasive technology. It is a functional, no-frills design that has proven splendidly adaptable and has therefore required few modifications over the aeons. That is one secret of cockroaches' survival. Another is the variety in their diet. Orthoptera, unlike some other orders of insects, have mouthparts that can chew. (Mayflies, in contrast, have useless vestigial mouths. Flies suck.) Because their mouthparts are unspecialized, cockroaches can ingest food whether it is soft, hard, or liquid. They seem willing to try out their versatile equipment on anything even vaguely edible. Archy, the cockroach who lives in the office of Don Marquis in the "Archy and Mehitabel" poems, complains that the paste is so stale he can hardly eat it. But he keeps trying.

Archy admits that some of his kind lead less-than-noble lives, but he asks if every man's hand must be against them. Apparently it must. Surely there is no insect more universally reviled than the cockroach. American naturalist Sue Hubbell quoted a college professor who confessed his irrational fear of them: "I see one in the kitchen and I am terrified, paralyzed, unable to speak or move. . . . Kill one? That would be impossible. It is, psychically, too big to kill." Even those who do not fear roaches find them difficult to kill. Because they will eat anything, happily live caged, and reproduce quickly, they are ideal test subjects in laboratories. They have suffered through experiments on insecticides, parasites, and hormones. But most famously they have been subjected to nuclear-war levels of radiation, with results that are sobering for their fellow tenants on this endangered ball of rock we both call home. Long, long after dogs and cattle and sheep and human beings succumb to radiation, cockroaches keep scurrying and chewing. The Blattidae may inherit the earth.

In recent years, the cockroach has received a lot of publicity for its survival virtues. On June 7, 1981, some U.S. newspapers ran a United Press International story about a group of people who had formed an organization called Metamorphosis. As their "alternative to the survivalists," the group proposed to inoculate themselves against Armageddon with daily cockroach-hormone pills. The leader pointed out that "the roach is the only species to survive every environmental change over a period of 350 million years, and it can survive 500 times the amount of radiation as man."

Of course this was all a hoax, and in his enthusiasm the gentleman exaggerated. Cockroaches are thought to date back about 250 million years. That still makes them the oldest living species of insect.

They were present in the jungles of the Carboniferous Period, before dinosaurs and *long* before humans. When the nonavian dinosaurs and many other creatures became extinct at the end of the Cretaceous, 65 million years ago, cockroaches seem to have gone on chewing as if nothing had happened. They respond stoically to everything except unequivocal squashing.

See also Kafka's vermin, 11/17.

Guest Stars

Ancient sky-watchers quickly noted any newcomer among the familiar constellations. Roman astronomers called such an upstart a *nova stella,* Latin for "new star." Nowadays, "nova" is the astronomical term for a star that has exploded and become many times brighter, frequently becoming visible where no star could be seen before at all. Early Chinese astronomers called them "guest stars." These are not as rare as one might imagine. The universe is a violent place, and every few years a nova appears that is bright enough to be seen with the naked eye.

Novas aren't really new, because we see stars as they were long ago. The night sky is a time machine. Every time we look at it we are seeing into the distant past. Light from the nearest star system takes almost 4 years to reach our eyes on Earth. In other words, if that star explodes today, we won't know it for another 4 years. Even light from our own star, traveling across 93 million miles of space at 186,000-plus miles per second, takes 8½ minutes to reach us. For that reason, the human life span precludes travel to even the nearer stars. At the fastest speed yet accomplished by an Earth-launched spacecraft, it would take us 40,000 years to reach even the nearest star.

The largest novas, giant new stars whose death throes outshine most other stars and sometimes even become visible during the daytime, are called supernovas. Approximately 30,000 years ago, there was a most impressive supernova in the night skies, probably striking fear into the hearts of Neolithic humans. A number of supernovas have been observed in historic times. One appeared in the constellation Taurus in 1054 and became what we now call the Crab Nebula. No European astronomers mentioned it, not that astronomy was a flourishing discipline in Europe during the Middle Ages. However, Muslim and Chinese observers recorded it, and a diagrammatic Anasazi painting may represent it. Cassiopeia was the scene of a supernova observed by the Danish astronomer Tycho Brahe in 1572. The next came shortly afterward, in 1604, observed by Brahe's German assistant Johannes Kepler.

The brightest "new" star since Kepler's appeared on June 8, 1918, in the constellation Aquila, the Eagle. The constellation lies against the backdrop of our own galaxy, the Milky Way, where, because of the concentration of stars, the sheer numbers make novas more likely. This supernova was 1,200 light-years away, which means that observers were seeing it as it was about the time that Suleiman ruled the Ottoman Empire.

The British science fiction writer Arthur C. Clarke wrote about a supernova in his story "The Star," which won a 1956 Hugo (science fiction's Oscar). The narrator is chief astrophysicist aboard a space mission to explore the neighborhood of a supernova. He learns upon arrival that the star had planets. On one of them a civilization, recognizing the warning signs that their sun was unstable, left a record of its last days. From there the story proceeds to its famous surprise ending, but the finding of the scorched planet is shocking enough. As recent discoveries have proven, other stars besides our own have planets. If one of the stars that exploded and became a nova in our night sky had planets circling it, populated with sentient beings that watched their sun and waited for the end, we would never know it.

---

9 JUNE 1892

One Hundred Aspects of the Moon

The Japanese term *ukiyo-e* means "pictures of the floating world." It was a flourishing genre of art during much of the time of the Tokugawa shogunate, which ruled Japan from the early seventeenth century to 1867, when the Meiji Restoration began. The term came from the first subjects of these realistic, decorative screen paintings—the Kabuki actors and courtesans of Edo's entertainment district. The *ukiyo-e* masters introduced the mass production possibilities of woodblock printing just in time to depict the changing interests of urban sophisticates.

Probably the best known *ukiyo-e* painters in the West are Hokusai and Hiroshige, both of whom flourished in the first half of the nineteenth century. One of their most distinguished successors, Yonejiro Yoshitoshi, was born in 1839 and died on June 9, 1892. When he joined the long tradition of *ukiyo-e,* with the publication of his first work at the age of fourteen, no one could have known that he was the artist who would bring a new realism, energy, and emotion to a relatively static and decorative genre.

The middle of the nineteenth century was a period of great unrest in Japan. In 1854, Admiral Perry forced the country to open its ports to the West or suffer the wrath of U.S. imperialism. In doing so he also helped reveal the decadent and crumbling structure of the shogunate. Yoshitoshi's notebooks from this violent time are filled with bloody themes. He published groups of prints entitled *Twenty-eight Murders with Verses* and *Yoshitoshi's One Hundred Warriors.* (Such series were common. Hiroshige's well-known works include *Sixty-nine Stations of the Kiso Highway.*) One picture featured, for example, a warrior holding a bloody, decapitated head impaled on his sword. Although Yoshitoshi has become famous for such horror, much of his work is free of it.

For a while, Yoshitoshi signed his name "Tsukioka Yoshitoshi." *Tsuki* is a Japanese word for "moon." That celestial body is the unifying symbol in one of Yoshitoshi's most interesting series of prints, *One Hundred Aspects of the Moon.* There, in picture after picture accompanied by verses, Yoshitoshi demonstrated his mastery of technique and variety of invention. The pictures differ widely in subject matter, from the thoughtful scene of a woman on the dock at Kyoto, dipping her foot in moon-dappled water, to a tableau of the Japanese hero Benkai in the prow of a boat, with the moon appearing from behind the crest of a wave. The moon does indeed exhibit a hundred aspects. It appears gibbous, crescent, waning, waxing. Plum blossoms are silhouetted against it, and slatted blinds and shorebirds. Its distant, celestial presence strangely unifies a wonderful cross section of Japanese society.

As in the real world, not all is happy under Yoshitoshi's moon. It appears high in the sky beyond the flames of a burning house. (The burning of the paper-walled houses was so common that the fires were called the "Flowers of Edo.") A soldier is about to commit *seppuku,* ritual suicide, unaware of the moonlight across the floor. An assassin approaches a man indoors, while the moon watches from behind the window. A soldier blows a huge conch-shell trumpet to sound attack.

Numerous historical and legendary figures appear in the series. One is Murasaki Shikibu, the "Lady Murasaki" who wrote *The Tale of Genji,* which is considered the first novel. According to one story, she retired to a temple overlooking a lake to write. In Yoshitoshi's picture, she is gazing at the moonlit mountains. The 100th picture beautifully wraps up the series with the appearance of the beloved haiku master Matsuo Basho, who leans on a staff and talks with two men who are celebrating the autumn festival. Scenes from Japanese folklore include a wrestling match between a rabbit and a monkey, and one of the magical foxes thought to lurk in the Musashi Plain near Tokyo. Perhaps most haunting of all is the sight of the legendary musician Toyohara Sumiaki, who, attacked by wolves and thinking he is about to die, begins to play his flute. His music charms the animals.

In some prints, the moon isn't visible, but Yoshitoshi cleverly evokes its presence. A Confucian acolyte reads by moonlight. A general wears the crescent "three-day moon" on his headgear. And, in one memorable and humorous scene, Hotei, the hairy-bellied god of luck and happiness, points at the sky in a reminder of an old adage that could be Yoshitoshi's motto for the whole series: "The wise man looks not at the finger, but at the moon to which it points."

---

10 JUNE 1818

"Thy Laurel"

Ovid tells the story in his *Metamorphoses.* Diabolically mischievous, Cupid shoots Apollo with a gold-tipped arrow that makes him love the beautiful Daphne. Then, in a gesture worthy of a Shakespeare comedy or a thirties Hollywood farce, he shoots Daphne with a lead-tipped arrow that makes her flee love. The outcome, like that of most myths, is tragic. Apollo unrelentingly pursues his quarry, and just as he is about to catch her, she prays for ugliness. Gradually her skin turns into bark, her arms become branches, her hair turns into leaves, and her feet take root in the ground.

Apparently with no remorse for driving her to this extreme, Apollo declares that the tree she became, the laurel, henceforth will be sacred to him. As a consequence, the priestesses at Delphi, the oracle dedicated to Apollo, chewed laurel's mildly narcotic leaves to induce visions. Nowadays we use laurel leaves as an herb in cooking; *Laurus nobilis* is also the sweet bay tree, which provides bay leaves. The Romans, too, revered laurel. Their city of Laurentium was named for its laurel groves, and its alleged purer air drew Nero there during outbreaks of pestilence. Thunderstorms terrified an earlier emperor, Tiberius. He wore a laurel crown for insurance but still hid under his bed. In time, a wreath of laurel became the award for excellence in everything from athletics to sculpture. Even now a poet's highest honor is "laureate."

When English poet John Keats published his first book of poems in the spring of 1817, he presented a copy to essayist and fellow poet Leigh Hunt, who predicted that the future would see a flow-

In this scene, worthy of Magritte but actually painted in the nineteenth century by George von Hoesslin, Fame crowns the artist who created her. Naturally, she uses the sacred laurel.

ering laurel on Keats's brow. Soon afterward, Hunt fulfilled his own prophecy. During dinner one evening, perhaps inspired by the wine they were drinking, Hunt suggested they crown themselves like Greek poets and write sonnets about the occasion. Keats was willing; surely no poet ever dreamed of greatness more than he. He may have remembered his youthful poem, "To a Young Lady Who Sent Me a Laurel Crown."

Hunt gave Keats a wreath of laurel, and Keats gave him one of ivy, another revered plant. Then, crowned, watching his companion scribble away, Keats could think of nothing to say during the time allotted. Finally, he wrote a lame poem about his inability to think of anything to write. When a servant entered to announce callers, Hunt whipped off his crown, but Keats, without explanation, calmly wore his laurels through the entire visit. As soon as the guests left, he wrote another sonnet, "To the Ladies Who Saw Me Crown'd."

Periodically, his impetuosity led Keats to declare that regret and embarrassment must be our punishments in hell. Over a year later, on June 10, 1818, he was still ashamed of the laurel incident, and alluded to it in a letter. But his most abject apology to the gods came in his "Ode to Apollo," in which he spoke of wearing "like a blank idiot . . . thy laurel."

See also Keats's nightingale, 5/12.

---

11 JUNE 1993

Jurassic Park

Dinosaurs have captured our imagination since their first discovered bones seemed to prove the biblical claim, "There were giants in the earth in those days." By the early twentieth century they were starring in books by Arthur Conan Doyle and Edgar Rice Burroughs. Godzilla was a dinosaur (albeit one with radioactive flamethrower breath), rudely awakened from its long sleep by an atomic blast. Such long-surviving dinosaurs have been proposed as the identity of both the Loch Ness monster and her Congo cousin, Mokele-Mbembe.

The improbable rise of extinct reptiles to celebrity status culminated on June 11, 1993, with the premiere of Steven Spielberg's adaptation of Michael Crichton's science fiction thriller *Jurassic Park*. Despite boasting a budget that made dinosaur researchers swoon with envy, the movie used only a few snippets of real science. "What I was after," Spielberg said, "was kind of like *Nova* meets *Explorer*, with a little bit of *Raiders of the Lost Ark* and *Jaws* mixed in." What he got was much more like the logical free-for-all of his own earlier films than like a scientific program. This loose approach is evident in Crichton's title. The stars hail mostly from the Cretaceous Period (65 million–145 million years ago) rather than the preceding Jurassic.

On a secluded island reminiscent of Kong's, a dotty old billionaire has built the ultimate theme park: a zoo featuring genetically engineered dinosaurs. The great beasts are resurrected by cloning. Technicians extract blood from the innards of mosquitos found encased in amber. In Ovid's story of Phaethon, amber is described as the tears of women turned into trees. In reality, it does indeed seep from plants, to harden as a translucent yellow-brown substance sometimes considered a semiprecious stone. Scientists have found many insects fossilized in amber, encased for the millions of years since they touched the sap.

The first assumption behind *Jurassic Park* is that on occasion, when a mosquito was trapped in amber shortly after imbibing blood, its victim's DNA was preserved in the insect's abdomen. This isn't merely plausible; it has happened. Scientists have extracted DNA from a bee that had been locked in amber for 40 million years. However, genetic material decays over time. None of the DNA found in amber, or in fossils, has amounted to more than 200 or 300 base pairs of genes. Unfortunately, a single dinosaur genome (the full set of chromosomes one parent could contribute) probably contained billions. These are not small holes that easily can be filled. It's like trying to rebuild a house with a few surviving bricks. In the film, missing DNA is supplied by frogs. Unfortunately, frogs are amphibians and dinosaurs were reptiles. Their ancestry, and thus their genetic makeup, diverged in the Carboniferous Period, over 100 million years before there were any dinosaurs.

It is axiomatic that horrific art derives its power from unleashed repressions, the resurrection of what should have stayed buried. Science fiction often spins cautionary fables about forbidden knowledge. This film just does so with a thin veneer of misrepresented chaos theory. For all its *Frankenstein* moralizing, *Jurassic Park* remains simply a monster movie dramatizing Lear's advice: "Come not between the dragon and his wrath." As winged serpents, dragons embodied the symbolism of both bird and snake; as avian progenitors, so do dinosaurs. Here, Saint George, played collectively by a troop of scientists, proves ineffectual against *Velociraptor*, *Dilophosaurus*, and that glamorous carnivore, *Tyrannosaurus rex*.

See also dinosaur eggs, 7/13; T. rex*, 8/12; and the perils of being a fossil, 9/3.*

Nabokov's Butterflies

Vladimir Nabokov had two professions. His eminence as a man of letters eclipses his credentials in another field—lepidoptery. He wrote not only novels, but numerous scientific papers. He was not only Professor of Slavic Languages at Cornell, but also Research Fellow in Entomology at Harvard's Museum of Comparative Zoology. "The pleasures and rewards of literary inspiration," Nabokov told an interviewer, "are nothing beside the rapture of discovering a new organ under the microscope or an undescribed species on a mountainside in Iran or Peru." His own account of his lifelong fascination appeared in the June 12, 1948, issue of the *New Yorker* and wound up a chapter in his autobiography, *Speak, Memory.*

Although spending hours daily peering through a microscope permanently damaged his eyes, Nabokov later described the Harvard years as "the most delightful and thrilling" of his adult life. At least one moth and several butterflies bear his name, and he revised the classifications of other species. "I discovered in nature," he wrote, "the non-utilitarian delights that I sought in art. Both were a form of magic, both were a game of intricate enchantment and deception."

Butterflies flit through most of Nabokov's work. Some of his early stories feature lepidopterists as protagonists. He used butterflies' names for his characters; "*Callophrys avis* Chapman" (the discoverer's name) became "Avis Chapman." He even described a bow tie as having "a crippled hind-wing." As a result, critics quibble over whether the white moths that drift into the headlights of Humbert Humbert's car in *Lolita* are spirits of the dead or symbols of deceased love. Impatient with such dissection, Nabokov would be amused to know that there is now an entire book on the lepidoptera in his fiction.

Nabokov pursued butterflies from St. Petersburg to Paris and from Telluride to Gatlinburg. For his projected study of the butterfly in art, he followed them through the museums of Europe, catching them in paintings by Bosch, Dürer, Breughel. He was interested not in butterfly symbolism, but in painters' precise delineation of known species. Were some less common then than now? Can a 500-year-old painted wing exhibit "the minutiae of evolutionary change"? The species he found in paintings more than any other was the red admiral, a favorite of his own that appears in more than one of his novels. Because many of them migrated from Africa to northern Russia the year Czar Alexander was assassinated, and marks on the underside of the hind wings seem to read "1881," Russians once called that particular species the "Butterfly of Doom." Nabokov also mentions in his autobiography a red admiral he saw in a Paris park, magically captive on a little girl's leash of thread.

Nabokov's entomological interests extended beyond butterflies. In one of his Cornell lectures, he demonstrated—with diagrams, no less—that the insect Gregor Samsa becomes in Kafka's *Metamorphosis* could not possibly have been a cockroach. ("Caress the details, the divine details!" he advised his literature students.) For him, C. P. Snow's two cultures of the sciences and the humanities were one. "There is no science without fancy," he said in his epigrammatical way, "and no art without facts."

See also Virginia Woolf and lepidoptera, 3/28.

---

13 JUNE 1991

"The Peculiar Haze"

In one of his letters in *The Natural History of Selborne,* English parson and naturalist Gilbert White described some alarming phenomena that he witnessed in 1783. He noted especially that the peculiar haze, or smokey fog, that prevailed for many weeks in the island, and in every part of Europe, and even beyond its limits, was a most extraordinary appearance, unlike anything known within the memory of man. . . . The sun at noon, looked as blank as a clouded moon, and shed a rust-colored ferruginous light on the ground, and floors of rooms; but was particularly lurid and blood-coloured at rising and setting. . . . The country people began to look with a superstitious awe at the red, louring aspect of the sun; and indeed there was reason for the most enlightened person to be apprehensive.

Benjamin Franklin, one of the first people to blame atmospheric effects on volcanic activity, was in Paris at the time, and he noted the strange fog in his diary. Meanwhile, White reported other disturbing phenomena, including earthquakes in Sicily and "a volcano sprung out of the sea on the coast of Norway." He was referring to the eruption of Laki, in Iceland. White's letter doesn't indicate whether he considered these various phenomena interrelated. However, the eruption in Iceland in 1783 not only caused the famous European fogs, but in its own region emitted poisonous gases that contaminated pastures and killed 75 percent of the country's livestock. The volcano is blamed for the resulting famine, which killed more than 9,000 people. Before its eight-month eruption was over, Laki rained an estimated 100 million tons of sulfuric acid back to earth.

However, Laki doesn't win the award for meanest volcano. The largest such eruption in historic times occurred in April of 1815. Tambora, a volcano on the island of Sumbawa in Indonesia, sent a column of ash and smoke and pumice 24 miles high into the atmosphere. The explosion was heard in Java, 300 miles away. For two days both Sumbawa and the nearby island of Lombok were engulfed in darkness, as 20 inches of pumice and ash fell, killing 10,000 people and burying crops and even trees. From the volcano's loss of more than 3,000 feet in height, geologists have calculated that Tambora cast at least 40 km^3 of fragments into the air. Heavier materials buried the ground or clogged the nearby sea for weeks. For years to come, the finer particles floated in the atmosphere, and the consequences were seen all over the world. The English landscape painter J. M. W. Turner was inspired by the sunsets that resulted. Of greater significance was the occurrence the next year of the coldest summer on record in Europe. In fact, 1816 is referred to as "the year without a summer."

In 1980, when Mount St. Helens erupted in Oregon, the American writer Ursula K. Le Guin had a ringside view from her home forty-five miles away. She documented the eruption's progress in her diary. "All morning there has been this long, cobalt-bluish drift to the east where the summit would be. . . . It is *enormous*. . . . It is so much bigger than the mountain itself." Although Mount St. Helens was a bantamweight in the volcano league, Le Guin was witnessing the first phase of what would nonetheless become widespread atmospheric aftereffects.

Obviously, this danger is still with us. In April of 1991, Mount Pinatubo in the Philippines began to experience minor eruptions. Because Pinatubo had been asleep at least since the Spaniards invaded the Philippines in 1541, everyone was understandably caught off guard. So peaceful did the mountain seem that the United States had built Clark Air Force Base at Pinatubo's feet, and Subic Naval Bay nearby. Minor eruptions and earthquakes followed over the next couple of months. On June 13, there was a lull. Then, as if the mountain had rested and gathered strength, Pinatubo began its full eruption. Typhoon Yunya arrived to help spread the ash farther about.

Pinatubo cast so much dust into the atmosphere that it endangered air travel. At high altitudes, volcanic dust clouds closely resemble normal water-vapor clouds, and over a dozen airliners suffered engine damage from flying through them. Nine were forced into emergency landings. Pinatubo cast into the upper atmosphere somewhere between 10 and 20 million tons of that toxic substance, and by the end of the year satellite mapping revealed that the cloud of it covered the entire planet. However, it is worth noting that even that total equals less than 25 percent of the toxic chemicals still produced annually by industries.

See also the year without a summer, 6/5.

---

14 JUNE 1494

Animals in Court

By comparison with some actual legal cases, the Knave of Hearts had a fair trial. Even Lewis Carroll's imagination can't compare with the history of the criminal prosecution of our fellow creatures. Accountability was taken to its limit. A pig was hanged for eating a consecrated wafer, a cock burned at the stake for allegedly laying an egg. Livestock, pets, even vermin, had their day in court. In the sixteenth century, an attorney made his reputation with an eloquent defense of a swarm of rats that failed to appear in court for their trial. Lest we smirk at the unenlightened past, we should remember that as recently as the 1920s, an elephant was hanged in the United States.

There is an embarrassment of precedents from around the world for such drastic measures. The Koran holds animals accountable in the next life for their misdeeds, and mad dogs are explicitly forbidden insanity pleas in the Persian Avesta. There is also a long Christian tradition; prosecutions usually came from the pulpit, and judges were usually religious officials. One council of learned divines tried and executed a hive of bees. Of course the sentence wasn't always death. Eels, moles, weevils, even dolphins, were banished or excommunicated. But those measures were found to be somewhat less effective than capital punishment.

So it is not surprising that, in France on June 14, 1494, a pig was arrested for murdering a child. There were almost as many pigs as children in urban Europe at that time. They were lucky enough to be the emblem of Saint Anthony of Padua, as a symbol of his defeat of his gluttony. Apparently children weren't the emblem of anything.

The plaintiffs were not the child's parents, but rather the monks who owned the land. Witnesses testified that, while the parents were out and their child was in its cradle, "the said pig entered during the said time the said house and disfigured and ate the face and neck of the said child, which, in consequence of the bites and defacements inflicted by the said pig, departed this life." The judge sentenced the pig, which was at that time held prisoner in the abbey, to be hanged. In a similar case in 1394, a pig's offense had been considered even worse because it ate a child "although it was Friday." And once, when a pig ate a young girl's ears, her father was legally sworn to provide a dowry so that her disfigurement might not end her chances for marriage.

During prosecution the defendants were treated as if they were human, even so far as to torture them on the rack to encourage confession. Not that the court actually expected a pig to confess, but the absolute letter of the law had to be upheld. Executions of animals were often performed in public with great solemnity. Bells were tolled and pronouncements read. More than once, human and animal were executed together if suspected of being partners in crime. The bodies of the unfortunate creatures were often displayed for some time to admonish the wicked—both human and beast.

See also an elephant hanged for murder, 9/13.

---

15 JUNE 1954

Them!

The first radioactive-mutant movie—*Them!*—premiered in New York City on the fifteenth of June, 1954. The *New York Times* admired its "unadorned and seemingly factual approach," but the leftist magazine *Twentieth Century* denounced it as allegorical propaganda promoting the extermination of Communists. Actually, with its external threat and responsible scientists advising soldiers, *Them!* isn't today considered one of the Communist paranoia films that began to appear in the fifties.

Bloodthirsty giant ants are discovered in New Mexico, only six miles from White Sands, where the first atomic bomb was tested in 1945. A father-and-daughter team of scientists arrive. When they are sure that they are dealing with giant ants, the elder Dr. Medford waxes biblical: "And there shall come a darkness upon the land. And the beasts shall reign over the earth."

Our heroes find a nest and note the characteristic colony odor. Scent is the primary medium of communication among ants, for everything from locating the nest to identifying strangers. These instructive scents, pheromones, are chemical messengers between organisms of the same species; hormones are chemical messengers inside the body of an organism.

Before the ants' nest is wiped out, empty eggs are found; a queen has escaped to reproduce elsewhere. A train is attacked, and a freighter at sea. The ants are multiplying. Medford explains their behavior with that favorite gimmick of science fiction movies, a film within the film, which was used effectively as recently as *Jurassic Park.* Through close-up footage, he demonstrates ants' herculean strength; their social organization, which is so cooperative that a colony is sometimes considered a "superorganism"; and the industry Solomon admired when he advised sluggards to emulate ants. Understandably, he omits the impossibility of their attaining such giant size.

Director Gordon Douglas built only two movable ant models for Them!*—and one of those consisted of merely the head and front legs. Wind machines waved the antennae of otherwise inanimate models.* Courtesy of Ronald V. Borst / Hollywood Movie Posters

Medford also emphasizes that ants are the only creatures other than humans known to make war. That reputation is preserved in the name of his own profession, which FBI agent James Arness stumbles over: "myrmecologist." Ants, and the study of them, are named for the Myrmidons, those unquestioning and ferocious Thessalian warriors who fought under Achilles in the Trojan War. Actually, ants are even more bellicose than humans. Several species devote themselves to imperialism and genocide. Had ants developed the atomic bomb rather than merely suffering its aftereffects, they would have destroyed the world by 1954.

For several reasons, mutant giantism in ants would be catastrophic. Estimates of ants' combined mass equal that of all humans; in the Amazon rain forests, they outweigh all land vertebrates combined. Many species are ferocious. In pre-Columbian Mexico, captives were tortured by tying them over the mounds of harvester ants. Both harvesters and driver ants are famed for their biblical swarms, which eat or at least kill everything in their path.

In the world of *Them!* the giant ants are finally subdued. However, their lesson lingers. Dr. Medford ends the film with a prophetic sermonette: "When man entered the atomic age, he opened a door into a new world. What we will eventually find in that new world, nobody can predict."

For other monster movies, see 2/9, 3/3, 3/23, and 11/1.

Montezuma's Zoos

Only twenty-seven years after Cristóbal Colón (Christopher Columbus) stood on a tiny Caribbean island and presumed to claim a quarter of the world's landmass for Spain, Hernán Cortés entered the Aztec city of Tenochtitlán. He was accompanied by several hundred soldiers, a couple of hundred native Americans, and Bernal Díaz del Castillo, who chronicled the campaign. The Aztec ruler, Montezuma II, cautiously welcomed them and showed off the city from atop a temple.

The Europeans were awestruck. Never had such beauty, Díaz wrote, "been heard of or seen before, nor even dreamed about." Tenochtitlán was built upon a constructed island the size of Manhattan, in the center of a vast complex of lakes. Historians estimate its population to have been 350,000—five times that of, say, London or Seville. In Europe, roadside ditches were public latrines, and cities were full of famine and plague victims. Here, a network of aqueducts piped in spring water, and there were hundreds of street cleaners. Most Europeans of the time bathed not once in their lives; the Aztecs used soaps, deodorants, even breath sweeteners.

Everywhere nature was incorporated into the city: irrigated orchards, vegetable gardens, aromatic groves. The Aztecs hadn't been defeated by the large marshy lagoon they found when they reached the area in the mid-1300s. They cut canals through the original reed swamps and wove the remaining floating vegetation into platforms to support beds of soil from the lake floor. The resulting array of moored floating gardens, some up to 300 feet long and 15–30 feet wide, was a spectacle reminiscent of the fabled hanging gardens of Nebuchadnezzar II, in ancient Babylon.

The zoos were equally impressive. Díaz wrote of a "large house where they kept many idols whom they said were their fierce gods, and with them every kind of beast of prey. . . ." The carnivores lived in roomy cages on a diet of deer, dogs, poultry, and the occasional human. Snakes slithered in pottery jars or in troughs of muddy water. The American bison, which these Spaniards were the first Europeans to glimpse, they called "the Mexican Bull, a wonderful composition of divers Animals." In cages overhead were owls, hawks, condors. Elsewhere, herons and white egrets stood among whole spectrums of parrots; there were splendidly colored flycatchers and hummingbirds, the copper-tailed trogon, the green jay. Hundreds of attendants scurried about. After the murmur of the many voices, the most impressive sound was the singing of the countless birds.

Montezuma finally expelled the arrogant invaders, but later he unwisely allowed them to return. At a festival where the Aztecs thought the gathered Spaniards were merely admiring their musicians and dancers, the massacre began. The soldiers decapitated and disemboweled at random. They destroyed the parks, the boulevards, the gardens, and then pushed rubble into the aqueducts to halt the water supply. On the sixteenth of June, 1521, in a campaign to terrorize and demoralize the city, Cortés set fire to Montezuma's zoos and aviaries. The shrieks of thousands of dying animals joined the screaming of the people. Soon Cortés had reduced to rubble what he himself described as "the most beautiful city in the world."

The Ape Man

After serialization, *Tarzan of the Apes,* the second novel by Edgar Rice Burroughs, was published as a book on June 17, 1914. The character struck a chord. Not only were pulp fiction readers thrilled, but soon film-goers saw the first screen version of the ape man. Twenty-six of the sixty-seven Burroughs novels would star Tarzan.

For background, Burroughs recalled Henry Stanley's *In Darkest Africa* and H. Rider Haggard's stalwart adventurers. But his hero was different. "How much would heredity influence character," Burroughs asked himself, "if the infant were transplanted to an entirely different environment and raised there?" Tarzan's upbringing resembled Mowgli's, the hero of Kipling's *Jungle Book* (1894), and that of Romulus and Remus, the legendary founders of Rome who were suckled by a wolf. The son of English nobleman John Clayton, Lord Greystoke, the orphaned Tarzan was raised in the African jungle by apes. But blood will tell. From the early days, clinging to his adoptive ape-mother's breast, Tarzan exhibits "that self-confidence and resourcefulness which were the badges of his superior being."

Burroughs stacked the deck for Tarzan, giving him blue blood but allowing him to grow up wild. In the jungle, in a scenario later reversed by William Golding in *Lord of the Flies,* the aristocratic young Tarzan reverts to a natural heroic goodness. The ape man was only one quirky twentieth-century incarnation of the "noble savage"—the idea, popularized by French philosopher Jean-Jacques Rousseau, that those close to nature retained a naive purity. Ernest Thompson Seton, in his book *Two Little Savages* and in countless speeches to the recently organized Boy Scouts, exhorted youngsters to emulate the virtuous American Indians. Soon Margaret Mead would idealize the Samoans. The idea is still popular. The "gentle Tasaday" hoax of the 1960s capitalized on our yearning for lost Eden, and Dian Fossey defended her gorilla family to the death.

In this illustration from Tarzan and the Jewels of Opar, *the ape man is accompanied by two simian sidekicks, euphoniously named Chulk and Taglat.*

Tarzan also embodies humanity's growing awareness of kinship with the great apes. The topic of evolution inspires in Burroughs a vision of time and adjectives: ". . . the dim, unthinkable vistas of the long dead past when our first shaggy ancestors swung from a swaying bough and dropped lightly upon the soft turf. . . ." One character thinking about evolution reaches the curious conclusion that "man" combines "all the vices of preceding types from invertebrates to mammals, while possessing few of their virtues." A character in a later novel is half human and half ape, a genetic hybrid with the feet of a man and the hands of a gorilla. He has become half simian by using ape genes to rejuvenate himself, a method reminiscent of the mad vivisectionist's in H. G. Wells's *Island of Dr. Moreau* (1896).

When Tarzan feels disgust for his fellow humans, it is expressed in warped evolutionary terms. "Most [animals] had courage and dignity of a sort; seldom did they stoop to buffoonery, with the possible exception of the lesser monkeys, who were mostly closely allied to man. Had he been impelled to theorize he would doubtless have reversed Darwin's theory of evolution."

---

18 June 1824

The "Companionship of Trees"

Mary Wollstonecraft Godwin met Percy Bysshe Shelley when she was seventeen years old. Although he was still married, they eloped two years later. After Shelley's first wife committed suicide, Mary married him. Their first two children died young, and in 1822 Shelley himself was drowned at sea. Mary Shelley's next few years were a struggle with grief and poverty, movingly recorded in her diaries and letters.

On June 18, 1824, she wrote in her diary about a solace that was beginning to soften the grief.

> What a divine night it is! I have just returned from Kentish Town; a calm twilight pervades the clear sky; the lamp-like moon is hung out in heaven, and the bright west retains the dye of sunset. If such weather would continue, I should write again; the lamp of thought is again illumined in my heart, and the fire descends from heaven that kindles it.

She addressed much of the entry to her deceased husband.

> Nature speaks to me of you. In towns and society I do not feel your presence; but there you are with me, my own, my unalienable! I feel my powers again, and this is, of itself, happiness; the eclipse of winter is passing from my mind. I shall again feel the enthusiastic glow of composition. . . . Study and occupation will be a pleasure, and not a task, and this I shall owe to sight and companionship of trees and meadows, flowers and sunshine.

Shelley was correct. She wrote again. Two years later, she published her science fiction novel of the twenty-first century, *The Last Man.* Hers is a familiar theme. Through poetry, fiction, and essay authors have written about the renewing, healing power of the natural world. Today, as always in our history, the poetic celebrate it and the philosophical analyze it: Is the notion of a healing nature illusion, escapism, or wishful thinking? Or is it a return to a deeper reality beyond the vanity and folly of society?

Henry David Thoreau, not surprisingly, had strong opinions on the matter. In 1853, he wrote in his journal, "The invalid, brought to the brink of the grave by an unnatural life, instead of imbibing only the great influence that Nature is, drinks only the tea made of a particular herb, while he still continues his unnatural life. . . . Drink of each season's influence as a vial, a true panacea of all remedies mixed for your especial use. . . . Why, 'nature' is but another name for health, and the seasons are but different states of health."

Suffering from tuberculosis, the New Zealand writer Katherine Mansfield took refuge in a diary that, when published after her death, became something of a feminist touchstone. In January of 1922, the year before her death, she recorded one of the little haiku moments that enliven her writings. "Little round birds in the fir-tree scouring the tree for food. I crumbled a piece of bread, but though the crumbs fell in the branches only two found them. There was a strange remoteness in the air, the scene, the winter cheeping. In the evening . . . I felt rested. I sat up in bed and discovered I was singing within."

---

19 JUNE 1306

Animals to the Rescue

Sometimes the best-known stories about historical figures cannot be verified. There is no evidence, for example, for a frequently told story about the hero of Scottish independence called Robert the Bruce. (The Norman family name was actually "de Bruis.") After the murder of his primary rival, which Robert probably either ordered or carried out himself, he was crowned king of Scotland in early March of 1306. On the nineteenth of June, the English soundly defeated Robert at the Battle of Methven. That is a decisive date in Robert's history. Afterward, he escaped and took refuge on Rathlin Island, off the northern coast of Ireland, where he licked his wounds. It is there, on that desolate island, that legend provides Robert the Bruce with an instructive little moral from natural history.

One day, so the story goes, Robert observed a spider spinning a web, trying to attach a thread to a beam. It failed. Six times in a row it failed. "Hmmm," Robert supposedly mused, "I also have failed six times to rout the English from my land." Then, on its seventh attempt, the spider succeeded. Encouraged, Robert went on to a series of successful battles culminating in his famous victory at Bannockburn in 1314.

By itself, this fable of perseverance is merely pat, not preposterous. It reveals not another of those coy hints with which God is supposed to nudge his favorites, but merely Robert's own interpretation of nature. However, it remains in the "almost certainly apocryphal" category. So does a similar story of entomological stick-to-itiveness concerning the fourteenth-century Mongol warlord Timur-i-leng, "Timur the Lame," frequently called Tamerlane. Supposedly, after a defeat and ignominious flight, the depressed warrior watched an ant carrying along something larger than itself. (Has anyone studied this tendency among soldiers to turn to entomology during hard times?) In one version of the story, the ant tries sixty-nine times to climb a wall. Finally, it succeeds, and by its commitment inspires Timur to go out and conquer some more.

Other legendary animals do more than merely inspire. They assist. The eighteenth-century English naturalist Thomas Pennant recorded an old story about Timur's illustrious predecessor, Genghis Khan.

> That prince, with his small army, happened to be surprised and put to flight by his enemies, and forced to conceal himself in a little coppice: an owl settled on the bush under which he was hid and induced his pursuers not to search there, as they thought it impossible that any man could be concealed in a place where that bird would perch.

Unfortunately, often real animals suffered even when their legendary counterparts were performing a service for people, as indicated by Pennant's addendum: "To this day the Kalmucs continue the custom on all great festivals; and some tribes have an idol in the form of an owl, to which they fasten the real legs of one."

Folklore attributes many such rescues to helpful spiders. The fugitive hides in a small space and for some reason a spider ("immediately," the stories claim) gets to work spinning a web over the entrance to the hiding place. The pursuers see the web and assume that no one could have hidden there because obviously the spider has been at work for some time. This popular scenario shows up in some strange places. It is told about a man who was fleeing Iroquois attackers during the Wyoming Massacre in Pennsylvania in 1778. It is told about no less a personage than King David of Israel. It is told about Mohammed, who was supposedly rescued by a spider while fleeing the Koreishites of Mecca.

A more likely anecdote is told about a spider that, while not rescuing Frederick the Great of Prussia, nonetheless saved his life. Each morning Frederick drank a cup of chocolate. One day, he received his usual cup but went out of the room for a moment before sipping it. When he returned, he found that a spider had fallen into the cup, and naturally he rang the bell for another. At that moment a shot rang out in the kitchen. Frederick soon found that his cook had killed himself. It turned out that the king's enemies had bribed the cook to poison Frederick's chocolate, and he had done so. When he heard the bell ring, he assumed his master had discovered the treachery. As a reminder of his good fortune, Frederick had a spider painted on the ceiling of that room—a tribute to nature's (sometimes unwittingly) helpful animals. Unfortunately, there is no evidence that this story is true.

---

20 June 1975

Jaws

In 1975, at least in the United States, sharks were the most popular animals in editorial cartoons. They represented Communism, inflation, even Ronald Reagan's threat to Gerald Ford's presidential candi-

An improbably hairy shark attacking a boat off the coast of Java. Then, as now, our most difficult task was seeing nature clearly.

dacy. Their teeth appeared in jewelry and their visages on T-shirts. Ever glad to coin a word, *Time* called the phenomenon *"Jaws*mania."

Film critic Pauline Kael called Steven Spielberg's adaptation of Peter Benchley's best-seller *Jaws* "cheerfully perverse." The director himself admitted it was a "primal scream" movie: "I read [the novel] and felt I had been attacked. It terrified me and I wanted to strike back." *Jaws* premiered on June 20 and became the summer's blockbuster. The opening shot of a swimmer attacked from underwater a few yards from a beach party has been compared with Alfred Hitchcock's shower scene in *Psycho.*

The eponymous villain was played by a twenty-four-foot polyurethane monster nicknamed Bruce. The size was not unrealistic. "Great" white sharks do reach over twenty feet in length, and at least one weighed over three-and-a-half tons. They have indeed attacked boats and left teeth in the hulls. Although the two largest species of sharks live on plankton, several are not picky eaters. Besides human body parts, their stomachs have been found to contain coconuts, rubber boots, dogs—and, in the film, an automobile license plate. In 1735 the pioneer systematist Linnaeus theorized that Jonah might have spent his three edifying nights in the belly of a white shark.

Another monster shark appears in *The Natural History of Barbados* (1750), in which local rector Griffith Hughes recounts the adventures of a group of sailors bathing in the sea.* "A Person on Board 'spyed a large Shark making towards them, and gave them Notice of their Danger." All escaped save one: "him the Monster overtook almost within Reach of the Oars, and griping [*sic*] him by the Small of the Back, his devouring Jaws soon cut asunder, and as soon swallow'd the lower part of his Body." The victim's best friend leaped into the water with a knife and fought a bloody duel. Finally killing the shark, he cuts it open and "unites and buries the sever'd carcase of his Friend in one hospitable Grave."

Much closer to the film's fictional town ironically named Amity was the New Jersey coast besieged in July 1916. One or more sharks attacked for days, usually biting the legs of swimmers. At least four people died. In 1960, again in New Jersey, three attacks came close together, but the victims survived. The shark in *Jaws* killed five.

However, such occasional shark horror stories are often misleading. Bears, the only truly dangerous American carnivores, have undergone an image makeover and are now considered cuddly. Such former villains as wolves and cougars hardly even impinge upon the consciousness of urban Americans. Apparently, with little *terra* still *incognita,* for titillating thrills we turn to that home of life and myth, the sea. Since its inception in 1958, the Shark Research Panel has received reports each year of about fifty

---

* For what it's worth, Hughes insisted he had "not represented one single Fact, which I did not either see myself, or had from Persons of known Veracity."

unpleasant encounters from around the world. Few are fatal. Many scientists declare that sharks are maligned, although not all would agree with the great naturalist William Beebe, who called sharks "harmless scavengers" and "indolent, awkward, chinless cowards."

See also **Jurassic Park, 6/11.**

The Connecticut Yankee's Saving Trump

In Mark Twain's novel *A Connecticut Yankee in King Arthur's Court,* Hank Morgan—the Yankee of the title—lives in Connecticut in the year 1879. During "a misunderstanding conducted with crowbars," he suffers a ferocious blow to the head and awakens in England in the time of King Arthur. A knight captures him, takes him to Camelot, and casually condemns him to be burned alive two days later. Our hero is stripped naked and thrown in a dungeon. For Morgan that is a mere stumbling block. Not only is he the very archetype of the resourceful Yankee, but he has the good luck to be a Mark Twain character, and his creator has made him a veritable encyclopedia of useful arcana.

Twain also thoughtfully provided Morgan with one of the more outrageous coincidences in all of literature. Not only does a total solar eclipse occur at the precise time of his scheduled execution, but he remembers the details in advance and is able to predict the event. "It came into my mind, in the nick of time, how Columbus, or Cortez, or one of those people, played an eclipse as a saving trump once...." It was Columbus. He used his foreknowledge of a lunar eclipse to convince Jamaican islanders that his god was angry with them for not supplying provisions. Morgan is inspired: "I could play it myself, now; and it wouldn't be any plagiarism,

Mark Twain's resourceful Connecticut Yankee foretells the eclipse that, a moment later, will save his life.

either, because I should get it in nearly a thousand years ahead of those parties." Morgan, too, makes a dire prediction. At the hour appointed for his execution, he says, he "will smother the whole world in the dead blackness of midnight. . . ."

Morgan is betting his life on his memory. "I knew that the only total eclipse of the sun in the first half of the sixth century occurred on the 21st of June, A.D. 528, O.S. [Old Style], and began at 3 minutes after 12 noon." *Why* the Yankee knew this handy astronomical tidbit, Twain didn't tell us. Morgan is an inventor and administrator, not an astronomer. The astronomy sounds convincing, but in reality, although lunar eclipses occurred in both February and August, there was no solar eclipse visible from Britain in A.D. 528.

Not content with that, Twain doubled the coincidence. Morgan plans to use the eclipse to impress his attempted executioners with his power as a wizard, but they move his execution forward a day. Then, as the executioner is about to apply the torch, somehow the eclipse begins anyway. It turns out that, when the Yankee had asked the date two days before, his informant had been mistaken. Now certain he will triumph, Morgan points up at the sky. "The rim of black spread slowly into the sun's disk, my heart beat higher and higher, and still the assemblage and the priest stared into the sky, motionless." The priests, the king, and Merlin are all impressed. Unfortunately, although Morgan remembered the precise date and time of the eclipse, he is unable to even guess the duration of a solar eclipse, and has to bluff his way through. In the end, he doesn't become ash, as he feared for a moment, but winds up the king's right-hand man.

See also Columbus's eclipse, 2/29; and other eclipses, 2/26 and 5/28.

---

22 June 1633

"Why Stand Ye Gazing Up into Heaven?"

Nowadays the Italian physicist, astronomer, and mathematician Galileo Galilei is acclaimed as one of the greatest scientists in all of history. He was born in 1564, the year that Michelangelo died, and died in 1642, the year that Isaac Newton was born. He perfected the Dutch invention of the telescope. With it, he observed spots on the Sun, and from their movement deduced its rotation. He discovered that the Milky Way is composed of countless individual stars and that the Moon illuminates the night by reflecting sunlight. Inviting the ire of countless scholastics, Galileo invalidated Aristotle by demonstrating that falling bodies of different weight do *not* descend at different rates. He observed that the path of a projectile is a parabola and discovered the reliability of pendulums in the exact measurement of time.

But to the Catholic Church of the seventeenth century, Galileo was a heretic. Among his other sins, he openly supported the Copernican notion that Earth revolved around the Sun rather than the other way around, which was thought to be a direct contradiction of Scripture. The Inquisition interrogated him twice. On June 22, 1633, in the church of Santa Maria Sopra Minerva in Rome, Galileo knelt before a Bible to renounce his observations. The Church wasn't seeking merely Galileo's denunciation of the doctrine of the geocentric solar system; it sought a public submission to its own supreme authority. Having learned at firsthand the ferocity of the Church when its doctrines were questioned, Galileo humbled himself completely. "With sincere heart and unfeigned faith, I abjure, curse, and detest my errors. I swear that in future, I will never again say or assert, verbally or in writing, anything to encourage this suspicion." Galileo was, of course, not sincere. He chose recantation rather than torture or death.

By a striking coincidence, even Galileo's family name, Galilei, played into the hands of his enemies. In 1613, a Dominican friar tried to dispose of the heretical astronomer once and for all, with a biblical quotation so apt it seemed planted by God as a warning. It appears in the account of the Ascension, in the first chapter of the Book of Acts: "And while they looked steadfastly toward heaven as [Jesus] went up, behold, two men stood by them in white apparel; which also said, Ye men of Galilee, why stand ye gazing up into heaven?" Naturally, the friar declaimed the words in Latin, and "men of Galilee" came out *Viri Galilaei.* No doubt his audience was impressed. If God himself would ask Galileo why he gazed into heaven, mere mortals knew enough to shy away from such a dangerous man.

Any account of Galileo's recantation must include the story that, in a stage-whisper aside worthy of Hamlet, he muttered a moment later, *"Eppur si muove."* ("But it does move.") Apparently, the story is apocryphal. Galileo probably thought it. He may have said it later. But it is unlikely that he risked muttering it after abasing himself. He might as well have said it, however, because in spite of his apologies he wasn't freed. He spent the remaining years of his life under house arrest.

The Church's behavior toward Galileo became emblematic of religion's opposition to science. Three-and-a-half centuries later, in Rome, Cardinal Paul Poupard announced the findings of the Vatican's commission on the age-old problem of Galileo. He insisted that those who forced Galileo to recant were mistaken. Scripture was not meant to be a literal description of the world, and Galileo himself had actually been the "more perceptive." Then the pontiff himself, Pope John Paul II, arose and expressed regret over the "tragic mutual incomprehension" characteristic of the Church's age-old relationship with the sciences. The pope did not condemn the actions of the Inquisition.

Galileo Galilei on his deathbed. He spent the last years of his life under house arrest.

"It's Official!" the headline in the *Los Angeles Times* announced in 1992. "The Earth Revolves Around the Sun, Even for the Vatican." On the other side of the continent, the *New York Times* headline was similar: "After 350 Years, Vatican Says Galileo Was Right: It Moves." One of the few newspapers to report the event without irreverence was the Vatican's own *L'Osservatore Romano.* The headline "Galileo Case Is Resolved" appeared inside, but on the front page was a statement that seemed to contradict the whole history of Galileo's relationship with the church: "Faith Can Never Conflict with Reason."

Galileo had never been forgotten by scientists. Through his telescope, he was the first human being to observe that Jupiter had satellites, as Earth did. In 1989, NASA launched a spacecraft intended to, among other tasks, send back images of Jupiter and its moons. It was named *Galileo*.

---

23 JUNE

"There Is Enough for All"

The popular American children's author Robert Lawson began his career as an illustrator. After graduating from the New York School of Fine and Applied Art in 1914, he drew for *Harper's Weekly* and *Vogue*, painted portraits, designed bookplates. To pay off his mortgage, he produced a Christmas card design every day for three years. Animals and the outdoors played a strong role in his work from the first. Naturally, the same favorite topics emerged when Lawson began illustrating books. His best-known illustrations for a book written by someone else are his strongly brushed ink drawings for Munro Leaf's 1936 tale *Ferdinand,* about a pacifist bull that understandably doesn't want to participate in a bullfight. Lawson also illustrated the classic *Mr. Popper's Penguins.*

In 1939, Lawson published his own first children's novel, *Ben and Me.* The narrator is a mouse and tells his sly rodent's-eye view of the American Revolution. Lawson followed this with other books approaching history in the same oblique and humorous way—*I Discover Columbus,* narrated by a parrot; *Mr. Revere and I,* told by Paul Revere's horse; and *Captain Kidd's Cat.*

Other books combined Lawson's unique blend of detailed and realistic drawings with outrageous stories. In *The Fabulous Flight,* a young boy named Peter Peabody Pepperell stops growing at the age of seven and begins to shrink. He winds up only a few inches tall. Employed by the government as a spy, he travels around the world on the back of an opinionated seagull named Gus. *Mr. Twigg's Mistake* is the story of Arthur Amory Appleton and his pet mole, General de Gaulle. Too much of the "miraculous, growth-producing Vitamin X" winds up in the Bities cereal that Arthur feeds the mole, and the creature grows as large as a rabbit, then rivals a dog, and finally winds up the size of a bear.

Lawson's most loved book, *Rabbit Hill,* is very different from these outlandish adventures. A gentle, utopian story of animals and human beings living in harmony, it won the 1945 Newbery Medal. All the Animal neighborhood watches anxiously as New Folks move into the long-vacant house, only to find that, unlike other humans they have known, this family believes all creatures can live peacefully together. First the people put up a sign: "Please Drive Carefully on Account of Small Animals." Then they refuse to poison the moles. They leave a section of stone wall unmended because it houses a woodchuck. When a rabbit named Little Georgie is hit by an automobile, the New Folks take him in and nurse him back to health.

On Midsummer's Eve, June 23, the people unveil a statue for the garden. Willie, the mouse, describes it for his blind friend, the Mole: "It's him, Mole, it's *him*—the Good Saint! . . . He's all out of stone, Mole, and his face is so kind and so sad. . . . And all around his feet are the Little Animals."

Spread nearby is a feast of clover and nuts and vegetables and even a cake of salt for the deer. At the base of the statue is an inscription, which Willie reads to his friend: "There Is Enough for All."

The Beast in James Thurber

When Gertrude Stein claimed that her famous line "Pigeons on the grass alas" was "a simple description of a landscape," James Thurber explained in three pages why pigeons can no more be alas than they can be hooray. It was only one of his countless quirky observations about the natural world. His repertoire included many topics, but animals were a specialty.

A representative Thurber title is *The Beast in Me and Other Animals: A New Collection of Pieces and Drawings about Human Beings and Less Alarming Creatures.* Some of those less alarming ones appear in a section entitled "A New Natural History," in which Thurber portrayed as animals such terms as 90-Year Lease and Pet Peeve and Bare-Faced Lie. There are flowers, too—a patch of I-Told-You-So, a clump of Marry-In-Haste. "A Gallery of Real Creatures" consists of surprisingly realistic (for Thurber) portraits of exotic animals that probably appealed to him for their names as much as for their appearance, including the Spider Muck-Shrew and Bosman's Potto.

Thurber joined the ranks of Aesop and La Fontaine with his *Fables for Our Time.* The humor comes from his cockeyed inversion of time-honored stereotypes. One of Aesop's many frogs, determined not to be outdone, tries to blow himself up to the size of an ox and kills himself in the process. In Thurber, a restaurateur flatters a vain frog until the amphibian swoons with self-esteem—and awakens without her succulent legs. Titles include "The Goose That Laid the Gilded Egg" and "The Bat Who Got the Hell Out." A lemming cries "Fire!" and starts a mass exodus into the sea. In another piece, a scientist interviews a lemming and learns that the animal cannot understand why human beings *don't* drown themselves. Thurber's morals are along the lines of one that wraps up a pointedly allegorical fight to the end among animals: "You can't very well be king of beasts if there aren't any."

Animals also swarm through Thurber's cartoons. Owls mysteriously strafe a table in a restaurant. An attorney in a courtroom holds up a kangaroo and says to a witness, "Perhaps *this* will refresh your memory." In one of the better-known cartoons, a woman demands of a huge beast, "What have you done with Mr. Millmoss?" At first, trying to amuse his daughter, Thurber had drawn only the animal. Then, "Something about the creature's expression when he was completed convinced me that he had recently eaten a man." Thurber's drawing style wasn't exactly formal, and occasionally viewers were uncertain about the identity of an animal. His two-year-old daughter immediately said of Mr. Millmoss's assailant, "That's a hippopotamus," but the *New Yorker* labeled the drawing for their files "Woman with strange animal."

As the body of his work grew and demonstrated staying power, Thurber attracted critical attention. On June 24, 1959, he complained in a letter to a friend that those who studied him were now overemphasizing his seriousness, although it was only a part of the whole. Inevitably animals came to mind.

"The power that created the poodle, the platypus, and people," he insisted, "has an integrated sense of both comedy and tragedy."

---

25 JUNE 1815

Joséphine's Roses

The historical figure most closely associated with roses was actually named Rose. Upon her birth in 1763, she was christened Marie-Josèphe-Rose Tascher de la Pagerie. Her family called her Rose until, at the age of thirty-three, she married her second husband, Napoléon Bonaparte.

Joséphine cultivated her famous rose gardens at their residence called La Malmaison. For the gardens, Joséphine emulated the unplanned look of her Martinique childhood in informal *jardins à l'anglais.* Wide expanses of lawn alternated with waterfalls and hidden glades. Her neoclassical greenhouse was filled with rare plants. With liberty unknown in zoos at the time, exotic animals wandered about—a zebra, emus, an orangutan, black swans, kangaroos. At his study window, Napoléon fed gazelles from his snuffbox. The halls of the house were raucous with caged birds.

Joséphine, first wife of Napoléon Bonaparte and an important patron of horticulture in Europe.

Joséphine's passion for roses seems to have quickened when she became empress in 1804. By the time of her death ten years later, she had over 250 varieties. She also cultivated many other plants, demonstrating her famous extravagance in gardening as in everything else. France was at war with England most of the time she lived at La Malmaison, but agents from London dodged blockades to deliver rare species to the empress. "I am happy to see these foreign plants flourish and multiply," she wrote. "I wish Malmaison soon to offer a model of good cultivation, and to become a source of riches for the rest of France." It was that impetus more than her own work that had lasting impact. Her heritage lives on in the names of such roses as *Brunsvigia josephinae* and *Souvenir de la Malmaison.*

It was at La Malmaison that the great French flower painter Pierre-Joseph Redouté, called "the Raphael of flowers," received his first commission from Joséphine: painting floral portraits for her bedroom. Eventually he helped create the book *Jardin de la Malmaison.* "Madame," the introduction purrs, "you have understood that a liking for flowers should not be a sterile study. You have gathered under your eyes some of the rarest plants on French soil. Tended by you, many plants that had never before left the deserts of Arabia and the scorching sands of Egypt . . . represent in the beautiful garden of Malmaison the sweetest memory of your illustrious husband's conquests, and the most agreeable evidence of your studious leisure."

Unlike Louis XIV, whose grounds were merely a stage for pageantry, Joséphine actually loved plants. A former lady-in-waiting complained about the empress's expertise. "When the weather was fine . . . the same walk was taken every day . . . the same subjects were talked over. The conversation generally turned on botany, upon Her Majesty's taste for that interesting science, her wonderful memory, which enabled her to name every plant. . . . I no sooner stepped onto that delightful walk, which I had so admired when I first saw it, than I was seized with an immoderate fit of yawning."

Napoléon divorced Joséphine in 1809 but allowed her to remain at her beloved home. On June 25, 1815, a year after her death, Napoléon returned to Malmaison. His first words were: "My poor Joséphine! I can see her now, walking along one of the paths and picking the roses she loved so well."

See also Peace rose, 5/2; and flowers, 7/30.

The Neck of the Giraffe

Scientists and nonscientists simply do not look at the world in the same way. Consider the response of a nineteenth-century English general named William Dyott to that strange and wonderful beast, the giraffe. Presumably Dyott first encountered the animals during his North African campaign in 1801. Years later, in his seventies, he saw them again back home in England. On June 26, 1836, he recorded a day's outing in his diary. After writing "I accompanied Lady Dickson to the Zoological Gardens to see the new curiosities lately added to the collection," he added with the practical mind of a military man, "the giraffes most surprising animals, but so shapen they can be of no use to employ, and whether eatable I did not inquire." Apparently, if the animal could not be employed or eaten, there was nothing else to say about it.

A biologist, on the other hand, looks at the giraffe's structure and asks, Why does that animal have that ridiculous cartoon neck and how did it acquire it? Because of its unique adaptations, the giraffe comes up often in the history of ideas about why animals are shaped the way they are. School texts and other books mention it especially in accounts of the evolutionary ideas of the early nineteenth-century French naturalist Jean-Baptiste-Pierre-Antoine de Monet, chevalier de Lamarck. The neck of the giraffe is presented as the perfect example of the shortcomings of the idea that the inheritance of acquired characteristics is the force that drives evolution. Although this notion is now dismissively called Lamarckism, Lamarck did not claim to have originated it. He was not, as he is frequently painted, a crank whose wild notions Darwin KO'd in the first round. He was a pioneer evolutionary thinker. He also coined the word "biology," from the Greek for "life" and "study."

As its appearance in everything from Saharan rock paintings to animated films indicates, artists have been unable to resist the cartoon charm of the giraffe.

Actually, Lamarck had little to say about the giraffe: "We know that this tallest of mammals living in arid localities, is obliged to browse on the foliage of trees. It has resulted from this habit, maintained over a long period of time, that in all individuals of the race the forelegs have become longer than the hinder ones, and that the neck is so elongated that it raises the head almost six meters [twenty feet] in height." He explained that the elongation is the result of countless generations of giraffes striving to reach ever higher leaves, and thereby stretching their necks, and then passing those stretched necks on to their offspring. To point out the error in Lamarck's reasoning, twentieth-century biologist Richard Dawkins offered the story of his mother's dog, which limped. A neighbor was convinced that her own dog, which had lost a leg in an encounter with a car, was the father of the lame dog. Obviously, she insisted, the animal had inherited its limp. A giraffe that spent its lifetime stretching its neck to reach ever higher leaves would not necessarily leave behind taller descendants, anymore than the crippled dog would transmit to its pups a misfortune acquired in its lifetime. Genetics doesn't work that way.

Darwin countered with an alternative theory of what he called the giraffe's "lofty stature" in the *Origin of Species*. First he pointed out how greatly individuals of a single generation may differ. Then he continued:

> These slight proportional differences, due to the laws of growth and variation, are not of the slightest use or importance to most species. But it will have been otherwise with the nascent giraffe, considering its probable habits of life; for those individuals which had some one part or several parts of their bodies rather more elongated than usual, would generally have survived. These will have intercrossed and left offspring, either inheriting the same bodily peculiarities, or with a tendency to vary again in the same manner; whilst the individuals, less favoured in the same respects, will have been the most liable to perish.

Lamarck offered no evidence for his speculation, and neither did Darwin. Obviously giraffes' long necks enable them to eat the topmost leaves of trees (usually acacias), but, technically, we do not know that they evolved for that reason. However it came to be so tall, the giraffe's surprising shape demonstrates the adaptability of the mammalian body pattern. Even though it reaches a height of sixteen feet or even taller, the giraffe has only seven neck vertebrae, the same number as almost all other mammals. Each one must simply grow larger than those of smaller animals to contribute to the giraffe's lofty stature.

27 June 1850

Certain Wild Legends of Whales

New York June 27th 1850

My Dear Sir,—In the latter part of the coming autumn I shall have ready a new work. . . . The book is a romance of adventure, founded upon certain wild legends in the Southern Sperm Whale Fisheries, and illustrated by the author's own personal experience, of two years & more, as a harpooneer.

In this letter to his English publisher, Herman Melville introduced an outlandish work-in-progress, a sharp departure from his early successful romances *Omoo* and *Typee,* or even the more recent *White Jacket* and *Redburn.* In the United States, the new book was entitled *Moby-Dick; or, The Whale;* in

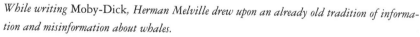

While writing Moby-Dick*, Herman Melville drew upon an already old tradition of information and misinformation about whales.*

England, the subtitle became the title. At the heart of the book are those wild legends about whales. The author did indeed speak from personal experience, but he supplemented it with a vast amount of research into materials at least purporting to be nonfictional.

Since the Dutch and British had created the whaling industry two centuries before, heavily armed ships had patrolled the watery portion of the globe in search of whales. Moby Dick is an albino sperm whale, *Physeter macrocephalus.* The species name means "large head," and it was from the oil in the whale's head that whalers derived spermaceti, a white waxy substance that provided cosmetics, ointments, and lighting fuel. At one point Ishmael exhorts, "For God's sake, be economical with your lamps and candles! not a gallon you burn, but at least one drop of man's blood was spilled for it."

The amount of spilled whale's blood Melville did not calculate. He went on at length about "the great power and malice at times of the sperm whale," but what creature thus tormented, speared with whole quivers of harpoons, would not summon all its power in self-defense? "I tell you, the sperm whale will stand no nonsense." Perhaps the whale would not, but fiction thrived upon it. The most nonsensical aspect of all was attributing ferocity and blood lust to an animal merely fortunate enough to be able to fight back. In the letter to his publisher, Melville remarked, "I do not know that the subject treated of has ever been worked up by a romancer." Actually, many of the stories of the maniacal fury of sperm whales feature romantic exaggeration, but not at the level of enthusiasm that Melville maintained throughout his long narrative. "Who would have looked for philosophy in whales," the English magazine *John Bull* asked in its review, "or for poetry in blubber?"

There have been several cinematic versions of Melville's tale. The first, *The Sea Beast,* appeared in 1926, but Melville's story is hardly discernible. Not only does John Barrymore's Ahab have a girlfriend, a brother, and a surname, but in a shameless reversal of the book's ending he triumphs over the papier-mâché whale. A 1930 version had basically the same plot. Finally, in 1956, there appeared John Huston's *Moby Dick,* with a script by Ray Bradbury. Gregory Peck made almost as unlikely an Ahab as John Barrymore, but at least the whale—who, as one review of the book described it, "abbreviated the captain's lower extremities"—bested the vengeance-obsessed Ahab and sent him and his ship down to the bottom of the sea.

A descendant of Melville's horrific whale appears in Walt Disney Productions' 1940 adaptation of Carlo Collodi's children's book *Pinocchio.* The filmmakers changed the book's Dog-fish into a whale. In the film, Pinocchio learns that his father, who went to sea searching for his lost puppet-boy, has been swallowed by a gargantuan whale. When Pinocchio, walking on the sea floor, asks the whereabouts of the animal, its very name, Monstro, makes the other denizens of the deep tremble and flee. Monstro turns out to be a curious cartoon hybrid, with the furrowed underside of a baleen whale such as a blue or finback, but with a flattened version of the square head of a sperm whale. Its rows of ferocious carnivorous teeth don't match the dental equipment of any known cetacean. Swallowed and reunited with his father, Pinocchio builds a fire. The whale sneezes them out, then chases them across the water like a speedboat. It is a terrifying scene, and fully worthy of Monstro's great white grandfather, Moby Dick.

"The Meaning of the Fishes"

As one would imagine from his writing, Robert Louis Stevenson traveled a great deal. His first two books were travel narratives. He saw much of both Europe and the United States, and finally the South Seas. In one of his essays, he wrote, "I began my little pilgrimage in the most enviable of all humours: that in which a person, with a sufficiency of money and a knapsack, turns his back on a town and walks forward into a country of which he knows only the vague reports of others." During his forty-four years, such pleasures became less and less common. Stevenson contracted tuberculosis at an early age, and much of his travel was spent in pursuit of better health. He wrote some of his books in sanitoriums.

Stevenson wrote a good deal about the outdoors, in both travel books and fiction. In the early *Travels with a Donkey in the Cévennes,* for example, one entire chapter is devoted to sleeping outdoors under pines. "Night is a dead monotonous period under a roof; but in the open world it passes lightly, with its stars and dews and perfumes, and the hours are marked by changes in the face of nature." He added, "I thought I had rediscovered one of those truths which are revealed to savages and hid from political economists: at the least, I had discovered a new pleasure for myself." Nor was his eye for such pleasures merely appreciative. He wrote a few scientific papers, including "On the Thermal Influence of Forests" and "On a New Form of Intermittent Light for Lighthouses." He read the latter before the Royal Society.

Finally, in search of both better health and adventure, Stevenson went to the Pacific. On June 28, 1888, aboard the *Casco,* he and his family departed San Francisco. Although he had crossed oceans before, it was his first trip to the South Seas. He did not enjoy most of the voyage. "[T]he sea is a terrible place, stupefying to the mind and poisonous to the temper, the sea, the motion, the lack of space, the cruel publicity, the villainous tinned goods, the sailors, the captain, the passengers—but you are amply repaid when you sight an island, and drop anchor in a new world." In late July, he found his new world in Polynesia. "The first experience can never be repeated. The first

Robert Louis Stevenson in 1893, the year before his death. The long struggle with tuberculosis had left its mark.

love, the first sunrise, the first South Sea Island, are memories apart and touched by the virginity of sense." They landed at Nuku-Hiva. He explored the South Seas awhile longer, and in 1889 bought Vailima, an estate on Samoa, where he lived the remaining five years of his life.

At the time, Samoans traditionally closed the day with household prayers and hymns. After Stevenson's death, his widow included in the volume of his collected works generally referred to as the *Vailima Papers* a number of the prayers he had written for these daily gatherings. A couple of the prayers are in response to the frequent tropical rains, and one of them emphasizes a point he made in many of his writings.

> Lord, Thou sendest down rain upon the uncounted millions of the forest, and givest the trees to drink exceedingly. We are here upon this isle a few handfuls of men, and how many myriads upon myriads of stalwart trees! Teach us the lesson of the trees. The sea around us, which this rain recruits, teems with the race of fish: teach us, Lord, the meaning of the fishes. Let us see ourselves for what we are, one out of the countless number of the clans of Thy handiwork. . . .

See also Travels with a Donkey in the Cévennes, *9/22.*

---

29 JUNE

A Journey to the Center of the Earth

In 1864, French novelist Jules Verne published his second novel, *Voyage au centre de la terre,* "Journey to the Center of the Earth." Emboldened by the success of its predecessor, *Five Weeks in a Balloon,* Verne turned from writing barely successful plays to writing fabulously successful fiction. He had launched his series of scientific adventure novels, collectively referred to as the *Voyages extraordinaires.*

Journey to the Center of the Earth tells the story of the German geologist Otto von Lidenbrock. Together with his nephew, Axel (the narrator), and a Danish guide named Hans, Lidenbrock attempts a daring expedition into the Earth itself. Many of the novel's ideas were in the air at the time of its composition. At a dinner party, Verne met the French geographer Charles Sainte-Claire Deville, and during the winter of 1863–64 they became friends. Deville had done what Verne only imagined, and his stories of exploring the volcanic craters of Stromboli and Tenerife inspired the novelist. During a lull in Stromboli's volcanic activity, Deville had actually descended into the volcano's crater. He theorized that some European volcanoes might be connected by passages underground.

Verne gave Lidenbrock the mad notion of entering a crater and descending all the way into the center of the Earth. He combined with Deville's accounts the ideas of American John Cleves Symmes, who theorized that the Earth was hollow and could be entered through openings at the poles. Symmes's hollow-earth scenario was so popular in the nineteenth century that the U.S. Congress had actually assisted an 1838 expedition to the Antarctic in search of proof. There had also been an earlier novel based upon Symmes's writings, *Symzonia,* by a Captain Seaborn, which may have been a pseudonym used by Symmes himself. A writer Verne admired, Edgar Allan Poe, had used some of Symmes's ideas in his *Narrative of Arthur Gordon Pym of Nantucket* a quarter century earlier.

In Verne's novel, the three men enter the crater of an Icelandic volcano on June 29. Axel is terrified, Hans calm, and the professor ecstatic. Like other Verne protagonists, the professor admits no barrier to the pursuit of knowledge. Although technically the expedition fails, because they do not reach the center of the Earth, Lidenbrock is amply rewarded for his persistence by glimpses of a world no other humans had seen. For as they

An early reconstruction of the megatherium, one of the fossils that inspired Jules Verne's evolutionary epiphany in Journey to the Center of the Earth.

journey farther into the Earth, they go ever backward in the planet's history. They witness a marine battle between a plesiosaur and an ichthyosaur. They find a skeleton of "Quaternary man," proving the description of a late Ice Age human fossil actually found in France while Verne was writing the novel. Finally, by entering the Earth in Iceland and exiting via the volcano Stromboli in Italy, they prove Deville's theory that the volcanoes connected.

Verne's characters are always exclaiming over the wonders of nature, but Alex experiences a powerful vision of the evolution of life. It is an uncharacteristically long outburst for a Verne character, and a daring one for its time. Darwin's *Origin of Species* had been published only five years before. "[M]y imagination carried me off into the wonderful theories of paleontology," Axel recalls. "Though awake, I was dreaming." He imagines a parade of the extinct animals that had only become known in that century—antediluvian turtles, giant tapirs, the megatherium, great-winged pterodactyls, birds, the earliest monkey.

> This entire fossil universe rolled through my imagination. It took me back to the biblical periods of creation, long before the birth of man, when the Earth was unfinished and not yet ready to sustain him. My dream then took me back even further, before the appearance of creatures with locomotion. The mammals disappeared, then the birds, followed by the reptiles of the secondary period, and finally the fish, crustaceans, mollusks, and arthropods; in last position, the zoophytes of the transitional period faded away one by one into oblivion. The entire story of the Earth passed by inside me, and mine was the only heart beating in this depopulated world.

For other Verne adventures, see 4/20 and 11/5.

700 Hiroshimas

On the morning of June 30, 1908, a fireball appeared over the Tunguska region of Siberia. Although it was larger than the rising sun, it could be looked at with the naked eye: a long flame splitting the sky in two. A hot wind blew the soil from the fields. Horses galloped away or fell to their knees. There was a loud boom, then smaller ones like nearby gunfire. Windowpanes shattered. Every tree within twenty miles of the blast site was flattened, and an entire herd of 500 reindeer was destroyed. Not only was the fireball seen for hundreds of miles in every direction, and the blast felt and heard even farther, but a pillar of fire and smoke rose into the air and formed a mushroom cloud.

It was the largest earthly explosion in history, estimated at the equivalent of 10 million tons of TNT—the force of 700 Hiroshimas. For two days, there was so much fine dust in the atmosphere that as far away as London one could read a newspaper at night by the scattered light reflected back from the sky. Two weeks later the debris was still arriving in California.

The explanation proposed at the time was that Earth had been hit by an unusually large meteorite. Meteors are leftover comet debris heated to incandescence by their passage through the atmosphere. Since most are tiny, they usually burn up long before reaching the surface. Large meteorites were not unknown—a mile-wide crater in Arizona is the result of one—but not until later observation of the Moon and Mars would we realize that they're relatively common, their evidence on Earth merely obscured by ocean or erosion.

But because the origin of a blast in Siberia wasn't high on the list of priorities in Russia at that time, it was almost twenty years before scientists penetrated the area and investigated. They didn't find a meteorite. Usually fragments are blasted from the crater and melt in the explosion, reconsolidating as black glassy droplets called tektites. No tektites were found. In their place were similarly formed objects whose chemical composition tested close to that of cosmic dust, as if they were extraterrestrial fallout from an explosion above Earth. Detonation in the air would explain the lack of an impact crater, but a meteor so large should have produced tons of debris, and apparently there was very little.

An accepted theory now is that a comet exploded. In 1908 Comet Encke changed its orbit slightly. The comet with the shortest known period of revolution, Encke circles the sun every 3.3 years. It is associated with, and perhaps the parent of, the annual Taurid meteor shower. In 1908 the Taurid shower peaked on June 30. Perhaps the culprit had been found. Meteors are described as "dirty snowballs"; mostly ice, with a rocky or metallic core, a meteor exploding miles above the surface would wreak havoc without leaving much residue. The issue still isn't settled, but probably we crossed paths with a wandering fragment of Encke.

See also the comet that struck Jupiter, 7/17.

Darwin and Wallace

Alfred Russell Wallace was born in England in 1823, fourteen years after Charles Darwin. Inspired partially by such books as Darwin's *Voyage of the* Beagle, which appeared when he was twenty-two, Wallace went off to explore the world. Over the years he made himself into a world-class naturalist. He was the first naturalist to study orangutans in the wild. He also named countless formerly unknown species of plants and animals. Wallace is especially remembered for his pioneer studies of the distribution of animals in the wild, including his discovery of what is now called "Wallace's Line." He noticed that there seemed to be two distinct groups of fauna in the Malay Archipelago, meeting along a line that runs, for example, between Borneo and Lombok. Geologists realized many years later that Wallace's Line marks the edge of the still-busy Indo-Australian tectonic plate.

Thanks to books proposing early concepts of evolution, Wallace started out with the idea of gathering evidence for and against the "development theory." In contrast, when Darwin left on his voyage, he had no such notions and was planning to settle down as a country parson upon his return. In 1855, Wallace, after exploring and analyzing the natural world for years, and reading avidly about concepts of change in nature, sent off from Malaysia a paper entitled "On the Law which has Regulated the Introduction of New Species." He stated clear evolutionary principles, arguing that species came into being "coincident both in space and time with a pre-existing, closely-allied species." However, Wallace did not suggest what the mechanism might be that drove such changes. Although the paper was published and important scientists read it, it attracted relatively little attention.

Four years later, still in Malaysia (or the Moluccas, as they were called at the time), Wallace was lying in bed with one of his recurring malarial fevers. Thinking over the ways that new species might originate, he remembered Thomas Malthus's *Essay on Population,* and the "positive checks" that the English economist had theorized might keep populations in balance. And "there suddenly flashed upon me the idea of the survival of the fittest . . . that in every generation the inferior would inevitably be killed off and the superior would remain. . . ." Over the next couple of days, Wallace carefully wrote out his ideas as a paper entitled "On the Tendency of Varieties to Depart Indefinitely from the Original Type" and mailed it to a scientist he had long admired—the already well-known Charles Darwin.

Darwin received the letter in mid-June of 1858. He was devastated. Ever since his return to England from the *Beagle* voyage in 1837, he had been quietly gathering information for the eventual publication of his own theory of natural selection. He was finally nearing that goal. Darwin wrote to the geologist Charles Lyell, "If Wallace had my MS. sketch written out in 1842, he could not have made a better short abstract!" Actually, there were significant differences in their thinking, but they were not apparent at first.

Wallace had sent the paper merely for Darwin's critique. However, crushed as he was, Darwin felt that he should immediately recommend its publication. Colleagues knew of Darwin's own work and had seen early abstracts from it as early as fifteen years before Wallace got the same idea. In their eyes, there was no question of Darwin's priority. Both grief-stricken by the death of yet another child and always willing to let his friends fight for him, Darwin left in their hands the decision of how to proceed. Lyell and botanist Joseph Hooker (who, with Thomas Huxley, would later form Darwin's support team when he scandalized both science and polite society) decided that they themselves would present Wallace's paper and an abstract of Darwin's huge book before the Linnaean Society. They did so on July 1, 1858, describing the papers as "the results of the investigations of two indefatigable naturalists." And Darwin redoubled his efforts to complete what appeared the next year as the *Origin of Species.*

The joint paper, "On the Tendency of Species to form Varieties; and on the Perpetuation of Varieties and Species by Natural Means of Selection," occupied only seventeen pages in the Linnaean Society journal. It was the first official pronouncement of what would turn out to be one of the greatest revolutions in scientific history, but that was not apparent at the time. At the end of the year, the president of the Linnaean Society editorialized, "The year which has passed has not, indeed, been marked by any of those striking discoveries which at once revolutionize . . . the department of science on which they bear; it is only at remote intervals that we can reasonably expect any sudden and brilliant innovation."

---

2 JULY 1874

"Out of Proportion to Man's Being"

Gustave Flaubert and Ivan Turgenev met in 1863. Turgenev was forty-four, Flaubert three years younger. Both were already well-known authors, and each was familiar with the other's work. Gradually they became friends. Over the next seventeen years, until Flaubert's death, they exchanged 230-odd letters, discussing such favorite themes as literature, the low nature of humanity, and, always, "Beauty."

In the summer of 1874, Flaubert was in Switzerland. His play *The Candidate* had flopped, he had just published *The Temptation of Saint Anthony,* and he was traveling for his health. He reported to Turgenev his response to his surroundings.

Kaltbad [sic] *Rigi Switzerland*
Thursday 2 July 1874

I came here as an act of obedience, because everyone said that the pure mountain air would decongest me and calm my nerves. . . . But so far, I only feel completely bored, owing to the solitude and idleness; and then I am not a *child of Nature:* "her wonders" move me less than those of the Arts. She crushes me without inspiring any "great thoughts" in me. . . . The Alps, moreover, are out of proportion to man's being. They're too big to be of any use.

Flaubert's lack of interest in scenery that did not inspire great thoughts was typical of his response to nature. He told Turgenev that he looked forward to moving on to Venice. In his essay on the architecture of that very city, John Ruskin reminded his readers that the most beautiful things in the world were the most useless. Peacocks and lilies were his examples, but Flaubert would have included mountains. It seems that Flaubert was forgetting the advice in one of his Russian friend's own books. "If you don't respond to beauty," Bersyenev tells Shubin in *On the Eve*, "if you don't love her wherever you meet her, beauty will elude you in your art." Of course, however much he was obsessed with "the beautiful," Flaubert's aesthetic sensibilities were more intellectual than visual.

He was not alone in his opinion of mountains. The Delectable Mountains in *Pilgrim's Progress* were mere allegory. Mountain scenery was one of the last orders of aesthetic appreciation to emerge in our evolving relationship toward the world around us. Mountains had long been described as warts and blisters on the landscape. England's hill named "the Divels-Arse" is a good example of the terminology. The detestation of mountains rose to what now seem absurd heights. Dante considered them the gates of hell. A century later, some Alpine travelers wore blindfolds to protect themselves against the potentially maddening scenery. Naturalist Conrad Gesner definitely voiced a minority opinion in his 1543 essay, *On the Admiration of Mountains*.

Gesner's esteem is doubly admirable, because familiarity can breed contempt even for one's own topography. No doubt the gods on Mount Olympus long since tired of the view. Olympus is a good example of the obverse of fear—awe. From Parnassus to Sinai to Qomolangma (called Mount Everest in the West), some mountains have been worshiped as the home of the gods or as even the gods themselves. Flaubert's complaint that mountains were out of proportion to humanity is one of the reasons that in some places they were revered. They inspire humility. In time, more people learned to admire what they had formerly despised. Mountains became the very emblem of a transcendental nature. And William Blake could write:

Great things are done when men and mountains meet;
This is not done by jostling in the street.

See also Mount Everest, 5/29.

Asta and His Ancestors

MGM released *The Thin Man,* based upon Dashiell Hammett's fifth detective novel, in June of 1934. *Variety* reviewed it in its July 3 issue and remarked that, surprisingly, the changes made in adapting the book to a film didn't harm the story. One significant change concerned the wirehaired fox terrier, Asta.

In the film, when Asta finds a body buried beneath floorboards, Nick Charles (William Powell) tells him, "You're not a terrier. You're a police dog." Not quite; at the first sign of trouble, Asta hides behind furniture. Although never a "police dog," Asta was originally a different breed—and a different gender. In Hammett's novel, while walking Asta, Nick "explained to two people that she was a Schnauzer and not a cross between a Scottie and an Irish terrier. . . ." Asta's dual metamorphosis doesn't affect the story, because both genders of both breeds have the playfulness and curiosity that distinguish terriers.

Knopf's publicity described Hammett as a man who "likes dogs and loves music." Actually, there is little evidence that he liked dogs. When an interviewer asked him about his hobbies, Hammett listed poker and—naturally—drinking, then added, "I had a dog once, but he died." However, when a California newspaper asked about his outline for a sequel to *The Thin Man,* Hammett replied, "In this sequel somebody must be killed—but I am at loggerheads to determine which character shall die. . . . I'm sure I will spare William Powell and Myrna Loy. . . . Who shall die? Shall it be poor little Asta, the wire-haired fox terrier? God forbid! It shall not be Asta!"

Asta, the true star of The Thin Man *movies, with his human assistants, Myrna Loy and William Powell.* Courtesy of Ronald V. Borst / Hollywood Movie Posters

Hammett wisely did not kill off Asta. Many viewers described the terrier as one of their favorite characters. Asta was played by a Hollywood veteran with the far less distinctive name of Skippy. Rudd Weatherwax trained Skippy, long before gaining fame and fortune with Lassie, who was actually a male dog named Pal.

Surprisingly, fox terriers also play a curious bit part in the history of evolution. In his column in *Natural History,* Stephen Jay Gould once speculated on why biology textbooks, when portraying the evolution of the horse, frequently refer to the early protohorse *Hyracotherium,* or *Eohippus,* as the size of a fox terrier. It is such a specific reference. Surely, Gould reasoned, not every writer on paleontology was a dog fancier, and even more certainly the comparison did not occur spontaneously to each of them. What perpetuated this canine image? Gould pointed out that, with the relative scarcity of fox terriers in the United States, the increasingly common comparison of *Eohippus* to them could only result from carbon-copy repetition by textbook authors too lazy to coin their own more vivid analogies.

The fox terrier's name describes its ancestry. Terrier is from *terra,* the Latin word for earth. In the age-old English ritual of the fox hunt, after the hounds pursued the quarry to its lair, it was the job of terriers to go in and evict the fox from its burrow. Hunters carried the dogs on their saddles, and breeders bred them to resemble horses as much as possible, down to the "saddle" pattern on their backs, which even today is considered desirable in the breed. American writer Roger Angell offered a possible solution to Gould's quandary about fox terriers and *Eohippus.* Perhaps the paleontologist who first used the fox terrier comparison unconsciously thought of it because of the old relationship between horses and Asta's ancestors.

See also Mary Stuart's terrier, 2/8.

Dodo in Wonderland

While rowing with friends on July 4, 1862, the Reverend Charles Lutwidge Dodgson began telling the tales that three years later became, under his pseudonym Lewis Carroll, *Alice's Adventures in Wonderland.* Dodgson and his fellow cleric Robinson Duckworth frequently went boating with the three young Liddell sisters—Lorina, Edith, and the soon-to-be-immortalized Alice. One of the incidents in the book grew out of a misadventure on a similar outing. "About a mile above Nuneham," Dodgson recorded in his diary, "heavy rain came on, and after bearing it a short time I settled that we had better leave the boat and walk: three miles of this drenched us all pretty well."

In Chapter Two of *Alice,* our heroine has shrunk almost to nothing and falls into the Pool of Tears she cried while she was nine feet tall. Other creatures accidentally join her: "There was a Duck and a Dodo, a Lory and an Eaglet. . . ." When they climb out of the water, a mouse tries to dry them by reading the driest prose he can find, and when that fails, the Dodo has them run in circles in a Caucus-race.

The scene was a transformation of that rainy day at Nuneham. The Lory, a kind of Australian parrot, was Lorina; Edith became the Eaglet; Duckworth naturally became a Duck. But the most interesting metamorphosis was the author's own. He was the Dodo. Like so many others from Demosthenes (and, legend says, Moses) to Somerset Maugham and Henry James, Dodgson was a lifelong stutterer. Frequently he had trouble with his own name, and it came out, "Do-Do-Dodgson." He was also a lover of wordplay who couldn't resist a joke, even on himself. Later he inscribed Duckworth's copy of a special edition of *Alice,* "The Duck from the Dodo."

Probably the dodo appealed to Dodgson for other reasons, too. As indicated by John Tenniel's illustration of the bird presenting Alice with her own thimble, the dodo was comically ungainly. Early accounts of its discovery on the island of Mauritius include the term *walckvogel,* "disgusting bird." This probably referred to its edibility, but similar terms were applied to its appearance. Tenniel portrays the dodo as realistically as he does the other unwilling swimmers. Its face was indeed as naked as a vulture's, its wings

The Dodo (Do-Do-Dodgson himself) returns the thimble to Alice (Alice Liddell). In the background, Alice's sisters, the Eaglet (Edith) and the Lory (Lorina), watch with the Duck (Reverend Duckworth).

like tiny ornaments, and its feet disproportionately huge. Of course, it neither leaned upon a cane nor had human hands emerging from under its wings.

An early description of this strange bird appears in the memoirs of English theologian Hamon L'Estrange:

About 1638, as I walked London streets, I saw the picture of a strange fowle hung out upon a clothe and myselfe with one or two more then in company went in to see it. It was kept in a chamber, and was a great fowle somewhat bigger than the largest Turky Cock, and so legged and footed, but stouter and thicker and of a more erect shape, coloured before like the breast of a young cock fesan, and on the back of dunn or dearc colour. The keeper called it a Dodo.

By the 1680s, the dodo was extinct. But only seventeen years before *Alice* was published, two Englishmen named Strickland and Melville published a classic of natural history detective work, *The Dodo and Its Kindred.* By Dodgson's time, the dodo was well known, and sometimes considered an example of nature's sense of humor, like the platypus. (Its early species name was *ineptus.*) The idea that the dodo became extinct because it was unable to adapt is pure slander, of course. It was certainly as well adapted to its insular habitat as was that curious Oxford don who chose the bird to play him in Wonderland.

See also Lewis Carroll on vivisection, 2/12.

---

5 JULY 1831

The Diary of Emily Shore

In England in the 1830s, a Romantic revival was making nature study one of the hobbies of choice. Much of it was motivated by delight in the works of the Creator, for Charles Darwin had yet to give biology a bad name in the eyes of the devout. In 1829, John Leonard Knapp published his *Journal of a Naturalist,* which summed up the attitude of the times with a single index entry: "Naturalist, pleasing occupations of the." And in 1831, on the fifth of July, in the little village of Woodbury, an eleven-year-old girl began keeping a diary.

Emily Shore's journal wasn't published until 1891, fifty-two years after her death from tuberculosis at the age of nineteen. Apparently sanitizing the family archives, Emily's sisters edited her voluminous diary to a fraction of its true length, sprinkling tantalizing ellipses throughout. Sadly, they seem to have destroyed the original. If it is unlikely that Emily was the model of Dickensian virtue and Mozartean precociousness that the sisters paint, still she was obviously a remarkable child. A pencil portrait faces the title page. Looking steadily at the viewer is a teenage girl with short dark hair and a mouth as delicate as her eyes are piercing. She looks tired. She died later that year.

The variety of entries that survived the sisters is still fascinating: "I have just tried to count the notes of the thrush. . . . I think I am now quite versed in the intimations of rain given by the swallows. . . . I found a honeysuckle leaf rolled up in a curious way by means of a gummy substance, and six or seven beautiful lady-birds comfortably lodged within it. . . . At a quarter past five a swallow was singing. I saw no chaffinches; I suspect them to be very lazy." Emily described the fur of a dead Norway rat, her dog's response to a bust of the Dog of Alcibiades, her father's indignation over the cruelty of foxhunters, and the sound of falling rose leaves. She asked a stargazer, "How near is Saturn's ring to the body of the planet, in its nearest part?" She said of a man who abhorred caterpillars, "Perhaps he may have a physical infirmity which makes him dislike this order of creation." Emily herself seemed to dislike no order, no individual, in creation.

Emily wrote several other (unpublished) books, some dating from before her teens, including three romantic novels and, in the words of her sisters, "an unfinished Conversation between herself and the Shade of Herodotus, in which she supposes herself to inform him of all the changes that have taken place in the world since his time." In the spring of 1835, she wrote in her diary, "The study of natural history seems to me to be one which belongs to the nature of man, and is born with him. . . . I believe that if I were chained for life to Woodbury, and never allowed to ramble from it more than three or four miles . . . —I believe that even in this situation I should for ever be discovering something new."

Buffalo Hunting

In 1846, Santa Fe trader Samuel Magoffin led a caravan of settlers into the southwestern territories. The Santa Fe Trail meandered from Independence, Missouri, across Kansas and part of Colorado to wind up in Santa Fe—which would not become a U.S. territory for two more years, until the end of the Mexican War. History remembers Magoffin because he was returning home with his new eighteen-year-old wife, Susan, who kept a vivid diary of her journey. Susan Magoffin had a sharp eye and a sense of adventure. She joked about her first home being a tent; she picked "the numberless flowers with which the plains are covered"; she reported the terrible plagues of mosquitos that attacked them near the Little Arkansas River. And she described living off the meat of the most common animal on the plains, the buffalo.

"It is a rich sight indeed," she wrote on the sixth of July, "to look at the fine fat meat stretched out on ropes to dry for our sustinence when we are no longer in the regions of the living animal." She worried that her husband would be harmed while hunting the buffalo. However, the meat was delicious. "I never eat its equal in the best hotels of N.Y. and Philada." They could not resist such abundant game.

This montage from an 1877 issue of Harper's Weekly
highlights the ongoing assault against the buffalo.

Long before the whites came, others were hunting the populous buffalo. There were many methods. The Plains Cree, Cheyenne, and Assiniboin, among others, "impounded" entire herds—drove them into a funnel composed of crouching, armed men who stood up one at a time to direct them into a corral. Once inside, the buffalo were killed with lances, arrows, rifles, and clubs. A party of returning Flathead hunters told a missionary in 1841 that one of them had killed three buffalo in unusual ways. He claimed he hit one between the horns with a rock, knifed the second, and speared the third, supposedly finishing it off by strangling. Another method was grass firing, which involved surrounding the herd with flames and slowly closing in on them, or leaving just enough of an opening in the ring of fire to allow the buffalo to run into a waiting ambush. Each of these methods came with its distinctive risks.

"The Indians," English explorer Richard Burton wrote in the late 1800s, "generally hunt the buffalo with arrows. They are so expert in riding, that they will, at full speed, draw the missile from the victim's flank before it falls." Whites didn't try to pluck the bullets from their victims, but their most common method—shooting with a rifle from horseback—had its own dangers. Four years before he became one of the best-known losers in U.S. history at the Little Big Horn River, George Armstrong Custer came close to death while hunting buffalo. He was riding his wife's horse, Custis Lee, when the buffalo he was chasing suddenly turned on him. Naturally the horse swerved, too. The sideways motion threw off Custer's aim, and he shot Custis Lee in the back of the head. The horse fell instantly to the ground, and Custer flew over him onto the grass. The buffalo glared at Custer for a moment and went on his way. It was just the sort of misadventure Susan Magoffin had feared might befall her own husband. In a letter to his wife, Custer described the death of her horse as a "most unfortunate occurrence."

7 JULY 1545

Europe's First Botanical Gardens

Flower gardening was not unknown in Europe during the Middle Ages, but its scope was limited. One historian estimated the number of cultivated plants in the year 1500 at a mere 200. By the mid-1800s, the total had climbed to 18,000, and much of the impetus for that growth came from the establishment of botanical gardens. Earlier there were specialized "physic gardens" for the cultivation of medicinal plants. In 1447, Pope Nicholas V designated an area on the Vatican grounds for a physic garden that could also be used in the teaching of medical botany. For a century or so it was the only sponsored garden devoted to study and teaching. We don't know exactly which plants Nicholas's gardeners cultivated, but, primarily because of its emphasis on medicine, most historians don't consider his a true botanical garden.

Before they adopted systematic classification by evolutionary kinship, codified in those nestled Chinese boxes of species-genus-family-order-class still called the Linnaean system, botanists classed plants by their own response to them. One herbalist's categories included "venomous, sleepy, and hurtful" and "strange and outlandish." Greeks such as the physician Dioscorides, author of the esteemed *De Materia Medica,* and philosopher/scientist Theophrastus classed plants by edibility and medicinal worth. One goal of botanical gardens was to group plants by their family relationships.

The first institution considered by contemporary historians to be a true botanical garden appeared in Italy in the mid-1500s. This isn't surprising, since no small contribution to the Late Renaissance was the influx of exotic plants and animals brought by Italians and Spaniards returning from their explorations, especially in the New World. The timing of its establishment indicates that the first

The cover of John Gerard's 1597 Herball, or Generall Historie of Plantes *features two patron saints of horticulture, Theophrastus and Dioscorides, both of whom contributed greatly to the study of what became horticulture.*

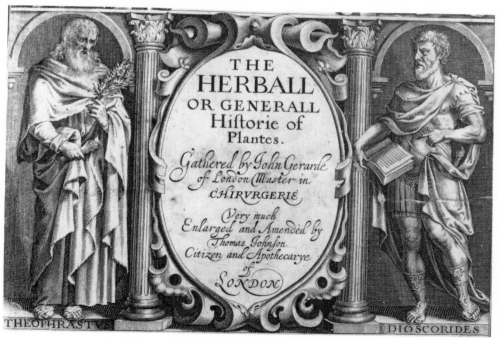

European botanical garden may have been inspired by the tales of explorers such as Hernán Cortés. His invasion of Mexico revealed—and demolished—such wonders as Montezuma's floating gardens at Tenochtitlán.

On July 7, 1545, the Venetian Senate announced that the San Giustina monastery in Padua had granted to the state lands designated for a botanical garden. Esteemed architect Giovanni Moroni da Bergamo was assigned the task of designing it, and the next year a director was appointed. In another expression of the Renaissance ideal, art was wed to science; the garden's design was elegant and formal. It was rectangular except for a central circle, which was subdivided into smaller spaces, each containing a single species of plant. The garden gradually added cacti, medicinal and culinary aromatics, and gingkos. Their innovative glasshouse still contains *La Palma di Goethe,* the tree that inspired Goethe's *Metamorphosis of Plants* (1790).

The Orto Botanico in Padua has one rival for the honor of first European botanical garden. A letter dated three days before the Venetian Senate's announcement on July 7 indicates that the garden in Pisa already existed. However, apparently their calendars differed at the time, and, unlike Pisa's, Padua's genesis is well documented. Whichever was first in a grand tradition, by the late twentieth century there were well over 500 botanical gardens in Europe.

See also Kew Gardens, 1/23.

---

8 JULY 1905

The Murder of Guy Bradley

In the 1880s, a distinguished ornithologist could be seen wandering the fashionable shopping district on 14th Street in New York City, peering closely at female passersby and scribbling in a notebook. His name was Frank M. Chapman. He was identifying the feathers on women's hats. New York, along with London and Paris, was a center of fashion, and in the late nineteenth century that included hats adorned with feathers and sometimes with the entire bodies of birds.

To a bird, a feather is a covering that insulates its high body temperature against the outside world, a lightweight and versatile flight mechanism, a disguise in a particular environment, an advertisement of species and gender, or all of the above. To a paleontologist, feathers are descendants of the scales that covered birds' reptilian ancestors. To the haut monde of the late nineteenth century, however, feathers were merely one of the supreme adornments in the milliner's art. No respectable headgear could be without them.

In 1892, the English humor magazine *Punch* ran a cartoon showing a well-dressed woman of fashion with extravagantly feathered wings hovering over dying shorebirds. That same year, a single feather dealer in Jacksonville, Florida, shipped to New York 130,000 bird skins. Plume hunters earned only $1.25 each for these "scalps," as they called the full skins with feathers still attached. It was the milliners who were making a fortune. In 1908 alone, London dealers sold 8,902 *tons* of kingfisher feathers and 15,000 tons of sooty tern feathers. Snowy and American egrets were nearing extinction in Florida. The birds sported their most prized plumage during nesting season, which meant that when they were killed their nestlings were left to starve.

Frank Chapman was author of the best field guide of his time and editor of the Audubon Society publication *Bird-Lore,* which later became *Audubon Magazine.* Soon after it appeared in 1899, the periodical began a crusade against the ravages of feather hunters. The (female) author of the first article maintained that any woman who wore a feather-decorated bonnet carried "a charnel house of beaks and claws and bones upon her fatuous head." Sometimes those wearing the hats were denounced as "murderers! Killers of baby birds!" The society endorsed an "Audubon hat," claiming its embroidered designs achieved beauty "without robbing the feathered kingdom of its plumage."

A late-nineteenth-century Punch *cartoon about the toll in avian lives resulting from the demands of fashion.*

The Audubon Society faced powerful opposition in their battle to protect what were often called "aigrettes." One major antagonist was Missouri senator James A. Reed. "Why worry ourselves into frenzy," Reed demanded, "because one lady adorns her hat with one of its feathers, which appears to be the only use it has? Let humanity utilize this bird for the only purpose that the Lord made it for, namely . . . so we could get aigrettes for bonnets of our beautiful ladies."

As so often happens, it took a tragedy to galvanize public awareness. In 1901, the Audubon Society succeeded in getting a nongame bird protection bill passed by the Florida legislature and immediately appointed four wardens to patrol the wild rookeries. Visiting Florida in 1904, the peripatetic Frank Chapman met one of those wardens. Young Guy Bradley was doing his solitary best to curb the annihilation of the birds of the mangrove and everglade swamps in Monroe County. When Chapman returned to New York, the *Sun* quoted his prediction: "That man Bradley is going to be killed sometime. He has been shot at more than once, and some day they are going to get him." He was sadly prescient. The very next year, on July 8, 1905, Guy Bradley heard shots over the Florida Bay. He grabbed his .32-caliber revolver—which more than one person had warned him was an inadequate weapon against the enemies he faced. He said a quick good-bye to his wife and children, got in his boat, and headed toward the gunshots. Hours later, someone found his body in his drifting boat. He had been shot through the neck.

Three years later, plume hunters murdered an Audubon warden in South Carolina. The national outrage over the killings helped push through new legislation. By 1910, New York State had outlawed the commercial use of wild bird feathers. Soon other states followed.

Charles Dickens and Grip

Charles Dickens published his novel *Barnaby Rudge* in 1841. Like *A Tale of Two Cities,* it was a story that, for many readers, came to define a tumultuous era—in this case, the bloody anti-Catholic uprisings of 1780, the so-called "Gordon riots." Readers of the weekly installments, in Dickens's own periodical *Master Humphrey's Clock,* eagerly followed the adventures of half-witted Barnaby and his constant companion, a garrulous raven named Grip.

Grip's oratory is memorable: "Halloa, halloa, halloa!" he cries in his first scene. "What's the matter here! Keep up your spirits. Never say die. Bow wow wow. I'm a devil. . . ." As he often did, Dickens was writing from personal experience. For years he had delighted in the antics of a pet raven. Its name was actually Grip, and its favorite exclamation was indeed "Halloa!" Dickens was so amused by the raven that, when it died, friends immediately sent him another. Eventually he owned a third.

Dickens began writing *Barnaby Rudge* in January 1841. That same month, he wrote to a friend that Grip had "waylaid and attacked a butcher, whose pantaloons have suffered considerably. He (the butcher) threatens to throw poison over the garden wall. . . ." Six weeks later, the raven became ill. The Dickens family thought Grip was probably suffering side effects of his diet. He had previously eaten the lining of a carriage and the paint from its wheels.

The raven, Grip, listening to the troubles of his imprisoned master, Barnaby Rudge.

Dickens's description of the bird's death is, well, Dickensian. "Grip is no more," he wrote to a friend. The pet shop owner Dickens summoned "administered castor oil and warm gruel," and under its influence Grip recovered his spirits enough "to be enabled to bite the groom severely." The bird "walked in a thoughtful manner up and down the stable till the clock struck Twelve at Noon; then staggered twice; exclaimed 'Hal-loa old girl'—either as a remonstrance with his weakness, or an apostrophe to Death: I am not sure which—and expired." Dickens was suspicious. The butcher wasn't even the only suspect, because Grip had also stolen a hammer from an ill-tempered carpenter. Dickens ordered an autopsy, but there was no sign of poison. Apparently the bird died of influenza.

The fictionalized Grip had many admirers. Four years after *Barnaby Rudge* appeared in England, Edgar Allan Poe published "The Raven" in the United States. His melancholy, talkative midnight visitor owes much to Grip. Almost thirty years later, Barnaby's raven was so well known that a humorous Canadian weekly used his name as its title. Other legacies include at least one portrait of the Dickens children with a raven.

After Grip's death, his owner wrote, "The Raven's body was removed with every regard for my feelings, in a covered basket. It was taken off to be stuffed. . . ." The bird was owned by various people after Dickens himself died. Mounted in a glass case, the stuffed Grip showed up on the auction block at Christie's in London. There, on July 9, 1970, for £126, someone took home the bird that had inspired one of Charles Dickens's most memorable characters.

See also Dickens's dinosaur, 2/28.

A Menace to Religion

Although William Jennings Bryan campaigned three times as the Democratic presidential candidate and was Woodrow Wilson's secretary of state, his most enduring mark on U.S. history comes from the boost he gave to the antievolution movement. His battle, although inspired by misconceptions about the nature of evolution, was a continuation of his reformist principles. He had always denounced "that damnable doctrine that might makes right," insisting that "such a conception of man's origin would weaken the cause of democracy and strengthen class pride and the power of wealth." During World War I, as Bryan had feared, the Germans expressed martial Darwinian views of their means and goals. Such pronouncements joined Bryan's fears of the moral weakness that would result from an abandonment of biblical principles, and galvanized him into becoming an antievolution crusader.

In the summer of 1925, before prosecuting Tennessee teacher John Scopes in what would be called "The Monkey Trial," Bryan sought advice from leading fundamentalists. One representative reply came from flamboyant evangelist Billy Sunday only a few days before the trial. A proudly nonintellectual former baseball player with a name worthy of a Sinclair Lewis character, Sunday had declared he wanted to spearhead a return to "old-time religion," because he felt that Americans were "groping through a fog of infidelism." Striking several fundamentalist bogeymen at once, he had called evolutionists "loud-mouthed, foreign-lingo-slinging, quack-theory-preaching bolsheviki." A later antievo-lutionist, Bernard Acworth, declared that "the *goal* of evolution, through psycho-analysis, is *moral degradation;* through organised mass birth control, and sterilisation, *extinction;* and through its social creed of communism, *revolution."*

Sunday expressed the views of many when he wrote to Bryan, "Atheism is a public enemy. Evolution is atheism. I do not believe a man can be an Evolutionist and a Christian at the same time. . . . Natural evolution is always downward and not up. If man evolved from a monkey, why are there any monkeys left? Why didn't they all evolve into humans?" He assured Bryan, "All the believing world is back of you in your defense of God and the Bible."

Perhaps not all the believing world, but many sided with Sunday and Bryan. They blamed the concept of evolution for every social ill, including the recent war. They said it undermined the God-ordained family structure, since an acceptance of the doctrine of "survival of the fittest" would lead to such abominations as men and women competing for the same job. In an article, Bryan quoted a letter that Charles Darwin wrote late in his life, chronicling his reluctant abandonment of Christianity. If Darwinism did that to Darwin, Bryan insisted, surely it would undermine tender young minds yearning to overthrow parental authority. "The evolutionary hypothesis is the only thing that has seriously menaced religion since the birth of Christ."

Such pronouncements led skeptical columnist H. L. Mencken to dismiss Bryan as "a tinpot pope in the Coca-Cola belt." But Bryan voiced growing concerns. A year earlier, an evangelist with another splendid name, Mordecai Ham, had declared: ". . . to hell with your science if it is going to damn souls." Bryan had that thought in mind as he entered the Dayton courtroom on the first day of the Scopes Trial, July 10, 1925.

See also the Scopes Trial, 7/21.

---

11 JULY 1754

Cat Overboard

As far back as 1275, dogs and cats were already so standard a part of an English ship's crew that the first Statute of Westminster ruled that a vessel was not abandoned as long as either was still aboard. A 1532 ship's log records that it had aboard both a dog and a cat, "with all other necessaries." It wasn't only commoners who observed this rule. When he was admiral under his brother King Charles II, the future James II took his dogs to sea with him. During a bad shipwreck James allegedly cried out, much to his later chagrin, "Save the dogs and Colonel Churchill!" In the ensuing scramble for safety, a duke's personal physician had to fight his employer's dog for the last available place.

Some of the stories of pets at sea turn out more pleasantly. In 1754, English novelist Henry Fielding undertook a trip to Portugal for his health. It was unsuccessful; two months after his arrival, he died. His last book was the posthumously published *Journal of a Voyage to Lisbon.* In the *Journal,* Fielding exhibited that affection for the common folk that suffuses such novels as *Joseph Andrewes* and *Tom Jones,* and also the simple morality that led Samuel Johnson to dismiss him as a "blockhead." Fielding loved scenes that had the moral ring of parables. He must have savored his story of the kitten that fell overboard.

The ship's cabin was home to four cats. They were there to prey upon the mice and rats that stowed away in every hold. Probably, like home owners, the ship's crew didn't feed them, because doing so would have weakened the animals' desire to hunt. On July 11, while the ship was under sail, a kitten fell into the sea. The captain received the announcement "with the utmost concern and many bitter oaths." He ordered the sails slackened. "I was, I own," Fielding said, "extremely surprised at all this; less indeed at the captain's extreme tenderness than at his conceiving any possibility of success; for if puss had had nine thousand instead of nine lives, I concluded they had been all lost."

The captain disagreed. To Fielding's astonishment, he ordered all hands to assist a rescue. The courageous boatswain stripped and dived into the water—returning a few minutes later, like a retriever, with the motionless cat *in his mouth.* The unfortunate animal was placed on the deck in the sunshine. At first it showed no signs of life, but in time it revived. Apparently neither it nor the boatswain lost even one life.

Fielding learned that this rescue effort was not as dangerous as it at first seemed to a landlubber. The captain's compassion nonetheless fell into the category the novelist elsewhere called "the more amiable weaknesses of human nature." Still, some of the crew felt that their captain had defied the venerable superstition that the best way to raise a favorable wind was to drown a cat at sea.

---

12 JULY 1794

Alexander Wilson, Bird of Passage

In the town of Paisley, Scotland, in 1766, a minister baptized an infant boy. The United States did not yet exist, but it soon would, and both man and child would become well known there. A decade later, the Reverend Dr. John Witherspoon was president of the College of New Jersey and became the only educator or minister to sign the Declaration of Independence. The baby, Alexander Wilson, grew up to become the second most famous ornithologist and bird painter in the New World, behind only the legendary Audubon.

No one observing Wilson's early life could have predicted his eventual fame. Later, the incurable wanderer described himself as a "bird of passage," and even as a child he liked to ramble far afield from Paisley. After a three-year apprenticeship as a weaver, young Alexander worked as a peddler and poet. He was one of the first subscribers to Robert Burns's volumes of poems and wrote in a similar vernacular style himself. After distributing several poems calling for political reform—or, in the eyes of their targets, libeling his fellow citizens—Wilson found himself imprisoned and finally burning his offensive poems in public. Inspired by the American Revolution, especially by the words of Thomas Paine, Wilson headed for the relative freedom in the New World. He was eighteen.

Wilson arrived in Delaware on July 12, 1794. Almost entirely self-taught, he nonetheless worked as a schoolteacher and as a surveyor in a small town in Pennsylvania. Back in Philadelphia, he encountered the garden of pioneer botanist John Bartram. (It still exists.) And he met the man who was going to point him in the direction of his eventual fame, Bartram's son, William, whose 1791 *Travels through North and South Carolina, Georgia, East and West Florida* is one of the monuments of natural history in the early nation.

From Bartram, Wilson learned the mix of romantic love of nature and accurate portrayal of its creatures that marks his work. In 1803, Wilson wrote to a friend back home in Scotland, "I am now about to make a collection of all our finest birds." In 1808, he published the first volume of his *American Ornithology,* nineteen years before Audubon's *Birds of America* began appearing. He vowed to travel "from the shores of the St. Lawrence to the mouth of the Mississippi, and from the Atlantic Ocean to the interior of Louisiana." Incredibly, over the next five years, he lived up to most of his promise. He traveled untold thousands of miles across half a continent, usually alone and mostly on foot.

Not counting the signature on his will, Alexander Wilson's last written words were a list of birds. One day in 1813, under "Undrawn," he listed twenty-one birds, including the turkey, swan, and albatross, and several gulls and pelicans. That very day, he collapsed from dysentery. Ten days later he died. "Alexander Wilson," noted the minister in his record book, "native of Scotland, but resident here for many years, author of *American Ornithology,* aged about forty years, not married." He was actually forty-seven, but everything else was correct. It was enough.

See also the ivory-billed woodpecker, 3/5.

---

13 July 1923

Dinosaur Eggs in Mongolia

During the 1920s, the president of the American Museum of Natural History, Henry Fairfield Osborn, sent several expeditions to Asia in search of fossil humans. Known as the "Missing Link" expeditions, they were both well funded and highly publicized. However, because of agreements with other paleontologists and the Chinese National Geological Survey, they were mostly restricted to the ancient wastes of Mongolia, the rocks of which were too old to be hoarding fossil humans. In that regard, the expeditions failed.

However, in other categories, they were a stunning success. Roy Chapman Andrews, who has been described as the Indiana Jones of paleontology, was a zoologist with the museum. He was chosen to head the Central Asiatic Expedition. Although he didn't succeed in his search for early humans, by the time Andrews left Mongolia for the last time the expedition's scientists had named over 1,000 animals and plants, both fossil and living, that were new to science. They brought to the United States a total of more than 26,000 fossil specimens. One of the most exciting discoveries was the first proof that dinosaurs laid eggs.

In September 1922, photographer J. B. Shackleford found a fossilized egg at a place called the Flaming Cliffs in Mongolia's Gobi Desert. The skeptical consensus was that it must be a fossilized bird egg. On July 13, 1923, an expedition member named George Olsen reported that he had found fossil eggs. Andrews and the others were still skeptical. Expecting the eggs to turn out to be some sort of geological concretion, they accompanied Olsen to the site. Andrews described the find in his 1932 book *The New Conquest of China:* "We saw a small sandstone ledge beside which were lying three eggs, partly broken. The brown, striated shell was so egglike that there could be no mistake." Admirably cautious, they tried to think of every objection to the items' being what they appeared to be. Finally, however, "we had to admit that eggs are eggs and we could make them out to be nothing else. It was evident that dinosaurs did lay eggs and that we had discovered the first specimens known to science."

In retrospect, it is not surprising that dinosaurs laid eggs. Most of their surviving relatives do, from the box turtle to the blue-footed booby. Nowadays, as the evidence pours in that birds are a surviving descendant of dinosaurs, scientists refer to those giant lizards beloved in film as "nonavian dinosaurs." In that case, not only did dinosaurs lay eggs long ago, but some still do. There is considerable evidence that a number of these creatures behaved much more like birds than like surviving reptiles such as crocodiles or lizards. For example, like many species of birds, apparently they even arranged their eggs in the nest with the broad end facing toward the center.

The dinosaur eggs proved to have more than scientific value. Andrews and the museum, ever in need of funds, decided to auction one of the eggs to publicize the research and encourage donations. One Colonel Austin Colgate was willing to pay $5,000 for the privilege of donating his own dinosaur egg to Colgate University. The funding campaign eventually raised over a quarter of a million dollars. In response, the governments of Russia, China, and Mongolia concluded that all the eggs found were of similar value. Their misconception that they had been robbed of a vast prehistoric treasure did not help the international climate, and eventually the expeditions had to be canceled.

For more on dinosaurs, see 8/12, 9/3, and 10/1.

"Grotesquest of Animals"

Mark Twain first made a name for himself with travel writing—*A Tramp Abroad, Roughing It, Innocents Abroad.* He returned to that genre late in his career, combining a lecture tour with research for a new book to relieve his bankruptcy. On July 14, 1895, he and his wife and one of their daughters left their home in Elmira, New York, for the trip around the world that in 1897 became *Following the Equator.*

Like most of Twain's books, the new one was filled with animal stories. One of the best is what Twain claimed was a naturalist's comments on "the opulently endowed *e pluribus unum* of the animal world," the duck-billed platypus, then called the *Ornithorhynchus.* "[I]n his opinion Nature's fondness for dabbling in the erratic was most notably exhibited in that curious combination of bird, fish, amphibian, burrower, crawler, quadruped . . . called Ornithorhyncus—grotesquest of animals, king of the animalculae of the world for versatility of character and make-up."

This creature, the naturalist maintained, "is clearly a bird, for it lays eggs. . . ." Of course, the platypus is not a bird, but it does lay eggs. The first authoritative confirmation of that astounding fact came in 1884, when English biologist W. H. Caldwell telegraphed from Australia his contribution to a meeting in Canada: "Monotremes oviparous, ovum meroblastic." Translation: Not only do monotremes lay eggs, but their eggs are more like those of reptiles and birds than like mammalian eggs that develop inside the body. The platypus and echidna are called monotremes ("one-hole") because they have a single orifice for their reproductive, urinary, and intestinal canals—another reptilian characteristic. Twain's naturalist declared the creature "clearly a mammal, for it nurses its young. . . ." True, the females have large mammary glands, but they lack nipples. They secrete milk through pores, and the babies lap it up.

For some time afterward, to the amusement of audiences on his lecture tour, Twain kept trying to write poems in which he could rhyme something with "Ornithorhyncus." The animal's other name, platypus, is Greek for "flat-footed," but the livelier *Ornitho-rhynchus* embodies a more obvious feature; it is from the Greek words for "bird" and "beak." That famous attribute, which European naturalists first thought was somehow sewn on as part of a hoax, is not avian. One of the many early questions about the platypus was why it had so many thick nerves running from the brain to the bill. We now know that countless tiny pores and projections in the bill house electroreceptors. Like many fishes and amphibians, which also live in wet environments, platypuses are extremely sensitive to electrical fields. That explains why they were observed swimming with their eyes closed: They don't need to see underwater.

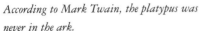

According to Mark Twain, the platypus was never in the ark.

Comedian Robin Williams imagined God piecing together the platypus while smoking marijuana and giggling to himself, with an attitude of "Hey, Darwin, watch this." Mark Twain also contemplated the creature's evolution. "It is a survival—a survival of the fittest. Mr. Darwin invented the theory that goes by that name, but the Ornithorhyncus was the first to put it to actual experiment and prove that it could be done. . . . It was never in the Ark; . . . it nobly stayed out and worked the theory."

See also Twain's animals, 1/20; and the Connecticut Yankee's eclipse, 6/21.

A Day's Work

The English word "journal" is simply a different pronunciation of the Old French *journal,* "daily," from the Latin with the same meaning, *diurnalis.* That in turn came from *dies,* "day." Our word for travel from one place to another, "journey," grew from precisely the same roots and once had the meaning of "a day's work." This is a fitting parallel, because for many people the keeping of a journal—a "diary," again ultimately from *dies*—has been the record of a day's work, or even the work itself.

"Do you keep a journal?" Ralph Waldo Emerson asked Henry David Thoreau. James Boswell wrote of Samuel Johnson, "He recommended me to keep a journal of my life, full and unreserved. He said it would be a very good exercise." John Locke aimed similar advice at lazy thinkers: "Nothing can contribute more to obviate the inconvenience and difficulties attending a vacant or wandering mind, than the arrangement and regular disposal of our thoughts in a well ordered and copious common-place book. . . ." Those words appeared in the front of the commonplace book used by Erasmus Darwin, England's prominent eighteenth-century poet, scientist, and evolutionist.

Erasmus's grandson Charles was a lifelong journal-keeper. From the days of the *Beagle* voyage, which he undertook at the age of twenty-two, Darwin's journal and notebooks were part of his day's work. Many of his entries in the purely science-oriented notebooks bear dates and form a journal of the progress of his thinking on evolution and other topics. A year after beginning his first notebook on what he called "Transmutation of Species," Darwin began a more specialized one. In his journal he wrote, "Opened note book connected with metaphysical enquiries." For Darwin, these were not separate topics. After designating other notebooks with various letters, he referred to this particular one as the "M" notebook. The first entry wastes no time.

> July 15, 1838. My father says he thinks bodily complaints /& mental disposition / oftener go with colour, than with form of body.—thus the late Colonel Leighton resembled his father in body, but his mother in bodily & mental disposition.—

His father was a physician. Darwin was always picking the brain of everyone around him and seeking out farmers, pigeon fanciers, rose growers, anyone who could cast light on the questions that plagued him. His journals and notebooks demonstrate the range of his interests. It is axiomatic that all art is self-portrait. So is much of science. And as Darwin recorded the progress of his thought on the many topics that interested him, he painted a vivid picture of himself.

In November of 1837, he wrote, "If all men were dead, then monkeys make men.—Men make angels." As his title page advertised (to himself only, he thought, but historians are shameless Peeping Toms), many of these remarks have philosophical overtones. That seems appropriate for a discipline addressing some of the most profound human questions, the sort Paul Gauguin would use for the title of one of his paintings half a century later—*Where did we come from? What are we? Where are we going?* Darwin wasn't presumptuous enough to tackle the last question, but he gave the other two his steadfast attention. In that vein, a month after beginning the "M" notebook, Darwin wrote, "Origin of man now proved.—Metaphysics must flourish.—He who understand baboon would do more toward metaphysics than Locke." So much for the patron saint of English empiricism—and of his grandfather's commonplace book.

In 1868, nine years after the publication of the *Origin* and three before *The Descent of Man,* Darwin took up a page of his notebook with a drawing of the evolutionary family tree of primates. Branches near the bottom are labeled "Lemurs" and "Old World Monkeys," while "Man" is only one of several branches that form the crown. He quoted some remarks by his sister about imagination, and added, "Children like hearing a story told though they remember it so well that they can correct every detail, yet they have not imagination enough to recall up the image in their own mind.—this may be worth thinking over." For Darwin, everything was worth thinking over, but he made his ultimate theme explicit in the manifesto he wrote in the "B" notebook:

> ((the grand Question which every naturalist ought to have before him when dissecting a whale or classifying a mite, a fungus or an infusorian is "What are the Laws of Life"))

---

16 July 1958

The Fly

"Did your brother ever experiment with animals?"
"Never."
"Or insects?"
"Insects?"

"There are things Man should never experiment with," the scientist in the film *The Fly* informs his wife in a note. "Now I must destroy everything—all evidence—even myself. No one must know what I discovered. It's too dangerous." Helene argues that he can't do that because he's a man with a soul. However, André has the rhetorical upper hand, because at the moment, soul notwithstanding, he's mainly a man with the head and arm of a fly. He has to communicate in writing because he can no longer talk.

"One strong factor of the picture," *Variety* remarked in its July 16, 1958, review, "is its unusual believability." That believability, such as it is, does help inspire sympathy for the plight of the inventor. André has foolishly tried his new invention, a matter transmitter, on himself. While he is disintegrating his atoms, in order to transport them across the room and reintegrate them, they become mixed with the atoms of a fly that wandered into the chamber. The fly winds up with the scientist's head and one arm, and the man receives the head and arm of the insect. (This technology hasn't improved by the far-future time of the first *Star Trek* series. When traveling via "transporter," the crew of Captain Kirk's *Enterprise* frequently find their particles scrambled in transit.)

In an earlier debacle which should have warned him, André grows impatient with experimenting on inanimate objects and places the family cat in the teleportation chamber. The animal vanishes but then does not reappear—although André can hear it meowing in the air around him. When he tells Helene, she articulates the implicit warning of many science fiction films: "It's—it's like playing God." The disintegration of her cat leads her to remark that life is moving too fast in the modern world.

Had André become a hamster or a canary it would have been inconvenient but not disgusting; his transformation is so horrific partially because flies are universally reviled. They were one of the plagues with which God punished Pharaoh. Heracles supposedly sacrificed to Zeus to rid Olympia of flies, and therefore the Eleans of ancient Greece called Zeus Apomysius, "who drives away flies." In Christian symbolism, flies usually represent evil and sin. One of the names for the devil, Beelzebub, comes from a derisive term the Israelites applied to other peoples' gods. They dismissed other deities as mere *baal zevuv* (or *zebub*), "lords of flies." In Milton's *Paradise Lost,* Beelzebub is Satan's lieutenant.

David Cronenberg's 1986 remake of *The Fly*—not to be confused with the much earlier sequel to the original—starred Jeff Goldblum. In another role, as the title character in Philippe Setbon's *Mr. Frost* (1990), Goldblum played Satan, or at least a serial killer who convinces a psychiatrist that he is Satan. Mr. Frost's Renfield-like fondness for flies is a quiet reminder of the old dark associations with these insects. Even without the mythological trappings, flies' reputations are forever tarnished by their association with disease and putrefaction. In reality, few of the 100,000 or so members of the order Diptera (which includes not only true flies but also mosquitos, midges, and gnats) are dangerous to humans.

In the famous climax of *The Fly,* Vincent Price and the police inspector are near a spiderweb when they hear a tiny high-pitched voice crying, "Help me." The web is a typically imperfect orb-weaver's job, with a zigzag pattern down the center like those spun by Argiope and other garden spiders. The spider itself turns out to be a menacing dark shape coming toward the source of the voice—a trapped, struggling fly with the head of Price's brother. With a huge stone, the inspector smashes web, spider, and yet another cinematic scientist whose fatal flaw was curiosity.

A Comet Hits Jupiter

Astronomers refer to it as 1993e—that is, the fifth comet discovered in 1993. Another well-known shorthand version is S-L9. Its full official name explains that abbreviation: Periodic Comet Shoemaker-Levy 9. The comet is named for a team of astronomers, Carolyn and Eugene Shoemaker and David Levy. The number denotes that this is the ninth periodic comet they have discovered. However, there are more than eight other comets bearing their names, because they have also discovered twenty-odd parabolic comets.

The Shoemakers and Levy discovered SL-9 in March of 1993. While looking over the photographs from a partly cloudy night of observing at California's Mount Palomar Observatory, they found what seemed to be a long smear in the sky near the bright glow of Jupiter. After their announcement, other astronomers went back and checked their photographic plates, and several discovered that they had photographed S-L9 and dismissed it as a smudge. Upon further examination, it turned out to be twenty or so objects apparently orbiting Jupiter. An extrapolated analysis of the comet's orbit revealed that, in July of the previous year, it had passed so near Jupiter that the planet's massive gravity had torn it apart. However, massive or not, Jupiter's gravity could not have crumbled a comet unless it was already a very loose coalition of particles ready to fragment.

No one had noticed the comet while it was near Jupiter. Usually astronomers don't try to photograph near the planet because its brightness blurs the image. Nonetheless, Swedish astronomers had photographed the area, and when the pictures from 1992 were examined, they showed no trace of the comet. Some astronomers suggest that S-L9 may have been there for a long time, but had not been bright enough to be detected until it broke apart and exposed a great deal more dust to sunlight.

Strictly speaking, by the time it was discovered Shoemaker-Levy 9 had already ceased to be a single comet. Probably it had orbited the sun for aeons before Jupiter attracted it. Scientists think that before it was torn asunder by Olympian gravity, S-L9 was no more than a few miles wide. Probably it was composed of rock, ice, and organic compounds. A series of photographic images of the comet, beginning in March of 1993, reveal its slow breakup. By July 17, the former comet has clearly separated into a chain of distinct particles. Two photographs taken precisely one year later, on July 17, 1994, show the dark spots in the southern hemisphere of Jupiter that resulted from the collisions of what were called Fragments C, A, and E. To put the matter in perspective, each of those spots was larger than the planet Earth. Tentative explanations of the nature of those spots include organic molecules that had been part of the comets, organic molecules synthesized by the impact, and matter thrown up from the forever-hidden lower levels of Jupiter's dense atmosphere.

Astronomers were able to predict exactly when the comet pieces would strike Jupiter. However, although guesses abounded, no one knew what effect the cometary particles would have on the planet. The results were more dramatic than astronomers had dared imagine. As millions of people watched either through telescopes or on television, each of the cometary particles crashed impressively into the Jovian atmosphere. For all its frightening nearness and its poignant reminder of our own vulnerability, SL-9 inspired absolute glee in sky watchers. The crash of Shoemaker-Levy 9 into the largest planet in the solar system was simply the most dramatic event to take place in our neighborhood in historic times.

---

18 JULY 1989

"The Demands of Luxury"

So geographers, in Afric maps,
With savage pictures fill their gaps,
And o'er uninhabitable downs
Place elephants for want of towns.

This late 1800s illustration portrays not merely ivory but the ivory of Siberian mammoths. As more and more of the ancient tusks surfaced, a thriving trade developed.

When Jonathan Swift wrote that, towns were scarcer in Africa than nowadays, and elephants more plentiful. Yet thousands of years of human depredation had already diminished the once continent-wide elephant population. Saharan rock-carvings from 5,000 to 11,000 years ago, before the desert was a desert, portray elephants. And yet, by the first century A.D., Pliny the Elder was bemoaning the herds that had fallen victim to "the demands of luxury."

Biologically, ivory is simply the modified teeth of various large mammals, including elephants and walruses. Although some have thought otherwise, it has no medical or other inherent value. But, usually fine-grained and always long-lasting, it's an ideal and prestigious medium for sculpture. The Greeks of 2500 B.C. sculpted in ivory and gold—chryselephantine, the combination was called—and China's ivory-carving is just as ancient. Sudanese chiefs paid tribute with ivory in the time of the Egyptian pharaohs. So many things have been made from it that at times "ivories" has been slang for false teeth, billiard balls, dice, and piano keys.

The invention of firearms placed elephants in greater peril than ever. A well-equipped hunter could kill 200 or more in a single safari. Surplus was abandoned in the bush. As the older elephants with larger tusks were killed, it took more and more of the smaller, younger ones to provide the same amount of ivory. The pace escalated, apparently on a sharp curve toward extinction.

Attempts to ban the ivory trade began as early as the 1880s. But it would be another hundred years before the elephant became the poster child for African conservation, achieving the celebrity status conservationists dub "charismatic megafauna." In 1989, the multinational Ivory Trade Review Group announced that Africa's 1.3 million elephants of 1979 had been reduced to only half that. This led to an international ban on ivory.

Then paleontologist-turned-conservationist Richard Leakey had an idea to publicize and gain support for the ban. He joined with Kenyan president Daniel arap Moi, whose conservation record hitherto had been less than inspiring. They hired a Washington, D.C., public relations firm to promote their plan. On July 18, 1989, representatives of news media from around the world gathered inside Nairobi National Park in Kenya. Various charismatic megafauna browsed against the Nairobi skyline, but most eyes and cameras were on a cone-shaped pile of ivory, twenty feet high and containing twelve tons of elephant tusks. Ivory traders had offered the Kenyan government $3 million for it, and arap Moi had refused. Millions around the world now watched as he set fire to it.

Many applauded; many did not. The burn was called both "moral" and "stupid." Detractors point out that the ban emphasizes ivory, not elephants. Here and there, greatly reduced prices have made ivory locally affordable, encouraging isolated poaching for the middle class. But in general the ban has been considered surprisingly effective. In 1990, Kenya lost only fifty-five elephants, a 99 percent reduction from the year before.

---

19 JULY 1941

Cat and Mouse

Early in the seventeenth century, Englishman Edward Topsell translated and annotated the Latin of Swiss naturalist Conrad Gesner, who had published his *Historiae Animalium* over half a century before. In Topsell's version, *The Historie of Foure-Footed Beastes,* the section on an age-old companion of human beings is marvelously phrased.

> The little mouse therefore is justly termed *Incola domus nostrae,* an inhabitant in our own houses, *Et rosor omnium rerum,* and a knawer of all things. . . . There is no creature that heareth more perfectly than a Mouse, they dwell in houses of men, especially neare supping and dyning roomes, kitchins or larders, where any meat is stirring. . . . In the day time they lye still, so long as they either see or heare a man, or any other beast harmeful unto them, for they discerne their enemies, not fearing an Oxe, though they run away from a Cat.

It was the mice's tendency to dwell near supping roomes and larders that led their human house-mates to keep a cat around. Two centuries after Gesner, the Swedish systematist who called himself Linnaeus dubbed the cat *Felis Catus,* and described it as "the lion of mice." One of Aesop's fables tells of an aging, decrepit cat that is no longer nimble enough to pursue his favorite prey. Hoping to lure the mice within reach of her arthritic paws, she hangs herself by the hind legs from a peg in a wall. Her old adversaries are not that gullible, however, and one of them mutters to the others, "I've seen many a bag in my day, but never one with a cat's head at the bottom of it."

A number of proverbs and phrases have resulted from this ancient conflict. "Cat and mouse" was a children's game in which one child chased another through the circle of their fellow players. It is easy to see why "when the cat's away, the mice will play." Because they didn't want their play rudely interrupted by the return of the cat, mice in another fable decide to hang a bell around its neck to alert them of its approach. Perhaps understandably, not one volunteered to "bell the cat" for the benefit of the others.

Understandably, the eternal rivalry of cat and mouse doesn't lend itself to live-action film. However, it is the perfect sort of relationship to thrive in the carefree world of animation, and beginning in 1940 it did so. That year, MGM released an animated short film entitled *Puss Gets the Boot.* It introduced early versions of two characters that would become popular cartoon stars— a cat, here named Jasper, and a nameless mouse. The cat's owner warns him that he will be evicted if he breaks anything, and every time he approaches the mouse, the wise rodent holds a fragile object ransom. Nonetheless, Jasper pursues the mouse with all the wicked glee of a real cat. They speak not a single word. Both they and we know the terms of their ancient feud.

Directed by Bill Hanna and Joe Barbera, who would later found their own studio, *Puss Gets the Boot* was a much greater hit than MGM expected. On July 19, 1941, the studio released a second

In a fable by Aesop, an arthritic old cat hangs herself up like a bag in hope of luring mice near. This is how B. te Gempt portrayed the scene for the 1755 French edition of La Fontaine's adaptation.

short cartoon, *The Midnight Snack,* starring the same characters. Jasper was renamed Tom, and the mouse became Jerry. In successive cartoons, taking place in a bowling alley, during a classical music concert, dancing with Gene Kelly, even swimming with Esther Williams, Tom and Jerry acted out the age-old game of cat and mouse.

---

20 JULY 1969

"Only One Earth"

Moments after the Landing Module touched the surface of the Moon, Neil Armstrong said into the radio, "Houston, Tranquillity Base here. The *Eagle* has landed." Beyond the Command Module, where Michael Collins orbited and watched, Earth hung in the sky over the heads of Armstrong and Edwin "Buzz" Aldrin. Back home on that blue and white ball, an estimated 600 million people watched the ghostly black-and-white broadcast of our first visit to another world. At 10:56 P.M. eastern daylight time, on July 20, 1969, Armstrong stepped onto the surface of the Moon. "That's one small step for man," he said, and paused, "and one giant leap for mankind."

The entire *Apollo 11* mission took only eight days, and within six months a second team had landed on the Moon. Others followed. Then, after *Apollo 17* returned in December 1972, it was over. In his 1939 science fiction story "Trends," Isaac Asimov envisioned American society vehemently resisting space travel; nonetheless, the first flight to the Moon takes place in the 1970s. The reality preceded Asimov's guess, but what no one foresaw is that soon after lunar flights became reality we would lose interest in them.

President Nixon took time out from the Vietnam War to sign a plaque that *Apollo 11* was to leave behind on the Moon: "We came in peace for all mankind." According to a treaty signed two-and-a-half years before, neither the Moon nor any other celestial body could belong to any nation on Earth. Nevertheless, the United States had long been in a race to the Moon with the Soviet Union, eager for the military clout due a technological front-runner. However, when Nixon called from Earth he avoided that narrow perspective. After reminding his global audience that he was making the most "historic" phone call ever made from the White House, Nixon said, "For one priceless moment, in the whole history of man, all the people on this Earth are truly one." Later astronauts remarked on the unity of humanity as viewed from space. "The first day or so we all pointed to our countries," a member of the Discovery 5 Space Mission recalled. "The third or fourth day we were pointing to our continents. By the fifth day we were aware of only one Earth."

After staying up late to watch the Moon landing, E. B. White wrote a quick paragraph for the *New Yorker.* He pointed out that although the childlike bounciness of Aldrin and Armstrong proved the Moon was a fun place to be, the flag looked awkward and unnatural. "Like every great river and every great sea, the moon belongs to none and belongs to all. It still holds the key to madness, still controls the tides that lap on shores everywhere, still guards the lovers that kiss in every land under no banner but the sky." He proposed that instead of a national flag snapping in an imaginary breeze, the astronauts ought to have planted a more universal emblem of humanity—perhaps a limp white handkerchief, symbol of that shared human experience, the common cold.

See also the flat Earth, 3/18.

---

21 JULY 1925

The Scopes Trial

In early 1925, partially because its sponsor hadn't had a bill passed recently, the Tennessee legislature approved a measure that made it illegal to teach evolution in the state's schools. No one expected it to become law. However, to the legislature's surprise, Governor Austin Peay chose to sign rather than veto. He called the bill "a protest against a tendency to exalt science, and deny the Bible," but added, "Nobody believes that it is going to be an active statute."

Shortly afterward, the recently founded American Civil Liberties Union advertised in the *Chattanooga Times,* offering free legal counsel for any teacher challenging the antievolution act. Boosters in nearby Dayton thought such a scandal might put their little town on the national map. They considered approaching their local biology teacher, but he was also the school principal and a conservative family man. However, John T. Scopes, the athletics coach and physics teacher, sometimes substituted for the older man, and he was a freethinking bachelor.

Scopes was playing tennis when a messenger invited him to the drugstore for a powwow with the town fathers. Although the current state-issued biology text addressed the concept of evolution, and although he himself had only assigned some review material while substituting and hadn't actually taught the hot topic, Scopes agreed to challenge the new law. His sponsors carefully publicized his arrest.

Famous defense attorney Clarence Darrow, fresh from the shocking *Leopold-Loeb* case, volunteered to defend Scopes. The World's Christian Fundamentalists Association got as prosecutor "The Great Commoner," three-time presidential candidate and antievolution crusader William Jennings Bryan. Reporters poured into the tiny town from all over the nation. Chicago's WGN radio station pioneered remote broadcasting to cover "the strange happenings in the Tennessee hills." Even archskeptic H. L. Mencken journeyed over from Baltimore to watch the show.

On July 21, 1925, the jury needed less than ten minutes to decide that Scopes was guilty. Darrow immediately began the appeals process, but it was thwarted. In January 1927, the Tennessee Supreme Court upheld the antievolution statute but basically declared it unenforceable. Then they also reversed the lower court's verdict on a technicality. The judge had fined Scopes $100, twice the penalty he could levy without a jury vote.

The Scopes Trial symbolized more than it accomplished. As the judge insisted, the question was, had Mr. Scopes violated the antievolution law or had he not? No one denied that he had. But for Darrow and Bryan, as for the millions of Americans who followed the trial, other issues were at stake. This was proved suddenly when, alarmed at the direction questions were taking, a member of Bryan's team demanded, "What is the meaning of all this?" The Commoner shook his fist at Darrow and shouted, "To protect the Word of God against the greatest atheist or agnostic in the United States!" The great atheist or agnostic replied in kind: "To show up Fundamentalism! To prevent bigots and ignoramuses from controlling the educational system of the United States!"

See also Bryan and Billy Sunday, 7/10.

---

22 JULY 1878

"The Night Is Very Large"

In the nineteenth century, when Gerard Manley Hopkins gazed at the night sky, he could hardly contain himself: "Look at the stars! look, look up at the skies! O look at all the firefolk sitting in the air!" With a solemn lack of exclamation points, Thomas Carlyle looked up at the stars and wrote, "A sad spectacle. If they be inhabited, what a scope for misery and folly. If they not be inhabited, what a waste of space." Walt Whitman tended more toward the Hopkins school of stargazing. His 1882 prose collec-

Walt Whitman saw the night sky as a criticism of human pride, glory, and ambition.

tion *Specimen Days* includes excerpts from his journal. On the evening of July 22, 1878, he wrote, "Now, indeed, if never before, the heavens declared the glory of God. . . . There, in abstraction and stillness, . . . the copiousness, the removedness, vitality, loose-clear-crowdedness . . . and I, though but a point in the centre below, embodying all." Elsewhere he asked, "Ah, where would be any food for spirituality without night and the stars?"

Like Huck and Jim floating down the Mississippi at night, most people throughout history have looked at the stars and wondered "whether they was made, or only just happened." It was a question of ultimate origins and meaning that some considered beyond the capabilities of science. "When I look at the stars," Thoreau wrote, "nothing which the astronomers have said attaches to them, they are so simple and remote." Walt Whitman agreed. In his brief poem "When I Heard the Learn'd Astronomer," he listens to a lecture, tires of the dry analysis, and wanders outdoors, where he looks up "in perfect silence at the stars."

Whitman also expressed a sense of the stars' vast size, so many orders of magnitude away from human concerns. "One can understand, such a night, why, from the days of the Pharaohs or Job, the dome of heaven, sprinkled with planets, has supplied the subtlest, deepest criticism on human pride, glory, ambition." Lord Dunsany said it simply in one of his fantasy stories: "A man is a small thing, and the night is very large and full of wonders."

American naturalist William Beebe agreed. He was a close friend of Theodore Roosevelt and frequently visited him at his home. They developed an odd little ritual to help them keep their lives in perspective with the rest of the universe. At bedtime, they went out on the lawn and looked up at the stars. "We searched," Beebe wrote, "until we found, with or without glasses, the faint, heavenly spot of light-mist beyond the lower left-hand corner of the Great Square of Pegasus. . . ." One of them would then recite something along the lines of this:

> *That is the Spiral Galaxy in Andromeda.*
> *It is as large as our Milky Way.*
> *It is one of a hundred million galaxies.*
> *It is 750,000 light-years away.*
> *It consists of one hundred billion suns,*
> *each larger than our sun.*

Then, after a moment's silence, the other would say, "Now I think we are small enough. Let's go to bed."

See also moonlight, 6/6.

Thoreau and Darwin

No doubt some of the people of Concord, Massachusetts, considered him a loafer and ne'er-do-well, but Henry David Thoreau stayed busy. He had many self-assigned tasks. He not only devoted himself to inspecting snowstorms and improving the nick of time, he read widely. Educated in the classics at Harvard, he read Virgil and Homer in the original. Thoreau knew the history of natural history and travel literature from throughout the ages, but he particularly admired Charles Darwin's *Voyage of a Naturalist round the World,* now referred to as the *Voyage of the* Beagle.

Thoreau first read Darwin in the summer of 1851 and scribbled page after page of notes. He liked the way the Englishman telescoped five years of crisscrossing the oceans and revisiting parts of the world into a single straightforward travel narrative. Later, as he constructed *Walden,* Thoreau turned his own two years and two months at the pond into a single yearlong circle of seasons. He went on to read many of the books Darwin quoted in the *Voyage.* And, as the iconoclastic Thoreau ambivalently watched the study of nature becoming a professional discipline, he admired Darwin's description of himself as "a person fond of natural history."

However, Thoreau and Darwin studied nature in different ways. Despite his adoring adjectives that, his children remarked, made him sound like a salesman, Darwin was not a poet. "Science," he wrote, "consists in grouping facts so that general laws or conclusions may be drawn from them." Thoreau found that definition inadequate. He noted in his journal, "I look over the report of the doings of a scientific association and . . . I cannot help suspecting that the life of these learned professors has been almost as inhuman and wooden as a rain-gauge or self-regulating magnetic machine." Darwin imagined that eventually "the terms used by naturalists . . . will cease to be metaphorical, and will have a plain signification." For Thoreau that was unthinkable. Metaphor was his very life. Walden Pond was the eye of the earth, and time not a spatial dimension but the stream in which he went a-fishing. Darwin reported the behavior of guinea fowl on the "Cape de Verd Islands," and Thoreau automatically transformed their skittishness into a metaphor for his own. "What sort of science is that," he asked, "which enriches the understanding but robs the imagination?"

Nonetheless, over the years, plenty of the time Thoreau could have spent writing poems he employed instead for fact noting and measuring. He complained to himself, "I fear that the character of my knowledge is from year to year becoming more detailed and scientific. . . ." Thoreau was not antiscience. He simply asked for something that science was already beginning to disclaim: meaning. On July 23, 1851, he wrote in his journal, "But this habit of close observation,—in Humboldt, Darwin, and others. Is it to be kept up long, this science? Do not tread on the heels of your experience . . . Poetry puts an interval between the impression and expression,—waits till the seed germinates naturally."

---

24 JULY 1609

The Storm Devil

The word "hurricane" comes from the Caribbean, where people knew enough to fear *Hurakan,* the Storm Devil. Back before storms were tracked with radar and satellites, hurricanes could lurk in the Atlantic with impunity, and many an unsuspecting mariner sailed right into them. One such encounter left a curious legacy. The *Sea Venture,* leading eight other ships, departed England in 1609 with supplies and colonists for the first English settlement in the New World, James Towne in Virginia. Severe weather sent them scurrying back to port, but finally they started across the ocean. Then, on Monday, July 24, they encountered a hurricane that raged for several days.

Of course, many ships have encountered storms. Aboard the *Sea Venture,* however, was William Strachey, a well-educated Englishman with a literary bent. He left a record of the battle against the hurricane. His memorable details include the crew checking for leaks by candlelight and stuffing holes with chunks of salted beef. For the next three days, as the ship was tossed about, the crew pumped water constantly just to remain afloat. Then, lost, without its fellows, the ship reached the formidable Bermuda coast. Other ships had wrecked there in the past by striking the coral reefs broadside and smashing apart. In this case, almost playfully, the waves lodged the *Sea Venture* head-on and held it between outcroppings. The vessel was ruined, but the crew, 150 passengers, and a dog survived. It was almost a year before the ship's carpenters could dismantle the hulk and build from it two smaller boats in which to cross the remaining 600 miles of sea to James Towne.

The following year, back home in England, Strachey published his account of the shipwreck, and it soon became well known. He wasn't the only survivor who told his story. A man named Silvester Jourdain published *A Discovery of the Bermudas, otherwise called the Isle of Divels,* but it didn't achieve the popularity of Strachey's well-written and dramatic account. A third author described the islands of the Bermudas as "rent with tempests."

At about this time a forty-six-year-old playwright named William Shakespeare set to work on what would be his last play. Act I, Scene I, begins with the stage direction, *"On a Ship at Sea.—A Storm, with Thunder and Lightning."* The story of the great storm, the separation of the lead ship from its fellows, the men miraculously delivered to languish on a fantastic island—all appear in *The Tempest.* One imagines Strachey's fellow sailors aboard the storm-tossed ship crying out in the tones of Shakespeare's characters as they fight to keep afloat: "All lost! to prayers, to prayers! all lost!"

The Tempest was produced at least by 1611, when it opened the Christmas season at Whitehall. Coleridge described the play as "a species of drama which owes no allegiance to time or space. . . ." True, Prospero's magical island doesn't appear on maps. However, besides the obvious parallels between his story and the *Sea Venture's,* Shakespeare even referred to "the still-vexed Bermoothes [ever stormy Bermudas]. . . ." There seems to be no question of the location of the islands that inspired the play, thanks to William Strachey's little encounter with a storm devil.

See also Hemingway's hurricane, 9/7.

"A Waterfall of a Dreadful Height"

Provoked by several factors, including British harassment of American shipping and fears that Indian attacks were fomented by the British, the United States again declared war on its former parent nation in 1811. Attacks on British installations in Canada followed. Although in the United States it is called the War of 1812, the fighting actually lasted into early 1815. The bloodiest battle of the entire conflict took place at an area called Lundy's Lane, near Niagara Falls, on the U.S.-Canadian border, on July 25, 1814. After five hours of fighting, both sides retreated behind their national borders, each with several hundred casualties.

Tempus, as an observant Roman remarked, *fugit.* Precisely 197 years later, with the United States and Britain firm allies and the U.S.-Canadian border long since demilitarized, there was nothing more violent going on at Niagara Falls than 122 million gallons of water plummeting 160 feet every minute. That in itself was enough to create a backdrop for one of those strange ways that human beings amuse themselves when they are not caught up in their favorite hobby, war. On July 25, 1911, a man named Bobby Leach went over the falls in a cast-metal barrel the size of a coffin but shaped more like a submarine. Unlike most of the men who fought the Battle of Niagara Falls, he survived without injury.

He was not the first. In 1901, a woman in dire need of funds to pay her mortgage exploited Niagara's already flourishing reputation for publicity stunts. She went over the falls in a padded barrel and survived. The falls had long been a magnet for attention seekers. One day short of this date in 1883, Captain Matthew Webb, the first man to successfully swim the English Channel, drowned while swimming above the rapids at Niagara Falls. During a tour of the United States, renowned French acrobat Charles Blondin, with the crowd expecting his death at any moment, successfully walked a tightrope that was stretched across the falls. It took him five minutes.

The figure of 122 million gallons per minute is an average, of course, the combined volumes of the two waterfalls, Horseshoe and American, which are separated only by a rocky outcrop called Goat Island. The amount of water also varies, depending upon everything from spring runoff to wind direction. Thanks to a drought, in 1903 the falls even stopped falling for a while. Horseshoe Falls pours nineteen times as much water over the edge as American Falls, because of the geological formation that gives it its name. An irregular semicircle, it is eroding at a much greater rate than American Falls, because the deepest, strongest channel of the Niagara River digs farther into it every day. (Technically, because it connects two large bodies of water—Lake Ontario and Lake Erie—the thirty-six-mile-long

Niagara River is actually a strait.) With its own fairly uniform edge, American Falls is eroding at a much slower rate. Nonetheless, it is thought to have begun its digging into the strata six miles away, after the retreat of the glaciers in the last ice age.

The natives of the region knew the falls well before, in 1603, the French explorer Samuel de Champlain learned from the locals of a waterfall downriver that was "somewhat high, and where little water flows over." It sounds like a local deliberately putting one over on a tourist. Elsewhere Niagara was explicitly described as "a waterfall of a dreadful height." Later in the seventeenth century, Champlain's countryman La Salle wrote in his report, "I leave you to imagine if it is not a beautiful cascade, to see all the water of the great river, which at its mouth is three leagues in width, precipitate itself from a height of two hundred feet." Notwithstanding his slight exaggeration of its height, La Salle's praise of the beautiful cascade is in the tone of how most people would respond to Niagara Falls over the next few centuries, whether they were there to honeymoon, walk a tightrope, fight a war, or simply go over the falls.

---

26 JULY 1938

The Syrian Golden Hamster

At the April 1839 meeting of the London Zoological Society, the curator, George Robert Waterhouse, presented a paper describing a formerly unknown species of animal—the Syrian golden hamster. Waterhouse described it from a single specimen, an old female someone had sent him from Aleppo. He contrasted it with the common European hamster, *Cricetus vulgaris,* and went on to describe the animal in the detail necessary to establish a type specimen.

Earlier, in 1797, English physician Alexander Russell had described the Syrian hamster in his *Natural History of Aleppo.* However, he mistakenly identified the specimen as a "common hamster," well known in the cultivated lands of western Asia and Europe but not found in the Middle East. Waterhouse erroneously cited Linnaeus and Buffon, and forfeited his chance to name a species. However, he described an adaptation that has certainly helped the rodent survive in its harsh native environment, a habit familiar to anyone who has worked with hamsters in the laboratory or kept them as pets—their ability to store foodstuffs in their expandable cheek pouches.

Of course, the hamsters didn't care if they were noticed. They were doing just fine—better, in fact, than they did after their laboratory virtues were recognized. One reason hamsters are valued for medical research is their reproductive rate. With a gestation period of only one to two weeks, and bearing several litters annually, they can produce as many as eighteen offspring per year. They are also clean, easily tamed, and demand little care. For all those reasons, plus the silky golden fur and charming personality, golden hamsters are also popular pets.

Almost a century after Waterhouse presented his paper, a scientist named Saul Adler set into motion the chain of events that would lead to the rediscovery of the golden hamster. Adler was a professor of parasitology at Hebrew University in Jerusalem. He couldn't persuade his laboratory's Chinese hamsters to reproduce in captivity, and found shipments of them from China unreliable and costly. He asked zoologist Israel Aharoni to look for native hamsters in the region.

Aharoni knew of the existence of the golden hamster and journeyed to Syria to find it in April of 1930. His Syrian guide, Georgius Khalil Tah'an, asked the assistance of a local sheik, who hired laborers to dig in a field known to be populated with hamsters. They unearthed a mother and 11 young. Tah'an placed them all together, and Aharoni was surprised to witness the mother decapitating the first pup that approached her. The biologist expressed a surprisingly sympathetic view of the hamster's infanticide: "Natural mother-love," Aharoni claimed, "led her to kill her dear child: 'It is better that my infant die than that it be the object of an experiment performed on it by a member of the accursed human race.' " Nonetheless, rather than allow the mother to kill the rest of her offspring, Tah'an put her in a jar of cyanide. The babies' eyes were not yet open. The Israeli and the Syrian became their foster parents.

Soon the hamsters escaped. All except one were recaptured, but then five of them gnawed their way out of a wooden box and escaped again. Aharoni was not optimistic. In all the world, there were exactly three golden hamsters in captivity. However, one of them was female. "Out of love for science and for the broadening of mankind," Aharoni wrote, "the Allpowerful nudged a single wheel of the uncountable wheels of nature—and a miracle happened!" Two of the hamsters committed incest and produced offspring.

The first golden hamsters to reach a U.S. laboratory arrived on July 26, 1938. Meanwhile, confident that he had supplied countless laboratory animals to assist humankind, Aharoni exulted: "And with the aid of God (not just by luck) the hamster that was brought from Aleppo proved to be incredibly prolific, and all from one mother! How marvelous are thy works, O Lord!"

---

27 JULY 1940

A Wild Hare

In the 1930s, Walt Disney dominated the field of animation. When Warner Brothers began distributing Looney Tunes shorts in 1930, the cartoons were not noted for their originality. Several of their animators were former Disney employees, and a number of their creations over the next few years owed an obvious debt to Disney characters. Two animators who worked on Oswald the Rabbit, Disney's predecessor to Mickey Mouse, re-created almost identical action scenes for their early Looney Tunes character Bosko. In 1931 there appeared the short-lived Foxy, who was obviously Mickey Mouse with a bushy tail and slightly pointed ears. He even wore spats and gloves. However, once Disney launched feature-length cartoons with 1938's *Snow White,* Warner Brothers soon took the lead in producing the short films.

The result was a revolution in animation and the creation of a whole zoo of unforgettable animal characters: Bugs Bunny, Daffy Duck, Wile E. Coyote, the Road Runner, Porky Pig, Sylvester the cat and Tweety Bird, Foghorn Leghorn, that romantic skunk Pepe LePew, and a south-of-the-border mouse named Speedy Gonzales. Porky Pig first appeared in 1935 and Daffy Duck arrived to plague him two years later.

Then came one of the most successful animated characters of all time. Disney's popular short *The Tortoise and the Hare* had starred a feisty, swaggering rabbit named Max Hare. Apparently the immortal Bugs Bunny was inspired by Max, although from the first, Bugs seemed a maniac beside Disney's creation. He first appeared in 1938, in *Porky's Hare Hunt,* as another of the obstacles in the way of Porky Pig ever having a successful hunting trip. (Later, Elmer Fudd would have the same trouble. Fortunately they didn't have little animated families to feed.) In this film, the big-eyed proto-Bugs was nameless, fatter, nowhere near as suave, and he even flew by spinning his long ears. He was feisty and smart-alecky to the point of annoying the audience.

A year later, in *Hare-um Scare-um,* Bugs looked like a missing link between his first incarnation and the Bugs we know today. But he was still scruffy and less refined. Again he failed to demonstrate star potential, although he did acquire prominent buck teeth. Only with *A Wild Hare,* which premiered on July 27, 1940, did Bugs Bunny come into his own. He still didn't look like he had quite achieved Bugshood, but he was acquiring his trademark suavity. For the first time, he glanced casually at Elmer Fudd's shotgun in his face and asked, "Eh, what's up, Doc?"

Bugs may have been descended from Max Hare on one side of his family, which would make Oswald the Rabbit his grandfather, but on the other he had nobler ancestors. In Aesop's fable of the tortoise and the hare, the rabbit is a smart aleck whose swaggering goads the tortoise into challenging him. The hare races madly ahead, becomes bored, and is dozing when the tortoise passes. By 1880, when Joel Chandler Harris published his first Uncle Remus stories, the hare was still a loudmouth but had become a clever rascal. Brer Rabbit defeats Brer Terrapin by employing several identical members of his (naturally populous) family to confuse his opponent.

The Remus stories are about cunning, against all odds, overcoming attempted oppression. That sounds solemn, but Brer Rabbit's exploits are full of the joy of flouting injustice while enjoying life to the fullest—the laugh of Robin Hood once again outwitting the Sheriff of Nottingham. Brer Rabbit's illustrious descendant, Bugs Bunny, inherited many of the family virtues. Every time he outwits Elmer Fudd and says to the camera "Ain't I a stinker?" he displays the family resemblance.

See also Tom and Jerry, 7/19; the Road Runner and the coyote, 9/16; and Mickey Mouse, 11/18.

---

28 JULY 1840

Edward Cope's Last Laugh

The first member of a new species to be described becomes its "type specimen," the representative by which the species' unique features are delineated. In 1758, in the tenth edition of his *Systema Naturae,* the Swedish systematist Linnaeus grandly named his own species *Homo sapiens,* "wise man." However, rather than designating and describing a type specimen, Linnaeus coyly supplied the Latin phrase, *Homo nosce Te ipsum,* "Man, know thyself." (Elsewhere, as motto for his section on the cold-blooded reptiles and amphibians he found repugnant, he wrote, "Terrible are Thy works, O Lord!")

By the standards now in use, because Linnaeus described the human species without designating a type specimen, the scientific name he chose could have been challenged at any time until a lectotype (an elected type specimen) could be appointed. That didn't happen until 1994. At least one historian had suggested that the type specimen most appropriate for the human race would have been the bones of Linnaeus himself. However, he was never formally nominated for the honor, and in time it fell to someone else.

That someone else was born in Philadelphia, Pennsylvania, on July 28, 1840, sixty-two years after Linnaeus died. His name was Edward Drinker Cope, and he grew up to become one of the foremost American paleontologists of the nineteenth century. Cope is remembered for numerous contributions to the field, but his aggressive pursuit of new finds and his underhanded methods for attaining them have made him notorious. Most famously, he had a long-running feud with rival paleontologist Othniel C. Marsh. Between them, Cope and Marsh described 136 new species of dinosaurs. Their rivalry boosted the fledgling science of paleontology and helped fill American museums with crucial early findings.

Cope died in 1897. Although he has remained legendary even among the eccentrics who populated the field of paleontology in the nineteenth century, his deathbed wish was the most eccentric of all. It was an extravagant last laugh that must have infuriated his surviving rival. Cope wanted his skeleton to become the type specimen for *Homo sapiens*. Unfortunately, after Cope's death in 1897 his skeleton was deemed unsatisfactory to fill the noble role for which he had volunteered. Apparently his bones exhibited the early stages of syphilis. *Home sapiens* proceeded into the tumultuous twentieth century without its diversity ever having been narrowed to a representative specimen.

Then the iconoclastic paleontologist Robert T. Bakker, famous for such coups as his early realization of the warm-blooded nature of some dinosaurs, renominated Cope for the position of human type specimen. In November of 1993, Bakker measured the volume of Cope's braincase. This procedure was to quantify the difference between the cranial capacity of this representative *Homo sapiens* and that of *Homo erectus*, our closest extinct cousin. Although cranial capacity varies widely among living humans, from under 1,000 cubic centimeters to over 1,800, that of *H. erectus* seldom exceeded our minimum. In 1994, ninety-seven years after his death, an amused scientific panel approved the nomination, and Edward Drinker Cope officially became the elected type specimen of *Homo sapiens*. At the same time, his place of birth became the representative human type locality—Philadelphia.

See also Cope versus Marsh, 10/1.

Teardrops of the Gods

Pliny the Elder, who said pearls were "wasteful things meant only for women," wrote that Cleopatra owned two extraordinarily fine ones. He also claimed that, in an effort to impress Mark Antony, she topped all her previous extravagance by dissolving a pearl earring in vinegar and then drinking the vinegar. Unfortunately, the pearl-dissolving story has been attributed to others, including Caligula. Also, acetic acid cannot dissolve pearls, and if it had it would have dissolved Cleopatra. The queen might have equally impressed Antony by simply swallowing the pearl, in which case its retrieval in due course was at least an option.

Antonio Pigafetta, a shipmate of Magellan's, also reported two perfect pearls. On July 29, 1521, he wrote in his diary, "The king of Burne [Borneo] has two pearls as large as two eggs, and they are so round that they cannot lie still on a table." The king acquired them as ransom for a ruler he had kidnapped. Many have gone even further for what Pliny called "the richest merchandise of all, and the most sovereign commodity throughout the whole world." Enemies of Julius Caesar cited his fondness for pearls as evidence of dangerous extravagance, and even suggested that lust for the freshwater variety inspired his invasion of Britain. Caesar's gift of a priceless pearl to Brutus's mother is one clue that Brutus might have been his illegitimate son.

Kino, the protagonist of John Steinbeck's novel *The Pearl,* finds the Pearl of the World, only to be almost destroyed by the evil it inspires. Saint Matthew compared the kingdom of heaven to a pearl of great price. In his Revelation, Saint John sees pearls as forming the gates of heaven *and* adorning the Mother of Harlots. That ambivalence is common. Both Queen Elizabeth I and Josephine Baker wore pearls. The former cascaded them down her unyielding royal dress as a symbol of purity and political power; the latter draped them around her otherwise naked breasts to represent femininity and sexual power. Pearls have decorated gloves for Frederick II and gowns by Erté. The wife of the thirteenth-century Chinese leader Shih Tsu wore them and so did Nancy Reagan.

Some people thought anything so beautiful had to have a supernatural origin. Pearls were the teardrops of the gods, or, in a clever union of fire and water, the result of lightning penetrating the oyster. Pliny thought oysters feared this meteorological rape and snapped shut when they heard thunder. Nowadays the genesis of pearls is well known. The narrator of Jules Verne's 1870 novel *Twenty Thousand Leagues Under the Sea* explains the process: "The pearl is nothing but a nacreous [mother-of-pearl] formation, deposited in a globular form, either adhering to the oyster-shell, or buried in the folds of the creature. On the shell it is fast; in the flesh it is loose; but always has for a kernel a small hard substance, may be a barren egg, may be a grain of sand, around which the pearly matter deposits itself year after year successively, and by thin concentric layers."

French ichthyologist Louis Roule told of opening a pearl oyster's shell and finding not a grain of sand immortalized but an entire mummified fish covered in mother-of-pearl. "Nature had built for it a tomb of rare and precious stone, a magnificent coffin: she had done for this little fish what the Egyptians used to do for the remains of their kings."

See also oysters, 9/28.

---

30 JULY 1889

"Solomon in All His Glory"

While preaching the Sermon on the Mount, Jesus advises his disciples to take no thought for their food or raiment because God will provide. He reinforces this point with one of his many analogies from nature: "Consider the lilies of the field, how they grow; they toil not, neither do they spin: and yet I say unto you, That even Solomon in all his glory was not arrayed like one of these."

Lesser figures have also nominated flowers as evidence of God's glory in a variety of contexts. One unlikely testimonial appears as an irrelevant aside in Arthur Conan Doyle's story "The Naval Treaty." On July 30, 1889, Sherlock Holmes answers an urgent summons to investigate a theft of important papers. After the client's recital of the circumstances, Holmes wanders around the room. "What a lovely thing a rose is!" he exclaims suddenly. He examines "the drooping stalk of a moss rose." Watson remarks to the reader, "It was a new phase of his character to me, for I had never seen him show any keen interest in natural objects." Then Holmes makes his sole explicit statement about religion:

> Our highest assurance of the goodness of Providence seems to me to rest in the flowers. All other things, our desires, our food, are really necessary for our existence in the first instance. But this rose is an extra. Its smell and its colour are an embellishment of life, not a condition of it. It is only goodness which gives extras, and so I say again that we have much to hope for from the flowers.

It is impossible, of course, to prove that flowers did not spend millions of years evolving showy and brightly colored blossoms for the future delight of the primate that would invent horticulture. Flowers' scent and color may not be a condition of *our* lives—they may be merely a delightful "embellishment"—but they are essential to the lives of the plants themselves. They are certainly not mere adornment. That notion ought to have been banished by the discovery of patterns visible only to insects that could perceive ultraviolet light, an embellishment hidden from us until the twentieth century. For thousands of years, we also overlooked the lilies' subtle toiling and spinning. The whole time, quietly, inside their leaves, underground in their roots, they were busily synthesizing energy from sunlight, mining nutrients from soil, and evolving irresistible lures for animals.

Because these activities were unknown to people, it came as a shock to many when flowers' true purpose was widely recognized in the eighteenth century. Technically, a flower is the reproductive structure of an angiosperm, the hugely diversified phyllum that, with gymnosperms (plants with "naked seeds"), constitutes the plant kingdom; more commonly, it is the blossom or bloom of any plant. In other words, flowers are sexual organs. This realization led to some elaborately gallant metaphors for the reproductive procedures of plants, language that seems more appropriate to the authors of romance novels. Linnaeus, whose system of plant classification was based upon sexual characteristics, published his *Praeludia Sponsaliorum Plantarum* in 1729. In it, he expressed his notion of botanical lusts and loves in appropriately flowery prose.

> The petals serve as bridal beds which the Great Creator has so gloriously arranged, adorned with such noble bed curtains and perfumed with so many sweet scents, that the bridegroom there may celebrate his nuptials with all the greater solemnity. When the bed is thus prepared, it is time for the bridegroom to embrace his beloved bride and surrender his gifts to her.

"To a Louse"

Robert Burns published his collection *Poems, Chiefly in the Scottish Dialect* on the last day of July, 1786. The next year, Dorothy Wordsworth thanked a friend for recommending the poems with the note, "I was very much pleased with them indeed, the one which you mentioned to me is I think very comical, I mean the address to a Louse. . . ." She was referring to a satirical meditation on the unnatural distinctions of class, "To a Louse, On Seeing one on a Lady's Bonnet at Church."

"Ha! whare ye gaun, ye crowlan ferlie!" Burns addressed *Pediculus humanus*—presumably the subspecies *capitis,* head lice, because they are larger than body lice and likelier to be visible on headgear. The bonnet it was climbing was a Lunardi, named after an Italian balloonist whose recent ascent from Edinburgh had been honored with a balloon-shaped bonnet. Thus it was the epitome of fashion, making the louse's presence that much more insulting.

> *Ye ugly, creepan, blastet wonner,*
> *Detested, shunn'd, by saunt and sinner,*
> *How daur ye set your sit upon her,*
> *Sae fine a* Lady!
> *Gae somewhere else and seek your dinner,*
> *On some poor body.*

Burns was not the first to immortalize lice; they have been reviled in literature ever since they were one of the plagues in the Bible. Aaron "stretched out his hand with his rod, and smote the dust of the earth, and it became lice in man, and in beast . . . throughout all the land of Egypt." Years after Burns, Tennyson alliteratively dismissed a fellow author as a "louse in the locks of literature." In James Joyce's *Ulysses,* Stephen Dedalus remembers his mother's fingernails "reddened by the blood of squashed lice from the children's shirts." These were body lice, which dine upon the body but reside in unwashed clothing. Lice helped Henry Miller establish his beloved squalor in the second paragraph of *Tropic of Cancer.* "Last night Boris discovered he was lousy. I had to shave his armpits and even then the itching did not stop." Such comments shock in the twentieth century, but they remind us how much this tiny creature tormented humanity in the past.

That history is preserved in language. The term "lousy" meant infested with lice as early as the fourteenth century, and in his 1755 dictionary Samuel Johnson defined it as both that and "low born." By the time of World War 1, anyone who seemed either filthy or vile might simply be described metaphorically as a "louse." Soldiers brought home from trenches another verbal legacy: To be "lousy with" meant to be "full of," as in "lousy with ammunition." Before World War II, one more meaning emerged; instead of botching a task, one might "louse up." Nowadays the most common usage is "I feel lousy."

Inevitably, lice have inspired jokes. After a fashionable hostess snubbed him, nineteenth-century English humorist Theodore Hook replied with an insulting quatrain reminiscent of Robert Burns.

> *Her ladyship said, when I went to her house*
> *She did not regard me three skips of a louse,*
> *I freely forgave what the dear creature said,*
> *For ladies will talk of what runs in their head.*

The Very Dead Sea

In the summer of 1986, U.S. vice president George Bush visited Jordan. It was, as usual, a tense time in the Middle East. The Iran-Iraq War was in its sixth year, and Jordan's relations with its neighbor Syria were strained by their support of opposing nations. Recently, King Hussein had expelled the Palestine Liberation Organization. However, on August 1, as Bush viewed troops and sights with the commander in chief of Jordan's military forces, Lieutenant General Zeid Bin Shaker, some of his questions were about older and less-controversial topics. One, in fact, concerned natural history.

"Tell me, General," Bush asked at one point, "how dead is the Dead Sea?"

Shaker replied thoughtfully, "Very dead, sir."

The general was correct. *Yam Ha-Melah,* the lake is called in Hebrew—"the Salt Sea." Neither animals nor plants can live there; only hardy bacteria survive in the incredibly salty water. Even along the shore of the Dead Sea only a few salt-loving plants (halophytes) eke out an existence. During the time of the dinosaurs, the Mediterranean Sea covered the region. Later, geological contortions created Africa's vast Rift Valley, the northern end of which became what is now called the Jordan–Dead Sea Trench. As a result, the Dead Sea is the lowest body of water on earth, 1,300 feet below sea level. It is dead because it is a landlocked lake in which, over the past 10,000 years or so, evaporation has exceeded precipitation.

Such a saline concentration gives the water of the Dead Sea an abnormal density several times that of the oceans. Swimmers have no trouble floating on the surface. Even the incoming freshwater of the River Jordan, which empties into the lake from the north, floats on the surface. In the spring, it can be detected atop the trapped salty water as far as thirty miles from where it enters the lake. There are two layers to the saltwater, too. The upper water, which dates from only a few hundred years after biblical times, has variable temperatures and a lower percentage of salt. The other, below a depth of 300 feet or so, maintains a uniform temperature of 72°F and is so dense with sodium chloride that it remains permanently on the bottom of the lake.

Naturally the region is as saturated with history as it is with salt. The Dead Sea lies on the contentious border between Jordan and Israel. Overlooking the western shore is the sheer face of fabled Masada, atop which the Hebrew Zealots resisted for two years before finally committing mass suicide rather than fall to the Roman siege in A.D. 73. Nearby, Mount Sedom looks down on the lake from its southwestern shore. The mountain was originally named Mount Sodom. The sites of Sodom and Gomorrah—upon which, in the Hebrew myth, God rained fire and brimstone as punishment for their wickedness—may lie submerged in the southern part of the sea. Historians think that the story of the transformation of Lot's wife into a pillar of salt, as punishment for glancing back at the burning cities, was invented to explain unique geological formations in the region. To this day columns of concentrated salt stand on Jebel Usdum, "the Hill of Sodom," a mountain of salt on the western shore of this ancient and very dead sea.

2 AUGUST 1877

The Attitudes of Animals in Motion

Eadweard Muybridge was already a well-known photographer when, in 1877, a former California governor and railroad tycoon, Leland Stanford, commissioned him to find out if a trotting horse ever had all four feet off the ground at the same time. Stanford offered the track at his farm for the photographic experiments. Muybridge rigged a dozen cameras down the track. The horse, named Occident, photographed itself by tripping a succession of strings attached to the cameras' shutters. The result surpassed even Muybridge's own expectations. It proved that, properly manipulated, the camera could be a tool for observing what the eye could not. The answer to Stanford's question was a resounding yes.

On the second of August, 1877, Muybridge wrote a letter to the editors of the San Francisco *Alta,* thanking them for their confidence in recommending him for the task of photographing Occident, and enclosing the print that resulted from the experiment: "The length of the exposure can be pretty accurately determined by the fact that the whip in the driver's hand did not move the distance of its diameter."

In October of 1878, a series of drawings based upon Muybridge photographs appeared on the cover of *Scientific American,* portraying a trotter and a walking horse. One man who became greatly interested in the work of Muybridge at about this time was the American painter Thomas Eakins, creator of such masterpieces of realism as *The Gross Clinic* and *Max Schmitt in a Single Scull.* In 1879, Eakins himself employed Muybridge photographs as the basis of his famous painting *A May Morning in the Park* (also called *The Fairman Rogers Four-in-Hand*). Although the horses' legs in the painting are frozen in their respective realistic positions, the spokes of the carriage wheels are, paradoxically, blurred. One reviewer remarked, "As a demonstration of the fact that the artist must fail when he attempts to depict what *is,* instead of what *seems to be,* this picture is of great value. . . ."

In 1881, Muybridge published his now-classic book, *The Attitudes of Animals in Motion.* From Philadelphia, Eakins wrote to suggest to Muybridge that he photograph the successive stages of human movement. Over the years, Muybridge recorded far more than just the motions of animals. The variety is impressive. In the photos, nude women, men, and children perform activities as diverse as carrying a water pitcher, wrestling, and climbing steps. One man throws and catches a baseball, another heaves a seventy-five-pound rock. A horse leaps over three others. A parrot flies against the measured background.

The last the public heard of Eadweard Muybridge during his lifetime was a letter he wrote to the *Encyclopaedia Britannica* in 1902, concerning illustrations accompanying an article by England's prominent Egyptologist, Flinders Petrie. Petrie had remarked of certain nameless Fourth Dynasty artists (c. 2550 B.C.) that they "did not make a work of art as such, but they rivalled nature as closely as possible." Muybridge himself could have been described that way. He commented on the ancient portrayal of motion: "This distinctive method of galloping was unknown, and, indeed, unsuspected by us moderns, until revealed by photographic investigation of animal locomotion; but it was apparently well known to the early artists of Egypt."

---

3 AUGUST 1934

"The Bird of the Devil"

An African folktale tells of a war between the beasts and the birds. First one group is in power, then the other. In time both realize that the bat is feigning allegiance to each in order to join whichever party is triumphant. Finally, the beasts win, and the bat is tried for his duplicity. His attorney points out that, though not a bird, the bat has wings and is perfectly at home in the air, and yet, with his fur and teeth, he is equally at home on the ground. Aesop uses a similar story to both warn against the dangers of neutrality and explain the bat's habitat. Condemned by each side for his nonpartisan status, in his shame the bat slinks away to cower in corners, never going out except after the other animals have retired for the day.

With angels sporting the wings of doves, demons were naturally assigned the flying equipment of those evil creatures, bats—as in Gustave Doré's illustration for the Divine Comedy.

Bats' refusal to fit snugly in one category seems to have worried many people. Alchemists sometimes employed the bat's well-known double nature to represent androgyny. In Japanese folklore, it symbolizes at the very least an uneasy restlessness. To Christians, the bat became "the bird of the devil," an incarnation of Satan himself. With angels wearing the white wings of doves, devils began to acquire the bat's leathery membrane. In Walt Disney's 1934 animated short cartoon *The Flying Mouse,* a mouse rescues a butterfly. The insect turns into a fairy godmother and grants the hero a wish. He wants to fly. She responds with taxonomists' reaction to bats: "A mouse was never meant to fly." Nonetheless, she grants his wish, and he discovers that birds reject him as a freak and his shadow frightens his own family.

One kind of bat particularly inspires fear. "*Vespertilio Vampyrus,*" Linnaeus called it, and added the chilling detail, "At night sucks in the blood of the sleeping, the combs of cocks, and the juice of palm trees." What could be more frightening than adding blood lust to an established reputation for defying natural laws? As early as 1565, the Italian historian Girolamo Benzoni was describing bats he encountered in Costa Rica: "There are many bats which bite people during the night. . . . While I was sleeping they bit the toes of my feet so delicately that I felt nothing, and in the morning I found the sheets and mattresses with so much blood that it seemed that I had suffered some great injury. . . ."

Members of the family Desmodontidae do not swoop down upon their prey, but prefer to land nearby and crawl toward the nearest exposed skin—usually that of livestock, but they don't hesitate to accost humans when they're handy. The tiny incisions are painless. Within twenty minutes or so, the bat is sated, sometimes so much that it is unable to fly. That explains the descriptive species name of one: *rotundus.* The bats, by the way, do not suck blood; they lap it up. Their saliva contains an anticoagulant so effective that sometimes victims later find the bleeding difficult to stop.

In 1933 and 1934, U.S. naturalists Raymond L. Ditmars and Arthur M. Greenhall studied vampire bats in Central America. They hoped to verify or disprove certain claims about them—that they first hovered over their victims and that they sucked the blood. Both turned out to be false. Ditmars and Greenhall observed the bats' feeding habits by capturing specimens and introducing them into observation pens containing goats and fowl. One bat swooped straight onto the back of the goat, returning each time to the same wound. A cock allowed a bat to lap blood from its leg, even as it walked.

On Friday, August 3, 1934, Greenhall observed a bat named Tommy, who had been under observation since May. Tommy landed lightly upon the goat's back and crawled about before settling on a picnic area. Even if the stories and films about them were disproven, the reality was enough to inspire horror. "The wandering of the bat upon the strangely tolerant host," Ditmars wrote, "the occasional lifting of the bat's head, the leer that disclosed its keen teeth, and the observer's realization that all of this pointed to a sanguineaous meal, produced a sinister and impressive effect."

See also **Dracula, 9/29.**

---

4 AUGUST 1837

"A Foul and Filthy Creature"

"Sweet are the uses of adversity
Which like the toad, ugly and venomous,
Wears yet a precious jewel in his head. . . ."

Duke Senior, in AS YOU LIKE IT

It is quite a leap from adversity's silver lining to the toad simile, but Shakespeare was nimble. From a natural history point of view, it is also an instructive image. Not only were frogs and toads long considered ugly and venomous, but they were thought to hide in their clammy little heads a mineral that cured poison—the "toadstone."

In a section of his *De Animalibus*, the thirteenth-century Dominican theologian and naturalist remembered as Albertus Magnus described a species of toad that "customarily bears a stone in its forehead, for which it is killed." Giambattista della Porta, a sixteenth-century Neapolitan natural philosopher, described the method of acquiring this useful bauble: "They say it is taken from living toads in a red cloth, in which colour they are much delighted; for while they sport themselves upon the scarlet the stone droppeth out of their head and falleth through a hole made in the middle into a box set under for the purpose. . . . But," even Porta must admit, "I never met with a faithfull person who said that he had found it; nor could I ever find one, though I have cut up many." Nonetheless, he insists that when swallowed this elusive stone "aswaggeth" poison. (The toadstone is not entirely mythical. Some amphibians, fishes, and invertebrates have in the vestibule of the ear small calcareous particles called otoliths, "ear stones," part of the hearing and equilibrium mechanism.)

Samuel Johnson defined the toad as a "small animal with four feet, living both by land and water, and placed by naturalists among the mixed animals, as partaking of beasts and fish." In other words, frogs refuse to stay in one category. (The prefix *amphi* in "amphibian" means "on both sides.") An English divine complained that the frog is "as we all know, a foul and filthy creature, abiding in foul places, as bogs and miry plashes, all the day long, and at night peeping out with the head above the water, making hateful noise with many others of his sort till the day appear again." To even bear a similarity to such a creature could mar another's appearance. A commentator remarked in the 1600s that many women "care not for dressing" a certain fish, because "he so resembles a toad."

When English naturalist Thomas Pennant saw frogs for sale in French markets, his "strong dislike to these reptiles prevented a close examination." The French habit of eating frogs was one trait the English found disgusting about their neighbors across the channel. "Toadeater," however, was a term for assistants who helped traveling medicine shows gull the bumpkins. The quack "doctors" employed toadeaters to pretend to consume frogs. This unsavory performance drew attention because toads were considered poisonous. After the assistant "swallowed" the toxic animal, the charlatan demonstrated the remarkable healing powers of his favorite elixir. "Toadeater" became a term for one who sucks up or flatters, thus willingly swallowing something unpleasant, and evolved into "toady."

Evidence that frogs were finally outgrowing the superstitions appears in Ralph Waldo Emerson's journal in 1837. On August 4, he wrote companionably, "The frogs that shoot from the land as fast as you walk along, a yard ahead of you, are a meritorious beastie. For their cowardice is only greater than their curiosity and desire of acquaintance with you." A year later, his remarks prove just how far these once despised mixed animals had come. "At night I went out into the dark and saw a glimmering star and heard a frog, and Nature seemed to say, Well do not these suffice?"

The Dognapping of Flush

Elizabeth Barrett and Mary Russell Mitford seldom met in person, but they carried on a correspondence for eighteen years. When they first met in 1836, Mitford was an established writer, and Barrett had published both translations and collections of poems. In the summer of 1840, four years into this epistolary friendship, Barrett suffered the most devastating loss of her life. Her adored brother died in a boating accident, his body lost until it washed up onshore three weeks later. Apparently Barrett never fully recovered from the shock.

A few months later, Mitford wrote to suggest that her friend needed an outlet for her grief and proposed her own favorite solace—a dog. She offered to give Barrett one of the new pups of her dog Flush. The six-month-old golden cocker spaniel pup arrived in January of 1841. Barrett named him after his father, and Flush's winning personality soon proved a sterling cure for depression. Barrett's unrestrained devotion to this dog suffuses her subsequent letters to Mitford. On August 5, 1841, for example, Barrett wrote a long letter babbling about his virtues.

Flush became the sultan of the household. He ate buttered bread and muffins. When he scorned mutton, he was served beef. Because the family physician warned the invalid Barrett to keep Flush clean, the dog received a daily bath. He spurned everyone except his goddess and her maid. Although her father and numerous siblings disagreed, Barrett thought Flush could do no wrong. Understandably, they pronounced her daft when she tried to teach Flush to read. She held out a book to the dog and said, "Kiss A, Flush—and now Kiss B."

In the fall of 1843, while the maid was walking him around the corner from the Barrett household in Wimpole Street, someone stole Flush. Barrett's brothers papered the neighborhood with handbills offering a reward. At the time there operated in London what Barrett described in a letter to Mitford as "the organised dog-banditti," an organization that called itself the Fancy, whose ill-gotten gains in the stolen dog trade came to £4,000 annually. Elizabeth's brother Alfred went to see the leader of the Fancy, a man named Taylor, who declared flatly, "You will never see your dog, sir, again."

"And why?" Alfred asked.

Taylor explained that thanks to the handbills the police were watching for the dog. Nonetheless, with some outside pressure, Alfred prevailed. At eight in the evening, while the Barrett household was at dinner—all except Elizabeth, who was upstairs—Taylor arrived. "I have found the dog. Give me five pounds and come in a cab with me to the place." When Barrett's father heard the terms, he arose from the dinner table, denounced Taylor as a rascal, and made it clear that two pounds was all the ransom they would pay. Taylor smiled and said, "You will never see your dog again."

Elizabeth's father admonished the others to tell her nothing of this encounter, but she had been eavesdropping. The next day, having heard that the Fancy cut the throats of dogs that earned them nothing, she sent her brother Henry to Taylor with three more sovereigns of her own. Taylor agreed to deliver the dog. Taylor remarked that the Fancy had had an eye on him for some time, and casually added, "If you lose your dog again whether in town or country, you may be sure that *I* am at the bottom of it."

Not surprisingly, Flush disappeared again a year later. This time the Fancy went to the trouble to employ a decoy to lure Flush from the front porch. Much calmer this time, Elizabeth asked her siblings to keep this matter secret from their father. She sent Alfred straight to Taylor, who declared that the ransom had gone up to seven guineas. Elizabeth paid it, and once again Flush was returned. He did not disappear again.

---

6 AUGUST 1945

"A Strange Kind of Half-Metal"

In Berlin in 1789, German chemist Martin Klaproth spoke to the Royal Prussian Academy of Science about a strange mineral he had been studying.

> The number of known metals has been increased by one—from 17 to 18. This I have called a metalloid, a new element which I see as a strange kind of half-metal. . . . I have chosen a name. A few years ago we thrilled to hear of the discovery of the final planet by Sir William Herschel. He called this new member of our solar system Uranus. I propose to borrow from the honor of that great discovery and call this new element—Uranium.

Not only did Uranus turn out not to be the "final" planet, but since Klaproth added the eighteenth, physicists have discovered seventy-six other naturally occurring elements and have created fifteen more in laboratories. For a long time the word "element" (from the Latin *elementum,* meaning "first principle") referred to any of the four substances that natural philosophers thought comprised all matter in the universe—earth, air, water, and fire. Nowadays an element is defined as a naturally occurring substance that cannot be broken down into further components by chemical means, one that consists of atoms of only one kind. In other words, a leaf can be broken down into the carbon and water and other substances that comprise it, and the water can then be split up further into hydrogen and oxygen. However, the process stops there unless we omit the qualifying phrase in the definition, "by chemical means." We have learned in our clever century that there are other ways to break down an element. We learned it partially through those elements that tend to "break down" all by themselves, such as uranium.

The story of uranium involves scientists from around the world. Although Klaproth discovered its existence, it was not until 1841 that France's Eugène-Melchior Péligot isolated it from its surrounding ore. In 1896, French physicist Antoine-Henri Becquerel discovered that uranium is what we now refer to as radioactive. Becquerel wanted to find out if uranium emitted the "X rays" recently discovered by Wilhelm Röntgen in Germany. He found that it performed similarly and wrote to the French Academy of Sciences, "There is an emission of rays without apparent cause." Becquerel later shared the

1903 Nobel Prize with Pierre and Marie Curie. It was the latter who coined the term "radioactivity" to describe this spontaneous emission of energy.

New Zealand–born Ernest Rutherford, working in England, discovered that what was happening was that uranium atoms were "bursting open, flinging off bits and pieces of their structure—constantly and without let-up." Rutherford admitted it sounded like the medieval dream of alchemists—transmutation—but it was true. In nature, he insisted, "Atoms throw off energy and bits of their structure and change from one element to another." In late 1938, Germans Otto Hahn and Fritz Strassmann discovered that bombarding uranium nuclei with a stream of neutrons produced radical changes in the neutron, a process now called nuclear fission. In time scientists learned that for that reason uranium could be a valuable fuel. It takes 3 *million* pounds of coal to produce as much energy as a single pound of uranium.

By far the most hazardous use of uranium is in nuclear weapons. American scientists created the first self-sustaining nuclear reaction in late 1942. In mid-July 1945, the first atomic bomb was exploded at Los Alamos in New Mexico. Then, on August 6, a U.S. B-29 Superfortress bomber named the *Enola Gay* dropped an atomic bomb on the mostly unmilitarized city of Hiroshima, Japan. Eighty thousand people died instantly, and 200,000 more were injured. Countless others would suffer the effects of the radiation. Klaproth's element had reached its ultimate use, and the world had entered a new age. Ringing in the ears of some scientists was the prescient question a worried Pierre Curie had asked Ernest Rutherford over forty years earlier: "We should ask—will mankind benefit from knowing the secrets of nature?"

---

7 AUGUST 1860

The Eighth Plague

In that great repository of irreverence, *The Devil's Dictionary,* Ambrose Bierce defined a plague: "In ancient times a general punishment of the innocent for admonition of their ruler, as in the familiar instance of Pharaoh the Immune." The story is in the Book of Exodus. To encourage Pharaoh to release the enslaved Israelites, God smites the Egyptians with all manner of inconvenience. The waters of the Nile turn into blood, frogs overrun even beds and ovens, the very dust of the land becomes lice, and swarms of flies torment everyone but the Israelites. Finally Pharaoh gives in, then backs out. Next comes a grievous murrain upon the cattle, boils attack people and beast, and hail pummels the land. Once again Pharaoh relents, only to change his mind when the pre-

Cicadas, crickets, and in this case grasshoppers have all been called locusts when they swarmed in great destructive masses.

cipitation stops. Then come locusts, darkness, and the midnight deaths of the Egyptians' firstborn. Only then does Pharaoh free Moses and his people.

The eighth plague—locusts—has become the symbol of God's warnings to the Egyptians. Flies, lice, frogs, even boils and hail, might occasionally be a problem. But nothing else could be as destructive as locusts. They "covered the face of the whole earth, so that the land was darkened; and they did eat every herb of the land, and all the fruit of the trees which the hail had left: and there remained not any green thing in the trees, or in the herbs of the field, through all the land of Egypt."

Locusts figure prominently in the Bible. God permitted the Israelites to dine upon locusts and grasshoppers; according to Matthew and Mark, John the Baptist lived on them in the desert. (Several grasshoppers, crickets, and cicadas are referred to informally as "locusts.") One didn't need to be as wise as Solomon to notice locusts' most important characteristic, but it was he who summed it up. They were third on his list of the four things "which are little upon the earth, but they are exceeding wise." Being a monarch himself, he was naturally surprised that, lacking a king, locusts still "go they forth all of them by bands." It was the combined appetite of their roving, marauding bands, eating everything in their path, that made them so destructive they seemed a deliberate punishment by God.

While traveling in central Africa in the late 1850s, British explorer Richard F. Burton encountered pink-and-green locusts that "rise from the earth like a glowing rose-colored cloud." Less than two years later, the peripatetic Burton was in the American West. He began his journal of his trip on Tuesday, August 7, 1860, and recorded his experiences in his usual exhaustive detail. One creature he encountered was the black cricket, *Anabrus simplex,* now called the Mormon cricket. It earned its new common name after devastating the crops of the newly arrived Mormons, especially in 1848, the year Brigham Young and his followers founded Salt Lake City. The plague of locusts seemed to the refugees a biblical test of faith, and they considered their constancy rewarded when a species of gull that lives near Great Salt Lake advanced in numbers to devour the insects.

Nowadays fewer people regard ecological misfortune as divine chastisement. It is just further evidence that there is no such thing as a balance of nature. Ambrose Bierce added to his definition: "The plague as we of to-day have the happiness to know it is merely Nature's fortuitous manifestation of her purposeless objectionableness."

---

8 AUGUST 1842

Barnum's Feejee Mermaid

In 1817 an enterprising Calcutta businessman offered for sale the dried body of a mermaid. He said that a Japanese sailor claimed to have netted the creature alive, only to see it die soon afterward. An American ship captain was so impressed he allocated to himself $6,000 of ship's funds, bought it, and went to England.

Soon 300 visitors daily were gawking at his prize in Piccadilly's Egyptian Hall. The July 1822 issue of *Gentlemen's Magazine* carried a story about the three-foot-long mermaid. "The head is turned back

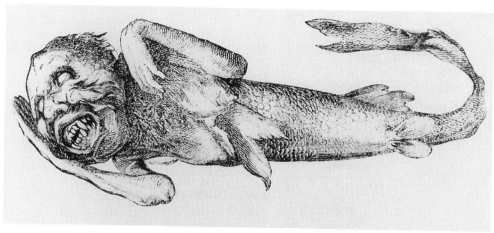

P. T. Barnum's notorious "Feejee Mermaid," made from the body of a fish and the torso of a monkey. Today the original resides, appropriately, at Coney Island.

and the countenance an expression of terror, which gives it the appearance of a caricature of the human face. . . . From the point where the human figure ceases, which is about twelve inches below the vertex of the head, it resembles a large fish of the salmon species. . . . The figure of the tail is exactly that which is given in the usual representation of the mermaid."

In time, interest waned. The ship captain returned to the United States. His son, who inherited the mermaid, sold it to the Boston Museum. Understandably reluctant to exhibit this questionable acquisition, in 1842 the director showed it to promoter and con man P. T. Barnum, at that time proprietor of Barnum's American Museum in New York. Barnum consulted a naturalist, who could not determine how the mammalian body had been joined to the fish body.

Barnum coolly asked, "Why do you suppose it is manufactured?"

"Because I don't believe in mermaids."

"That," Barnum replied, "is no reason at all. I'll believe in mermaids and hire it." He assigned his collaborator Levi Lyman, who would later assist Brigham Young, to prepare this new hoax. A series of letters in New York papers claimed that the celebrated English scientist Dr. Griffin was returning from a stopover in South America with a Fiji Island mermaid he had discovered. As Griffin, Lyman permitted glimpses of his treasure in Philadelphia, and by the time he reached New York the papers were begging for more information.

Barnum prepared promotional illustrations and gave them to editors, saying that since he wasn't able to acquire the famous mermaid they were of no use to him. Neither they nor the pamphlet that then appeared mentioned Barnum. The latter claimed that, in response to "numerous and urgent solicitations from scientific gentlemen in this city, MR. J. GRIFFIN, proprietor of the Mermaid . . . has consented to exhibit it to the public, *positively for one week only!*" Beginning August 8, 1842, thousands flocked to hear Griffin's learned dissertation on the creature. After the promised week, Barnum moved the mermaid to his museum, the first time it had been linked with him. He advertised the preserved half-monkey and half-fish carcass under an eighteen-foot banner depicting a beautiful, classical mermaid.

Lyman continued to hold forth on the Feejee Mermaid. One visitor protested, "But I lived two years on the Fiji Islands and I never heard of any such thing as a mermaid."

Lyman shrugged. "There's no accounting for some men's ignorance."

See also Barnum's elephant, 2/22.

---

9 AUGUST 1846

"Murders in the Rue Morgue"

"These tales of ratiocination," Edgar Allan Poe wrote to a friend on August 9, 1846, "owe most of their popularity to being something in a new key." The new key was a whole new genre. Poe had fathered the detective story. In this letter, he referred to the first of his three tales featuring the eccentric C. Auguste Dupin. "In the 'Murders in the Rue Morgue,' for instance, where is the ingenuity of unravelling a web which you . . . have woven for the express purpose of unravelling?"

"EXTRAORDINARY MURDERS," shouts a headline in the story. "This morning, about three o'clock, the inhabitants of the Quartier St. Roch were aroused from sleep by a succession of terrific shrieks. . . ." Neighbors had trouble breaking in because all the doors were locked. They found the body of Mademoiselle L'Espanaye in the chimney, and her mother's almost decapitated corpse sprawled in the courtyard. On the floor lay a bloody razor. "To this horrible mystery there is not as yet, we believe, the slightest clew."

Here in its initial appearance, in the April 1841 issue of *Graham's,* the mystery story features a locked-room double murder, an unofficial investigator, and an admiring narrator. There is also an unlikely villain. As Dupin deduces, the perpetrator of the carnage in the Rue Morgue was not human. Equipped with his owner's razor, an escaped orangutan was innocently trying to shave the old woman, as he had seen his master shave. Understandably, Madame resisted beautification by an armed primate, and the ape (accidentally?) slashed her throat. Then, finding the daughter's screams disquieting, he stuffed Mademoiselle up the chimney.

Orang utan is a Malay phrase meaning "man of the woods." Dutch naturalist Jacob de Bondt, who had supposedly seen an orangutan walking upright, described it as a "wonderful monster with a human face." Of course, he also said he saw a female orangutan weeping and modestly covering her private parts. English sea captain Daniel Beeckman observed the "Oran-ootan" in Borneo in 1712. "The Natives really do believe," he wrote, "that these were formerly Men, but Metamorphosed into Beasts for their Blasphemy."

In a simian lineup, the ungodly old man of the woods would look suspiciously capable of these murders. No other ape is taller, and only the gorilla is heavier. Orangutans are the most arboreal of the great apes, and highly intelligent. With a seven-foot span of very powerful arms, probably one wouldn't balk at the acrobatics required to enter the fourth-floor L'Espanaye apartment. Nevertheless, orangutans are famously peaceful, and there is no record of unprovoked attacks on humans.

Although described in grisly detail in newspaper reports, the murders occur offstage; we never glimpse the villain. However, Dupin makes us witness the events in retrospect. His sole antecedent in literature, the observant but nondetective hero of Voltaire's *Zadig* (1747), performs similar marvels. Voltaire's description of Zadig's method applies to Dupin: ". . . He chiefly studied the properties of plants and animals; and soon acquired a sagacity that made him discover a thousand differences where other men see nothing but uniformity."

Homo Sylveſtris. Orang Outang.

An early portrayal of the orangutan. The Latin Homo sylvestris, *like the Malay* orang outang, *means "man of the woods." From Tulpius,* Observationes Medicae, *1641*

---

10 AUGUST 1774

"Largest and Most Surprising"

Robert Jamieson, the captain of the herring ship *Janet* out of Glasgow, signed the deposition himself. So did his entire crew of nine. All swore that the preceding autumn, around noon on August 9 or 10, 1774, someone called the captain up on deck to observe "an island which had just made its appearance in the sea. . . ." They gave the precise location off the coast of Scotland. Jamieson couldn't estimate how broad the "island" was, but it seemed about a mile and a half long and finally rose to a height of perhaps thirty feet above the surface. For "five or six Minutes" the crew watched, until the island slowly sank beneath the waves.

Numerous Scandinavian legends concern a gigantic marine creature called the kraken. Sixteenth-century Swedish historian Olaus Magnus reported floating islands that rose from the ocean only to disappear shortly afterward. Two centuries later, Danish theologian Erik Pontoppidan, in his *Natural History of Norway,* called the kraken "the largest and most surprising of all the animal creation." Supposedly, a Finnish regiment performed military maneuvers on one island, and a bishop raised an altar and performed a Mass on another, only to watch the "land" sink underwater afterward. The tale of the maritime wanderings of the sixth-century Irish ecclesiastic Saint Brendan includes an adventure with a kraken. He and his companions are cooking a meal on a small island when the very land beneath

According to the eleventh-century Navigation of St. Brendan, *the cleric and his shipmates built an altar and performed religious services upon what they* thought *was an island.*

them begins to move. Presumably the heat woke the kraken that they had mistaken for land. It tilts, the cauldron slides into the sea, and the men scramble for their lives.

As recent a scientist as Linnaeus believed for a while in the kraken and included it in the first edition of his classification system. He designated it *Sepia microcosmos. Sepia* is the Greek word for cuttlefish; the pigment was originally prepared from the inky fluid they secrete. Linnaeus could confidently label a myth because, like so many myths, it had a foundation in reality. The kraken of legend doesn't appear solely as wandering real estate. Many stories tell of huge tentacles shooting up out of the sea and pulling sailors, and sometimes entire ships, under the waves. For that reason several scholars think that the kraken was based upon the giant squid, or upon a combination of the squid and the whale.

Some biblical references to Leviathan seem to concern the crocodile; others may describe whales. However, Jewish legend describes the great sea beast as Jehovah's most awesome creation. Rivaled in size only by Behemoth, the largest animal on land, it supposedly led God to reconsider his own handiwork. Naturally he had made a pair of the monsters. However, because they were so large, he destroyed one before they reproduced and ate the rest of his new planet. He allowed one to live. It was, after all, his magnum opus. Not surprisingly, some stories identify the kraken with Leviathan. As with the biblical beast, supposedly there were only two krakens alive and they lived until the end of the world. That life span alone explained away the absence of physical evidence.

Such stories inspired Alfred, Lord Tennyson to describe the kraken:

> *Below the thunders of the upper deep,*
> *Far, far beneath in the abysmal sea,*
> *His ancient, dreamless, uninvaded sleep*
> *The Kraken sleepeth . . .*

See also Verne's giant squid, 4/20.

Gifford Pinchot's Common Sense

When Gifford Pinchot was born on August 11, 1865, in Simsbury, Connecticut, the profession that he would make famous did not yet exist in his native land. No U.S. educational institution offered courses—much less degrees—in forestry. Therefore, in 1900, at the age of thirty-five, he went to France to study at the National School of Waters and Forests.

Long before then, however, Pinchot had demonstrated his knowledge of forestry and conservation. In 1891, park designer Frederick Law Olmsted asked him to come to North Carolina as forester for the vast Biltmore estate. There Pinchot began the first systematic program of forest management in America, with a private budget larger than that of the Agriculture Department at the time. For some years afterward he worked as a private consultant in the new field of forestry and conservation. When the National Academy of Sciences appointed a Forest Commission, Pinchot was naturally a member. The commission, convinced that unrestricted lumbering and other exploitation would result in the destruction of America's forests, recommended that the U.S. government create official forest reserves.

During the brief time Theodore Roosevelt was governor of New York State, Pinchot had advised him on conservation issues. Then, to the dismay of the hard-core Republican establishment, William McKinley's assassination in 1908 promoted the radical Roosevelt to the most influential office in the United States. Roosevelt proved to be what would later be called "an environmental president." He proved what can be done against all opposition if there is a committed innovator in the White House. Conservation was one of Roosevelt's progressive weapons against the abuses, both social and economic, of unrestricted industrialization and urbanization.

As head of the Forest Service, Pinchot became Roosevelt's conservation deputy. In 1901, when Pinchot took over their administration, there were 51 million acres of what would become the national forests. By the time William Howard Taft, Roosevelt's successor, dismissed Pinchot in 1910, the amount had more than tripled, to 175 million acres. That same year, in order to pursue his conservation agenda, Pinchot founded the National Conservation Association. He founded the Society of American Foresters and headed numerous other private and government institutions. He was even governor of Pennsylvania. Pinchot voiced the radical notion that the common people had the first claim to the natural resources of America: "Better help a poor man make a living for his family than help a rich man get richer still."

Back in 1910, the year Taft dismissed him, Pinchot expressed his convictions in his book *The Fight for Conservation.*

> The central thing for which conservation stands is to make this country the best possible place to live in, both for us and for our descendants. . . . Conservation . . . holds that people have not only the right, but the duty to control the use of the natural resources, which are the great sources of prosperity. And it regards

the absorption of these resources by the special interests, unless their operations are under effective public control, as a moral wrong. Conservation is the application of common-sense to the common problems for the common good.

---

12 AUGUST 1902

Tyrannosaurus Rex

In 1901, W. T. Hornaday, the director of the New York Zoological Park, was hunting deer along the banks of the Missouri River in eastern Montana. He came across the exposed fossil bones of several giant animals, but, since he wasn't exactly outfitted for a dinosaur dig, he simply photographed them. Back in New York City, he took the photos to a man who is remembered as one of the great dinosaur collectors in U.S. history, Barnum Brown, at the American Museum of Natural History. Brown identified the bones as those of the dinosaur *Triceratops.*

The first of the now legendary Hell Creek collecting expeditions took place in 1902. A paleontological treasure trove, the site has since provided many of the world's most spectacular fossils. Almost immediately upon arrival, Brown found the *Triceratops* fossil Hornaday had photographed. And during that first remarkable season, he unearthed what would become the type specimen (the first recognized example, by which a new species is described) for a dinosaur that was to capture the world's imagination.

On August 12, 1902, Brown wrote to Henry Fairfield Osborn, the museum's director: "Quarry No. 1 contains the femur, pubes, part of the humerus, three vertebrate, and two indeterminate bones of a large carnivorous dinosaur. . . . I have never seen anything like it from the Cretaceous." Three years later, he officially described the creature and named it *Tyrannosaurus rex,* "king of the tyrant lizards." In 1908 Brown found a second specimen, even more complete than the first. It would be over half a century before any other specimens of *Tyrannosaurus* would be found, and even now there are only a dozen or so.

During World War II, the American Museum of Natural History sold Brown's *Tyrannosaurus* type specimen to the Carnegie Museum, supposedly so that the two skeletons wouldn't be housed together in case the Germans bombed New York. In 1993, the museum began remounting the remaining specimen in a pose suitable to its reputation. With one foot lifting off the ground, the outstretched tail high and straight like a rudder, and the heavily armed head held low, *T. rex* looks like the ultimate lean, mean killing machine.

It is a reputation that has sometimes caught our imagination in unpredictable ways and built an impressive fame. In 1967, rock-and-roll musicians named their band Tyrannosaurus Rex, only to shorten it to the less-cumbersome and just as recognizable T. Rex three years later. After the explosion of interest in dinosaurs in the 1980s, their popularity culminated in the book and film *Jurassic Park.*

Understandably, the destructive force of such an animal appeals to children. When Calvin, the eponymous antihero of Bill Watterson's comic strip *Calvin and Hobbes,* is in a particularly troublesome mood, he imagines himself a carnivorous dinosaur sowing mayhem among the lumbering herbivores of the Cretaceous. His usual weapon of choice is *Tyrannosaurus*. Once, taking the matter a step further, he imagined the ultimate destructive fantasy his six-year-old mind could conjure: "Tyrannosaurs in F-14s!!" Snug in their cockpits, the begoggled raptors even have silhouettes of their dinosaur prey stenciled on the fuselage of their fighter jets.

For other dinosaurs, see 7/13, 9/3, and 10/1.

Al Capp's Menagerie

Before Calvin met a stuffed tiger named Hobbes, before Opus the penguin came to Bloom County, before a philosophical possum named Pogo met the enemy, the comics page of newspapers was already the habitat of some curious animals. Several of them were invented by Al Capp, whose comic strip *Li'l Abner* began appearing in the *New York Mirror* on August 13, 1934. It was wildly popular and generated several fads. One was Sadie Hawkins Day, on which women, for the novelty of it, were authorized to accost the men of their choice. The outrageous characters—Abner Yokum, his Mammy and Pappy, the lovesick Daisy Mae—have been compared to everything from Jewish folktales to Paul Bunyan stories. Capp retired the strip on Sadie Hawkins Day, 1977.

Capp's animals are as memorable as his people. The bald iggle stimulates everyone around it to speak the truth. The meat of the fatoceros is not only irresistible, it makes whoever consumes it grow steadily thinner and waste away. Swarms of turnip termites plague the village of Dogpatch. Capp's take on the "Emperor's New Clothes" was the Bashful Bulganik, which is nonexistent but people believe it's merely invisible.

In one series, Abner inherits 50 million Kigmies from an Australian relative. These creatures say, "We is a nice, safe li'l minority to kick around—*We* don't kick back." A man plans to make a fortune by selling them to Americans, who can kick them and quit kicking each other. Of course, it doesn't work out that way: "Wif pests like *them* aroun', folks stops *fightin'* each other—an thet throws lawyers, generals an' liniment makers *outa work!!*" Finally the masochistic Kigmies learn that the only pleasure greater than being kicked is kicking someone else. Then, of course, they are shipped back to their native land.

Meanwhile, high atop Mount Neverbin, Tiny Yokum and his boss Fatback discover creatures called Abominable Snow-hams. Aromatic and tasty, they seem the perfect animal, except that they appear intelligent. A question of what it means to be human results. When Tiny points out that the creatures build homes, carry their young, and love each other, Fatback replies testily that beavers build their homes, kangaroos carry their young, and rabbits love each other. The fight goes to court. Attorney Bagpipe deliberately slips on a banana peel and, when everyone laughs except the Snow-ham, he declares that that proves it isn't human.

Then, in 1948, there emerged from the Valley of the Shmoon a shapeless two-legged beanbag of a creature that is the greatest boon to humankind imaginable. The Shmoo wants above all else to make people happy. It gives milk already labeled "Grade A" and lays eggs neatly packaged by the dozen. Its hide provides either leather or lumber, depending on how thickly it's sliced. Broil a shmoo and you get steak; fry one and it comes out chicken. Even its eyes and whiskers are useful, for suspender buttons and toothpicks. Like the Kigmies, Shmoos could wreck civilization. However, their selflessness knows no bounds, and they kill themselves rather than risk the trouble their devotion might incite.

Of course, Li'l Abner and the other folks of Dogpatch learn nothing from the altruism of Shmoos, anymore than they do from the bald iggle's honesty, the Kigmies' pacifism, or the humanity of Snowhams. Despite the parade of their fellow creatures sporting morals as obvious as a bestiary's, in the world of Al Capp, people never learn.

---

14 AUGUST 1942

Bambi

The Hungarian writer Siegmund Salzmann, who used the pen name Felix Salten, wrote novels, criticism, essays, journalism, and plays. However, many people remember him primarily for a single children's book, *Bambi: Eine Lebensgeschichte aus dem Walde.* It was published in 1923. Five years later, a young American named Whittaker Chambers translated it into English—*Bambi: A Life in the Woods.* Salten also published *Florian, the Emperor's Stallion* (1934) and *Bambi's Children* (1940), but neither achieved the lasting fame of *Bambi.*

The deer's story, like David Copperfield's, begins with his birth:

> He came into the world in the middle of the thicket, in one of those little, hidden forest glades which seem to be entirely open, but are really screened in on all sides. There was very little room in it, scarcely enough for him and his mother. . . .
>
> "What a beautiful child," cried the magpie.

In his introduction to the American edition, novelist John Galsworthy wrote, "I do not, as a rule, like the method which places human words in the mouths of dumb creatures, and it is the triumph of this book that, behind the conversation, one feels the real sensations of the creatures who speak." Once the reader grants the initial premise of creatures that talk and feel in humanlike ways, the greatest risk to the suspension of disbelief comes from some of their interactions. Salten's novel is both realistic and surreal. Like a real deer, Bambi must flee hunters. But then he converses with grasshoppers and butterflies. Elsewhere, leaves speculate on the meaning of their impending fall to the ground.

The Walt Disney studio began working on an animated adaptation of *Bambi* in 1937, but the completed film didn't arrive in theaters until five years later. It required so much detailed advance work that Disney shunted it to a sidetrack while producing *Pinocchio, Fantasia,* and *Dumbo.* Instructors regularly held art classes at the studio, but special classes were added to assist the animators in the realistic portrayal of familiar forest animals. As soon as Disney announced that *Bambi* was in production, the studio received from the Maine Development Commission two fawns as models. The animators' portrayal of Bambi's growth from birth to adulthood followed the fawns' development over the next couple of years. In time the crew added other animals to the studio zoo. For the scenes of Bambi learning to skate on the "stiff water," animators photographed the contrived tumbles of ice-skaters. Avian accents were mostly provided by a woman who specialized in birdcalls.

Salten's novel was, naturally, European in setting and tone. Nonetheless, Disney dispatched a photographer to the Maine woods to record local color that could be transmuted into appropriately lyrical backgrounds for the action. He recorded a variety of sylvan phenomena that the animators would have been unable to conjure without his help—sunlight angling through the forest and glistening on spiderwebs, raindrops splattering, the shadows cast by lightning, tree branches filled with snow. When the result appeared, it was the most "realistic" animation ever attempted.

The world premiere of *Bambi* was held at Radio City Music Hall. The next day, August 14, 1942, the *New York Times* reviewer complained that Disney was trying to take naturalism too far, and if he did that, "why have cartoons at all? . . . Because Bambi and his mother are naturalistically conceived, the fact that they speak like people becomes widely incongruous. . . ." There were other complaints. For every reviewer who found the film too cuddly for adults, another proclaimed it too dark and disturbing for children. Some disliked the too-cartoonish forest fire, or the broad slapstick of Thumper and Flower, who have no counterparts in the book.

Thanks to the carefully contrived naturalism of the setting, departures from reality are unsettling in ways that the big-eared flying elephant of *Dumbo,* secure in his circus fantasy world, is not. The age-old method of placing "human words in the mouths of dumb creatures" has always had its paradoxes, and they grow more sharply defined the greater the attempt at a naturalistic treatment. But that doesn't seem to inhibit writers from doing it. The lure—the altered perspective, the sheer otherness of these other lives—seems to be too strong.

---

15 AUGUST 1962

Spider-Man

Spider-Man's debut on August 15, 1962, was a one-shot gamble in the last issue of a dying comic book. The publisher worried that readers would find the idea of spiders distasteful, but modern youngsters proved less squeamish than Miss Muffett. Spider-Man became Marvel Comics' most popular hero.

At a scientific demonstration, seventeen-year-old Peter Parker is bitten by a spider that was accidentally irradiated. This is not an uncommon sort of occurrence in the comic book universe. Like primitive hunters who donned the skins of their prey, many superheroes and -villains owe their powers to animals or choose animals as their totems. More fortunate than the hero of the film *The Fly,* Parker acquires only the spider's beneficial characteristics. He discovers his new powers when he is almost run-down by an automobile and instinctively leaps far out of the way and clings to the side of a building.

Spiders do have impressive skills. Many have acute vision; hairs on the legs of some are extremely sensitive to vibration; and several species are powerful jumpers. However, Spider-Man did not acquire the ability to paralyze and liquefy his prey. Even comic books have limits.

The original story refers to the "dying insect" that bit Peter Parker. Of course, spiders aren't insects. Like insects, they're arthropods, creatures with jointed legs and external skeletons. There are 30,000-plus species named, with countless others waiting to be discovered. Spiders' class name, Arachnida, has an interesting history. Ovid, in his *Metamorphoses,* told the story of Arachne, who arrogantly tried to outweave the goddess Athena. Later, Arachne hanged herself and was turned into a spider, her descendants cursed to dangle forever from their webs as Arachne had from her noose.

A reluctant hero, Spider-Man is also a misunderstood one, considered little more than a criminal himself. This fits the pattern of spider stories. Arachnids in literature and folklore are untrustworthy. In Mary Howitt's 1821 poem, a spider artfully invites a fly into its parlour. The spider Ananse, protagonist if not exactly hero of Ashanti folktales, aims higher: By trickery he obtains the Sky God's stories and reads his thoughts. In such tales the spider's hypocrisy is a given. "O what a tangled web we weave," Sir Walter Scott admonished, "When first we practise to deceive!"

Peter Parker supplemented his new abilities with web-shooting wrist sacs, which he invented. He had not acquired the spider's signature talent: spinning a filament out of its own substance. "Nowhere, in the whole animal kingdom," wrote the French entomologist J.-Henri Fabre, "has the need to eat inspired a more cunning industry." It was an industry so cunning the gods usurped it. Athena wasn't the only one who considered weaving a divine pastime; goddesses of fate and time were usually weavers. The Great Mother, as weaver of destiny, was sometimes portrayed as an actual spider. More recently, in E. B. White's *Charlotte's Web,* Charlotte A. Cavatica uses her humble web—like Spider-Man—to right a wrong. She reweaves the destiny of Wilbur, the pig.

See also Batman, 1/12.

---

16 AUGUST 1948

Alger Hiss's Warbler

As a teenager, Alger Hiss spent summers at Camp Wildwood in Maine, where popular nature writer Ernest Thompson Seton expounded upon the glories of nature. Nevertheless, Hiss didn't develop an interest in birding until one day years later, when a goldfinch appeared at the window of his law office in Boston. Hiss examined it through a coworker's binoculars and found himself charmed. Soon he was an ardent bird-watcher.

In the summer of 1948, Whittaker Chambers testified before the House Un-American Activities Committee (HUAC). A Communist party member from 1924 to 1937, and now a senior editor at *Time,* Chambers claimed that he had known many high-level Washingtonians who were secretly Communists.

Prominent among the list was a Harvard Phi Beta Kappa who had been at Yalta with Roosevelt and had recently been secretary general to the conference that created the United Nations—Alger Hiss. Chambers claimed that Hiss had passed him 200 state documents.

The most important question for the HUAC was Chambers's credibility. He insisted that he had known Hiss well when they were in the party together, and he offered intimate knowledge to prove it. He knew some of the Hisses' nicknames for each other; that they had a cocker spaniel and a particular Audubon print; and that Hiss's Quaker wife used "thee" and "thou" at home. But most damning of all, in the eyes of the House committee, especially Richard Nixon and John McDowell, was the apparent inside knowledge of Hiss's hobby, bird-watching. "They used to get up early in the morning . . . to observe birds," Chambers said. "I recall once they saw, to their great excitement, a prothonotary warbler."

On August 16, still unaware of the nature of his accuser's testimony, Hiss was asked about his hobbies. "Tennis and ornithology," he replied. ". . . Maybe I am using too big a word to say an ornithologist because I am pretty amateur, but I have been interested in it since I was in Boston. I think anybody who knows me knows that." McDowell, a birder himself, asked Hiss if he had ever seen a prothonotary warbler. Hiss replied enthusiastically, "I have, right here on the Potomac. . . . Beautiful yellow head, a gorgeous bird." Hiss insisted that such casual knowledge could easily have been acquired during his single brief contact with Chambers; his enthusiasm for discussing birding was apparent in his response to McDowell. But for the committee, and later for Hiss's prosecutors at his trial, the warbler was the clinching detail.

The prothonotary warbler became the most debated issue of a national cause célèbre. Alger Hiss was convicted of perjury rather than treason, spent forty-four months in prison, and wound up an office-supplies salesman. His trial's momentum propelled the career of Richard Nixon and helped prepare for Joseph McCarthy. During the investigation, an FBI agent visited famed ornithologist Roger Tory Peterson, who recognized Hiss from a photo as a man he had sometimes met birding in the mornings along the Potomac. Years later, Peterson said, "It was a miserable prothonotary warbler . . . that was responsible for Nixon."

See also Nixon's "Checkers speech," 9/23.

---

17 August 1786

Frederick's Greyhounds

Frederick the Great of Prussia liked animals. In spite of, or perhaps because of, the legendary hunting fervor of his father, Frederick William I, he didn't enjoy hunting or hunters. "The butcher," he said, "kills for the necessities of man but he does not enjoy killing; the sportsman kills for pleasure and should therefore be classed below the butcher." When asked why he disapproved of spurs for horsemen, he replied, "Try sticking a fork into your naked stomach and you will soon see why."

Most of all, like many a monarch before and after him, Frederick loved dogs. He particularly favored Italian greyhounds, which were his constant companions throughout his life. One romps in the foreground of a portrait of Frederick at the age of two. They appear in statues that still grace his palace, Sans Souci ("Without Tears") in Potsdam. Inside Sans Souci, the dogs had free rein. They tore the chairs

Frederick the Great, whose passions in life included his beloved Italian greyhounds.

and curtains and considered the floor their toilet. On sunny days, after Frederick dealt with the day's royal business, with perhaps a little time devoted to the flute, he went into his garden with a book. The hounds cavorted around him. Frederick called them "his Marchionesses de Pompadour," after the mistress of Louis XV, but remarked that they cost less money to maintain.

Frederick wasn't the only ruler who enjoyed Italian greyhounds. So did Maximilian I of Austria, France's King Charles VIII, and James II of England. The dogs originated not in Italy but in Egypt, where greyhound-like dogs were buried in tombs with royalty. The name comes from their popularity during the Italian Renaissance, when various artists portrayed them in paintings. They show up in the work of van der Weyden, Memling, and Bosch, and even in Vatican statuary.

However much he was known as a military tactician, Frederick had two habits that worried his generals. He liked to reconnoiter alone, and he liked to take a greyhound with him on his horse, under his coat. During one of the several wars with Austria, he was forced to hide under a bridge while Austrian soldiers rode over it. At every moment he expected his dog to bark or his horse to neigh. Neither made a sound. Later, he buried both on the grounds of Sans Souci.

Frederick's last act concerned one of his dogs. In the summer of 1786, at the age of seventy-four, he lay dying. He awoke from his stupor late on his last evening and observed that one of his hounds, seated nearby, was shivering. He ordered a quilt thrown over it. That was his next-to-last utterance. His final words were, *"La montagne est passee, nous irons mieux."* ("We are over the hill, we shall go better now.") He died in the wee hours of 17 August. Frederick wanted to be buried at Sans Souci, near the graves of his horses and dogs, but he was placed in a church beside his father. In 1991, when the Berlin Wall came down, his body was returned to Sans Souci and laid to rest beside his dogs.

---

18 AUGUST 1939

The Cowardly Lion

The lion hath roared, who will not fear?

—Amos 3:8

Sometimes the best way to examine a long-held notion is to reverse it. The myth of the lion as noble and brave is well demonstrated by the one lion who thought he was neither. He first appeared in L. Frank Baum's novel *The Wonderful Wizard of Oz* in 1900. Dorothy and her newfound companions are following the yellow brick road to the Emerald City when "a great Lion" attacks them. He knocks down the Scarecrow and the Tin Woodman, but Dorothy slaps his nose before he can harm Toto. Her refusal to be bullied crumbles his ferocious act. Then Dorothy asks him the key question: "What makes you a coward?"

"I suppose I was born that way," the Lion replies. "All the other animals in the forest naturally expect me to be brave, for the Lion is everywhere thought to be the King of Beasts." The Cowardly Lion thinks he is the exception. On August 18, 1939, the day after the New York pre-

In The Wizard of Oz, *Bert Lahr played a lion who has trouble living up to his noble heritage.* Courtesy of Ronald V. Borst/ Hollywood Movie Posters

miere of the film version, the *Times* said of Bert Lahr's portrayal of the Lion, "As he mourns in one of his ballads, his Lion hasn't the prowess of a mow-ess; he can't sleep for brooding; he can't even count sheep because he's scared of sheep." Actually, of course, the Lion turns out to be just as impressive as his cousin who, earlier, roars majestically over MGM's title sequence.

There clings to the lion an irresistible prestige. Killing the Nemean lion is a task so daunting as to be worthy of the first labor of Heracles, who afterward wears its skin as a badge of his strength and courage. In honor of this feat, Zeus places the lion in the heavens as the constellation Leo. To this day, astrologers attribute extraordinary boldness to those born under this sign. The English could come up with no better name for their famously brave Richard I than Lion-Hearted. Heinrich Schliemann found lion sculptures protecting the gate of ancient Mycenae, and even today they guard the New York Public Library. The ruler of the Island of Misfit Toys in *Rudolph the Red-Nosed Reindeer* is a lion. Significantly, C. S. Lewis didn't choose a hedgehog or goldfinch as king of Narnia. In literature and myth, other animals seem to know their place by comparison. In Disney's animated film *The Lion King,* the cub's future subjects respectfully await his birth.

Reputation is everything. "I learned," the Cowardly Lion tells Dorothy, "that if I roared very loudly every living thing was frightened and got out of my way." In reality, as such patient and careful observers as George Schaller have reported, what humans might consider nobility or bravery is not a prominent characteristic of leonine behavior. Lions are notoriously lazy animals. They get as much of their food as possible by scrounging, either finding animals felled by disease or stealing from hyenas. When there isn't enough food to go around, the adults keep it to themselves. Many of the cubs that don't starve from such treatment are abandoned by their mothers. Lions also ignore certain cherished notions of gender roles. The males come and go from family to family, while the females maintain the pride through a close-knit sisterhood. Killing is not, as it is sometimes portrayed, a quick and merciful affair. In one favored method, the big cat clamps its jaws on the prey's throat and slowly drags the animal down as it strangles. The females do most of the hunting, only to find the males charging up for the first share.

The phrase "lion's share" comes from Aesop's fable in which a lion hunts with companions, then demands a disproportionate amount of the kill. And the kingly status of the lion is nowhere so clearly demonstrated as in another fable by Aesop, one about the value of quality over quantity. Animals are vying with each other to produce the largest litter of offspring. After they have squabbled over the size of their families, they ask a lioness how many children *she* has.

"One," she replies, "but that one is a lion."

See also Dorothy's tornado, 4/3.

---

19 AUGUST 1909

The Millionaire's Dinosaurs

Andrew Carnegie contributed millions of dollars to the infant science of paleontology and earned lasting fame in the field.

Andrew Carnegie, the Scot who immigrated to the United States and became one of the richest men in the world, was as much philanthropist as steel magnate. In 1895, he endowed the Carnegie Museum in Pittsburgh. Among that institution's many projects was a search for fossils to fill the Dinosaur Hall. Carnegie was used to the best of everything, and therefore he wanted the biggest dinosaurs that could be found. (Most people are understandably more impressed with the giants, but many of those creatures we lump together under the term "dinosaurs" were smaller than chickens.)

Carnegie hired geologist Earl Douglass to go to the American West and find bones. Douglass went to the Morrison Formation. It is composed of fossil-rich late Jurassic stone that was formed from mud and sand deposited by rivers in Mississippi Delta–like floodplains many millions of years ago. The fabled Bone Cabin Quarry in Wyoming—so named because fossils were so common there that a local sheepherder built his cabin out of them—is also part of the Morrison Formation.

On August 19, 1909, Douglass found in the sandstone of the Uinta Basin, near the town of Jensen, Utah, eight tailbones of the dinosaur *Apatosaurus (Brontosaurus)*. Carnegie poured money into the site, hiring dozens of workers who toiled even through the bitter Utah winters. The site eventually became one of the most productive in paleontology's history, yielding more than 400 Jurassic dinosaur specimens from nearly a dozen genera, including 20 skeletons complete enough for museum mounting. In 1958, a building was erected over the site of what came to be called Carnegie Quarry. Nowadays almost half a million people per year visit the monument to admire the monstrous bones.

Carnegie's legacy can be found throughout the last century of paleontology. A relatively smallish, graceful dinosaur from the quarry was named for Carnegie himself, *Diplodocus carnegii,* and the larger *Apatosaurus louisae* bears the first name of his wife. There are interesting little footnotes to the history of both. Carnegie was so proud of "his" *Diplodocus* that he had ten metal copies of it cast and sent to museums around the world—Mexico, Austria, England, Argentina. And, at seventy-seven feet, the one mounted in the museum in Pittsburgh and named for his wife is the longest mounted dinosaur in the world.

Funded by Carnegie, Earl Douglass collected another impressive creature that has achieved a new fame in recent years. In 1991, the American Museum of Natural History installed a gigantic 140-million-year-old skeleton of *Barosaurus* in the main hall. It was mounted in a controversial pose, rearing high on its hind legs to defend its young from an attacking *Allosaurus*. There is no proof that such events took place, but a variety of evidence confirms it as a reasonable conjecture. Although its bones lay scattered in three different museums for a while, the *Barosaurus* came from the Carnegie Quarry, yet another legacy of the businessman who has been called the patron saint of paleontology.

---

20 AUGUST 1811

"Of Gardens"

"God Almighty first planted a garden," Francis Bacon wrote in his essay "Of Gardens." Gardening, Bacon maintained, "is the purest of human pleasures. It is the greatest refreshment to the spirits of man; without which, buildings and palaces are but gross handyworks; and a man shall ever see, that when ages grow to civility and elegancy, men come to build stately, sooner then to garden finely: as if gardening were the greater perfection."

Bacon described his ideal garden in detail. There were certain evergreens for winter, then particular flowers for each season, even each month. He discussed his favorite aromatics, his dislike of topiary, and why pools are not good for a garden. Bacon's essay "Of Suspicion" took two pages; "Of Vainglory," three. His thoughts on gardening, on the other hand, took several times as much space. Obviously he knew whereof he spoke. So, too, did Shakespeare, if the ring of authority in the politically charged garden scene in *Richard II* can be trusted.

(Enter a *Gardener* and two *Servants*.)

Gardener. *Go, bind thou up yond dangling apricocks,*
which, like unruly children, make their sire
Stoop with oppression of their prodigal weight:
Give some supportance to the bending twigs.—
Go thou, and like an executioner
Cut off the heads of too-fast-growing sprays,
That look too lofty in our commonwealth:
All must be even in our government.—
You thus employed, I will go root away
The noisome weeds, that without profit suck
The soil's fertility from wholesome flowers.

A couple of centuries later, when he built Monticello, Thomas Jefferson intended it to be his hermitage, where he could evade the pressures of life in public, where he could write and invent and correspond—and garden. However, his increasing fame encroached ever more upon his time. Now and then, when the demands of family and friends became too much for him, he fled to his other estate, Poplar Forest, ninety miles away. On the twentieth of August, 1811, Jefferson wrote to artist Charles Willson Peale from Poplar Forest: "No occupation is so delightful to me as the culture of the earth, and no culture comparable to that of the garden. Such a variety of subjects, some one always coming to perfection, the failure of one thing repaired by the success of another, and instead of one harvest a continued one throughout the year. . . ."

Later in the same century, Victorian novelist Charles Kingsley said his garden had replaced for him the need to travel and see the world. It was the world in miniature. "For there it is, friend, the whole infinite miracle of nature in every tuft of grass, if we have only eyes to see it, and can disabuse our minds of that tyrannous phantom of size. . . ." As his essay "My Winter-Garden" progresses, Kingsley sounds like Walt Whitman, in his declaration that "the fly who basks upon one of the trilithons of Stonehenge, is in truth infinitely greater than all Stonehenge together." Then, reminiscent of Thoreau, he expresses the glories of gardening in a single rhetorical question: "Is it not true wealth to have all I want without paying for it?"

---

21 AUGUST 1921

Winnie-the-Pooh

In 1921, a young father named A. A. Milne bought a teddy bear in Harrod's and gave it to his son for his first birthday, on the twenty-first of August. Christopher Robin usually called his inseparable companion either Bear or Teddy Bear, but occasionally he introduced him formally as Mr. Edward Bear. (To add to his aliases, Pooh lived in the forest under the name of Sanders.) Milne traced in his introduction the etymology of the bear's more famous name. Christopher Robin once named a swan Pooh, and he enjoyed visiting a bear named Winnie in the London Zoo. Winnie was an American black bear, a former mascot donated by a Canadian regiment when they proceeded to France in World War I. The swan was at the Milnes' country getaway in Arundel.

For Christmas 1921 Christopher Robin received a stuffed donkey he named Eeyore. It was undistinguished until a wire in its neck broke and the now-drooping head gave it a melancholy air. That hanging head inspired a glum temperament reminiscent of that "lone, lorn creetur," Mrs. Gummidge, in *David Copperfield.* When Milne began writing stories about the animals, and working with illustrator Ernest H. Shepard, he returned to Harrod's on a character quest and came home with a toy kangaroo and its joey, which became Kanga and Roo. The characters most realistically drawn, Owl and Rabbit, Milne simply imagined. Pooh received from Shepard the slightly humped back that was then a standard feature of teddy bears, which lent him something of Eeyore's thoughtful look.

Pooh could only have been a modern incarnation in bears' long trek from savage monsters to nursery companions. In the Bible, they are considered the essence of wildness, even personifying God's uncontrollable anger, as when he sends two to kill forty-two children merely because they mock Elisha's baldness. But the reputation of bears, like that of wolves later on, slowly improved as they became further removed from daily experience. Winnie-the-Pooh was only the latest bear of very little brain. Aesop's gullible bears inspired the medieval story cycle *Roman de Renart,* in which the naive bear is always duped. In the nineteenth century, slow-witted but not unkind bears populated fairy tales such as "Goldilocks." Renart's foe was reincarnated in 1881 as Brer Bear in Joel Chandler Harris's *Tales of Uncle Remus.* Then, in 1902, the teddy bear was invented, and bears were poised for the deification led by Pooh.

Inspired by toys, the characters were already once removed from real animals. But Shepard portrayed them in a forest that looks natural rather than cartoonish, based upon the Milnes' nearby woodland. Every character except Rabbit, who has a burrow, lives in a tree—even the boy. Asked decades later about his father's arboreal obsession, Christopher Robin Milne explained that as a child he actually spent much of his time in trees, especially one ancient walnut. "The tree was hollow inside and a great gash in its trunk had opened up to make a door. . . . There was plenty of room for a boy and his bear."

See also the teddy bear, 11/16.

---

22 AUGUST 1485

The Wars of the Roses

Let him that is a true-born gentleman
And stands upon the honor of his birth,
If he suppose that I have pleaded truth,
From off this brier pluck a white rose with me.

This famous scene in the Temple garden, in Shakespeare's *Henry VI, Part One,* pretends to depict the origin of what came to be called the Wars of the Roses. The English civil wars of the 1400s occupy several of Shakespeare's plays, but this scene, like many others, he invented from whole cloth. Finding that no one is openly siding with him, Richard Plantegenet proposes that each man choose either the white rose of the House of York, which would mean they were aligning themselves with him, or the red rose of the House of Lancaster, which had its own claim to the throne.

Although they are the best known, roses were by no means the only symbols the royal families employed. They reworked and incorporated their ancestors' insignias, as if cultivating heraldic hybrids. The favorite badge of the Lancastrian Henry VI was actually an antelope. Various rivals employed a black bull, a boar, and a sunburst. Richard of York used a falcon. The symbols of Henry Tudor, inherited from his mother and father and other sources, included a red dragon and a dun cow.

The Yorkist white rose appears in various documents—for example, peeking from behind the elaborate initial letter of Bristol's town charter—but it became a prominent symbol only during the wars. The Lancaster leader, Henry Tudor, didn't employ the red rose at all until after he became Henry VII. Even then, his Yorkist wife holds a white one in a portrait. Referring to Henry's defeat of Richard III at the famous Battle of Bosworth Field in Leicestershire, a contemporary wrote, "In the year 1485 on the 22nd day of August the tusks of the boar were blunted and the red rose, the avenger of the white, shines upon us." Henry not only won the crown, but displayed the naked corpse of Richard as a trophy.

Apparently Henry VII was a master of symbolic propaganda equal to the image consultants of our own time. He determined to reunite a divided land. The following April, during his first official "progress" northward through England, he issued orders to his advance men about his reception in York. In the first of many pageants, a complicated mechanical device was to show "a royal, rich, red rose conveyed by a vice, unto which rose shall appear another rich white rose, unto whom all the flowers shall lout [bow] and evidently give sovereignty, showing the rose to be principal of all flowers, and there upon shall come from a cloud a crown covering the roses." York and Lancaster were symbolically (and, with his later marriage to Elizabeth of York, officially) united in the person of this new king.

John Skelton, court poet to Henry VII and tutor of the future Henry VIII, summed up this floral union succinctly: "The rose both white and red / In one rose now doth grow." Intertwined, the two roses still adorn the Tudor stained glass of Westminster Abbey.

See also Shakespeare and the Lupercalia, 2/15; and starlings, 3/6; and the northern star, 3/15.

---

23 AUGUST 1960

Spoiling for a Fight

"Bulls are noble in appearance," Pliny the Elder wrote, "with a grim brow and shaggy ears; while their horns are threatening and seem to spoil for a fight." Actually, the ones who spoil for a fight are, as usual, humans. The bulls don't round up people and torment them literally to death. Probably the bulls' viewpoint is more accurately expressed by Munro Leaf's children's book *Ferdinand,* memorably illustrated by Robert Lawson. It tells the story of a young bull that is a pacifist and wants simply to sniff the flowers and enjoy the sunshine.

According to Pliny, the Thessalians invented the sport of bullfighting. On horseback, they raced alongside the bull, grabbed its horns, and twisted its neck. It sounds like a diversion potentially gory enough to amuse the bloodthirsty sporting types of the time, and the encyclopedist says that that old crowd-pleaser, Julius Caesar, was the first to bring bullfighting to Rome. Pliny claimed the bull goads itself into a rage by pawing the sand so that it hits its stomach. Actually, there is a long, established tradition of acceptable means by which human beings may goad a bull into a suitably dangerous rage. Danger is, of course, the spice. The threat of bloody death hangs over every wave of the cape. The pre-occupation with killing a bull is complex and ancient. Frequently in mythology and primitive art the bull symbolizes the masculine principle of nature, the procreative power of the male.

The one nation in the world particularly associated with bullfighting is Spain. Although its origins are ancient, the "sport" doesn't extend backward in an unbroken line to the mists of antiquity. After the barbarian invasions of the fifth century, the tradition languished, at least in the urban areas, for several hundred years. The sport was revived in the eleventh century, as part of the festivities surrounding occasions of importance to the nobility. Legend says the first person to impale a bull in front of a crowd as part of the rediscovered entertainment was the Spanish soldier Rodrigo Díaz de Vivar, remembered as El Cid.

Bullfights were popular entertainment for thousands of years before Pablo Picasso and others portrayed the "sport."

One prominent twentieth-century artist is particularly associated with bullfights—Pablo Picasso. They were a favorite social occasion. He attended bullfights with a succession of lovers and wives, accompanied by his children and such friends as Jean Cocteau. After buying the villa La Californie overlooking Cannes, in 1955, he entertained there the famous Spanish bullfighter Luis-Miguel Dominguín. A photograph of one of those visits shows Picasso holding a wicker bull's head, with Dominguín grasping the horns as if explaining the risks he has faced.

Inevitably, like almost every experience that passed before his eyes, bullfighting appeared in Picasso's work. Numerous ink-wash studies exist, mostly vibrant silhouettes. One, painted at Vauvenargues on August 23, 1960, portrays the matador swirling the cape while a spear-wielding man rides up behind the bull on a rearing horse. In a famous series of lithographs created in December of 1945 and January of 1946, Picasso portrayed his chosen totemic animal in a succession of drawings.

In a way, the eleven drawings of bulls mimic Picasso's own growth as an artist. The first has a realistic air, although the figure is already simplified almost in the manner of a cave drawing. The second bull is monumental, the fourth almost cubist, the eighth arbitrarily fractured into its component planes. In the last, the eleventh in the series, the head is a tiny ball with horns consisting of a single curve, the legs mere sticks, and the genitals conveyed by a single loop and dash. It is difficult to imagine how Picasso could have carried the drawing to any greater extreme of simplicity and still so readily conveyed the subject. It was the result of many years of watching bulls in the arena.

24 AUGUST A.D. 79

The Fall and Rise of Pompeii

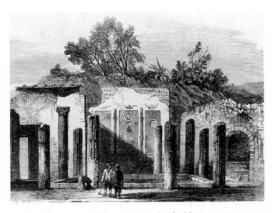

Buried for over a millennium and a half, Pompeii was one of the great archeological finds of all time. The busy lives of ancient Romans were preserved—and their catastrophic end offered a pointed moral.

The Romans considered volcanoes chimneys of the god Vulcan, who was perpetually stoking his subterranean fires. Although Lucretius suggested a more scientific origin, volcanoes remained the mouths of hell. Among Vulcan's best-known chimneys is Vesuvius, one of a string of Mediterranean volcanoes responsible for over 150 eruptions in recorded history. Vesuvius looks down upon what is now the Bay of Naples, which the Greeks settled around 800 B.C.

Crops flourished on the mountain's fertile green flanks—figs, almonds, pomegranates. The Romans conquered the irresistible area in 88 B.C. and built the cities of Herculaneum and Pompeii into jewels of the empire. After an earthquake in A.D. 62, Nero and the Senate funded reconstruction. Pompeii had public baths, gladiators' barracks, a 16,000-seat amphitheater, and, complete with lewd graffiti, 118 taverns.

On the morning of August 24, A.D. 79, another earthquake struck. Vesuvius was erupting. Blazing ash shot upward, creating a cloud of smoke and debris that rose high into the sky. White-hot stones rained down. Buildings crumbled. Running, trying to hide or escape or save their loved ones, the Pompeians were blinded by ash and choked by noxious fumes. Nearby Herculaneum was buried under a river of pumice and mud.

Much of the information we have about the eruption is archaeological. But an eyewitness account comes from the nephew of the naturalist Pliny. In nearby Misenum when his uncle died in the eruption, the younger Pliny thought he was witnessing the end of the world. Years later, he wrote an account of the event for the Roman historian Tacitus.

Civilizations rose and fell while Pompeii lay buried. After its gradual rediscovery in the 1700s, Pompeii became de rigueur on the European grand tour. Such an Old Testament sort of apocalypse captured the public's imagination. Figures eerily preserved included gladiators in chains, a dog on its leash, children holding hands. Skeletons still lying where they fell offered the same admonitory thrill as the melancholia of the Graveyard poets or the skulls watching over Dutch *vanitas* still lifes. In 1787, renamed Monte Somma, the mouth of hell was growling and spitting during Goethe's visit; later he said that to visualize the entombment of Pompeii one should imagine a mountain village buried in snow. Mark Twain wrote of a shortcut worn between temple pillars "by generations of time-saving feet," a skeleton with a necklace bearing the owner's name, and inscriptions over doors warning *cave canem,* "beware the dog."

Naturally, the mournful scene excited the imagination of Charles Dickens, who wrote about it in *Pictures from Italy:* "The chafing of the bucket-rope in the stone rim of the exhausted well; the track of carriage-wheels in the pavement of the street; the marks of drinking vessels on the stone counter of the wine shop . . . —all rendering the solitude and the deadly lonesomeness of the place, ten thousand times more solemn than if the volcano, in its fury, had swept the city from the earth, and sunk it in the bottom of the sea."

See also Pliny's death, 8/25.

Vesuvius Kills Pliny the Elder

Pliny the Elder was a man of his time. He believed in the owl's prophetic ability and the fatal gaze of the basilisk. He wondered why miners didn't encounter hell. The newly discovered ostrich he considered the offspring of a giraffe and a gnat. He claimed that lions spare prey who humble themselves and that eels are sexless and reproduce by rubbing against rocks.

Nevertheless, after Aristotle, Pliny was the most influential naturalist of the ancient world. He made genuine contributions to, and he is the primary source of information on, the botany and agriculture of his time. If he claimed a drop of bat's blood under a pillow is an aphrodisiac, he countered that with a useful analysis of the effects of lake-draining on crops. He described the phoenix as if he held it in his hand, but he also assumed the earth is round.

Obviously, unlike Aristotle, Pliny had little empirical bent. He was an encyclopedist, and he tackled the cataloging of everything in nature with energy worthy of his ambition. He slept only a few hours each night. When he had to stop studying to eat or bathe, his servants read to him. Once he reproached his nephew for walking, reminding him that if he were carried he could spend the time learning. Although his thirty-seven-volume *Natural History* would be enough for any career—and unfortunately that's all that survives—Pliny also wrote biography, history, even a grammar. But most of his time was taken up with civic duties. A wellborn gentleman, he was a lawyer and a career soldier; indeed, his first book was *On Throwing a Lance from Horseback.*

In the year 79 he was commander of a fleet in the Bay of Naples. On the twenty-fourth of August, nearby Vesuvius erupted. Pliny led his ships straight for the volcano, both to rescue the locals and to witness the spectacle. Through a growing cloud of smoke, flames were visible on the side of the mountain. Ash and pumice fell from the sky. But Pliny calmly dictated notes, and when the helmsman suggested turning back, his commander quoted Terence: *Fortis fortuna adiuvat* ("Fortune favors the courageous"). He was mistaken.

When finally they made it to shore, they debated whether the risk was greater indoors or out. Pliny chose indoors and went to sleep. We know he actually slept, because he was stout and the soldiers heard his loud snore. Outdoors, his trembling men tied pillows over their heads for protection against falling rock and awaited dawn.

The next morning the waves were too fierce to allow departure. Pliny, who already suffered from respiratory problems, was overwhelmed by sulfurous fumes. His slaves roused him, but he collapsed again. They fled without him. Two days later, when the eruption had subsided, Pliny was found where he had fallen, his body intact and seemingly uninjured. He looked, we are told, not dead but asleep.

See also the eruption of Vesuvius, 8/24.

---

26 AUGUST 1859

"The Devil's Tar"

In 1818, at the mouth of the aptly named Troublesome Creek, on the Big South Fork of the Cumberland River in Kentucky, two men used a pole and an auger to drill a hole 5 inches wide and 536 feet deep. They were looking for salt. What they found instead was oil, a great black seeping mess of it. This was not unprecedented; the first encounter with an "oil spring" in the New World occurred as early as 1627, in New York. But because they were unaware of any use for what they called "the Devil's tar," the two men plugged the troublesome hole with sand. They directed the oil itself into the river, where it formed a 35-mile-long oil slick which, in a foreshadowing of twentieth-century events, caught fire and caused extensive damage not only to the nearby forest but to the region's thriving salt-works.

But oil had been lurking under the surface of the earth for millions of years and could wait patiently for a few more. Finally, in 1859, along came a man named "Colonel" Edwin L. Drake, who became the first person in history to tap petroleum at its source. In Titusville, Pennsylvania, on August 26, using parts of a steam engine, Drake drilled a mere 60 feet into the earth. He struck oil. Soon the well was pumping 20 barrels daily, and within three years the new industry had produced 128 million gallons. An oil rush began, with boomtowns materializing as they had during the gold rush, only a decade before.

The new industry owed its existence to natural circumstances that occurred millions of years before humans appeared on Earth. The word "petroleum" comes from the Latin *petra,* "rock," and *oleum,* "oil"; indeed, the first petroleum development corporation was called the Pennsylvania Rock Oil Company. The oil had taken a long time to wind up in the rock, but the earth has always had plenty of time on its hands. Long ago, the bodies of prehistoric creatures became trapped by the deposition of sedimentary particles in ancient waterways. Anaerobic bacteria (bacteria that work without the presence of oxygen) decomposed the organisms. Petroleum is a naturally occurring fossil hydrocarbon in liquid form, derived from the crude soups that result from aeons of geological action on such long-decaying organic matter.

Thanks to massive advertising, throughout much of the twentieth century Americans have understood the link between dinosaurs and petroleum better than they comprehend most prehistoric phenomena. For decades, the Sinclair Oil and Refining Corporation advertised its products with a dinosaur mascot. "Dino" adorned gas pumps, billboards, and finally television commercials. Nor did Sinclair's link with paleontology cease with the manufacture and distribution of fossil fuels. When the company's president, Harry Sinclair, wasn't presiding over board meetings or fighting his indictment in the Teapot Dome Scandal—itself a battle over oil fields—he was funding dinosaur research.

A clever paleontologist had had the foresight to exploit the link between oil and dinosaurs. Barnum Brown, one of the most celebrated dinosaur collectors in U.S. history, cultivated Sinclair's acquaintance. In time, the millionaire agreed to fund a succession of dinosaur digs. Not one to waste an opportunity, he incorporated the results of each year's fieldwork into his ongoing advertising. In time, Brown reciprocated by designing dinosaur memorabilia, such as stamps and cards, which Sinclair stations across the country gave away as promotions. (As of 1980, collectibles associated with dinosaurs are officially called "dinosaurabilia.")

Brown and Sinclair became quite a team. Not surprisingly, a paleontologist of Brown's caliber was also an eagle-eyed geologist. The first man to survey from the air, Brown searched for both oil fields and likely fossil sites from Sinclair's airplane *Diplodocus.* The result of one such expedition was the skeleton of an extinct crocodile of the genus *Phobosuchus,* which as a consequence acquired the species name *sinclairi.*

Banneker's Almanac

Benjamin Banneker was born in Ellicott, Maryland, in 1731, the son and grandson of slaves. His father was named Bannka or Bannaka, which in time was corrupted to the surname Banneky and then Banneker. Toward the end of the seventeenth century, Bannka's owner freed him and then, defying custom and law, married him. When young Benjamin was six years old, his father purchased over 100 acres of land in the name of himself and his son. From an early age, therefore, Benjamin Banneker had extraordinary advantages.

From childhood he exhibited a strong interest in mathematics and statistics. His white English grandmother had had greater opportunities than her daughter's interracial family, and she was able to teach Benjamin to read and write. For a while he attended a small local school where black and white students were taught together. A classmate, a fellow "free Negro," later remembered that Benjamin cared little for play and that even then "all his delight was to dive into his books." Unfortunately, as soon as he was old enough to work full-time alongside his father, he had to leave school. As he grew up, he alternated his precious spare time between reading and exploring the nearby woods.

At the age of twenty-two, the extent of Banneker's abilities became apparent. He borrowed a pocket watch, analyzed its complex mechanism, and with that as his only guide constructed a large clock that actually struck the time. This was considered a miraculous accomplishment. Then as now, timekeeping devices were the domain of skilled craftsmen. Banneker's mechanical and mathematical aptitude led to work with the white owners of a local mill, and then to his learning surveying. He even helped survey the site of the District of Columbia.

Most impressive of all were his astronomical calculations. From 1792 to 1802, he published *Banneker's Almanac,* providing such information as the precise dates and times of eclipses. He was sixty when the first one appeared. The printer's preface introduced their "COMPLETE and ACCURATE EPHEMERIS for the Year 1792, calculated by a sable Descendant of Africa, who, by this Specimen of Ingenuity, evinces, to Demonstration, that mental Powers and Endowments are not the exclusive Excelence [*sic*] of white People, but that the Rays of Science may alike illumine the Minds of Men of every Clime. . . ." Banneker became a regional celebrity.

Over the years, Banneker was plagued with troubles. When he rented out parcels of his unused farm, his tenants frequently resisted or even refused to pay their debts. In 1790, someone—later he obliterated the name in his diary—stole both his "horse and Great Coat," and threatened his life. Local boys stripped his orchards bare. Both Banneker's social problems and his devotion to scientific observation are apparent in a single entry in his journal:

> *August 27, 1797.* Standing by my door, I heard the discharge of a gun, and in
> 4 or 5 Seconds of time after the discharge, the Small Shot came rattling about
> me, one or two of which Struck the house, which plainly demonstrates that the
> Velocity of Sound as [*sic*] much greater than that of a Cannon-Bullet.

The next year, "two Black men with a gun" discharged a round near his door. In 1802, someone ransacked his home and stole several articles. Did the burglars imagine his modest acclaim had brought him riches? Or was the burglary racially motivated? Finally, sadly hoping it was the source of the ill will toward him, Banneker sold most of his land. Eventually he was no longer able to even ride his horse. Age and infirmities forced him to abandon the burdensome tobacco farming. As the demands on his time dwindled, he turned to intellectual pursuits.

Banneker didn't marry. He devoted himself to his orchard, his bees, and the stars. Although never a member of a particular sect, Banneker was a religious man. His favorite church was a nearby Friends (Quaker) meetinghouse. After Banneker's death, a fellow Friends churchgoer described him: "His life was one of constant worship in the great temples of nature and science."

---

28 AUGUST

"A Little Night Music"

Tucker Mouse lives in a drainpipe in the Times Square subway station. He is watching Mario Bellini work his parents' newsstand when both boy and rodent hear a strange sound. "It was like a quick stroke across the strings of a violin, or like a harp that had been plucked suddenly." Mario follows the sound and finds a cricket.

Admirers compare the humor, warmth, and sparkling dialogue of George Selden's children's novel *The Cricket in Times Square* (1960) to *Charlotte's Web*. Chester Cricket hops into a picnic basket in the Connecticut countryside and hops out in New York City. Underneath the surging crowds of Times Square, worlds away from his countryside, Chester learns to play the human compositions he hears on the radio. He begins with the "Blue Danube Waltz." The first evening, he "memorized three movements from different symphonies, half a dozen songs from musical comedies, the solo part for a violin concerto, and four hymns." Later, Mario's mother is about to banish Chester when he absentmindedly plays a few bars of her favorite song, "Come Back to Sorrento."

A local music teacher hears the phenomenal insect and writes a letter to the *New York Times* on August 28: "Rejoice, oh New Yorkers—for a musical miracle has come to pass in our city!" When music lovers read the story, they converge on the newsstand. Chester responds with the most appropriate work imaginable for a virtuoso cricket, Mozart's *Eine Kleine Nachtmusik* (A Little Night Music). Soon the Bellinis are making a profit. Unfortunately, Chester longs to return to Connecticut. For his farewell performance, he chooses the sextet from Donizetti's opera *Lucia de Lammermoor*.

Other than his conversations with his new friends, his understanding of humans, and a certain prodigious musical talent, Chester behaves realistically. He doesn't drive an automobile, for example, as Mr. Toad does in *Wind in the Willows*. He dines on lettuce. He is the size a cricket should be. A French cousin of Chester starred in an even more convincing slice-of-nature story, *The Curious Adventures of a Field Cricket,* by Ernest Candeze (1881). The protagonist encounters such horrifying but natural sights as ichneumon grubs devouring larvae, and a war between ants. And, of course, there is the Talking-cricket in Carlo Collodi's 1883 novel, who became Jiminy Cricket in Disney's film.

Naturalist Loren Eiseley once encountered a subterranean musician reminiscent of Chester. "A few days ago, passing through one of the less frequented corridors of Pennsylvania Station," he wrote in his journal in 1958, "I heard the wonderful loud trilling of a single cricket apparently all alone in this great rumbling place. Was he calling for a female in his loneliness or merely singing an autumn song to himself?" Eiseley's rhetorical question wasn't published until many years later, but it was answered in 1960, by George Selden. The cricket was practicing Mozart.

---

29 AUGUST 1914

The Dove of Peace

In common usage, the heavier birds are called pigeons and their more svelte brethren doves, although scientists use the terms interchangeably. Scattered throughout temperate and tropical regions, and probably the first domesticated birds, the nearly 300 species have played roles as diverse as messenger for the Hindu god Yama and the emblem of King Arthur's Knights of the Grail. Fluttering in the air over

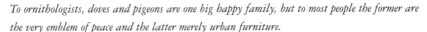

To ornithologists, doves and pigeons are one big happy family, but to most people the former are the very emblem of peace and the latter merely urban furniture.

Mary, a dove represents the Spirit of God in the *Annunciation*s of both Jan van Eyck and Nicolas Poussin. Even now Picasso's *Dove of Peace* can be found on Christmas cards. Carrying an olive twig, it harks back to the bird that, in the biblical myth, brought Noah an olive branch when the Flood waters receded.

That symbol was memorably employed in New York City in 1914. On August 29, a few months after the assassination of Archduke Franz Ferdinand of Austria launched World War I, over 1,500 women gathered in New York City to protest the threat of U.S. involvement in the war. Dressed in solemn black, accompanied by muffled drums, they marched down Fifth Avenue. They carried with them a white flag bearing a figure that everyone present understood as a universal symbol of peace: a dove holding an olive branch.

The legend of the neighborly goodwill of these birds apparently predates Aesop's fable of the ant and the dove. In that story, a thirsty ant climbs down a blade of grass to drink from a spring and loses his grip and falls into the water. It would have drowned if not for a nearby dove. Perched in a tree, the bird notices the ant's plight, plucks a leaf from a twig, and drops it into the water as a life preserver. The ant climbs aboard, and soon the leaf floats to shore and he is safely home again. Unfortunately, a hunter has seen the dove and is setting up a net with which to catch it. The ant notices this, and, in a quick repayment of his debt, bites the hunter on the heel. When the hunter drops his net, the dove flies away. Moral: "One good turn deserves another." In another fable, Aesop described what happens to a flock of foolish pigeons when they agree to allow a hawk to be their king, hoping that in turn he will protect them. Immediately he extorts frequent squab sacrifices as tribute in his protection racket.

The most common symbolic reference to doves recalls that march in 1914. In political parlance, a "dove" is one who prefers diplomacy in a confrontation, as opposed to a "hawk," who emphasizes brute military strength. The terms achieved wide currency in the 1960s, first in the United States and then in Europe and elsewhere.

The Bavenda people of Africa told a wonderful just-so story of how hawks and doves came to be at odds. It involves some uncharacteristic discourtesy on the part of the dove. Once upon a time, the hawk, the dove, and the vulture were friends. One day the dove's mother died, and his friends mourned with him. Then the vulture's mother died, and the hawk and the dove came to share his grief. Finally, the hawk's own mother died. However, when the other birds came to his home they were unkind. "Was she a queen?" the vulture asked scornfully, and the dove said, "Are we to mourn for such a miserable old thing?" Ever since then, understandably, the hawk has been the enemy of the dove.

See also Picasso's doves, 4/19.

Cleopatra's Suicide

"The real truth nobody knows," Plutarch wrote of Cleopatra's death. Even though one of his sources was the report of Cleopatra's physician, Plutarch himself was writing a century or more after Cleopatra's death. Two thousand years later, the truth is even more elusive.

Octavian, who became Caesar Augustus, defeated Mark Antony and Cleopatra at the Battle of Actium. Later, mistakenly thinking Cleopatra dead, Antony stabbed himself. Cleopatra, queen of Egypt, was now Octavian's prisoner. When she learned that he intended to parade her in his triumph in Rome, she planned her suicide. Octavian's sentries were unaware that they were guarding the scene of the first locked-room mystery. It was August 30, 30 B.C.

As soon as he received Cleopatra's note asking to share Antony's tomb, Octavian sent soldiers. In perfect B-movie style, they ran up the stairs and burst open the door. The carefully staged scene they found was re-created in Victorian *tableaux vivant* almost two millennia later. Cleopatra was already dead. She had mutilated herself after Antony's death, she was half starved, but she was lying on a golden couch, crowned and arrayed in full royal robes. Two maids were dying beside her.

Octavian had seized Cleopatra's weapons after her attempt to stab herself, yet somehow she had robbed him of his glory. The room was searched, the guards interrogated. A peasant had entered with a basket of figs. The guards had examined the fruit and allowed him to pass. A guard remembered the queen's cryptic remark upon the arrival of the food: "So here it is!" Supposedly Cleopatra's arm bore faint puncture marks. Had the peasant smuggled in a snake under the figs? A search revealed no snake, but they did find what one soldier thought was a serpentine trail in the sand.

Legend declares the culprit to have been an "asp." Several vipers of northern Africa are called asps, and one is even nicknamed "Cleopatra's asp." But the decorum of Cleopatra's death indicates the snake was not a viper. Viper venom is a blood poison that can cause blotches, swelling, vomiting, and even uncontrolled urination and defecation before death. This would not have been a departure befitting the descendant of so many kings. Cobra venom, however, is a nerve poison. It does not disfigure; it causes a slow paralysis that results in coma and an easier death.

Like a twentieth-century politician, Cleopatra understood the power of the image. The Book of the Dead said that the snake, because it could shed its skin and emerge renewed, was the symbol of immortality. The Egyptian cobra was both the emblem of the royal house of Egypt and the personal totem of the goddess Isis, whose earthly incarnation was none other than Cleopatra. Hood spread, ready to strike, the cobra coiled around the royal headdress. A suicide weapon worthy of a goddess/queen, it helped Cleopatra influence the interpretation of her own death. Some of her followers decided that she didn't die. She merely rejoined the gods.

In this etching after the painting by seventeenth-century Italian Guido Reni, Cleopatra, like a cross between Eve and a Madonna, holds the fatal asp to her breast.

Dog Days and Summer Soldiers

Now welcom somer, with thy sonne soft,
That hast this wintres weders overshake.

—Chaucer

"This is the last day of August," Virginia Woolf wrote in her diary in 1928, "and like almost all of them of extraordinary beauty." Her description of summer is familiar to most people who live in temperate regions; those in the Southern Hemisphere simply experience it in different months. "Each day is fine enough and hot enough for sitting out; but also full of wandering clouds; and that fading and rising of the light which so enraptures me in the downs; which I am always comparing to the light beneath the alabaster bowl. . . . Sometimes I see the cattle galloping 'like mad' as Dostoievsky would say, in the brooks. The clouds—if I could describe them I would; one yesterday had flowing hair on it, like the very fine white hair of an old man. . . ."

In his Eighteenth Sonnet, William Shakespeare compared his love to a summer's day, and his love rated higher. For one thing, she was more temperate. "Sometimes," he complained, "too hot the eye of heaven shines." There's no denying that, but summer's peak of growth and beauty has still been praised by poets and artists throughout history. According to Edith Wharton, Henry James thought the season held life's finest moments. "Summer afternoon—summer afternoon," he sighed; "to me those have always been the two most beautiful words in the English language." The word "summer," like the German *Sommer,* derives from the Sanskrit *sama,* meaning season or year. We still use "summer" in that sense on occasion, as in Tennyson's "after many a summer dies the swan."

Of course, for connoisseurs of summer, August is the end of the splendor. The month has its disadvantages. Meteorologists consider it the beginning of the hurricane season. The hottest days of summer usually occur in July and August. The Romans called a six-week period overlapping the two months *caniculares dies,* "dog days," and we still use the term. They thought that, since it rose and set with the sun at this time, Sirius, the Dog Star (so called because it is in the constellation of the Big Dog, Canis Major), must be contributing to the heat. In Robert Louis Stevenson's *A Child's Garden of Verses,* the narrator of the poem "Bed in Summer" points out one of the injustices of summer that is cured by adulthood:

303

In winter I get up at night
And dress by yellow candle-light.
In summer, quite the other way,—
I have to go to bed by day.

Summer is the time of laziness and lethargy, supposedly when, as the song from *Porgy and Bess* says, "the livin' is easy." One of the more amusing comments associated with this season is the infamous (and possibly apocryphal) notation scribbled across a paper and accidentally read aloud before England's House of Lords: "This is a rotten argument, but it should be good enough for their lordships on a hot summer afternoon." As the very emblem of the easy life, summer has occasionally provided some negative imagery. When Thomas Paine was calling American colonists to arms in *The Crisis* in 1776, he wrote that "the summer soldier and the sunshine patriot" might shrink from their duty, but not the true-blue citizen. *The Summer Soldier* is also the English title of Hiroshi Teshigahara's 1971 film about military desertion.

One of naturalist Edwin Way Teale's most significant accomplishments was his American Seasons series. In *Journey into Summer,* he wrote, "This is the season of gardens and flowers, of haying and threshing. Summer is the period when birds have fewer feathers and furbearers have fewer hairs in their pelts. Through it runs the singing of insects, the sweetness of ripened fruit, the perfume of unnumbered blooms."

The Death of Martha

Just before 1:00 P.M. on the first day of September, 1914, a twenty-nine-year-old bird named Martha died in the Cincinnati Zoo. Although she attracted attention as she aged, the story that a flock of ornithologists attended her last moments is fiction. Martha's last known wild cousin had been shot in Ohio in 1900. None has been reported since, and the story has become conservation's premier cautionary tale. Scarcely a century after pioneer naturalist Alexander Wilson estimated a migrating flock of them to be 1 mile wide and 240 miles long, the last passenger pigeon was dead.

To the Narragansett the bird was *wuskowhan,* "wanderer," and that is echoed in both the later "passenger" and the species name *migratorius.* The earliest European settlers called them simply wild pigeons or wood pigeons, and they were overwhelmed by the numbers of them. Since the birds gathered by the millions in huge colonies, all a hunter had to do was pick up the squabs that fell from the flimsy nests or reach up and knock them down with long poles.

Soon the pigeons were prized as food, and avarice designed more ingenious killing methods. The birds were fed grain soaked in alcohol and then picked up drunk, or suffocated with burning sulfur, or had their heads crushed in pincers after being netted. A favorite ploy, and the source of the term "stool pigeon," was to sew a bird's eyes shut so it wouldn't fly and then set it out on a stool as a decoy.

There were so many of the birds that legislatures wouldn't consider trying to protect them. Later, when they did, the laws were ignored. Even Audubon, after witnessing an all-night killing spree, still thought the species inexhaustible. In one year, 15 million were shipped from one Wisconsin colony. Twenty thousand squabs were taken from their nests and shipped to Coney Island for a pigeon shoot sponsored by the New York State Association for the Protection of Fish and Game.

But slowly the numbers were dwindling and the odds against the pigeons were growing. For one thing, a pair produced only a single young at each nesting. And, like many social species, they needed the protection of large numbers for breeding. This, and their incessant foraging for acorns and beechnuts, demanded vast tracts of deciduous woodland. So it wasn't just the hunting itself that destroyed them. As the numbers ran out, the slaughter was no longer economically feasible; it was stopped while there were still tens of thousands of pigeons in the wild. But that was still too few

305

"Suddenly there burst forth a general cry of 'Here they come!'" Audubon wrote. "The pigeons arriving by thousands, alighted everywhere, one above another. . . . Even the reports of the guns were seldom heard."

birds and too little land. They simply couldn't regain a foothold anywhere. Martha stands as a reminder that it isn't essential to kill the last member of a species in order to drive it to extinction.

The reports of witnesses sound portentous in retrospect. "When an individual is seen gliding through the woods and close to the observer," Audubon noted about passenger pigeons, "it passes like a thought, and on trying to see it again, the eye searches in vain; the bird is gone."

See also the cahow, 1/8; and the dodo, 7/4.

---

2 SEPTEMBER 1963

Bear Attack

"Under ordinary circumstances," Albertus Magnus wrote in the twelfth century, "a bear will not deliberately attack a man, unless the man inflicts a wound which enrages the beast." Hundreds of years later and thousands of miles away, the record of the Lewis and Clark Expedition in the early 1800s labeled the bear "a creature of extraordinary ferocity." Both these points of view are correct. In the first place, there are many different kinds of bears, living on every continent except Australia. Another problem in resolving the question of their temperament seems to be that bears have a broad definition of what constitutes ordinary circumstances.

In the summer of 1963, the blueberry crop in Alaska was smaller than usual. Cranberries, another staple food of the local black bears, had not yet ripened. The food shortage may have been what goaded the normally peaceful bears to forage outside their usual range, not to mention outside their usual diet. Surprisingly, more than one tried to add people to its menu. On September 2, 1963, Alaska newspapers reported four attacks by black bears. Two men were wounded and one killed. One was dragged from his sleeping bag by a bear and apparently survived only because a fellow camper shot the animal. Another man found the mauled body of his brother with a bear standing over it. One man had to race up a tree to escape, and another fled his tent when a bear entered it. Both were clawed or bitten.

These incidents were not what Albertus Magnus would have called ordinary circumstances. Apparently the bears in question were not provoked. Nor, by most definitions of provocation, were the grizzlies that killed two young women in Glacier National Park in August of 1967. The national outcry that arose from that incident was enlightening. The tone was mostly along the lines of "The parks are for people, not for bears!"

Those are very rare cases. Although they are interesting, both for their drama and what they reveal about our thinking, most of the occasional unpleasant encounters with bears occur because of human irresponsibility. Every day, for example, visitors to American national parks are caught teasing, abusing, or simply foolishly cavorting with wild bears. Tourists' tendency to feed the animals, which is strictly and with good reason forbidden, results in the bears lumbering down to peer in automobile windows and paw at the drivers. In a Canadian park, a ranger probably prevented a disaster by coming upon a family just in time. The woman had lured a bear with a candy bar, and, while the man aimed his camera, she was placing their one-and-a-half-year-old son on the bear's back.

Why did our ancestors worship bears as old men of the forest? Why are we so determined nowadays to regard them as harmless clowns? Bears' appeal seems to have a basis in their biology. Like us, they can walk on their hind legs. Like their cousin the raccoon, they have paws that are more manipulative than most animals'. Like other omnivores, they have a diverse diet and thus, constantly foraging, eagerly explore the world. We translate this as a charming, almost human curiosity. However, whether standing up in a humanlike posture or shuffling along in their flat-footed way, bears remain, at least on the North American continent, the only truly dangerous carnivore.

Much of our relationship with bears has been colored by our perception of them as some sort of cuddly version of ourselves.

See also Winnie-the-Pooh, 8/21; the teddy bear, 11/16; and the slain bear ceremony, 12/2.

---

3 SEPTEMBER 1943

Bombing Dinosaurs

After spending its few allotted years in the Mesozoic fighting for its life like every other creature, a dinosaur lies trapped in stone for millions of years. Then, after it is unearthed and becomes the object of admiring exclamations from museum-goers, it finds that its troubles *still* aren't over. Even fossilized, serenely inanimate, it is subject to the vicissitudes that plague every other physical object. One of those is the same that threatens the great architecture and art of the world—the large-scale destruction that accompanies war.

Again and again in this century, dinosaur skeletons have been carefully reconstructed only to then be bombed into dust. World War II, especially, destroyed many prized specimens. All over Europe, museums were destroyed, resulting in the loss of a sizable portion of our prehistoric legacy. Sometimes forethought rescued a few precious skeletons. On other occasions, there was no time even for caution, and the scientists who did not themselves fall victim were left to contemplate the ruins of their work.

Foreseeing the potential risk to their collection early in the conflict with Germany, the British Museum of Natural History in London wisely hid its prized dinosaur specimens in chalk caves in nearby Kent. Thus the bones survived the war undamaged. Others, however, were not so lucky. A skeleton that did not survive was that of one of the first dinosaurs discovered. A German raid on Bristol reduced to rubble the Bristol City Museum, and with it the reconstructed skeleton of the venerable *Thecodontosaurus*—just over a century after it had been named in 1836.

Nor did the opposition leave all the destruction to the Germans. A typical bombing took place on the third and fourth of September, 1943. While Allied planes dropped their payload on Berlin, the glass skylight of Humboldt University's Natural History Museum collapsed and fell in shards to the floor below. This prompted the curators to take drastic action. Their most prized specimen was the largest dinosaur on exhibit in the world, the seventy-foot-long *Brachiosaurus.* They dismantled it and stashed it in the basement. A little over two months later, their caution was vindicated. Another Allied raid left fires in its wake that reduced the Reptile Hall to smoldering rubble. In the ashes were the bones of several dinosaurs, including *Kentrosaurus* and *Dysalotosaurus lettowverbecki.* The latter was not only a fine skeleton but the type specimen, the example by which a new species is described.

Another great loss to paleontology occurred during a Royal Air Force raid on Munich. The Bavarian State Collections for Paleontology and Historical Geology housed the type specimens of *Carcharodontosaurus, Bahariasaurus,* and *Aegyptosaurus.* Another skeleton destroyed, that of a sail-backed carnivore named *Spinosaurus,* was not only the type specimen but the only known skeleton. Other such stories are common. In some cases, the exent of the loss can't be determined. Firebombing during the invasion of Normandy, for example, resulted in the destruction of the museum in Caen, France. At least two of the specimens lost were new to science and not yet named.

Nature's machinery of decay is so efficient that the odds are against any creature ever winding up preserved as a fossil. That's why the geological record of life is so spotty—and so precious. It is ironic but perhaps only natural that a creature could evade such odds and then, millions of years later, be utterly destroyed by the dominant animal of a different time.

See also Jurassic Park, *6/11;* T. rex, *8/12; and* Brontosaurus, *10/1.*

Peter Rabbit and
Beatrix Potter

When Beatrix Potter's governess married, she and her former charge remained friends. Potter wrote letters to all of the woman's children, but she got along especially well with her son Noel. Then, at the age of five, Noel was stricken with a long illness. Potter wrote him letters about her life and her adventures with her pet rabbit, Peter. Sometimes, when there was no news to report, she invented stories. On the fourth of September, 1893, she wrote a letter that has become legendary in children's literature.

My dear Noel,

I don't know what to write to you, so I shall tell you a story about four little rabbits whose names were Flopsy, Mopsy, Cottontail and Peter. . . .

Mrs. Rabbit warns all four of her children to avoid Mr. McGregor's garden because their father had an accident there; "he was put in a pie by Mrs. McGregor." However, while the others gather blackberries, Peter sneaks into McGregor's garden and consumes an unwise amount of greenery. Naturally, he stumbles into McGregor himself and has to flee for his life. Peter finally escapes and rushes home, minus his tiny jacket and shoes, which McGregor hangs up as a scarecrow. Potter avoided a moral, but no child misses the detail that Peter went to bed sick while his siblings ate milk and blackberries.

The letter/story contained seventeen black-and-white drawings, and fans would recognize most of them as early versions of the book's illustrations. Eight years later, Potter wrote to ask if the boy had kept the letter. He had. Potter copied the drawings and added more. One of the new illustrations showed a realistic-looking English robin peering at one of the doll-size shoes Peter loses in his flight. The book exhibits many of those odd contradictions that often appear in children's books. Peter and McGregor behave like a real rabbit and a real gardener, except for the vivid detail of Peter's tiny clothes. The rabbits live in a burrow, but there is Mrs. Rabbit cooking at a fireplace. The children eat blackberries—with milk.

Potter based many of her characters on her own pets. Almost from birth, she had animals around, and she was always drawing them. Her childhood sketchbooks are filled with drawings and watercolors of caterpillars, flowers, a wolf skull, a dead bird, and, always, her pets—a dormouse, a bat, a turtle, an owl. She portrayed her ailing mother as a mouse tucked in bed, with her doctor as a mole. Young Beatrix included her pet lizard Judy in a painting of a fresh pineapple that was eaten a few hours later. When she decided to try to sell some animal illustrations, Potter bought a rabbit and named him Peter Piper. He later served as model for her illustrations of the White Rabbit in *Alice* and Brer Rabbit in *Uncle Remus.* In time, she also acquired Benjamin Bunny. Potter based her animals' appearance and lifestyle upon her pets, but admitted that some of their personalities were "harmless" caricatures of acquaintances.

"I have never quite understood the secret of Peter's perennial charm," Potter admitted. However, she may have revealed the secret in another remark: "I have just made stories to please myself, because I never grew up."

---

5 SEPTEMBER 1987

"No Sex, Please"

An alien visiting the planet Earth would quickly be able to discern the chief preoccupation of the human race—sex. The evidence is everywhere, from the lewd graffiti adorning the walls of Pompeii to the satirical drawings of William Hogarth, from *Portnoy's Complaint* to the play *No Sex, Please—We're British.* The durability of the latter alone is proof of the topic's appeal. The longest running comedy in the world, it finally closed on September 5, 1987, after 6,671 performances over a 16-year period.

Over the centuries, there have been countless satirical commentaries on human sexuality. In 1929, in their sole book together, James Thurber and E. B. White brought their combined lack of scientific training to bear on the matter. In such chapters as "The Nature of the American Male: A Study of Pedestalism," Thurber and White lampooned the humorless sex books clogging the market with such titles as *The Doctor Looks at Love and Life.* Convinced that human sexuality is not only a morass but a Slough of Despond, the authors skipped what they called the sexologist's traditional cross section of the human body and replaced it with something they considered more useful—"a chart of the North Atlantic, showing airplane routes." The subtitle comfortingly promises to explain *Why You Feel the Way You Do,* but it is the title that asks an important question often overlooked in the rush of hormones: *Is Sex Necessary?*

Nature's answer is an equivocal "Not always." As Cole Porter pointed out, birds, bees, and even electric eels do it. However, not all creatures do it the same way. Biologists estimate that more than half of the world's organisms make do with a single parent—literally a single parent, because it takes only one to reproduce. Asexuality is rampant. Orchids employ their Circean wiles to lure insects; dandelions depend upon the whims of the wind; and yet Bermuda grass reproduces by simply sending out runners. To make generalizations even more suspect, many creatures (rose aphids, for example) reproduce asexually for generations, and then for some arcane reason decide to mate with the opposite sex and reproduce in what we would think of as the "normal" way. Nature is not known for its family values.

Someone once defined a human being as a device invented by water to transport it from one place to another. In a similar way, biologists maintain, a human being exists in order to reproduce its DNA. If that sounds pointless and mindless, it is no more so than the lives of our wildly mating brethren. It is true of other creatures, and we must reluctantly admit it seems true of us. We exist to reproduce ourselves. That our complex brains have invented so many ways to amuse themselves in the meantime is not nature's goal, but it's a nice little bonus.

However, as the hypothetical alien of the first paragraph would quickly observe, sex requires a huge investment from the individual. The peacock's tail, the bowerbird's elaborate rituals, and humans' sports cars and perfume all use a great deal of energy that could be spent in other ways. Most animals spend their days securing territories and announcing parental virtues. If asexual reproduction is simpler, and allows *Entamoeba hystolytica* to skip the mating rituals that so preoccupy *Homo sapiens,* what exactly is sex for? Why did some animals evolve fusion, and others fission?

There are many theories of the nature and origins of sex, but the bottom line of most is that sexual reproduction provides genetic variety. Instead of the identical carbon copies of asexual reproduction, organisms wind up with genetic packages that vary from one generation to the next, beautifully uniting the biological heritage of one parent with that of the other. The resulting variety of individuals creates a more adaptable gene pool for the species over all, and results in more offspring—or, in nature's view, the successful manufacture of a greater amount of DNA. If all environments were identical and unchanging, such variations would have no adaptive virtue and sexual reproduction might not have evolved. Therefore, those of us who choose not to reproduce, or who choose when to do so, may be cheating our biological imperative. But it isn't the first time culture has overruled biology.

The Royal Oak

"Generations pass while some trees stand," Sir Thomas Browne wrote, "and old families last not three oaks." In Shropshire, England, in a field that was once a forest, with a fence around it to keep out climbers, is an oak that has seen many generations pass. Thanks to it, one family lasted longer in England than it might have—the Stuarts, royal line of Mary, Queen of Scots, and of Charles II.

In 1651, two years after his father was beheaded, Charles was defeated at Worcester by Oliver Cromwell. Disguised, he escaped with a trusted Royalist to Boscobel House in Shropshire. As Charles dictated to Samuel Pepys after he was restored to the throne, the family was "Romane Catholick" and had "hideing-holes for Preistes." When search parties neared, Charles hid in a nearby tree, "a greate Oake that had been Lop't some 3 or 4 Yeares before, and being growne out again very Bushy and Thick, could nott be seene through."

Ensconced in the old tree with a Royalist named Careless (or Carlis), the fugitive could see soldiers on the highway. Saturday, September 6, was a long day. Charles slept awhile with his head in the other man's lap. Then, his arm numb from supporting Charles, Careless gently woke the king for fear both would fall down among the searchers. When the soldiers moved on, Charles and Careless climbed down. Shortly afterward, Charles embarked upon his nine-year exile on the Continent.

The royal hiding place entered legend. For 200 years, Charles's birthday, May 29, was celebrated as Oak Apple Day, with leaves on hats and boughs over doors. Even before the Restoration, medals issued abroad showed Charles on the obverse and an oak on the verso. But there was a symbolic Royal Oak before Charles hid in a real one. The oak has so long been a symbol of a strong and ancient British identity that, in heraldry, when leaves are designated but no tree specified, oak is assumed. The medal issued when Charles became a Knight of the Garter in 1638 bore an oak under a prince's coronet. Later, anti-Puritan illustrations showed "The Royal Oak of Britain" cut down by Cromwell, and predicted that it would sprout again.

The symbolism was rooted in tangible value. Oaks were crucial for shipping, building, and millwork. Acorns fattened swine and poultry; leaves had medicinal value; the bark was favored in tanning. Even cork comes from one of the nearly 500 species of *Quercus*. As late as the 1890s, Gladstone equated the cutting of forests with England's progress as a nation. When he visited Germany, a wiser Bismarck gave him an oak sapling.

Long before Charles, the Druids venerated oaks. Before that the Greeks awarded a crown of oak leaves to soldiers who saved a comrade's life. The oak was said to have been Thor's Tree of Life and the Hebrew Tree of the Covenant, its wood credited with both the club of Hercules and the cross of Jesus. Vienna was supposedly built around a sacred oak grove, one tree of which remains in the city's center. And Zeus, a far more powerful king than Charles, spoke through an oak whose leaves moved when there was no wind.

"Nothing Could Give an Idea of the Destruction"

Of all natural disasters, hurricanes are undoubtedly the most dangerous to humans. One that roared out of the Bay of Bengal in 1737 is thought to have drowned about 300,000 people. Completely disobeying all the usual rules of behavior, the hurricane that almost destroyed Galveston, Texas, in 1900 continued across the United States, stomped the Great Lakes and the East Coast, tore across the Atlantic, wrecked parts of Europe, and finally wore itself out over Siberia. That was considered the greatest natural disaster in U.S. history until Hurricane Andrew struck south Florida with the force of an atomic bomb.

As an example of the power of these great storms, in 1938 earthquake seismographs in Alaska picked up the roar of the sea crashing against the New England coast. In 1972, flooding from Hurricane Agnes swelled the waters of the Susquehanna until, for a day, it was the second-largest river in the world, after only the Amazon. Just before it became a nation in 1970, Bangladesh lost half-a-million people to a hurricane—far more than the number of people killed at Hiroshima and Nagasaki combined. In fact, meteorologists claim that a single run-of-the-mill hurricane releases energy equivalent to the explosion of much of the world's nuclear arsenal.

In September of 1935, a relatively small but nonetheless savage hurricane struck the Florida Keys. Winds reached 200 miles per hour—over twice the official hurricane-force wind speed of 74 mph. The barometric pressure fell to 26.35, the lowest ever recorded on the ground in the Western Hemisphere. Many survived only by perching in the tops of palm trees and clinging for dear life as the waves tried to wash them away. Some had to hang on all night. That hurricane became the model for the ferocious storm in Maxwell Anderson's 1939 play *Key Largo,* which John Huston turned into a film in 1948. The cinematic version was scary enough, but apparently trapping Humphrey Bogart and Edward G. Robinson in a resort hotel was the least of the hurricane's accomplishments.

Ernest Hemingway weathered the 1935 Florida hurricane from his house in Key West. Immediately afterward, on September 7, 1935, he described it in a letter to his editor at Scribner's, Maxwell Perkins: "Imagine you have read it in the papers but nothing could give an idea of the destruction. . . . Saw more dead than I'd seen in one place since the lower Piave in June of 1918." Hemingway said that between 700 and 1,000 died, but later estimates hovered around 400. He reported that not a single building was left standing, and the foliage was stripped off every plant as if by fire. "There is over thirty miles of the R.R. completely gone and there will probably never be another train in to Key West." He was correct. The over-the-seas railway to Key West was gone forever. It was only one of countless human structures that have surrendered to the fury of a hurricane.

See also a certain tempest, 7/24.

Star Trek and Superman

Among the original *Star Trek*'s scientific gaffes, which are legion, the most obvious is the presence of aliens who look surprisingly like human beings. The show's most conspicuous alien is the prim science officer with the quizzical eyebrows but otherwise frozen facial muscles, Mr. Spock. The eyebrows alone are a considerable stumbling block to the suspension of disbelief. Presumably we are to believe that Vulcans and Romulons and Klingons, like Terrans, evolved from mammalian ancestors whose protective body covering has shrunk to a few scattered vestigial patches—hair, eyebrows, mustaches, and presumably less conspicuous areas.

Mr. Spock comes from a distant planet named, for some reason, after the Roman god of the fiery underworld, and he himself bears the name of a prominent Earth pediatrician. However, we know he is not of our planet because he has pointed ears. Spock's father came from Vulcan, his mother from Earth. This interplanetary miscegenation is one of the series' worst scientific heresies. As Carl Sagan has remarked, "Such a cross is about as likely as the successful mating of a man and a petunia." It ignores everything that is known about molecular biology and evolution, about how we came to be shaped the way we are and how that must inevitably differ under the demands of a different world.

The original *Star Trek* series premiered on September 8, 1966. Seven years later, an animated version appeared. With special effects limitations removed, animators advanced slightly in the envisioning of alien life-forms. However, most still resembled humans. Communications officer M'Ress, for example, was a "felinoid," equipped with a long catlike tail and a purr. She seemed like a cat-human hybrid out of Egyptian mythology. Less derived from Earth creatures was Lieutenant Arex, who had the charmingly un-Terrestrial distinction of possessing three arms and three legs.

Of course, alien misconception isn't limited to *Star Trek*. Like Spock, Superman (whose name back home was Kal-El) also comes from a planet named after an Earth word, in this case the element Krypton. Either as the caped hero or disguised with eyeglasses, he looks like a man from Earth. In the Superboy adventures, the young hero has a super*dog* that, when not lifting trucks or repelling bullets, looks basically like a Dalmatian without spots. How did this happen? The stories don't maintain that Kal-El took the form of an Earthman when he discovered that on this planet he had extraordinary powers. It seems that, by a curious coincidence, the people of Krypton are indistinguishable from white Americans on Earth. At least Spock has pointed ears.

American science fiction writer Larry Niven, in his notorious essay "Man of Steel, Woman of Kleenex," speculated upon the physiological results should Superman, after decades of celibacy, surrender to his superhormones and consummate his long-running flirtation with Lois Lane. Similar interplanetary problems might have plagued Spock's parents. Tongue firmly in cheek, Niven remarked that Kal-El's external similarity to humans is "doubtless the result of parallel evolution, as the marsupials of Australia resemble their mammalian counterparts."

Even as a joke, that remark highlights the shaky reasoning behind many representations of extraterrestrials. Australian marsupials resemble their cousins because they share the same origin. Australia and its tenants became separated from the Asian mainland and the rest of mammalian history only after sharing millions of years of evolution, like siblings that grew up together and then went off to their separate adulthoods. Only by a similar shared genesis could the people of Krypton and Vulcan and Earth bear the family resemblance they exhibit in science fiction.

---

9 September 1737

"This Uncommon Species"

The advertisement in the London *Daily Post* announced the opportunity to view, "at One Shilling each, the Surprising Fish of Maremaid, taken by eight Fishermen on the 9th of September last." That would have been 1737. "This uncommon Species of Nature represents from the Collarbone down the Body what the Antients called a Maremaid. . . ." The creature had the tail of a dolphin and wings like a cherub; the back of its head was like that of a "Lyon."

Mermaids—half woman, half fish—cavort through much of our history. *Meerfrau,* Germans call her; the Irish, *Merow.* In Denmark she is *Maremind,* and in Iceland *Marmenill.* Like other commentators, Danish theologian Erik Pontoppidan, in his eighteenth-century *Natural History of Norway,* sneered at the fanciful embellishments of the simpleminded but didn't doubt the creature's existence.

Over the centuries, whenever thoughts turned to the deep, mermaids came to mind.

Although presumably few of us now believe in mermaids, they show up frequently in the arts. In Ray Bradbury's 1958 short story "The Shore Line at Sunset," two men find the body of a mermaid washed ashore on the California coast. She is either unconscious or dead. One man wants to sell her to a museum or an aquarium, but in his absence his companion allows the magical creature to float back out to sea where she belongs. Poul Anderson, an American well versed in his Danish descent, began a fantasy series in 1973 with "The Merman's Children." He spun variations on the medieval ballad of Agnete, a mortal woman who married a merman, bore him seven sons, and then returned to her Christian life on land. These Christians are wary of merfolk, who are as soulless as animals.

Equally doomed are the creations of another Dane—Hans Christian Andersen. His 1837 fairy tale "The Little Mermaid" is probably the best-known literary incarnation of these creatures. Lacking souls, when they die they vanish, as one of them says, like so much sea foam. They can attain the immortality of humans only through the love of one. Even after trading her beautiful voice for legs, the nameless heroine fails to achieve that goal. Unwilling to kill the man she loves to free herself from her contract, she dies.

A century and a half later, the Walt Disney Company adapted Andersen's story into a hugely successful animated film. The question of soullessness does not arise, and, inevitably, the mermaid and prince marry. That movie was preceded by 1984's *Splash,* in which Daryl Hannah's mermaid comes ashore naked at the Statue of Liberty and learns English from televisions on display in Bloomingdale's. She has human legs while she remains dry, but reverts to half fish when wet. The Tom Hanks character renounces society and joins his true love in her world, from which, unlike Agnete, he will be unable to return.

Apparently most of Hans Christian Andersen's tales were his own inventions, but the early "Little Mermaid" he based upon traditional Danish folklore. Most stories about mermaids include two standard elements: their yearning for human souls and their beautiful voices, which hint at their kinship to the sirens who captivated sailors. In numerous medieval stories, priests overhear the songs of mermaids and cruelly taunt them with damnation until the mermaids burst into tears.

See also Barnum's mermaid, 8/8.

---

10 September 1850

"The Schemes and Wonders of Nature"

The letter was one of two Charles Darwin wrote to Richard Owen that day in 1850.

> Down Farnborough Kent
> Sept 10th
>
> My dear Sir
> You are aware that I have been employed for a considerable time on a Monograph on the Cirripedia. . . .

The Latin *cirri* is the plural of *cirrus,* "curl"; *pedia* means "foot." Cirripedia is an order of curl-footed crustaceans that, in their adult stage, attach themselves to rocks, to other creatures, or to such inanimate objects as the hulls of ships. The common name of the best-known group comes from the Middle English word for "goose," *barnakylle,* which has become "barnacle." The barnacle's gooselike shape inspired the myth that rotting ships spawned a worm that hung by its beak until it grew into a goose.

Darwin tackled this obscure topic partially because he needed to establish a firm grounding in the minutiae of science, before undertaking the colossal task that he knew awaited him on what became the *Origin of Species.* His barnacle studies required detailed work in taxonomy and anatomy. Darwin's reputation was already such that the British Museum lent him their entire barnacle collection. Louis Agassiz sent barnacles from the United States. A colleague from the *Beagle* days shipped several from New South Wales. Because of Darwin's refusal to abandon a problem before he mastered it, a task he expected to require a few months wound up occupying eight long years. The resulting four-volume monograph is still a standard reference.

Victorian novelist Edward Bulwer Lytton parodied this preoccupation with matters he considered not only irrelevant but distasteful. In 1858, a few years after Darwin completed his barnacle research, Bulwer Lytton published his novel *What Will He Do with It?* In one chapter, the Gatesboro Athenaeum and Literary Institute offers a "Lecture on Conchology" by one Professor Long, author of *Researches into the Natural History of Limpets.* "Conchology," a character observes, "is a subject which requires deep research, and on which a learned man may say much without fear of contradiction. . . . If limpets were but able to read printed character in the English tongue, this work would have more interest for them than the ablest investigations upon the political and social history of man. But," he adds dryly, "the human species is not testaceous [hard-shelled],—and what the history of man might be to a limpet, the history of limpets is to a man."

Obviously Darwin disagreed. He found barnacles fascinating. Many species were hermaphroditic (bearing both male and female sex organs). Some males were so tiny they seemed like parasites on the females. One female, Darwin wrote, "had two little pockets, in *each* of which she kept a little husband. . . . Truly the schemes and wonders of nature are illimitable." His enthusiasm for barnacles amused his children. When he described a larval cirripede as having "six pairs of beautifully constructed natatory legs, a pair of magnificent compound eyes, and extremely complex antennae," they said he sounded like a salesman. The younger children hadn't seen their father at work on anything else. They came to regard barnacles as what men worked at. Darwin discovered that misconception when one of his offspring asked a visiting child, "Where does your father do *his* barnacles?"

---

11 SEPTEMBER 1894

The Red Planet

Mars. The very word seems exotic and alluring. As numerous works of art attest, no other planet has so captured our imagination as our nearest neighbor. The first novel by Edgar Rice Burroughs, *A Princess of Mars,* tells the story of John Carter, an Earthman of the manly, two-fisted sort, who journeys to "Barsoom," as the natives call it. He battles with green giants who have as many arms as Hindu gods and ultimately marries Dejah Thoris, the royalty of the title. In Ray Bradbury's famous story "Mars Is Heaven," astronauts from Earth arrive on Mars and find that it resembles a small midwestern town back home. That turns out to be an illusion, of course, and Mars actually proves to be a kind of hell. A kinder, gentler version appeared in the 1960s in the U.S. television series *My Favorite Martian.*

Because the planet glimmered blood-red in the night sky, the ancient Romans named it after their god of war. Presumably for the same reason, the Babylonians called it Nirgal, "Star of Death." With the invention of the telescope, the planet was slowly demoted from celestial deity to a fellow ball of rock spinning through space. Its surface, unlike that of Venus, was not obscured by clouds. Other than the Moon, it was the first planetary surface we were able to observe.

As early as 1659, the Dutch astronomer Christian Huygens was sketching the Martian surface features that his modest telescope revealed. He and others soon distinguished the planet's striking polar caps, which grew and dwindled over time. In the late seventeenth century, William Herschel, the man who discovered Uranus, determined that the axial tilt of Mars is almost identical to that of Earth. Sky watchers began to think of its dark and light patches as analogous to Earth's own mix of land and sea.

These accumulating revelations led to the notion that, if it was so similar to Earth, Mars might also be inhabited. Herschel himself casually remarked that the inhabitants of our sister planet "probably enjoy a situation similar to our own." The stage was set for one of the stranger chapters in the history of our ideas about Mars. In 1877, an Italian astronomer named Giovanni Schiaparelli announced that he had observed *canali* on Mars. The word translates into English as "channels," but the features, assisted by the sharp pencil lines of Schiaparelli's drawing, became known as "canals." Schiaparelli himself remarked in 1893, "It is not necessary to suppose them the work of intelligent beings," but soon he was adding the afterthought that such a concept was not absurd. The French astronomer Camille Flammarion began wondering aloud if Mars could possibly experience its climatic changes over the aeons "without giving birth to the smallest blade of grass." Finally, the American millionaire, adventurer, and astronomer Percival Lowell built the Lowell Observatory near Flagstaff, Arizona, to search for life on Mars.

Other scientists were not convinced. On September 11, 1894, the American astronomer Edward Emerson Barnard wrote to a colleague:

> I have been watching and drawing the surface of Mars. . . . To save my soul I can't believe in the canals as Schiaparelli draws them. . . . I verily believe . . . that the canals as depicted by Schiaparelli are a fallacy and that they will so be proved. . . .

Barnard was correct. The *canali* were discredited. However, their hold on the public imagination was firmly established. One result, well before either Burroughs's or Bradbury's series about Mars, was H. G. Wells's prototypical story of alien invasion, *The War of the Worlds,* which appeared in 1898. It begins ominously.

> No one would have believed in the last years of the nineteenth century that this world was being watched keenly and closely by intelligences greater than man's and yet as mortal as his own; that as men busied themselves about their various concerns they were scrutinized and studied. . . .

Actually, thanks to decades of far-fetched speculation, many people found that scenario easy to believe. And forty years later, when Orson Welles adapted the story to the eastern United States and broadcast it as a Halloween special, enough people believed it to inspire widespread panic.

Cave Artists

The tale has appeared in countless news stories and even made its way into school textbooks. Four French schoolboys—Marsal, Ravidat, Agnel, and Coencas—were wandering in the countryside. Robot, a dog belonging to one of them, fell into the narrow opening of a cave. When the boys went in after it, they found the walls and even the ceiling of the cavern covered in paintings of animals. The dog had led the boys into what would become the best-known gallery of prehistoric art in the world, Lascaux Grotto. It was September 12, 1940. Hitler's troops had invaded France only months before, and the rest of the world learned little about the amazing artwork until after the war.

All of that story is true except for the dog. Incredibly, reporters thought it necessary to add the dog to squeeze more "human interest" out of one of the great artistic and archaeological finds of all time. Lascaux is one of over 200 caves, nine-tenths of them in France and Spain, that contain, depending upon what a scholar chooses to regard as a single work, at least 10,000–15,000 engravings, paintings, and drawings. Unlike those caves that have miles of narrow passages, Lascaux consists of three galleries, the largest slightly over 100 yards long. The second largest, called the "side gallery," boasts 60 or so drawings, including cows and a horse painted on the ceiling.

Animals parade across the walls of Lascaux and its fellow galleries. Rhinoceroses form a frieze along a wall. Deer, both individuals and herds, are adorned with elaborately branching treelike antlers. Some artists cleverly exploited their medium, as in the horse-head-shaped curve at the end of a rock that becomes the head of a spotted horse painted on the stone. One figure has the feet and legs of a human and the trunk and head of a bison. No one knows whether the figure represents a shaman wearing the totemic robe of a sacred animal, or a human-beast hybrid like the Minotaur of Greek mythology.

Such artwork appears in all kinds of caves, from the spacious high-ceilinged caverns that even a tourist can comfortably navigate to those accessible only to devotees willing to scale sheer walls and crawl on their bellies through narrow tunnels. One turn-of-the-century illustration portrays three cave artists at work. All are men, of course, one sitting beside a boulder and sculpting what appears to be clay, another lying on the floor and carving a stone, the third drawing on the wall and leaning back to admire his handiwork. All three artists are clad in animal skins, but their calm industry is reminiscent of the workshop of Verrocchio or some other busy studio.

The reality may have been a bit messier, and was probably accompanied by religious ritual. Magical rather than aesthetic goals might explain why some paintings appear over others, like a palimpsest, even when bare wall was available nearby, and why many are hidden in inaccessible corners. Certainly much of the work required the expenditure of greater effort than is visible in that illustration. We know that, for example, 15,000 years ago in the Pyrenees of southern France, a Cro-Magnon artist entered a cave, crawled on her belly through claustrophobia-inducing tunnels, and navigated an underground river. There, by the flickering light of a carefully guarded torch, deep in what is surely the least-accessible studio any artist ever occupied, she carved two relief sculptures of bison. The figures emerge from the clay around them. They are highly stylized, now dramatically cracked but still powerful, long after the artist herself joined her models in the earth.

An Elephant Hanged for Murder

The elephant is the largest land animal humans have encountered since mastodons and mammoths became extinct. Apparently we recognized their virtues and drafted them very early in our history. They have carried building materials during peacetime and soldiers in war, but frequently we have simply kept them around for amusement. Elephants' comical antics enlivened lulls between bouts of slaughter in the Roman Colosseum. To amuse the citizenry on one memorable occasion, troupes of elephants reminiscent of the tutu'd pachyderms in Walt Disney's *Fantasia* danced together in flowered dresses.

Although elephants have symbolized patience, endurance, and self-restraint, their great size and strength can be dangerous. There are many stories of circus or zoo elephants trampling or otherwise harming humans. One of the more tragic involved an elephant named Mary.

In September 1916, while they were in Virginia on their autumn loop through the southern United States, the Sparks Circus hired a young man named Walter Eldridge. Immediately he was riding high astride the star performer, Mary, who was advertised as "The Largest Living Land Animal on Earth," supposedly three inches taller than P. T. Barnum's legendary Jumbo. Two days after Eldridge was hired, the circus was performing the afternoon show for a crowd of 5,000 in Kingsport, Tennessee, when Mary began to turn slightly off course. To make her behave, Eldridge struck her head.

In response, Mary grasped Eldridge with her trunk, threw him to the ground, gored him, and tossed his body into the crowd. Even though they were presumably just out to enjoy an afternoon at the circus, many in the crowd happened to have brought along their handguns. Several fired at the elephant, but didn't kill her. Mary was soon under control and no one besides the abusive attendant was harmed.

Nonetheless, after serious deliberation, the town fathers declared Mary guilty of murder and sentenced her to die. On September 13, 1916, two days after Eldridge's spectacular death, another crowd of 5,000 gathered to witness Mary's execution. In a famous incident in Georgia only a few years before, a circus elephant trampled her trainer and ran through the streets, only to be brought down by a police rifle. In spite of this well-known precedent, Mary's accusers rejected shooting as a means of execution. They also decided against poison. Instead, a chain was fitted around Mary's vast neck, and, as thousands of local country folk stared openmouthed, Mary was hanged from a crane belonging to a nearby railroad.

Once the spectacle was over and Mary's body was taken down, a doctor helped saw off her tusks (for souvenirs) before she was buried. That's when he discovered that, due to neglect, Mary had several abscessed teeth. Presumably that was why she responded so violently when Eldridge struck her face. Apparently the true culprit was immediately punished by his victim, which makes Mary's execution an even greater parody of justice than it first appears.

See also animal trials, 6/14.

---

14 SEPTEMBER 1937

Bringing Up Baby

Howard Hawks picked Katharine Hepburn as the female star for *Bringing Up Baby* long before he settled on a leading man. Finally, on September 14, 1937, he hired a popular young actor who had changed his name from Archibald Alexander Leach to Cary Grant. Grant played David Huxley, a bumbling, absentminded, divorced-from-the-real-world paleontologist with the Stuyvesant Museum of Natural History. You can tell he's an intellectual by his dark-rimmed glasses. As one reviewer observed, the film is like a movie-cliché quiz. Huxley's white lab coat is wrapped around him as tightly as a straitjacket. Both his museum and his fiancée seem arid and inert. Apparently Hawks didn't care for scientists. However, although the mad scientist in *The Thing from Another World* is a coldhearted monster, Huxley is merely an idiot.

Even though his profession was chosen for what someone considered its humorous possibilities, there are interesting traces of science strewn through the film. In the opening scene, Huxley is sitting atop the scaffolding that surrounds a huge dinosaur skeleton, described in the film as a "brontosaur." Although that is a common term, the long-necked, long-tailed lizards are more accurately called "sauropods." Chin on fist as if posing for Rodin, Huxley is muttering to himself about the fossil bone he holds. When he suggests it belongs in the tail of the dinosaur, his fiancée reminds him that he tried it in the tail yesterday and it didn't fit. While hardly typical of the methods of paleontologists, this error is also not inconceivable. There is an exact parallel in history.

In the late nineteenth century, American paleontologist Edward Drinker Cope assembled a skeleton of a long-tailed, long-necked marine reptile named *Elasmosaurus*. His archrival O. C. Marsh gleefully pointed out that Cope had mounted the head on the wrong end. Mortified, Cope not only reassembled the skeleton, but hurried to destroy every copy he could of his erroneous illustration. He didn't know that Marsh was hoarding some copies. In a similar mistake, for decades the *Apatosaurus* in the Carnegie Museum in Pittsburgh—and, as a consequence, *Apatosaurus* skeletons around the world—bore the head of a different dinosaur, *Camarasaurus*.

In that first scene in *Bringing Up Baby,* Huxley receives a telegram announcing that a museum expedition has found the brontosaur's only missing bone, the "intercostal clavicle." A gag writer added that fictional bone to what a reviewer called "the ominous tread of deliberative gags" at the last moment. In human beings the clavicle is the collarbone. We have two, and they form part of the "pectoral girdle" that extends from the sternum (breastbone) to the scapula (shoulder blade). In some animals the arrangement is similar, while in others the clavicle is rudimentary or even absent. In birds, the two fuse and become the wishbone. The adjective *intercostal* means "between ribs," and if there is one place a clavicle never shows up it is between ribs. However, in some crocodiles and lizards, and in extinct reptiles such as brachiosaurs, there is a bone called the *interclavicle,* which attaches from the sternum to the underside of the clavicle. "Intercostal clavicle" may be a nonsensical expression, but it was coined by someone who was at least familiar with the terminology.

The idea of a dog stealing a valuable dinosaur bone and burying it came from Knerr's popular comic strip "Professor Dinglehoofer und His Dog," and RKO paid King Features Syndicate $1,000 for the right to use it. Skippy, who played Asta in *The Thin Man* and Mr. Smith in *The Awful Truth,* played George, the larcenous dog in *Bringing Up Baby.* The title character was played by a leopard named Nissa.

Presumably, Cary Grant's character is named after Thomas Huxley, trailblazing paleontologist and friend of Darwin. Interestingly, there is another cinematic tribute to Huxley. In the 1932 comedy *Horse Feathers,* Groucho Marx becomes dean of Huxley College, which battles nobly for the athletic championship sought by its rival—Darwin College.

---

15 SEPTEMBER 1835

"That Mystery of Mysteries"

The Galápagos Islands straddle the equator, 600 miles west of Ecuador. HMS *Beagle* arrived there on September 15, 1835. Now almost four years away from England, the *Beagle* had just come from surveying down the Brazilian coast, through the Strait of Magellan at the southern tip of the continent, and up the coast of Peru. Charles Darwin was only twenty-six years old. Judging from his journal and his later comments, he had not yet begun to think about what he would eventually call "the species question."

Darwin was impressed by "the strange Cyclopean scene." He wandered the black rocks, collected plants, shot birds. He grasped an iguana by the tail and flung it into the water again and again, watching it return to shore until he was satisfied that they were land animals that entered the water only for food. (One commentator later remarked about this method of research, "It was a simpler time.") The ponderous giant land tortoises seemed to Darwin "like some antediluvian animals"; he rode their backs and timed their perambulations. He encountered a locally famous mad hermit and found the "bleached skull of a ship's captain, killed by his mutinous crew."

He also found some strange birds. For their role in his thinking about evolution, they are now referred to as "Darwin's finches." However, Darwin himself labeled some of them finches, some grosbeaks, one a wren, and put several in the family that includes orioles and blackbirds. He noticed that the beak of each was precisely shaped for its unique function—prying out plant seeds, catching insects, foraging on the ground—but he didn't yet realize that their peculiarities were specific to each island. Nowadays it is well known that oceanic islands, with their limited competition and predation, are evolutionary laboratories. Elsewhere several species would have filled the ecological niches into which finches radiated in the Galápagos.

On Darwin's last day in the Galápagos, the official supervising the nearby British penal colony declared that he could tell on which island a tortoise originated by its distinctive shell pattern. "I did not for some time pay sufficient attention to this statement," Darwin wrote, "and I had already partially mingled together the collections from two of the islands." He had noted that the archipelago's mockingbirds varied, but even riding the tortoises' backs he overlooked their distinctive markings. Later he wrote that the distribution of Galápagos animals, combined with the similarities between South American fossils and living species in the same region, were "the factual origin of all my views."

Although the fossils nagged at him from the beginning, other naturalists back home in England had to point out the significance of the finches. In time, Darwin would write of the Galápagos in the 1839 edition of his *Journal of Researches:* "The natural history of these islands is eminently curious, and well deserves attention. Here, both in space and time, we seem to be brought somewhat near to that great fact—that mystery of mysteries—the first appearance of new beings on this earth."

---

16 SEPTEMBER 1949

The Road Runner and the Coyote

Warner Brothers released a new Looney Tunes animated short film, *Fast and Furry-ous,* on September 16, 1949. It starred Chuck Jones's cartoon versions of two familiar animals of the American Southwest—the roadrunner and the coyote. From this first encounter, the formula was set. In his unswerving determination to capture and eat the Road Runner, Wile E. Coyote employs every gadget the Acme mail-order company can devise. Yet the bird always triumphs.

When the characters first appear, joke scientific names accompany them. The Road Runner is *Accelerati Incredibus.* One of many later names was the Sophoclean pun *Speedipus Rex.* In reality, the greater roadrunner is named *Geococcyx californianus.* The suffix in the genus name doesn't refer to the little bone at the bottom of the human spine; *coccyx* is the Latin word for "cuckoo." That bone is so named because it resembles the cuckoo's beak, and the roadrunner's name identifies it as a ground cuckoo. When a naturalist from Holland asked Roger Tory Peterson where he could see the "American cuckoo that runs on the ground," Peterson was momentarily stumped. It is easy to forget that the roadrunner *is* a cuckoo.

Although the bird does indeed run throughout much of the American Southwest, it seldom exceeds twenty miles per hour. That is an unusual speed for a bird, but hardly *incredibus.* It earned its name by running down roads ahead of horse teams, but nowadays it can be seen dashing across highways. Speed is the rule in the desert. Most creatures leap or scamper or swoop. In other ways, the real bird resembles the cartoon Road Runner considerably less. Its crest is smaller and stiffer, its tail straighter. Although it seldom flies, its short rounded wings are capable of it. And it does not run up to other animals, peer thoughtfully at them, and exclaim, "Beep! Beep!" Its song consists of a series of descending dovelike coos, but when excited it utters a rattlelike *brrr.*

Curiously, the roadrunner's unique personality has inspired a reputation for cunning that Wile E. Coyote would admire. One recurring story dates back at least to a 1756 book by a man with the splendid name of Ignaz Pfefferkorn. He wrote that the roadrunner—the *paisano,* he called it, which is still one of its names—builds a corral of cactus around sleeping rattlesnakes and taunts them until they impale themselves on the spines. Naturalists attest to the roadrunner's agility in outmaneuvering its opponents. One was seen dashing around a bush, avoiding each leap of, yes, a coyote. Another was observed adroitly dodging a pair of marsh hawks that had teamed up against it.

In *Fast and Furry-ous,* the animal so easily avoided by roadrunners is given the Latin name *Carnivorous Vulgaris.* It's appropriate. Coyotes certainly eat meat, and Wile E. would if he could catch any. Although many regard the coyote as vulgar, *vulgaris* means "common," which is why the starling has the same species name. A later episode identifies Wile E. as *Famishus-famishus,* which is no wonder, but scientists know coyotes as *Canis latrans.* A clue to the meaning of the species name is the obsolete adjective *latrant,* which meant "barking." After a few asides in earlier cartoons, Wile E. kept his thoughts to himself, but his real cousins are famously noisy. Probably their calls have been dubbed into Westerns more than any other sound effect.

Wile E.'s specialized diet is surprising, because coyotes are virtually omnivorous. Their scat has been found to contain—besides the bones of practically every desert creature—paper, rubber from a tire, and a harness buckle. Also, desert carnivores frequently must survive without freestanding water, and one thing besides food that the coyote might be seeking in the roadrunner is moisture.

Although they have never been caught ordering guided missiles from the Acme Company, coyotes are known for their cleverness. They have adapted with casual aplomb to the presence of their most dangerous fellow predator, *Homo sapiens.* In several Native American mythologies of the Southwest, Coyote plays the role that Raven fills in the Northwest and Rabbit in the East—Trickster. On that point, Wile E. Coyote shames his ancestors. The Road Runner outwits him every time.

Barnard's First Comet

Edward Emerson Barnard was an example of that rare species, a genuinely self-made man. Like David Copperfield, he was born with a caul. Since he felt this biographical tidbit worthy of mention, Barnard must have been familiar with the superstition that a child entering the world still wrapped in a membrane would have good luck. However, that particular brand of luck was conspicuously absent from his early life, and he made the belief come true by sheer willpower.

Born in Nashville, Tennessee, three years before the Civil War began, Barnard spent his infancy in an occupied city. His father died three months before he was born. His mother began his education at home. He refused to allow either poverty or an environment struggling painfully through Reconstruction to prevent him from achieving his goals. By the time he was nine years old, Barnard was working in a photography studio, acquiring skills he would use for the rest of his life.

American astronomer Edward Emerson Barnard was a genuine self-made man, rising from a poverty-stricken Civil War childhood to the summit of his profession.

Surely few astronomers have had a more pains-taking initiation into their field. One of the new apprentice's tasks was to operate the huge solar camera that was mounted on the roof of the studio. The silver then in use on photographic paper lacked the sensitivity of today's emulsions and required an intense light to produce an image. This was achieved by focusing the sun's rays through the giant camera. (The photographer also used images thus enlarged for portrait painting.) However, this only worked if the image produced remained constant. To achieve that, someone had to continually turn the wheels that kept the giant camera oriented toward the celestial light source. Failure to do so could result in the intense light touching the wooden frame and setting it afire. This tedious and potentially dangerous job fell to young Edward. With it he supported himself and his now invalid mother. And, as he performed his mechanical task, he began to think about the astronomical motions he was tracking.

When an acquaintance gave him a book as security against a loan, Barnard discovered that it contained star charts. Soon he had identified the major constellations. A coworker built Barnard's first telescope for him, with a paper tube and a one-inch spyglass found in the street. Gradually Barnard began to expand his studies. His first publication reported his observations of the transit of Mercury in 1878. In time he began to focus his interest on comets, and then particularly on a quest for the $200 prize promised to everyone who discovered a comet in 1881. In May of that year, he thought he spotted a comet at about three o'clock one morning, but neither he nor any other astronomer was able to find it again.

Then, not long after sunset on Saturday, September 17, he found another one. The next night, in between scurrying clouds, he confirmed another position for it. Soon he and others had still more confirmation. The fifth comet discovered that year, it was designated *1881e.* It turned out to be a relatively humble phenomenon, but it was only the beginning. E. E. Barnard went on to discover many comets. He worked at both Lick and Yerkes Observatories and taught at the University of Chicago. He discovered the fifth satellite of Jupiter, determined that thirty-six stars were actually double-star systems, and pioneered celestial photography. No matter what signs there may have been at his birth, good fortune in Barnard's life ran a distant second to energy and commitment. He seems to have drawn exactly one lucky card: His visual acuity was legendary. Repeatedly he observed extremely subtle phenomena that remained invisible to others until technology improved enough to catch up with him.

See also Barnard and Mars, 9/11.

---

18 SEPTEMBER 1954

"It Was the Little Octopus"

"I will now speak of bloodless fish," Pliny wrote in his *Natural History*, introducing his section on mollusks. He described the octopus simply: "They have their head between their feet and belly and have eight small feet." Like the squid, the octopus is a mollusk without a shell. Both are in the class Cephalopoda, from the Greek words for "head" and "foot." The word "octopus" means "eight-footed."

In his 1940 book *Inagua,* Gilbert C. Klingel described his first encounter with one of these mysterious creatures. He was diving at the base of a barrier reef. Reaching for a yellow rock, he saw that it had "a cold dark eye" that didn't blink. Many writers have described the curious movements of an octopus. Klingel's effort is vivid: "Before my gaze the rock started to melt, began to ooze at the sides like a candle that had become too hot." Within seconds, Klingel's creature had flushed from yellow to mottled brown to white to gray and maroon. Klingel was worried, because the octopus had a five-foot tentacle span. However, he backed away slowly and escaped without mishap.

Although many octopuses are harmless, not every encounter ends so happily. In his 1975 book *Dangerous to Man,* naturalist Roger Caras reported an encounter with the little blue-ringed octopus, *Octopus* (or *Hapalochleana) maculosa.* On September 18, 1954, two Australian skindivers, John Baylis and Kirke Dyson-Holland, were diving near Port Darwin. They were just about to leave the water and go up on shore when Baylis spied a small blue octopus. He scooped it up out of the water and put the eight-armed creature on his own shoulder. Apparently undisturbed, it crawled around on his arms. Then Baylis threw it to Dyson-Holland. It clung to his arm, then crawled across his back and fell back into the sea. As it swam away, the two divers left the water.

Almost immediately, Dyson-Holland began to experience strange symptoms. He couldn't swallow. His mouth was dry. He was quickly losing muscular control. Finally he vomited and collapsed upon the sand. Baylis got his companion into a car and rushed him to a hospital, but it was too late. Dyson-Holland died shortly after doctors began trying to save him—less than two hours after playing with the octopus. On his back, where the octopus had paused, was a small bleeding puncture wound. During the drive, before he lost consciousness, Dyson-Holland had muttered, "It was the little octopus."

Physicians fairly confidently identified the octopus that killed Dyson-Holland as a little blue-ring. It is the only species known to pose a serious risk to human beings. Not all octopuses are venomous. Some use their venom—sometimes merely ejected into the water nearby—to paralyze prey such as crabs. To harm a human being the little blue-ring has to bite with its famous parrotlike beak and then spit venom into the wound. Sometimes, not surprisingly, it does the former without the latter, and the resulting wound is far less serious. Apparently the one Dyson-Holland handled performed both functions, in response to what it perceived as a threat.

After Dyson-Holland's death, three other men were made dangerously ill by what was thought to be the little blue-ringed octopus. Then, in 1967, an Australian soldier was bitten by a little blue-ring that was less than four inches wide. He died within an hour and a half. Although not typical of encoun-

325

ters with most octopuses, such stories are reminders of how little is known about these strange and alien animals.

See also giant squid, 4/20; and kraken, 8/10.

---

19 SEPTEMBER 1783

"Unimagined Arts"

Because seemingly they could elude the bonds of gravity, birds have often been part of our fantasies. In a moving story in Ovid's *Metamorphoses,* Daedalus and his son Icarus yearn to escape the island of Crete, where the Minotaur is lost in the labyrinth and Daedalus himself confined to a tower. Daedalus realizes that although King Minos watches all else, he doesn't control the air.

So then to unimagined arts
He set his mind and altered nature's laws.

Father and son attach bird feathers to their arms with wax and fly away. But, for daring to soar too close to the sun, Icarus is punished: The wax melts, the feathers abandon him, and he plunges into the Aegean.

This cautionary fable was often quoted in the 1780s in France. Brothers Joseph-Michel and Jacques-Étienne Montgolfier were setting their minds to "unimagined arts" in their own attempt to alter, or at least to circumvent, nature's laws. As would two brothers in the early twentieth century, they shared a dream of flying like the birds. They pursued their scientific experiments while running their father's prosperous paper manufactury. In 1782, they discovered that heated air, collected in a lightweight bag, would force the bag to rise. They learned that the least-substantial and most efficient fuel was straw mixed with carded wool. Rather than silk, which would become the material of choice for hot-air balloons, the Montgolfiers made the bag from the product with which they were most familiar—paper.

In early June 1783, with the local nobility crowding around them in the marketplace, the Montgolfier brothers sent aloft a balloon. It was thirty-five feet in diameter and had no basket and no passengers. But it rose a mile into the sky, remained airborne for almost ten minutes, and landed over a mile away. Some sources claim the local peasantry thought the moon had fallen.

Joseph and Étienne were heroes. The Académie des Sciences invited them to repeat the performance in Paris before Louis XVI. Bad weather ruined their first effort, but on September 19, 1783, before the entire royal court at Versailles, they succeeded. For the command performance, a larger balloon was extravagantly decorated. Underneath it the Montgolfiers suspended a wickerwork basket. Just as animals would precede humans into outer space almost 200 years later, so they led us into the upper atmosphere. Before risking their own lives, the brothers wanted to test the possibly disastrous effects of ascending to such fearful heights. They placed in the basket a duck, a rooster, and a sheep.

In their wicker capsule, the animals were probably unaware of their unique experience. Soon the straw and wool burned up; after only eight minutes, the balloon came down in woodland a couple of miles away. When the Montgolfier brothers reached the site, they found that the passengers had survived the celestial realm and their rough landing unharmed. Once again animals had served as our ambassadors and poison tasters.

It was settled. Earth-dwelling creatures could endure flight. Humans would be next.

---

20 SEPTEMBER 1863

The Brothers Grimm

Although the Brothers Grimm were close in life and are now inseparable in legend, they were not twins. Jacob Ludwig Carl was born in 1785, and Wilhelm Carl followed a little over a year later. Both were born in Hanau, in Hesse-Kassel, and died in Berlin. After Jacob died on September 20, 1863, Wilhelm lived almost another quarter century. He labored for years to polish away roughness and improprieties, in order to make the stories more suitable for Christian children. Fortunately, he wasn't entirely successful. The tales retain the raw, unprocessed flavor of folktale rather than the blandness of moral fable.

Both Jacob and Wilhelm wrote numerous works on language and folklore. Jacob is considered one of the founders of comparative philology, and formulated what is still called Grimm's law, a correspondence between Germanic words of Indo-European origin and their cognates (words with shared ancestries) in other Indo-European languages. They were experts in their field, and they didn't merely wander about jotting down folktales. However, outside scholarly circles the two brothers are best known as joint authors of a series of volumes called *Kinder- und Hausmärchen* ("Children's and Household Tales"), issued from 1812 to 1815 and translated a few years later as *Grimm's Fairy Tales*.

The stories have become part of the world heritage of folklore—"Cinderella," "Briar Rose," "Puss in Boots," "Little Red Cap," "Rapunzel," "Hansel and Gretel." The list isn't endless, but sometimes it seems that way. The Grimm brothers collected and published 210 tales in their famous collections, and omitted 40 more that have only recently appeared in English. They are full of animal characters, sometimes as individuals but often merely enacting their time-honored stereotypes. The variety is wonderful. Just-so stories follow horrific nightmares. Some are as brief and pointed as those of Aesop or Bidpai.

For their efforts to gather and preserve them, Jacob and Wilhelm Grimm will always be associated with folktales.

In one tale, a fox snubs an obsequious cat and demands to know how many skills it has mastered. The cat admits his only skill is running up a tree to avoid dogs. The fox scoffs and claims to possess "over a hundred skills and have a bagful of tricks besides." Naturally, at that moment a pack of dogs attack. The cat exploits its sole talent and leaps into a tree, and, of course, the fox's hundred skills do not save him. In a different story, another fox encounters a flock of geese and warns them to prepare to die. Their last request is a final prayer so they won't die in sin. One after the other, they begin praying. The story ends: "After they have finished praying, the tale shall be continued, but at the moment they are still cackling away."

One story, "The Animals of the Lord and the Devil," reads like an old fable from the Talmud or Koran. God makes all the other animals, and the Devil makes the goat. Tiring of disentangling goats' tails from brush, where they get caught, the Devil bites off their tails, leaving the stump we see today. Then the goats graze on fruit trees and grapevines, and God sends wolves to kill them. The conversation is amusing.

"Your creatures," the Devil complains childishly, "have torn mine apart." God wants to know why the Devil created goats to be harmful. The Prince of Darkness replies that his creations share his own destructive nature, and he demands monetary compensation. "I'll pay you as soon as the oak leaves fall," God counters. In the autumn the Devil comes to claim reparation, and God replies that there is a single tree in Constantinople that still bears its leaves. The Devil goes to see for himself, and by the time he returns it is spring and all the other oaks have their leaves again.

---

21 SEPTEMBER 1541

Paracelsus, Nature's Child

*For it is so ordered that we see but half of man and all the
other creatures, and therefore must explore them further.*
—Paracelsus

Philippus Aureolus Theophrastus Bombastus von Hohenheim was born in Einsiedeln, Switzerland, the year after Columbus stumbled upon North America. His alias, Paracelsus, meant "better than Celsus." Celsus was a first-century Roman physician, whose only surviving work, *De Re Medica,* was the first such work to be printed in Europe, in 1478. He was a revered encyclopedist on the order of Pliny, and for Theophrastus to call himself better was not only shameless self-promotion but a declaration that he would stand on his own research.

As his alias indicates, Paracelsus did not suffer from a lack of confidence. In his inaugural lecture at Basel in 1527, he proclaimed:

I will not defend my monarchy with empty talk but with arcana. And I do not take my medicines from the apothecaries. Their shops are but foul kitchens from which comes nothing but foul broths. . . . Every little hair on my neck knows more than you and all your scribes, and my shoebuckles are more learned than your Galen and Avicenna, and my beard has more experience than all your high colleagues.

Paracelsus, alchemist and magician, physician and scientist.

His credo begins, "I am different." He was indeed. "Nothing created," he insisted, "is beyond man's fathoming." Although Paracelsus was not a man of science in the modern sense, he was moving in that direction. He rejected the humoral theory of disease then prevalent. Convinced that particular diseases require particular treatments, he insisted that "only ignoramuses allege that Nature has not provided a remedy against every disease." He entreated his colleagues to cease their attempts to turn other metals into gold and to begin a search for medicines.

At the end of his life, Paracelsus was offered asylum back in Salzburg, from which he had been banished for his heretical theories. Settled finally, after decades of travel, he wrote to a friend, "Evening has come, the faces of people at the windows grow more melancholy. The snow of my misery has come. Summer is over." The next year, on September 21, 1541 (which is thought to have been his forty-eighth birthday), Paracelsus dictated his will. His ointments and surgical instruments he left to the barbers of the town. Although he mentioned manuscripts, he didn't appoint an executor to superintend them. After throwing himself upon the mercy of the divine judge, and listing the psalms he wanted sung at his church service, he stipulated that a coin should be given to every poor man at the door of the church—a last bit of charity he felt it necessary to mention in his own epitaph.

Three days later, Paracelsus died. The epitaph is no more humble than anything else he wrote: "Here lies buried Philip Theophrastus, the famous doctor of medicine who cured wounds, leprosy, gout, dropsy, and other incurable diseases of the body with wonderful knowledge, and who gave his goods to be divided and distributed among the poor. . . ."

Paracelsus became firmly a part of the Renaissance with his belief that experimentation and inquiry are more important than received opinion. All things were part of nature, he was convinced—even humanity. "Only he is the enemy of nature," he wrote, "who fancies himself wiser than nature, although she is the greatest school for all of us." And elsewhere he argued, "God could surely have created man out of nothingness by merely saying: 'So be it!' This he did not do, but took him from nature, placed him in nature, left him to nature, and subjected him to nature as her child."

Travels with a Donkey

Robert Louis Stevenson's account of a canoe trip in France and Belgium, *An Inland Voyage,* was published in 1878. Favorable response nudged him to undertake the walking tour in the south of France that became his next book, *Travels with a Donkey in the Cévennes.* He departed on Sunday, September 22, 1878. Stevenson's elaborate "sleeping sack" and other impedimenta required a beast of burden. He bought a donkey for sixty-five francs and a glass of brandy, less than the cost of his other gear. He said that that was appropriate because the donkey was only an appurtenance of his bedding.

For contemporary readers, this attitude toward his companion can sour Stevenson's otherwise charming travelogue. He names the donkey Modestine, and the tone of his relations with her sounds at times like Victorian pornography. Her obstinacy drives him to immediately use his staff on her; otherwise she won't move ahead at more than a snail's pace. He claims his own violence revolted him. "God forbid, thought I, that I should brutalize this innocent creature; let her go at her own pace, and let me patiently follow."

The frontispiece of Robert Louis Stevenson's second book, Travels with a Donkey in the Cévennes, *portrays him dreaming about his rambles.*

He soon abandons this pledge. He beats Modestine's rear until the exertion tires him. "The sound of my own blows sickened me. Once, when I looked at her, she had a faint resemblance to a lady of my acquaintance . . . and this increased my horror of my cruelty." Much of Stevenson's regret stems from the animal's gender. He finds her gait dainty and her gaze adoring. Later he observes, "Her faults were those of her race and sex; her virtues were her own." Stevenson dismisses an admiring male donkey as unworthy of Modestine because he doesn't fall upon her abuser "tooth and hoof" to end her pain.

An amused peasant sees the creeping donkey and gives "excellent, if inhumane" advice. He warns against pity, cuts a switch, and shows Stevenson how to switch Modestine's "sternworks." Another helpful native provides a goad, a "plain wand, with an eighth of an inch of pin." Stevenson is pleased because it spurs the donkey without tiring him. "Blessed be the man who invented goads! . . . And what although now and then a drop of blood should appear on Modestine's mouse-colored wedge-like rump?"

In Stevenson's time, only a few progressive thinkers demanded compassion for animals. Anna Sewell's plea for horses' humane treatment, *Black Beauty,* had been published only the year before. Stevenson plays his struggles with Modestine as comedy. (Over a century earlier, the English novelist Tobias Smollett traveled the same region and didn't find the abuse of mules and donkeys amusing.) In an argument with monks, Stevenson, a freethinker himself, defends his family's zealous Calvinism. But apparently he forgets Calvin's injunction to treat beasts gently even though they are "in subjection to us."

When Stevenson is advised that the exhausted donkey needs two days of rest, he doesn't want to wait. "I determined to sell my lady friend." He says he had kept his patience in spite of her obstinacy and she had come to regard him as a god. He cries at their parting.

23 SEPTEMBER 1952

Nixon's "Checkers Speech"

"He cannot be a gentleman," an eighteenth-century proverb declared, "who loveth not a dog." The opposite is also considered true: "He's kind to his dog," we say; "he must be a nice guy." Not surprisingly, public figures long ago added these popular symbols to their repertoire. Of course, not all of them were faking their affection for dogs. Theodore Roosevelt kept a pack of them at the White House for the amusement of himself and his children. Lyndon Johnson had his famous beagles, which had to suffer being lifted by their ears. Richard Nixon, on the other hand, disliked dogs but considered them effective props, like flags or babies or Elvis Presley. He kept an Irish setter at the White House, and he loved to be seen with it, although he hardly ever spent any time with it when the news media weren't watching.

Nixon went so far as to work his family dog into a speech. On Tuesday, the twenty-third of September, 1952, advisers from an advertising agency helped him rehearse his poses and gestures, then seated him before a bookcase full of painted wooden books. "My fellow Americans," he said into the camera, "I come before you tonight . . . a man whose honesty and integrity have been questioned. . . ." Nixon was Dwight Eisenhower's vice presidential running mate, and questions about his campaign fund had led to demands that Eisenhower drop him. In response, Nixon was baring a carefully packaged soul for an audience of 60 million. He detailed his financial situation, and even mentioned again his wife's "cloth coat" that distinguished her from the mink-clad wives of Democrats.

But most famously of all, he described one gift he admitted receiving: "A man down in Texas heard Pat on the radio mention the fact that our two youngsters would like to have a dog." Soon, he said, they received a gift from Texas. "It was a little cocker spaniel dog in a crate. . . . Black-and-white-spotted. And our little girl—Tricia, the six-year-old—named it Checkers. And you know, the kids, like all kids, love the dog, and I just want to say this right now, that regardless of what they say about it, we're gonna keep it."

Thus was born what would ever after be called the "Checkers speech." The coat story, the intimate fiscal revelations, the fake humility, the dog-and-children combination—each played its role in

Nixon's political recovery. Later, he admitted that he had based the use of his family dog on Franklin Roosevelt's similar reference to his Scottish terrier, Fala. In 1944, Roosevelt complained that Republicans had gone so far in their dirty campaign as to slander even his dog. *"I don't resent the attacks,"* Roosevelt had said, "and my family doesn't resent the attacks, but Fala *does* resent them." Nixon bragged: "Using the same ploy as FDR would irritate my opponents and delight my friends. . . . I'll needle them on this one, I said to myself."

Overnight, Nixon was transformed into a political asset for Eisenhower. But that evening he thought he had tragically flubbed his last chance. As he left, slumped dejectedly beside Pat, an Irish setter bounded along beside the car. Nixon watched it run and said bitterly, "Well, we made a hit in the dog world, anyway."

See also Alger Hiss's warbler, 8/16.

---

24 SEPTEMBER 1870

"Delightful Fear"

The poetry of Gerard Manley Hopkins is suffused with his view of nature as the manifestation of God. His diaries and notebooks reveal a similar devout attention to the power and beauty of even such simple experiences as watching violets age and wither and cloud patterns flow. No wonder the grander and lesser-known phenomena hit him with the force of revelation. On September 24, 1870, Hopkins wrote in his journal, "First saw the Northern Lights." He described the translucent shimmer and dance of color with a poet's eye. His response is typical: "This busy working of nature wholly independent of the earth and seeming to go on in a strain of time not reckoned by our reckoning of days and years but simpler and as if correcting the preoccupation of the world by being preoccupied with and appealing to and dated to the day of judgment was like a new witness to God and filled me with delightful fear."

Hopkins would have found the hard facts behind the aurora just as wonderful. The Latin word for "dawn" is *aurora. Borealis* is Latin for "north"; the same phenomenon in the Southern Hemisphere is called *australis,* "south." Naturally, a wide variety of explanations were advanced for the mysterious northern lights, from distant forest fires to the glow of sunset reflecting off ice and back into the sky. In reality, the aurora works like a neon sign, which lights up when an electrical current passes through a gas. In a streetlight, the gas might be sodium vapor; in a bar sign, neon. In the northern sky, it is largely oxygen, which produces the greens and reds, with nitrogen behind the occasional violet. The electricity comes from solar flares, which send pulses of electrons streaming through the solar system. When they reach Earth, its magnetic field traps them and forms them into patterns.

The aurora borealis may help explain a period called the Little Ice Age. Roughly a thousand years ago, the world climate was somewhat warmer than now. During this time, the Vikings ventured far afield from Scandinavia, exploring Iceland, then on over to Greenland, Newfoundland, and even the North American mainland. For a couple of hundred years, the Scandinavians were able to maintain agriculturally independent colonies on Greenland. Then, during the thirteenth century, the temperature began to drop. Records of Japanese festivals and Chinese harvests, glacial evidence in mountains as far apart as the Rockies and the Alps, archaeological evidence of the Vikings' settlements—all combine to indicate a considerable change in the world climate. The Vikings were unable to stay in contact with their Greenland colonies, and the settlements crumbled.

One theory of why the world climate changed emerges from hints of fluctuations in solar activity at the time. The variations in the northern lights follow the eleven-year sunspot cycle of solar flares. Chinese notes about sunspots in the thirteenth century combine with contemporary Scandinavian records of changes in the aurora borealis—and even fluctuations in the amounts of various carbon atoms in tree rings at about the same time—to explain the Little Ice Age. It may be that the sun's energy output varied enough to cause the drop in temperature.

Gerard Manley Hopkins would have been most impressed.

---

25 SEPTEMBER 1890

"Silver Blaze"

"Sometimes I have got upon dangerous ground," Arthur Conan Doyle admitted, "where I have taken risks through my own want of knowledge. . . ." When he wanted a snake as a murder weapon in "The Adventure of the Speckled Band," he simply invented one, not caring that its behavior was unrealistic. "I have never been nervous about details, and one must be masterful sometimes."

Likewise, Conan Doyle didn't bother to research horse racing before writing the Sherlock Holmes story "Silver Blaze." Many fans nevertheless consider this one of the great detective's finest moments. Conan Doyle must have agreed. He bet his wife a shilling that she would be unable to guess the identity of the villain in what Watson described as ". . . the singular disappearance of the favourite for the Wessex Cup, and the tragic murder of its trainer."

"Silver Blaze," Holmes explains to Watson on Thursday, September 25, 1890, on the train to the scene of the crime in Devonshire, "is from the Isonomy stock." Some American editions misprint that as "Somomy." One Conan Doyle biographer, long on theory and short on research, confidently asserted that either version of the horse's name was a sly allusion to "sodomy," and therefore a jab at Victorian England's whipping boy, Oscar Wilde. Unfortunately for that claim, Isonomy—actually Greek for "equality of privilege"—Conan Doyle did *not* invent. He was a famous racehorse. Isonomy won many prizes, and his son, Isinglass, founded the Blandford line, from which descend such honored horses as Donatello. Of Isonomy's missing descendant, Holmes says, "Enormous sums of money have been laid upon him. It is obvious, therefore, that there were many people who had the strongest interest in preventing Silver Blaze from being there at the fall of the flag. . . ."

The police inspector, like Conan Doyle's wife, does not deduce the identity of the murderer. He arrests a suspicious stranger, theorizing that the man drugged the stable boy's mutton so that he could sneak the horse out. Holmes demurs. In a famous exchange, he points out to the inspector "the curious incident of the dog in the night-time."

With his hand on Silver Blaze's neck, a top-hatted Sherlock Holmes reveals to his client the identities of both the horse thief and the murderer. Illustration by Sidney Paget, *Strand Magazine*, 1892

"The dog did nothing in the night-time."

"That," Holmes replies, "was the curious incident."

Holmes knew that if a stranger had entered the barn, the dog would have barked. Therefore the person who led away Silver Blaze was not the stable boy but the head groom himself, John Straker. But Straker was murdered, and the horse is nowhere to be seen. Straker himself drugged the boy's food and removed the horse, planning to inflict subcutaneous nicks on the horse's tendons, so that it would be unable to run. Frightened, Silver Blaze killed Straker with a kick to the head, then wandered off across the moor. After using a snake as a weapon, Doyle had topped that by using a horse as a murderer.

Two real-life incidents parallel this story. In New Zealand in 1920, the solution to a famous mystery lay in a dog doing nothing in the night-time. The dog had once belonged to the criminal, so the animal didn't alert its current owners when its old master appeared. And in 1956, in Kent, a detective remembered "Silver Blaze" and realized a victim was "murdered" by a horse.

---

26 SEPTEMBER 1774

John Chapman's Birthday

Emanuel Swedenborg was an eighteenth-century Swedish mystic. A scientist at first, from the age of fifty-nine he devoted himself to religion, claiming he was regularly having visions and even ascending to heaven to chat with the angels. Swedenborg himself didn't organize a sect. However, his followers founded the Church of New Jerusalem, or more properly "the New Church signified by the New Jerusalem in the Revelation," a few years after his death in 1772. A couple of years later, on September 26, 1774, there was born in Massachusetts a man who would become Swedenborg's best-known disciple in the New World. His name was John Chapman.

Chapman wandered on foot throughout the Midwest, carrying a Bible and pamphlets on Swedenborgianism, and proclaiming God's love. He held séances and, like his prophet, claimed to converse with celestial beings. Apparently he was a powerful preacher. One woman described his voice as "rising denunciatory and thrilling—strong and loud as the roar of the wind and the waves, then soft and soothing." Chapman dressed with exaggerated simplicity, wearing over his rough trousers a coffee sack with holes cut for his arms and head. He owned nothing. Usually he was barefoot, not because he never had shoes, but because poverty and hardship on Earth assured his spiritual luxury in the New Jerusalem.

Chapman held the revolutionary notion that all creatures on Earth conceal within them the spark of divinity and therefore should not be harmed. Naturally he was a vegetarian. Legend has it that he once put out his campfire when he saw that mosquitoes were dying in it. Apparently he killed only one animal in his entire life—a rattlesnake—and regretted it ever after. As if all these quirks were not enough, Chapman had a mission. On all his wanderings, he traded herbs, bartered seeds, and planted trees. Apparently numerous orchards and groves all across the American Midwest owe their inception to his handiwork, although his religious beliefs prevented him from even pruning a tree, because he feared it might experience pain during the surgery. (One wonders how he rationalized his inconsiderate habit of eating plant products.) He particularly loved apples, presumably because of their role in the Bible, and planted innumerable apple trees. In time this unsolicited arboriculture earned Chapman the nickname "Johnny Appleseed."

His ways were so strange that even in his own lifetime the myths threatened to obscure the reality. It has been a long time since one could clearly see the man behind the folk hero. Chapman is honored annually in numerous places around the United States. There are Johnny Appleseed monuments, festivals, and parks. As late as the 1940s, magazines were still publishing photographs of old apple trees supposedly planted by America's beloved itinerant treeman. In 1966, Chapman's hometown of Leominster, Massachusetts, was the site of issue for the first postage stamp in the American Folklore series. A black-and-white Johnny strides purposefully in front of a big red apple.

Swedenborg influenced a number of prominent figures in the nineteenth century, including Coleridge, Balzac, and Whitman. Later, Helen Keller was a believer. The pantheon of latter-day Swedenborgian Vachel Lindsay included the apple tree planter. It was Lindsay's 1928 *Johnny Appleseed and Other Poems* that inspired renewed interest in the fading folk hero. The title poem includes these deathless lines:

> *Loving every sloshy brake,*
> *Loving every skunk and snake*
> *Loving every leathery weed*
> *Johnny Appleseed, Johnny Appleseed.*

See also Arbor Day, 4/10.

---

27 SEPTEMBER 1960

Travels with Charley

In 1960, John Steinbeck wrote to friends: "In the fall . . . I'm going to learn about my own country. I've lost the flavour and taste and sound of it." He outfitted a pickup truck for what turned out to be an eleven-week loop through the United States—alone. Steinbeck was fifty-eight. He had suffered a stroke only months before, and both family and friends hinted that his upcoming trip was quixotic at best. He began calling it "Operation Windmills" and lettered on his truck in sixteenth-century Spanish script *Rocinante,* the name of the loyal steed that carried the man of La Mancha on his quests.

Steinbeck had always owned dogs: a Belgian shepherd named Ozymandias and called Oz, Jodie the Irish terrier, Toby the setter, and a sheepdog named Willie. At this time the Steinbecks had a standard poodle named Charles le Chien and called Charley. Steinbeck's wife worried about him traveling alone, but one day he said, "This is a big favor I'm going to ask, Elaine. Can I take Charley Dog?"

"What a good idea!" his wife exclaimed. "If you get into any kind of trouble, Charley can go get help!"

Steinbeck replied, "Elaine, Charley isn't Lassie."

Charley wasn't Lassie, but he was a remarkable dog. He became Steinbeck's ambassador, opening conversations, extending welcomes. A "mind-reading dog," he hid in the truck days before departure. On the twenty-seventh of September, 1960, only a few days into the trip, Steinbeck wrote to Elaine about Charley: "This is his favorite kind of life. What stories he will have." Perhaps Charley's best story for the dogs back home was his first encounter with a bear, in Yellowstone National Park. To Steinbeck's astonishment, this cowardly poodle who would "turn his steps rather than disturb an earnest caterpillar" saw his first bear and "shrieked with rage. His lips flared, showing wicked teeth that have some trouble with a dog biscuit. . . ."

Riding along in Rocinante, Charley became Steinbeck's Sancho. They conversed. "Does all America so far smell alike?" Steinbeck asked. "Or are there sectional smells?" Crooked teeth enabled Charley to pronounce the letter *F;* the statement "Ftt" meant "he would like to salute a bush or tree." Gradually Charley became something of an arborist, but nothing prepared him for the towering redwoods. After Charley "lifted his leg on a tree that was fifty feet across, a hundred feet high, and two thousand years old," Steinbeck asked friends he was visiting, "What's left in life for that poor dog?"

Elaine said on the phone that Steinbeck's diarylike letters home reminded her of Robert Louis Stevenson's *Travels with a Donkey in the Cévennes.* "I think of them as 'Travels with Charley.' "

Steinbeck said, "You've just given me my title."

Travels with Charley, subtitled *In Search of America,* was published in 1962. It was Steinbeck's last book and one of his most popular. Charley died in the spring of that year, "full of years but leaving a jagged hole nevertheless." The Steinbecks planted a willow over his grave. When they returned a few hours later, they found that someone—they never learned who—had planted flowers all the way around the tree.

---

28 September (Date Approximate) 1942

Oyster Shells and History

Thomas Porter was a farmer in the county of Hampshire, in southern England. One day in late September of 1942, he unwittingly earned a footnote in both history and natural history. He was digging out a ferret that had taken refuge in a rabbit burrow. The farther he dug, the more puzzled he became. There seemed to be no end to the rabbits' burrow. Then he realized that the rabbits had made use of something that already existed there, some kind of buried buildings. And perhaps strangest of all was another finding—a large number of oyster shells.

Alice fell down a rabbit hole and found herself in a different world. Thomas Porter almost did the same. Within a few days, Porter showed the shells to an archaeologist, A. T. Morley-Hewitt, who identified them as a kind of oyster that the Romans were known to have cultivated at the harbor at nearby Poole. Although World War II slowed his progress, Morley-Hewitt began performing what occasional excavations he could manage. By the end of the war it was apparent that the site included several buildings.

Eventually Morley-Hewitt bought the land and began his excavations in earnest. He found dozens of rooms, built of the same flintstone in use in the region today. Apparently the Romans had occupied the villa from the first to the sixth centuries A.D. Thousands of coins dated from the third century alone. There was considerable evidence of the high state of Roman civilization—lost and forgotten after the Romans withdrew from England—including a bronze safety pin that still had spring in its coil.

One interesting discovery was a clay-lined pool. At first the excavators were puzzled about its purpose. Gradually, as evidence fell together, they formulated the theory that it was designed for the cultivation of live oysters transported from the harbor at Poole—source of the shells Thomas Porter had found when he followed the ferret downward into the rabbit hole and backward into history. "Oysters," Pliny the Elder wrote in the first century A.D., "have long since taken pride of place as a delicacy for our tables." He quoted the Roman administrator Mucianus, whom he called the greatest expert of their time. The extent of Roman enthusiasm for this mollusk is apparent in Mucianus's roll call: "Oysters from Cyzicus are larger than those from the Lucrine Lake, fresher than the British variety, sweeter than those from Medullae, sharper than oysters from Ephesus, fuller than those of Spain, less slimy than ones from Coryphas, softer than those from Histria and whiter than oysters from Circeii."

The Romans began farming oysters. According to Pliny, who is (to say the least) not always to be trusted, the first Roman to cultivate oysters—that is, to prepare oyster beds—was one Sergius Orata. "His reason," Pliny added, "was not gluttony but monetary greed." From the moment they arrived in Britain, the Romans cultivated oysters, lining the channel coast with beds, some of which are still in use two millennia later.

Oysters have other virtues, of course. One of the most prized of all nature's creations is the pearl, the oyster's answer to life's minor irritations. Suetonius claimed that rumors of the pearls from British oysters inspired Caesar's invasion of Britain. Oysters were also the subject of an early attempt to envision the progression of evolution. The early-nineteenth-century evolutionist Lamarck examined fossil oysters, compared them with living species, and concluded that rather than actually becoming extinct the former had developed into the latter. Although oyster shells may have helped English archaeologists determine the age of a Roman villa, the shells themselves were a reminder that wherever evidence of human civilization is found, it is always only a recent development in an ancient neighborhood.

See also pearls, 7/29.

Dracula

Probably the best-known portrayal of a vampire is by Bela Lugosi in Tod Browning's version of *Dracula,* which began filming in Hollywood on September 29, 1930. That single movie exhibits most of the nature folklore that vampire stories have accrued over the centuries. The topic may be so popular because it partakes of many preoccupations in our culture.

Take blood, for example. "I never drink—wine," Lugosi says memorably. The basic assumption in the vampire story is the same as that in ritual cannibalism: that the consumption of the flesh or blood of another passes on the attributes of the victim, whether courage, strength, youth, or life itself. The same idea underlies the Christian ritual of communion. Saint Leo stated it flatly: "Nothing else is aimed at in our partaking of the Body and Blood of Christ than that we change into what we consume. . . ." This you-are-what-you-eat notion has fueled cannibals' raids upon their neighbors and encouraged the consumption of particularly brave prisoners of war. In a similar vein was the sixteenth-

Bela Lugosi as filmdom's favorite sanguivorous fiend. Courtesy of Ronald V. Borst / Hollywood Movie Posters

century Transylvanian noblewoman Erzebet Bathory, whom legend accuses of bathing in the blood of young women in the hope of prolonging life. Numerous scholars have remarked that it is no coincidence that the unprecedented popularity of vampire imagery in the 1980s accompanied the spread of that wasting, sex- and blood-related disease, AIDS. They point out that many of the trappings of vampire lore arose during similar plagues in the Middle Ages.

Bela Lugosi's Dracula is as much werewolf as vampire. At his castle in Transylvania, he hears wolves howling and says appreciatively, "Listen. Children of the night. What music they make." After he leaves a house in England, others glimpse a wolf crossing the lawn. Thanks to the limited special effects of the time, Lugosi performs his metamorphoses offscreen. Later, wolves howl, and Dracula's omnivorous henchman Renfield howls back at them.

However, vampires' association with wolves is less pronounced than their link with another animal—the bat. In the Lugosi film, dim-witted Jonathan Harker sees Dracula departing in winged-mammal guise and observes, "My, that's a big bat." Surprisingly, in Bram Stoker's 1897 novel, Dracula changes into an unclassifiable winged creature described as simultaneously resembling a bat, a bird, and a lizard. Bats, like wolves, come equipped with enough slanders and myths to endow a whole genre. One kind will forever be linked with vampires. It gets its name from them. Vampires are not named after vampire bats; it's the other way around. When Europeans first encountered gargoyle-faced, blood-drinking creatures of the night in South America, they named them for these fictional creatures that have haunted the human imagination for centuries.

Because of his lupine tendencies, Dracula is repelled by the wolfsbane Van Helsing holds up like a crucifix. An actual plant of the *Aconitum* clan, wolfsbane is prescribed for a bad case of lycanthropy (the fictional condition, not the medical disorder in which patients merely *believe* they are werewolves). The 1935 film *Mark of the Vampire* featured an imaginary plant called "bat thorn," which is as harmful to vampires as wolfsbane is to werewolves. A real plant associated with Dracula is garlic, a versatile vampire repellent that can be worn as a medallion or hung above doors and rubbed around windows. Thanks to its supposed immunization and purification properties, garlic has long been a popular folk remedy, and modern medicine recognizes its antifungal and antibacterial virtues.

Even as Dracula fears certain plants, he needs the soil in which they grow. In Greek mythology, Heracles defeats Antaeus only after breaking the giant's contact with the earth that gives him strength. Apparently the undead, too, share this need for the revivifying soil. Expatriate vampires fill their coffins with dirt from their native land, in order to successfully rampage abroad. It seems to work.

*See also **vampire bats**, 8/3; and* **The Wolf Man**, *12/10.*

---

30 SEPTEMBER 1644

"An Incomparable Meate"

John Evelyn was famous in seventeenth-century England as the author of, among other things, *Sylva, or a Discourse of Forest Trees,* and his natural history *Kalendarium.* His renown in several fields was established long before his death. However, his name acquired new luster after his long-lost diary was found being used as kitchen wastepaper in the early nineteenth century. It was published in 1818. Since then, Evelyn has been remembered primarily as a diarist on the order of his friend Samuel Pepys—detailed, informed, gossipy, and ever curious. Wherever he went, he recorded the human society and natural world around him.

In 1644, Evelyn was traveling in France. His diary records his first encounter with a certain prized food.

> Sept: 30
>
> . . . Dauphine: This is an Archbishoprick and the Province gives title to the Heyre apparent of France; here we lay, and supp'd; having (amongst other dainties) a dish of Truffles, which is a certaine earth-nut, found out by an hogg, train'd up to it, and for which those Creatures, are sold at a greate price.

Countless admirers have agreed with Evelyn's assessment of this subterranean fungus: "It is in truth an incomparable meate." Frequently the response is ecstatic. Colette called truffles "jewels of the poor soil." Balzac claimed that "if a truffle falls on my plate . . . it immediately hatches ten characters for my *Comédie Humaine.*" Nowadays admirers pay up to $500 per pound. *Tuber melanosporum,* a black truffle from the Périgord region, is the most prized and is considered as essential as goose liver in the best pâté de foie gras. Truffles are unlikely ever to become an inexpensive food; the farmers have too large an investment in their harvest. First they must plant a grove of oaks and beeches, around the roots of which truffles grow. Only when the trees have grown to some height do the farmers place pieces of truffles in the ground nearby. It can be a decade before the first harvest. Meanwhile, it takes years for pigs to be "train'd up" for the hunt.

Only the female pig yearns for truffles. Scientists have discovered that the earthnut contains twice the level of the hormone androsterone than is found in male pigs. Presumably the sow isn't merely craving a favorite food; she imagines she is in hot pursuit of some pungent boar. As each digging reveals merely an unattractive tuber, no doubt she finds these field trips frustrating. The pig is performing the purpose for which nature makes the truffle so alluring. Its scent encourages forest creatures to dig it up and scatter its spores. Nor are pigs the only animals moved by the scent. Sardinian goats, Russian bear cubs, Italian dogs—all are used in the harvesting of the seventy-odd varieties around the world.

Interestingly, the chemical composition of androsterone is similar in pigs and humans. In numerous experiments, women responded more favorably to men or even to photographs of men if they had been scented with androsterone. This may help explain truffles' age-old reputation as an aphrodisiac. "Sensual men of fashion," an Italian wrote in the 1400s, "consume them to whet their appetite for lovemaking." Perhaps it genuinely enhanced not only their appetite but their appeal.

Brontosaurus versus *Apatosaurus*

At Walt Disney World in Orlando, Florida, on the first day of October, 1989, the U.S. Postal Service cashed in on what is surely one of the stranger cases of celebrityhood on record—the late-twentieth-century status of dinosaurs as cultural icons. The post office issued a set of four 25-cent stamps honoring *Stegosaurus, Tyrannosaurus, Pteranodon,* and *Brontosaurus.*

A question of nomenclature ensued. "Furious purists," the *New York Times* reported, "point out that the 'brontosaurus' is now properly called 'apatosaurus.' " Critics pronounced the postal service scientifically illiterate, and some concerned citizens actually demanded the recall of the misnamed stamps. True, the sanctioned name is *Apatosaurus,* but most adults grew up referring to the animal in question as *Brontosaurus.* Familiar from museums, from the comic strip "Alley Oop," and even from brontoburgers on *The Flintstones,* it was also the logo and animated mascot for Sinclair Oil. However, the name change wasn't new. Scientists designated *Brontosaurus* and *Apatosaurus* synonymous as long ago as 1903.

Official scientific names must obey the International Code of Zoological Nomenclature, which follows the modern version of the scheme devised by the pioneer systematist Linnaeus, in the tenth edition of his *Systema Naturae* in 1758. A capitalized genus name precedes an uncapitalized species name, both in italics, both in our one truly international tongue, Latin. Some names are descriptive, such as *Pachycephalosaurus,* which means "bone-headed lizard," or a tick branded *sanguineus.* Some allude to mythological characters, as in *Hyacinthus,* which refers to a dying youth whose blood Apollo turned into flowers as the boy's head lolled like a broken blossom. Others designate discoverers (*darwini, andersoni*). A few, for whatever reason, honor someone who had nothing to do with the find (*garylarsoni*).

The confusion between *Brontosaurus* and *Apatosaurus* resulted from a famous feud. Two important nineteenth-century American paleontologists, Edward Drinker Cope and Othniel C. Marsh, were bitter rivals. In a rush to best the other, each performed shoddy work that their successors had to correct. They described and named skeletons before they were fully unearthed and they named fragments. In this case, Marsh named the same animal more than once. In 1877, he described a new find and dubbed it *Apatosaurus ajax.* The genus name means "deceptive lizard," and the species appropriately refers to the gigantic but dim-witted soldier who fought beside Achilles in the Trojan War. Two years later, Marsh described *Brontosaurus,* which means "thunder lizard." In time the two turned out to be the same species, and priority determined that the former name become the official one.

However, a species' name is derived from, and forever linked with, a "type specimen," the particular fossil from which it was described. *Brontosaurus* kept its original moniker, even after being renamed *Apatosaurus,* because the skeleton from which Marsh described the creature was simply the most complete ever found. To this day, Marsh's *"Brontosaurus"* stands in the Smithsonian Institution.

See also Cope, 7/28; and the devil's tar, 8/26.

---

2 OCTOBER 1787

The Degenerate New World

The forty-four-volume *Histoire naturelle* of Georges-Louis Leclerc, comte de Buffon, is considered the premier natural history work of the eighteenth century. But Buffon's descriptions of the Americas, which he had not visited, inspired much debate. Such writers as Chateaubriand and Rousseau considered America a second chance at Eden, but Buffon was the most prominent of several European naturalists who maintained that nature in the New World was "degenerate." This unfortunate condition was primarily due to America's (mythical) greater humidity and fiercer cold—which, they theorized, resulted from a deluge "many centuries later than Noah's."

Buffon said that animals common to both Old and New Worlds were smaller in the New; if unique to America, smaller than their nearest European counterparts; if domesticated in both, smaller in the Americas; and that there were fewer species in the corrupt New World. American animals were "imperfect," "awkward," "ill-proportioned." Buffon didn't ignore the human populace, either; the male "savage" was feeble, cowardly, and stupid, and had a small penis.

Thomas Jefferson, in his *Notes on Virginia,* tackled Buffon. Providing heights and weights for living or recently killed animals, he contrasted them, category by category, with Buffon's European figures. He also refuted each of the Frenchman's slanders of native Americans. In 1784, Jefferson replaced the ailing Benjamin Franklin as minister to France, where he remained until the eve of the Revolution in 1789. He took with him the skin of a panther large enough to impress the scientist. Buffon admitted he had been mistaken regarding the panther, but refused to concede other points. When Jefferson said that the American deer and moose were much larger than their European relatives, Buffon scoffed. When Jefferson claimed that the tiny European reindeer could stand up under an American moose, Buffon laughed aloud.

Jefferson requested from the States the largest moose available. Hunters snowshoed the winter woods, finally killing a huge buck in a thicket so dense that ten men couldn't remove the corpse. Finally, a team hacked a twenty-mile road and hauled the moose out by sleigh, but the ship scheduled to deliver it to Jefferson left without it. Finally, on another ship, it reached Jefferson on the second of

October, 1787. The body was not intact, and thanks to inadequate taxidermy much of the hair had fallen off, but the size of the skeleton was irrefutable. Included were antlers of various related species.

Jefferson sent the bedraggled trophy to his adversary. Buffon graciously replied, "I should have consulted you before publishing my natural history, and then I should have been sure of the facts." He said he would rectify matters in his next edition, but he died a few months later.

Over two hundred years later, Ismail Merchant and James Ivory were in France filming their 1995 motion picture *Jefferson in Paris.* For the encounters with Buffon, the film crew borrowed from a science museum a huge moose skeleton on a wheeled cart. Then someone noticed what seemed a good omen: Its label, in French, read *Gift of the United States of America to the People of France, 1787.*

---

3 OCTOBER 1800

"The Leech Gatherer"

Dorothy Wordsworth and her renowned brother William moved to Dove Cottage at Grasmere in the last weeks of 1799. It was a poor area, and many beggars came their way. On October 3, 1800, Dorothy recorded in her journal an encounter that inspired William to write a poem. "When Wm & I returned . . . we met an old man. . . ." He was a former soldier who told of his wife and ten children, all dead. He had been hurt driving a cart, and now his trade "was to gather leeches but now leeches are scarce & he had not strength for it—he lived by begging. . . . He said leeches were very scarce partly owing to the dry season, but many years they have been scarce—he supposed it owing to their being much sought after, that they did not breed fast, & were of slow growth."

Two years later, assisted by Dorothy's distilled memories, William transmuted the experience into a poem. In "The Leech Gatherer," later retitled "Resolution and Independence," he called the old man's vocation "employment hazardous and wearisome." The famously rainy Lake District would have been a better leech-gathering site than many, but it isn't surprising that they were scarce. The nineteenth century would see one European leech driven almost to extinction. It was so much in demand for medicinal purposes that England and other countries passed game laws to protect it. The very word "leech" derives from the Anglo-Saxon *læce,* meaning "physician." Originally the word referred to those for whom bloodletting was a professional service, but gradually it came to name their favorite tool.

Leeching and other methods of bloodletting were once a requisite medical practice. When dark humors clouded the system, bleeding off some of that sullied blood was frequently the prescription. Gilded ceramic jars from the nineteenth century survive, with airholes in the lid and the elegantly written label *Leeches.* As leeches became scarce, some pharmacies rented them. Sufferers applied the creature to the skin. When it finished its meal, it dropped off, and the patient returned it to the pharmacy, where it was rented to someone else. An infection could not have devised a better method for spreading itself.

George Washington was bled by leeches only a day or so before his death. In the twentieth century, both Adolf Hitler and Joseph Stalin were leeched. Bleeding is no longer a common practice, but leeches are still in demand. In the genus *Hirudo,* there is a species tellingly named *medicinalis.* It not only provides hirudin, the strongest known natural anticoagulant, but contains an anesthetic that usually makes the bite painless. Oncologists have found that an extract from the salivary gland of another leech inhibits the spread of cancer.

These parasites, reviled from the time of ancient Rome to *The African Queen,* don't always match their reputation. Not all species live only in water. Nor do all require warmth; there are more in Antarctic waters than anywhere else. One species reaches eighteen inches in length and can live twenty years. And not all are bloodthirsty. While exploring Mormon territory in the American West, Sir Richard Burton complained about the inefficient leeches. "The American hirudo, however, has a serious defect in a leech—it will not bite. . . ."

---

4 October 1582

Caesar and the Pope

Presumably the first unit of time noticed by primitive humans was the one most easily observed by us—the day. It isn't difficult to discern a pattern in the recurring circuit of the sun across the sky. However, the day's very frequency limits its utility as a measurement. If a year of days were numbered consecutively to form a calendar, it would take only a few to lose track of events.

The next most obvious natural pattern is the waxing and waning of the second-brightest light in the sky, the Moon. It grows to full glory and vanishes to nothing and returns in a regular number of days. Therefore, "moons" became a second measurement of time. Unfortunately, the Moon's full cycle comes to slightly more than 29½ days. That means that there is no handy numerical relationship between the two ways of measuring time. If one unit can't be subdivided by the other, they will conflict at times.

The third conspicuous natural pattern is the year. It takes longer to become aware of it, but it measures much bigger chunks of time. An entire human life can be marked off with it. Nature, however, is not concerned with human pattern-recognition. Once again there is no handy ratio to express the lunar and solar periods. The time it takes the Moon to go through twelve full cycles does not exactly equal the time it takes Earth to revolve around the Sun. Inevitably, calendars based upon a lunar year will have discrepancies and require periodic updating if they are to have any valid correspondence with the solar year.

A good example of such a calendar was the one in use in Rome in the first century B.C. According to the tradition of the time, the calendar had been introduced by none other than Romulus himself, the city's legendary founder, in 738 B.C. No matter how old it actually was, it was decrepit. For a long time it had consisted of ten months totaling 304 days, with a rather vague unmeasured time in the winter, when its agricultural relevance vanished. Finally, two more months had been added, but they did not erase the discrepancies.

When Julius Caesar came to power, the calendar was so off kilter that January came in autumn, and few could predict the length of a year. In Egypt, however, Caesar encountered a more exact system. The

Egyptian year consisted of 365 days, twelve 30-day months with 5 feast days thrown in at the end. Caesar determined to revise Rome's calendar. He brought the Greek astronomer Sisogenes from Alexandra and assigned him the task of making the calendar as self-correcting as possible. Sisogenes calculated that the solar year was roughly 365¼ days long. To make up the difference, he inserted one extra day every four years. The Julian calendar went into effect in 45 B.C.

However, Sisogenes made an error. The year is actually eleven minutes and fourteen seconds less than 365¼ days long. That doesn't seem like much, but over the centuries it adds up. By the sixteenth century, the vernal equinox was occurring around March 11. Not only did the discrepancy create problems in civil record-keeping, but the uncertain computation of holy days left the Church looking less than infallible. Using Copernicus's impressive new calculations of the motions of the Sun and Earth, astronomers under the aegis of Pope Gregory XIII revised the Julian calendar. The Julian discrepancy was dealt with by suppressing three leap years every four centuries. Officially, October 4, 1582, was the last day of the Julian calendar. The next day, however, was not October 5. It was October 15. For religious reasons, Gregory wanted to restore the mean vernal equinox to March 21, its date at the time of the Council of Nicaea that had begun the process of setting the official date of Easter. To do so he simply lopped off 10 days.

Taking place during the Protestant Reformation, the Catholic pope's arbitrary rearrangement of the very days of our lives was slow to find acceptance. In some places it was centuries before the need for greater accuracy won out over factional rivalry. Of course, even the Gregorian system isn't perfect. It overcorrects by about twenty-six seconds per year, which means that every 3,323 years we will have to add another day.

See also the north star, 3/15; and the solstice, 12/21.

Old Possum's Book of Practical Cats

T. S. Eliot liked variety. Shortly after the premiere of his play *The Family Reunion,* and upon the heels of his nonfiction work *The Idea of a Christian Society,* he published *Old Possum's Book of Practical Cats.* The British edition appeared in London on October 5, 1939. It was a difficult time for nonsense verse; Britain had declared war upon Germany only a month before. Nonetheless, the book received glowing reviews and sold well.

Eliot wrote several of the verses to amuse his publishers' children. Over three years before the book was published, Faber and Faber advertised "Mr. Eliot's Book of Pollicle Dogs and Jellicle Cats as Recited to Him by the Man in White Spats." However, by the time the book appeared, the cats had taken over. The role of the Pollicle Dogs was reduced to a single poem, "The Pekes and the Pollicles," and even there it is the Great Rumpuscat that triumphs. The man in white spats also vanished, although his footwear shows up on that feline Beau Brummell, Bustopher Jones. "The truth," Stephen Spender wrote in his review of *Old Possum* for the *Listener,* "is that poets have always shown a marked preference for cats. . . . Dogs are themselves too like little satiric poems on the behaviour of their masters to need much interpreting. But cats are mysterious. . . ."

Eliot's cats are very English. An expatriate American and rabid Anglophile, he places his characters firmly in London, sometimes apparently just for the joy of sounding the words—Kensington Square, Victoria Grove. The characters are almost Dickensian. Take, for example, Gus, the Theatre Cat, who has even sat by the bedside of Little Nell. Or consider that social activist, Jennyanydots, the Gumbie Cat. Convinced that her household's vermin can be rehabilitated with a little remedial breeding, she forms the cockroaches into a scout troop and teaches the mice tatting and music. Perhaps the most realistic cat in the book is the Rum Tum Tugger, who is never satisfied with anything his human masters do.

Even their names delight the ear—Mr. Mistoffelees; Skimbleshanks, the Railway Cat; Old Deuteronomy. Indeed, the first poem addresses that subtle art, "The Naming of Cats." In this matter, the poet succumbed to cuteness. Eliot himself owned cats named Wiscus and Pettipaws. He entered crossword puzzle competitions under the name of another of his pets, George Pushdragon. (Even this degree of preciousness can't compare with the poet Robert Southey's name for his cat: "The most Noble the Archduke Rumpelstiltzchen, Marquis Macbum, Earl Tomlemagne, Baron Raticide, Waowhler, and Skaratch.")

Old Possum's cats grew out of Eliot's lifelong admiration for his own pets. His "serious" poems demonstrate a similar interest in the rest of nature. As a child in St. Louis, he watched birds and examined the world through a microscope. He planned, but didn't write, a memoir of childhood to be entitled *The River and the Sea.* At Harvard, Eliot enjoyed the antics of animal characters in comic strips such as *Mutt and Jeff* and *Krazy Kat.* He admired nonsense verse, too, especially the masters, Edward Lear and Lewis Carroll, whose way with inventive names and bouncy rhythms he equaled.

Eliot died in 1965, years too early to witness the hoopla surrounding a later adaptation of *Old Possum.* In 1981, the musical stage production *Cats* opened in London, and the next year it took New York by storm. It's a shame the reserved, intellectual poet wasn't around to record somewhere his opinion of the energetic, gaudy musical. What would the cats themselves have thought of it? No doubt that illustrious scene-stealer, Gus, would compare it unfavorably to his history-making performance as Firefrorefiddle, the Fiend of the Fell.

"Ivy Day in the Committee Room"

Charles Stewart Parnell was the most popular Irish hero in the late nineteenth century—Ireland's "uncrowned king." In 1875, he was elected to Parliament, where he forced his fellow representatives to at least discuss, if not approve, home rule for Ireland. He was idolized by the Irish poor. In time Parnell both helped bring about the fall of Gladstone's Liberal government and joined with him when he was restored to power. However, after a scandalous affair with a colleague's wife, Parnell lost much of his following. He died in 1891.

The English remember Charles II on Oak Apple Day, his birthday. The Irish memorialize Parnell with another plant-linked holiday, Ivy Day, on the anniversary of his death, October 6. Although apparently he disliked the color, Parnell chose a sprig of green ivy as a memorial badge to himself and his country's struggles with British rule. Parnell, and his ivy, come up often in Irish literature. For example, there is the scene in James Joyce's story "Ivy Day in the Committee Room," which appears near the end of his collection *Dubliners*.

Charles Stewart Parnell gave yet another boost to that already popular plant, ivy.

Mr. O'Connor tore a strip off the card and, lighting it, lit his cigarette. As he did so the flame lit up a leaf of dark glossy ivy in the lapel of his coat. . . . "This is Parnell's anniversary," said Mr. O'Connor. . . . We all respect him now that he's dead and gone—even the Conservatives. . . ."

Unwittingly, those ivy-sprigged patriots were commemorating more than the death of Parnell. Like so many other plants woven into history, ivy has a remarkable heritage. Along with, naturally, the grapevine, ivy was sacred to Dionysus, the god of wine and revelry equivalent to the Greek Bacchus. When Tyrrhenian pirates tried to abduct Dionysus to sell him in Asia, he confounded them by metamorphosing into a lion and magically filling their ship with ivy. His antics drove them to madness, and they leaped overboard and were transformed into dolphins. It is said that Alexander the Great, in imitation of Bacchus, returned from India with his victorious army adorned with ivy. Thalia, the Greek muse of comedy, wore an ivy wreath. Pliny the Elder found it surprising "that any honor has been accorded to ivy," because it destroys tombs and walls and "is very popular with cold-blooded snakes." He also said that its berries would cure everything from disorders of the spleen to tapeworms.

Apparently due to its determined clinging, ivy has become a symbol of friendship and constancy. However, now and then the same characteristic is interpreted quite differently. In *The Tempest,* Prospero derides his brother as "The ivy which had hid my princely trunk / And sucked my verdure out on 't." Prospero was mistaken. Technically, although it does damage buildings, ivy is not a parasite, because it derives its nourishment from the soil in which it is rooted rather than the stone on which it climbs.

Many plants besides the English ivy, *Hedera helix,* are called ivy. There are Boston, Mexican, German, West Indian, ground, and poison "ivies." The one that festoons institutions of higher education in the United States, and which lent its name to the Ivy League of northeastern universities, is not a true ivy but a member of the grape family. A native of central China and Japan, it was introduced into the United States in 1862, where it was sold as Japanese ivy. Much hardier than the English version, and not evergreen, it thrived in the northeastern United States, and in time came to be called Boston ivy. It is now as cherished a part of the cityscape in the United States as is Parnell's ivy in Joyce's Ireland. In the spring of 1982, Harvard University's plans to rid several buildings of Boston ivy resulted in picketers waving signs demanding "Hell, No! Let the Ivy Grow!" It was an ancient sentiment.

See also Keats's laurel, 6/10; and the Royal Oak, 9/6.

---

7 OCTOBER 1959

The Far Side of the Moon

In the first half of the seventeenth century, during the years he was imprisoned for his heretical notions about the universe, the aging Galileo Galilei developed a cataract condition and finally became totally blind. Only when there was no hope of saving his sight did the pope allow him to visit a physician. During the last few months before the man who had so expanded the human conception of the universe completely lost his vision, he again turned his ailing eyes to the sky. Galileo could no longer see the stars, but he could still discern the Moon. Through the film that was creeping across his eyes, he determined that the Man in the Moon doesn't always show the same face. Although the face always seemed to be there, it turned a little up or down or left or right.

Galileo was correct. Nowadays scientists call these oscillations the Moon's "librations." The word comes from the same origin as the name of one of the constellations (the Latin *libra,* "scales") and refers to the oscillating motions of the beam of a balance before it comes to rest. Thanks to the combination of its rates of rotation and revolution, the Moon does present roughly the same side toward Earth at all times. However, its slight librations reveal a little more or less along what is, from our perspective, the edge of the disk. That is the extent of the Moon that we are able to observe from home.

Naturally, ever since Galileo and others helped establish that the Moon is a globe, people have wondered what the back of it might look like. Scientists assumed that it would be roughly the same as the front—barren and cratered by meteorites—but artists and science fiction writers toyed with the notion that it would reveal a Looking-Glass sort of face.

Finally, after hundreds of years of speculation, the human race developed the capability to launch a vehicle that would fly around to the back of the Moon and let us see for ourselves. Following the success of *Sputnik 3* in the spring of 1958, the Soviet Union changed the emphasis of its embryonic space program from merely analyzing the upper atmosphere to aiming for the Moon. Their first several attempts to launch a Moon probe did not succeed. Then came the first object to ever escape Earth's gravity. In the first few days of 1959, *Lunik* (Luna) *1* was aimed straight at the Moon, armed with micrometeoroid and radiation detectors and a magnetometer. However, a guidance error sent it arcing past and *Lunik* wound up captured by the irresistible gravity of the Sun, where it went into orbit. Following a disappointing failure, another spacecraft was launched that autumn, and it crashed into the surface of the Moon, in Mare Imbrium near the crater Archimedes.

Only three weeks later, the Soviets launched another craft. Equipped with a 35mm camera and both narrow- and wide-angle lenses, plus an automatic developing system, *Lunik 3* flew over the Moon's south pole on October 7, 1959. From a height of about 40,500 miles, it took over two dozen photographs of the far side of the moon. The procedure took forty minutes, and then the automatic system developed the negatives. Immediately afterward, when television cameras scanned the photos and transmitted images back to Earth, scientists got their first glimpse of the far side of the Moon. The pictures were grainy and faint, but they proved that the back of the Moon's head looked the same as its face. The scientists named the features the Gulf of Cosmonauts, the Sea of Moscow, and, appropriately, the Sea of Dreams.

See also moonlight, 6/6; Moon landing, 7/20; and fictional trips to the Moon, 10/14.

Celestial Cows

"Cows are my passion," says the Honourable Mrs. Skewton in Dickens's novel *Dombey and Son.* She is not alone. Cows do more than merely jump over the moon. In Gary Larson's "Far Side" universe, they ring doorbells as pranks, joyride in stolen cars, and have their own religion—Cowintology. For some reason, cows were a favorite disguise of the Greek gods. To prevent Hera, his long-suffering wife, from learning of his philandering with the youthful Io, Zeus turns the maiden into a white cow. Taygete, one of the seven Pleiades sisters, resists the amorous advances of the same swaggering god, and Artemis metamorphoses her into a cow. And Pasiphae, whose passion for a certain bull is not as pure as Mrs. Skewton's, has Daedalus construct a hollow and anatomically detailed wooden cow in which she can hide.

Cows have left their stodgy legacy all over our language. As a noun, the word now refers not only to female cattle (and sometimes to cattle in general), but also to female whales, elephants, and other animals. We have cowboys, cowgirls, cowherds, cowpokes, cowpunchers, and cowcatchers. The latter was not a person, but a wedge-shaped device on the front of a train, to keep tracks clear. Cowards are not so named because they behave like cows; nor does cowering or being cowed have bovine connotations. However, there are plenty of other derisive references to these animals. One dictionary definition of "bovine" contains the adjectives "dull" and "sluggish" (itself a comparison to another animal). An entry on "cattle" includes "human beings in the mass: used in contempt or reproach." As an example of the cow's importance in our economies and cultures, every square inch of its body has a name, from the brisket to the thurl.

Because over the centuries we have allowed no animal to be onstage without performing in the play, cows have acquired certain symbolic roles. In Scandinavian mythology, the primordial cow sculpted the first man by licking ice. In India, the wish-fulfilling cow-goddess Nandi provides holy milk (except, of course, when Nandi appears in the form of a bull). However, the most common cow figure is nicely expressed in a statue carved in the late Twenty-sixth Dynasty of ancient Egypt, which dates it roughly as the seventh century B.C. The pharaoh Psamettichus I, who founded the dynasty, stands under the protective gaze of the Great Mother goddess, Hathor, who happens to be portrayed as a large ungodly cow. The disk of the sun, symbol of divinity, nestles cozily between her horns. Egypt's herd of bovine symbols included a two-headed cow representing Upper and Lower Egypt. Another sky goddess, Nut, was also sometimes portrayed as a celestial cow. Her legs represented the four corners of the world and she bore the firmament on her belly.

Painted in northern India around the end of the eighteenth century, this portrait of the Hindu goddess Parvati shows her riding one of many versions of divine cows and bulls, Nandi (or Nandini). Vanderbilt University Fine Arts Gallery / Photo by Denny Adcock

Speaking of cows' bellies, to a biologist a cow is an ungulate and a ruminant. The first word places it in the group of mammals that have hoofs, which are simply the horny structures that form the ends of digits, and which have their parallel in our own fingernails. The second term narrows the cow's classification to the four-legged, even-toed hoofed mammals such as giraffes, deer, and camels, all of which have four stomachs. (For the record, they are the rumen, reticulum, omasum, and abomasum.) This alimentary redundancy enables ruminants to swallow their food unchewed, regurgitate it, chew it thoroughly, and reswallow it. While this procedure may not be appetizing, it ensures that food is fully divested of all nutrients before passing on to its ultimate fate, which itself has led to a vulgar term for deceitful nonsense. Meanwhile, the four-stomach process results in the thoughtful-looking practice of chewing the cud and has led to "ruminate" being used as a verb meaning "to ponder or meditate." With that etymology in mind, Dryden's line "Mad with desire, she ruminates her sin" becomes considerably less attractive.

Obviously, most of the time cows are not assigned the role of villain. However, in one incident that may well be apocryphal, a cow is blamed for a disaster. On October 8, 1871, a fire broke out in a barn owned by a Chicagoan named Patrick O'Leary. It raged out of control through the mostly wooden structures, killing 300 people and destroying four square miles of the city. With the speed of the fire itself, the story spread that flames had been started by the O'Learys' cow kicking over a lantern in the barn.

---

9 OCTOBER 1778

"A New Constellation"

In 1778, Benjamin Franklin and John Adams were both U.S. ministers to France, where Franklin negotiated an alliance between England's former colony and its age-old enemy. Understandably, numerous matters had not been attended to prior to the break with England. One was an official symbol for the new nation. The king of the Two Sicilies, as the regions around Sicily and Naples were called at the time, asked the Americans how ships during wartime might be recognized as from their country. On October 9, 1778, Franklin and Adams jointly replied:

> It is with pleasure we acquaint Your Excellency that the flag of the United States of America consists of thirteen stripes alternately red, white, and blue; a small square in the upper angle, next the staff, is a blue field, with thirteen white stars, denoting a new constellation.

More than a year before, in a list of routine business, the Continental Congress had passed a resolution including that telling phrase designating stars to represent their "new constellation." They didn't specify either the design of the stars or their arrangement. Previously there had been various symbols of the union—the famous rattlesnake, the Liberty Tree, clasped hands, thirteen links. The flag resolution was vague enough to inspire a number of designs. Most were variations on the single theme, but occasionally the stars outshone the stripes. Charles Willson Peale's 1779 portrait of George Washington at the Battle of Trenton depicts a flag with a circle of six-pointed white stars on a stripeless blue field.

The United States isn't the only country to have stars on its banner. They are present in a huge percentage of national flags, including the British "Meteor Flag," from which the first U.S. flag was adapted. Nations as diverse as Iraq, Morocco, and Israel chose star symbolism. On Yemen's flag, stars are accompanied by a sword; on Lybia's and others, by a crescent moon. Many employ the sun, which, although it has different associations, is certainly a star.

The symbolism is firmly rooted in history. Earlier generations knew the night sky as a powerful presence; we have always aspired to the heavens. Stars' lights amid darkness have symbolized hope, righteousness, perseverance. They have naturally represented multiplicity, and in clusters they expressed order. The Pole Star, the one apparently fixed position in the heavens, became a symbol of constancy, and some Hindu marriage rites still employ it as such. Ironically, due to the precession of the equinoxes, supposedly reliable old Polaris hasn't always been the North Star. To Tutankhamen, for example, it was Thuban, the second-brightest star in the constellation Draco.

Star symbolism isn't confined to flags, of course. The character for "star" was in the Egyptian hieroglyph for the verb "to educate," and today it is all around us—in the asterisk, the name Stella, the aster, the symbol for Judaism, and even our label for prominent thespians. Incidentally, in his 1863 story "The Man without a Country," Edward Everett Hale helped preserve the myth that each star in the U.S. flag represents a particular state, when his dying protagonist asked someone to name the stars. Actually, from the first the stars represented the new national constellation collectively, not singly.

See also stars, 7/22.

---

10 OCTOBER 1881

Darwin's Orchestra

Early in 1881, Charles Darwin took a new manuscript to his loyal publisher, John Murray of London. "Here is a work," he said, "which has occupied me for many years. I fear the subject will not interest the public, but will you publish it for me?"

The Formation of Vegetable Mould, through the Action of Worms, with Some Observations on their Habits was published on October 10, 1881. Although not a topic calculated to grab the Victorian reading public by their starched collars, within three years the book had sold 8,500 copies. Darwin was in his seventies, and, as usual, in poor health. He knew this might be his last book. (He died six months later.) Rather than a weighty summation of his life and thought, it is the last chapter in a lifelong habit of pursuing whatever interested him.

The ecological and evolutionary effects of earthworms had fascinated Darwin for decades. In 1837 his uncle Josiah Wedgwood, founder of the pottery dynasty and the man who persuaded Robert Darwin to allow his son to travel on the *Beagle,* showed young Charles objects found buried in his yard that had formerly been upon the surface. A few months later Darwin wrote his first paper on earthworms as agents in the formation of "vegetable mould" (topsoil).

Darwin studied the burial rates of fallen sarsen at Stonehenge, the floor of an excavated Roman villa, even an incrementally marked "Wormstone" in his own yard. Worms lived in pots in his study. He held red-hot pokers near them and poured water into the soil. He and his family even subjected them to various noises. On one memorable occasion, son Francis played a bassoon, grandson Bernard blew a whistle, and wife Emma played the piano. The audience barely reacted, but Darwin's little orchestra is remembered as one of the more amusing experiments in the history of science.

The study of earthworms combined Darwin's interests in biology and geology, and the very nature of the observations required his specialty: patient observation and experiment over many years. Soon after he and Emma settled at Down House, he had a layer of chalk "laid on the land." After twenty-nine years a trench was dug and examined, and layers of chalk were found beneath the soil at regular depths. As Darwin observed, the worms and turf were indeed "in close partnership." Like his early work on coral reefs, the earthworm inquiry studied the action of organic upon inorganic. The point of this research was the same as that on evolution: the implications of incremental changes over a long period of time.

Few naturalists had considered the cumulative effects of the earth's industrious earthworms. But as one reviewer observed, Darwin rehabilitated their reputation. He discovered that earthworms spend most of their time swallowing. Much of the earth passes through their intricate guts. They grind rocks ever smaller. Their castings glue crumbs together and nurture vegetation. Darwin's last book demonstrated the ecological "utility" of earthworms so successfully that one reader wrote asking if she could still kill snails in her garden, or were they "as useful as worms?"

This 1881 cartoon of a childlike Darwin appeared in the British humor magazine Punch. *The spine of the book slyly refers to the 1521 church ruling, or* diet, *at Worms, Germany, which led to declaring Protestant Martin Luther a heretic.*

---

11 OCTOBER 1492

A Mysterious Light

The sailors accompanying Christopher Columbus on his first voyage to what would come to be called a New World announced on several occasions that they had seen land. Each time was a false alarm. The first "sighting" was late in September. On that day, the three little ships were tossing about in the mid-Atlantic, so we know that the man was mistaken. Again, early in October, only three days before the fateful landfall, sailors aboard the *Niña* were so certain that they had glimpsed land that they fired a signal gun and ran up a flag. Apparently they, too, were mistaken.

The most interesting false alarm, however, came at roughly 10:00 P.M. on October 11, 1492, the day before the actual landfall. Columbus was pacing the quarterdeck, peering as usual into the darkness ahead of the *Santa Maria.* Suddenly he thought he saw a light, as he described it in his journal, like "the flame of a small candle alternately raised and lowered." Columbus called to some of his men. Pedro Gutiérrez thought he could discern the light. Rodrigo Sánchez could not, but that didn't overrule the sighting, because as Columbus noted, Sánchez "was not in a position where he could see anything." Then Pedro Yzquierdo cried, "A light! Land!" The captain's page boy replied haughtily, "My master has already seen it," and Columbus himself couldn't resist mentioning that he had pointed out the light quite some time before. Soon they could no longer see it. Four hours later they sighted land, and this time there was no question that it was real.

What, many historians have asked, was the source of that mysterious light? Some have suggested that Columbus glimpsed a campfire or torches on a beach. However, based upon the time of actual landfall, the ships' recorded speed indicates that at 10:00 P.M. they must have been about thirty-five miles offshore. Even the powerful 170-foot-high lighthouse now on San Salvador isn't visible from thirty-five miles out to sea. Some writers have suggested that Columbus saw a light from a boat carrying fishermen. However, the likelihood of natives fishing that far from land, in those deep waters, during a gale, is slight to say the least.

In 1935, a British biologist named L. R. Crawshay suggested another alternative explanation. His paper, "Possible Bearing of a Luminous Syllid on the Question of the Landfall of Columbus," appeared in the October 5 issue of the scientific journal *Nature.* Crawshay had recently returned to England from government work in the Bahamas. He had seen a strange creature there, and as he contemplated its life cycle he thought of Columbus's mysterious light. He thought what the captain might have seen that night was the luminous mating display of the Atlantic fireworm *Odontosyllis.* It is a genus of marine annelids (segmented worms) in the family Syllidae, many of which are phosphorescent.

Several characteristics of the display fit the circumstances of Columbus's sighting. Although the illumination doesn't occur throughout the year, Crawshay saw it several times in October. In the species he observed, the display always occurred close to the moon's last quarter, and on October 11 the moon's last quarter was one day away. Furthermore, "the period of illumination is always very brief, usually not exceeding 5–10 minutes from first to last. . . ."

There are objections to Crawshay's thesis. For one thing, *Odontosyllis* performs its mating display in relatively shallow water probably no more than a few fathoms deep. Historians nominate a number of locations for the sight of Columbus's first landfall, and their speculative charts only include one possible area where shallow water extends far enough to offer likely fireworm mating grounds. It would require that Columbus had sailed near another island and missed it in the dark, which is certainly not impossible.

Of course, Columbus was never certain that he saw an actual light. Perhaps he decided it was a sign from the God who had given him this great mission in life, and with whom he claimed to be in constant contact. Some historians have decided that the simpest explanation is most likely. Even in mariners who are not exhausted, who haven't been resisting mutinies, and who aren't desperate to find land soon, optical illusions are not uncommon.

"Espanola Is a Marvel"

Near the end of *The Great Gatsby,* F. Scott Fitzgerald imagined that "for a transitory enchanted moment man must have held his breath in the presence of this continent, compelled into an aesthetic contemplation he neither understood nor desired, face to face for the last time in history with something commensurate to his capacity for wonder." Fitzgerald was certainly correct about the magnitude of the discovery. Visible even through the greed and cruelty of the early explorers are expressions of that sort of wonder. "New World" wasn't a casual phrase.

There were many opportunities for a first exposure to the splendors of the Americas. Asians migrated across the Bering Strait during the ice ages and gradually scattered across two continents that had never before known human beings. Norse mariners were exploring the northern islands by the year 1000. Other adventurers may have successfully crossed the Atlantic or Pacific. However, the European arrival in the New World is considered to have begun with the arrival of Christopher Columbus, and for that event we know the precise date. On October 12, 1492, at about 2:00 A.M., he and his men first glimpsed land.

Columbus himself raved about the lands he had discovered in the Caribbean, in a letter he wrote a few months later to his sponsors, the king and queen of Spain. His tone was akin to what Fitzgerald must have had in mind.

> This island and all the others are very fertile to a limitless degree, and this island is extremely so. In it there are many harbours on the coast of the sea, beyond comparison with others which I know in Christendom, and many rivers, good and large, which is marvelous. Its lands are high, and there are in it very many sierras and very lofty mountains, beyond comparison with the island of Teneriffe. All are most beautiful, of a thousand shapes, and all are accessible and filled with trees of a thousand kinds and tall, and they seem to touch the sky. . . . The harbours of the sea here are such as cannot be believed to exist unless they have been seen, and so with the rivers, many and great, and good waters, the majority of which contain gold.

A fanciful, John-Wayne-storming-the-beaches reconstruction of Columbus's landing on Guanahani in the Bahamas.

He summed up his feelings in a single sentence: "Espanola is a marvel." In the same letter, he described the friendliness and generosity of the people they met. His response, however, was decidedly not appreciative wonder. He immediately took several prisoner and kept them with him as translators and guides. The treatment of the natives foreshadows the attitude toward other living things. Columbus declared that God's blessing had made the expedition such a success for the glory of the king and queen, and that everyone in Europe should celebrate "the turning of so many peoples to our holy faith, and afterwards for temporal benefits, for not only Spain but all Christians will have hence refreshment and gain."

Columbus was already planning that right on the heels of the conversion of the natives would come the exploitation of them for the temporal benefits of Europeans. The land itself would not even have the interlude of a conversion. Perhaps F. Scott Fitzgerald's vision should be tempered with a remark by Samuel Johnson, who wrote to a correspondent in 1773, "I do not much wish well to discoveries, for I am always afraid they will end in conquest and robbery."

For more about Columbus, see also 2/29, 10/11, and 11/6.

---

13 OCTOBER A.D. 54

The Death of Claudius I

After the assassination of his nephew Caligula, in A.D. 41, Tiberius Claudius Drusus Nero Germanicus was found hiding in the palace by the Praetorian Guard and proclaimed emperor of Rome. We remember him as Claudius I. Only his reputation for weak-mindedness saved him from the fate of Caligula, and his generosity to the troops that spared him began a practice that soon got out of hand. Apparently Claudius was not a model ruler.

In the year 48, persuaded by advisers, Claudius married his fourth wife, his niece Agrippina. A year or so later Claudius adopted her thirteen-year-old son, Nero. Agrippina persuaded Claudius to wed Nero to his own daughter Octavia, thus promoting Agrippina's son to the line of succession ahead of his own son Britannicus. It was Claudius's undoing. Soon he repented the adoption, and, urging Britannicus to "grow up quickly," he took steps toward restoring his own son. But it was too late. On October 13, A.D. 54, Claudius was poisoned. He was sixty-three.

Most historians think Agrippina murdered Claudius. In his classic history *The Twelve Caesars,* the Roman biographer Suetonius, who was born only fifteen years after Claudius's death, expressed the confusion that already surrounded the events of the emperor's last night.

> Some say that the eunuch Halotus, his official taster, administered the drug while he was dining with the priest of Jupiter in the Citadel; others, that Agrippina did so herself at a family banquet, poisoning a dish of mushrooms, his favorite food. . . . According to many of my informants, he lost his power of speech, suffered frightful pain all night long, and died shortly before dawn. A variant version is that he fell into a coma but vomited up the entire contents of his stomach and was then poisoned a second time. . . .

Seutonius added the telling detail, "Claudius's death was not revealed until all arrangements had been completed to secure Nero's succession."

Opinions vary as much about the poison as about the poisoner. One mycologist proposes that Claudius was merely eating the harmless mushroom *Amanita caesarea*, and that Agrippina or Nero doctored it. Actually, Agrippina would not have had to poison her husband's favorite food. She could have replaced it with a similar mushroom. The deadly *Amanita phalloides*, for example, closely resembles the innocuous favorite *Boletus edulis*. Both were widespread in Italy at the time, and it was not uncommon for mushroom gatherers to confuse the two—with fatal results. Many commoners died of mushroom poisoning, but, of course, their deaths are not so well documented as those of rulers. But Claudius's death was no accident. It seems unlikely that his attendants would accidentally serve food of questionable edibility.

Several scholars agree that *A. phalloides*, the notorious "death cap," seems a likely culprit. Usually its effects appear within 10–30 hours after ingestion, although shorter and longer periods have been recorded. It attacks the liver, causing blood sugar levels to plummet, and also affects the heart and kidneys. Violent vomiting is followed by diarrhea and hemorrhaging. Then there is a round of dehydration and profuse sweating. The face turns blue and the body becomes cold. If the story that Claudius appeared to rally is true, he would not have had to be poisoned again. A short-lived false recovery is a common phase of mushroom poisoning, usually followed by coma and death.

Claudius's death did not leave Agrippina free of problems. Years later, in a reversal of fortune worthy of Sophocles, Nero sent soldiers to assassinate his mother. When Agrippina saw them she knew she was doomed. Legend claims that she bared her abdomen and uttered some of the most powerful last words on record: "Smite my womb."

---

14 OCTOBER 1899

Bound for the Moon

Voyages to the Moon are a common theme in literature. The two earliest surviving accounts are both by the great satirist Lucian, who lived in the second century. In his *True History*, a whirlwind blows fifty ship passengers to the moon. There are no women there; the men bear children in their thighs, sweat honey, and battle the sun people for colonization of Venus. In Lucian's *Icaromenippus*, Menippus (only one of many caricatures of the real Menippus, a third-century-B.C. Cynic philosopher) wants to fly to the Moon. He imitates the legendary Icarus by donning wings, one of an eagle and one of a vulture, "the only kinds equal to a man's weight." Because the vulture is lower in the mythological hierarchy, Menippus holds its wing in his left hand. It tires first, forcing the flier to bank leftward as he alights on the Moon.

Fifteen centuries later, the same Johannes Kepler who formulated the famous laws of planetary motion also wrote a science fiction story, *Somnium* ("Dream"). Although his hero, Duracotus, journeys to the Moon with supernatural rather than technological assistance, Kepler astutely envisioned side effects of space travel. Duracotus has to be drugged so his limbs won't be torn off when he's catapulted moonward. Kepler also understood the need to aim a vehicle not at the Moon's location at launch time but at where it would be when the traveler arrived. He even foresaw the dangers of unfiltered solar rays. But his advice for enduring airlessness was less than inspired: "One has to hold a wet sponge over nose and mouth."

The protagonist of Francis Godwin's *Man in the Moone* (1638) is carried there by birds. In the spirit of his age, Oliver Cromwell's brother-in-law, John Wilkins, insisted in his *Discovery of a World in the Moone* that England must colonize Earth's satellite before some other nation did. Their contemporary John Donne simply thought the Moon a good place to send the Jesuits.

Evaporation was the vehicle in a story by Cyrano de Bergerac. His hero strapped bottles of dew to his legs, and when it was drawn up by the sun, so was he. In Edgar Allan Poe's "The Unparalleled Adventures of One Hans Phaall" (1835), Hans escapes his creditors by inflating a balloon with a buoyant gas he invented and floating to the Moon. Jules Verne's *From the Earth to the Moon* (1865) finds several Americans in an air-conditioned, artificially lit capsule fired from a cannon in, yes, Florida. It achieves the necessary escape velocity of seven miles per second, loops around Earth, and heads for the Moon. Verne's interest was in the trip as much as the destination; his characters circle the Moon and return to Earth.

In 1901 H. G. Wells published *The First Men in the Moon,* featuring his daft scientist, Mr. Cavor. "The object of Mr. Cavor's search was a substance that should be 'opaque' to all forms of radiant energy," including gravity. He succeeded on October 14, 1899. Then, in a capsule treated with "cavorite," he and the narrator flew to the Moon—and into the century that would see real lunar visits.

---

15 OCTOBER

The Hound of the Baskervilles

When his doctor prescribed a holiday, a tired Arthur Conan Doyle retired to the Regency resort of Cromer in Norfolk to play golf with his friend Fletcher Robinson, a journalist and folklorist. One wild afternoon, as they sat with cigars by the fire and listened to the wind howling in from the sea, Robinson told Conan Doyle a story. An old family was supposedly still haunted by a ghostly hound that prowled Dartmoor. Before he left Cromer, Conan Doyle wrote to his mother about his plan to write a "real Creeper" entitled *The Hound of the Baskervilles.* Only later did he incorporate Sherlock Holmes into the story.

In a letter to Holmes headed "Baskerville Hall, October 15th," Watson describes the baying of the spectral Hound of the Baskervilles. "It came with the wind through the silence of the night, a long, deep mutter, then a rising howl, and then the sad moan in which it died away. Again and again it sounded, the whole air throbbing with it, strident, wild, and menacing."

Watson is in the wilds of Dartmoor without Holmes because of the concerns of Holmes's client, Sir Henry, heir to the Baskerville fortune. Two-and-a-half centuries earlier, black-hearted Hugo Baskerville died the death he deserved: "Standing over Hugo, and plucking at his throat, there stood a foul thing, a great, black beast, shaped like a hound, yet larger than any hound that ever mortal eye has rested upon." Recently the latest heir died of fright on the moor, with huge dog tracks nearby. Sir Henry's friend James Mortimer hires Sherlock Holmes to investigate the death.

The first installment of Conan Doyle's new novel, in the August 1901 *Strand,* ended with Mortimer's exclamation, "Mr. Holmes, they were the footprints of a gigantic hound!" That was the power of suggestion speaking. Paw-print size would limit the nominees, of course, as would indications of fur long enough to show in a track, but not even Holmes could deduce a dog's breed from its prints.

Earlier, Holmes examines the teeth marks on Mortimer's stick and describes him as "the possessor of a favourite dog, which I should describe roughly as being larger than a terrier and smaller than a mastiff." That much is not unreasonable. Then, "It may have been—" he begins, and adds as he sees it in the street, "yes, by Jove, it *is* a curly-haired spaniel!" Later, he finds the skeleton of a dog and at a glance declares it to be that of Mortimer's pet. Holmes prides himself on knowing anything that might be useful in his field, but even had he studied the comparative anatomy of dogs he couldn't perform that particular feat, especially since there is no such dog as a curly-haired spaniel.

A descendant of Conan Doyle's spectral hound haunts one of the children's books of Phyllis A. Whitney. In *The Mystery of the Crimson Ghost* (1969), twelve-year-old Janey Oakes finds her summer vacation interrupted by a dog that, surrounded by a crimson glow, bays in the ruins of a burned hotel. Of course, in accordance with the rules of mystery novels, Whitney's dog has a natural explanation— as does the allegedly supernatural Hound of the Baskervilles.

See also the speckled band, 4/6; and "Silver Blaze," 9/25.

"The Only Common Ground of Communication"

Understandably, fiction writers are preoccupied with the subtleties of speech. In his note at the beginning of *Huckleberry Finn,* Mark Twain defended the distinctions between the dialects of his characters. "I make this explanation," he added, "for the reason that without it many readers would suppose that all these characters were trying to talk alike and not succeeding." Surprisingly, many authors attend to the language of their animal characters with a comparable sociological precision.

In fiction, the language spoken by animal characters is human, but like any other language it reflects the character's background. In Margery Sharp's children's books about the heroic rescue efforts of the Mouse Prisoners' Aid Society, beginning with *The Rescuers* in 1959, the well-spoken ways of the aristocratic white mouse Miss Bianca are part of her class consciousness. When she excuses the bad manners of field mice because they haven't seen better examples, one of them exclaims, "The lady says we never learnt no manners! Hands up who goes to dancing class!" Father, the patriarch of the Rabbit clan in Robert Lawson's *Rabbit Hill,* is a "Southern gentleman." For some reason he migrated northward. Long since settled in Connecticut, Father thinks longingly of the glories of his youth: "I would really relish an occasional chase with a couple of highly bred hounds. Why down in the Bluegrass Country where I was born—" At which point his long-suffering friends usually depart.

The more "realistic" the behavior of characters—the less fantastic their adventures—the more fragile the spell in their use of human language and behavior. In *Charlotte's Web,* the animal characters are humorous and fanciful but not out of character as animals, with the truly fantastic restricted to their ability to understand human language—and even, in the case of Charlotte herself, to read and write it. Rudyard Kipling, in *Thy Servant, a Dog,* uses a surreal patois, a kind of canine baby-talk, to convey the mental processes of his narrator, an Aberdeen terrier: "There is walk-in-Park-on-lead. There is off-lead-when-we-come-to-the-grass." Anna Sewell's fictional horses in *Black Beauty* convince the reader primarily because they possess no unequine abilities other than the (naturally Victorian) sensibility apparent in their humanlike thought and language.

Equally convincing are the canine protagonists of Richard Adams's 1977 novel *The Plague Dogs.* Outdoing Twain, Adams even appended a glossary; occasionally the dialogue is as incomprehensible to those born outside the British Isles as the more vernacular asides of Robert Burns. Burns, in fact, wrote a

In Rudyard Kipling's Thy Servant, a Dog, *the narrator Boots communicates his canine thoughts in a slangy baby-talk.*

poem about two such canine adventurers, "The Twa Dogs." However, Adams's Snitter and Rowf undergo far worse troubles than Burns's Caesar and Luathe. With only their own canine wits, they escape on October 16 from an animal research facility where they have been routinely tortured in the name of science. Soon the two dogs encounter a tod (a fox) who offers to teach them the ways of the wild if they will join him. He speaks in northern England's Geordie dialect: "Noo yer reet, hinny. . . . Crrunshin bait's th' bonniest." Rowf complains to Snitter, "I can't understand a word he says."

In such realistically constructed tales, no character could carry off the self-awareness possessed by the narrator of O. Henry's story "Memoirs of a Yellow Dog." A slangy lower-class urbanite from the first sentence, he is nonetheless aware of the problem of language: "I don't suppose it will knock any of you people off your perch to read a contribution from an animal. . . . But you needn't look for any stuck-up literature in my piece. . . . A yellow dog that's spent most of his life in a cheap New York flat . . . mustn't be expected to perform any tricks with the art of speech." However self-deprecating he may be, he astutely observes that "humans were denied the speech of animals. The only common ground of communication . . . is in fiction."

The Potato Famine

Elizabeth Smith was born in Edinburgh three years before the end of the eighteenth century and lived until 1885. In India she met and married an Irishman, and returned to settle down with him in County Wicklow. As a record for her daughter, she kept a diary of most of the rest of her life. Those pages portray a kind, intelligent woman who observed the alien culture around her with a mixture of sympathy and exasperation. Smith saw herself as an outsider in Irish society, but in time she shared a catastrophe with her neighbors.

In 1847, Smith wrote in her diary:

> *17 October.* . . . People are oppressed by this frightful amount of bankruptcies, almost everyone either themselves or their friends affected by some of these numerous failures. . . . The destitution is expected to be wider spread than last year for the very poor will be very nearly as ill off while the classes above which then relieved them are all this year in serious difficulties. . . . The Queen has ordered the begging box to go round all the English churches for us!

Elizabeth Smith was living through what the Irish would later call the Hungry Forties. It was the result of the potato blight, which struck the most important agricultural crop in Ireland. At first it appeared to be simply a crop failure, probably no worse than a couple in the 1830s. But it didn't take long to bring Ireland to its knees. Less than a year before, Smith had written the first ominous note in her diary: "Hal has just brought in two damaged potatoes. . . ."

Overpopulated and barely industrialized at all, Ireland was used to famine. Other disasters had struck the potato crop in the past—dry rot, mold, and an aphid-transmitted disease called "curl." However, none of those compared with "blight," the common name for the fungus *Phytophthora infestans*. It appeared in August of 1845 in every country in Europe, presumably from the United States, where it was reported two years earlier.

Potatoes are native to the high plateaus of the Andes, where the Incas cultivated them for hundreds of years before European invaders arrived. There is some question about how the plant migrated to Europe, to play such a critical role in the fortunes of Ireland. A likely scenario involves England's favorite sea dog, the pirate Francis Drake. In 1586, Drake tried to overtake the annual shipment of treasure leaving Colombia on its way to Spain. He missed it by only a few hours. When he returned to England, he carried in the ship's hold something considerably more important than the gold he had sought—the potato.

Solanum tuberosum is a member of the nightshade family, Solanaceae, a diverse clan of shrubs, herbs, and trees that includes tomatoes, eggplant, and tobacco. Various family members produce drugs, including belladonna. Even potato sprouts left in sunlight manufacture a poisonous alkaloid called solanine. No matter how humans and other animals may regard the potato, in nature's view it, like all tubers, is a storehouse in which the plant can overwinter its energy stores safely underground.

Because humans, who are themselves unable to synthesize nutrients from the soil, also covet that stored energy, the potato—like so many plants, including cotton and sugar—has had a dramatic effect on history. Not long after its introduction to Europe, the impoverished people of Ireland had developed it into a staple of their diet. It is a versatile and low-maintenance crop. Without it, after the ravages of Cromwell and other English invaders, the Irish peasantry would have starved. Historians have estimated that over half of Ireland's population depended upon the potato for as much as three-quarters of its nutritional needs.

The blight returned on occasion, but the peak was that first year, 1845–46. Estimates of the deaths resulting from famine and its attendant diseases reach 1 million. As a consequence, countless Irish peasants emigrated from their home country to the United States. Like all such migrations, it affected the history of both the new country and the one left behind. One historian has remarked that John F. Kennedy was born in the United States rather than Ireland because of the potato famine.

---

18 October 1980

"All Kernel and No Husk"

The American naturalist Edwin Way Teale was born Edwin Alfred Teale in Joliet, Illinois, in the last year of the nineteenth century. He grew up exploring the Indiana Dunes, studied at Columbia, and went to New York City to write about nature for magazines. In time he wrote books as well, and became one of the most popular and influential naturalists of the twentieth century.

Finally, after years of working in the city, Teale escaped to his beloved countryside in the summer of 1959, when he and his wife, Nellie, found a farm of roughly a hundred acres near Hampton, Connecticut. They named it Trail Wood, and Teale called their lives there "all kernel and no husk." When a lost visitor from the city stopped to ask directions, she looked around at the lack of farm equipment and the variety of wild animals and asked, "What kind of farm is this?" Before they could answer, she said, "Oh, I get it. It's a fun thing." It was indeed. Teale recounted their adventures in finding and exploring this long-awaited paradise in his 1974 book *A Naturalist Buys an Old Farm*. The Teales bequeathed Trail Wood to the Audubon Society as a nature sanctuary.

Four volumes following the progress of the American seasons from coast to coast won Teale the first Pulitzer Prize ever awarded to a "nature book." Eventually he also won the highest honor in his field—the Burroughs Medal, named for American naturalist John Burroughs. In the late 1960s, Teale and Nellie journeyed across the Atlantic to chronicle the progress of the English spring. For Teale it was a pilgrimage to the sacred haunts of his heroes, from Gilbert White's Selborne to Darwin's home in Downe.

Two of Teale's many books are arranged as books of days, compilations of his observations of nature, most of them taken from his journals. *Circle of the Seasons: The Journal of a Naturalist's Year* came out in 1953. In his entry in that book for October 18, Teale described several encounters with one of his favorite insects, the praying mantis. Unlike most insects, the mantis can turn its head. That talent combined with its reverent posture gives it what most insects conspicuously lack—a personality. Teale described one of these creatures apparently hypnotized by a swinging leaf, turning its head right and left as if watching a tennis match. Recently he had seen a courageous mantis fighting off a blue jay, striking at it, turning to fend off a succession of attacks, until the bird admitted defeat and flew away.

A quarter century after *Circle of the Seasons,* Teale published another book of days, this one entitled *A Walk through the Year.* Consisting of excerpts from his Trail Wood journals, these essays are longer than the first book's and, if possible, even more delighted with the natural world. It was Teale's last book. Its entry for October 18 begins with a quotation from the Swiss philosopher Henri Amiel: "One feels the hours gently slipping by, and time, instead of flying, seems to hover." Teale admitted that in May he considered spring the finest time of year, but every new October reminded him that autumn days were best. "In them, as in the days of spring, there is beauty, sunshine, genial conditions. But here there is an added quality, a sense of maturity, of having experienced more, a greater sense of knowing, a sense of ripening, of fulfillment, of acceptance." Teale enjoyed the autumn of his life as he enjoyed the autumn of every year. He died on October 18, 1980.

---

19 OCTOBER 1752

"The Regions of Thunder"

With its commitment to reasoned scrutiny of nature and human institutions, the Enlightenment was a time of experimentation—social, philosophical, and scientific. Some natural philosophers, as scientists were known, began to think of themselves as experimental philosophers. Prominent among them was Benjamin Franklin. Like Thomas Jefferson, Franklin was a man of many talents. Social reformer, humorist, politician, aphorist, inventor, he was also endlessly curious about the natural world. His letters prove that no aspect of nature was too large or too small to intrigue him. He studied marsh gas and the Gulf Stream, waterspouts and the aurora borealis, the habits of turkeys and the nature of lightning.

Until Franklin's time, lightning remained as mysterious as it had been in the ancient world, when every religion had a storm deity and every storm deity had lightning as weapon or attendant. Franklin was not the first to suggest that lightning was a form of electricity; he was merely the first to devise an experiment that would prove it. Several of his most important experiments concerned the nature of electricity. He coined such terms as *capacitor, discharge, conductor,* and even the electrical meanings of *positive* and *negative.* He shocked himself while trying to kill a holiday turkey with electricity and knocked unconscious six men who were naive enough to participate in one of his experiments. But his most famous experiment involved a kite, a key, and a thunderstorm.

In the *Pennsylvania Gazette* on October 19, 1752, Franklin published a murky account of his kite experiment. Curiously, he didn't identify himself as the person who performed it, and not until 1788 did he claim credit. Europeans had proven Franklin's thesis in a similar experiment weeks before, but eighteenth-century communication was slow, and it is unlikely that Franklin knew that. Familiar as he was with electricity's deadly attributes and the destructive force of lightning, it is surprising that Franklin invited it to strike him. Several people have died imitating him.

Some historians suspect that the whole event may be apocryphal. However, Franklin's English friend Joseph Priestley provided a detailed contemporary account of the experiment in his 1767 *History and Present State of Electricity.* According to him, Franklin at first waited for a church steeple to be completed, then realized that with a kite "he could have a readier and better access to the regions of thunder than by any spire whatever." About the time he was going to give up, Franklin noticed that threads on the string were standing out away from each other. He touched his knuckle to the key and felt a spark. As Priestly said, "When the rain had wet the string, he collected electric fire copiously."

The French statesman Turgot wrote an inscription for a bust of Franklin that sounds worthy of Zeus: "He snatched the lightning shaft from heaven, and the sceptre from tyrants." Byron employed similar Olympian images for his apotheosis of Franklin in "The Age of Bronze":

> *And stoic Franklin's energetic shade,*
> *Robed in the lightnings which his hand allayed. . . .*

---

20 OCTOBER 1967

Bigfoot: The Motion Picture

Roger Patterson told the story many times. He said that he and his friend Bob Gimlin were riding on horseback up Bluff Creek Valley in northern California on October 20, 1967. Armed with rifles and a movie camera, they were looking for Bigfoot, also called Sasquatch. Patterson claimed that they found one.

Patterson's years in rodeo didn't prevent his horse from throwing him at first sight of the beast. But he had his movie camera handy. The initial frames of the well-known film are jostled, as if shot, as Patterson claimed, while running over rough terrain. Gimlin hung back with his .30/.06 rifle at the ready. But the creature, as usual in Bigfoot reports, showed no sign of aggression when it saw them. At first she (her gender was apparent in the large hairy breasts) was striding along the far side of the streambed, swinging her arms widely. Then, as Patterson approached, she turned to the camera. Her shoulders and chest were massive, she had little waist or neck, and her entire body was extravagantly furred. Her face was bare but dark, her palms and soles lighter. From the moment she looked at him, Patterson didn't move. Finally, turning her back on the two men, the creature disappeared into the forest.

Life magazine was interested in stills from Patterson's film until the American Museum of Natural History pronounced it fake. Finally, the photographs showed up in the men's magazine *Argosy.* Over the next few years, innumerable scientists viewed the film. Biologist and scholar John Napier viewed it at least eighteen times and distilled his and other scientists' analyses. He concluded that, although he "couldn't see the zipper," the creature was a human in a Bigfoot suit.

Its stride seemed very like that of a human male. The broad steps and arm swinging, Napier suggested, might be the result of the man's attempt to lengthen his stride to more closely approximate that of the usual Bigfoot reports. If so, it was unsuccessful. More than one scientist said the stride simply didn't match the purported height, and concluded that the tracks or the film or both were faked. Judging from its movements, the creature's center of gravity seemed to be that of a modern human male, perhaps slightly above normal height. One expert on the human gait declared of the creature, "Its walk is human in type and, possibly, identical with that of modern man."

There were other points. For one thing, no matter how hirsute the rest of a mammal's body, breasts themselves are not hairy. Heavy legs rose to prominent buttocks, a feature unique to humans. Also, the top of the creature's head was somewhat conical. In gorillas and orangutans, that skull shape forms an anchor for the powerful jaw muscles required to chew the heavy roughage of their diets. However, a side effect of that diet is a potbelly large enough to hold all that material during its slow digestion. Bigfoot showed no sign of a potbelly. Individually, these points are not conclusive, but taken together they add up to a strong refutation of Patterson's claims.

---

21 OCTOBER 1955

A Poet Names a Car

The value of symbolism hasn't been lost on automobile manufacturers. They outgrew such meaningless appellations as "Model T" and "Model A" early in their evolution. Many of their most successful models have been named after animals or other aspects of nature, with hood ornaments and trunk logos suspiciously reminiscent of the animal carvings that once graced the prows of ships.

The Volkswagen ("people's car"), which Hitler promoted as Germany's answer to Ford's Model T, was elsewhere nicknamed the Beetle, and later even the Bug. When Volkswagen wanted to convey a sense of maneuverability and unpretentiousness for a new make of car, they chose the name Rabbit. Early animal models included the Hudson Wasp and Hornet. Nowadays whole orders of animalian automobiles race past each other every day. There are Jaguars and Cougars, Mustangs and Pintos, Eagles and Falcons. A Bobcat chases a Python. An Impala outruns a Viper. Mythical animals zoom by—the Firebird, the Thunderbird. Other aspects of nature appear, including the desert wind Sirocco and its cousin the Zephyr, and such astronomical phenomena as Nova, Eclipse, and Galaxy.

In the 1950s, fully aware of what's in a name, the Ford Motor Company appealed to an expert in symbolism, the animal-obsessed U.S. poet Marianne Moore. "Dear Miss Moore: This is a morning we find ourselves with a problem which, strangely enough, is more in the field of words and the fragile meaning of words than in car-making. . . ." Ford needed a name for a new series of automobiles. They didn't want a mere label; they wanted a symbol of a highly evolved creature, fleet and elegant. The author of the letter explained that in their search Ford already had amassed some 300 hopelessly pedestrian nominees, and would offer generous remuneration should Miss Moore rescue them.

On October 21, 1955, Moore replied that she was flattered to be consulted on such a "high matter." She promised she would try, and, of course, being Marianne Moore, she derived many of her ideas from nature. The Silver Sword was her first suggestion, named after a plant native to Tibet and Hawaii. Then, although she imagined it difficult to top Ford's own admirable Thunderbird, she proposed a bird series, perhaps combining bird names with "Hurricane," for such names as the "Hurricane aquila" (Latin for eagle) and the "Hurricane accipiter" (Latin for bird of prey). She even suggested one in the series named after the swallow genus *Hirundo,* the "Hurricane Hirundo."

One can easily imagine Ford's Marketing Department despairing as the list of suggested names poured in from Moore. She came up with The Intelligent Whale; the Arcenciel, from *Arc-en-Ciel,* French for "rainbow"; the Thunder Crester; Aeroterre; Chaparral; the Mongoose Civique. She sent a note proposing the Turcotingo, a name derived from the turquoise cotinga, a South American finch. Her final suggestion is in a brief note: "May I submit UTOPIAN TURTLETOP? Do not trouble to answer unless you like it." Ford gallantly replied with two dozen roses, accompanied by the inscription, "To our favorite Turtletopper." However, they did not choose a Moore-inspired symbol. In time, Ford informed Moore of the final choice of name for their new car—the Edsel.

---

22 OCTOBER 1837

"Do You Keep a Journal?"

In retrospect, one can see David Henry Thoreau and his fellow Concord native Ralph Waldo Emerson moving toward each other in 1837. The Concord Public Library records show that Thoreau checked out Emerson's recent Transcendentalist manifesto *Nature* in April and again in June. In late August, Emerson gave the Phi Beta Kappa commencement address at Thoreau's graduation from Harvard. Within a month, Thoreau had acquired a teaching position in the Concord Public Schools and left it because he refused to cane his students. At about that time, he reversed the order of his given names to Henry David. He was twenty, and the already distinguished Emerson was only thirty-four.

Later, Emerson said that it was in the fall of 1837 that he and Thoreau began to become friends. One day during that season, Thoreau picked up a volume of lined manuscript paper, turned to the front page, dipped his pen in an inkwell, and wrote in a flowing and elegant script:

Oct 22nd 1837

"What are you doing now?" he asked.
"Do you keep a journal?"
So I make my first entry today.

And below that Thoreau inscribed his mantra: "Solitude."

It was the beginning of one of the most famous diaries in history. Samuel Pepys, Dorothy Wordsworth, James Boswell—all kept vivid, anecdotal accounts of their lives, but Thoreau did more. He made of his journal a storehouse for the future and a place for wrestling with angels. It was also his commonplace book, in which he jotted quotations from poets, including his lifelong favorites Goethe and Virgil. In time, Thoreau began to realize the journal's own worth, and sometimes wrote preliminary drafts of the entries, polishing and refining them until they best represented his thought and experience. He reminded himself, "Improve every opportunity to express yourself in writing, as if it were your last."

Emerson's influence on Thoreau didn't end with the suggestion that the young man keep a journal. It was Emerson who later allowed Thoreau to construct a cabin on his land beside Walden Pond. By early 1838, the two were taking long rambling walks through the fields and woods of Concord. Sixteen miles west of Boston, a four-hour stage ride, Concord was a thriving town with a population of some 2,000. From this early age, in the search for his own best way of living, Thoreau was critiquing the lives of those around him. "[E]verything that boy says," Emerson noted, "makes merry with society." Thoreau's merrymaking had a serious intent. He noted in 1856, "Lectured in basement (vestry) of the orthodox church, and I trust helped to undermine it."

Most of the region was pasture or tilled farmland, with woodland relatively scarce. But it didn't seem to matter where Thoreau was. Somehow he always saw the world as if it had just been created. "I wonder that I ever get five miles on my way, the walk is so crowded with events and phenomena. How many questions there are which I have not put to the inhabitants." The day-to-day record of his life allowed Thoreau to observe his own development as a thinker and a lover of life. "We hear and apprehend only what we already half know. . . . Every man thus tracks himself through life in all his hearing and reading and observation and travelling. His observations make a chain." As late as 1851, Thoreau wrote, " 'Says I to myself' should be the motto of my journal."

Thoreau died in 1862, at the age of forty-five. In his lifetime he published only two dozen articles and two books. Neither *Walden* nor *A Week on the Concord and Merrimack River* sold well. He would be surprised to find that his journal has been published in whole and in part several times. Many readers have agreed with his own estimation: "I do not know but thoughts written down thus in a journal might be printed in the same form with greater advantage than if the related ones were brought together in separate essays. They are now allied to life, and are seen by the reader not to be far-fetched."

See also Thoreau and a forest fire, 4/30; and Darwin, 7/23.

---

23 OCTOBER 4004 B.C.

"The Archives of the World"

"Time we may comprehend," Sir Thomas Browne wrote, "'tis but five days elder than ourselves." It was a typical seventeenth-century conviction. If the world had been created only days before humans, its history and ours were one. Thus Christianity had abridged to a few thousand years the cosmic cycles of Hindu

An alternative view of the origin of the world. When it appeared in McClure's Magazine, *the cartoon was captioned: "ZEUS: 'Fore!' "*

and Islamic and Greek conceptions of time. Over the centuries, sharing Browne's assumption, scholars tried to determine exactly how many years had elapsed since God's busy first week.

Eusebius of Caesarea, who chaired the Council of Nicaea that Constantine convened in the year 325 to decide Christian doctrine, calculated that the time between Adam and Abraham was precisely 3,184 years. In the eighth century, the Benedictine monk remembered as the Venerable Bede estimated the date of creation at 3952 B.C., which left the earth a mere toddler, less than 5,000 years old. (He also initiated the practice of designating historical events from Christ's birth, with the phrase *anno Domini,* "in the year of the Lord.") One of Thomas Browne's contemporaries, Archbishop James Ussher of Ireland, went even further. In 1650 he published his *Annals of the Old Testament, Deduced from the First Origin of the World,* in which he declared that "the beginning of time . . . fell on the beginning of the night which preceded the 23rd day of October, in the year . . . 4004 B.C." Within fifty years, Ussher's chronology was appearing in many Bibles, a practice which continued until quite recently, and even now crops up on occasion.

For its time, Ussher's attempt to calculate a chronology addressing all of human history was a respectable intellectual effort. He did not, as detractors claim, merely total up the ages in the "begats." That could have accounted for the span from the Creation to Solomon, but not for the reigns of the kings. Nor would it cover the 400-odd years between the end of the Old Testament and the birth of Christ. Of course, Ussher did start with an assumption long since invalidated by discoveries in geology and biology—that the Bible's Creation tale was historically accurate. And yet even this was no more naive than the medieval devotion to the untested theories of the philosophers of Greece and Rome.

However, as knowledge of the world slowly grew, thinkers were beginning to turn away from the certainties of sacred books and ancient naturalists. "Speak to the earth," Job advised, "and it shall teach thee." Shakespeare wrote of books in the running brooks and sermons in stones. In the eighteenth century, French zoologist Georges-Louis Leclerc, comte de Buffon, summed up a new attitude. It was he who insisted that, just as historians analyze human artifacts, "so in natural history one must dig through the archives of the world, extract ancient relics from the bowels of the earth, [and] gather together their fragments."

Estimates of the age of our planet have varied widely over the last couple of centuries. Hundreds of millions and even billions of years were proposed in the eighteenth century, only to shrink to tens of millions in the nineteenth and return to the former heights in the twentieth. The longer the history of the earth turned out to be, the more time was available for slow evolutionary change, and the less God seemed required to explain away the intricacies of nature. Buffon expressed that idea, too, when he said, "Nature's great workman is time."

See also Noah's Ark, 5/26.

Fer-de-Lance

Rex Stout's immortal detective Nero Wolfe leads an indoor, sedentary life. Although he spends part of every day tending the orchids in his rooftop greenhouse, he seldom encounters animals other than those cooked to perfection by his chef. However, in his first recorded case, he met a creature as formidable as some of his human enemies.

When *Fer-de-Lance* was published on October 24, 1934, Wolfe's interests were all present—beer, literature, gourmet food, and orchids. Already he seldom leaves the old brownstone on West 35th Street for pleasure and never for business. In Chapter One, a client sits in the famous red leather chair and hires Wolfe to find her brother. After Wolfe discovers why a man who died while golfing had snake venom in his veins, the murderer hides the snake in the great detective's desk drawer. Wolfe smashes its head with a couple of his ever-present beer bottles. His intrepid Watson, Archie Goodwin, measures the corpse: six feet, three inches long, and in the middle almost as thick as his wrist. "It was a dirty yellowish brown, and even dead it looked damn mean." Then, at Wolfe's direction, Archie wraps the dead snake in excelsior and mails it to the murderer.

"Fair-duh-lahnss," Archie pronounces laboriously, and Wolfe says, "Too much *n* and not enough nose." He explains, "*Bothrops atrox.* Except for the bushmaster, it is the most dreaded of all vipers."

When Arthur Conan Doyle wanted a snake as a murder weapon in "The Speckled Band," he simply invented one. Rex Stout expended a little more effort. The fer-de-lance is a real snake—as Wolfe said, one of the most poisonous in the world. Found mostly in tropical forests between Brazil and the Yucatán, its clan, which includes the bushmaster, claims credit for most of the dangerous snakebites in the Americas. Its northern cousins include rattlesnakes and copperheads. The common name is French for the iron tip of a lance. *Bothrops* comes from the Greek words for "pit" and "eye"; like the rattlesnake, it's a pit viper. The "pits" are heat sensors that enable the snakes to detect infrared radiation so they can accurately strike at warm-blooded prey in darkness.

Snakes make dramatic murder weapons. Their venom is a complex substance that apparently evolved from saliva. Snakes can't chew their food, and therefore they developed powerful digestive secretions that begin the breakdown of tissue. Finally the saliva reached the level of toxicity. Injected with venom, poisoned tissues prepare to become snake food. Blood vessels weaken, fats and proteins break down. Evolution, with its practically infinite time and resources for Research and Development, has refined venom to the point of overkill. One (fortunately rare) snake's glands contain enough venom to kill a quarter of a million mice. Although the frequency of fatal bites is exaggerated, one of the few snakes genuinely to be feared is the one that Nero Wolfe tackled in his first recorded case.

The Icebergs of
Frederic Church

Frederic Edwin Church was born in Hartford, Connecticut, in 1826, at about the time the Hudson River school of painting was founded. Art historians consider that group of American landscape painters to have had its origin the year before, with Thomas Cole's move to New York City. Church studied with Cole, and joined him and other artists such as Asher B. Durand in trying to express on canvas their visionary, romantic sense of the divine glories of the American landscape, all the power and mystery inherent in the phrase "the New World."

Although he created many works about North and South America and even the Near East, Church is probably best known for two monumental paintings, *Niagara* (1857) and *The Heart of the Andes* (1859). The year he completed the latter, Church embarked on a natural history voyage. Like most of his many travels, this one was motivated as much by his interest in science as his artistic pursuits. One of his heroes was the German explorer and naturalist Alexander von Humboldt. In his 1845 study of the natural world, *Kosmos,* Humboldt had announced that the world needed a new kind of art, one that could express the grandeur of such breathtaking scenery as that of the Amazon and the Andes. For years, Church had been trying to do just that, and his 1859 trip had the same goal.

The first response of earlier observers to the sight of icebergs had often been astonishment, followed by an almost spiritual sense of an alien and hostile environment that was somehow still beautiful. The ultimate result of Church's own encounter was a painting that was destined to occupy a strange place in art history. Almost six feet high and nearly ten feet wide, *The Icebergs,* like many of its predecessors, was painted on a scale appropriate to its subject.

Critics responded with excitement, as in the New York *World* in 1861: ". . . The 'Icebergs' leads us at once to the inner arcana of that mysterious temple which sits forever upon the forehead of the world. We can but stand at the base of that towering cliff of ice, broken into huge crystallizations of form, streaked with mingled tints of azure, emerald and gray, kindling here and there into cold, instense gleams of dazzling luster, and look out along the lazy folds of water towards the white pinnacles, uplifted against the horizon, and confess the picture is above and beyond criticism." And the New York *Knickerbocker* wrote, "None need be told that Church is great—that he is national. Has he not given us his 'Niagara' and his 'Heart of the Andes,' and is he not treating us this summer with his refrigerating 'Iceberg'? How those dazzling mountains of ice freeze into the very soul, awing us with the mystic revelations of another sphere!"

On its 1863 trip to England, *The Icebergs* met with ecstatic proclamations of the wonders of both nature's and Church's art. It was in England that a Mr. Watkins quietly purchased the painting. Church's star faded over the years until his death, and the location of the painting was forgotten. It did not reappear for over a century, when it was found hanging on a wall in Watkins's former home. At that time, it was quickly purchased and brought to the United States. At an auction held by Sotheby's on

October 25, 1979, Lot 34 was *The Icebergs.* The bidding lasted less than four minutes, beginning at $500,000 and advancing by $50,000 increments. *The Icebergs* sold for $2.5 million. At the time, it was the highest price ever paid for a painting in the United States.

---

26 OCTOBER 1984

The Baboon's Heart

In 1871, in *The Descent of Man,* Charles Darwin wrote of the similarities between human beings and their relatives. "It is notorious that man is constructed on the same general type or model as other mammals. All the bones in his skeleton can be compared with corresponding bones in a monkey, bat, or seal. So it is with his muscles, nerves, blood-vessels, and internal viscera." He listed some of the diseases and ailments from which humans and other primates suffer, from cataracts to syphilis, then moved on to behavioral similarities.

Among the apes Darwin studied was the baboon. Like most of its cousins, baboons are famously clever. In South Africa, they have been trained to dig up edible bulbs. In the same country, a disabled railway station attendant trained his pet baboon to operate signal switches on command. Darwin quoted one biologist who claimed that natives of northeastern Africa captured wild baboons by leaving out strong beer, which they drank. Apparently they got happily smashed. "On the following morning they were very cross and dismal; they held their aching heads with both hands, and wore a most pitiable expression; when beer or wine was offered them, they turned away with disgust, but relished the juice of lemons." Allowing for exaggeration, the story still fits with many others about the similar tastes and attitudes of humans and other apes.

"At the Cape of Good Hope," Darwin wrote, "an officer had often plagued a certain baboon, and the animal, seeing him approaching one Sunday for parade, poured water into a hole and hastily made some thick mud, which he skilfully dashed over the officer as he passed by, to the amusement of many bystanders. For long afterward the baboon rejoiced and triumphed whenever he saw his victim." Darwin himself rejoiced in such stories. Revenge, drunkenness, manual dexterity, intelligence—it was beginning to sound familiar.

He dwelled upon the famously humanlike maternal instincts of apes. "One female baboon had so capacious a heart that she not only adopted young monkeys of other species, but stole young dogs and cats, which she continually carried about. . . . an adopted kitten scratched this affectionate baboon, who certainly had a fine intellect, for she was much astonished at being scratched, and immediately examined the kitten's feet, and without more ado bit off the claws." Darwin added in a footnote that a critic disputed that choice anecdote. "Therefore I tried, and found that I could readily seize with my own teeth the sharp little claws of a kitten nearly five weeks old."

One wonders what Darwin would have had to say about a surgical operation that took place 102 years after his death. On October 26, 1984, an American surgeon named Leonard Bailey, at the Loma Linda University Medical Center in California, replaced the malformed heart of a twelve-day-old human infant with the healthy heart of a seven-month-old baboon. The surgery aroused a great deal of controversy about both the ethics of interspecies transplantation and the race to the limelight that might result between physicians with a greater lust for fame than a sense of Hippocratic responsibility. Few thought the child would survive. Not surprisingly, they were correct. With the heart of a distant relative pumping her blood, "Baby Fae" lived a little less than three weeks before her body rejected the transplant.

---

27 October 1858

Pink Flamingos

Theodore Roosevelt was born on October 27, 1858, in New York City. From childhood he enjoyed being outdoors more than any other activity. By the age of nine, he was writing in his diary about the local birds. Thanks to his family's money, he was able in his teens to explore such exotic locales as the banks of the Nile. Roosevelt grew up to be an enthusiastic outdoorsman, and an eloquent writer on nature and conservation. He did not forget these passions when he reached high political office.

Roosevelt served as vice president under William McKinley. Upon McKinley's assassination in September of 1901, he became president. Only a couple of months later, in his first message to the assembled Congress, he said, "The preservation of our forests is an imperative business necessity." In 1905, he arranged the transfer of federally owned forest reserves from the General Land Office, a unit of the Department of the Interior, to the Forest Service, which answered to the Department of Agriculture. Two years later, they were renamed "national forests." He approved the Newlands Reclamation Act. Many later regional resource-development projects grew out of the Roosevelt-sponsored Inland Waterways Commission. The first White House governor's conference, which Roosevelt hosted in 1908, helped promote nationwide interest in conservation.

Roosevelt's many books weren't the sanitized memoirs of a person in office. He had been writing long before he became president. His interests are evident in such titles as *Ranch Life and the Hunting Trail* (1888), *The Strenuous Life* (1900), *Hunting the Grizzly* (1905), and *Through the Brazilian Wilderness* (1914). Not all were merely hunting and fishing escapades. A devoted naturalist, Roosevelt was up-to-date on scientific explanations of nature's ways, as one of his lesser-known publications proves.

In 1911, three years after ending his second term in office, Roosevelt broke off from the Republicans and organized the Progressive (Bull Moose) party. Of course he didn't know that his actions would ensure both parties' defeat by Woodrow Wilson the next year, so he devoted his impressive energy to it. Somehow, during that busy year he published a 100-page article about the evolution of protective camouflage, entitled "Revealing and Concealing Coloration in Birds and Mammals."

He was writing in response to a theory proposed by the naturalist and artist Abbott H. Thayer. Naturalists had long observed that many animals' colors and patterns help camouflage them against certain backgrounds. Thayer, however, claimed that all animal coloration was aimed at that goal, and went to elaborate lengths to twist nature to fit his theory. For the frontispiece to one of his books, he painted a flamboyantly patterned peacock made invisible against a carefully chosen forest background. He even claimed that flamingos' pink coloration makes them disappear against sunrise and sunset. Since it was obvious that any creature standing against such bright skies would be silhouetted, Thayer had to point out that the birds' pink hue made them invisible *from the opposite direction.*

Early in 1912, Roosevelt wrote:

> There is in Africa a blue rump baboon. It is also true that the Mediterranean Sea bounds one side of Africa. If you should make a series of experiments tending to show that if the blue rump baboon stood on its head by the Mediterranean you would mix up his rump and the Mediterranean, you might be illustrating something in optics, but you would not be illustrating anything that had any bearing whatsoever on the part played by the coloration of the animal in actual life.

Thayer did manage to correctly identify a method of concealment now called "countershading." It is the principle evident in, for example, a common trait of shorebirds. Their darker upper halves and lighter undersides combine to reduce the dimensional effect of shadows. There is an amusing footnote to Thayer's story. Although he failed to convert the scientific community to his other notions, his writings had a considerable effect on the history of military camouflage. One ship painted according to Thayer's countershading advice was twice rammed by its fellow ships—because they couldn't see it.

Redefining "Human"

We have spent much time over the centuries dismissing the rest of creation as hopelessly below us. As a result, frequently new discoveries about primate behavior necessitate revisions of the definition of human uniqueness. Such provocative revelations about human origins and behavior are possible in the field of primate research because apes are our closest relatives.

Until recently tool and language use were considered hallmarks of humanness. But even those ramparts have fallen. In 1960, at her research compound at Gombe, near Lake Tanganyika, Jane Goodall observed a chimpanzee trimming a wide blade of grass so it could be inserted into a termite mound to draw out lunch. This proved to be widespread behavior and showed that chimps not only use tools but even make them. Goodall's mentor, paleontologist Louis Leakey, responded to the news with a famous telegram: "Now we must define *tool,* redefine *Man,* or accept chimpanzees as human."

Similar pronouncements greeted revelations in the early 1970s about an orangutan named Abang. Primate researcher R.V. S. Wright showed Abang how to use a flint knife to cut a rope that bound a food container. Within an hour, Abang had learned to cut the rope. Wright then taught him to make a flint knife himself by chipping away flakes. Although it is a precise skill, and one formerly attributed

Shall we add this to the family album?

solely to humans, Abang learned in only a few lessons.

Famous moments from ape research include the chimpanzee Lucy pouring herself a drink and turning on the television before signing to herself while leafing through a magazine, and a chimp named Washoe signing her human surrogate mother's name after eleven years apart. Chimpanzees' heavily publicized success with sign language in the early 1970s encouraged a Stanford University graduate student named Francine Patterson to test gorillas for the same aptitude. The result was the famous Koko. By the end of the decade, Patterson claimed, Koko had surpassed her chimpanzee rivals and learned over 400 signs.

Most animals, lacking our emphasis on the spoken word, are more attuned to body language. Skeptical scientists dismiss many animal language studies because they suspect the results are tainted with the "Clever Hans phenomenon," the unconscious influencing of an experimental subject by such hints as expression and posture. A famously "intelligent" German circus horse in the early part of the century, Hans was acclaimed for his counting abilities. Then observers realized that his questioners relaxed once Hans reached the correct answer, subtly signaling the horse to stop at that point. If the questioner was hidden, or ignorant of the question's answer, Hans too was stumped. Even Herbert Terace, whose pioneer research with the chimpanzee Nim Chimpsky attracted so much attention to ape language studies, later reexamined and disavowed his findings.

In response to this skeptical climate, a primate researcher named Sue Savage-Rumbaugh began some of the most rigorous language tests yet performed on primates. While she was trying to teach sign language to a bonobo named Matata, the chimp gave birth to the most recent star in the field. Kanzi was born on October 28, 1980. Bonobos are pygmy chimpanzees. Technically, because of the two distinct species, the more familiar chimpanzees should be distinguished—but not diminished—by the adjective "common."

In the 1970s, while working with the Yerkes Primate Center in Georgia, Savage-Rumbaugh was considered eccentric because she helped clean bonobos' cages, and because in general she spent more time with the apes than was necessary to merely collect data. But, as she had hoped, the bonobos learned to trust her. She learned an amazing array of information. Bonobos exhibit surprisingly perceptive responses to human body language; the females enjoy a high status due to the importance of child rearing; and "lesbian" relationships are common among those same females.

Humans and chimpanzees share 99 percent of their DNA structure. As a result, we even suffer many of the same diseases. Jane Goodall tells the moving story of a chimpanzee troop's rejection of a polio-deformed youngster. It is this astounding similarity to us that makes apes, especially chimpanzees, prized in medical research. But that very closeness raises important ethical issues. Ought we cage and maim our family members? Often chimpanzees live their entire lives, which can be as long as fifty years, in sterile cages, deprived of everything they seem to value—freedom, movement, family. Chimps kiss, mourn, cry, laugh, and fight. They react in ways similar to our own when deprived of social contact, parental love, or normal sexual development. In their power struggles they exhibit a corporate intrigue worthy of humans. Louis Leakey was right. Our definitions of humanity may have to broaden. Chimpanzees are too close even to be patronizingly called our cousins. We are siblings.

---

29 OCTOBER 1982

The Dingo Baby Murder Case

There are many kinds of wild canines around the world, all distantly related, all cousins of *Canis familiaris,* the domesticated dog. Besides the familiar wolves, foxes, and coyotes, they include the Andean wolf, the dark reddish dholes of India, the so-called Simian fox of Ethiopia, the cape hunting dogs of Africa, and the jackals that prowl much of the Old World.

On rare occasions, one of these wild dogs is accused of attacking a human being. In 1962, the Madras (India) *Mail* reported, "Nine children have been lifted away during nights by beasts of prey, believed to be Hyenas in six weeks in Bhagalpur town and its outskirts." A few years later, a hyena attacked a four-year-old boy in his tent in Kruger National Park in South Africa and dragged him 100 feet or so before he was rescued. (Actually, although they are almost always referred to as wild dogs, the hyena of southern Asia and Africa is not a true canine, but apparently closer to felines. It occupies the family Hyaenidae.)

One well-established canine that has been accused of such crimes is the Australian wild dog called the dingo, or sometimes the warrigal. It is one of the few mammals in Australia today that is not a marsupial. Apparently it arrived there from Asia with adventurous Aborigines between 5,000 and 8,000 years ago. Some Aborigines still use the dingo as a hunting dog. Like most canines, they make affectionate pets. They can also be affectionate with other kinds of dogs, as proven by the rate of interbreeding. Nowadays, in southeastern Australia, it seems that all the dingoes being seen are actually dog-dingo hybrids.

In 1980, an Australian woman named Lindy Chamberlain reported that her baby daughter Azaria, the youngest of her three children, had been stolen by a dingo. Chamberlain and her husband Michael, a Seventh-Day Adventist pastor, presented the police with a bloody, torn jumpsuit as evidence. The child's body was never found. However, when a forensics expert examined the clothing, he concluded from the bloodstains that the baby's throat had been cut. Lindy Chamberlain was charged with murder, and her husband with being an accessory after the fact.

One of the problems Chamberlain's defense attorneys faced was experts' failure to reach a consensus on the likely behavior of a dingo. That the adult dog would be physically capable of carrying off a human infant few seemed to doubt. Dingoes are about four feet long and two feet tall or so at the shoulder. They hunt alone or in small groups, usually preying upon rabbits and, when convenient, livestock. Because of the latter dietary supplement, they have been considered enemies of farmers ever since the European settlement of Australia brought tasty poultry and sheep to their home turf.

Nor was the dingo's popularity boosted by the initial reports of the baby's death. However, the dingo's unpopular reputation was not enough to indict it by hearsay. Although the prosecution failed to establish a motive for the alleged murder of Azaria Chamberlain, a jury in Darwin returned a verdict of guilty on October 29, 1982. Lindy Chamberlain was sentenced to life imprisonment.

---

30 OCTOBER 1938

Bug-Eyed Monsters

As epigraph to his 1898 science fiction novel *The War of the Worlds,* H. G. Wells included a quotation from the German astronomer Johannes Kepler. It asked a question that was attracting a lot of attention in the late nineteenth century: "But who shall dwell in these worlds if they be inhabited?" For some time, astronomers such as Giovanni Schiaparelli, Camille Flammarion, and Percival Lowell had been speculating with great publicity about the existence of intelligent life on Mars. As Wells and his wife rode around southern England on a bicycle built for two, he enthusiastically plotted his battles. "I wheeled about, marking down suitable places and people for destruction by my Martians." In the tradition of stories ever since Homer, he imagined monsters and described them with gleeful distaste.

> Those who have never seen a living Martian can scarcely imagine the strange horror of its appearance. The peculiar V-shaped mouth with its pointed upper lip, the absence of brow ridges, the absence of a chin beneath the wedge-like lower lip, the incessant quivering of this mouth, the Gorgon groups of tentacles . . . —above all, the extraordinary intensity of the immense eyes—were at once vital, intense, inhuman, crippled, monstrous. There was something fungoid in the oily brown skin, something in the clumsy deliberation of the tedious movements unspeakably nasty. Even at this first encounter, this first glimpse, I was overcome with disgust and dread.

It turns out, of course, that the creatures are deadly. But Wells's narrator is describing his first glimpse of the creature as it emerges from the cylinder in which it just crash-landed. For all he knows, for all the reader knows, the visitor may be an interplanetary traveling salesman seeking directions to a mechanic. However, "A sudden chill came over me." And he adds a detail that remains a required ingredient in science fiction and horror films today: "There was a loud shriek from a woman behind."

Wells described his Martian partly in terms of its differences from human beings. It had a mouth, but it was "peculiar." It lacked a chin and brow ridges. Wells applied three telling adjectives—*inhuman, crippled,* and *monstrous.* The first is redundant, but sums up the sheer otherness of the alien; the second is shocking, and again indicts the creature for its shortcomings. The root of the third word, "monstrous," is enlightening. Originally, "monster" referred to an animal or a plant that departed greatly from the usual structure of its kind. In time, it acquired several meanings gathered around the sense of strangeness. All of this is summed up in the word we now use for both hypothetical beings from other planets and illegal immigrants. The word "alien" comes from the Latin *alienus,* which derives from *alius,* "other," also the root of "alias." And we are back to the fear of otherness.

H. G. Wells had just introduced a character that would almost take over the genre soon to be called science fiction. The Bug-Eyed Monster had arrived. BEMs, the in-crowd would call them, and even pronounce it "bims." (Further initialese would appear for their cousins, LGMs, the Little Green Men.) Interestingly, it was a dramatization of *The War of the Worlds* that would give the infant genre of science fiction a boost. On October 30, 1938, CBS Radio broadcast an adaptation of *The War of the Worlds* on "The Mercury Theatre of the Air," directed and narrated by twenty-three-year-old Orson Welles. The young Welles had been producing radio plays for four years already and had founded the Mercury Theatre in 1937, but none of his earlier works caused such an uproar as this Halloween special performance.

Welles transferred the site of Wells's story from southern England to the northeastern United States. Even though the radio play was clearly identified as fiction, it inspired widespread panic. Telephone lines were overwhelmed. Hospitals and police stations were besieged. Parents piled their children into cars and drove madly away from the purported landing sites. Besides an example of the imaginative power of a medium that, like reading, forces the mind to imagine the action, it was dramatic proof of the ease with which mass hysteria could be incited. The uproar was also an indication of the number of people who believed that alien creatures might be out there somewhere, waiting for us, even coming for us. And the scariest thought of all was that they wouldn't be like us.

See also **The Andromeda Strain,** *2/5.*

Halloween

The Romans consecrated a particular temple, the Pantheon, to all of their gods. In the year 609, the Christians converted it to a temple honoring Mary and all martyrs, where a festival was held every May. Eventually the church expanded Mary's holiday to include saints and moved it to November 1, probably to supplant lingering pagan rituals performed then. It was the time of the Celtic New Year, the feast of "Samhain." Hilltop bonfires encouraged the waning sun while frightening evil spirits. Just as the festival of Beltane, half a year away, observed the herds' move to pasture, so did the first of November mark their return. It was the time to celebrate the end of summer and prepare psychologically for the rigors of winter.

Pope Gregory IV established "All Saints' Day" in the early ninth century and required the observance of a vigil the night before. The Christian habit of adapting preexisting observances to new purposes is evident in a decree by Gregory: "They are no longer to sacrifice beasts to the Devil, but they may kill them for food to the praise of God. . . ." In time All Hallows' Eve (or Evening) was shortened to Hallowe'en. Thus the holiday's name is partly Christian, although many of its traditions originated among the Druids and their conquerors, the Romans.

With the sanctified getting their due on All Saints' Day, the night before became the playtime of the Prince of Darkness. He was said to hold an unholy feast of his own. Someone got the idea that those hardy souls brave enough to peer through a church window on Halloween could glimpse the future. The devil himself, ever the Looking-Glass version of God, would be in the pulpit, reading aloud the names of those who would die before the next Halloween. Divination was rampant. Local superstitions varied so much that Scottish vernacular poet Robert Burns appended explanatory footnotes to his poem "Halloween."

Theories vary regarding the origins of trick or treat and Halloween costumes, with credit going to everything from the English custom of "soul cakes" for remembering the dead to the masquerading associated with Guy Fawkes Day on November 5. Some historians suggest that both customs grew from pagan feasts. After carousing with the spirits that were thought to be gathered invisibly around, people dressed as ghosts led them away from the living for another year. The Celtic festival of Samhain, like many other New Year celebrations around the world, was a time in which the dead were thought to revisit the living. The Celts believed that the souls of those who died sinful went into animals. It was Samhain who judged the degree of sinfulness and determined the soul's next abode.

The figures that now decorate store windows at Halloween grew out of those dark rites. Naturally the devil's attendants would accompany him on All Hallows' Eve. Witches would bring their own familiars, among whom were cats, those poor animals unfortunate enough to become associated with such nonsense. Although the Romans forbade human sacrifices, and Christians prohibited most others, cats were still being burned alive in the Middle Ages. Another familiar Halloween icon is the bat, which—nocturnal, aerial, and distinctly un-cuddly—became "the bird of the devil," and eventually one of his incarnations.

Because Halloween wasn't a particularly English or Protestant holiday, at first only scattered Irish settlements observed it in the New World. Then, when the potato famine of the 1840s brought a vast influx of Irish emigrants to the United States, they imported Halloween as part of their Celtic heritage. The potato, along with the turnip and the rutabaga, was one of the original jack-o'-lanterns, hollowed out and grotesquely carved, and lit from within by a candle. American pumpkins proved to work even better.

Largely taken over by children, Halloween's reputation for innocent mischief has been tarnished in recent decades by vandalism and violence. However, it is still the one day in the United States when death may be laughed at and honored. It is no longer a time of supernatural fear, but its masks and dark associations still inspire seasonal thrillers such as the film *Halloween* and its sequels.

See also "the bird of the devil," 8/3.

"An Intellectual Carrot"

Shortly after 6:00 P.M. on November 1 of an unnamed year during the Truman administration, American military seismographs and magnetometers pick up the presence of a large, fast-moving object near the North Pole. Upon arrival the next day, soldiers find a flying saucer crashed in the ice. Trying to free it with thermite bombs, they accidentally destroy it. However, Geiger counters detect another source of odd radiation, which turns out to be an inhabitant of the saucer, entombed in ice. "What'll we do now?" one soldier asks. "Defrost him?" Accidentally, a dim-witted soldier does just that, with an electric blanket.

The prototypical 1950s monster film *The Thing from Another World,* usually just called *The Thing,* is decidedly hawkish. In this scenario, the military are right to dismiss the very idea of communicating with the Thing, and the fuzzy-minded scientists are not only ludicrous but turn out to be dangerous. "Knowledge is more important than life, Captain," mad Dr. Carrington declares. "We owe it to our species to stand here and die." Later, the Thing (surprise!) kills him.

The Thing escapes and the compound's sled dogs attack it, tearing off its arm. The scientists examine the limb and report, "It seems to be a sort of chitinous substance, something between a beetle's back and a rose thorn. Amazingly strong." It has no arterial structure and no apparent nerve endings. The reporter almost winks at the audience with his famous line, "An intellectual carrot. The mind boggles." After the Thing's escape, soldiers find a sled dog's shrunken body, drained of blood. Carrington identifies seedpods in it, plants them, and drenches them with stored blood meant for humans. He quickly cultivates a tableful of drooping, pulsating, young Things. A scientist holds a stethoscope to one and hears a sound like the wail of a newborn.

The single token woman in the film is tough and witty. However, triumph over the Thing results from her more traditional womanly skills. One of the men asks in desperation, almost rhetorically, "What do you do with a vegetable?" She replies, "Boil it? Stew it? Bake it? Fry it?" First they throw kerosene on the Thing and set it afire; in the end they fry it—with electricity. The film ends with a much-quoted parody of paranoia that makes a good motto for science fiction films: "Watch the skies everywhere! Keep looking! Keep watching the skies!"

The Thing bears little resemblance to its inspiration, John W. Campbell's 1938 novella "Who Goes There?" That story takes place at the South, not North, Pole. Scientists thaw an alien that has been frozen in ice for millions of years. Science fiction fans were understandably disappointed when Campbell's loathsome three-eyed shape-shifter became in the film merely James Arness with the forehead of Frankenstein's monster. A film historian later called the Thing "sort of an evil Green Giant." It is not the only villainous vegetable in film. Obviously the pods in *Invasion of the Body Snatchers* are botanical aliens, as are the creatures in *The Day of the Triffids*. Even the centerpiece of *The Little Shop of Horrors* is a monstrous plant that demands, "Feed me!" Finally, in 1978, this entire botanical subgenre was spoofed in *Attack of the Killer Tomatoes*.

---

2 NOVEMBER 1938

An Elysian *Pastorale*

In 1809, Ludwig von Beethoven published his Symphony no. 6 in F Major, op. 68, under the title *Sinfonia Pastorale, No. 6*. There are five movements. The first, "Awakening of pleasant feelings upon arriving in the country," sets the tone. There follows a scene at a brook, the merrymaking of peasants, and a thunderstorm. The symphony ends with a shepherd's hymn of thanksgiving following the storm.

In 1940, Leopold Stokowski adapted the *Pastorale* for a segment of Walt Disney's anthology film, *Fantasia*. Disney had long planned to include a segment featuring characters from classical mythology. Originally he intended to use as accompaniment Gabriel Pierné's *Cydalise*, but it didn't work with the action that developed. In a story meeting on November 2, 1938, Disney abandoned the use of Pierné. His search for accompaniment with what he called "the right class" resulted in the choice of Beethoven's symphony.

When *Fantasia* first appeared, most critics agreed that the *Pastorale* was the film's nadir. It might have worked had the animators replaced Beethoven's country folk with gods and creatures of classical stature. They chose instead to populate the Elysian Fields with the most cartoonish figures in the whole movie, making them run around as if lost in an Olympian Silly Symphony. One wishes Zeus would simply smite them all.

Sketches from Walt Disney Productions' Character Model Department reveal a devolution from classical to cartoonish. Apollo was originally an impressive, truly godlike figure driving his wild stallions across the sky. Vulcan dwindled from a bearded giant to a lump-nosed rube in a diaper. Perhaps the turn for the worse can be dated to the note on a model sheet that read, "Bacchus should look like the balloon in Macy's parade."

The segment is both a roll call and a parody of Greek mythology. Pegasus, the winged horse who helped Bellerophon defeat the Amazons and Chimera, appears first. In this bucolic scene, he is accompanied not by a warrior but by a female of his own kind. They swoop out of the cotton-candy clouds and settle onto a lake, folding their wings like swans. Pegasus is black, his mate white. Not one of their pastel-hued foals resembles them. That can't be due to recessive genes, because Pegasus was born of the

Gorgon's blood. Incidentally, a curious bit of mythological natural history appears when the animators reveal that winged horses sleep in wickerlike nests in trees.

Elsewhere, fauns cavort like children, and cupids hover overhead. (Cupid was the Roman version of Eros, the Greek god of love. There was actually only one, not a whole nursery of them. Later representations of cherubim are similar.) Baby unicorns radiate all the mythic allure of Care Bears. Coquettish nymphs waist-deep in a stream wade out and reveal themselves as female centaurs—"centaurettes," the animators called them. The Hays Office, always able to find even cartoon animals too sexy for the public good, insisted that, in close-up, the centauresses were to wear garlands over their dangerously provocative breasts. Cupids, however, were allowed to show their backsides.

Awkwardly joined, the centaurs lack the grace of their classical counterparts. Still, surprisingly, one of the centauresses nicely demonstrates the dual nature—the conflicting urges of human and

This is how Walt Disney could have portrayed the centaurs and other characters of ancient mythology— as regal, impressive hybrids of humans and other animals. Instead he opted for the hopelessly cute.

horse—that might plague a real centaur. The moment occurs in the storm scene following the slapstick bacchanal that replaces Beethoven's merry peasants. As Zeus flings lightning from on high, and rain scatters the celebrants, a centauress gallops toward a hedge. Like a horse, she hesitates, afraid to jump. Then her human side takes over. She whips her own equine flank and leaps the hedge in a single bound.

In *Fantasia,* the spirit of mythology emerges best in the way the gods enact the simplest natural phenomena. They *cause* nature. No supercooling and ionization for Zeus; he personally hurls every thunderbolt. The rainbow flows from Iris's diaphanous gown as she arches across the sky. Morpheus, imagined here as a dark-haired woman, draws her purple twilight robe across the sunset. And, finally, Diana uses the crescent moon as a bow and fires a comet that becomes a shower of falling stars.

See also Rite of Spring *segment of* Fantasia, *1/4.*

---

3 NOVEMBER 1957

"Muttnik"

On November 3, 1957, a month after they began the space age with *Sputnik,* the Soviet Union launched *Sputnik 2.* It was equipped to perform observations on cosmic rays and ultraviolet radiation, and a few of its 1,120 pounds of payload were taken up by a special passenger. In the Western press, the satellite was nicknamed "Muttnik," because nestled in the tight space of a pressurized cabin was a dog. She was herself Russian, a young female Siberian husky named Laika. Photographs taken prior to the launch show her peering curiously out of her tiny cubbyhole, with one paw draped over the edge. Actually, since she had an official role to play, Laika was more crew than passenger. Electrodes attached to her body relayed back to earth some of the earliest biomedical data about the effects of space travel on living creatures. Technicians back on earth noted with satisfaction that, although the dog's respiration and heartbeat were affected by the acceleration required to attain escape velocity, they soon returned to normal rates.

The Russian scientists knew when they sent Laika into space that they would be unable to recover *Sputnik 2*. After a week, the life-support system ran out, and Laika was, as the press said at the time, "put to sleep." Laika's pioneer role and tragic fate caught the imagination of a thirteen-year-old Swede named Reidar Jönsson, who grew up to write the 1983 novel *Mit Liv som Hund* ("My Life as a Dog"). His narrator, Ingemar Johansson, who is also thirteen, remarks, "But Laika we must all feel sorry for, because she symbolizes human progress. She circled around in space without knowing why. . . . I am sure she would have begged to be taken down—if she could." Swedish filmmaker Lasse Hallström adapted Jönsson's novel for the screen in 1985.

In spite of some outcry over the death of Laika, the Soviet Union continued to send cosmonaut-surrogates into space before they were willing to risk the lives of human beings. One example of the practical information collected occurred with the Soviet mission called *Korabl Sputnik 2*. (*Sputnik* is the Russian word for satellite, and this new series of flights was given the prefix *Korable,* which means "vessel" or "ship.") Launched into space in 1960, it orbited the planet for a day before its controllers fired its retro-rockets to return it to earth. Aboard were plant seeds, adult plants, algae, fungi, and a veritable zoo—flies, mice, rats, and two dogs.

None of the other animals (and presumably none of the plants) were honored with names, but the dogs were called Strelka and Belka. Perhaps that was because the scientists knew the fate of the other creatures. After the satellite reentered the atmosphere, only the dogs were ejected from the capsule before it burned up on its way to the surface. They landed safely. Scientists then analyzed the medical data from the trip and discovered that one of the dogs had undergone convulsions during the fourth orbit. On that basis the authorities decided that the upcoming first manned flight should be limited to a single orbit.

The next canine cosmonauts were not so lucky. A few months later, *Korabl Sputnik 3* carried two more dogs, Pchelka and Mushka. They, too, orbited their home planet for a day. Then, as the satellite reentered the atmosphere, a retro-rocket malfunction sent it into a trajectory too steep for it to withstand. It broke apart and burned up. Subsequent missions, however, ended happily. In 1961, a dog named Chernushka orbited and landed successfully, as did one named Zvezdochka a few weeks later. The Russians decided that they had learned how to keep creatures alive in space and safely return them to earth. In mid-April of 1961, cosmonaut Yuri Gagarin became the first human being to venture into space.

See also chimpanzees in space, 1/31; and the Montgolfiers' balloon, 9/19.

4 November 1869

The Agnostic Pope

Nature! We are surrounded and embraced by her: powerless to separate ourselves from her, and powerless to penetrate beyond her.

With that quotation from Goethe's aphorisms, Victorian biologist and educator Thomas Huxley
launched a new periodical, the first magazine-format journal devoted to science. Its title was *Nature,*
and the inaugural issue was dated November 4, 1869. One mathematician responded, "What a glorious title, *Nature.* It is more than Cosmos, more than Universe." Charles Darwin, however, complained
that Huxley's florid, passionate introduction to his new journal read "as if written by the maddest
English scholar."

Thomas Huxley was at the peak of his career. The secularization of education was under way, and no
one was fighting harder for it than Huxley. Exactly as religious leaders had feared, the new discoveries
and ideas of science were having a powerful effect on attitudes toward the church. One result was an
increasing prestige for the first generation of university-trained professional scientists. The year he
launched *Nature,* Huxley was elected president of the Geological Society and the Ethnological Society.
(Shortly after he took over the latter, this soldier for intellectual freedom restricted the participation of
women to special events, because of their obvious intellectual inferiority.)

It was also in 1869 that Huxley was invited to attend a meeting of the recently founded Metaphysical Society, a group of scientists, theologians, and other thinkers who met in London to discuss such
matters as the nature of knowledge. The occasion led to the coining of an important new term. At the
dinner, Huxley later wrote, he was surrounded by "-*ists* of one sort or another; and . . . I, the man without a rag of a label to cover himself with." He complained that the "one thing in which most of these
good people were agreed was the one thing in which I differed from them. They were quite sure they
had attained a certain 'gnosis'—that is, a revealed knowledge of the truth about existence."

Gnosis was the Greek word for "knowledge." The second- and third-century Gnostic sect was an
early rival to more established versions of Christianity. Gnostics believed that they in their openness to
revelation were the only truly spiritual beings. Huxley took that ancient term, added the prefix *a-*
("non"), and coined the word *agnostic.* "It came into my head as suggestively antithetic to the 'gnostic'
of church history, who professed to know so much about the very things of which I was ignorant. . . ."

The term was controversial, of course, and then as now agnostics spent much time defining it.
Huxley had rejected that traditional invitation to opprobrium, *atheist.* For one thing, it, too, was a
statement of faith, since disproving the existence of a ruling deity was just as impossible as proving
it. For another, his role as leader of the revolution didn't need to draw unnecessary fire. Agnosticism,
for Huxley, was a method of examining the world. It meant that convictions must be founded upon
evidence. In a lecture to the Young Men's Christian Association, Huxley explained that science was
"neither Christian, nor Unchristian," but "Extra-christian." He would have agreed with the scientific manifesto of Thomas Jefferson, who advised his nephew to "question with boldness even the

existence of a God, because if there is one, he must more approve the homage of reason, than that of blind-folded fear."

Huxley's confident, unswerving leadership of the increasing secularism led commentators to wonder if he, like the head of a much older sect in Rome, thought himself infallible. They began calling him "Pope Huxley." It was an appropriate title. There is no question that Huxley was driven partially by a secular version of evangelical zeal. Perhaps it is not surprising that he later entitled a collection of his essays *Lay Sermons.*

See also doubting Thomas, 5/4.

---

5 November 1867

"The Contemplation of So Many Wonders"

Jules Verne's characters travel far afield. In the first few years of his writing career, he sent several aloft for five weeks in a balloon and others on a journey to the center of the Earth, and launched still more from the Earth to the Moon. Then, in 1870, he sent his favorite character, Captain Nemo, and three passengers adventuring for 20,000 leagues under the sea.

"For some time past, vessels had been met by . . . a long object, spindle-shaped, occasionally phosphorescent, and infinitely larger and more rapid in its movements than a whale." Ships sight the creature all over the world. "There appeared in the papers caricatures of every gigantic and imaginary creature, from the white whale, the terrible 'Moby Dick' of hyperborean regions, to the immense kraken. . . ."

The narrator of *Twenty Thousand Leagues under the Sea,* French zoologist Pierre Arronax, accepts an invitation to join the U.S. frigate *Abraham Lincoln*'s expedition to pursue the monster. They find it on November 5, 1867. When the creature rams the ship, the impact tumbles Arronax, his servant Conseil, and Canadian harpooner Ned Land into the sea. The creature rises to the surface, rescuing them from drowning, and Land discovers that his harpoon did not penetrate because the monster is made of iron. They have encountered the first and best-known submarine in literature—the *Nautilus.* The master of this strange vessel, Captain Nemo, is a bitter refugee from society who describes himself as "a man who has broken all the ties of humanity." Now that these three know his secret, they must remain prisoners.

With his unquenchable curiosity about the sea, captivity rests easily on Arronax. Nemo knows this: "You are going to visit the land of marvels. . . . The sea is everything. . . . Upon its surface men can still exercise unjust laws, fight, tear one another to pieces, and be carried away with terrestrial horrors. But at thirty feet below its level, their reign ceases. . . ." No one knew greater freedom than Nemo. This was long before sonar; there were no other practicable submarines; even the first successful transatlantic telegraph cable went into operation the very year that Arronax boarded the *Nautilus.*

The zoologist finds aboard the submarine natural history collections that rival the greatest European museums, but the true treasures are in the sea itself. The book is suffused with Verne's love of the ocean. In a protective suit prefiguring those of the twentieth century, Arronax walks upon the ocean floor. He dodges giant sea spiders and great sharks, finds the hulls of sunken ships, and witnesses an underwater burial. He eats turtle fillet, dolphins' livers, and anemone preserves. He watches a squid migration, as the *Nautilus* propels for miles through millions of them, and sees Captain Nemo attack a shark to save an endangered pearl diver.

Washed ashore after surviving the maelstrom that forms the climax of the book, like Ishmael surviving the wreck of the *Pequod,* Arronax expresses a wish for the misanthropic Captain Nemo: "May the contemplation of so many wonders extinguish for ever the spirit of vengeance! May the judge disappear, and the philosopher continue his peaceful exploration of the sea!"

See also Verne's giant squid, 4/20; and* Journey to the Center of the Earth, *6/29.

---

6 NOVEMBER 1492

"A Foul and Pestiferous Poison"

In October 1492, Christóbal Colón (Christopher Columbus) claimed for Spain a small island in the Bahamas. The people who lived there called their home Guanahani, but Columbus named it San Salvador.

Three days later, he noted in his diary that a man he encountered had in his boat "a few dried leaves which must be something of importance to these people, because they brought me some in San Salvador." Then some of the Spaniards explored inland Cuba. On November 6, Columbus recorded that his "two men met many . . . men and women, carrying in their hand a burning brand and herbs which they use to produce fragrant smoke." It was the first European encounter with what the natives called *tabaco.* Eighty years later, in his *Historio del Nuovo Mondo,* historian Girolamo Benzoni would describe what the Europeans had observed:

John Gerard, in his 1597 Herball, *included one of the earliest scientific representations of the noxious weed that Columbus had encountered in the New World.*

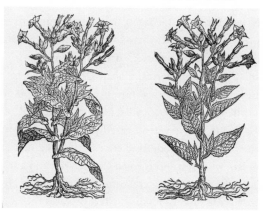

> When the leaves are mature they are gathered and hung in bunches over a fire until they are thoroughly dry, and when the people want to use them they take a leaf of their corn and roll up one of these other leaves inside it like a tube. . . . They suck in all they

can, and take pleasure in it, filling themselves with this bitter smoke to the extent of losing their wits. Some of them inhale so much that they fall down as if dead. . . . Consider what a foul and pestiferous poison of the Devil this is!

If this sounds like exaggeration akin to the horrors of marijuana in the film *Reefer Madness,* it should be noted that the tobacco in question had a far higher percentage of nicotine than today's relatively gentle blends. A poisonous alkaloid that works as a nerve toxin, like alcohol, nicotine was used by shamans to induce the "ecstatic-visionary" state that is almost always part of the shamanic job description. They smoked it, chewed it, ate it, even absorbed it through their skin. It was prescribed to reduce pain, cure disease, and exorcise demons. Tobacco became a recreational drug after its diffusion to the Old World, but only when it had circled the globe and penetrated tribal Siberia did it regain its religious and magical status.

There are sixty-odd species of *Nicotiana,* occurring naturally in Australia, Oceania, and Africa. (The genus is named for Jean Nicot, French ambassador to Portugal, who brought tobacco to France in the mid-1500s.) A dozen or more kinds were cultivated in the New World. At least two of them grew all the way from southern Chile to Canada—as widely distributed as the maize whose leaves were used to wrap it. Actually, even these two were already hybrids, cultivated strains that may date back to the origins of agriculture, perhaps 8,000 years ago. Tobacco use is portrayed in such pre-Columbian documents as the *Codex Vindobonensis* of the Mixtec people.

The genus is a member of the Solanaceae family, which includes eggplant but also the deadly nightshade, belladonna, and mandrake. The kinship of another plant, the petunia, is apparent in its name, which derives from *petún,* the Tupian word for those dried leaves that puzzled Columbus.

See also Columbus's eclipse, 2/29; and his mysterious light, 10/11.

---

7 NOVEMBER

A Lost World

When Professor George Challenger returns to the Amazon Basin, to prove his claim that he glimpsed prehistoric animals there, reporter Edward Malone tells him, "You are a Columbus of science who has discovered a lost world." Arthur Conan Doyle's 1912 novel *The Lost World* was the first of the Professor Challenger stories. Conan Doyle hoped to be remembered for more than just Sherlock Holmes. Besides such historical novels as *Micah Clarke* and *The White Company,* he also wrote this series of tales in the genre we now call science fiction.

Conan Doyle was inspired partially by the works of Jules Verne, the Frenchman who is considered the founder of modern science fiction. Verne's 1864 novel *Journey to the Center of the Earth* follows geologists who descend into an extinct volcano and go backward in time as they go deeper into the earth. They find surviving creatures that elsewhere are extinct. Today the idea of hidden corners of the earth harboring "living fossils" still captivates the imagination. In his 1993 book *Drums along the Congo,* U.S.

The narrator of The Lost World *finds himself face-to-face with a prehistoric ancestor.*

travel writer Rory Nugent pursued Africa's hypothetical leftover dinosaur, Mokele-Mbembe. Loch Ness Monster proponents theorize that the legendary lake monster might be a plesiosaur whose family somehow survived since the Mesozoic.

Conan Doyle had his own way around extinction. "An area, as large as Sussex," Challenger explains, "has been lifted up *en bloc* with all its living contents. . . ." Its granite cliffs isolating it from

387

the ravages of time, on this plateau the "various checks which influence the struggle for existence in the world at large are all neutralized or altered." A pterodactyl snatches dinner from the campfire; *Iguanodons* prowl the land; plesiosaurs swim the lakes. Eventually the explorers find ape-people. Contrasting one of them with Challenger, Malone remarks smugly that "the sloping forehead and low, curved skull of the ape-man were in sharp contrast to the broad brow and magnificent cranium of the European."

The climax of *The Lost World* is memorable. On November 7, after two days back in England, the adventurers present their findings to the Zoological Institute. Hecklers challenge their outrageous claims, and finally Malone and others bring out a box and set it onstage. Challenger snaps his fingers and says, "Come, then, pretty, pretty." A young pterodactyl climbs out of the box. "The face of the creature," a reporter writes the next day, "was like the wildest gargoyle that the imagination of a mad mediæval builder could have conceived. . . . It was the devil of our childhood in person. . . ." Frightened by the crowd, the flying lizard takes to its ten-foot wings. Before Challenger can shut the window, the prehistoric trophy, "beating and bumping along the wall like a huge moth within a gas shade," flies out the window.

Passersby see the creature perched on the roof of the hall. Later, a soldier claims that he saw the devil between himself and the moon, and a ship sights a flying monster at sea. "If its homing instinct led it upon the right line," Malone adds, "there can be no doubt that somewhere out in the wastes of the Atlantic the last European pterodactyl found its end."

---

8 NOVEMBER 1798

Treasure Island

Nauru was once an isolated island, near the equator north of New Zealand, 165 miles from its nearest neighbor. Its living coral reef discouraged the landing of even the occasional wandering ship. Isolation encouraged seabird colonies, and many generations of nesting birds left a legacy. Hills of guano made four-fifths of the island's eight square miles inhospitable. Guano is excrement that accumulates under favorable conditions. Bat guano can be found in caves worldwide; seal guano is understandably less common, its most noteworthy accumulation on some islands off the coast of Peru. Bird guano, more valuable because of its higher percentages of nitrogen and phosphorus, is also found near Peru, and in Baja California and Africa. But nowhere else in the world is it as rich as on Nauru.

Phosphorus is a crucial element in the balance of nutrients necessary for life. It had come a long way to pile up on Nauru. First, nitrogen and phosphorus from the ocean create a rich environment in which microscopic zooplankton flourish. Link by link up the food chain, the nutrients accumulate in ever larger concentrations, through fish to the birds that eat fish, especially pelicans, gannets, and cormorants. These birds use some of the phosphorus in their own metabolism, of course, but the rest is excreted. In the right climates, it accumulates. Ammonia and other unstable components fade away, leaving a residue of phosphates. These stored nutrients can be returned to the soil in the form of fertilizer, and that's why phosphate deposits have been Nauru's blessing—and curse.

On November 8, 1798, Captain John Fearn and the crew of the English ship *Hunter* became the first recorded Westerners to visit Nauru. They called it Pleasant Island because unarmed natives paddled out with gifts of fruit. European gifts in return included firearms and venereal diseases. Fortunately for its inhabitants, Nauru was ignored by Europe until whaling began in the region in the 1830s, and interest was slight until the turn of the century. Then a mining employee in Sydney noticed a Nauruan doorstop composed of almost pure phosphates. Illegal licenses were issued, and the Pacific Phosphate Company formed.

Not until after World War I did the Nauruans receive much profit from the sale of their bounty. But ever since independence in 1968, they have had the highest income per capita of any nation in the Pacific, and one of the highest in the world. Because the phosphate deposits were not infinite, Nauru invested abroad, in real estate, in shipping, in Australian condominiums.

Of course, prosperity brought demons. By the 1990s, thousands of automobiles jammed the perimeter road, as the population neared 10,000. Presumably because of their diet of processed foods and alcohol, nearly half have diabetes and many are alcoholics. In addition, mining has turned more than 80 percent of Pleasant Island into what has been described as a lunar waste.

---

9 NOVEMBER 1936

The Giant Panda

When they first examined the giant panda, some taxonomists maintained that it was a bear. Others thought that it was more closeley related to the raccoon. A third group insisted that because of anatomical peculiarities it deserved a family of its own. Finally, biochemical analyses indicated that the giant panda is more closely related to bears than even to the lesser panda, and it is now included in the Ursidae family of bears.

The Chinese hunted the unclassifiable creature for centuries. They called it the *beishung,* and farmers paid their taxes with its pelt. Like the elephants whose ivory once served as tribute money to the pharaohs, the *beishung* has come a long way. Also like the elephants, it may be too late. The panda once occupied a considerable territory across China and parts of Myanmar (formerly Burma), but its range is now limited to protected reserves in central China and eastern Tibet. As its thick coat with its woolly underlayers indicates, it lives in a cold climate, wisely hiding out in inaccessible mountain forests.

Europeans first observed the giant panda in the wild during an exploratory expedition in 1913–15, although a Jesuit missionary had seen its pelt in 1869. The coat the Chinese coveted—a white body with black limbs, ears, and eye patches—has made the panda a favorite zoo animal. It weighs over 200 pounds and reaches a length of five feet, so it is an impressive creature. On November 9, 1936, a baby panda was captured in China and named Su-Lin. Within six weeks, it arrived in San Francisco, California. At a tender age, and weighing a scant 5 pounds, she became the first giant panda to be seen in the United States. Chicago's Brookfield Zoo purchased Su-Lin for almost $9,000, and she immediately became a popular exhibit. Unfortunately, she did not last long in her adopted country and died in the spring of 1938. Slowly, others followed, although they do not breed readily in captivity. There are perhaps 100 in zoos worldwide, and fewer than 1,000 in the wild.

The giant panda is now so well known that it has become a poster child for international conservation. It is even the logo of the World Wildlife Fund, which, outside the United States, is called the Worldwide Fund for Nature. All fund drives need a glamorous chairperson, and the giant panda is unwittingly heading the struggle to save the unique ecosystem of the Chinese bamboo forests. *Panda* may be a corruption of a Nepalese word meaning "bamboo eater," and although it also eats other plants and some animals, it lives mostly on bamboo.

The panda's diet and anatomy have worked together to create a unique adaptation. Its unusually short intestine reduces the efficiency of its digestive system, and it must devote practically every waking minute to stripping bamboo stalks. In doing so over a long period of time, one of its wrist bones has evolved into a sort of extra digit, a makeshift "thumb." Such evolutionary imperfections demonstrate the haphazard way that nature, rather than perfectly suiting an animal to its environment, simply makes do with what is available. Indeed, Harvard paleontologist Stephen Jay Gould calls this tendency "the panda principle," and it has become a central theme in his long-running series of essays in *Natural History.* His second collection of essays was entitled *The Panda's Thumb.*

Such imperfections refute creationists' claims that the supposed balance of nature could not have come about without divine guidance. The early-nineteenth-century English theologian William Paley proposed the classic expression of this belief. In 1802, he published *Natural Theology, or Evidences of the Existence and Attributes of the Deity.* The book opens with an "argument from design," insisting that just as a watch's intricate design implies a watchmaker, so does nature's own complexity require a "Master Creator." Evolutionists, who study nature's Rube Goldberg inventions every day, have little patience with that theory. British evolutionary biologist Richard Dawkins wrote an entire book entitled *The Blind Watchmaker,* filled with examples of nature's awkward ways, including the ersatz thumb of the panda.

---

10 NOVEMBER 1926

Hirohito the Biologist

Upon the death of his father in 1926, Micho-no-miya (Prince Micho) Hirohito became the 124th God Emperor of Japan, supposedly a lineal descendant of the demigod Jimmu, who had come to Earth over twenty-six centuries ago. His formal coronation ceremony, however, was not held until November 10, 1926. He was twenty-five years old. Hirohito's reign was remarkable for many reasons. At sixty-two years, it was longer than any other in Japanese history, lasting until his death in

1989. Also, contrary to the Japanese code of *bushido,* which held that the courageous fight to the death, Hirohito surrendered Japan to the Allies following the bombing of Hiroshima and Nagasaki. Then, perhaps even more shocking, he renounced his traditional divine status and tried to democratize his office.

However, biologists remember Hirohito for still another reason. After his father's death, Hirohito announced that the new Imperial Era was to be called *Showa,* meaning a time of peace and enlightenment. Although peace would evade his grasp, Hirohito continued to pursue a form of enlightenment that had delighted him since childhood—the study of natural history. He soon found that his carefree days were over. Still, when he wasn't presiding over state functions or national or Shinto holidays, he managed to find time to study nature. The intrigue of office stimulated Hirohito less than the observation of nature. When Fukiage Garden, with its elaborate ponds and fountains and teahouse, was destroyed during air raids in World War II, Hirohito decided that rather than rebuild it he wanted to plant it in native grasses from the Musashino Plain. More traditional Japanese objected, and Hirohito replied, "I am free do to as I wish only within the confines of this garden."

From the beginning, the military objected that natural history was an unseemly diversion for a monarch. Once, while the emperor was diving, a young naval officer aboard his boat looked in disgust at the accumulating seaweed and shellfish and complained to the imperial staff, "That stuff doesn't belong in a boat like this." His superiors were even more outraged. Because of the opposition, even before the war Hirohito worked in his laboratory only on Saturday mornings, and eventually he hesitated to escape to his microscope for even a few hours. During the war, he rarely turned to biology at all. Afterward, he permitted himself two half days and all day Saturday.

Hirohito's scientific mentor was the biologist Kotaro Hattori. It was he who advised the young emperor, who had ranged throughout biology from cytology to genetics, to narrow his studies. Even this choice was limited by the strictures of office. Hattori suggested that it might be unwise for an emperor to intrude upon another scholar's work. Finally, they decided that Hirohito would devote his spare time to the study of the slime molds and hydrozoa. Although his staff replied to disgruntled officers that Hirohito's biological interests were only a hobby, in reality it was always far more. In time, his studies resulted in several books, including *The Opisthobranchia of Sagami Bay, The Myxomycites of Nasu District,* and *Some Hydroids of the Amakusa Islands.*

With Hattori's guidance, Hirohito exhibited the systematic thinking of a future scientist even in early childhood. His brother Chichibu—said to be, because of his relative freedom, the one person Hirohito envied—reminisced about their childhood: "When the emperor was about ten years old, we went to the mountains and caught a large number of butterflies and other insects. . . . From beginning to end, no matter how many insects there were, he carefully checked and recorded the name of each one." Some years later, collecting on a beach after a storm, Hirohito found a red prawn he couldn't identify. His reference books didn't show it. When he took it to an expert he learned that, at the age of seventeen, he had discovered a new species, and in his honor the prawn acquired the name *Sympathephae imperials.* It was only the first of many such discoveries. By the time of Hirohito's death, he had identified over 100 new species of animals and plants.

Humble Pie

The English diarist Samuel Pepys recorded several years of his life in informative detail. His diary not only paints an unflinching self-portrait, but provides a wealth of information about seventeenth-century London. For example, on November 11, 1667, "a most cold and foggy, dark, thick day," Pepys noted that he had been to see John Dryden's play *The Indian Emperour,* that he feared he had caught a cold while working in a damp room, and that his bookseller had just died. Then he added, "This day I had a whole doe sent me, which is a fine present, and I had the umbles of it for dinner."

What Pepys was eating was humble pie. Originally "umble pie," it was a meat dish made from entrails, which included such organs as the kidneys, liver, and heart. Some historians have described umble pie as a meal scorned by the better off, a dish for the poor, who could afford no loftier fare than the cast-offs of their betters. However, etymologists think that the bad reputation of umble pie resulted from folk etymology linking unrelated words.

Pepys referred to this dish on other occasions, and always with approval. Five years before he received the "whole doe," he wrote: "I having had some venison given me a day or two ago, and so I had a shoulder roasted, another baked, and the umbles baked in a pie, and all very well done." Pepys not only enjoyed the dish himself. He was in the Naval Office, and on that occasion he served umble pie to Admiral Sir William Penn. Present also was the admiral's son, who would later become a Quaker, immigrate to the New World, and found Pennsylvania. Obviously Pepys did not regard umble pie as a food for peasants. A year or so later, he wrote that a woman brought "an umble pie hot out of her oven, extraordinarily good, and afterwards some spirits of her making, in which she has great judgment, very good," and he went on to add the cheery Pepysian coda "and so home, merry with this night's refreshment."

The etymology of "humble pie" is fascinating. The Latin word for loin was *lumbus,* which led to *lumbulus* for a cut of meat. In Norman French that evolved into a word for an animal's edible viscera, *nombles,* and as early as the fourteenth century that had become in English "numbles." By the next century the English word was "humbles," and by the next "umbles." The earliest recorded use of the actual term "umble pie" dates to only four years before Pepys received the deer and ate its umbles for dinner. That he ate the umbles first is further evidence that the food was perhaps a delicacy rather than a last resort. Incidentally, although Pepys referred explicitly to a doe, for centuries the word "deer" meant any animal, as in Edgar's remark in *King Lear* that "mice and rats and such small deer / Have been Tom's food for seven long year."

The first recorded usage of "humble pie" appears in 1830, in a vocabulary book that defines the phrase "make one eat humble pie" as meaning "to make him lower his tone, and be submissive." The author linked the term with the supposed low status of umble pie. By that time folk etymology seems to have securely linked "umble" with "humble," perhaps partially through the frequent omission of the initial letter *h* in English pronunciation. Witness the slimy and most un-humble Uriah Heep in *David Copperfield,* who continually says of himself and his mother, "We are so very 'umble." But *umble* and *humble* are unrelated. "Humble" and "humility" mean meek or not proud, and come—again via the French—from the Latin *humilis,* which meant low or slight. That in turn derived from *humus,* "earth," and is still the term for the organic material in soil, decayed vegetable matter, once called "vegetable mould."

Apparently, that Samuel Pepys was eating an umble pie did not necessarily make it a humble meal.

The Loch Ness "Monster"

Loch Ness is a lake in north-central Scotland, south of Inverness. Although one American wrote of "Lake Loch Ness," *loch* is the Gaelic word for a lake or firth (an estuary or sea inlet). Many people believe that Loch Ness is the home of "monsters," creatures hitherto unknown to science unless they are surviving plesiosaurs that somehow avoided the extinction of their comrades. Most scientists scoff. In the legitimate news media, "Nessie" inhabits cartoons and jokes. There is even a roller-coaster ride called the Loch Ness Monster.

Lake monsters are common in folklore. It is said that *skrmsl* lurk in Irish waters and Ogopogo in Canada's Lake Okanagan. Old maps of Scotland portray *Loch-na-Beistie,* "lochs of the beast." Nessie has been linked with the legendary Gaelic water horse, *Eigh-Uisge,* and with water-kelpies, malevolent sprites that inhabit streams and lakes. Occasional sightings predate this century, but widespread publicity began in the spring of 1933, when a new road provided access and views of the lake.

That year, on Sunday, November 12, a man named Hugh Gray was walking along the shore after church when he noticed a disturbance on the water. He grabbed his camera. His photo is extremely blurry, and analysis proves that he was much closer to the motion than he admitted. Believers say it is Nessie. Others say it looks more like an otter rolling on the surface or even a dog fetching a stick.

Most snapshots of Nessie turn out to be either completely faked, tampered with afterward, or so blurry they might just as well prove the existence of the Abominable Snowman. At best, few could have been taken from the distances or vantage points claimed, sometimes not even with the cameras and lenses supposedly used. That casts doubt on the photographers' estimates of distance and motion, if not on their veracity. The famous underwater close-ups of the creature's flipper turned out to be composites of photos greatly "enhanced" by computer. One shot claimed as a view of the creature's head apparently recorded a stump on the lake bottom.

As criminal studies have proven, eyewitnesses are unreliable. "There is no occurrence," Pliny the Elder remarked, "so fabulously shameless that it lacks a witness." Innumerable phenomena explain the sightings without recourse to leftover plesiosaurs. There is the desire to believe. No visitor is unaware of the legend, and most admit hoping to sight the creature. Also, on Loch Ness and other lakes at similar altitudes, temperature inversions over the surface create a mirage effect on sunny, still, warm days—exactly what believers call "good Nessie weather," when visits peak.

Few researchers question the eyesight of witnesses, or their qualifications for estimating size, speed, and distance. From the prevalence of sightings at twilight, one researcher concluded, not that eyesight might be fooled at the murkiest time of day, but that the creature was nocturnal. Those "monsters" occasionally seen on land, as well as cavorting in water, behave like otters, whose tails also match accounts of the monster's head. Occasional descriptions of "horns" sound like the velvet-covered antlers of young deer, which swim in the lake. Gases produced by decaying vegetable matter on the lake floor sometimes lift large masses bobbing to the surface.

However, there is at least one bit of anecdotal evidence that believers reject—a man's claim to have started the uproar in 1933 as a publicity stunt to attract people to the new resort by the lake.

See also Bigfoot, 10/20.

---

13 NOVEMBER 1787

Coleridge's White Phantom

"We have been on another tour," Dorothy Wordsworth wrote in her diary on November 20, 1787; "we set out last Monday evening at half-past four . . . William and Coleridge employing themselves in laying the plan of a ballad. . . ." The previous Monday was November 13. The poem that William Wordsworth and Samuel Taylor Coleridge were planning was the latter's "Rime of the Ancient Mariner." The next year it took its place in their joint effort, *Lyrical Ballads.*

The Mariner's shipmates regard the fateful albatross, which has perched on the rigging for a staring match.

Already Coleridge had been toying with an image from a friend's dream—a ghostly ship and crew. During their walk with his sister, Wordsworth told a story from George Shelvock's 1726 *Voyage round the World.* Once, in the Antarctic, the crew saw not one creature "except a disconsolate black Albitross [*sic*], who accompanied us for several days, hovering about us as if he had lost himself." A sailor decided that the bird was an ill omen and shot it. Coleridge thought both the setting and the crime appropriate for his new poem. At this time, he hadn't been to sea, but he knew travel writing and the natural sciences. He turned to Shelvock for details, and used images, even entire phrases, from Erasmus Darwin's biological epic, *The Botanic Garden.*

No longer thought to embody the souls of drowned sailors, albatrosses survive as symbols mainly due to Coleridge's poem. From the mariner's penance for shooting the bird, we get the current meaning of an "albatross" as a crippling burden. But Shelvock's bird was black, not white. This was probably the sooty albatross. The wandering albatross—the best known, and apparently the one Coleridge had in mind—is white, but it also has a wingspan of eleven feet. It could hardly dangle from a sailor's neck.

In Captain James Cook's *Journal,* albatrosses are killed with no report of an eerie aftermath. Baudelaire, in 1841, saw sailors killing albatrosses. He said that, dead, the former kings of the sky were comical and ugly, and he made of that a symbol of the poet. Less poetic sailors baited fishing lines with salt pork and dragged them behind the ship. The webbing between the birds' feet made tobacco pouches; their long wing bones became pipe stems. Darwin brought back from the *Beagle* voyage an albatross-leg-bone pipe.

On land, the klutzy animals earned one of their nicknames, "gooney bird." Hunters simply approached the amicable birds and tipped them backward off their nests, robbing them of their one-pound eggs before they could regain their balance. Albatrosses are also awkward as they run across the water to become airborne. But they are elegant fliers. Herman Melville rhapsodized about the albatross, calling its bill Roman and sublime, and referring to those "vast archangel wings." Because Coleridge's bird was sacrificed, even shot with a *cross*bow, some commentators speculate that it represents Christ. No, says another, it is the breast, the Mother. But Melville simply declared the albatross "that white phantom [that] sails in all imaginations."

See also Shakespeare's starling, 3/6; and Keats's nightingale, 5/12.

---

14 November 1916

Saki and the Birds of War

Hector Hugh Munro began his writing career as a journalist, serving as a correspondent for the *Morning Post* in Europe and Russia. He wrote stories, which frequently involved strange animals, and eventually a novel and a book on Russian history. For his pseudonym, he chose "Saki," the name of a servant in one of Edward FitzGerald's numerous versions of the Rubáiyát of Omar Khayyám:

> *And when like her, O Saki, you shall pass*
> *Among the Guests Star-scatter'd on the Grass. . . .*

Munro was a conservative man who spent most evenings playing bridge at his club. But, as his alter ego, he became famous for satirical sketches, tightly plotted horror stories, and the adventures of such characters as Clovis and the unbearable Bassington. Frequently either writing about nature or sketching it, Munro filled his stories with animals, including the much-anthologized talking cat Tobermory, whose story appears in the collection *Beasts and Super-Beasts.*

With the arrival of the Great War, Munro refused offers of a commission and enlisted as a private. He went to France in 1915. He had enlisted in high spirits, but as he lost friends and fellow soldiers he was soon bitter about the war. "Invalided out" with malaria, he returned sooner than doctors advised. To cheer himself up, he wrote "Birds on the Western Front" for the *Westminster Gazette.*

". . . I once saw a pair of crows engaged in hot combat with a pair of sparrow-hawks," he wrote, "while considerably higher in the sky, but almost directly above them, two Allied battle planes were engaging an equal number of enemy aircraft."

In wartime, "Saki" reported, the normally "gun-shy and nervous" rook could be seen "sedately busy among the refuse heaps of a battered village, with shells bursting at no great distance and the impatient-sounding, snapping rattle of machine guns going on all round him." He saw hovering kestrels "not in the least disconcerted, apparently, when a promising mouse area suddenly rises in the air in a cascade of black or yellow earth." No matter how well the hawks and owls "mobilized," unfortunately there were always enough of the mice and rats "to populate one's dug-out and make a parade-ground and race-course of one's face at night. . . ."

Munro didn't compile bird lists; he described how he felt in terms of what he saw. "In the chill, misty hour of gloom that precedes a rainy dawn, when nothing seemed alive except a few wary water-logged sentries and many scuttling rats, the lark would suddenly dash skyward and pour forth a song of ecstatic jubilation that sounded horribly forced and insincere."

A few days later, Munro was in the attack on the German stronghold at Beaumont-Hamel. In the predawn darkness of November 14, 1916, a soldier was lulled enough by the pause in shelling to light a cigarette. Munro shouted, "Put that bloody cigarette out!" But the light and shout had pinpointed their location, and a moment later a sniper shot Munro through the head.

---

15 November 1280

Of Animals and Albertus Magnus

Albertus Magnus died on November 15, 1280. Over six-and-a-half centuries later, in 1931, Pope Pius XI proclaimed him a saint and doctor of the church. A Dominican philosopher and bishop, Albert had long been recognized as one of the premier scholars of medieval Europe. He was influential in bringing the learning of Aristotle and other Greeks to the attention of medieval scholars. However, Albert's accomplishments were not limited to those dusty fields, as indicated by a second tribute paid him by the Catholic Church. A decade after his predecessor's proclamation, Pius XII further promoted the shade of Albert to the post of patron saint of students of natural history.

Albertus Magnus is Latin for "Albert the Great." He was called that even before his death, the only scholar of his time to be thus honored. Albert was born in the 1190s, in Lauingen an der Donau, in Swabia, a historically important region in what is now southwestern Germany. His father was a wealthy German nobleman, and Albert was able to study liberal arts at the University of Padua. It was there, in 1223, that he took his vows for the Dominican order, which Dominic had founded only seven years before. At the University of Paris, he encountered the newly translated works of Aristotle.

For at least a quarter of a century, Albert taught in numerous schools. At Cologne a young man named Thomas Aquinas was his pupil. By the time he wrote his famous work *De Animalibus* ("Of Animals"), which took him two decades or so, Albert had realized the need for some sort of systematic introduction to the available knowledge about the natural world. He tried to provide it.

The first nineteen books of Albert's magnum opus consist of translations of and commentaries on Aristotle's own nineteen books concerning animals—four of *The Parts of Animals,* five of *The Generation of Animals,* and ten of *The History of Animals.* However, Albert's work is three times as long as Aristotle's original, because he included asides and parentheses by many other naturalists. The next two books in Albert's monumental work were further commentaries and appendices, clarifying issues raised earlier. But, finally, in his last five books, Albert diverged from what he called "the usual method of a philosopher." He dared to present his own scholarship, rather than continuing the reorganizing of others'. Albert called his personal contribution a "systematic inventory of animals and the peculiarities of each species."

Some of these peculiarities, like those that enliven Pliny's first-century-A.D. *Historia Naturae* and even Gesner's sixteenth-century *Historia Animalium,* seem ludicrous to us now. Albert declared that war horses sometimes shed tears for their fallen riders—unless gelded, which leaves them "timorous and fainthearted" and unfit for the rigors of battle. "The king snake," he wrote, "kills by its gaze and the sound of its hissing." Of the ass, he said, "Having a melancholic nature, it possesses stronger and harder bones at its lower end where the melancholic humor is seated. . . ." He quoted a claim that may yet make its way into magazine advertisements—that the blood of a slain mole, if rubbed on the scalp, encourages hair growth.

However, after quoting the claims of his contemporaries or even of his illustrious predecessors, frequently Albert added disclaimers such as "I do not believe this story is true" and "But I think it is a fable." And, although his worth as a naturalist can't be measured by how often he was correct by our standards, he did make many observations that are incontestable today. He noticed, for example, that birds do not urinate, "despite the fact that every one seems to imbibe liquids." That is true. Birds, like lizards and many other animals, possess a cloaca, a single passageway through which pass combined liquid and solid wastes. (The unusual presence of that sort of canal in the platypus and echidna, by the way, earned them their scientific name, *monotreme,* "one-hole.") He corrected Pliny's mistake about the nightingale ceasing to sing after mating. He reported Aristotle's observation on the "king bee," *rex apum,* which was thought to be the parent of all the bees in a hive. Nowadays we call her the queen, but despite her gender change her lofty status, like Albert's, remains secure.

---

16 NOVEMBER 1902

"Teddy's Bear"

In late 1902, U.S. president Theodore Roosevelt went south to resolve a boundary dispute between Mississippi and Louisiana. He took four days off to hunt, but game was scarce. Finally, a single bedraggled black bear was surrounded by the dogs and roped and held for the president to shoot. Roosevelt indignantly denounced the idea of shooting a captive animal. Reporters, eager for stories after the expedition's bad luck, played up his refusal. On November 16, the *Washington Star* published a C. K. Berryman cartoon portraying Roosevelt refusing to shoot the bound bear, captioned "Drawing the Line in Mississippi."

An enterprising Russian emigré named Morris Michtom, who owned a toy store in Brooklyn, saw the cartoon. He and his wife constructed a brown plush bear and placed it in their shop window with a sign that read, "Teddy's Bear." It sold immediately. So did the next one they made, and the next. Soon Michtom was seeking facilities for mass production and permission from the president to use his nickname on the new toy. Roosevelt replied that he didn't know how useful his name would be in the stuffed animal business, but that Mr. Michtom was welcome to use it. Soon advertisements appeared for "Teddy's Bears," and finally for "Teddy Bears."

Stuffed animals were not new; there had been even a few stuffed bears. But manufacturers had assumed that such a ferocious animal was unlikely to become a popular toy. They were mistaken. Bears

After C. K. Berryman's cartoon appeared, the ensuing "bear craze" reached such heights (or depths) that a parody of Longfellow starred a teddy bear:

> *The Shades of night were falling fast*
> *As through an Alpine village passed*
> *A creature covered all with fur,*
> *A Teddy Bear whose contents were*
> *EXCELSIOR!*

DRAWING THE LINE IN MISSISSIPPI

were the most dangerous carnivore on the continent, but with the real animals banished to the hinterlands, Teddy—and, later, Smokey and Pooh and Paddington—helped bears assume the cuddly mien they wear now.

By 1906, trade magazines were trumpeting, "There has never been anything like the Bear Craze!" Teddy bears appeared dressed in swimsuits, baseball uniforms, and inevitably a Rough Rider uniform. Dancers in vaudeville shows, even clowns and dogs at Madison Square Garden, sported teddy bear costumes. In chic display windows they wore jewels over evening gowns. "Grammbear" was spoken, a coy dialect composed of puns: "celebriteddy," "bearadise lost." Soon teddy bear images appeared on water pistols and rocking horses, card games and squeeze balls. One bear whistled; another had electric eyes ("Shake the right paw, eyes light up").

There was even a backlash. Editorial writers lamented the sight of their little girls playing with teddy bears instead of dolls. A priest in Michigan claimed that teddy bears destroyed the maternal instinct and would therefore be responsible for the suicide of the human race. But the tide was not reversed. Michtom's earnings founded the Ideal Toy Company.

When William Howard Taft succeeded Roosevelt in 1908, manufacturers thought they could repeat their success. A dish called "possum and taters" was served to Taft at a Georgia banquet, and his purported fondness for it inspired the creation of a new stuffed animal, Billy Possum. But Billy did not seriously challenge Teddy. Nor did a patriotic raptor named Billy Owlett. Teddy bears were quite secure, and they remain so today.

See also Winnie-the-Pooh, 8/21.

"The Metamorphosis" of Franz K.

Franz Kafka began writing *Der Verwandlung* (The Metamorphosis or The Transformation) on November 17, 1912. On that day, in a letter to his fiancée, he mentioned the story's genesis: It "occurred to me in bed in my misery, and now troubles me and demands to be written." A few days later he warned her that the story might scare her, and added that his "story's hero has had a very bad time today, and yet it is only the last lap of his misfortune, which is now becoming permanent."

What Kafka called "this exceptionally repulsive story" was published in the periodical *Die Weissen Blätter* in October 1915 and as a book a month later. No doubt Kafka did not foresee that its first sentence would become one of the best known in literature: "As Gregor Samsa awoke one morning from uneasy dreams, he found himself transformed in his bed into a gigantic insect." Samsa, a traveling salesman who until last night led a normal life, is lying on his curved, armored back. He can clearly see his segmented abdomen and his six skinny legs. There is a lovely detail: The bed quilt is sliding off. Yes, thanks to his creator, Gregor Samsa is having a very bad day. Kafka once confessed, ". . . If I didn't write I felt like a piece of garbage on the floor, ready to be swept out the door." That is ultimately the fate of Samsa.

It is frequently said that Samsa was transformed into a cockroach. However, Vladimir Nabokov, armed with his considerable entomological skills, explained from the internal evidence exactly why the vermin into which Gregor Samsa was transformed could *not* have been a cockroach. Nabokov insisted it was a creature that, in human terms, is even lower and more "Kafkaesque"—the dung beetle. That is what the maid calls Samsa in the story. Kafka's publisher, Kurt Wolff, referred to "The Metamorphosis" as "the bedbug story." Kafka himself used the term *ungeheuren Ungeziefer,* roughly "monstrous vermin." He left the species unidentified.

Kafka also knew the power of his imagery would fade if made too literal. When Wolff informed him that he had commissioned a cover for the book, he responded in a panic: "It occurred to me . . . that [the artist] might want to draw the insect itself. Please, not that—anything but that!" The final cover portrayed a man emerging from a room with his head in his hands. There are no insects in sight.

Some of Kafka's stranger literary descendants include science fiction and fantasy stories. Take, for example, Kit Reed's 1968 story "Sisohpromatem." Like its title, the plot is a reversal of *The Metamorphosis:* "I, Joseph Bug, awoke one morning to find that I had become an enormous human." Michael Bishop's 1975 story "Rogue Tomato" spins a more space-operatic variant. The title of the first section, "The Metamorphosis of Philip K.," pays tribute to both Kafka ("K." is the protagonist of both *The Castle* and *The Trial*) and the science fiction writer Philip K. Dick. "When Philip K. awoke," Bishop's story begins, "he found that overnight he had grown from a reasonably well shaped, bilaterally symmetrical human being into . . . a rotund and limbless planetary body circling a gigantic gauzy-red star. In fact, by the simple feel, by the total aura projected into the seeds of his consciousness, Philip K. concluded that he was a tomato. . . ."

---

18 NOVEMBER 1928

"Of the Vulgar Little Mouse"

From bison on the wall of Lascaux to *Apollo 10*'s lunar orbiter named *Snoopy*—with a command module that defied the gods by being named after that legendary failure, Charlie Brown—animals real or symbolic have attended many new technologies. Thus it isn't surprising that they were present at the birth of animation. The verb "animate" means to bring to life; its root, *anima,* the Latin word for breath or soul, is also the root of "animal." Many animals have been brought to life by animators, but true stardom was reserved for, surprisingly, a mouse.

The sixteenth-century naturalist Conrad Gesner titled a discourse "Of the Vulgar Little Mouse." One of these unpopular rodents taught Robert Burns that the best-laid schemes gang aft a-gley, and one ran up a clock, and three blind ones had their tails cut off with a carving knife, and on Christmas Eve in Clement Clark Moore's poem, not one was stirring (a line apparently adapted from a remark by Hamlet). A mouse was miracle enough to stagger Walt Whitman, and Aesop's fable of the Lion and the Mouse ends with the moral, "Little friends may prove great friends." Mice played a relatively minor artistic role among the world's animals.

Until 1928, that is. Late in the previous year, Al Jolson in *The Jazz Singer* actually *sang,* and cinema changed forever. Producers scurried to make "talkies." One young man quickly realized the impact sound could have on his own specialized field, and started over on an animated cartoon he had begun as a silent. An unscrupulous distributor had stolen his silent character Oswald the Rabbit, but Walt Disney wasn't beaten yet. He wed the new technology to a new creation, and *Steamboat Willie* premiered in New York City on November 18, 1928. Its star, Mickey Mouse, was similar to Oswald, but more elegant and even more simply drawn. Unlike Oswald, he spoke. Like Jolson, he even sang. Minnie already accompanied him, resisting his lechery but abetting his sadism as they played, among other improvisations, a cow's teeth as a xylophone and her udder as a bagpipe. Later, the moral watchdogs at the Hays Office demanded that Disney cows be either udderless or clothed.

Mickey's slapstick was patterned on the antics of Mack Sennett's Keystone Kops, who had grown out of French knockabout comedies. His only serious rival, Felix the Cat, was soon left behind, his silent gestures simply not as commanding as Mickey's high-pitched voice. Both Franklin Roosevelt and George V insisted that all film showings they attended include a Mickey Mouse cartoon. His likeness saved a watch company from bankruptcy and was painfully created in mosaic in the front teeth of certain African tribesmen. The Allied code word on D-Day was "Mickey Mouse," which lent Mickey the distinction of being denounced by Adolf Hitler as "the most miserable ideal ever revealed," because "mice are dirty."

Over the years, Mickey metamorphosed from wily rascal to avuncular straight man. The public demanded the evolution, and Disney understood that the character who was evolving into his corporate logo could not behave like a brat. So Mickey was tamed, and the role of rapscallion assigned to the crotchety and incomprehensible Donald Duck.

---

19 NOVEMBER 1808

A Sea Serpent

In Edinburgh, at the November 19, 1808, meeting of the Wernerian Natural History Society, a man named Patrick Neill presented a paper describing in detail a creature that he considered new to science. He named it *Halsydrus.* Neill thought he was describing a "sea monster," as his summation indicates: "No doubt could be entertained that this was the kind of animal described by Ramus, Egede, and Pontoppidan, but which scientific and systematic naturalists had hitherto rejected as spurious and ideal."

Neill's examples are well-known accounts of sea serpents. The Norwegian historian Johann Ramus wrote in his 1689 history of Norway of "a large Sea-snake" observed by many witnesses only two years before. He claimed that the creature moved very quickly and took some time "in stretching out its many folds." Hans Egede was a Norwegian Lutheran missionary to Danish Greenland in the first half of the eighteenth century. In his *Description of Greenland,* he admitted that of many reputed sea monsters there was only one that he or his acquaintances had observed. It surfaced off the coast of Greenland in 1734. Not only was it seen by a number of sailors, but its proximity to their ship provided a handy frame of reference. Supposedly the monster's body was as bulky as the ship's and at least three times as long, and its neck reached out of the water to the height of the masthead. The third source in Neill's list was another clergyman, the Danish theologian Erik Pontoppidan. In his 1755 *Natural History of Norway,* Pontoppidan described a number of monsters. One had a horselike head with a long white mane, and it too posed with a number of "folds, or coils" visible.

By the time of Patrick Neill, there were many such stories. With such a legacy, it is small wonder that his imagination ran away with him. Neill had based his account upon the report of a farmer named John Peace. Earlier in the year, Peace had spied what he thought was a whale washed up on the rocky coastline of Stronsa (now Stronsay), one of the Orkney Islands off the northern coast of Scotland. Approaching in his boat, he found not a whale but an unidentifiable carcass, battered by the crashing waves and greatly decomposed. It appeared to have only one genuinely bony body part, the spine; the rest of the skeleton was cartilage. Peace somehow estimated its length at 55 feet. As drawn by a man accompanying Peace, the creature had six legs, a long tail and neck, and a fin down its back. Hence Neill's designation *Halsydrus,* which means "sea water snake."

As the American naturalist Richard Ellis pointed out, in his account of the story in his book *Monsters of the Sea* (1995), unfortunately for Neill's place in the history of science others disagreed with his findings. In England, a part-time naturalist named Everard Home examined bits of the creature's cartilage and skin, and analyzed Peace's and the artist's descriptions. He recognized the supposed monster as a creature already well known—the basking shark. At a confirmed length of up to 40 feet, it is one of the largest of all fishes, as its species name *maximus* indicates. The basking shark does not have six legs, but it has two pelvic fins and two pectoral fins, and a male would have been equipped with two "claspers," organs unique to sharks. The first part of the shark's skeleton to decompose probably would have been the cartilaginous gill rakers, which would have left what appeared to be a serpentine neck. Although Home's analysis didn't dismiss the stories of the trio that Neill cited, it demonstrated how easily ignorance can spur the imagination, and it effectively discredited Neill's own paper. Yet another "sea monster" had turned out to be less monstrous, if no less fascinating, than people like to imagine.

---

20 November 1971

Banning DDT

In 1940 a Swiss chemist created a new insecticide related to that era's infamous nerve gases. Its chemical name, dichlorodiphenyltrichloroethane, was abbreviated DDT. Many officials declared it a boon to agriculture and public health on the order of the recently discovered penicillin. Soon it protected soldiers on Pacific islands from insect-borne diseases, controlled typhus by killing the body lice that transmitted it, and destroyed mosquitos so effectively that by 1951 malaria had been virtually wiped out in the United States.

Not surprisingly, such a fierce poison proved dangerous to more than just the targeted insects. One beach was sprayed to kill flies, and a week later there were so many dead fish that flies came just to feast. In Bolivia a village was sprayed to kill malarial mosquitos, but most of the local cats died, too, and an uncontrolled new population of vermin carrying black typhus killed hundreds of the villagers.

Then it was discovered that not only does DDT kill outright, but it also accumulates. Those concentrated dosages are what made it dangerous and caused a delay in linking cause and effect. A synthetic product that natural decomposers were unable to digest, it was nearly insoluble. Aquatic plants and microscopic animals absorbed it, and they in turn were eaten by a succession of animals higher in the food chain. At each level, DDT wasn't excreted but instead built up in the animal's fatty tissues.

Shrimp in Lake Michigan were found to have 70 times the DDT concentration of the water in which they lived. As the shrimp were eaten by fish that were in turn eaten by larger fish, the herring gulls higher in the chain wound up with a concentration 7,000 times that of the lake itself. Thus, those most threatened were the birds of prey at the top of the pyramid, and they have long life spans in which to absorb poisons.

The behavior of birds was also affected by DDT. Sometimes it made them so jumpy they abandoned their nests or young. However, the greatest danger came from the way it altered calcium production during egg laying. Sometimes eggs were so thin they couldn't support the parent bird during brooding. One DDT-poisoned bald eagle laid an egg that had no shell at all, just a membrane.

Some of these problems were known quite early. Soon after its introduction, entomologists warned that the new pesticide was dangerous. But as usual the poison makers and the Department of Agriculture ignored the evidence. They produced more and more DDT. Ever since the publication of Rachel Carson's *Silent Spring* in 1962, the public had known about the dangers, but it took years of protests to finally force national hearings. Although manufacturers, farmers, and public health officials predicted mass starvation and plagues, residential use of DDT was finally banned on November 20, 1971. A year later, a more comprehensive ban on all domestic use went into effect. Of course, DDT was replaced with stronger poisons such as malathion, but they didn't linger long enough to do as much damage. And it could still be exported. But another small battle had been won by conservationists.

---

21 November 1555

Agricola

The name Agricola has been a popular and illustrious one in history. To begin with, there was the first-century Roman general Gnaeus Julius Agricola. Besides rampaging about in Britain—and being the first to effectively conquer it—he also happened to be the father-in-law of Tacitus. Agricola was his real name; others later took it as a pseudonym. In fifteenth-century Europe, Dutch humanist Roelof Huysmann, who euphoniously redubbed himself Rodolphus Agricola, was influential in spreading about the (relatively) liberal notions of the Renaissance. About the time Huysmann died a child was born in Germany, christened Martin Sohr, who would become an important musical theorist under the surname Agricola. A few years later, Johannes Schnitter was born in the same country, where, under the alias Agricola, he would grow up to be a colleague of Luther and one of the founders of Protestantism. Fifteenth-century Europeans must have found all this confusing.

At about the same time, there was yet another man writing and stirring things up under the name of Agricola, and he is the one important in the history of natural history. He was born Georg Bauer, in Glauchau in the 1490s, and died on November 21, 1555. Bauer seems to have had a varied career. For some years he was rector of a school in Zwickau. In 1527 he shows up as a physician in Joachimstal, and then, for twenty years, in Chemnitz, where he also served as the city's burgomaster. However, by 1531, he was also studying mining in Chemnitz. In that field he seems to have found his niche, and he proceeded to become Europe's first systematic mineralogist.

Agricola's era was just beginning to outgrow medieval alchemical notions of the origin and behavior of minerals. Agricola is considered the father of mineralogy. He was one of the first Europeans to build his scientific writings upon a firm foundation of personal observation rather than upon the slavish quotation of the ancients, which constituted most scholarship at the time. In the mid-1550s he published his magnum opus, *De re metallica,* considered the first masterpiece of technological writing as well as a pioneer work of geology. Agricola examined the entire craft and science of mining and metallurgy—smelting, casting, the extraction of saltpeter, the production of gunpowder, the purification of mercury, even the making of glass. He classified minerals according to their chemical and physical attributes, and described over eighty. Twenty of them were previously unknown.

This tentative trust in reason and observation instead of received opinion is of course one of the hallmarks of that flowering of culture that we call the Renaissance. Just as Leonardo was doing in Italy at about the same time, Agricola compared the structure of the earth to that of the human body. Discussing minerals, he wrote, "The term vein is borrowed from that used for animals, for just as their veins are distributed through all parts of the body, and just as by means of the veins blood is diffused from the liver throughout the whole body, so also the veins traverse the whole globe, and more particularly the mountainous districts; and water runs and flows through them." Elsewhere, he said, "There are three forces which loosen and demolish the mountains, for in this case, to the power of the water and the strength of the wind we must add the fire in the interior of the earth." Such observations reveal the characteristic common sense that made Agricola so revolutionary in his time, and so well remembered in ours.

---

22 NOVEMBER 1977

Celebrating the Little Things of the World

"Most children have a bug period," Edward O. Wilson wrote in his autobiography. "I never grew out of mine." As a child, the future naturalist was drawn to the natural world. He was interested in everything, from the creatures of the sea to the birds overhead, but other factors interfered to narrow his focus to a particular aspect of nature. While fishing from a dock, Wilson yanked too hard on his line and a fish flew out of the water and into his face. A spine on its dorsal fin pierced his right eye. He lost most of the vision in that eye, but in his left it was so acute at close range that he could perceive the hairs on the bodies of small insects. During his early years Wilson also lost most of his ability to hear in the higher registers, which prevented him from appreciating, or even overhearing, most bird-songs. His view, he said, turned downward. "I would thereafter celebrate the little things of the world. . . ."

Wilson grew up on the Gulf Coast, prowling the aptly named Paradise Beach, near Pensacola, Florida. It was indeed paradise, at least for a child who loved the outdoors. He also explored the edge of the ocean, which turned out to be the edge of an alien world. "I became determined at an early age to be a scientist," he wrote, "so that I might stay close to the natural world." He caught snakes and ants and butterflies and frogs. He read *National Geographic* articles on the discoveries of scientists in far places and longed to grow up and join them.

Wilson turned his childhood interests into a career. He became an entomologist and an ecologist, and actually managed to travel to those remote parts of the world whose photographs he had once pored over. Over the years, he has won many awards, including two Pulitzer Prizes and the Crafoord Prize, which was established because the Nobel doesn't honor such fields as ecology. One mark of his success is the number of terms associated with him. "Biodiversity" is linked to him, although he did not coin it. In fact, he resisted it as too catchy, but his colleagues won him over. He did, however, coin a related word, *biophilia,* which he defines as "the inborn affinity human beings have for other forms of life." And a third word is so completely associated with him that he might as well have coined it: sociobiology, the study of the biological roots of human behavior. It is that topic that has caused the most uproar. It has always been controversial, since Darwin himself first examined the issue in *The Descent of Man.*

On November 22, 1977, President Jimmy Carter awarded Wilson the National Medal of Science for his work in sociobiology. In August, the cover of *Time* had carried the headline "Why You Do What You Do." The accompanying illustration depicted a man and a woman being manipulated by mari-onette strings from above, a misrepresentative simplification of the instinctive drives that influence human biology and hence human society. When Wilson lectured on the topic a few months later, a demonstrator emptied a pitcher of ice water over his head and with other demonstrators chanted, "Wil-son, you're all wet!" Nonetheless, Wilson has on his desk at Harvard a larger-than-life-size model of an ant carrying the banner "ONWARD SOCIOBIOLOGY!"

In 1980, *Harvard Magazine* invited seven Harvard professors to comment on what they regarded as the most perilous doom facing humanity in the next decade. Wilson was the only one to address envi-ronmental issues. "The worst thing that can happen, will happen, is not energy depletion, economic collapse, limited nuclear war, or conquest by totalitarian government. . . . The one process ongoing in the 1980s that will take millions of years to correct is the loss of genetic and species diversity by the destruction of natural habitats. This is the folly our descendants are least likely to forgive us."

Wilson says that for years one form this realization seemed to take in his mind was a recurring dream. He is on an island. He has been there for weeks and has done no natural history researches. Now that it is time to depart, he realizes he knows nothing about the plants and animals of the island. He tries to figure out where to begin. But it is too late. "The dream ends, and I awaken knotted with anx-iety and regret."

"The Inconvenience
of the Air"

Dr. Watson describes the scene in the Sherlock Holmes story, "The Adventure of the Bruce-Partington Plans":

> In the third week of November, in the year 1895, a dense yellow fog settled down upon London. From the Monday to the Thursday I doubt whether it was ever possible from our windows in Baker Street to see the loom of the opposite houses. . . . [F]or the fourth time, after pushing back our chairs from breakfast we saw the greasy, heavy brown swirl still drifting past us and condensing in oily drops upon the window panes.

Although the word for it had not yet been coined, Watson was observing more than fog. It was smog. The term was formed in 1905, when British physician Harold Des Voeux grafted the front of "smoke" to the rear of "fog." It was the phenomenon to which John Evelyn was referring in his 1661 tract *Fumifugium, or, the inconvenience of the air, and smoke of London dissipated.* He wrote of a day when "a presumptuous smoke issuing from near Northumberland house, and not far from Scotland Yard, did so invade the Court, that all the rooms, galleries and places about it, were filled and infested with it, and that to such a degree as men could hardly discern one another from the cloud. . . ."

Obviously, smog is not merely a recent phenomenon. In casual usage, the term refers to any kind of visible air pollution, particularly if it irritates our lungs or eyes or reduces visibility. Ever since early humans began to use fire, such pollution has been an occasional, localized phenomenon. As cities grew, and more and more people burned greater and greater amounts of fossil fuels, it became a health hazard not only to people but to other animals and plants. Smog inspired the first recorded legislation aimed at protecting the environment, an edict by England's King Edward I. Around the end of the thirteenth century, when not busy invading Scotland and Wales, Edward was prohibiting English merchants from burning coal while Parliament was in session. Coal burns much less efficiently than wood, but by comparison it was inexpensive and handy. The businessmen, as usual, won out over concerns about health, and the pollution continued to worsen, as Evelyn's *Fumifugium* indicates.

Fogbound in Baker Street, Holmes remarks to Watson that such weather is a godsend to criminals. "The thief or the murderer could roam London on such a day as the tiger does the jungle, unseen until he pounces, and then evident only to his victim." Actually, although it did hide the crimes of Jack the Ripper, far worse dangers lurk in smog. One modern demon that most urbanites have witnessed is a specialized variety called "photochemical smog," the kind of ugly brown haze that sunny days produce over large, automobile-crowded cities such as Los Angeles.

A photochemical reaction is one in which the energy comes from light. In photosynthesis, for example, plants absorb sunlight and transform its energy into chemical energy. (Ozone is formed by a similar sort of photochemical reaction. In the stratosphere, it helps insulate the earth from radiation, but lower in the atmosphere it is a chemical pollutant formed from ultraviolet radiation reacting with combustion gases.) Photochemical smog results from the action of sunlight upon hydrocarbons and nitrogen oxides suspended in the air, which converts them to toxic pollutants called photochemical oxidants.

Smog continues to plague cities, but in the twentieth century procedures have been enacted to reduce it. In 1929, for example, Des Voeux, the man who named the problem, formed the Coal Smoke Abatement Society in England. After a high-pressure system kept London choked and blinded for several days in 1952, killing 4,000 people and permanently endangering the health of many thousands of others, the British government finally enacted the Clean Air Bill in 1956. It prohibited the combustion of soft coal within London, and that was all it took to banish the deadly smogs. Environmentalists are now battling the photochemical pollution of Los Angeles and other cities.

---

24 November 1859

"A Gospel of Dirt"

"When on board H.M.S. *Beagle,* as naturalist," the book began, "I was much struck with certain facts in the distribution of the organic beings inhabiting South America, and in the geological relations of the present to the past inhabitants of that continent. These facts . . . seemed to throw some light on the origin of species. . . ." Charles Darwin's *On the Origin of Species by Means of Natural Selection, or the Preservation of Favoured Races in the Struggle for Life* was published on November 24, 1859. To Darwin's astonishment, the first printing of 1,250 copies was oversubscribed and sold out the first day. One of the most controversial books in history was off and running.

Nowadays, while there are disagreements about the mechanisms that drive the process, no reputable scientist questions the fact of evolution. It is too well documented. New fossil, anatomical, molecular, and behavioral evidence accumulates daily. However, what is now the foundation of biology and the cornerstone of ecology was at that time scandal and heresy.

Darwin was not the first to suggest that species evolve. He was the first to marshal an irresistible array of evidence that evolution had indeed occurred. Also, even without knowledge of genetics, he proposed a reasonable mechanism to explain evolution—"natural selection." Put simply, it meant that in each generation some individuals in a species are better suited to their environment than others, and that species thus fortunate would be likelier to survive and reproduce, passing on their survival virtues. That this "selection" was entirely "natural," with a hands-on God nowhere in sight, was what most offended Darwin's opponents. Thomas Carlyle called Darwin's ideas "a gospel of dirt."

The original caption to this cartoon began with the Defrauded Gorilla crying, "That Man wants to claim my Pedigree. He says he is one of my Descendants." In response, Henry Bergh, founder of the American Society for the Prevention of Cruelty to Animals, demands, "Mr. Darwin, how could you insult him so?"

Darwin disagreed. He thought there was a "grandeur" in the view that, "from so simple a beginning, endless forms most beautiful and most wonderful have been, and are being evolved." And he made his idea's ecological implications explicit: "If we choose to let conjecture run wild, then animals—our fellow brethren in pain, disease, death, suffering and famine, our slaves in the most laborious works, our companions in our amusements,—they may partake from our origin in one common ancestry, we may be all netted together."

Not everyone condemned Darwin. Victorian novelist and rector Charles Kingsley wrote to applaud the *Origin*. Although he admitted that "if you be right I must give up much that I have believed," still, it was "just as noble a conception of Deity, to believe that He created primal forms capable of self development . . . as to believe that He required a fresh act of intervention" for each new kind of animal. In the United States, a long-time Darwin reader named Henry Thoreau wrote in his journal, "The development theory implies a greater vital force in nature, because it is more flexible and accommodating, and equivalent to a sort of constant *new* creation."

Darwin's sole remark about the place of *Homo sapiens* in his vision of nature was "Much light will be thrown on the origin of man and his history." However, most readers understood that Darwin had posed, and answered, a secular version of Pascal's great question, "For in fact what is man in nature?" If all other creatures derived from a common origin, humanity must have also. Immediately there were expressions of disgust at the thought of our neighbors in the family tree. Objections arose not because the kinship was unthinkable, but because it was quite thinkable, and people had been thinking it since their first encounters with monkeys and apes. In the third century B.C., the Roman poet Ennius remarked, "The ape, vilest of beasts, how like to us!" Almost 2,000 years later, the English Restoration playwright William Congreve admitted, "I could never look long upon a monkey, without very mortifying reflections."

One of the concerns of even the more open-minded Victorians was that the widespread realization of our animal origin might result in a surrender to our beastly nature—as if other worldviews had kept it in check. The classic remark along those lines is attributed to the wife of the Anglican bishop of Worcester: "Descended from apes! My dear, let us hope that it is not true, but if it is, let us pray that it will not become generally known."

"So Thick a Mist and Fog"

The reality is straightforward enough. When humid air cools to its dew point, the water vapor suspended in it condenses into droplets, forming a cloud near the ground. Yet something about fog tugs at the imagination. Carl Sandburg's Chicago fog comes on little cat feet. T. S. Eliot employed similar feline imagery in "The Love Song of J. Alfred Prufrock," in which yellow fog rubs its back and muzzle upon the windowpanes, licks its tongue into the corners of the evening, and finally curls about the house and goes to sleep. In the less domesticated world of Ray Bradbury's short story "The Fog Horn," a new lighthouse broadcasts its warning horn into the coastal fog until one night a plesiosaur, drawn from its ancient home in the deep, replies.

Most fog is neither so metaphorical nor so mysterious. Ground fog, or radiation fog, as meteorologists call it, forms when the ground, which warms during the day, radiates its heat upward, cooling both the ground and the air close to it. This requires a clear night with little or no breeze, because stronger winds mix cold and warm air and prevent the conditions under which fog might form. As cool air moves in to replace the departing warmth near the ground, the air is cooled to its dew point and condenses into fog. The morning mists that burn off within a couple of hours are of this kind.

There are other species, but all recognizably in the same genus. Advection fog, for example, is the sort that shuts down airports and harbors in wintertime, when wind pushes horizontal masses of humid warm air inland across cool ground. It can cover large areas and last for days. John Evelyn described a dramatic experience of it in his diary on November 25, 1699.

> There happen'd this weeke so thick a mist and fog that people lost their way in the streetes, it being so intense that no light of candles or torches yielded any (or but very little) direction. I was in it and in danger. Robberies were committed between the very lights which were fix'd between London and Kensington on both sides, and whilst coaches and travellers were passing. It began about four in the afternoone, and was quite gone by eight, without any wind to disperse it. At the Thames they beat drums to direct the watermen to make the shore.

Many areas of the world experience dramatic fogs, but England's are legendary. They occupy their own meteorological classification in literature. After the witches in *Macbeth* determine where they three will meet again, they chant in unison: "Fair is foul, and foul is fair: / Hover through the fog and filthy air." The early scenes in *Great Expectations,* in which Pip sneaks food to the felon hiding in the marsh, would not be half so chilling if fog didn't disguise his familiar surroundings and allow everything to jump out at him as he nears it. And where would the Sherlock Holmes stories be without fog? The chase across Grimpen Mire in *The Hound of the Baskervilles* is a frightening scene partially because fog has isolated the moor in a Coleridgean realm: "As we watched it the fog-wreaths came crawling round both corners of the house and rolled slowly into one dense bank, on which the upper floor and the roof floated like a strange ship upon a shadowy sea."

Fog can also be a powerful device in cinema, as proven by films from *Dracula* to *Casablanca.* It won the title role in John Carpenter's 1979 supernatural thriller *The Fog* and shared top billing in Woody Allen's *Shadows and Fog* in 1992. Both exploit the shadowy unearthliness of fog for its ability to disorient, for its clammy nighttime terrors, in the spirit of Browning's line that expresses a great deal more than water vapor condensation: "Fear death?—to feel the fog in my throat, / The mist in my face."

---

26 November 1922

Tut's Animals

Tutankhamen was an Egyptian pharaoh of the Eighteenth Dynasty in Egypt. He had already been a king for several years when he died at the age of eighteen, in the middle of the fourteenth century B.C. For over three millennia, his tomb lay underneath the sands of Egypt's barren Biban el Moluk, the Valley of the Kings. He was largely forgotten. Then, after years of investigating the few scattered mentions of the boy king, an English archaeologist named Howard Carter found the tomb and made Tutankhamen's name a household word in a much larger world than he had ever known.

Carter described November 26, 1922, as "the day of days, the most wonderful that I have ever lived through, and certainly one whose like I can never hope to see again." A second sealed doorway had been reached in the excavations. Watched by his backer, Lord Carnarvon, and others, Carter slowly made a hole in the door large enough for him to hold a candle inside. As ancient air escaped, the candle flickered. The first thing Carter noticed was the glint of gold all about the room.

"Can you see anything?" Carnarvon asked.

It was all Carter could do to speak the words: "Yes, wonderful things."

Among the wonderful things in the tomb were many animal figures, reminders of the primitive, intertwined origins of art and religion. These creations that nowadays we regard as beautiful works of art were to the ancient Egyptians figures of enormous religious significance. All creatures had a symbolic role to play in the great drama of the cosmos. Nothing underlines that more than the variety of animal representations in Tut's tomb.

Carter immediately saw three couches, "their sides carved in the form of monstrous animals, curiously attenuated in body, as they had to be to serve their purpose, but with heads of startling realism." Eventually he and his workers found a gold cloisonné pendant of Nekhebet, the vulture goddess of Upper Egypt; a stylized recumbent lion made of stone; and many versions of the winged scarab, symbol of resurrection. An alabaster jar bore on its lid a carving of a bird just emerged from an egg. The legs of Tut's folding stool and headrest were shaped like the long necks of geese. He himself took the form of the jackal-headed god Anubis, and appeared in the guise of an alabaster lion atop an unguent jar decorated with a hunting scene. Another such container, again carved of alabaster, was in the shape of a kneeling ibex, with one real horn (the other was missing). There were representations of Thoth, the overworked god of magic and learning and time, who had the head of an ibis. Statues of the king wore upon their foreheads the sacred cobra with spread hood, the universal symbol of Tutankhamen's divine authority.

For all the many centuries it lay cozy in its nestled sarcophagi, Tut's body was surrounded by animal figures. Entwined cobras wrapped around his temple and over the crown of his shaven head, which was also adorned with a vulture with spread wings—all, of course, made of gold. A long golden serpent lay stretched out beside his left leg. These animals were to help the boy king voyage to the other world. Whether or not he achieved his planned-for resurrection in the next world, thanks to Carnarvon and Carter he was resurrected in this one. It is no wonder that the last resting place of the boy king captured the world's imagination. His own funerary inscriptions include a reassurance of the power of remembering: "To speak the name of the dead is to make them live again."

---

27 November 1712

"War with the Snakes"

One might imagine the honor would go to Benjamin Franklin or Thomas Jefferson. But no, the first American member of Britain's prestigious Royal Society was the Puritan divine, Cotton Mather. Although he is best known for his involvement in the Salem witch trials, and for his *Memorable Providences relating to Witchcraft and Possessions,* it was his *Curiosa Americana* that prompted the Royal Society to invite him to join.

In more than fifty letters, Mather wrote to the society about the birth of Siamese twins, the influence of the phases of the moon upon tree cutting and weather, the ubiquity and edibility of passenger pigeons, the insensibility of a family of "idiots," a calf born with a disturbingly human visage—and, appropriately, the power of imagination. And, on the twenty-seventh of November, 1712, he wrote about one of his most curious bits of Americana, an animal that European natural philosophers found fascinating. "The Rattle-snakes have their Winter-habitations on our Hills, in hideous Caves, and the Clefts of Inaccessible Rocks. In the Spring they come forth, and ly a Sunning themselves, but still in pretty feeble circumstances. Our Trained Bands [the militia, later called Minute Men] in some of our Countrey towns, take this time, to carry on a *War* with the *Snakes,* and make the killing of them, a part of their Discipline."

For Mather, the snake was not a mere animal, if indeed he regarded any animal as lacking spiritual significance. It was plain from the Bible that snakes were Satan's earthly manifestation, and therefore the enemy of both man and God. In an essay with a title straight from a hiking guide, "The Right Way to Shake Off a Viper," Mather talks about how Jesus was ill-treated. "Thus a Generation of vipers, the most remarkable set of the Seed of the serpent that had been in any generation, stung the *Holy, Harmless,*

The common opposition to snakes is exemplified in the biblical myth of the Garden of Eden, in which Satan, in the guise of a chatty and persuasive serpent, dares Eve to ignore God's dietary restrictions.

Undefiled JESUS!" According to both Matthew and Luke, Jesus called several crowds a generation of vipers. (American author Philip Wylie couldn't resist the powerful phrase for the title of a 1942 work of nonfiction.) Although Job refers to one, only a single snake described as a viper actually appears in the Bible. It comes out of a fire and fastens itself to Paul's hand. When he merely shakes it off and suffers no swelling, the crowd decides he is a god. This is one of the passages cited as biblical authority by Christians who believe snake handling proves their faith.

Like their ancestors, the New World Puritans saw nature's every move as the meaningful gesture of a compulsively symbol-minded God. Massachusetts governor John Winthrop described in his journal a battle several people claimed to have witnessed between a mouse and a snake, which the mouse won. As if the world were one big fable by Aesop, a minister interpreted this alleged showdown: "That the snake was the devil; the mouse was a poor, contemptible people, which God had brought hither, which should overcome Satan here, and dispossess him of his kingdom." It was such simpleminded attitudes that kept alive the biblical notion, still to be found in places, that humanity was engaged in an ongoing war with the snakes.

---

28 NOVEMBER 1967

Little Green Men and the Nobel Prize

Jocelyn Bell was born in 1943, in Belfast, Northern Ireland. Her parents were Quakers, and she claimed that it was growing up in that faith that instilled in her the importance of education. Quakers have produced a disproportionate number of scientists. Bell was destined to join them.

During Ireland's Catholic-Protestant strife in the 1950s, Bell's parents sent her to a boarding school in York, England. Her father was an architect, and on visits back home she visited one of his projects. He was renovating the Armagh Observatory. Soon Bell was devouring everything she could find on astronomy. She planned to major in her new passion in Glasgow, Scotland, one of the few places in Great Britain where she could earn a degree in astronomy. However, the limited professional opportunities led her to choose physics instead. Soon she was the only woman in her class. Men kidded her; women told her she was getting more education than a woman needed. In 1965, she graduated with honors.

At the time, female astronomers were scarce, and the field seemed determined to keep them that way. In the United States, women were simply not permitted to use important telescopes such as the one on Mount Palomar. In Britain, they were shunted into research on the sun because such daylight work avoided the risk of immorality resulting from men and women staying up late together to look at the sky. Nonetheless, Bell went into graduate studies at Cambridge, with astronomer Anthony Hewish. Hewish was building a radio receiver to eavesdrop on radiation coming from space, especially those sources that produced variable amounts of it. His telescope was a vast network of wires that eventually covered almost five acres, and Bell was in charge of much of its installation.

In 1967, when the radiotelescope went into operation, Hewish placed Bell in charge of operating it and analyzing the results. The sensitivity required to detect cosmic radiation sources meant that the telescope also gathered every kind of local radio noise, from aircraft flying over to television transmissions from across the channel. Bell spent her time meticulously analyzing every squiggle on the receiver's endless output of graph paper. After only two months, she noticed that a half-inch-long "bit of scruff" was recurring. Bell kept checking and finally saw the characteristic scruff again. On November 28, 1967, the machine drew a series of pulses that were 1⅓ seconds apart. More precise measurement revealed a beacon in the sky sending out a signal precisely every 1.3373011 seconds. It was the fastest and most precise variable radiation ever detected.

It was a conundrum. Analysis indicated that the source must be far beyond the solar system and was probably no larger than a small planet. "We had to face the possibility," Hewish remarked later, "that the signals were, indeed, generated on a planet circling some distant star and that they were artificial." The first radiation source was nicknamed LGM-1. Initialese is rampant in astronomy, but this example stood for Little Green Men.

Shortly afterward, however, Bell discovered a similar signal coming from another part of the sky, and it was even more frequent than the first. Soon she found two more. Hewish decided to announce the discovery and sent a paper to *Nature,* with Bell as one of five coauthors. In 1974, the Nobel Prize for Physics was awarded, for the first time, to astronomers—Anthony Hewish and Martin Ryle. Jocelyn Bell was not mentioned. Many scientists were outraged on her behalf, and she has won numerous honors since.

What Bell had discovered was what we now call "pulsars." Apparently, the term, a rear-end collision between "pulsating" and "star," was coined by an English science reporter. Bell declared it "a ghastly name," but by coincidence it was close to the Latin root of "pulsate"—*pulsare,* meaning to beat like a heart. The existence of pulsars had been predicted as early as the 1930s. Stars of different sizes come to different ends. Smaller ones may end up as burned-out white dwarfs. Larger stars may collapse in upon themselves and form an astonishingly dense clump of matter called a neutron star. Spinning ever faster on its axis as it becomes more dense, the former star emits radio waves from its magnetic poles. From elsewhere in the universe—for example, from a radio telescope in a field in England—the spin appears as a pulsating broadcast of radiation. Although there are now more than 600 known pulsars, no little green men seem to be involved. However, as Carl Sagan has pointed out, such regularly blinking natural sources of radiation would make great interstellar navigation beacons.

The Cardiff Giant

The Great
CARDIFF GIANT!
Discovered at Cardiff, Onondaga Co., N.Y., is now on Exhibition in the
Geological Hall, Albany,
For a few days only.

Below these exclamations, the broadsheet lists "His Dimensions," a strange hodgepodge of statistics including

Length of Body,	10 feet, 4 1-2 inches.
Length of Nose	6 "
Across the Nostrils	3 1-2 "
Length of Right Arm	4 feet, 9 1-2 "
Length of Foot	21 "

And, most impressively, the last item in the list:

Weight	2990 pounds

At the bottom, in small print, the broadsheet is dated November 29, 1869. Scarcely a month earlier, a farmer named William Newell, of Cardiff, New York, had announced the discovery of a prehistoric giant. He claimed he and others were digging a well behind his barn when they accidentally dug into the resting place of a stone giant. The figure was nude, lying on his back, his right arm folded across his abdomen. Crowds of the curious flocked to the area. It was no surprise to anyone to find Newell, assisted by his cousin George Hull, charging admission. First the Syracuse newspapers picked up the story, then the national and finally the international papers joined in.

Both experts and nonexperts, including some who had not seen the item in question, readily pontificated. Most agreed it could not possibly be a fossil human being, because fossilization simply does not turn the entire bodily structure into stone while preserving all the soft body parts. Others declared that it was an ancient statue—which, while not rating up there with proof of prehistoric giants, was still a wonderful find. The opinion of a third group is nicely represented by the words of Yale paleontologist Othniel C. Marsh, who said flatly, "It is of very recent origin and a decided humbug."

Nonetheless, Newell and Hull took their show on the road. They went to Albany, then Syracuse, and finally on to New York City. Inspired by so many conflicting opinions on the authenticity of the Cardiff Giant, reporters went to work exhuming its secret history. They found several juicy items, including witnesses who had observed a suspiciously large box aboard a cart headed toward the Newell farm not long before the discovery. It turned out that Hull had masterminded the scheme, securing a massive block of gypsum from a quarry in Iowa. Finally a sculptor confessed that he had carved the figure.

In the meantime, naturally, P. T. Barnum couldn't let anyone challenge his role as premier con man of his era. As soon as the showman got wind of Newell's "find," he determined to cash in on it. Newell turned down Barnum's offer of $60,000 for a three-month lease on the giant, so Barnum merely commissioned a sculptor to copy it. By the time Hull and Newell took their prize to New York City, Barnum was already exhibiting his own. They sued him. However, when their scam fell apart and the papers were full of stories about the fraud, Barnum once again dodged the law by pointing out that he was merely showing a fake fake.

A photograph from 1948 shows the gypsum giant being lowered into a grave at the Farmer's Museum in Cooperstown, New York. Hats over their hearts, the workmen struggle to feign solemnity, but two or three are grinning. A half century later, now covered by a shed, the statue is still on display, mute testimony to P. T. Barnum's estimate of the birthrate of a certain portion of the populace.

These 1869 illustrations for Harper's Weekly *portray the "excavation" of that great American fake, the Cardiff Giant.*

---

30 NOVEMBER 1974

Woman from Afar

There were three good reasons to stay in camp that morning: The temperature was over 100°F, the end of the fossil-digging season was near, and there was paperwork to do. It was the latter, paleoanthropologist Donald Johanson said later, that drove him and graduate student Tom Gray back out for another look around. Their dig was in the Hadar region of the Afar Triangle in Ethiopia, in the northern end of Africa's vast Rift Valley that stretches from Tanzania to the Red Sea. Farther south, the valley includes such fossil-rich sites as Olduvai Gorge and Koobi Fora.

That morning, Johanson and Gray found fossil antelope and horse teeth and a monkey jaw. Then, before heading back at midday, they returned to a gully they had scrutinized twice before. "Along the way," Johanson wrote later, "I glanced over my right shoulder. Light glinted off a bone. I knelt down

415

for a closer look." It was an arm bone. In a few minutes they found a thigh bone, ribs, even a piece of a skull. The bones were obviously of human ancestry. Johanson and Gray jumped for joy and hugged. It was November 30, 1974.

The skeleton might well have been named Hadar Woman, joining such traditional names as Java Man and the Taung Child. (Thirteen skeletons found nearby the next year were dubbed the First Family.) Instead, that evening, the team examined the jigsaw pieces of the skeleton by the light of butane lamps, while playing a Beatles cassette over and over. No one remembers who named the skeleton after "Lucy in the Sky with Diamonds." Reporters loved the name "Lucy"; it was certainly catchier than her later scientific designation, *Australopithecus afarensis*. She soon made world headlines. Cartoons and magazine covers followed. Lucy attained the role of an almost Eve-like ancestor of humanity. In a recent chronology of women's history, she is the first female mentioned.

Lucy is now thought to be a million years or so younger than the first age estimate of 4 million years. Still, she embodies the oldest evidence of bipedalism. Free hands and a taller posture were adaptive virtues even then. Although the Turkana Boy would break her record twelve years later, in 1974 Lucy's was the most intact fossil hominid ever found. Her curved fingers and toes indicate she still may have been partially arboreal. Because her braincase was only slightly larger than that of a modern six-year-old, scientists describe her as a sort of upright chimpanzee. Lucy was evidence on behalf of the theory that bipedalism evolved before brain enlargement.

Lucy accompanied Johanson home to the United States in January 1975. "Each fragment of her precious skeleton was wrapped in toilet paper and stored in a bulging carry-on suitcase." Flying over the curved earth in which Lucy had remained hidden for so long, Johanson marveled at how "the scrawny primate whose remains were tucked under my feet had evolved into a species capable of constructing the Boeing technology that carried me home."

---

1 DECEMBER 1959

Two Treaties

On the first of December, 1959, representatives from twelve nations signed a treaty supposedly designed to preserve Antarctica from the greed and shortsightedness that had ravaged every other continent. The signers were Argentina, Chile, New Zealand, Australia, Norway, France, Britain, the Soviet Union, the United States, Japan, South Africa, and Belgium. All except the last three claimed parts of Antarctica, but agreed to freeze those claims for the time being. The Soviet Union and the United States proclaimed in unison that they would establish no territories in Antarctica, and that furthermore they would not respect the territorial claims of other nations.

The Antarctic Treaty was also the first international arms control treaty to reach fruition since the end of World War II. No military bases were to be built. Because the relative seclusion and lack of population might tempt the irresponsible, the treaty became the first to specify an area in which no nuclear weapons could be tested and no nuclear wastes dumped. The continent was to be considered open to all nations for scientific inquiry. Of course, as soon as scientific bases are established, they are considered an unofficial claim to the area by virtue of squatters' rights. For example, the number of scientific territories that converge at the South Pole are often considered to be outvoted by the U.S. research base situated at the pole itself.

As soon as the Antarctic Treaty was enacted, countries began violating both the spirit and the letter of it. In the summer of 1961–62, the U.S. Navy hauled to Antarctica a portable nuclear reactor actually nicknamed "Nukey Poo." Although in use for the next eleven years, it deliberately released radioactive gases and accidentally leaked radioactive liquids. And, finally, in 1979, satellites and radio antennae detected a telltale flash in the neighborhood of Prince Edward Island, a region claimed by South Africa. The next year a U.S. government panel proclaimed the source of the explosion to be "technically indeterminate," but at the same time the U.S. Navy described it as a "nuclear event." Only in 1991 did South Africa finally admit that they had indeed tested a nuclear weapon in Antarctica. The optimistic Antarctic Treaty had gone the way of most of its ancestors.

Not surprisingly, the treaties easiest to enact and uphold concern lands not coveted by anyone at the moment. History proves again and again that these documents, like other promises, are made to be broken. Yet they are better than nothing. In 1967, in both Moscow and Washington, representatives of several nations signed a treaty with more far-reaching consequences than the one for the Antarctic. Both the Soviet Union and the United States were regularly sending human beings into outer space. It was apparent that in the near future the human race would set foot on the Moon, and then on other planets. The worry was that whoever got there first would not do so in the name of the entire human race, but on behalf of the area of Earth marked off with the imaginary lines they had been taught to revere. Therefore the signers of the 1967 treaty solemnly declared that no nation on Earth could claim any part of another planet.

This treaty thinks farther ahead than politicians usually do, perhaps because many of them consider it a document never to be challenged. The less myopic, however, realize that as soon as trips to the Moon begin again, nationalism will rush to the fore. The Moon is in our backyard. We have been there before, and we will return. Voyages to Mars are completely within the capabilities of current technology, lacking only funding and public enthusiasm. There are other planets in our solar system besides Mars. And, in 1995, astronomers proved that there are indeed planets circling some nearby stars. Like the Antarctica Treaty, the Planetary Treaty will be relevant before we know it.

Killing the Dear Little Divine One

The onset of winter, with the disappearance of animals and the apparent death of the plants that had been so busy in the autumn, filled primitive cultures with dread. They knew they were themselves in for a difficult time during the next few months. Every winter, like every sunset, was a symbolic death, and apparently one of the few constants throughout human history is the human brain's determination to perceive the world in symbolic terms.

Because of its distinctive biological rhythms, one animal came to represent the life force itself. Bears retreat into the earth for an apparent death, reemerge just ahead of spring as if causing it, and give birth to cubs very early. Like so many aspects of nature, bears' lives seemed to their human neighbors like a ritual enacted for their instruction. The result of this magical thinking was, naturally, most unfortunate for the bears. For many centuries, one of the enduring winter rituals of cultures of the Northern Hemisphere was the festival of the slain bear. Like most such rites, this one had a practical side to it. Taken from the earth during its sleep, roused and fêted and ceremoniously killed, the bear's body then offered nourishing red meat and fat, and even gave its fur to warm its human brethren.

In some cultures, hunters found a mother bear with a cub, killed the mother, and took the cub home to their village. It was then raised by a childless couple, who treated it as one of their own. They even allowed it to sleep in a bed. Then, after three years, it was released into the forest. Some peoples, however, did not free the cub but raised it to adulthood to be ritually sacrificed. One such group was the

Ainu of mountainous Japan, who held their bear celebration in early December. If they captured a cub that was very young, Ainu women nursed it as if it were a human baby. Then, for the next two or three years, it was treated as an honored guest. When the time came for its death, it was tied up, ritually beaten and tormented with goads, and finally strangled. The bear's human foster mother, who had nursed and cared for it since its infancy, performed the ceremonial grief.

An Ainu invitation to friends, preserved from as late as 1888, indicates the tone of the bear ritual:

> I . . . am about to send away the dear little divine one whose home is among the mountains. My friends and masters, come yet to the feast and we will unite in the great joy of sending him off. Come!

The bear's form was thought to be merely the body it wore while among humans. Its fur and meat were ultimately gifts to humanity, which it left behind when death freed it to return to its true divine form. That belief is evident in an Ainu

Like most other animals, bears have suffered endless violence for no other reason than religious ritual.

prayer led by a shaman (the translation of which has been glaringly couched in the tone of the King James Bible): "O divine One, we present Thee with these fetishes, cakes and dried fish. Take them to thy parents and say, 'I have been brought up by an Ainu father and mother, and have been kept free from harm and trouble. I am now grown big and am come back to you. I have also brought cakes, dried fish, and fetishes with me. Let us rejoice.'"

---

3 DECEMBER 1775

"Don't Tread on Me"

Snakes show up in the strangest places. In a nineteenth-century sculpture from southern India, a serpent representing creative energy emerges from an extremely private part of a goddess. The Hopi snake dance required a rattlesnake to be held between the teeth. A T'ang dynasty pottery figurine from seventh- or eighth-century China portrays a berobed human figure with piously clasped hands and the long-necked head of a snake, representing the Year of the Serpent. Christian zealots in the American South handle poisonous snakes to prove their faith in Jesus. Practically every hospital displays somewhere a caduceus, the staff of Asclepius with two snakes wound around it.

Snakes have been our familiar neighbors throughout history, and their behavior provides ready images. Plumbers call their pipe-cleaning tools "snakes," and a roll of two ones in dice is called "snake eyes." In his *Essay on Criticism*, in a withering description of predictable verse, Alexander Pope described an Alexandrine sonnet, "That, like a wounded snake, drags its slow length along." (Because of the common habit of attacking any snake we encounter, the sight of a wounded one is not uncommon.) Presumably it was some snakes' habit of hibernating en masse, and the vivid images that inspires that led to the association with mental institutions immortalized in M. J. Ward's 1947 novel *The Snake Pit,* and the film version the following year. Steven Spielberg made the image just a bit more explicit in such herpephobe's nightmares as Indiana Jones's tumble into a railway car full of snakes.

Found in almost all parts of the world, the more than 2,000 species of snakes have played an astonishing variety of symbolic roles in folklore and mythology. In the few places where there are none, there are stories about them; the Irish regard its snakelessness as one of the Emerald Isle's prime virtues. Because our own fright can inhibit reflexes, humans have claimed snakes possess the ability to immobilize their prey with their hypnotic eyes. For its habit of shedding its old skin and appearing in a new one, the snake became a symbol of rebirth, as in Keats's grotesque simile "The earth doth like a snake renew." Snakes have been cast in a villainous light from the Genesis myth of the Garden of Eden to Kaa in *The Jungle Book* to the unintentionally campy film *Ssssssss* (also known as *Sssnake.*) One familiar usage probably predates Virgil's *Latet anguis in herba,* "There's a snake hidden in the grass."

One strange place where a snake can be found is on early American flags. The best known depicted a coiled rattlesnake in the center of a yellow field, and underneath it the warning "Don't Tread on Me." That challenge first flew over the American ship *Alfred,* on December 3, 1775, when Commander in Chief Esek Hopkins took command of the Congress's new fleet. A rattlesnake appeared on a different flag raised on another ship the very same day, crawling across the familiar thirteen stripes. "Liberty or Death" was the slogan under the coiled rattlesnake on the flag of the Virginia Minutemen. Other colonial flags portrayed, for example, a snake coiled around a pine tree. All of these were unlikely sights, but powerful symbols, and for snakes just another job to list on a crowded résumé.

---

4 DECEMBER 1882

"The Stupendous Background"

"This slightly built romance," Thomas Hardy wrote in his preface, "was the outcome of a wish to set the emotional history of two infinitesimal lives against the stupendous background of the stellar universe, and to impart to readers the sentiment that of these contrasting magnitudes the smaller might be the greater to them as men." *Two on a Tower* was published in October of 1882. On December 4 Hardy sent a copy to a friend, the writer Edmund Gosse. A few days later, he wrote to Gosse, "I get most extraordinary criticisms of T. on a T." He complained that in private critics told him his new novel was the most original thing he had done, but in public they denounced him as immoral. Like most of Hardy's novels, this little-known one was first denounced as improper.

The tragicomic story concerns the love affair between Lady Viviette Constantine, an older woman who has been abandoned by her husband, and Swithin St. Cleeve, a younger man with a passion for the stars. Although the tower of the title belongs to Lady Viviette, until her arrival young Swithin had secretly used it as an astronomical observatory. At their first meeting, he confesses his ambition: "I aim at nothing less than the dignity and office of Astronomer Royal. . . ." Their romance seems inevitable from the moment she arrives unannounced at the tower and says, "You said you would show me the heavens if I could come on a starlight night. I have come." Readers were shocked by Viviette's later calculated marriage to a bishop so that her child would be born in wedlock. However, "strange behavior," as the *Saturday Review* described it, "is less startling on top of an astronomical tower than in an ordinary drawing room."

Swithin, like many stargazers before him, draws humbling lessons from the heavens. He points out that only 3,000 or so stars are visible with the naked eye and asks Viviette how many she thinks are visible with a telescope. She refuses to guess. "Twenty millions," he informs her. "So that, whatever the stars were made for, they were not made to please our eyes." She replies, "I think astronomy is a bad study for you. It makes you feel human insignificance too plainly."

On those rare occasions when astronomers show up in fiction, that sense of insignificance is usually a theme. It appears, for example, in Saul Bellow's novel *The Dean's December,* published 110 years after Hardy's. Albert Corde, the dean of the title, is married to an astronomer. At the end of the novel, he accompanies her to California, where she has won time to use the telescope at Mount Palomar. "The hugeness of the dome referred you—far past mosques or churches, Saint Paul's, Saint Peter's— to the real scale of the night. We built as big as we could for investigating the *real* bigness. . . . And what he saw with his eyes was not even the real heavens. No, only white marks, bright vibrations, clouds of sky roe, tokens of the real thing, only as much as could be taken in through the distortions of the atmosphere. Through these distortions you saw objects, forms, partial realities. The rest was to be felt."

Huge, domed like sky-worshiping cathedrals, observatories inspire such epiphanies by their very architecture. So, on occasion, do places that resemble them. In an essay about the movies that meant so much to his small-town childhood, Italian author Italo Calvino described a cinema in his hometown that provided fresh air through a metallic dome that opened like an observatory's in the middle of the vaulted ceiling. During the intermission between the first and second reels, the management would open the cathedral-like dome. "The sight of the sky in the interval would give pause for thought, with the slow passing of a cloud that might perfectly well have come from other continents, other centuries. On summer evenings the dome would stay open during the film itself; the presence of the firmament enclosed everything remote in a single universe."

The Disappearance
of Peking Man

Near Beijing is a region called Chou Kou Tien, "Hills of the Dragons." The name comes from artifacts long familiar from the quarries and limestone caves of the region—ancient bones and teeth that earlier generations called "dragon bones." Supplying the dragon bone trade has been a lucrative cottage industry in China for centuries. Even today some Chinese apothecaries sell such fossils. Ground into fine powder, they are a prized ingredient in medicines.

Although Darwin had predicted in 1871 that humanity's ancestors would be found in Africa, the discovery of Java Man in the late 1800s redirected attention to Asia. In the early decades of the twentieth century, paleontologists flocked to China and elsewhere in the region, seeking proof that humanity had first evolved there. (The dramatic African discoveries of the Leakey clan, Donald Johanson, and others would not come to light for several decades.) In 1926, a paleontologist announced to his fellow scientists that he had found two humanlike fossil teeth in the ancient strata of Chou Kou Tien. He didn't publicize the discovery, because the find was so modest. Then, in the 1930s, a group of paleontologists found several skulls of prehistoric humans there.

Photographs from the time reveal the extent of the excavations. Much of the hillside is scored with a grid to guide the digging. Down on the floor of a surprisingly deep hole, scientists measure and document every scrap of material in what was a cave before it collapsed. In the background, beyond the former homes of cave people, modern houses perch on hillsides, testimony to the passage of aeons and the evolutionary success of Peking Man's descendants.

The new fossil resembled Java Man, *Pithecanthropus erectus* ("Upright Walking Ape Man"), but it received its own name, *Sinanthropus* ("Man from China") *pekinensis*. Finally, paleontologists determined that both were the same species, and during the 1950s they were merged into the single designation that stands today, *Homo erectus*. Fossils of this mid-Pleistocene species have since been found in Africa, Europe, and Asia. Apparently it died out roughly 400,000 years ago. Some of the Chou Kou Tien skulls were broken at the base, which may indicate cannibalism. The common presence of ashes proves the use of fire.

H. erectus fossils are known from many places, but those of Peking Man that caused the original excitement in China in the 1930s are, simply, gone. After spending millions of years hidden away, they were unearthed for a few years and lost again. After the Japanese invasion of China, paleontologists hesitated to ship the fossils out because they belonged to the Chinese government. However, they prepared careful casts, which they shipped safely to the American Museum of Natural History in New York. Finally, the original bones were packaged for shipment out of harm's way.

Their ultimate fate is unknown. Stories vary. Apparently the bones were placed aboard a train carrying U.S. Marines from Beijing by way of the Manchuria railroad to Chinwangtao, a small town on the coast of China. From there they were to sail from Shanghai aboard the U.S. liner *President Harrison*.

The train departed Peking at 5:00 A.M. on December 5, 1941, but that was the last the scientific community ever saw of the bones of Peking Man. Two days later, the Japanese bombed Pearl Harbor, and the region was at war. One story claims that the Japanese took over the train, the marines wound up in Japanese concentration camps, and the bones vanished. Another story says the bones actually made it safely aboard the *President Harrison.* At least the first scenario permits the faint possibility that the ancient relics might turn up some day in China. The second is hopeless, because the *President Harrison* was attacked, and wound up on the bottom of the Pacific Ocean.

---

6 DECEMBER 1851

"The Whale Is a Fish"

On December 6, 1851, London's comprehensive *Literary Gazette and Journal of Science and Art* published its review of a new American book entitled *Moby-Dick; or, The Whale.* "The author has read up laboriously to make a show of cetalogical learning. . . . He uses it as stuffing to fill out his skeleton story. Bad stuffing it makes, serving only to try the patience of his readers, and to tempt them to wish both him and his whales at the bottom of an unfathomable sea." Herman Melville's zoological asides on whales are certainly more than mere stuffing, although some readers do abandon the voyage when they reach the first encyclopedic exposition.

One of the tasks Melville assigned himself was the determination of his title character's place in the natural order of things. What, exactly, is a whale? "As no better man advances to take this matter in hand," Melville's narrator, Ishmael, says modestly, "I hereupon offer my own poor endeavors." He quotes Linnaeus playing Adam: "I hereby separate the whales from the fish." Ishmael says he submitted Linnaeus's evidence to a couple of his former messmates, and one of them went so far as to profanely hint that the opinion of the immortal systematist might be humbug. There are more scientific ways of settling the matter, but nonetheless Ishmael concurs: "Be it known that, waiving all argument, I take the good old fashioned ground that the whale is a fish, and call upon holy Jonah to back me up."

The tale of Jonah's sea change occupies four short chapters in his own book in the Bible. The word "whale" does not appear. "Now the Lord had

It took naturalists (and artists) a long time to make up their minds about whales. In André Thevet's illustration from the 1574 Cosmographie Universelle, *the whale has a fishlike shape but the breasts of a mammal.*

prepared a great fish to swallow up Jonah. And Jonah was in the belly of the fish three days and three nights. Then Jonah prayed unto the Lord his God out of the fish's belly. . . . And the Lord spake unto the fish, and it vomited out Jonah upon the dry land." Not that the word "whale" doesn't appear in the King James Bible at all. Elsewhere, when the Pharisees ask Jesus for a sign, he predicts that, "for as Jonah was three days and three nights in the whale's belly; so shall the Son of man be three days and three nights in the heart of the earth." Like Jonah and Jesus, the seventeenth-century translators working for King James did not distinguish between fish and aquatic mammals.

Any system of classification reflects the worldview of its inventors. Only recently have we devised such categories as "mammal." The Israelites knew nothing of evolutionary kinship, and it wasn't relevant. They defined animals by behavior and habitat, and in both the whale naturally fell in with fish rather than with bears or horses. The Bible, Melville's final arbiter regarding whales, holds other examples of categories that have changed. In Leviticus, speaking through Moses, God lists the bat among the unclean "birds" the Israelites are prohibited from eating. "Taxonomies," Stephen Jay Gould has observed, "are guides to action, not passive devices for ordering."

The Brazilian fabulist Jorge Luis Borges parodied the human urge to categorize. He claimed that a "certain Chinese encyclopedia" divides animals into such helpful categories as Belonging to the Emperor, Embalmed, Tame, Innumerable, and That from a Long Way Off Look Like Flies. Melville would have laughed. His own final definition fits right in: "To be short, then, a whale is *a spouting fish with a horizontal tail.* There you have him."

See also 6/27.

---

7 DECEMBER 1942

Cat People

In 1942, American film producer Val Lewton released the first of his stylish, famously understated horror films, *Cat People,* directed by Jacques Tourneur. A sequel, *Curse of the Cat People,* appeared two years later (not to be confused with the 1982 remake of the original, which could never be accused of understatement.) Lewton said he had a simple formula: "A love story, three scenes of suggested horror and one of actual violence." There's a bit more to *Cat People* than that. The film boasts some of the most famous scenes in the genre, especially the unseen creature stalking a woman who is trapped in a swimming pool in sudden darkness, and, for late-twentieth-century urbanites, the wonderful, terrifying scene of Jane Randolph's character running from the safe little island of light under each streetlight into the terrifying darkness between it and the next.

On December 7, 1942, in a review entitled "Purrrr," the *New York Times* dismissed *Cat People* as "tedious," and added, "And Miss Simon's cuddly little tabby would barely frighten a mouse under a chair." Enthusing for the trade, *Variety* disagreed. In the weekly's signature jargon, the reviewer predicted, "Exploitation-minded exhibs have a good subject here to play with to hypo b.o. returns." Box office returns were respectable, but the film's reputation has grown over the half century and more since its release.

The main character, Irena, played by Simone Simon, is a New York fashion designer. She seems outwardly "normal," whatever that means. However, she is riddled with anxiety, fearing that she has inherited the bestial traits of the medieval Balkan people from whom she is descended. The women of this sect have the inconvenient habit of turning into rampaging black panthers when their sexual passions are aroused. (This is a curious choice of animal, since panthers are not found in the Balkans. They are simply darkly patterned leopards, a cat native to both southern Asia and Africa, although seldom found in the latter region in their black phase.) In spite of the feline tendency—from, one assumes, her mother's side—Irena falls in love and marries. However, fear of a homicidal hormone imbalance prevents her from consummating the relationship.

Other events only enforce her fear. In public, Irena notices an alarmingly feline woman give her a glance of what could only be shocked recognition. Meanwhile, she finds herself drawn to a caged black panther. These incidents, and her tendency to swat at caged birds and claw sofa arms, are what a detective would call clues. If she is not a were-cat, she needs professional help, and her understandably frustrated husband provides it. But, of course, the therapy is unsuccessful.

Like poor Larry Talbot, Lon Chaney Jr.'s werewolf in *The Wolf Man,* Simone Simon's were-panther Irena is not evil. She is guilty of nothing. The cartoon genetics of horror films is to blame, a kind of "unto the seventh generation" racial curse. Some of this seems an armature to support yet another version of that old cinematic bogeywoman, the dangers of unleashed feminine sexuality. The core of Irena's anxiety is her own fear of what she may do if she experiences too much pleasure. However, the film's poster followed Hollywood's usual tradition by titillating with exactly those traits for which the woman would ultimately be punished. Under the heading "She Knew Strange, Fierce Pleasures That No Other Woman Could Ever Feel!" the ad copy read "She was one of the dreaded 'Cat People'—doomed to slink and prowl and court by night . . . fearing always that a lover's kiss might change her into a snarling, clawing *killer!*"

Lewton and Tourneur had planned to present the film as a study of a woman who actually might be no more than psychologically disturbed. For a long time in the film, there is no proof that Irena is genuinely a were-cat. However, fearing that the last thing American audiences could comprehend was subtlety, the studio insisted that the filmmakers insert footage of an actual black panther into certain scenes.

---

8 DECEMBER 1859

"Portable Ecstacies"

No aspect of our lives better demonstrates humanity's integral place in nature than our ability to go through the world and ingest so much of it, like Hansel and Gretel nibbling the gingerbread house. Because we are a part of their world—because we are each a different recipe whose main ingredients are carbon, oxygen, and other staples—we can consume asparagus and squid, and can be consumed by crocodiles and sharks. We are able to extract calcium from milk. A tiger can extract protein from us. It seems that every plant or animal on the planet is on somebody's menu.

Of course, as parents try to teach their children as early as possible, not everything in the world that will fit in the mouth is harmless. Plants have all sorts of effects on us. Coffee stimulates; chamomile calms. Foxglove provides digitoxin that can jump-start the heart or stop it completely. Lurking in many plants are chemical compounds that enter the human body and set off alarms, even tricking the innocent brain into counterfeiting experiences. The seemingly transcendent experiences produced by some of these plants have been praised by groups as diverse as Indian shamans and San Francisco hippies.

One man who wrote memorably about some of these mind-altering effects was the nineteenth-century Englishman Thomas De Quincey. Fans of the outré remember him for "Murder Considered as One of the Fine Arts," and Shakespearean commentators for "On the Knocking at the Gate in Macbeth." He wrote on theology and economics. He wrote fiction and poetry. But ever since its appearance in 1821, his best-known work has been the autobiographical *Confessions of an English Opium-Eater.* In the essay, which he later expanded into a book, De Quincey described opium as "a panacea for all human woes" and "portable ecstacies corked up in a pint bottle." Naturally, such ecstacies were not without a price. De Quincey also said that after a while a "shadow as of sad eclipse sat and rested upon my faculties." His descriptions of his long addiction to opium, especially its effect on his dreams, are haunting.

Opium is derived from the opium poppy, *Papaver somniferum.* Its species name indicates its narcotic qualities, which have long been known, and which show up in a book as different from De Quincey's as it is possible to imagine—L. Frank Baum's *Wonderful Wizard of Oz.*

> They now came upon more and more big, bright scarlet poppies, and fewer and fewer other flowers; and soon they found themselves in the midst of a great meadow of poppies. Now it is well known that when there are many of these flowers together their odor is so powerful that anyone who breathes it falls asleep, and if the sleeper is not carried away from the scent of the flowers he sleeps on and on forever.

Medical books and lists of medicinal herbs from ancient Assyria include references to both opium and the poppy from which it is made. It is described in Dioscorides' first-century Greek pharmacopoeia, *De Materia Medica.* Although opium existed in various forms, apparently its users didn't smoke it until after the discovery of the New World, from which European and other explorers brought back, with tobacco, the concept of the pipe. Purified opium alkaloids include codeine and morphine; the latter also produces heroin. Although synthetic substitutes for opium and its various alkaloids are in common use today, the world medical demand during the 1980s still surpassed 1,700 *tons.*

De Quincey was merely the most eloquent of countless opium addicts in his time. The plant's popularity had long-lasting effects on world history. When De Quincey died, on December 8, 1859, the Second Opium War was in progress. Earlier in the century, Britain had been illegally importing opium into China. The First Opium War began when the Chinese government confiscated 20,000 chests of opium the British had warehoused in Guangzhou (Canton). Britain quickly won the war, and as a result China paid a heavy indemnity, opened five ports, and, most significantly, ceded Hong Kong to Britain. (With the 1984 accord, Britain agreed to return the colony to China in 1997.)

That the opium trade was a flourishing industry in the nineteenth century is demonstrated by these bronze elephants in graduated sizes, which were used as balancing weights for measuring the drug. Vanderbilt University Fine Arts Gallery / Photo by Denny Adcock

The Second Opium War began three years before De Quincey's death, when Chinese officials boarded an English ship and lowered its flag. Claiming the murder of a French missionary as provocation, France joined the British in these hostilities. Again China lost, and the extensive concessions forced upon the country are now called the Unequal Treaties. Yet another effect of opium on history was the result of one of these treaties. It led to the origin of international trade's now-common "most favored nation" status.

9 DECEMBER 1899

The Story of Babar

French artist and children's author Jean de Brunhoff was born on December 9, 1899. By his early twenties, he was studying art in Paris. Besides his artistic abilities, he was also known for his tact and consideration, two traits that would later be prominent in a fictional character he would create. In 1924, Jean married Cécile Sabouraud, and in 1925 their son Laurent was born. A second son, Matthieu, followed the next year.

Cécile de Brunhoff liked to read books to her children—Beatrix Potter, La Fontaine, A. A. Milne. One day in 1930, she decided to invent a tale instead. Although it was not a sad story over all, it began with a tragedy: "A little elephant was happily playing in the jungle when a hunter shot his mother. . . ." Laurent and Matthieu were spellbound. When Jean fleshed out the story and illustrated it, he suggested to Cécile that she be listed as coauthor. She refused.

Cécile had always referred to the central character of her story as simply a *bébé éléphant.* Besides illustrating the story, Jean also named the elephant, filling a spiral-bound notebook with the story and illustrations. When *L'Histoire de Babar* appeared in 1931, it began, "In the great forest a little elephant is born. His name is Babar." (Jean also provided Babar with a mate, whose name, Celeste, is suspiciously close to his own wife's.) Reproduced exactly as Jean had written and drawn and painted it, the book had an easy informality and elegance that became the hallmark of the series.

In an early scene, Babar rides on his mother's back across a cartoon version of the African savannah. From behind some bushes, a pith-helmeted hunter shoots Babar's mother. It is the beginning of a long series of adventures, not all of them pleasant. Like many young children who have lost their parents, the elephant simply proceeds with life without looking back. In Paris, Babar meets the Old Lady, who becomes his patron. She gives him the money to buy a new suit, and in a spending spree Babar discovers that clothes make the pachyderm. Comforted by material wealth, he joins the world of human beings. He takes to standing on his hind legs and preening in front of the mirror. He sits comfortably on Directoire chairs and poses for photographers. He drives happily along in the long, elegant automobiles of the thirties. In time, of course, Babar comes to grieve both for his mother and for the life he left behind.

Jean went on to write and illustrate six more books about his peripatetic hero, taking Babar on adventures around the world. Then, in 1937, Jean died of tuberculosis. Ordinarily that would be the end of a series, but the de Brunhoffs were not an ordinary family. In 1946, a year after the end of World War II, Jean's son Laurent, who had grown up to become an abstract painter, resurrected his father's adventurous character. Beginning with *Babar's Cousin: That Rascal Arthur,* the series was off and running again. In the later books, Babar exhibits the same human behavior invented by his creator. On the grounds of his castle, he rides a tractor mower. When he visits the United States, he walks the streets of New York, flies over Los Angeles in a helicopter, attends a drive-in movie. But Laurent takes Babar farther afield. He rides a boat on an underground river and even journeys to another planet.

Throughout both artists' work, the series exhibits the usual paradox of children's books. Some children's authors resolve the question of their characters' bestial nature by populating the world strictly with animals. De Brunhoff *père* and *fils* both scorned such homogeneous societies. Babar is fitted for clothes and photographed by human beings, but rescued from an island of cannibals by a friendly whale. His friends are monkeys and birds, but when he walks the streets of New York he is surrounded by people who, with classic Big Apple unflappability, pay no attention to the green-suited beast in their midst. Babar's talent for remaining true to his nature while living in society may be his most endearing trait.

10 DECEMBER 1941

The Wolf Man

The Wolf Man premiered in Hollywood on December 10, 1941. One review began with "Universal, which must have a veritable menagerie of mythological monsters, all with an eye on stardom and a five-year contract . . ." The reviewer described Lon Chaney Jr.'s werewolf as "a sort of Mr. Hyde badly in need of a shave." Actually, he looks more like a were-warthog, but the comparison was apt; Robert Louis Stevenson's *Dr. Jekyll and Mr. Hyde* is itself a version of the werewolf story. Dracula, besides being a vampire, was also a werewolf. In the Bela Lugosi film, Van Helsing keeps Dracula at bay with wolfsbane.

To their great misfortune, wolves have long been associated with evil. Plagues and wars left the European countryside littered with corpses during Europe's Hundred Years' War, in the thirteenth and fourteenth centuries. Wolves, which prefer to scavenge when such easy food is available, came at night to feed.

People immediately linked this behavior with the devil. *Wargus,* the Germanic word for wolf, soon also referred to one who disturbed the dead, and finally to one possessed. The term "werewolf," however, comes from the Anglo-Saxon *wer,* "man," and *wulf,* "wolf." Elsewhere, other animals fill the wolves' role. Around the world, folklore abounds with stories of metamorphoses into whichever animal is considered the most dangerous predator. Thus there are versions of were-jaguars, even were-crocodiles.

All werewolves are evil, Ambrose Bierce wrote, but some "are as humane as is consistent with an acquired taste for human flesh." That describes Lon Chaney's unwilling werewolf, Lawrence Talbot. In this film, Chaney plays most scenes without his usual dramatic makeup. When he accompanies friends to a gypsy fortune-teller, they encounter a flowering bush of wolfsbane, and a woman recites the horror genre's only famous poem:

Lon Chaney Jr. as the unfortunate Larry Talbot, who is innocently entertaining a date when a werewolf ruins the evening. Courtesy of Ronald V. Borst / Hollywood Movie Posters

> *Even a man who is pure in heart*
> *And says his prayers by night*
> *May become a wolf when the wolfsbane blooms*
> *And the autumn moon is bright*

Wolfsbane is a widespread member of the buttercup family. The name is a translation of the Latin *lycoctonum,* from the Greek for "wolf" and "to kill," which survives in its scientific name, *Aconitum lycoctonum.* Another insurance against werewolves is also used against vampires—silver, which in Christian symbolism represented purity. The Wolf Man is finally bludgeoned to death with a cane, the head of which is a silver wolf.

In his 1983 *Thriller* video, just before he metamorphoses into a werewolf, Michael Jackson says to his date, "I have something I want to tell you. I'm not like other guys." Or is he? Lawrence Talbot seems just like other people until nighttime. Do the werewolf and Mr. Hyde imply a universal darker side of humanity? ("Even a man who is pure in heart . . .") Claude Rains, as Talbot's father in *The Wolf Man,* explains the myth: "It's probably an ancient explanation of the dual personality in each of us." In Abbott and Costello's 1948 romp with the monsters of filmland, Costello jokes about that universality. He disagrees with Michael Jackson. When a clean-shaven Lon Chaney says, "You don't understand. When the moon rises, I'll turn into a wolf," Costello replies, "Yeah, you and about five million other guys."

See also Hitler's wolves, 3/10; and Dracula, 9/29.

The White-Tailed Deer

Deer are a diverse and adaptable family, found throughout much of the world. From moose to caribou, from the roe and fallow deer of Europe to the Indian chital and sambar, counting species, subspecies, and local races, there may be as many as 100 varieties. As prehistoric representations reveal, they have been familiar to human beings throughout our history. The white-tailed deer, *Odocoileus virginianus,* is the most widespread variety in the New World and has been an important game animal for thousands of years.

Shy, perfectly camouflaged, and with a hair-trigger alarm system, the white-tailed deer was never easy prey until the advent of modern weaponry. Lacking the long-distance killing capabilities of the firearms later imported by European colonists, the early North Americans were more adept at luring game. The Ojibwa and Cree in the Great Lakes region used sheets of rolled birch bark as megaphones to amplify moose calls. Deer would come to the simplest lure of all. Blowing across a blade of grass held between two fingers imitated the distress call of a fawn, which could draw concerned does to their death. Hunters among the Timucua people of Florida disguised themselves with deer hides and sneaked close enough to hunt. To channel deer toward them, some hunters in northeastern North America planted hedges that were up to a mile long. Elsewhere, the same sort of controlled fires used against buffalo served to flush

Despite being a favorite (and sometimes easy) target for hunters, the white-tailed deer has flourished in North America.

deer. The Cherokee, Choctaw, and other southeastern tribes hunted deer with darts fired from blowguns like those still in use in Amazon rain forests, or with spear-throwers that increased their range.

In spite of all of these methods of predation, deer were plentiful when European colonists arrived in the New World. From the moment English colonists reached what would later become Massachusetts, and founded a colony nostalgically named Plymouth, deer were a staple of their diet. The following year, on December 11, 1621, a colonist named Edward Winslow wrote a letter to a friend back home in England, describing the first of the annual New World harvest feasts that would come to be called Thanksgiving. In the course of the letter he mentions an animal that had already proven a crucial part of the colonists' diet and provided clothing, even coverings for their feet and heads. The governor he mentions was William Bradford, and the captain Miles Standish.

> Our harvest being gotten in, our Governor sent four men on fowling that so we might after a more special manner rejoice together after we had gathered the fruit of our labors. . . . And they went out and killed five deer which they brought to the plantation and bestowed on our Governor and upon the Captain and others.

Over the nearly four centuries since the founding of the Plymouth Colony, the deer population has not diminished in response to growing urbanization and the loss of forests. Always frequenters of meadows and brushy woodland, deer have found the margins of human habitation quite agreeable, like gray squirrels and cottontail rabbits and American robins. As a result, unlike some animals that were abundant when European depredations were added to those of natives, white-tailed deer are now so widespread that they are still hunted annually in the United States. They are the most populous large mammal in North America. This creature that was one of the first to be protected by law turned out to need it the least.

---

12 DECEMBER 1851

The "Flower of the Holy Night"

In 1823, President James Monroe, in the doctrine named for him, announced to Europe and the rest of the world that the United States would tolerate no meddling in the Americas. The United States was fully capable of doing enough meddling for everyone. As part of established governmental policy at the time, the government sent a number of meddlesome representatives both north and south of the border. One was the first U.S. minister to Mexico, Joel Robert Poinsett.

Poinsett was born in South Carolina in 1779. In 1810, as a special U.S. agent, he opened diplomatic and business contact with two Spanish territories in South America, Chile and Buenos Aires, and also encouraged their struggle to break free of Spain. (Not that he was a proponent of liberty and peace. He also directed the Second Seminole War.) It was in 1822, while a member of the U.S. House of Representatives, that Poinsett was sent on a special diplomatic mission to Mexico. Two years later he published his well-known *Notes on Mexico.* Apparently he was such an inveterate meddler that his reputation earned him an eponym. The Mexican government coined a word for meddlesome, officious behavior—*poinsettismo.*

Probably few people have had two words named after them, but Poinsett has that distinction. His several scientific interests, which led to his helping launch the institution that became the Smithsonian, included plants. Poinsett was a knowledgeable amateur botanist, and he brought many plants home to the United States. One of those was subsequently renamed for him, the poinsettia. Some areas of the American Southwest still celebrate the day of his death, December 12, 1851, as Poinsettia Day.

The Mexicans called the plant *Flora de la Noche Buena,* "Flower of the Holy Night." Its crimson, vaguely star-shaped bracts reminded someone of the Star of Bethlehem. The plant blooms in the winter, and it became associated with Christmas. One legend tells of a village that, like most others, displayed a crèche in its church on Christmas Eve. It was the custom to bring gifts and place them before the infant in the manger. One poor boy who could afford no gift instead knelt to pray in the snow outside the church. When he stood up, the poinsettia grew instantly where his knees had touched the ground. A clever lad, he could take a hint from above, and he took the plant into the church and gave it to the Christ doll, who had no use for it whatsoever. (One aspect of the plant that goes against its Nativity associations is its reputation as a poison. Apparently that is exaggerated, although its leaves and stems produce a milklike latex that can irritate the skin.)

The poinsettia, *Euphorbia pulcherrima,* was in Mexico long before the Spaniards imported Christianity. It grows wild there and in portions of Central America, on hillsides and in damp woodland ravines. Under the right conditions, in the wild it can reach a height of ten feet, but most people north of the border know it as a potted plant. The poinsettia is not a red-petaled flower. Its flowers are tiny and yellow, and cluster at the center of the bright red leaflike bracts that make the plant so striking. But, whether by virtue of its petals or bracts or leaves, the poinsettia is now a perennial sight at Christmas throughout the United States and elsewhere, one of the legacies of the man who was so meddlesome he couldn't bear to even leave a plant where he found it.

For other Christmas plants, see 12/25.

---

13 DECEMBER 1945

Beauty and the Beast

Mme. Leprince de Beaumont's eighteenth-century love story between a woman and a beast who was once a man has proven an irresistible fable. On his way home one night, an old man encounters a magical castle that, apparently without human assistance, provides bed and board for him. Before departing, he plucks a bunch of roses for his daughter, who is so beautiful she is called simply Beauty. "At that moment he heard a terrible noise, and saw coming toward him a Beast so hideous that he nearly fainted."

For his ungrateful theft of the flowers, the Beast condemns the merchant to die unless one of his daughters takes his place. Like most such tales, Mme. de Beaumont's original occupies itself with action rather than description. She contents herself with that sole adjective "hideous." The nature of the beast is left to the imagination.

There have been a number of recent attempts to envision that nature. In an uninspired 1976 version, George C. Scott played the Beast, looking like an ill-starred hybrid of a pig and, perhaps, a buffalo. In the eighties, the Beast starred in his own television series, as a glamorous, feline, Broadway-stage-looking fellow who tended toward the poetic. In Walt Disney's 1991 animated incarnation, the disneyfied Beast is tusked and extravagantly maned, and appropriately depressed and possessive, but seldom appears exactly bestial. None of these versions compares with the classic cinematic portrayal of the Beast by Jean Marais, in Jean Cocteau's 1946 film *La Belle et la Bête*.

In La Belle et la Bête, *Jean Cocteau created the only cinematic version of the story that captures the spirit of Mme. Leprince de Beaumont's original.* Courtesy of Ronald V. Borst / Hollywood Movie Posters

Cocteau closely followed Mme. de Beaumont's original story, with a similar offhand realism—a style he called "documentary"—except for such surrealistic touches as candelabras held by arms that emerge from the walls. His diary of the film's production records not only his determination to express his own vision of a perennial fable, but also the problems of making a movie in France only months after the Liberation. Just as they began filming the scene in which the Beast proves himself a predator, no deer carcass could be found because the game markets went on strike.

One evening, preparing for that scene, Cocteau wrote in his diary:

December 13th, 1945, 6 p.m.

While I write this on the marble-topped make-up table, at my right Marais and [the make-up man] start on the head and tear the shirt with the enormous shoulders (Marais's head make-up throws his normal shoulders off balance).

The torn shirt was for the moment in which Beauty gets her most shocking glimpse of the Beast's animal nature. Earlier, when he scented a stag, his ears pricked up and he excused himself. Now, she sees him and demands, "What are you doing outside my room at such an hour?" Bloody, his clothes in tatters, and—a lovely magical touch—his fur smoking, the Beast is returning from a wild nocturnal hunt. He has proven himself more animal than man.

Cocteau and Marais were determined to make the Beast convincing. With the masochistic resolve of a Lon Chaney, Marais suffered terribly under his makeup, as he described in his autobiography: "Because of the fangs attached to my teeth, all I could eat was mush, and that by the spoonful. Between takes I scarcely dared open my mouth lest the makeup become unglued. . . ." Marais's beloved dog Moulouk often accompanied him to the mask maker. Together the two men studied the animal, and "the dog taught [them] things: the unevenness and shagginess and spottiness of the fur that make it seem so alive are due to Moulouk." The rest was a triumph of acting over special effects. When Lawrence Olivier remarked that he would not have submitted to such pains, Cocteau commented, "In my opinion, one must have Marais's passion for his work and his devotion to his dog, to persevere as he did in deserting the human race for the animal race."

---

14 DECEMBER 1911

Amundsen's Strategy

The South Pole is the southern end of the Earth's axis, the point at which the axis would emerge if it were tangible. It is not to be confused with the south magnetic pole, which, like the north, doesn't quite align with the axis. The Earth's $23\frac{1}{2}°$ axial tilt creates seasons even at the poles, but their respective summers remain cold. Surrounded by a seemingly endless Antarctic wilderness, the South Pole is one of the most inhospitable places on Earth. Only astronomical observations can even reveal its precise location.

Nevertheless, in 1911 the Norwegian Roald Amundsen and the Englishman Robert Scott led teams racing to be the first to set foot at the South Pole. The two men had little in common except an urge to explore. Robert Falcon Scott was born in 1868, and between 1900 and 1904 commanded an expedition that explored the Ross Sea area of Antarctica. Roald Engelbregt Gravning Amundsen was born in Norway when Scott was four years old. In 1903, while Scott was still exploring Antarctica on his first expedition, Amundsen took off to sail the legendary Northwest Passage. It took him a year and three months. In 1910, Scott announced his intention to reach the South Pole and outfitted the aptly named whaler *Terra Nova.* Having decided from his previous expedition that sledge dogs were not adequate to his needs, he carried aboard his ship nineteen ponies.

Two months after Scott left England in June, Amundsen and company departed on their own trip, ostensibly headed around Cape Horn and into the Pacific. Only in early September did Amundsen's famous cable reach Scott: "BEG LEAVE TO INFORM YOU PROCEEDING ANTARCTICA." It had become a race. They proceeded toward the pole from different directions. On December 14, 1911, Amundsen hoisted the Norwegian flag at the South Pole.

Nothing was heard from Scott's team. Eight months later, they were found dead, lying in their sleeping bags. They had reached the pole in mid-January of 1912, only to find that Amundsen had come and gone. Turning back, exhausted and disappointed, they encountered raging snowstorms. Scott kept a diary during the ordeal, and the last page reads:

We shall stick it out to the end, but we are getting weaker, of course, and the end cannot be far.

It seems a pity but I do not think I can write more.

R. Scott

For God's sake, look after our people.

In his 1927 autobiography, Amundsen explained why he survived and Scott did not. "All my experience in Polar work had convinced me that dogs were the only practicable draught animals for use in snow and ice. They are quick, strong, sure-footed, intelligent, and able to negotiate any terrain that man himself can traverse." Scott used impractical motor sledges and ponies. "I was confident that this was a fatal mistake, and much to my sorrow it was in part the cause of Scott's tragic end."

Of crucial importance, Amundsen maintained, was his method of beginning with a number of short trips, stashing provisions and erecting shelters along the way, leaving at each a carefully calculated minimum weight of supplies for the return. And he had an ingenious (if, to some, distasteful) solution to the question of provisions. He reduced "the weight of provisions to be carried by calculating the flesh of the dogs which carried it as part of the food supply of us men." Every Eskimo dog meant fifty pounds of food. "In my calculations before the start for the final dash to the Pole, I figured out exactly the precise day on which I planned to kill each dog as its usefulness should end for drawing the diminishing supplies on the sleds and its usefulness should begin as food for the men. This schedule worked almost to the day and the dog. Above everything else," Amundsen concluded, this strategy "was the essential factor in our successful trip to the Pole and our safe return to the base camp."

---

15 December 1762

Cockfighting

One evening in 1663, Samuel Pepys attended a public entertainment that had been popular in England for at least 500 years. He "took Coach, and being directed by sight of bills upon the walls, did go to Shooe lane to see a Cocke-fighting at a new pit there—a sport I was never at in my life." Cockfighting wasn't considered merely a sport for the riffraff. Pepys was himself a gentleman; on that first visit, he recognized a member of Parliament. However, the crowd was largely made up of the working class—apprentices, butchers, clerks. All had one thing in common: a thirst for blood. The pain of the animals was not a concern. The brute creation was here for our sustenance and diversion. "Christianity," a contemporary of Pepys said of cockfighting and bearbaiting, "gives us a placard to use these sports."

"I soon had enough of it," Pepys wrote of his first encounter; "and yet I would not but have seen it once, it being strange to observe the nature of those poor creatures, how they will fight till they drop down dead upon the table and strike after they are ready to give up the ghost. . . ." The cocks were carefully bred as fighters, raised on prescribed diets. Their wings were clipped and their wattles

Cockfighting is an ancient pastime, and it still thrives in many corners of the world.

and cockscombs removed. Then, to make the contest still more vicious, they were armed with sharp metal spurs. Pepys observed that men who looked like they could ill afford bread were placing hefty bets.

It turned out that Pepys had not had enough, after all. He returned to the "Cocke pitt." (The name for an airplane pilot's cubbyhole derives from these small enclosed arenas.) Five years later, we find him marveling at "two battles of cocks, wherein is no great sport, but only to consider how these creatures without any provocation do fight and kill one another. . . ."

A century later, cockfighting was still a popular sport. On Wednesday, December 15, 1762, another great diarist recorded his adventures at the festivities. "The enemies of the people of England who would have them considered in the worst light," James Boswell wrote, "represent them as selfish, beef-eaters, and cruel. In this view I resolved today to be a true-born Englishman." He ate beef, ate it alone to be selfish, and "saw cock-fighting for about five hours to fulfill the charge of cruelty." At the cockpit, seats rose around the circular arena. "The cocks, nicely cut and dressed and armed with silver heels, are set down and fight with amazing bitterness and resolution." Few lasted long, but one prodigy held out for forty-five minutes. The shouting and swearing were deafening. It was customary to bet at each stage of the fight.

At least Boswell felt a small measure of sympathy: "I was sorry for the poor cocks." Apparently he was the only one. "I looked round to see if any of the spectators pitied them when mangled and torn in a most cruel manner, but I could not observe the smallest relenting sign in any countenance. . . ." In time, as higher-class sensibilities became more refined, cockfighting was judged too barbaric for gentlemen, but it would not be prohibited in England until 1849. Not that illegal status wiped it out. Even today, cockfighting is a popular illicit entertainment in many parts of the world.

---

16 December 1773

The Boston Tea Party

In the mid-1600s, three new products arrived in London—coffee, cocoa, and tea. Tea was known in Lisbon by 1580, but took a while to reach the rest of Europe. A 1660 English description of tea explains much of its appeal: "It makes the body active and alert. . . . It banishes tiredness and cleanses the vital fluids and the liver. . . . One infusion is sufficient to allow one to work through the night, without doing injury to one's body." That last fallacy has resulted in many a jittery truck-driver and college student. Apparently there is no such thing as a popular drink that doesn't contain some sort of thrilling drug—if not alcohol, at least caffeine.

Although there are many additives and blends, most true teas—a distinction that excludes caffeine-free herbal concoctions—derive from a plant called *Camellia* (formerly *Thea*) *sinensis,* "Chinese camellia." The leaves, flowers, and even the buds of the plant are used, carefully dried and blended in appropriate proportions. Of course, tea provides caffeine as much as taste. Caffeine is a multitalented plant alkaloid that stimulates respiration, heart rate, and even the nervous system. It is also a powerful diuretic. Besides caffeine, tea also contains tannin, a bitter and astringent substance found in the fruit and bark of certain plants, and used in the tanning of leather. Like most substances, tea doesn't sound appetizing when analyzed.

At the time of the American Revolution, Europeans and their colonies had to get their tea from Canton, the single Chinese port open to foreigners. In May of 1773, the English Parliament passed a law expressly designed for the financial benefit of the nation's largest tea importer. Parliament basically granted the East India Company a monopoly on the American tea trade. Thereafter the company was permitted to ship its product directly to England's American colonies, thus eliminating the distributor and allowing the huge corporation to price their tea below even smugglers' best offers.

Although the lower prices were easier on their purses, the colonists resented the imposition of a monopoly. Not only were colonial tea merchants endangered, but colonial businessmen saw looming on the horizon the risk of further monopolies on such prized commodities as spices and silks. Separationists also welcomed more fuel for the fires of revolution. Conservative merchants, who had formerly dreamed of a resolution of the colonies' problems with England, found themselves uneasy allies with the radical Sons of Liberty. The more cautious proposed less dramatic means of reprisal, and some ships were sent back to England while other shipments of tea were warehoused and allowed to rot. Nonetheless, on the night of December 16, 1773, from thirty to sixty colonists disguised as "Indians" threw £10,000 worth of tea into Boston Harbor. This was not the worst vandalism. In Annapolis Harbor, colonists burned not only the *Peggy Stewart*'s cargo of tea but the ship itself.

Throughout the eighteenth century, what Thomas Jefferson called "that obnoxious commodity" had become steadily more affordable. Tea was so popular in colonial America that one critic blamed the colonies' economic problems on tea drinking, claiming it both wasted time and encouraged dependence on a market economy rather than good old-fashioned self-reliance. He blamed women for this problem, and declared that in his home, "The tea kettle shall be sold." But it was the patriotic anti-English sentiment that finally affected the popularity of tea, and after the Revolutionary War it never quite regained its former popularity in the United States. The per capita consumption of tea in Canada has averaged four times that of its southern neighbor. Tea is the most popular nonalcoholic drink among people of Anglo-Saxon ancestry everywhere in the world—except in the United States.

Saturnalia, Best of Days

In one of his quirky, informal verses, the first-century-B.C. Roman poet Catullus complained, "I've wasted my whole Saturnalia, my favorite day of the year." That's a loose modern translation; Catullus actually called the Saturnalia *optimus dierum*, "the best of days." He wasn't the only one who thought so. It was the most popular Roman holiday, happily anticipated throughout the year.

Saturn was an ancient Italian deity, the Roman version of the Greek god Cronus. Supposedly he emigrated from Greece when Zeus, whom the Romans called Jupiter, evicted him from Olympus. He founded a village named Saturnia on the Capitol, long before Rome existed. The Romans later referred to Saturn's reign as the Golden Age. There was no need for doors then because there was no such thing as theft. It hadn't occurred to anyone to kill a fellow creature, so everyone was a vegetarian. The gods strolled among the people. For that reason, the adjective "Saturnian," when not referring to the second-largest planet in the solar system, now means contented or prosperous.

"Saturnalian," on the other hand, implies orgiastic revelry. The Romans liked their festivals festive. The public celebration began in fine style with a sacrifice. Attire was formal—togas only. There followed a more relaxed banquet that was open to the public. Schools, courts, and stores were closed, and gambling was allowed in public. Unrestrained merriment was the order of the day. There was even a mock king who ruled for a week. But perhaps the most famous aspect is the reversal of the social hierarchy that took place in the home, where master waited upon slave.

In later days, the Temple of Saturn (which was also the Roman treasury) rose impressively in the Forum, at the base of the Capitol. Inside stood, naturally, a statue of the deity. It was filled with oil, perhaps as a preservative, and bound with woolen bonds that were removed on the Saturnalia. Tentative explanations for this ritual suggest that it symbolized either the child emerging from the womb or plants coming to fruition. Some scholars think the latter is likelier, because apparently Saturn was a god of agriculture.

As originally established, the Saturnalia took place on December 17. That remained the official date, but over the years the festivities began to extend for several more days, through the twenty-third of December at least. That way the observance came on each side of the winter solstice, a time in many cultures for celebrating the successful completion of the harvest and the year, and the gradual lengthening of the days. The Latin poet Publius Papinius Statius, who lived in the first century A.D., wrote of the Saturnalia, "Time shall not destroy that holy day, so long as the hills of Latium endure, and father Tiber, while your city of Rome and the Capitol remain."

The hills are still there and the Tiber still flows through them, but the Rome of Statius and Catullus has long since passed. However, aspects of their favorite holiday endure. Most historians agree that the date of December 25 was chosen for Christmas because it replaced the hugely popular Saturnalia. Furthermore, the Roman emperor Aurelian, who temporarily reunited a crumbling empire, dedicated a temple to Sol Invictus, the god of the sun, in 274, and a feast was held in his honor every December 25. The first record of Christmas falling on that date comes only sixty years later. The Christians were able to replace two pagan holidays for the price of one. And they kept one of the most popular aspects of the Saturnalia—the tradition of giving gifts.

Piltdown Man

Charles Dawson was a country solicitor and amateur archaeologist in the English county of Sussex. In 1912, he journeyed to London to visit his friend Arthur Smith Woodward, the Keeper of Palaeontology at the British Museum (Natural History). Dawson took with him some bone fragments and a story about them. He said that a few years before, at a gravel pit in Piltdown, Sussex, he had found a piece of a human cranium that had been unearthed by workmen. As an archaeologist he was of course intrigued. In 1911, Dawson told the paleontologist, he found another fragment; like the first, it seemed unusually thick for a human skull. Smith Woodward was fascinated. Worn and stained, the bones seemed genuine, and, of course, Smith Woodward had no reason to doubt Dawson's story.

During the summer of 1912, the two men spent many hours sifting through piles of earth the laborers had removed from the gravel pit. During one of their excavations, Dawson found a broken mandible. It appeared apelike, in contrast with the human-looking cranium. Disappointingly, the parts of the jaw that would have revealed more clearly whether its origin was human or simian were broken off. Still, with these pieces of what appeared to be a pretty little puzzle, Smith Woodward attempted a reconstruction, buttressing his argument for the specimen's age with other fossils found in the pit.

On December 18, 1912, at a meeting of the Geological Society of London, Smith Woodward and Dawson presented their findings. Smith Woodward named their prize *Eoanthropus dawsoni,* "Dawson's dawn man." Among the headlines that soon appeared was "MISSING LINK FOUND—DARWIN'S THEORY PROVED." Although not every paleontologist was convinced, many English scientists responded with enthusiasm to the notion that the earliest humans might have evolved right there on their own island. That bias was amply demonstrated in the title of Smith Woodward's later book *The Earliest Englishman.* Because Peking Man, for example, had lived in Asia, the appearance of Piltdown Man in Europe fit cherished notions that different races evolved in different parts of the world. Naturally, in this scenario, Piltdown's larger brain would imply that white Europeans were an earlier and therefore more highly developed race.

By and large, Piltdown was accepted as genuine. Then, as other findings in Africa and Asia clinched the identities of established fossils and painted the anomalous Piltdown finding into a corner, paleontologists began to reexamine the evidence. And, like a mystery novel's denouement, the investigation explained previously overlooked clues. It turned out that the cranium and mandible were so different because they were from two different species, a human and an orangutan. The jaw's well-placed breaks were not bad luck; they were the result of a carefully contrived forgery. The bones had been stained, the jaw filed. Even the other mammal fossils in the gravel pit had been placed there, imported from elsewhere. The whole affair was a forgery. There were many red faces in museums around the world, especially in England.

Of course, creationists guffawed. They were delighted with what they saw as proof of the gullibility of their longtime enemies and declared that it proved the essentially fictive nature of paleoanthropology. *Au contraire,* replied the scientists; such highly publicized admissions merely proved the self-policing nature of science.

Who perpetrated the hoax? Obviously it was fashioned by an expert. However, no smoking gun was found. Investigators have nominated several culprits, but no one has yet amassed more than circumstantial evidence. Naturally, Dawson himself is a suspect. But did he have accomplices? Thanks to the controversial investigations of Harvard paleontologist Stephen Jay Gould, another suspect is Pierre Teilhard de Chardin, the French Jesuit philosopher and paleontologist known for his idea that *Homo sapiens* is evolving toward greater spiritual unity with God. Teilhard had worked side by side with Dawson, and it was he who found a handily corroborative canine tooth in 1913. One recent book even points the finger at Arthur Conan Doyle. The creator of Sherlock Holmes lived near Piltdown. (For that matter, the site was also near the former home of Charles Darwin, an irrelevant giblet but still satisfying.) As a passionate spiritualist, Conan Doyle also had bones to pick with several antispiritualist scientists and might have enjoyed their discomfiture.

Apparently there has never been a hint of any dishonesty on the part of Arthur Smith Woodward. It appears that the man who named "Dawson's dawn man" was fooled as much as the rest of the scientific community.

---

19 DECEMBER 1967

Doctor Dolittle

Alice's Adventures in Wonderland grew out of the impromptu stories the Reverend Charles L. Dodgson invented to amuse his young friends, especially Alice Liddell. Kenneth Grahame's letters to his son Alastair became in time *The Wind in the Willows.* The Peter Rabbit stories began with Beatrix Potter's letters designed to amuse a child during his long-term illness. So, when a young soldier named Hugh Lofting put pen to paper to invent stories that would amuse his children Elizabeth and Colin back home, he was following in a fine tradition. The difference was that Lofting was writing from the trenches in World War I. Born in England, he had settled in the United States, then joined the English army at the beginning of the war. He served in France and Flanders. After he was wounded and invalided out, he returned to the United States.

As Lofting's own son later remarked, he had "a strange affinity for animals." As a child, he had little contact with his parents and spent much of his time alone. He climbed mountains and fished and watched birds. He kept a small natural history museum in a linen closet, an arrangement that would show up later in the Dolittle books. During the war, Lofting witnessed the agonized deaths of horses that, unlike the soldiers, couldn't be protected from poisonous blister gases. Later, on a camping trip, Lofting attacked three men—one of whom was armed with a knife—who had hobbled a herd of wild horses. He single-handedly bested all three, used the knife to cut the horses' bonds, emptied the men's

rifles, and returned to his own camp to read a story to his son. Apparently Dr. Dolittle's frequent heroism came as naturally to his creator as did the travel. Lofting worked on railways in Cuba and West
Africa, and surveyed and prospected in Canada.

Dr. Dolittle is not a veterinarian. He is a physician. His new career is forced upon him when his
growing menagerie of pets begins to drive away his human patients in the little town of Puddleby-on-
the-Marsh. Once he learns "the animals' ABC" from his parrot Polynesia, he is able to ask the creatures
where it hurts. Since the names of the characters—Dab-Dab the duck, Too-too the owl, Gub-Gub the
pig, Chee-Chee the monkey—aren't assigned by humans, they must be their true animal names, which
indicates a rampant echolalia in nature. Thankfully, there are also such names as Jip, the good doctor's
dog; Cheapside, a swallow; and, of course, the world's most indecisive beast, the Pushmi-pullyu.

The Story of Doctor Dolittle was published in 1920. Lofting wrote about a dozen more books in the
series, and died in 1947. (The year before, the actor who most resembled Lofting's portraits of Dolittle—W. C. Fields—also died.) When the film version premiered on December 19, 1967, readers were
shocked to find their hero both more eloquent and more elongate. Rex Harrison, while looking
nothing like the pudgy fellow in Lofting's original illustrations, nonetheless captured the dignity and
sense of frustration with the world that are the doctor's hallmarks. The film is a collage of adventures
from several Dolittle books, plus certain superfluous cinematic additions, such as a romantic interest
with a woman half the doctor's age. The film certainly has a different look. Nowhere does a pig sit
decorously on a stool at the dining table, its trotters drawn under it and its tail in a tidy curl, while a
duck on the tabletop stands on one leg to hold out the toast caddy. Worst of all, in the movie all of Lofting's smiling giraffes and zebras and ducks have been replaced by real animals that never seem to smile.

See also **Wind in the Willows, 5/10; Alice in Wonderland, 7/4; and Peter Rabbit, 9/4.**

Household Gods

Charles Dickens edited several publications, including *Household Words* and *Master Humphrey's Clock.*
For a while he entertained the idea of a new one to be titled *The Cricket on the Hearth,* but in time abandoned the idea. In the summer of 1845, he wrote to his friend John Forster about a notion that had
grown from that title. "It would be a delicate and beautiful fancy for a Christmas book, making the
Cricket a little household god—silent in the wrong and sorrow of the tale, and loud again when all
went well and happy."

The Cricket on the Hearth appeared on the twentieth of December. Dickens had published two other
Christmas tales—*A Christmas Carol in Prose* and *The Chimes*—during the preceding holiday seasons.
Like much of Dickens, *Cricket* now seems artificially sweetened. Ebenezer Scrooge's midnight rehabil-
itation by spirits is far better known now, but after the 1845 holiday season Dickens reported that "The
Cricket . . . has beaten my two other Carols out of the field. . . ." He followed these successes with two
other holiday fantasies over the next three years, *The Battle of Life* and *The Haunted Man.*

The cricket has long been a symbol of the domestic hearth and the blessings of home. Mrs. Peery-bingle exclaims, "To have a Cricket on the Hearth is the luckiest thing in all the world!" Annual festivals honor crickets and other musical insects. Crickets invade homes to avoid cold weather, so our hero's presence on the hearth is not surprising. Most crickets are sensitive to fluctuations in temperature. Someone actually figured out that the number of their chirps in fifteen seconds plus 37 approximates the temperature in degrees Fahrenheit.

The title character's music, Dickens says, is "astoundingly disproportionate to its size." It debuts in a musical duel with the whistling tea kettle, but soon races ahead of it. "Good heaven, how it chirped! Its shrill, sharp, piercing voice resounded through the house, and seemed to twinkle in the outer darkness like a star." Of course, crickets don't have voices; they make their music by rubbing one leg across another. However, even naturalists refer to their courtship calls as "song." Crickets have other sounds for aggression or that general alarm that will suddenly make all insects in an area stop signaling. In most species, the calls are made by males only, and they are able to vary the pitch. That's one of the traits that distinguish them from grasshoppers, whose sounds are more mechanical. Also, each species has a distinctive music. Crickets in chorus are the very sound of an autumn night, but, as many homeowners know, a soloist can be maddening.

Naturally, Dickens's isn't the only musical cricket in the arts. Unlike the Talking-cricket in Carlo Collodi's *Pinocchio* (1883), Jiminy Cricket in Walt Disney's 1940 animated adaptation croons Pollyanna metaphysics. In George Selden's *The Cricket in Times Square* (1960), Chester Cricket hops into a picnic basket in the Connecticut countryside and hops out in New York City. There he learns to perform human compositions—symphonies, musical comedies, hymns. And the title character in Joyce Maxner's 1989 picture book *Nicholas Cricket* is a "banjo picker" in the Bug-a-Wug Cricket Band.

See also musical insects, 5/22.

---

21 December

The Sun Stands Still

The earth is tilted on its axis at an angle of 23½° from the plane in which our solar system's bodies travel around the sun. Because of that axial tilt, combined with the earth's orbit being an ellipse rather than a circle, the amount of solar radiation that reaches any spot on the planet may vary greatly in the course of a year. That variation causes seasons. We divide the seasons according to the apparent motion of the sun. From our viewpoint on earth, the sun seems to shift to the northern part of the sky for some months, and back to the south at the opposite end of the year. The northern limit of that apparent migration is the Tropic of Cancer, and the southern limit the Tropic of Capricorn. As a result, each tropic is the same number of degrees north or south of the equator as the earth tilts—23½. The Arctic and Antarctic Circles are similarly determined by astronomy. They mark the line beyond which the sun does not rise above the horizon during that region's winter.

Every six months during its annual migration, the sun appears to cross the celestial equator (an imaginary band of the sky directly above the planet's equator) and shines directly down upon the equator. These are the vernal (from *vernus,* "belonging to spring") and autumnal equinoxes. From two Latin words meaning "equal-night," *equinox* refers to the twelve hours each of daylight and darkness everywhere on the earth. The other two milestones of the year, marking it into quarters, are called solstices, from the Latin *solstitium,* meaning "sun standing still." It refers not to Joshua's astronomical miracle during the battle between the Hebrews and the Amorites, nor to equally unlikely exploits by Superman, but to the moment at which the sun, from our point of view, reaches its northernmost position, seems to pause and reconsider, and begins its return.

Because of the inadequacy of calendars, rather than the inconstancy of the sun itself, the solstice does not invariably take place on the same day of the year. Whenever it doesn't fall upon the twenty-first of December, it is the day before or after. The solstice is the official beginning of winter. As such, many cultures have regarded it as a timely occasion for thanking the gods of the harvest and perhaps appeasing those of the upcoming cold. The Romans, for example, chose that time to celebrate the intemperate Saturnalia. To some it seemed a time when the beneficent and evil gods warred with each other. Marduk, a god of the Mesopotamians, renewed his everlasting struggle against the forces of darkness. The worshipers of Mithra, who vied with the early Christians for most popular cult in Rome, called the solstice *dies solis invicti nati,* "the birthday of the invincible sun."

In most places, winter was a harsh time. The source of the word is uncertain. It may have originally come from a word meaning white or one meaning wet. The name for the other solstice is more firmly established. "Summer" ultimately comes from the Sanskrit *sama,* which means season or year. Appropriately, the names of the two more active seasons derive from verbs. They are used correctly in the mnemonic for remembering how to set clocks during daylight saving time: "Spring forward, fall back." The English word "spring" is indeed from its meaning that describes shooting upward, and refers to the season's most charming and symbolic trait, the way plants seem to leap out of the ground. "Autumn" comes from the Latin *autumnus,* a synonym for our other word for the season, "fall." Both refer to plants and to gravity—the autumn's falling leaves. A 1545 source describes the seasons as "Spring tyme, Somer, faule of the leafe, and winter."

---

22 DECEMBER 1823

"The Homer of the Insects"

> This is what I wished for . . . : a bit of land, oh, not so very large, but fenced
> in, to avoid the drawbacks of a public way; an abandoned, barren, sun-scorched
> bit of land, favoured by thistles and by Wasps and Bees.

This unusual wish was expressed by the French entomologist J.-Henri Fabre, in one of the many volumes of his classic work of natural history, *Souvenirs Entomologiques.* His lifelong dream of a place in which he could quietly study insects evaded him until he was fifty-five. Plagued by poverty, supporting a wife and five children by teaching and writing, he worked on, worrying that his dream would never be a reality. Finally, after scrimping and saving for decades, he was able to afford the first plot of land he had ever owned, on the outskirts of the village of Sérignan. He described it in *The Life of the Fly.* "It is a *harmas,* the name given, in this district, to an untilled, pebbly expanse abandoned to the vegetation of the thyme. It is too poor to repay the work of the plough; but the sheep passes there in spring, when it has chanced to rain and a little grass shoots up." It was less than three acres. Nevertheless, Fabre called it "the Eden of bliss where I mean to live henceforth alone with the insects."

Jean-Henri Casimer Fabre was born on the twenty-second day of December, 1823, in Saint-Léons, France. The next year, Charles X tried to reestablish the *ancien regime.* When Fabre died ninety-two years later, in 1915, France was the bloody battleground of World War I. During nine tumultuous decades, Fabre spent every spare moment observing the natural world. Inevitably, he asked himself the question that no doubt others had asked about him: "Is it really worth while to spend our time, the time which escapes us so swiftly, this stuff of life, as Montaigne calls it, in gleaning facts of indifferent moment and of highly contestable utility?" But for him, the myriad melodramas around him were of great moment, and nothing could have had greater utility than the slowly fitting together pieces of the greatest puzzle of all—the complex, subtle, interwoven lives of his fellow creatures.

Fabre's work was so impressive, his dedication so complete, that he became a legendary figure. Victor Hugo called him "the Homer of the insects." When Louis Pasteur tackled the very costly problem of silkworm disease, he naturally made a pilgrimage to Fabre. A minister of education under Napoléon III met Fabre, and was so fascinated by him that he introduced him to the emperor. Fabre received the Legion of Honor and other decorations. Although pleased, he had little interest in such notice and returned to his barren weedlots to lie in the sand and watch caterpillars. Interestingly, he was much more of an observer than a theorist. Although he and Darwin corresponded and respected each other, Fabre never accepted the Englishman's ideas on the evolution of animals.

In his old age Fabre wrote to a friend, "Here I am, run wild, and I shall be so till the end." He was. Decades later, before English naturalist Gerald Durrell visited Fabre's grave in Provence, he worried that admirers might have erected an inappropriately ornate monument to the reclusive scientist. He was relieved to find instead a simple stone slab with an urn. And then he saw that nature had provided a fitting tribute of its own. Under a handle of the urn, a wasp had built a little mud nest.

---

23 DECEMBER 1823

"Eight Tiny Rein-deer"

There are two kinds of reindeer: real and imaginary.

Real reindeer have been associated with human beings since the ice ages. Paleolithic humans' favorite prey, their likeness adorns cave walls, and their bones became ornaments and tools. Indeed, the retreat northward, around 15,000 years ago, of the glaciers that dominated northern Europe is sometimes called the Reindeer Age. As the ice migrated, so did reindeer, and today they are the most common deer in many areas of the frozen north. Fortunately for the reindeer, humans find their preferred environment inhospitable.

Imaginary reindeer, by contrast, are semi-aerial and fond of games, their habitat is limited to the North Pole, and at least one has an effulgent nose. In the popular imagination they accompany Christmas. The first public link of reindeer and Christmas was in the Tuesday, December 23, 1823, edition of the *Troy* (New York) *Sentinel.* On the same page as a story about a farmer's 1,232-pound pig was an unsigned poem.

> *'T was the night before Christmas, when all through the house*
> *Not a creature was stirring, not even a mouse . . .*

The previous Christmas Eve, New York professor Clement Clarke Moore had read the poem to his six children. A relative copied it and gave it to a friend, who published it anonymously the next year. Probably Moore never saw a reindeer, much less a sleigh pulled by them. He adapted his Santa from Saint Nicholas, the fourth-century bishop whose legends were brought to New York by Dutch settlers as Sinterklaas.

Modern illustrations portray Santa Claus as a rotund adult and his team as deer-sized, but in Moore's version they are diminutive. What appeared to his narrator's wondering eyes was a *miniature* sleigh, drawn by eight *tiny* reindeer. In the illustrations for the 1848 edition, Santa himself is appropriately miniature, as befits an elf who frequents chimneys. His reindeer are the size of chihuahuas. In his late nineteenth-century illustrations, cartoonist Thomas Nast gradually enlarged Santa and his deer.

In 1939, the Montgomery Ward Department Store asked its advertising writer Robert L. May to create a Christmas story for the annual customer gift. "Rudolph the Red-Nosed Reindeer" is almost a parody of Moore's poem. It even opens with "'T was the day before Christmas, and all through the hills . . ." Rudolph, who is a reindeer but not one of Santa's, lives in a city far south of the pole. Christmas Eve is so foggy that Santa steers by street lamps. While stumbling about in a house, he sees a glow from Rudolph's bedroom and realizes the young reindeer's navigational potential. Heretofore there has been no hint that Rudolph can fly, but off they go to save the holiday.

The 1964 film relocates Rudolph and his abusive playmates to the North Pole. It also imports

> *The moon on the breast of the new-fallen snow,*
> *Gave the luster of mid-day to objects below,*
> *When, what to my wondering eyes should appear,*
> *But a miniature sleigh and eight tiny rein-deer . . .*

Illustration by T. C. Boyd, from *A Visit from St. Nicholas,* 1848

the Abominable Snow Monster, half Yeti and half parody of King Kong. No less relevant than an aerial reindeer in need of rhinoplasty, perhaps the Snow Monster will be the next animal to join the holiday tradition.

---

24 DECEMBER

"Come; See the Oxen Kneel"

Christmas Eve, and twelve of the clock.
"Now they are all on their knees,"
An elder said as we sat in a flock
By the embers in the hearthside ease.

We pictured the meek mild creatures where
They dwelt in their strawy pen,
Nor did it occur to one of us there
To doubt they were kneeling then.

So fair a fancy few would weave
In these years! Yet, I feel,
If someone said on Christmas Eve,
"Come; see the oxen kneel,

"In the lonely barton by yonder coomb
Our childhood used to know,"
I should go with him in the gloom,
Hoping it might be so.

Thomas Hardy's poem "The Oxen" sums up one of the countless superstitions associated with the behavior of animals around Christmastime. Supposedly, on Christmas Eve, our fellow creatures were overcome with the holiness of the anniversary, even though December 25 was an arbitrary date chosen to replace a pagan holiday. Variations on this theme are widespread, although some attach to the eve of Old Christmas, January 5. Many stories involve a version of farm animals chatting in the barn. One appealing belief was that anyone born between 11:00 P.M. and midnight on Christmas Eve would possess the ability to join in these dialogues, a Christmas version of the age-old desire to converse with the animals. In these superstitions, it isn't only domestic animals that celebrate Christ's birth. Ignoring cold and precipitation, bees exit their hives to observe the holiday, although presumably they do not kneel.

In the United States, inhabitants of the Ozark Mountains believed that cocks all crowed together at three o'clock on Christmas morning. (That would be a good time for such a choir. F. Scott Fitzgerald claimed that in the dark night of the soul it is always three o'clock in the morning.) Shakespeare wove

Christmas animal superstitions into his plays—along with, apparently, every other passing thought of the Elizabethan Age. One concerns just such a Chanticleer. In the first scene of the first act of *Hamlet,* the ghost of Hamlet's father returns to Horatio and the two officers for a second close encounter. Horatio interrupts his comparison of recent portents to those presaging the death of Julius Caesar in order to ask the ghost to share any handy supernatural knowledge it might have. A cock crows, and the ghost flees. Horatio mentions the common belief that at the cock's warning of impending daylight spirits return to their confines. Marcellus adds an interesting Christmas twist to the superstition:

> *Some say that ever 'gainst that season comes*
> *Wherein our Saviour's birth is celebrated,*
> *The bird of dawning singeth all night long:*
> *And then, they say, no spirit can walk abroad;*
> *The nights are wholesome; then no planets strike,*
> *No fairy takes, nor witch hath power to charm;*
> *So hallow'd and so gracious is the time.*

The ever rational Horatio replies grudgingly, "So have I heard, and do in part believe it."
See also Christmas, 12/25; and other holidays, 2/2, 3/17, 3/24, and 12/17.

---

25 DECEMBER

Christmas Greenery

Most stories of the origin of the Christmas tree are both entertaining and questionable. The custom of bringing greenery indoors has been common in many cultures, including even ancient Egypt, and apparently the Romans decorated trees during the Saturnalia. However, attempts to attribute the "first Christmas tree" to a particular person strain credulity. Saint Boniface replacing Odin's sacred (but pagan) oak with a more appropriate fir tree seems an unlikely genesis. Surely it is not probable that, while walking home one Christmas evening, Martin Luther saw starlight twinkling on the boughs and determined to mimic the phenomenon with candles.

However, the German origin of the modern Christmas tree seems well established. As early as 1561, an ordinance in Alsace forbade burghers to "have for Christmas more than one bush of more than eight shoes' length." A 1605 description is unequivocal: "At Christmastime in Strassburg they set up fir trees in the rooms, and they hang on them roses cut of many-colored paper, apples, wafers, gilt, sugar. . . ." By the 1700s the practice was becoming common in Germany. In 1850, in the first Christmas issue of his own periodical, *Household Words,* Charles Dickens referred to the Christmas tree as "that pretty German toy." In England the custom of bringing trees indoors for Christmas had been popularized recently by the German-born prince consort, who had married Victoria a decade before.

Several other plants besides the Christmas tree are associated with the holiday, including mistletoe and holly. The ancient appreciation of mistletoe is apparent in a description by Pliny the Elder. He claimed

Supposedly, a single sprig of mistletoe will elicit a kiss. What this young woman may have hoped to inspire with this impressive bundle is not recorded.

that its seed didn't grow unless it passed through a bird. He pointed out "the veneration shown to the mistletoe by the provinces of Gaul." The Druids held it sacred. Pliny claimed they prepared a sacrifice and banquet beneath a tree in which mistletoe was growing. "They think that mistletoe given in a drink renders any barren animal fertile and is an antidote for all poisons. So great is the power of superstition among most people," the famously gullible encyclopedist couldn't help adding, "in regard to relatively unimportant matters."

Apparently the Druids burned mistletoe as a sacrifice and also hung sprigs of it indoors. Some sources make the unlikely claim that enemies lay down their arms and embraced when they passed under the mistletoe, and that from that custom we get the usage for it that Washington Irving described in his 1822 book *Bracebridge Hall.* At that venerable manse Irving saw "the mistletoe, with its white berries, hung up, to the imminent peril of all the pretty housemaids." He added the footnote, "The mistletoe is still hung up in farmhouses and kitchens at Christmas, and the young men have the privilege of kissing the girls under it, plucking each time a berry from the bush. When the berries are all plucked, the privilege ceases."

Holly has a more pious heritage. Unlike mistletoe, which was reviled by Christians because of its pagan associations, holly was pure enough to enter churches. In time its prickly leaves came to symbolize the crown of thorns and its red berries the blood of Jesus. One legend claimed that the holly's berries had originally been white, but that when the crown of holly was pressed on Jesus's head they turned blood-red. Some people even managed to see in the supposedly flame-shaped leaves a symbol of Mary's fiery love for God, and from there it was a short step to allowing this versatile plant to represent the burning bush. Nonetheless, not everyone loved it. A novel use for holly was proposed in Charles Dickens's *A Christmas Carol.* "If I had my will," Ebenezer Scrooge exclaims to his nephew, "every idiot who goes about with 'Merry Christmas' on his lips should be boiled with his own pudding, and buried with a stake of holly through his heart."

---

26 December 1909

"The First Mourner"

After a month in Bermuda, Samuel Clemens returned to Stormfield, his home in Connecticut, a few days before Christmas 1909. The man known as Mark Twain had turned seventy-four in Bermuda, he was unable to shake his preoccupation with the villainy and folly of the human race, and he was still grieving over the death of his beloved wife, Olivia, five years before. Clemens's daughter Jean met him at the dock and tried to inspire some enthusiasm for the approaching holiday. Over the next few days, with her characteristic energy, she decorated Stormfield and bought and wrapped gifts. Christmas Eve morning, Jean was up early to complete her holiday plans. She prepared a bath. An hour later, she had not reappeared. The maid went up to check and found Jean drowned in the tub, apparently the victim of an epileptic seizure.

Clemens had been working on his autobiography. While notifying his remaining daughter, Clara, who was in Germany, and preparing for the funeral, he turned as he had always turned to the written word. The last chapter in the book is about Jean's death. "Why did I build this house, two years ago?" he wrote to himself. "To shelter this vast emptiness?"

As Clemens wandered alone in the emptiness, he encountered what appeared to be a fellow mourner. ". . . I came upon Jean's dog in the hall downstairs, and noted that he did not spring to greet me, according to his hospitable habit, but came slow and sorrowfully; also I remembered that he had not visited Jean's apartment since the tragedy." Until Jean's death, the dog had always followed Clemens up- and downstairs at a gallop. Generally he didn't care for dogs, because, he said, they bark when there is no reason to. But this one was quiet, and because Jean adored him Clemens did also—especially now.

On Christmas Day, Jean's body lay in its coffin in the library. "They told me the first mourner to come was the dog. He came uninvited and stood up on his hind legs and rested his fore paws upon the trestle and took a last long look at the face that was so dear to him, then went his way as silently as he had come. He *knows*." As soon as Clemens picked up a pen, he became Mark Twain, and Twain was never above exaggerating for effect. He was also inclined to see his own grief reflected in everything around him. Nonetheless, his account of Jean's dog echoes countless other stories of the response of such pets to the loss of their owners.

Jean was buried on December 26, 1909. That morning, Clemens wrote, "The dog came to see me at eight o'clock in the morning. He was very affectionate, poor orphan! My room will be his quarters hereafter." The dog didn't have long to shift his affections. Early in January, Clemens departed again for Bermuda, leaving both the house and Jean's dog in the care of friends. He did not return for three months, and by late April he had followed Jean to the grave.

---

27 December 1831

Seeking a Naturalist
for the *Beagle*

The most surprising aspect of Charles Darwin's momentous voyage around the world was that it ever took place. A long chain of unlikely circumstances led to it, and had any one not fallen into place Darwin might have ended up a country parson pursuing natural history on the side.

In the summer of 1831, Her Majesty's Ship *Beagle* was almost ready for its second expedition, and its new captain wanted a companion. Robert Fitzroy was only twenty-six, and he had in mind another young man who might share the captain's table and provide civilized discourse. In time a letter asking recommendations came to John Stevens Henslow at Cambridge, and briefly he toyed with the idea of accepting the offer himself. Thanks partially to the expression on his wife's face when he mentioned it, he did not. Henslow passed the letter on to Leonard Jenyns. That scientifically minded young parson had recently accepted a parish, but he went so far as to pack his clothes before summoning the willpower to refuse. Henslow then passed on the invitation to another skilled young naturalist—Charles Darwin.

The letter reached Darwin in late August. It described the upcoming voyage to Tierra del Fuego and back by way of the East Indies. Its captain, Henslow emphasized, "wants a man (I understand) more as a companion than a mere collector & would not take anyone however good a Naturalist who was not recommended to him likewise as a *gentleman*." Although he lived for geology, insects, and partridge shooting, Darwin fit the bill. He was twenty-two and a Cambridge graduate. Having failed at medicine, he hoped to secure a quiet country parsonage and pursue natural history in his considerable free time. His father was a respectable Shrewsbury physician, his grandfather the famous poet and scientist Erasmus Darwin. Henslow knew that young Charles was not "a finished Naturalist, but as amply qualified for collecting, observing, & noting any thing worthy to be noted in Natural History."

Darwin immediately prepared to accept. Unfortunately, his father was not so sure. The next morning, Darwin sadly wrote to Henslow that he would not be comfortable accepting the offer without his father's approval. However, perhaps because he was impressed by the esteem in which the Cambridge colleagues held his son, Dr. Darwin left an opening: "If you can find any man of common sense who advises you to go, I will give my consent."

That sensible man was right there in the family—Josiah Wedgwood, son of the founder of the pottery dynasty and Charles's uncle. Dr. Darwin wrote to his brother-in-law, enclosed Charles's itemized list of his father's objections, and begged Wedgwood's opinion. In reply, his uncle addressed each point. No, he did not think the voyage would be a detriment to Charles's eventual career, convinced that "the pursuit of Natural History, though certainly not professional, is very suitable to a Clergyman." He summed up with "The undertaking would be useless as regards his profession, but looking upon him as a man of enlarged curiosity, it affords him such an opportunity of seeing men and things as happens to few."

A good loser, Dr. Darwin promised his support. There was only one hurdle left. Charles had to be accepted by the man with whom he expected to spend the next two years. (In reality, the voyage lasted almost five years.) Meanwhile, during the time his invitation had been passed from hand to hand, Captain Fitzroy had reconsidered. He had asked someone else. A colleague persuaded him to consider Darwin, but at their first meeting the captain did his best to convince Charles of the pitfalls and discomforts of the voyage. However, they got along well together, and in the end Fitzroy accepted Darwin. Only later did Fitzroy reveal a last obstacle of which Darwin had been unaware. The captain was an ardent believer in phrenology and physiognomy, which judged character by the bumps on the head and the shape of facial features. "[H]e doubted," Darwin later wrote, "whether anyone with my nose could possess sufficient energy and determination for the voyage."

Happily, the captain overcame his doubts. For weeks Darwin wandered uselessly about the docks in Plymouth while Fitzroy supervised repairs to the ship. Finally, on December 27, 1831, the *Beagle* left England on what was to become one of the most famous voyages in history, one that turned a promising young man into a seasoned naturalist with some revolutionary ideas.

---

28 December 1985

"Magnificent Condescension"

"Neither destiny nor fate took me to Africa," Dian Fossey wrote. "Nor was it romance. I had a deep wish to see and live with wild animals in a world that hadn't yet been completely changed by humans." She lived that wish from 1967, when she first moved to the Karisoke compound in the high volcanic mountains at the juncture of Zaire, Rwanda, and Uganda, until her death in 1985. After a childhood in which she was forbidden any pets save goldfish, then a period as an occupational therapist in Kentucky, untrained in the natural sciences, she went on to become one of the best-known figures in conservation and biology.

On her first visit to Africa in 1963, Fossey met the grand old man of paleontology, Louis S. B. Leakey. He became her mentor. She became one of his "ape women," joining Jane Goodall, whose work with chimpanzees would soon be famous. Later, also launched by Leakey, Birute Galdikas would devote herself to studying orangutans.

Fossey had a lot to learn. Ardent pacifists, mountain gorillas are nonetheless masters of the bluff. The first time a big male charged her, Fossey held on to a tree, closed her eyes, and lost bladder control. The next time, she flung herself into a blackberry thicket. Then *she* learned to bluff, and when another came roaring toward her she stood her ground and made a frightful face at it. The ape looked puzzled, sat down, and began eating. When Fossey didn't leave, he did. The rest of the obstacle course she learned the same way—by confrontation. Critics accused her of anthropomorphism, fanaticism, boorishness, and insensitivity to the native cultures, but no one questioned her courage or endurance. Those attributes may have saved the mountain gorilla from extinction.

After years of obscurity, Fossey's exposure on a *National Geographic* television special and on the *Tonight Show* increased funding for her research. Her book *Gorillas in the Mist* appeared in 1983. The next year, having alienated most of her supporters, she returned to the United States to try to raise money. Then she returned to her favorite place on earth. Soon, however, she made headlines again. On December 28, 1985, Rwandan authorities descended upon the Karisoke compound, and the next day the reason was known worldwide. Late on the night of the twenty-sixth or in the early hours of the twenty-seventh, someone had crept into Fossey's tent and killed her with a bush knife she had once taken from a poacher. No doubt many poachers wished her dead, but various clues indicated that she knew her assailant. On the last day of 1985, on a rare sunny morning, Dian Fossey was buried in a wooden coffin beside the dozen gorillas already in the cemetery she had made. The first word on her grave marker is what the locals called her—*Nyirmachabelli,* "the woman who lives alone on the mountain."

A local minister performed the graveside ceremony, surely one of the more extraordinary eulogies on record. He mentioned that only a week before, Christians had honored Christ's birth on Earth as a man. "We see at our feet a parable of that magnificent condescension—Dian Fossey, born to a home of comfort and privilege she left by her choice to live among a race facing extinction." Then he added: "And if you think the distance that Christ had to come to take the likeness of man is not so great as that from man to gorilla, then you don't know men. Or gorillas. Or God."

------

29 DECEMBER 1946

The Torpid Poorwill

In one of the letters preserved in his *Natural History of Selborne,* English parson-naturalist Gilbert White responded to an inquiry about swallows "being found in a torpid state during the winter." He replied flatly, "I never heard any such account worth attending to." His contemporary Samuel Johnson expressed in his own colorful way the consensus about how birds deal with cold weather. "Swallows certainly sleep all winter," he told Boswell in 1768. "A number of them conglobulate together, by flying round and round, and then all in a heap throw themselves under the water, and lie in the bed of the river." His view is reminiscent of Pliny the Elder, who said birds had been found hiding in the mountains, completely featherless. In time, as scientists began to understand migration, White's view won out over Johnson's. Some creatures slept all winter, but not birds; they flew away.

The first exception to that rule was found on December 29, 1946. California naturalist Edmund Jaegar, accompanied by two students, was in a Chuckwalla Mountains canyon when he noticed a bird resting in a rock niche about two feet above the desert floor. Its feathers had the color and pattern of the stone. Cozy in its bird-size niche, the poorwill didn't respond when Jaegar touched it. It didn't move when he picked it up. He shouted. No response. Finally, as he placed it back in its bed, one of the bird's eyelids flickered.

Jaegar banded the bird, and for the rest of that winter and the next three, he regularly observed the same poorwill. He weighed and measured and photographed it. He could detect no heartbeat even with a stethoscope. The bird's chest didn't move; its breath didn't show on a mirror; its body temperature had sunk from the normal 106°F to 64.4°F. Once, when Jaegar checked the bird, it had one eye open, but a flashlight held two inches away provoked no response. Nor did a hailstorm that battered its feathers. However, because its only source of energy was its own stored fat, even with its metabolic needs reduced by nine-tenths the bird slowly lost weight each winter.

The poorwill is the western relative of the better-known eastern whippoorwill, and the chuck-will's-widow. One was named for what its call sounded like; others are variations on a theme. They and their cousin the nighthawk comprise the Caprimulgidae family. The name derives from the Latin word for goat, *caper.* Because in folklore they are said to milk goats during the night, their common name is "goat-sucker." Poorwills were the first bird species known to hibernate, but we now know that others become dormant for short periods. The metabolism of some hummingbirds is so high—demanding almost constant feeding—that some species sink beyond sleep into dormancy every evening, only to slowly reemerge come morning. If their life processes didn't diminish, they might starve during the night.

Scientists may have been slow to realize the uniqueness of the poorwill, but apparently the Hopi have known for quite some time. They call the bird "The Sleeping One."

---

30 DECEMBER 1816

"The Poetry of Earth"

> Nature is a language, and every new fact that we learn is a new word; but rightly seen, taken all together, it is not merely a language, but the language put together into a most significant and universal book. I wish to learn the language, not that I may learn a new set of nouns and verbs, but that I may read the great book which is written in that tongue.

So Ralph Waldo Emerson wrote in his journal in 1833. That nature is a book from which we never cease to learn is one of the enduring metaphors by which we have tried to understand the world around us. The image recurs frequently throughout literature. In Shakespeare's *Antony and Cleopatra,* for example, the queen's attendant Charmian asks the Soothsayer, "Is't you, sir, that know things?"

"In nature's infinite book of secrecy," the Soothsayer modestly admits, "a little I can read."

Shakespeare returned to a version of that image in *As You Like It,* where Duke Senior speaks of "tongues in trees, books in the running brooks, / Sermons in stones, and good in everything." The speech is reminiscent of the advice of Job: "But ask now the beasts, and they shall teach thee; and the fowls of the air, and they shall teach thee: or speak to the earth, and it shall teach thee; and the fishes of the sea shall declare unto thee."

Edward Jenner, the English physician who pioneered immunology, said of his studies, "The great book of nature is open to all." Sometimes, nature is presented not only as a book, but as actual poetry or music. "All nature," Alexander Pope wrote in *An Essay on Man,* "is but art unknown to thee." Thomas Browne agreed, and went further: "All things are artificial, for nature is the art of God." Robert Osserman's 1995 book on the mathematical analysis of nature is entitled *Poetry of the Universe.*

It is interesting how often the arts and the natural sciences find themselves in the same sentence. We are ourselves an example of nature's restless creativity, and art seems to be our modest answer to it. The metaphors intermingle. "So near is man to the creative pageant," the American nature writer Henry Beston wrote, "so much a part is he of the endless and incredible experiment, that any glimpse he may have will be but the revelation of a moment, a solitary note heard in a symphony thundering through debatable existences of time. Poetry is as necessary to comprehension as science." Beston expressed what may underly the perception of nature in terms of creative arts: "It is as impossible to live without reverence as it is without joy."

No artist agreed more than John Keats. In his best poems, he conveyed his reverence for the natural world in the form of what at first appear to be direct transcriptions of experience. On December 30, 1816, he wrote a poem entitled "On the Grasshopper and the Cricket." Through the example of a grasshopper providing music in summer, and a hearthside cricket taking over in winter, he expressed a sense of the undying artistry of the natural world. He summed up the sentiments of artists and others with a single line: "The poetry of earth is never dead. . . ."

---

31 December 1995

"There's More to This World Than People"

In November of 1985, a new comic strip began appearing in U.S. newspapers. In the first strip, a little boy baits a tiger trap with a tuna fish sandwich. By the last panel, a tiger is eating the sandwich as he hangs upside down by one leg. It was the beginning of a beautiful friendship. *Calvin and Hobbes,* by Bill Watterson, ran until December 31, 1995, and during that decade the six-year-old and his possibly imaginary tiger explored the world together.

Sometimes it seemed that Hobbes's mission was to adjust humanity's opinion of itself. The tiger explains that animals seem content while people are crabby because animals know they're superior and people know they're not. He claims that children don't have fleas because fleas can't stand the smell of children. Calvin wonders why animals don't wear clothes, and Hobbes explains that if they had "naked pink butts" like ours, they probably would.

Despite his affection for Calvin, Hobbes is unable to overcome his feline instincts. The best he can do is keep his claws retracted when he pounces—and pounce he does, constantly. It simply reminds Calvin that it is his curse to suffer through life without the advantages of the animals he admires. He lacks wings, a prehensile tail, fangs, even opposable toes. When he informs Hobbes that he is letting his fingernails grow, Hobbes reminds him that *his* are retractable.

Evolution was a frequent theme in the strip. In one of his many dinosaur fantasies, Calvin envisions natural selection—in this case, a pack of playground-haunting *Deinonychus* dinosaurs weeding out the "weak and stupid," starting with his archenemy Susie. Calvin builds a snowman with a snowball in its twig hand, and explains that it is contemplating snowman evolution and the morality of shoveling one's genetic material off the sidewalk. When Calvin asks Hobbes if he thinks humans evolved from monkeys, the tiger says no, he can't really see any difference.

While admitting that in the real world colors are less intense and people are uglier than on TV, still Calvin finds the universe interesting. Like most six-year-olds, he is quick to invent theories to explain the mysterious phenomena around him. When he finds angel patterns in the snow, he theorizes that they are fallen angels and explains to Hobbes that usually they burn up in the atmosphere. He says that in this case one must have vaporized upon impact, leaving an angel-shaped crater in the snow. Calvin's knowledge of natural history is frequently inadequate. When he is assigned a school report on bats, he refuses to waste time on research and writes a piece entitled "Bats: The Big Bug Scourge of the Skies." As he reads it, his entire class cries out in unison, "Bats aren't bugs!"

Nature is not unrealistically pretty in the strip. One series begins with a dead bird on a sidewalk. Another has the boy and his tiger finding a baby raccoon, only to have it die on them, eliciting Calvin's comment, "What a stupid world." Like most people, Calvin is alternately awestruck and repelled by nature. Reciting a poem about the loveliness of a gossamer web in the grass, he is horrified to observe the spider sucking out the vital juices of its prey. Calvin often meditates on the nature of the universe, the lack of accountability, the waste and inefficiency. He complains that nothing ever gets fixed in nature because there's no toll-free customer service line. Nonetheless, when Calvin wonders if there's an afterlife, if this crazy world is all we get, Hobbes looks around and says, "Oh, what the heck. I'll take it anyway."

One of Watterson's recurring themes—and a sentiment that could become a conservation motto— is summed up in Calvin's school assignment to design a traffic-safety poster. Hobbes suggests a warning against looking into car headlights because you might freeze and get run over or shot. When Calvin says he doesn't think that happens to too many people, Hobbes replies, "There's more to this world than people, you know."

Further Reading

The pioneer English printer William Caxton said it better than I can, in the preface to the second (1484) edition of his beloved Chaucer's *Canterbury Tales.*

> Great thanks, laud, and honour ought to be given unto the clerks, poets, and historiographs that have written many noble books of wisdom . . . by which we be daily informed and have knowledge of many things whom we should not have known if they had not left to us their monuments written.

This is not a full bibliography; it lists only a small percentage of sources consulted. It consists of suggested further readings for those topics that may have piqued your interest. To save space, I omit such invaluable reference works as encyclopedias and dictionaries, which are as much a given as paper, and I exclude all works mentioned in the text. Occasionally I list a source that contributed little to my essay but that contains rich material on the topic. The publisher and date are of the first edition in English when I could find it, and otherwise of the edition consulted.

1/1

Larson, Gary, *The Pre-History of the Far Side: A Tenth Anniversary Exhibit,* Andrews and McMeel, 1989

Shute, Nancy, "Scientists Meet Their Alter Ego on the Far Side," *Smithsonian,* April 1984

1/2

Holroyd, Michael, *Bernard Shaw,* 3 v., Random House, 1988–91

Pearson, Hesketh, *G. B. S.: A Full Length Portrait*, Harper & Brothers, 1942

1/4

Culhane, John, *Walt Disney's* Fantasia, Abrams, 1983

1/5

Morton, Eugene S., and Jake Page, *Animal Talk: Science and the Voices of Nature*, Random House, 1992

Nalven, Nancy, *The Famous Mister Ed: The Unbridled Truth about America's Favorite Talking Horse*, Warner, 1991

1/6

Clark, Ella E., and Margot Edmonds, *Sacagawea of the Lewis and Clark Expedition*, U. of California, 1979

Howard, Harold P., *Sacajawea*, U. of Oklahoma, 1971

1/7

Bonta, Marcia Myers, *Women in the Field: America's Pioneering Women Naturalists*, Texas A & M U., 1991

Brooks, Paul, *The House of Life: Rachel Carson at Work*, Houghton Mifflin, 1972

1/8

Matthiessen, Peter, *Wildlife in America*, Viking, 1987

1/9

Marais, Eugene, *The Soul of the White Ant*, Penguin, 1973

Quammen, David, *Natural Acts*, Schocken, 1985

1/10

Degler, Carl N., *In Search of Human Nature: The Decline and Revival of Darwinism in American Social Thought*, Oxford U., 1991

Thomas, Tony, *The Films of Ronald Reagan*, Citadel, 1980

1/11

Desmond, Adrian, and James Moore, *Darwin: The Life of a Tormented Evolutionist*, Warner, 1991

Kohn, David, ed., *The Darwinian Heritage*, Princeton U., 1985

1/12

Fleisher, Michael L., and Janet E. Lincoln, *The Encyclopedia of Comic Book Heroes,* v. 1, *Batman*, Macmillan, 1976

Reynolds, Richard, *Super Heroes: A Modern Mythology*, U. Press of Mississippi, 1992

1/13

Morton, Eugene S., and Jake Page, *Animal Talk: Science and the Voices of Nature*, Random House, 1992

1/14

Warner, Sylvia Townsend, *T. H. White: A Biography*, Viking, 1967

1/15

Rose, Phyllis, *Jazz Cleopatra: Josephine Baker in Her Time*, Doubleday, 1989

1/16

Carpenter, Humphrey, *The Letters of J. R. R. Tolkien*, Houghton Mifflin, 1981

Milner, Richard, *The Encyclopedia of Evolution: Humanity's Search for Its Origins*, Facts On File, 1991

1/17

Peary, Danny and Gerald, *The American Animated Cartoon: A Critical Anthology*, Dutton, 1980

Smoodin, Eric, *Animating Culture: Hollywood Cartoons from the Sound Era*, Rutgers U., 1993

1/18

South, Malcolm, ed., *Mythical and Fabulous Creatures: A Source Book and Research Guide*, Greenwood Press, 1987

1/19

Bonner, W. N., and D. Walton, eds., *Antarctica*, Pergamon Press, 1985

Stewart, John, *Antarctica: An Encyclopedia*, McFarland, 1990

1/20

Emerson, Everett, *The Authentic Mark Twain: A Literary Biography of Samuel Clemens*, U. of Pennsylvania, 1984

Kaplan, Justin, *Mark Twain and His World*, Simon & Schuster, 1974

1/21

Richardson, Robert D., Jr., *Henry Thoreau: A Life of the Mind*, U. of California, 1986

Wilson, Edward O., and Bert Hölldobler, *Journey to the Ants: A Story of Scientific Exploration*, The Belknap Press of Harvard U., 1994

1/22

Christianson, Gale E., *Fox at the Wood's Edge: A Biography of Loren Eiseley*, Henry Holt, 1990

Heuer, Kenneth, ed., *The Lost Notebooks of Loren Eiseley*, Little, Brown, 1987

1/23

King, Ronald, *The World of Kew*, Macmillan, 1976

Turrill, W. B., *The Royal Botanic Gardens at Kew: Past and Present*, Herbert Jenkins Ltd., 1959

1/24

Weyr, Thomas, *Reaching for Paradise: The Playboy Vision of America*, Times Books, 1978

1/27

Brunvand, Jan, Several books, especially *The Vanishing Hitchhiker*, Norton, 1981

1/29

Meyers, Jeffrey, *Edgar Allan Poe: His Life and Legacy*, Scribner's, 1992

Silverman, Kenneth, *Edgar A. Poe: Mournful and Never-Ending Remembrance*, HarperCollins, 1991

1/31

Arnold, H. J. P., *Man in Space: An Illustrated History of Space Flight*, Smithmark, 1993

2/1

Dickson, Lovat, *H. G. Wells: His Turbulent Life and Times*, Atheneum, 1969

Suvin, Darko, *H. G. Wells and Modern Science Fiction*, Bucknell U., 1977

2/2

Shepard, Paul, and Barry Sanders, *The Sacred Paw: The Bear in Nature, Myth, and Literature*, Viking, 1985

2/3

de Rocher, Gregory David, trans. and ed., *Popular Errors*, U. of Alabama, 1989; *The Second Part of the Popular Errors*, U. of Alabama, 1995

2/4

James, Peter, and Nick Thorpe, *Ancient Inventions*, Ballantine, 1994

Officer, Charles, and Jake Page, *Tales of the Earth: Paroxysms and Perturbations of the Blue Planet*, Oxford U., 1993

2/7

Desmond, Adrian, *Huxley: The Devil's Disciple*, Michael Joseph, 1994

Norell, Mark A., et al., *Discovering Dinosaurs: In the American Museum of Natural History*, Knopf, 1995

2/8

Fraser, Antonia, *Mary, Queen of Scots*, Delacorte, 1969

Thomas, Keith, *Man and the Natural World: A History of the Modern Sensibility*, Pantheon, 1983

2/9

Clair, Colin, *Unnatural History*, Abelard-Schuman, 1967

Weaver, Tom, *Interviews with B Science Fiction and Horror Movie Makers: Writers, Producers, Directors, Actors, Moguls and Makeup*, McFarland, 1988

2/10

Cousteau, Jacques-Yves, and Frédéric Dumas, *The Silent World*, Harper & Row, 1953

Hamilton-Paterson, James, *The Great Deep: The Sea and Its Thresholds*, Random House, 1992

2/11

Calder, Nigel, *Comets: Speculation and Discovery*, Penguin, 1982

Flaste, Richard, et al., *The New York Times Guide to the Return of Halley's Comet*, Times Books, 1985

2/12

Collingwood, Stuart Dodgson, *The Life and Letters of Lewis Carroll*, Gale Research, 1899

French, Richard D., *Antivivisection and Medical Science in Victorian Society*, Princeton U., 1975

2/13

Lum, Peter, *Fabulous Beasts*, Pantheon, 1951

2/15

Grant, Michael, and Rachel Kitzinger, *Civilization of the Ancient Mediterranean*, Scribner's, 1988

Scullard, H. H., *Festivals and Ceremonies of the Roman Republic*, Cornell U., 1981

2/16

Fricke, Hans, "Coelacanths: The Fish That Time Forgot," *National Geographic,* June 1988

Thomson, Keith Stewart, *Fossil Fish: The Story of the Coelacanth*, Norton, 1991

2/17

Crick, Bernard, *George Orwell: A Life*, Secker & Warburg, 1981

Smyer, Richard I., *Animal Farm: Pastoralism and Politics*, Twayne, 1988

2/18

Croswell, Ken, "The Pursuit of Pluto", *American Heritage of Invention and Technology,* Winter 1990

Sheehan, William, *Worlds in the Sky: Planetary Discoveries from Earliest Times through Voyager and Magellan*, U. of Arizona, 1992

2/19

Caras, Roger A., *Dangerous to Man*, Holt, Rinehart and Winston, 1975

2/20

Diolé, Philippe, *Under-water Exploration: A History*, Elek Books, 1954

2/22

Wallace, Irving, *The Fabulous Showman: The Life and Times of P. T. Barnum*, Knopf, 1959

Werner, M. W., *Barnum*, Harcourt, 1923

2/23

Finch, Christopher, *The Art of Walt Disney: From Mickey Mouse to the Magic Kingdoms*, Abrams, 1995

2/24

Cikovsky, Nicolai, Jr., *Winslow Homer*, Abrams, 1990

2/25

Bedini, Silvio A., *Thomas Jefferson: Statesman of Science*, Macmillan, 1990

Milner, Richard, *The Encyclopedia of Evolution: Humanity's Search for Its Origins*, Facts On File, 1991

2/27

Sparks, John, and Tony Soper, *Owls: Their Natural and Unnatural History*, Facts On File, 1989

2/28

Gould, Stephen Jay, et al., *The Book of Life*, Norton, 1993

2/29

Morison, Samuel Eliot, *Admiral of the Ocean Sea: A Life of Christopher Columbus*, Little, Brown, 1942

Taviani, Paolo Emilio, *Columbus: The Great Adventure: His Life, His Times, His Voyages*, Orion, 1991

3/1

Clark, Ronald W., *Benjamin Franklin: A Biography*, Random House, 1983

Uman, Martin A., *Lightning*, Dover, 1969

3/3

Morris, Ramona and Desmond, *Men and Apes*, McGraw-Hill, 1966

Rensberger, Boyce, *The Cult of the Wild*, Doubleday, 1977

3/5

Adams, Alexander B., *Eternal Quest: The Story of the Great Naturalists*, Putnam, 1969

Hunter, Clark, *The Life and Letters of Alexander Wilson*, American Philosophical Society, 1983

3/6

Feare, Christopher, *The Starling*, Oxford U., 1984

Laycock, George, *The Alien Animals*, Natural History Press (Doubleday), 1966

3/7

Beaglehole, J. C., *The Life of Captain James Cook*, Stanford U., 1974

3/8

Kohn, David, ed., *The Darwinian Heritage*, Princeton U., 1985

3/9

Bruce, Evangeline, *Napoleon and Josephine: The Improbable Marriage*, Scribner, 1995

Thomas, Keith, *Man and the Natural World: A History of the Modern Sensibility*, Pantheon, 1983

3/10

Alexander, Sidney, "Jack London's Literary Lycanthropy", *The Reporter,* 24 June 1957

Wilcox, Earl J., *The Call of the Wild: A Casebook with Text, Background Sources, Reviews, Critical Essays, and Bibliography*, Nelson-Hall, 1980

3/12

Clair, Colin, *Unnatural History: An Illustrated Bestiary*, Abelard-Schuman, 1967

Lewinsohn, Richard, *Animals, Men, and Myths: An Informative and Entertaining History of Man and the Animals around Him*, Harper, 1954

3/13

Peterson, Ivars, *Newton's Clock: Chaos in the Solar System*, W. H. Freeman, 1993

Sheehan, William, *Worlds in the Sky: Planetary Discovery from Earliest Times through Voyager and Magellan*, U. of Arizona, 1992

3/14

Hubbell, Sue, *Broadsides from the Other Orders: A Book of Bugs*, Random House, 1993

Stein, Sara, *Noah's Garden: Restoring the Ecology of Our Own Back Yards*, Houghton Mifflin, 1993

3/18

Berthon, Simon, and Andrew Robinson, *The Shape of the World: The Mapping and Discovery of the Earth*, Rand McNally, 1991

3/19

Sinyard, Neil, *The Films of Alfred Hitchcock*, Gallery Books, 1986

Sterritt, David, *The Films of Alfred Hitchcock*, Cambridge U., 1993

3/20

Cartwright, Frederick Fox, *Disease and History*, Crowell, 1972

Clarkson, Leslie, *Death, Disease, and Famine in Pre-Industrial England*, St. Martin's, 1975

3/21

Eriksson, Paul S., et al., *Treasury of North American Birdlore*, Eriksson, 1987

Kastner, Joseph, *A World of Watchers: An Informal History of the American Passion for Birds*, Knopf, 1986

3/22

Bruccoli, Matthew J., *Ross Macdonald*, Harcourt Brace Jovanovich, 1984

Sokolov, Raymond A., "The Art of Murder", *Newsweek,* 22 March 1971

3/23

LaValley, Al, ed., *Invasion of the Body Snatchers: Don Siegel, Director*, Rutgers U., 1989

Schelde, Per, *Androids, Humanoids, and Other Science Fiction Monsters: Science and Soul in Science Fiction Films*, New York U., 1993

3/25

Shattuck, Roger, et al., *Henri Rousseau*, Museum of Modern Art, 1985

3/26

Brent, Peter, *Charles Darwin: A Man of Enlarged Curiosity*, Harper & Row, 1981

3/27

Bonta, Marcia Myers, *Women in the Field: America's Pioneering Women Naturalists*, Texas A & M U., 1991

Kastner, Joseph, *A Species of Eternity*, Knopf, 1977

3/28

King, James, *Virginia Woolf*, Hamish Hamilton, 1994

Richter, Harvena, "Hunting the Moth: Virginia Woolf and the Creative Imagination," in *Critical Essays on Virginia Woolf*, ed. by Morris Beja, G. K. Hall, 1985

3/29

Lee, Lynn, *Don Marquis*, Twayne, 1981

White, E. B., "Don Marquis," in *Essays of E. B. White*, Harper & Row, 1977

3/30

Blount, Margaret, *Animal Land: The Creatures of Children's Fiction*, Morrow, 1974

Lansbury, Coral, *The Old Brown Dog: Women, Workers, and Vivisection in Edwardian England*, U. of Wisconsin, 1985

3/31

Paine, Albert Bigelow, *Thomas Nast: His Period and His Pictures*, Pyne, 1974 (1904)

Shikes, Ralph E., *The Indignant Eye: The Artist as Social Critic in Prints and Drawings from the Fifteenth Century to Picasso*, Beacon, 1969

4/2

Benson, Jackson L., *The True Adventures of John Steinbeck, Writer*, Viking, 1984

Parini, Jay, *John Steinbeck: A Biography*, Heinemann, 1994

4/3

Williams, Jack, *The Weather Book*, Vintage, 1992

4/4

James, Peter, and Nick Thorpe, *Ancient Inventions*, Ballantine, 1994

Temple, Robert, *The Genius of China,* Simon & Schuster, 1986

4/5

Dennis, Arnett S., *Weather Modification by Cloud Seeding*, Academic Press, 1980

Hess, W. N., ed., *Weather and Climate Modification*, Wiley, 1974

4/6

Baring-Gould, William S., *The Annotated Sherlock Holmes,* 2 v., Clarkson N. Potter, 1967

Eyles, Allen, *Sherlock Holmes: A Centenary Celebration*, Harper & Row, 1986

4/7

Browne, Janet, *Charles Darwin: A Biography,* v. 1, *Voyaging*, Knopf, 1995

Clark, Ronald W., *JBS: The Life and Work of J. B. S. Haldane*, Coward-McCann, 1968

4/8

Calder, Nigel, *The Comet Is Coming! The Feverish Legacy of Mr. Halley*, Penguin, 1982

Flaste, Richard, et al., *The New York Times Guide to the Return of Halley's Comet*, Times Books, 1985

4/9

Bowen, Catherine Drinker, *Francis Bacon: The Temper of a Man*, Atlantic–Little, Brown, 1963

Farrington, Benjamin, *Francis Bacon: Philosopher of Industrial Science*, H. Schuman, 1951

4/11

Danly, Robert Lyons, *In the Shade of Spring Leaves: The Life of Higuchi Ichiyo, with Nine of Her Best Stories*, Norton, 1981

4/12

Jenkins, Alan, *The Naturalists*, Mayflower, 1978

Teale, Edwin Way, *Springtime in Britain*, Dodd Mead, 1970

4/13

Lewin, Roger, *Bones of Contention: Controversies in the Search for Human Origins*, Simon & Schuster, 1987

Willis, Delta, *The Hominid Gang: Behind the Scenes in the Search for Human Origins*, Viking Penguin, 1989

4/15

Crane, David, "Below the Tip of an Iceberg", *Geographical,* December 1993

Lord, Walter, *The Night Lives On*, Morrow, 1986; *A Night to Remember*, Henry Holt, 1955

4/17

Johnson, Donald S., *Charting the Sea of Darkness: The Four Voyages of Henry Hudson*, McGraw-Hill, 1993

4/18

Officer, Charles, and Jake Page, *Tales of the Earth: Paroxysms and Perturbations of the Blue Planet*, Oxford U., 1993

4/19

Gilot, Françoise, and Carlton Lake, *Life with Picasso*, McGraw-Hill, 1964

Laporte, Genevieve, *Sunshine at Midnight: Memories of Picasso and Cocteau*, Macmillan, 1973

4/20

Clair, Colin, *Unnatural History: An Illustrated Bestiary*, Abelard-Schuman, 1967

Lum, Peter, *Fabulous Beasts*, Pantheon, 1951

4/21

Callicott, J. Baird, *A Companion to* A Sand County Almanac, U. of Wisconsin, 1987

Meine, Curt, *Aldo Leopold: His Life and Work*, U. of Wisconsin, 1988

4/22

Shabecoff, Philip, *A Fierce Green Fire: The American Environmental Movement*, Hill & Wang, 1993

4/23

Churcher, Peter B., and John H. Lawton, "Beware of Well-Fed Felines," *Natural History,* July 1989

Martin, John Bartlow, *Adlai Stevenson of Illinois*, Doubleday, 1976

4/24

Davidson, Basil, *The African Past: Chronicles from Antiquity to Modern Times*, Little, Brown, 1964

Schivelbusch, Wolfgang, *Tastes of Paradise: A Social History of Spices, Stimulants, and Intoxicants*, Pantheon, 1992

4/25

Kaplan, Justin, *Mr. Clemens and Mark Twain: A Biography*, Simon & Schuster, 1966

Robinson, Alan James, ed., *The Celebrated Jumping Frog of Calaveras County*, Cheloniidae, 1985

4/26

Desmond, Adrian, and James Moore, *Darwin: The Life of a Tormented Evolutionist*, Warner, 1991

4/27

Sagan, Carl, and Ann Druyan, *Comet*, Random House, 1985

4/28

Carpenter, Humphrey, ed., *The Letters of J. R. R. Tolkien*, Houghton Mifflin, 1981

4/30

Harding, Walter, *The Days of Henry Thoreau*, Knopf, 1970

Hough, Henry Beetle, *Thoreau of Walden: The Man and His Eventful Life*, Simon & Schuster, 1956

5/2

Coggiatti, Stelvio, *Simon & Schuster's Guide to Roses*, Simon & Schuster, 1986

Schneider, Peter, *Peter Schneider on Roses*, Macmillan, 1995

5/4

Desmond, Adrian, *Huxley: The Devil's Disciple*, Michael Joseph, 1994

Irvine, William, *Apes, Angels, and Victorians: The Story of Darwin, Huxley, and Evolution*, McGraw-Hill, 1955

5/5

Oliver, Douglas, *Return to Tahiti: Bligh's Second Breadfruit Voyage*, U. of Hawaii, 1988

Wenkam, Robert, and Byron Baker, *Micronesia: The Breadfruit Revolution*, East-West Center Press, 1971

5/6

James, Peter, and Nick Thorpe, *Ancient Inventions*, Ballantine, 1994

5/7

Wilson, John Harold, *Nell Gwyn: Royal Mistress*, Pellegrini & Cudahy, 1952

5/8

Williams, Jack, *The Weather Book*, Vintage, 1992

5/9

Asimov, Isaac, *Asimov's Annotated* Gulliver's Travels, Clarkson N. Potter, 1980

5/10

Grahame, Kenneth, *My Dearest Mouse: "The Wind in the Willows" Letters,* ed. by David Gooderson, Pavilion & Bodleian Library, 1988

Prince, Alison, *Kenneth Grahame: An Innocent in the Wild Wood*, Allison & Busby, 1994

5/11

Bonta, Marcia Myers, *Women in the Field: America's Pioneering Women Naturalists*, Texas A & M U., 1991

Nice, Margaret Morse, *The Watcher at the Nest*, Macmillan, 1939

5/12

Gittings, Robert, *John Keats*, Heinemann, 1968

Wilson, Katherine M., *The Nightingale and the Hawk: A Psychological Study of Keats' Ode*, Allen & Unwin, 1964

5/13

Elledge, Scott, *E. B. White: A Biography*, Norton, 1984

White, E. B., *Letters of E. B. White,* ed. by Dorothy Lobrano Guth, Harper & Row, 1976

5/14

George, Uwe, *In the Deserts of This Earth*, Harcourt Brace Jovanovich, 1977

Laycock, George, *The Alien Animals*, Natural History Press (Doubleday), 1966

5/16

Kastner, Joseph, *A World of Watchers: An Informal History of the American Passion for Birds*, Knopf, 1986

5/18

Avery, Peter, and John Heath-Stubbs, trans. and eds., *The Ruba'iyat of Omar Khayyam*, Penguin, 1979

Dashti, Ali, *In Search of Omar Khayyam*, Columbia U., 1971

5/19

Thomas, Keith, *Man and the Natural World: A History of the Modern Sensibility*, Pantheon, 1983

5/20

Clarke, T. H., *The Rhinoceros from Dürer to Stubbs*, Sotheby's, 1986

5/23

Devlin, John C., and Grace Naismith, *The World of Roger Tory Peterson: An Authorized Biography*, Times Books, 1977

5/24

Elledge, Scott, *E. B. White: A Biography*, Norton, 1984

Neumeyer, Peter F., *The Annotated* Charlotte's Web, HarperCollins, 1994

5/25

Root, Nina J., "Victorian England's Hippomania," *Natural History,* January 1993

Schwartz, David M., "Snatching Scientific Secrets from the Hippo's Gaping Jaws," *Smithsonian,* March 1996

5/26

Gould, Stephen Jay, *Hen's Teeth and Horse's Toes*, Norton, 1983

Numbers, Ronald L., *The Creationists: The Evolution of Scientific Creationism*, Knopf, 1992

5/27

Davenport, Marcia, *Mozart*, Scribner's, 1932

West, Meredith J., and Andrew P. King, "Mozart's Starling," *American Scientist,* March–April 1990

5/28

Burke, James, *The Day the Universe Changed*, Little, Brown, 1985

Lloyd, G. E. R., *Early Greek Science: Thales to Aristotle*, Norton, 1970

5/29

Berthon, Simon, and Andrew Robinson, *The Shape of the World: The Mapping and Discovery of the Earth*, Rand McNally, 1991

Jerome, John, *On Mountains: Thinking about Terrain*, Harcourt Brace Jovanovich, 1978

5/30

Jones, Kathleen, *A Glorious Fame: The Life of Margaret Cavendish, Duchess of Newcastle, 1623–1673*, Bloomsbury, 1988

Phillips, Patricia, *The Scientific Lady: A Social History of Women's Scientific Interests, 1520–1918*, Weidenfeld & Nicolson, 1990

5/31

Mossiker, Frances, *The Queen's Necklace*, Simon & Schuster, 1961

6/2

Shreeve, James, *The Neandertal Enigma: Solving the Mystery of Modern Human Origins*, Morrow, 1995

Trinkaus, Erik, and Pat Shipman, *The Neandertals: Of Skeletons, Scientists, and Scandal*, Knopf, 1993

6/3

Clarke, T. H., *The Rhinoceros from Dürer to Stubbs*, Sotheby's, 1986

6/4

Collins, Ace, *Lassie: A Dog's Life: The First Fifty Years*, Penguin, 1993

6/5

Laskin, David, *Braving the Elements: The Stormy History of American Weather*, Doubleday, 1996

Officer, Charles, and Jake Page, *Tales of the Earth: Paroxysms and Perturbations of the Blue Planet*, Oxford U., 1993

6/9

Segi, Shinichi, *Yoshitoshi: The Splendid Decadent*, Kodansha, 1985

Stevenson, John, *Yoshitoshi's One Hundred Aspects of the Moon*, San Francisco Graphic Society, 1992

6/10

Bate, Walter Jackson, *John Keats*, Oxford U., 1963

Ward, Aileen, *John Keats: The Making of a Poet*, Viking, 1963

6/11

Gould, Stephen Jay, "Dinomania", *New York Review,* 12 August 1993

Wollen, Peter, "Theme Park and Variations", *Sight and Sound,* July 1993

6/12

Nabokov, Vladimir, *Lectures on Literature,* ed. by Fredson Bowers, Harcourt Brace Jovanovich, 1980; *Speak, Memory*, Putnam, 1966; *Strong Opinions* (interviews), McGraw-Hill, 1973

6/13

Officer, Charles, and Jake Page, *Tales of the Earth: Paroxysms and Perturbations of the Blue Planet*, Oxford U., 1993

Scarth, Alwyn, *Volcanoes*, Texas A & M U., 1994

6/14

Evans, E. P., *The Criminal Prosecution and Capital Punishment of Animals*, Heinemann, 1906

Thomas, Keith, *Man and the Natural World*, Pantheon, 1983

6/15

Slasser, George, et al., *Shadows of the Magic Lamp: Fantasy and Science Fiction in Film*, Southern Illinois U., 1985

Wilson, Edward O., and Bert Hölldobler, *Journey to the Ants: A Story of Scientific Exploration*, Harvard U., 1994

6/16

Stannard, David E., *American Holocaust: Columbus and the Conquest of the New World*, Oxford U., 1992

6/17

Holtsmark, Erling B., *Edgar Rice Burroughs*, Twayne, 1986

McWhirter, George T., *The Burroughs Dictionary*, U. Press of America, 1987

6/20

Caras, Roger A., *Dangerous to Man: The Definitive Story of Wildlife's Reputed Dangers*, Holt, Rinehart and Winston, rev. ed., 1975

Taylor, Philip M., *Steven Spielberg: The Man, His Movies, and Their Meaning*, Continuum, 1992

6/22

Drake, Stillman, ed., *Discoveries and Opinions of Galileo*, Anchor, 1957

Reston, James, Jr., *Galileo: A Life*, HarperCollins, 1994

6/24

Grauer, Nail A., *Remember Laughter: A Life of James Thurber*, U. of Nebraska, 1995.

Holmes, Charles S., *The Clocks of Columbus: The Literary Career of James Thurber*, Atheneum, 1972

6/25

Bruce, Evangeline, *Napoleon and Josephine: The Improbable Marriage*, Scribner, 1995; *Roses for an Empress: Josephine Bonaparte and Pierre-Joseph Redouté*, Sidgwick & Jackson, 1983

6/26

Dawkins, Richard, *The Blind Watchmaker: Why the Evidence of Evolution Reveals a Universe without Design*, Norton, 1986

Laufer, Berthold, *The Giraffe in History and Art*, Field Museum (Chicago), 1928

6/27

Vincent, Howard P., *The Trying-Out of Moby-Dick*, Houghton Mifflin, 1949

6/28

McLynn, Frank, *Robert Louis Stevenson: A Biography*, Random House, 1993

6/29

Fuye, Marguerite Allotte de la, *Jules Verne*, Staples, 1954

Lynch, Lawrence, *Jules Verne*, Twayne, 1992

6/30

Steel, Duncan, *Rogue Asteroids and Doomsday Comets*, Wiley, 1995

Whipple, Fred L., *The Mystery of Comets*, Smithsonian Institution, 1985

7/1

Kohn, David, ed., *The Darwinian Heritage*, Princeton U., 1985

McKinney, H. Lewis, *Wallace and Natural Selection,* Yale U., 1972

7/2

Beaumont, Barbara, trans. and ed., *Flaubert and Turgenev: A Friendship in Letters*, Fromm, 1985

7/3

Gould, Stephen Jay, "The Case of the Creeping Fox Terrier Clone," in *Bully for Brontosaurus*, Norton, 1991
Layman, Richard, *Shadow Man: The Life of Dashiell Hammett*, Harcourt Brace Jovanovich, 1981

7/4

Fuller, Errol, *Extinct Birds*, Facts On File, 1987
Gardner, Martin, ed., *The Annotated Alice*, Clarkson N. Potter, 1960

7/5

Gates, Barbara Timm, ed., *Journal of Emily Shore*, U. Press of Virginia, 1991

7/6

McHugh, Tom, *The Time of the Buffalo*, Knopf, 1972

7/7

Hyams, Edward, *Great Botanical Gardens of the World*, Macmillan, 1969

7/8

Brookfield, Charles M., "The Guy Bradley Story," *Audubon Magazine,* July–August 1955
Kastner, Joseph, *A World of Watchers: An Informal History of the American Passion for Birds*, Knopf, 1986

7/9

Ackroyd, Peter, *Dickens*, HarperCollins, 1990
Kaplan, Fred, *Dickens: A Biography*, Morrow, 1988

7/10

Gatewood, Willard B., Jr., ed., *Controversy in the Twenties: Fundamentalism, Modernism, and Evolution*, Vanderbilt U., 1969
Gould, Stephen Jay, *Hen's Teeth and Horse's Toes*, Norton, 1983

7/12

Adams, Alexander B., *Eternal Quest: The Story of the Great Naturalists*, Putnam, 1969
Hunter, Clark, *The Life and Letters of Alexander Wilson*, American Philosophical Society, 1983

7/13

Psihoyos, Louie, with John Knoebber, *Hunting Dinosaurs*, Random House, 1994
Reader, John, *Missing Links: The Hunt for Earliest Man*, Little, Brown, 1981

7/14

Gould, Stephen Jay, "To Be a Platypus," in *Bully for Brontosaurus*, Norton, 1991

Gregory, Ed, "Tuned-in, Turned-on Platypus," *Natural History,* May 1991

7/15

Gruber, Howard E., *Darwin on Man: A Psychological Study of Scientific Creativity*, bound with Paul H. Barrett, ed., *Darwin's Early and Unpublished Notebooks*, Dutton, 1974

7/17

Sagan, Carl, *Pale Blue Dot: A Vision of the Human Future in Space*, Random House, 1995

Steel, Duncan, *Rogue Asteroids and Doomsday Comets: The Search for the Million Megaton Menace That Threatens Life on Earth*, Wiley, 1995

7/18

Adams, Jonathan S., and Thomas O. McShane, *The Myth of Wild Africa: Conservation Without Illusion*, Norton, 1992

Bonner, Raymond, *At the Hand of Man: Peril and Hope for Africa's Wildlife*, Knopf, 1993

7/19

Maltin, Leonard, *Of Mice and Magic: A History of American Animated Cartoons*, New American Library, 1980

7/20

Arnold, H. J. P., *Man in Space: An Illustrated History of Space Flight*, Smithmark, 1993

Chaikin, Andrew, *A Man on the Moon: The Voyages of the Apollo Astronauts*, Viking Penguin, 1994

7/21

Numbers, Ronald L., *The Creationists: The Evolution of Scientific Creationism*, Knopf, 1992

Scopes, John, *Center of the Storm*, Holt, Rinehart and Winston, 1967

7/23

Christie, John Aldrich, *Thoreau as World Traveler*, Columbia U., 1965

Richardson, Robert D., Jr., *Henry Thoreau: A Life of the Mind*, U. of California, 1986

7/24

Fisher, David E., *The Scariest Place on Earth: Eye to Eye with Hurricanes*, Random House, 1994

Hume, Ivor Noël, *The Virginia Adventure: Roanoke to James Towne*, Knopf, 1994

7/26

Siegel, Harold I., ed., *The Hamster: Reproduction and Behavior*, Plenum, 1985

7/27

Maltin, Leonard, *Of Mice and Magic: A History of American Animated Cartoons*, New American Library, 1980

Schneider, Steve, *That's All Folks! The Art of Warner Brothers Animation*, Henry Holt, 1988

7/28

Psihoyos, Louie, with John Knoebber, *Hunting Dinosaurs*, Random House, 1994

7/30

Schiebinger, Londa, "The Loves of the Plants," *Scientific American,* February 1996

7/31

Lindsay, Maurice, *Robert Burns: The Man, His Work, the Legend*, St. Martin's, 2nd ed., 1968

Zinsser, Hans, *Rats, Lice and History*, Little, Brown, 1935

8/2

Haas, Robert Bartlett, *Muybridge: Man in Motion*, U. of California, 1976

Hendricks, Gordon, *Eadweard Muybridge: The Father of the Motion Picture*, Grossman, 1975

8/4

Clair, Colin, *Unnatural History*, Abelard-Schuman, 1967

Thomas, Keith, *Man and the Natural World: A History of the Modern Sensibility*, Pantheon, 1983

8/5

Forster, Margaret, *Elizabeth Barrett Browning: A Biography*, Doubleday, 1989

Raymond, Meredith B., and Mary Rose Sullivan, eds., *Women of Letters: Selected Letters of Elizabeth Barrett Browning and Mary Russell Mitford*, Twayne, 1987

8/8

Wallace, Irving, *The Fabulous Showman: The Life and Times of P. T. Barnum*, Knopf, 1959

Werner, M. W., *Barnum*, Harcourt, 1923

8/9

Silverman, Kenneth, *Edgar Allan Poe: Mournful and Never-Ending Remembrance*, HarperCollins, 1991

8/10

Costello, Peter, *The Magic Zoo: The Natural History of Fabulous Animals*, St. Martin's, 1979

Lum, Peter, *Fabulous Beasts*, Pantheon, 1951

8/11

Shabecoff, Philip, *A Fierce Green Fire: The American Environmental Movement*, Hill & Wang, 1993

8/12

Norell, Mark A., et al., *Discovering Dinosaurs in the American Museum of Natural History*, Knopf, 1995

8/13

Berger, Arthur Asa, *Li'l Abner: A Study in American Satire*, Twayne, 1970

8/14

Bingham, Jane M., ed., *Writers for Children: Critical Studies of Major Authors since the Seventeenth Century*, Scribner's, 1988

Maltin, Leonard, *The Disney Films*, Crown, 1973

8/15

Benton, Mike, *The Comic Book in America*, Taylor, 1989

Daniels, Les, *Marvel: Five Fabulous Decades of the World's Greatest Comics*, Abrams, 1991

8/16

Cook, Fred J., *The Unfinished Story of Alger Hiss*, Morrow, 1958

Smith, John Chabot, *Alger Hiss: The True Story*, Holt, Rinehart and Winston, 1976

8/17

Asprey, Robert B., *Frederick the Great: The Magnificent Enigma*, Ticknor & Fields, 1986

Burnside, Dennis, "The Italian Greyhound: Renaissance Elegance in Miniature," *Dogworld,* May 1995

8/18

Rensberger, Boyce, *The Cult of the Wild*, Doubleday, 1977

8/19

Milner, Richard, *The Encyclopedia of Evolution: Humanity's Search for Its Origins*, Facts On File, 1991

Psihoyos, Louie, with John Knoebber, *Hunting Dinosaurs*, Random House, 1994

8/21

Shepard, Paul, and Barry Sanders, *The Sacred Paw: The Bear in Nature, Myth, and Literature*, Viking, 1985

Thwaite, Ann, *A. A. Milne: The Man Behind Winnie-the-Pooh*, Random House, 1990

8/22

Gillingham, John, *The Wars of the Roses: Peace and Conflict in Fifteenth-Century England*, Louisiana State U., 1981

Pollard, A. J., *The Wars of the Roses*, St. Martin's, 1988

8/24

Etienne, Robert, *Pompeii: The Day a City Died*, Abrams, 1992

Scarth, Alwyn, *Volcanoes: An Introduction*, Texas A & M U., 1994

8/27

Bedini, Silvio A., *The Life of Benjamin Banneker*, Scribner's, 1972

8/30

Hughes-Hallet, Lucy, *Cleopatra: Histories, Dreams and Distortions*, Harper & Row, 1990

Weigall, Arthur, *The Life and Times of Cleopatra*, Putnam's, 1924

9/1

Fuller, Errol, *Extinct Birds*, Facts On File, 1987

Verney, Peter, *Animals in Peril: Man's War against Wildlife*, Brigham Young U., 1979

9/2

Caras, Roger, *Dangerous to Man*, Holt, Rinehart and Winston, 1975

9/3

Psihoyos, Louie, with John Knoebber, *Hunting Dinosaurs,* Random House, 1994

9/4

Taylor, Judy, *Beatrix Potter: Artist, Storyteller and Countrywoman*, Frederick Warne, 1986; *Beatrix Potter's Letters*, Frederick Warne, 1989; *That Naughty Rabbit: Beatrix Potter and Peter Rabbit*, Frederick Warne, 1987

9/6

Matthews, William, ed., *Charles II's Escape from Worcester: A Collection of Narratives Assembled by Samuel Pepys*, U. of California, 1966

Pearson, Hesketh, *Charles II: His Life and Likeness*, Heinemann, 1960

9/7

Baker, Carlos, *Ernest Hemingway: Selected Letters, 1917–1961*, Scribner's, 1981

9/9

Clair, Colin, *Unnatural History*, Abelard-Schuman, 1967

Lum, Peter, *Fabulous Beasts*, Pantheon, 1951

9/10

Darwin, Charles, *A Monograph of the Sub-Class Cirripedia,* 4 v., John Murray, 1850–58

Desmond, Adrian, and James Moore, *Darwin: The Life of a Tormented Evolutionist*, Warner, 1991

9/11

Baker, Carlos, ed., *Ernest Hemingway: Selected Letters, 1917–1961*, Scribner's, 1981

Fisher, David E., *The Scariest Place on Earth: Eye to Eye with Hurricanes*, Random House, 1994

9/12

Collins, Desmond, *The Human Revolution: From Ape to Artist*, Dutton, 1976

Pfeiffer, John E., *The Creative Explosion: An Inquiry into the Origins of Art and Religion*, Harper & Row, 1982

9/13

Daniel, Pete, *Standing at the Crossroads: Southern Life Since 1900*, Hill & Wang, 1986

9/14

Mast, Gerald, ed., *Bringing Up Baby: Howard Hawks, Director*, Rutgers U., 1988

9/15

Browne, Janet, *Charles Darwin: A Biography,* v. 1, *Voyaging*, Knopf, 1995

Desmond, Adrian, and James Moore, *Darwin: The Life of a Tormented Evolutionist*, Warner, 1991

9/16

Maltin, Leonard, *Of Mice and Magic: A History of American Animated Cartoons*, New American Library, 1980

Schneider, Steve, *That's All Folks! The Art of Warner Brothers Animation*, Henry Holt, 1988

9/17

Sheehan, William, *The Immortal Fire Within: The Life and Work of Edward Emerson Barnard*, Cambridge U., 1995; *Planets and Perception: Telescopic Views and Interpretations, 1609–1909*, U. of Arizona, 1988

9/18

Caras, Roger, *Dangerous to Man*, Holt Rinehart Winston, rev. ed., 1975

Ellis, Richard, *Monsters of the Sea: The History, Natural History, and Mythology of the Ocean's Most Fantastic Creatures*, Knopf, 1995

9/20

Zipes, Jack, *The Brothers Grimm: From Enchanted Forests to the Modern World*, Routledge, 1988

9/21

Jacobi, Jolande, ed., *Selected Writings*, Princeton U., 1979

Pachter, Henry M., *Paracelsus: Magic into Science*, H. Schuman, 1951

9/22

Hennessy, James Pope, *Robert Louis Stevenson*, Simon & Schuster, 1974

McLynn, Frank, *Robert Louis Stevenson: A Biography*, Random House, 1994

9/23

Mazo, Earl, *Richard Nixon: A Political and Personal Portrait*, Harper, 1959

Morris, Roger, *Richard Milhous Nixon: The Rise of an American Politician*, Henry Holt, 1990

9/25

Baring-Gould, William S., *The Annotated Sherlock Holmes,* 2 v., Clarkson N. Potter, 1967

9/27

Benson, Jackson L., *The True Adventures of John Steinbeck, Writer*, Viking, 1984

Parini, Jay, *John Steinbeck: A Biography*, Heinemann, 1994

9/29

Skal, David J., *The Monster Show: A Cultural History of Horror*, Norton, 1993; *V Is for Vampire*, Plume, 1995

9/30

Ackerman, Diane, *A Natural History of the Senses*, Random House, 1990

Lake, Max, *Scents and Sensuality: The Essence of Excitement*, John Murray, 1989

10/1

Gould, Stephen Jay, *Bully for Brontosaurus*, Norton, 1991

Norell, Mark A., et al., *Discovering Dinosaurs: In the American Museum of Natural History*, Knopf, 1995

10/2

Bedini, Silvio A., *Thomas Jefferson: Statesman of Science*, Macmillan, 1990

Martin, Edwin T., *Thomas Jefferson: Scientist*, Collier, 1952

10/3

Gill, Stephen, *William Wordsworth: A Life*, Clarendon, 1989

Wordsworth, Dorothy, *The Grasmere Journals,* ed. by Pamela Woof, Clarendon, 1991

10/5

Ackroyd, Peter, *T. S. Eliot: A Life*, Simon & Schuster, 1984

10/6

Swain, Roger, *Field Days*, Scribner's, 1983

10/9

Guenter, Scot M., *The American Flag, 1771–1924: Cultural Shifts from Creation to Codification*, Fairleigh Dickinson U., 1990

Quaife, Milo M., et al., *The History of the United States Flag*, Harper & Row, 1961

10/10

de Beer, Gavin, *Charles Darwin: Evolution by Natural Selection*, Doubleday, 1964

Keith, Arthur, *Darwin Revalued*, Watts & Company, 1955

10/11

Crawshay, L. R., "Possible Bearing of a Luminous Syllid on the Question of the Landfall of Columbus," *Nature,* v. 136, pp. 559–60

Taviani, Paolo Emilio, *Columbus: The Great Adventure: His Life, His Times, His Voyages,* Orion, 1991

10/13

Grant, Michael, *The Twelve Caesars,* Scribner's, 1975

Ramsbottom, John, *Mushrooms & Toadstools: A Study of the Activities of Fungi,* Collins, 1953

10/14

Arnold, H. J. P., *Man in Space,* Smithmark, 1993

Brueton, Diana, *Many Moons: The Myth and Magic, Fact and Fantasy, of Our Nearest Heavenly Body,* Prentice-Hall, 1991

10/15

Hardwick, Michael, *The Complete Guide to Sherlock Holmes,* St. Martin's, 1986

Higham, Charles, *The Adventure of Conan Doyle: The Life of the Creator of Sherlock Holmes,* Norton, 1976

10/17

Blythe, Ronald, ed., *The Pleasures of Diaries,* Pantheon, 1989

Hobhouse, Henry, *Seeds of Change: Five Plants That Transformed Mankind,* Sidgwick & Jackson, 1985

10/19

Clark, Ronald W., *Benjamin Franklin: A Biography,* Random House, 1983

Wright, Esmond, *Benjamin Franklin: His Life as He Wrote It,* Harvard U., 1990

10/20

Green, John, *Sasquatch: The Apes among Us,* Hancock House, 1978

Napier, John, *Bigfoot: The Yeti and Sasquatch in Myth and Reality,* Dutton, 1972

10/21

Molesworth, Charles, *Marianne Moore: A Literary Life,* Atheneum, 1990

10/22

Richardson, Robert D., *Henry Thoreau: A Life of the Mind,* U. of California, 1986

10/23

Albritton, Claude C., Jr., *The Abyss of Time: Changing Conceptions of the Earth's Antiquity after the Sixteenth Century,* Freeman, Cooper, 1986

Gould, Stephen Jay, *Eight Little Piggies,* Norton, 1993

10/24

Caras, Roger A., *Dangerous to Man: The Definitive Story of Wildlife's Reputed Dangers*, Holt Rinehart Winston, rev. ed., 1975

Palmer, Thomas, *Landscape with Reptile*, Ticknor & Fields, 1992

10/25

Carr, Gerald L., *Frederic Edwin Church: The Icebergs*, Dallas Museum of Fine Arts, 1980

Kelly, Franklin, et al., *Frederic Edwin Church*, Smithsonian Institution, 1989

10/27

Gould, Stephen Jay, *Bully for Brontosaurus*, Norton, 1991

10/28

Goodall, Jane, *Through a Window: My Thirty Years with the Chimpanzees of Gombe*, Houghton Mifflin, 1990

Savage-Rumbaugh, Sue, and Roger Lewin, *Kanzi: The Ape at the Brink of the Human Mind*, Wiley, 1994

11/1

Lucanio, Patrick, *Them or Us: Archetypal Interpretations of Fifties Alien Invasion Films*, Indiana U., 1987

Schelde, Per, *Androids, Humanoids, and Other Science Fiction Monsters: Science and Soul in Science Fiction Films*, New York U., 1993

11/2

Culhane, John, *Walt Disney's* Fantasia, Abrams, 1983

11/4

Desmond, Adrian, *Huxley*, Michael Joseph, 1994

11/6

Bedini, Silvio A., ed., *The Christopher Columbus Encyclopedia*, Simon & Schuster, 1992

Cummins, John, trans. and ed., *The Voyage of Christopher Columbus: Columbus' Own Journal of Discovery*, St. Martin's, 1992

11/8

Malik, Michael, "Ruined Republic," *Far Eastern Economic Review,* 29 June 1989

Viviani, Nancy, *Nauru: Phosphate and Political Progress*, U. of Hawaii, 1970

11/10

Hoyt, Edwin P., *Hirohito: The Emperor and the Man*, Praeger, 1992

Kanroji, Osanaga, *Hirohito: An Intimate Portrait of the Japanese Emperor*, Gateway, 1975

11/12

Bauer, Henry H., *The Enigma of Loch Ness: Making Sense of a Mystery*, U. of Illinois, 1986

Campbell, Steuart, *The Loch Ness Monster: The Evidence*, Aberdeen U., 1991

11/13

Lowes, John Livingston, *The Road to Xanadu: A Study in the Ways of the Imagination*, Princeton U., 1927, 1986

Rowland, Beryl, *Birds with Human Souls: A Guide to Bird Symbolism*, U. of Tennessee, 1978

11/14

Langguth, A. J., *Saki: A Life of Hector Hugh Monroe*, Simon & Schuster, 1981

11/16

Cockrill, Pauline, *The Teddy Bear Encyclopedia*, Dorling Kindersley, 1993

Miller, Nathan, *Theodore Roosevelt: A Life*, Morrow, 1992

11/17

Karl, Frederick R., *Franz Kafka: Representative Man,* Ticknor & Fields, 1991

Stern, J. P., ed., *The World of Franz Kafka*, Holt Rinehart Winston, 1980

11/18

Lawrence, Elizabeth A., "In the Mick of Time: Reflections on Disney's Ageless Mouse," *Journal of Popular Culture,* Fall 1986

Updike, John, "The Mystery of Mickey Mouse," in *The Best American Essays, 1992*, Ticknor & Fields, 1992

11/19

Ellis, Richard, *Monsters of the Sea: The History, Natural History, and Mythology of the Oceans' Most Fantastic Creatures*, Knopf, 1995

11/20

Brooks, Paul, *The House of Life: Rachel Carson at Work*, Houghton Mifflin, 1972

Ehrlich, Paul and Anne, *Extinction: The Causes and Consequences of the Disappearance of Species*, Random House, 1981

11/23

Officer, Charles, and Jake Page, *Tales of the Earth: Paroxysms and Perturbations of the Blue Planet*, Oxford U., 1993

11/24

Brent, Peter, *Charles Darwin: A Man of Enlarged Curiosity*, Harper & Row, 1981

Desmond, Adrian, and James Moore, *Darwin: The Life of a Tormented Evolutionist*, Warner, 1991

11/26

Carter, Howard, and A. C. Mace, *The Tomb of Tut Ankh Amen,* 3 v., Cassell, 1923–33

Desroches-Noblecourt, Christiane, *Tutankhamen: Life and Death of a Pharaoh*, New York Graphic Society, 1963

11/27

Palmer, Thomas, *Landscape with Reptile*, Ticknor & Fields, 1992

Silverman, Kenneth, ed., *Selected Letters of Cotton Mather*, Louisiana State U., 1971

11/28

McGrayne, Sharon Bertsch, *Nobel Prize Women in Science: Their Lives, Struggles, and Momentous Discoveries*, Birch Lane, 1993

11/29

Gould, Stephen Jay, *Bully for Brontosaurus*, Norton, 1991

Milner, Richard, *The Encyclopedia of Evolution*, Facts On File, 1990

11/30

Johanson, Donald C., and Maitland A. Edey, *Lucy: The Beginnings of Humankind*, Simon & Schuster, 1981

Willis, Delta, *The Hominid Gang: Behind the Scenes in the Search for Human Origins*, Viking Penguin, 1989

12/2

Shepard, Paul, and Barry Sanders, *The Sacred Paw: The Bear in Nature, Myth, and Literature*, Viking, 1985

12/5

Reader, John, *Missing Links: The Hunt for Early Man*, Collins, 1981

Shapiro, Harry, *Peking Man*, Simon & Schuster, 1974

12/9

Weber, Nicholas Fox, *The Art of Babar: The Work of Jean and Laurent de Brunhoff*, Abrams, 1989

12/10

Skal, David J., *The Monster Show: A Cultural History of Horror*, Norton, 1993

South, Malcolm, ed., *Mythical and Fabulous Creatures: A Source Book and Research Guide*, Greenwood, 1987

12/13

Cocteau, Jean, Beauty and the Beast: *Diary of a Film*, Dover, rev. trans., 1972

Sprigge, Elizabeth, and Jean-Jacques Kihm, *Jean Cocteau: The Man and the Mirror*, Coward-McCann, 1968

12/14

Amundsen, Roald, *My Life as an Explorer*, Doubleday, Page, 1927

"The Last Frontiers," *The Encyclopedia of Discovery and Exploration,* Doubleday, 1971

12/16

Hobhouse, Henry, *Seeds of Change: Five Plants That Transformed Mankind*, Sidgwick & Jackson, 1985

Schivelbusch, Wolfgang, *Tastes of Paradise: A Social History of Spices, Stimulants, and Intoxicants*, Pantheon, 1992

12/17

Scullard, H. H., *Festivals and Ceremonies of the Roman Republic*, Cornell U., 1981

12/18

Blinderman, Charles, *The Piltdown Inquest*, Prometheus, 1986

12/19

Bingham, Jane M., ed., *Writers for Children: Critical Studies of Major Authors since the Seventeenth Century*, Scribner's, 1988

Schmidt, Gary D., *Hugh Lofting*, Twayne, 1992

12/20

Ackroyd, Peter, *Dickens*, HarperCollins, 1990

Kaplan, Fred, *Dickens: A Biography*, Morrow, 1988

12/22

Hays, H. R., *Birds, Beasts, and Men: A Humanist History of Zoology*, Putnam, 1972

Teale, Edwin Way, ed., *The Insect World of J.-Henri Fabre*, Dodd Mead, 1949

12/23

Kennedy, X. J., "The Man Who Hitched the Reindeer to Santa Claus's Sleigh," *The New York Times Book Review,* 5 December 1993

Pond, Caroline, "The Truth about Reindeer," *New Scientist,* 22/29 December 1990

12/27

Browne, Janet, *Charles Darwin,* v. 1, *Voyaging*, Knopf, 1995

Desmond, Adrian, and James Moore, *Darwin: The Life of a Tormented Evolutionist*, Warner, 1991

12/28

Hayes, Harold T. P., *The Dark Romance of Dian Fossey*, Simon & Schuster, 1990

Mowat, Farley, *Woman in the Mists: The Story of Dian Fossey and the Mountain Gorillas of Africa*, Warner, 1987

12/29

Kirk, Ruth, *The Desert: The American Southwest*, Houghton Mifflin, 1973

Teale, Edwin Way, *Wandering through Winter*, Dodd Mead, 1965

12/31

Watterson, Bill, *The Calvin and Hobbes Tenth Anniversary Book*, Andrews and McMeel, 1995

Acknowledgments

There is no question who is at the head of the list. While writing this book, I have been encouraged and assisted by my intrepid in-house horticulturist and favorite human being to hang out with, my wife, Chris Matasick. The dedication is insufficient to express my gratitude, admiration, and love.

Many thanks to Paula Kakalecik, my editor at Henry Holt, who is invariably patient, helpful, and entertaining. Without her, this book—if it existed at all—would be much diminished. Ken Wright shepherded *Darwin's Orchestra* into publication with expertise and good humor beyond the call of duty. I'd also like to thank others who contributed to the book's content or appearance. Raquel Jaramillo designed the jacket; Paula R. Szafranski designed the book itself; and Annette Corkey copyedited the manuscript. Joseph Mella provided invaluable assistance and lunchtime company.

Shortly after selling *Darwin's Orchestra,* my agent, Diane Cleaver, suddenly died. I miss her. However, her friend and colleague, Heide Lange, took over as my agent and has been a joy ever since.

Late-in-coming gratitude to the *other* NRA (the unarmed one). This book and this author owe a debt to Jim Young, friend and teacher, who even gave me the fossil that held down the growing pile of pages. The ever-enthusiastic Steve Womack helped especially on matters cinematic. Alana White started the ball rolling by mentioning my project to Diane Cleaver. And thanks to their cohorts: Phyllis Gobble, Martha Whitmore Hickman, Nancy Hite, Amy Lynch, Madeena Spray Nolan, and Ronna Wineberg-Blaser.

Jon Erickson commented on essays, and discussed everything from 32-bit addressing to poetic metaphor. Ann Shayne provided source materials and her patented Shaynesque perspective. James Laffrey read and commented upon a sizable portion of the manuscript. The committee is also proud to present special lifetime awards to Jeff Hood and Sally Schloss.

My thanks to those who readily shared their expertise in various fields. Science historian William Sheehan critiqued essays on astronomical topics and wrote wonderful letters from the wilds of darkest Minnesota. Mark A. Norell at the American Museum of Natural History answered questions about a certain fictional dinosaur bone. Arleen Tuchman critiqued some of my interpretations of Darwin's thinking. James Epstein discussed especially English history. Needless to say, any errors that may remain are entirely my own.

The staff of the Nashville Public Library, especially the Green Hills branch, was unfailingly helpful. I found several treasures in the library of Cheekwood Botanical Garden. But without the fine people who run the Jean and Alexander Heard Library at Vanderbilt University, I would have to write fiction. Although everyone was helpful, I especially thank Dale Manning and Daisy Whitten. Some kind of merit badge should go to Peggy Earheart, who is unfailingly helpful and gracious. Dewey James provided frequent advice and a joke du jour.

"Nothing corrupts a man as deeply as writing a book," Nero Wolfe remarks somewhere; "the myriad temptations are overpowering." One of those temptations is to pick the brains of everyone around you. I have shamelessly done so. I hope I haven't forgotten anyone who helped. If so, please forgive me, and write your name in.

Illustration Credits

Denny Adcock expertly reproduced illustrations from the fragile volumes I carried to him and photographed a number of artifacts. (And thanks, Denny, for four years of helping me plot where to hide the bodies.) Ronald V. Borst of Hollywood Movie Posters advised me about illustrations from films and provided those that appear in this book. Carla Stiff, on behalf of the Universal Press Syndicate, arranged permission for me to reproduce the "Far Side" cartoon. Joseph Mella, curator of the Vanderbilt University Fine Arts Gallery, provided artifacts from Vanderbilt's collections. Obviously, a number of illustrations came from old books, and the source should be apparent from the illustration itself or its caption. However, I found many illustrations in European and American periodicals of the eighteenth and nineteenth centuries, and I want to thank those publications, even though some no longer exist: *Harper's Weekly* (United States), *La Illustración Artística* (Spain), *The Illustrated London News* (England), *The Illustrated News of the World* (England), *Le Magasin Pittoresque* (France), *McClure's* (United States), and *Punch* (England). Occasionally, when I could not get access to the original of an illustration that is obviously in the public domain, I copied it from reproductions in more recent sources.

INDEX

Page numbers in *italics* refer to illustrations.